THE BATTLE FOR CHINA

The Battle for China

ESSAYS ON THE MILITARY HISTORY
OF THE SINO-JAPANESE WAR OF 1937–1945

Edited by Mark Peattie,
Edward J. Drea, and
Hans van de Ven

STANFORD UNIVERSITY PRESS

STANFORD, CALIFORNIA

Stanford University Press
Stanford, California

Maps produced by David Rennie.
Japan photographs reproduced with permission of AFLO/Mainichi Shimbun.

Printed in the United States of America

Library of Congress Cataloging-in-Publication Data

The battle for China : essays on the military history of the Sino-Japanese War of 1937–1945 / edited by Mark Peattie, Edward Drea, and Hans van de Ven.
   p. cm.
   Includes bibliographical references and index.
   ISBN 978-0-8047-6206-9 (cloth : alk. paper)
   ISBN 978-0-8047-9207-3 (pbk.   )
   1. Sino-Japanese War, 1937–1945—Campaigns—China. 2. China—History, Military—1912–1949. 3. Japan—History, Military—1868–1945. I. Peattie, Mark R., 1930– II. Drea, Edward J., 1944– III. Van de Ven, Hans J.
  DS777.53.B337 2011
  940.54'251—dc22   2010042047

Typeset by BookMatters in 10/12.5 Sabon

There is no instance of a nation benefiting from prolonged warfare.

—Sunzi

Contents

List of Illustrations   xi

List of Tables   xiii

Contributors   xv

Introduction   xix

Acknowledgments   xxiii

Part I. Overviews of the War   5

     Chronology of the Sino-Japanese War, 1937–1945   7
     HANS VAN DE VEN AND EDWARD J. DREA

     1. An Overview of Major Military Campaigns during
     the Sino-Japanese War, 1937–1945   27
     EDWARD J. DREA AND HANS VAN DE VEN

     2. The Dragon's Seed: Origins of the War   48
     MARK R. PEATTIE

Part II. The Two Armies on the Eve of the War   81

     3. The Nationalist Army on the Eve of the War   83
     CHANG JUI-TE

     4. The Japanese Army on the Eve of the War   105
     EDWARD J. DREA

Part III. From the Fighting at the Marco Polo Bridge,
July 1937, to the Fall of Wuhan, October 1938   139

     5. Chiang Kai-shek and the Battles of Shanghai
     and Nanjing   143
     YANG TIANSHI

6. Japanese Operations from July to December 1937   159
   HATTORI SATOSHI WITH EDWARD J. DREA

7. The Defense of the Central Yangtze   181
   STEPHEN MACKINNON

8. The Japanese Eleventh Army in Central China,
   1938–1941   207
   TOBE RYŌICHI

*Part IV. The Middle Years and the Search for
Military Solutions*   233

9. The Japanese Air Campaigns in China, 1937–1945   237
   HAGIWARA MITSURU

10. The Great Bombing of Chongqing and the
    Anti-Japanese War, 1937–1945   256
    EDNA TOW

11. China's Quest for Foreign Military Aid   283
    ZHANG BAIJIA

12. Nationalist and Communist Guerrilla Warfare in
    North China   308
    YANG KUISONG

13. Japanese Combat Morale: A Case Study of the
    Thirty-seventh Division   328
    KAWANO HITOSHI

*Part V. The Later Japanese Offensives: The Burma and
Ichigō Campaigns*   357

14. Japanese Operations in Yunnan and North Burma   361
    ASANO TOYOMI

15. Chinese Operations in Yunnan and Central Burma   386
    ZANG YUNHU

16. The Ichigō Offensive   392
    HARA TAKESHI

17. The Battle of Hunan and the Chinese Military's
    Response to Operation Ichigō   403
    WANG QISHENG

Part VI. Historical Perspectives 421

18. The Strategic Correlation between the Sino-Japanese
and Pacific Wars 423
TOHMATSU HARUO

19. The Sino-Japanese War in History 446
HANS VAN DE VEN

20. The Sino-Japanese War in the Context of
World History 467
RONALD SPECTOR

Notes 485

Bibliographies: Explanatory Note 569

A Selected Bibliography of English-Language Sources 571
STEVE PHILLIPS

A Selected Bibliography of Chinese-Language Sources 577
STEVE PHILLIPS

A Selected Bibliography of Japanese-Language Sources 583
EDWARD J. DREA AND TOBE RYŌICHI

Character List 587

Index 595

List of Illustrations

Maps (following page 26)

1. Political China
2. Japanese Army Order of Battle, July 1937
3. Outline of Operational Progress in North China, July 1937–June 1941
4. Pingxingguan Pass, 25 September 1937
5. Shanghai Campaign, August–November 1937
6. Nanjing Campaign, November–December 1937
7. Japanese Army Movements in the Xuzhou Operation
8. Wuhan Operation, June–November 1938
9. Military Situation, Early 1939
10. Japanese Offensives in China, July 1937–December 1941
11. Nationalist War Zones, August 1937
12. Japanese Air Operations, May 1939–December 1941
13. Ichigō Operation, April 1944–February 1945
14. Chinese Operations in North Burma, October 1943–March 1945

Photographs

CHINA PHOTOGRAPHS *(following page 136)*

1. Chinese antiaircraft battery at Nanjing, 1937
2. Battle of Changsha, 1939

3. Chinese trenches during Battle of Taierzhuang, 1938

4. Chongqing bombed

5. Victory celebration in Chongqing, 1945

JAPAN PHOTOGRAPHS *(following page 418)*

6. Aerial photo of the Marco Polo Bridge

7. Japanese tanks moving through a village near Nankou, Hubei Province

8. Japanese bombers on a mission over the Chinese interior

9. Japanese infantry returning from fighting outside Guangzhou, 1938

10. Japanese infantry clearing a village in central China

11. Japanese infantry counterattacking across the Peking–Wuhan rail line in central China

List of Tables

3.1 The organization and equipment of a Nationalist and
     a Japanese division   89

3.2 Educational background of ranking officers before
     1937   100

3.3 Educational background of military officers in the
     Nationalist army (1936)   101

3.4 Educational background of colonels and lieutenant
     colonels (1936)   101

4.1 Development of the firepower of the Japanese squad
     over time   114

4.2 Standard artillery and armor in Japanese army
     inventories   120

6.1 Japanese losses during the Shanghai campaign   175

10.1 Japanese air raids on Chongqing, June to
     August 1941   263

10.2 Population of Chongqing, 1937 to 1944   269

13.1 The Organization of the Thirty-seventh Division   338

13.2 Equipment and weapons of the Thirty-seventh Division   340

16.1 Losses incurred during the Ichigō offensive   394

16.2 Transportation of Japanese military stocks,
     November 1944   394

Contributors

ASANO TOYOMI is Professor at the School of International Liberal Studies, Chukyo University. He is the author of *Teikokunihon no Shokuminchi Housei* (The colonial legal system of Japanese empire), which took both the Masayoshi Ohira Memorial Prize and the Yoshida Shigeru Prize in 2009. In 1998–2000 he was a Research Associate at the Asia-Pacific Research Center in Waseda University and in 2006–2007 a visiting scholar at the Sigur Center of the Elliot School of International Affairs at George Washington University.

CHANG JUI-TE is Professor of history at Chinese Culture University and Adjunct Researcher at the Institute of Modern History, Academia Sinica, Taipei. He is author of *Ping-Han tielu yu Huabei di Jingji fazhan, 1905–1937* (The Peking–Hankou Railroad and economic development in north China, 1905–1937); *Zhongguo jindai tielu shiye guanli di yanjiu: zhengzhi cengmian di fenxi, 1876–1937* (Railroads in modern China: Political aspects of railroad administration, 1876–1937); and *Kangzhan shiqi di guojun rensi* (Anatomy of the Nationalist army, 1937–1945).

EDWARD J. DREA is a military historian who has taught at the U.S. Army Command and General Staff College and the U.S. Army War College and worked at the U.S. Army Center of Military History in Washington, DC. His published works include *MacArthur's ULTRA: Codebreaking and the War against Japan, 1942–1945* and *In the Service of the Emperor: Essays on the Imperial Japanese Army*. His latest book is *Japan's Imperial Army: Its Rise and Fall, 1853–1945*. In 2003 he received the Society for Military History's prestigious Samuel Eliot Morison Prize for lifetime achievement.

HAGIWARA MITSURU is a dean and professor at Kushiro Public University of Economics in Kushiro, Hokkaido, Japan. He received his Ph.D. in Economics from Hokkaido University Graduate School of Economics.

After serving as a post-doctoral fellow in the Department of Economics at Hokkaido University, he joined the Kushiro Public University faculty where he specializes in modern Chinese economic history. Professor Hagiwara's recent research interests include the history of Chinese companies and the history of modern Chinese transport policy.

HARA TAKESHI is a researcher in the Japanese Defense Agency Research Bureau, specializing in the general history of the Japanese Imperial Army. He is a graduate of the Japanese Defense Academy. He is the author of a study of defense history during and after the Bakumatsu Period (1988), as well as of *Japanese Military and Naval Affairs* (1997). He teaches self defense at the Japanese Defense Agency.

HATTORI SATOSHI is an instructor at Osaka University. His interests include general military history, the diplomatic history of the period between the two world wars, and the histories of Japanese foreign and trade policies in the 1930s, subjects on which he has published various scholarly articles. His work on the diplomacy of Matsuoka Yōsuke, 1940–1941, is in press.

KAWANO HITOSHI is Professor of sociology in the Department of Public Policy at the National Defense Academy, Yokosuka, Japan. His research interests include military history, sociology of combat and peacekeeping, and civil-military relations in post–cold war Japan, and he has published various articles on these subjects. He is the author of *GyokusaiI no Guntai, Seikan no Guntai* (The army of death, the army of life).

STEPHEN R. MACKINNON is Professor of history at Arizona State University. He is author most recently of *Wuhan, 1938: War, Refugees, and the Making of Modern China*. He is the editor, with Diana Lary and Ezra Vogel, of *China at War: Regions of China, 1937–45*, as well as an earlier volume with Diana Lary, *Scars of War*, among other books.

MARK R. PEATTIE is Visiting Scholar, Shorenstein Asia/Pacific Research Center, Stanford University, and Research Fellow, Hoover Institution on War, Revolution, and Peace, Stanford University. His publications include *Ishiwara Kanji and Japan's Confrontation with the West* and *Nan'yō: The Rise and Fall of the Japanese in Micronesia, 1885–1945*. He edited, with Ramon Myers, *The Japanese Colonial Empire, 1895–1945*. His book with David Evans, *Kaigun: Strategy, Tactics, and Technology in the Imperial Japanese Navy, 1887–1941*, was named book of the year by the Society for Military History in 1999.

RONALD SPECTOR is Professor of history and international relations in the Elliott School of International Affairs, George Washington University. His book *Eagle against the Sun: The American War with Japan* was a main selection of the Book of the Month Club and winner of the Theodore and Franklin Roosevelt Prize in Naval History. His most recent book is *In the Ruins of Empire: The Japanese Surrender and the Battle for Post-war Asia*. Other books include *After Tet: The Bloodiest Year in Vietnam* and *At War at Sea: Sailors and Naval Combat in the Twentieth Century*, which received the 2002 Distinguished Book Award of the Society for Military History.

TOBE RYŌICHI received his B.A., M.A., and Ph.D. from Kyoto University, specializing in political studies. He was a professor at Japanese Defense University, specializing in Japanese political and diplomatic history. He also taught at the International Research Center for Japanese Studies. He coedited *Nitchū Sensō no Gunji-teki Tenkai* (Military Development of the Sino-Japanese War, 1937–1945) in 2005 and coauthored *Senryaku no Honshitsu* (Essence of Strategy) in 1999.

TOHMATSU HARUO is Professor of diplomatic and war history at the National Defense Academy of Japan. His research interests include international administration of territories focusing on the League of Nations mandate and United Nations trusteeship systems, history of Anglo-Japanese relations, the Russo-Japanese War, the Manchurian Incident, Japan's Micronesian mandates, the Sino-Japanese War of 1937–1945, and United Nations peacekeeping operations. He has edited *Nicchū sensō sairon* (The Sino-Japanese War of 1937–45 revisited).

EDNA TOW is a PhD candidate in Chinese history at the University of California, Berkeley. Her doctoral dissertation examines the political, social, and cultural impact of mass aerial bombardment on the Chinese state and society during the Sino-Japanese War, 1937–1945. She documents the Chinese government's response to Japan's air raid campaigns against the wartime capital of Chongqing and situates the air war as a critical front in the broader conflict waged between China and Japan that significantly shaped political, military, and diplomatic developments of the period.

HANS VAN DE VEN is Professor of modern Chinese history at Cambridge University. He is the author of *From Friend to Comrade* and *War and Nationalism in China*. He has also edited *Warfare in Chinese History* and *New Perspectives on the Chinese Communist Revolution*. He is currently working on a history of globalization as it has affected China.

WANG QISHENG is Professor of history at Peking University. His major areas of expertise are the history of the Republic of China and the history of the Chinese Nationalist Party (or Kuomintang, KMT). He is the author of books including *Party Members, Party Power and Party Struggle—the KMT Organization in 1924–1949* and *KMT-CCP Cooperation and the Nationalist Revolution.*

YANG KUISONG holds two professorships, one at Peking University and one at East China Normal University. Previously he worked at the Central Party School as editor of Party History Research and was a researcher at the Chinese Academy of Social Sciences. He is the author of 11 books, including *A Re-assessment of the Xi'an Incident (Xi'an Shibian Xintan)* and *Lost Chance? A True Record of CCP-KMT Wartime Negotiations (Shiqu de Jihui? Zhanshi Guo-Gong Tanpan Shilu).*

YANG TIANSHI is a Researcher at the Institute of History of the Chinese Academy of Social Sciences. Following graduation from Peking University in 1960, he taught at a middle school in Peking, joining the Chinese Academy of Social Sciences. His studies have straddled philosophy, including monographs on Wang Yangming and Zhu Xi, and Republican History, including a general history of the Northern Expedition period and important articles on Chiang Kaishek. He holds numerous awards, including that of Academician of the Chinese Academy of Social Sciences, and he is the editor of *Century Tide (Bainian Chao).*

ZHANG BAIJIA is a research professor at the Party History Research Center of the Central Committee of the Chinese Communist Party. He has authored several books on Chinese foreign policy, Chinese Communist Party history, and China's policy-making process, including *Lengzhan yu Zhongguo* (The cold war and China) and *Zhongguo Gaige Kaifang Shi* (History of the reform and opening). He has also authored numerous articles and policy papers.

ZANG YUNHU is Associate Professor of history at Peking University. He has worked in the Department of Military History of the Military Science Academy of the People's Liberation Army. His research interests include the modern history of Sino-foreign relations and the history of the Republic of China.

Introduction

Five days after the minor firefight at the Marco Polo Bridge (Lugou-qiao/Rokōkyō) outside Peking, a noted Japanese left-wing intellectual and China watcher, Ozaki Hotsumi, wrote that he was "convinced that [the incident] can hardly fail to develop on such a scale as to prove of utmost significance in world history." Ozaki was to expand on this prediction and, until the day of his death in 1943, insisted that the critical theater in World War II was not the Pacific but China. Certainly, the Sino-Japanese War of 1937–1945 had titanic and tragic consequences for both countries and has shaped postwar Asia in ways that continue to be obvious today.

Yet it is clear that, despite its scale and import, the Sino-Japanese War has long been overshadowed by the European and Pacific theaters in Western military history, while issues such as the Chinese Revolution, economic modernization, and cultural change have dominated histories of China and Japan. A few specialized studies of the conflict exist, largely centered on diplomatic and political matters, mass mobilization in China, major incidents such as the Nanjing Massacre, and Japanese counterinsurgency efforts in China. But a general history of military operations during the war based on Japanese, Chinese, and Western sources does not exist in English. Only when our ignorance is repaired will the basis exist for a more balanced understanding of World War II, for nuanced and textured analyses of the significance of the conflict in East Asia, and for an accurate assessment of Ozaki's claim.

This was the central motivation of the organizers of a general project on the history of the war. Ezra Vogel of Harvard University sponsored the first stage of a long-range effort to subject the war to broad scholarly investigation. Two China specialists, Steven MacKinnon of the Arizona State University and Diana Lary of the University of British Columbia, organized an international conference at Harvard University as the first step in the reassessment. The papers from that conference are published by the Stanford University Press.

Vogel approached the general editor of this volume to organize an inter-

national conference on the military dimension of the conflict. With the
counsel and assistance of Edward J. Drea, an authority on the Japanese
army, and Hans van de Ven, a specialist in Chinese military history, and
working with Yang Tianshi of the Chinese Academy of Social Sciences,
Yamada Tatsuo of Waseda University, Hatano Sumio of Tsukuba University, and a number of Western scholars of China and Japan, the structure
of the project took shape. The result was a four-day conference on the
military dimension of the war, sponsored by the Asia Center of Harvard
University and held at the Sheraton Hotel on the island of Maui in Hawaii
in January 2004.

In organizing the conference the members of the editorial committee
made several decisions that were critical to the atmosphere of the discussions and the composition of the subsequent volume. The first two are easily
stated. First, the organizers asked the participants to focus their papers on
military operations because a military history of the war did not exist and
would have enduring value. Second, they believed the emphasis on military
operations and strategy would not only sharpen the focus of the study but
also illustrate that, in this period, warfare drove much of what happened
in the political, economic, social, and cultural spheres in China and Japan.

Third, the organizers believed that a volume of high caliber could result
only from close collaboration between Chinese, Japanese, and Western
scholars. Much of the best scholarship on World War II in East Asia is
naturally produced in China and Japan. To bring the fruits of Chinese
and Japanese work to the attention of a wider public is one of the aims of
this volume. At the same time, opportunities for productive collaboration
between Chinese and Japanese scholars have been limited for many years
due to historical and political reasons, and also because of the enormous
sensitivity that the Sino-Japanese War holds in East Asia. The organization of the conference out of which this volume has grown was driven by
the commitment to scholarly dialogue and debate, and by the belief that
advances in understanding and interpretation will come from that.

It was only natural that occasionally Chinese participants would become
vexed at flat-footed comments by some Japanese participants and that
some Japanese would become irritated with Chinese insistence on fuller
Japanese apologies for Japanese wartime behavior. Perhaps more surprising was the irritation of some American scholars when the significance or
the purpose of the U.S. role in China, especially as embodied by General
Joseph Stilwell, was questioned. Nonetheless, the forty-plus scholars from
several nations who were brought to Maui all shared a basic commitment
to cooperative scholarship. Of benefit also was the salubrious atmosphere
of the conference venue. The result was the production of a set of conference papers that collectively provide an authoritative introduction to the
military course of one of the greatest conflicts of the twentieth century.

As with all such collaborative efforts, not all topics of obvious interest in such a history could find a place in these pages. To a large extent this was due to the inability of the organizers to find specialists qualified and willing to write essays on such subjects. To an extent, we have been able to bridge these gaps by providing a general overview of the military campaigns, an accompanying chronology, and introductions to the several sections into which the chapters are grouped.

Although Japan's record of war crimes is a topic of great current interest, Japanese atrocities are mentioned only if pertinent to a particular campaign or strategy. Thus, no paper specifically addresses war crimes, in part because the topic is a subject unto itself that has been dealt with in a range of books, monographs, and journals. The recently published National Archives and Records Administration report to Congress on the subject is a good place to start for those interested in Japanese war crimes.

The editors of this volume are aware that the beginning date of World War II in East Asia is subject to debate. Recently, most scholars in China have taken the Japanese occupation of Manchuria in 1931 as the beginning of what they refer to as the War of Resistance against Japan. The United States became involved after the Japanese bombed Pearl Harbor on 7 December 1941. It was only after this that China officially declared war on Japan, not having done so until then for diplomatic and legal reasons. Most American scholarship has focused on the period after 1941. As to the end date of the war, on 15 August 1945 Emperor Hirohito of Japan announced the Japanese acceptance of the Declaration of Potsdam, demanding unconditional surrender. In China today, the formal commemoration of the ending of the war takes place on 2 September, when Japanese representatives signed the surrender instrument aboard the USS *Missouri* anchored in Tokyo Bay. This volume takes the Marco Polo bridge Incident of 7 July 1937 as the beginning date of the Sino-Japanese War. For the purposes of this volume, whether the end date is defined as 15 August or 2 September 1945 is irrelevant.

The bibliography, like the volume, is not exhaustive. Instead, it provides an entry for students interested in pursuing a long-neglected topic that merits careful research and study.

This book uses the pinyin transliteration system, with a few arbitrary exceptions. In the case of the few well-known Chinese proper and place names, we have used commonly accepted English usage such as Peking, Chiang Kai-shek, Whampoa, and Kwantung Army. In the case of Japanese, we have used the Hepburn system.

Acknowledgments

The origin of the project of which this book forms a part was a series of communications early in this decade with Ezra Vogel, Professor Emeritus at Harvard University, distinguished sociologist, and lifelong friend of both China and Japan. Professor Vogel—who has lived and traveled extensively in both countries, who uses their languages with utmost facility, who has acquired a host of friends and acquaintances in the Chinese and Japanese academic communities, and who has written of the societies and cultures of both countries with authority, insight, and verve—has been central to the organization of this project. His enthusiastic encouragement, his wise counsel, his introductions to a number of influential members of Chinese and Japanese scholarly circles, and his initiative in identifying and then making representations to important sources of funding for the project have been invaluable assets to the work of the organizational committee and editorial board.

In obtaining financial support for both the conference and the editing of this volume, our gratitude to the Andrew W. Mellon Foundation is profound. Quite simply, without the material assistance of the foundation, this project would have remained only a concept. With it, we have the ability to achieve a full measure of success.

We have been fortunate in being able to assemble the roster of specialists who appear in these pages, and we are grateful to all the authors who have contributed chapters to this volume. That we have been able to obtain their contributions is largely due to the organizational and collaborative efforts of influential scholars in China and Japan. Among these we should particularly cite Yang Tianshi of the Institute of Modern History, Chinese Institute of Social Sciences, Beijing; Yamada Tatsuo, University of the Air, Tokyo; and Hatano Sumio, Dean of the Graduate School of Political Economy, Tsukuba University.

Particular recognition must be given to those translators and interpreters in the project whose skilled and tireless efforts enable Chinese, Japanese, and Western participants to understand one another's presentations and viewpoints. In the former category we identify and thank Theodore Cook of William Paterson University, New Jersey; Edward Dreyer of the University of Miami, Florida; Joshua Fogel of the University of California, Santa Barbara; Lyman Van Slyke of Stanford University; and Daqing Yang of the George Washington University. We are also delighted to recognize the expert and demanding work of the interpreters at our Maui conference: Mei June, Mei Jiangzhong, Reiko Farrelly, Sato Fujiko, and Utsunomiya Satoko.

Expert and constructive comment on scholarly presentations is a major necessity for the success of any project such as ours. Here we greatly benefited from the observations of Michael Barnhart, Stony Brook University; Chang Jui-te, Academia Sinica, Taipei; Parks Coble, University of Nebraska; Theodore Cook; Edward Dreyer; Joshua Fogel; Diana Lary, University of British Columbia; Alice Miller, Naval Postgraduate School, Monterey, and the Hoover Institution, Stanford University; and Douglas Porch of the Naval Postgraduate School.

The conference was also fortunate in having the participation in its deliberations of a number of other fine scholars from China, Japan, and the United States: Baba Takeshi of Aichi University; Li Yuzhen of the Institute of Modern History, Beijing; Liu Fenghan of the Academica Sinica, Taipei; Ma Zhendu, Second Historical Archives of China, Nanjing; Momma Rira of the Japanese Ministry of Education; Tuo Ping of the Central Institute of Documents, Beijing; Masahiro Yamamoto of the University of Wyoming; and Maochun Yu of the United States Naval Academy.

No editors of a collection of scholarly papers can lay claim to their final production as an intellectual resource without a usable and instructive bibliography. In this regard, we have been ably and expertly served by Steven Phillips, Towson State University, Maryland. Professor Phillips has brought his scholarly knowledge and archival skills to the selection of the most important titles and archival sources relevant to the military history of the Sino-Japanese War of 1937–1945 in the three primary languages essential to our project. We were also expertly served by David Rennie for his fine work on the maps included in this volume.

Without a written record of the proceedings of our Maui conference we would have been hindered in reviewing and contemplating the results of that gathering. Thankfully, we had the illuminating notes taken by Brad Glosserman of the Pacific Forum CSIS, Honolulu, and Andrew Wilson of the Naval War College.

Thanks to Tarryn Li-Min Chun and Admiral Koda Yoji for their able assistance in refining the character list found at the back of this book. Thanks to Mike Mollett for the heroic task of copyediting the works of so many writers, and Anne Smith for her excellent work proofreading the typeset version of the same. Samantha Miller did a thorough job of indexing the book, and navigating the many demands of all the hands at the helm. Thanks to David Peattie and his staff at BookMatters for managing the entire cast of characters involved in putting this book together.

Finally, our special thanks go to Holly Angell on the staff of the Asia Center, Harvard University. For months before the conference, as the organizers of the conference were laboring to pull together the arrangements, and in the months after it, as the editors were engaged in the task of compiling this volume, Ms. Angell, with industry, cheer, and remarkable efficiency undertook a range of administrative tasks essential to the success of our efforts.

THE BATTLE FOR CHINA

Part I

OVERVIEWS OF THE WAR

The first two chapters in part I, the "Chronology of the Sino-Japanese War" and chapter 1, "An Overview of Major Military Campaigns during the Sino-Japanese War," provide the reader with an overview of the military operations of the Sino-Japanese War and establish the context for the essays in the volume. They are also useful because the contributors could not address all the campaigns of the eight-year-long struggle in a detailed, complete, or exhaustive manner.

In chapter 2, "The Dragon's Seed: Origins of the War," Mark Peattie's essay on historical perspective identifies the political and military origins of the war with the decline of the classical Chinese empire in the nineteenth century and the concurrent rise of a modernizing, expansionist, and aggressive Japan. But where others have seen Japan's nineteenth-century intrusions into China as the genesis of a rational, coordinated, smoothly working government or military plan, Peattie stresses the dysfunctional nature of Japan's China "policy." Although he implicitly acknowledges that Japan's decision to go to war with China in 1894 had concrete and well-planned objectives, he argues that subsequent Japanese actions in China were the unintended, often haphazard consequences of the actions of various contenders: the general staffs of the military services, the Foreign Ministry, business interests, the political parties, belligerent army field officers, reformist zealots, and individual idealists, adventurers, and ultranationalists, who collectively sought to bully China into agreeing to Japanese hegemony over the country, beginning with the infamous Twenty-one Demands of 1915. Ultimately, in his view, it was the Japanese army field officers stationed in China who played the most active and pernicious role in this regard. For that reason, he devotes considerable space to exploring the knowledge, outlook, and activities of these officers. He notes that although they had a detailed and accurate knowledge of Chinese garrisons and warlords, their arrogance and prejudices blinded them to the most salient fact about China in the 1920s and '30s: the swelling tide of Chinese antiforeign nationalism caused by foreign, and particularly Japanese, intervention.

Peattie's discussion of Chinese nationalism covers ground familiar to Western readers: the first faltering steps toward national reform under Sun Yat-sen, in the post–World War I decade; the fragmentation of China into warlord satrapies in the ensuing years; the rise of Chiang Kai-shek and his Northern Expedition to unify China; and the establishment of Chiang

Kai-shek's Nationalist regime balanced on a shaky coalition of regional military power holders and reformist bureaucrats. He takes note, too, of Chiang's ongoing efforts to deal with internal challenges—the bureaucratic infighting of his domestic political rivals and combat operations to crush a Communist insurgency—while concurrently implementing a Fabian strategy against Japanese military incursions on China's borders. In this sense, he argues, the conflict's origin lay in the volatile mixture of decades-long bullying by the Japanese military services in China and the explosive Chinese resentment of this abuse. He sees the 1936 Xi'an Incident, Chiang's humiliation at the hands of activist elements of the Chinese National Army, as the catalyst for the ultimate explosion of violence in July 1937. The tragedy, he believes, was that this confrontation occurred when the Japanese government, including some in its military leadership, was belatedly rethinking its obdurate hostility to Chinese nationalism and considering greater accommodation with Chiang's government.

Chronology of the Sino-Japanese War, 1937–1945

HANS VAN DE VEN AND EDWARD J. DREA

1937

July 7: Clash at the Marco Polo Bridge (Lugouqiao in Chinese; Rokōkyō in Japanese) near Peking between Japanese soldiers on night maneuvers and Chinese units under Song Zheyuan.

July 9: At Lushan, Jiangxi Province, Chiang Kai-shek convenes an emergency conference of prominent national figures in preparation for war.

July 17: Zhou Enlai and other Chinese Communist Party (CCP) leaders arrive at Lushan for discussions with the Nationalists and other national leaders.

July 27: The Japanese cabinet, following an emergency meeting, declares that it is determined to establish a "New Order" in Asia. The Chinese Foreign Ministry states that China has exhausted all its efforts to maintain peace.

July 29–30: The Japanese capture Peking and Tianjin.

August 13: Chiang Kai-shek opens a second front at Shanghai, beginning the Battle of Shanghai.

August 14: The Chinese Nationalist air force attempts to sink Japanese warships in Shanghai, but the bombs hit the city, killing many civilians.

August 21: China and the Soviet Union sign a Mutual Nonaggression Pact and the Soviets begin to aid China. Nationalist and Communist representatives carry on negotiations in Nanjing.

August 24: Japanese forces attack Nankou (northwest of Peking).

August 28: Chiang Kai-shek appoints Li Zongren, the leader of the Guangxi Clique, as commander in chief of the Fifth War Zone in north China.

September 5: Japanese Second and Third fleets blockade much of the Chinese coast.

September 8: After the arrival of reinforcements, Japan begins a general offensive at Shanghai.

September 13: Japanese forces take Datong in Shanxi Province.

September 16: Japanese forces break through Chinese defenses north of Shanghai, inflicting heavy losses.

September 19–20: Major air battle takes place over Nanjing (Nanking).

September 23: Chiang Kai-shek recognizes the legality of the Chinese Communists, thus establishing the Second United Front.

September 25: Chinese Communists claim victory over the Japanese Fifth Division under General Itagaki Seishirō at Pingxingguan Pass, Shanxi Province.

October 5: The League of Nations condemns Japan for violating the Nine-Power Treaty.

October 9: Japanese forces in north China begin an offensive toward Shijiazhuang, Hebei Province, which is taken on 10 October.

October 12: Chinese Communist forces south of the Yangtze are organized into the New Fourth Army; General Ye Ting is appointed its commander.

October 13: Battle of Xinkou in north central Shanxi Province begins. This massive three-week battle ends in a major Japanese victory, opening up routes of advance south toward Taiyuan.

October 14: A Chinese counteroffensive north of Shanghai fails.

October 25: Japanese compel Chinese forces to retreat to Suzhou, Jiangsu Province, and Suzhou Creek in Shanghai, where the Chinese form a new defensive line.

October 30: The Chinese government announces the removal of its capital to Chongqing in Sichuan Province. Some government agencies establish temporary offices in Wuhan, Hubei Province.

November 3: The Brussels Conference of the signatories of the Nine-Power Treaty opens. Japan is condemned, but the conference rejects collective action.

November 5: Japanese troops land at Hangzhou Bay, south of Shanghai, to begin encirclement of Shanghai. On 9 November, Chiang Kai-shek orders a general withdrawal

November 9: Japanese complete the occupation of Taiyuan, capital of Shanxi Province.

November 11: First Soviet supplies reach Lanzhou, Gansu Province.

November 29: After their naval forces enter the Yangtze River area in force, the Japanese begin a four-pronged offensive toward Nanjing.

December 5: Chiang Kai-shek announces that he will not begin peace negotiations until Japan has withdrawn its forces from China.

December 13: Japanese forces enter Nanjing and begin an extended series of atrocities.

December 24: Hangzhou, capital of Zhejiang Province, falls to the Japanese.

December 25: Following the unauthorized retreat of General Han Fuju, the Japanese capture Jinan, the capital of Shandong Province. Han will be court-martialed and executed.

December 31: Implementing a scorched-earth policy, the Chinese evacuate Qingdao, Tsingtao, Shandong Province, burning the city.

1938

January 5: One hundred Soviet volunteer pilots arrive in Wuhan.

January 16: Following a second mediation effort by Trautmann, the Japanese government issues a formal statement that it will no longer recognize or deal with the Nationalist government (*aite ni sezu* statement).

February 5: The Japanese undertake first terror bombing of Guangzhou (Canton).

February 20: Japanese forces cross the Yellow River at Kaifeng.

Mid-March: Opening phase of the Battle of Xuzhou. The Japanese North China Area Army and the Central China Army attempt to encircle and annihilate 600,000 Chinese troops of the Fifth War Zone headquartered at Xuzhou in north Jiangsu Province. The Japanese will take Xuzhou, but the Chinese defenders manage to break through the encirclement after Chiang Kai-shek orders a withdrawal on 15 May.

March 23: Beginning of the Battle of Taierzhuang, which ends in Chinese tactical victory on 6 April.

March 19-April 1: Kuomintang (KMT) National Congress convenes in Wuhan, leading to the adoption of a wartime constitution and the establishment of a National Consultative Conference.

April 7: Japanese high command reorganizes Xuzhou front.

April 29: Major air battle over Wuhan, in which Soviet volunteers participate on the Chinese side.

May 21: Germany recalls its advisers in the Nationalist army.

May 29: Fierce air battle over Wuhan in which both sides suffer losses.

June 1: Chiang Kai-shek takes the decision to break the dikes of the Yellow River at Huayuankou, Henan Province, to prevent westward movement of Japanese forces from Xuzhou toward Zhengzhou, Henan Province, along Longhai Railway.

June 6: The Japanese capture Kaifeng, capital of Henan Province. Nationalists invite seven CCP members, including Mao Zedong, to attend the National Consultative Conference.

June 12: Japanese occupation of Anqing, Anhui Province, in preparation for the Battle of Wuhan.

July 4: Japanese high command reorganizes the Central China Expeditionary Army for a general offensive against Wuhan.

July 31: Soviet and Japanese forces clash at Zhanggufeng (Changkufeng) but sign an armistice in mid-August.

August 6: Japanese foreign minister states that Japan aims for a New Order in East Asia, which would include China, French Indochina, and the Dutch East Indies.

August 22: The Japanese high command issues an order for the offensive against Wuhan. While the Japanese navy forces its way up the Yangtze River, Japanese army units advance along both the north and south shores of the Yangtze.

September 27: Japanese air units attack Kunming.

September 29–November 6: Following Comintern instructions, the CCP convenes Sixth Central Committee Plenum, leading to the approval of Mao Zedong's wartime policies and condemnation of his rival Wang Ming.

September 30: Munich: Britain and France agree to German annexation of the Sudetenland.

October 21: The Japanese Twenty-first Army takes Guangzhou (Canton).

October 22: Wang Jingwei sends emissaries to Shanghai for discussions with the Japanese.

October 25: The Nationalist government orders the evacuation of Wuhan.

November 3: The Japanese cabinet declares that it is willing to cooperate with China if it abandons its policy of resistance.

November 8: The Japanese bomb Hengyang and Changsha in Hunan Province.

November 12: Japanese forces take Yuezhou in west Hunan Province.

Believing (wrongly) that the enemy had already arrived, Nationalist authorities order Changsha to be set on fire.

November 25–28: The Nationalists convene the Nanyue Military Conference, at which they establish ten war zones and two field headquarters. They declare that a second phase, in which the fighting will be decentralized, has been opened.

December 18: Wang Jingwei breaks with Chiang Kai-shek and leaves Chongqing to pursue an accommodation with Japan. He reaches Hanoi on 21 December.

December 22: Prime Minister Konoe Fumimaro of Japan issues statement proposing "three principles" for settlement of the war and calls for the establishment of a "new order in East Asia."

1939

January: The Nationalists begin a policy of terrorism and assassinations in urban centers, including Shanghai.

January 13: The CCP establishes a Chongqing Liaison Office under Zhou Enlai.

January 15: Japan launches first air attack on Chongqing.

February 10: Japanese land on Hainan Island off the Guangdong coast.

February 20: A fierce air battle takes place above Lanzhou, Gansu Province, involving Soviet pilots.

February 23: Zhou Enlai transmits to the CCP New Fourth Army in Anhui the instruction that it should extend its area of operations. Hostilities between Nationalist and Communist forces intensify.

March 17: The Battle of Nanchang, Jiangxi Province, begins.

March 30: Britain and France guarantee Poland's independence.

April 29: After the Chinese counteroffensive, Japanese force seizes Nanchang.

May 4: The heavy bombing of Chongqing leads to widespread fire and numerous casualties.

May 5–28: The Chinese Fifth War Zone under General Li Zongren begins offensives toward Zaoyang and Suixian, Hubei Province, to establish bases in mountainous north Hubei and disrupt the Peking–Wuhan Railway. The Japanese will take both cities, but they cannot dislodge Chinese forces from the area.

June 14: Japanese forces blockade the French and British concessions in Tianjin.

July 7: Night bombardment of Chongqing takes place.

July 25: Japan closes the Pearl River.

August 20: Fighting begins between Japanese and Soviet troops near Nomonhan (Khalkhin-Gol) on the Manchurian-Mongolian border. Following skirmishes during the summer, Soviet General Georgy Zhukov uses tanks to surround and destroy three Japanese divisions of the Kwantung (Guandong) Army 20–31 August. A cease-fire is arranged, and the Japanese and Soviets will not go to war again until August 1945. Japanese from then on will concentrate on eliminating Chinese resistance before waging war on the Allies.

August 23: In Moscow, Germany and the Soviet Union sign a nonaggression treaty. The Soviets claim eastern Poland, Finland, Latvia, Estonia, and Bessarabia. Germany takes western Poland and Lithuania.

September 1: Germany invades Poland. With Britain and France having promised to assist Poland, the Second World War begins in Europe.

September 23: Japan establishes the General Headquarters of the Chinese Expeditionary Army in Nanjing to unify military command in China. Japan declares that it is willing to negotiate with Chongqing.

September 29–October 6: Bitter fighting takes place between Nationalist and Japanese forces in the First Battle of Changsha in Hunan Province. A Chinese counteroffensive under General Xue Yue, supported by Nationalist operations in northern Jiangxi and southern Anhui, is successful.

September 24: The Japanese begin an offensive in southern Shanxi Province.

October 29: Nationalists convene the Second Nanyue Military Conference to prepare for a winter offensive involving most war zones.

November 4: The Japanese bomb Chengdu, Sichuan Province.

November 19: After landing at Qinzhou, Guangxi Province, the Japanese begin an offensive toward Nanning, Guangxi Province, which they take on 24 November.

November 29: Shanxi warlord Yan Xishan begins a major anti-Communist offensive.

December 12: The Nationalist army begins a winter offensive, which lasts until approximately 20 January 1940 but proves a failure.

December 19: KMT forces retake the Kunlun Pass in Guangxi Province. The Japanese dislodge them two days later and take Longzhou.

December 30: Wang Jingwei and the Japanese sign Guideline for the Readjustment of Relations between Japan and China.

1940

January 8: The Japanese cabinet approves the establishment of the Wang Jingwei national government at Nanjing.

February 21–25: The Nationalists convene the Liuzhou Military Conference to review the winter offensive. Chiang Kai-shek issues an apology for failing to have anticipated the Japanese Guangxi landings. Leading generals, including Chen Cheng and Bai Chongxi, are punished.

February 25: Yan Xishan and the Communists agree to an armistice in Shanxi.

March 30: Establishment of the "Republic of China" at Nanjing under Wang Jingwei.

April 11: The Japanese begin anti-Communist mopping-up operations in central Hebei, Anhui, and around Shanghai.

April: The Japanese naval air service launches Operation 101 to knock out Chinese airpower in Sichuan Province generally, and military facilities around Chongqing in particular.

May 1: The Japanese undertake substantial offensives in central China, leading to the Battle of Zaoyi in Hubei Province. The Japanese aim is to dislodge Fifth War Zone forces in north and central Hubei, secure the fertile Hubei plains, and seize Yichang in west Hubei to choke off communications between Sichuan and China's war zones.

May 10: Germany begins a major offensive in Western Europe. Churchill succeeds Chamberlain as British prime minister.

May 22: A massive air battle takes place over Chongqing.

June 3: The Japanese take Yichang.

June 8: The Japanese occupy Shashi.

June 20: The French close the Yunnan–Hanoi Railroad.

July 15: Under Japanese pressure, the British close the Burma Road, China's last link with the outside world.

July 31: The Japanese begin a massive air campaign against the Nationalists. Chongqing, Chengdu, Xi'an, Lanzhou, and other cities are attacked continuously throughout the summer and autumn.

August 1: Japan, under new prime minister Konoe Fumimaro, declares its aim to be the creation of a Greater East Asia Co-Prosperity Sphere, involving Japanese leadership of China, India, Burma, Siam, Malay, the Philippines, Dutch East Indies, Australia, Pakistan, French Indochina, Afghanistan, and Siberia.

August 13: The Battle of Britain begins with 1,485 Luftwaffe sorties against British harbors and airfields in preparation for a German invasion of the United Kingdom.

August 19: Japanese Zero fighters appear for the first time over Chongqing. The French permit the Japanese use of Cam Ranh Bay Naval Base in French Indochina.

August 20: The first engagement begins in the Battle of the Hundred Regiments, a four-month-long series of local offensives by Communist forces in Hebei, Shaanxi, Honan, and Chahar against Japanese and puppet troops. One-hundred-seventy Japanese aircraft firebomb Chongqing. The Japanese take the Hongkou section of the International Settlement at Shanghai.

September 7: The Japanese begin a second massive offensive on Changsha, which ends in failure.

September 15: Germany loses the Battle of Britain and postpones the invasion.

September 22: Japanese land forces occupy Tonkin in northern French Indochina.

September 27: Germany, Japan, and Italy sign the Tripartite Pact, aimed at keeping the United States out of the war.

September 30: The Japanese launch air strikes against Kunming, Yunnan Province.

October 1–6: Large-scale clashes take place between KMT and CCP forces at Huangqiao in central Jiangsu.

October 10: A large air battle takes place over Kunming.

October 8: Nationalist forces penetrate into Yichang, Hubei Province, but Japanese forces manage to drive them out. Churchill agrees to the reopening of the Burma Road.

October 18: The British reopen the Burma Road.

October 19: The Nationalists order the removal of the CCP New Fourth Army to north of the Yellow River and substantial reduction in its force strength.

October 29: Japanese forces retreat from Nanning and Longzhou, Guangxi Province.

November 19: The Nationalists cease providing financial support to the CCP Eighth Route Army

December 8: The Nationalists repeat their order to the New Fourth Army to remove its forces from Anhui and Jiangsu.

1941

January 1–7: The Anhwei, or New Fourth Army, Incident. Nationalist forces annihilate one division of the New Fourth Army, killing large numbers, including Commander Xiang Ying. The remaining New Fourth Army units move north.

January 24: The Japanese begin the Henan Offensive to clear the Peking–Wuhan Railway.

January 28: New Fourth Army headquarters is reestablished in northern Jiangsu with a force of 90,000 troops.

March 6: The KMT rejects CCP demands regarding the New Fourth Army Incident, but declares that no further military actions will be taken against the Communist forces.

March 15: The Battle of Shanggao between Japanese and Nationalist forces begins. Japanese forces aim to destroy the Ninth War Zone forces of Luo Zhuoying in Jiangxi Province, forces that threaten the Yangtze and block Japanese approaches from Jiangxi to Changsha. In mid-April, the Japanese retreat with heavy losses.

April 13: Japan and the Soviet Union sign neutrality agreement.

April 18: The Japanese attack Chongqing by air.

April 19: The Japanese seize Fuzhou, Fujian Province.

April 20: The Japanese seize Ningbo, Zhejiang Province.

May 3: A massive air bombardment of Chongqing takes place.

May 6: Roosevelt extends Lend-Lease to China.

May 7: A large Japanese offensive drives Nationalist forces under General Wei Lihuang from the Zhongtiao mountains in southern Shanxi; the forces had protected the approaches to Xi'an and cut Communist lines of communication from Yan'an to bases in north and central China.

May 9–10: The Japanese air assault on Chongqing continues.

May 11: The Wang Jingwei national government begins military operations to "clear the countryside" in lower Yangtze area. Zhou Enlai meets Chiang Kai-shek in Chongqing.

May 16: The Japanese continue bombing Chongqing.

June 5: During the Japanese night air bombardment of Chongqing, thousands die in an air raid shelter as a result of oxygen deprivation. The American and British embassies are hit during raids over the following weeks.

June 22: Germany begins Operation Barbarossa against the Soviet Union.

July 2: The Japanese Imperial Council decides against joining the

German-Soviet war and in order to concentrate on the offensive in
Southeast Asia.

July 30–31: Massive Japanese air raids strike Chongqing and other places
in Sichuan.

August 1: Roosevelt prohibits oil exports to Japan. American Volunteer
Group (AVG, or the Flying Tigers of Claire Chennault) are formally
incorporated in Chinese air force.

August 7: Japan begins a campaign of continuous night and day bombing
of Chongqing.

August 15–October 26: Large-scale Japanese anti-Communist mopping-
up operations take place in north China.

September 7: The Japanese second offensive against Changsha. Japanese
forces launch a massive and rapid strike on Changsha, but logistic
difficulties and determined opposition again compel their withdrawal
on 1 October. General Chen Cheng seeks to use this opportunity to
retake Yichang. Although he is able to encircle the city and the Japanese forces run out of rations, a Japanese relief force made up of units
participating in the Second Battle of Changsha rushes to Yichang and
breaks the siege.

October 24: The Soviet Union ends aid to China.

December 7–8: The Japanese begin an offensive seeking to occupy Southeast Asia within 150 days. A two-pronged attack aims at first occupying the Philippines and Malaya and then converging on the Dutch
East Indies. The attack on Pearl Harbor aims to prevent intervention
in those plans by the U.S. Pacific Fleet. Japanese forces occupy the
Shanghai International Settlement and British and American concessions at Tianjin.

December 9: Thailand surrenders to Japan.

December 10: HMS *Repulse* and HMS *Prince of Wales* are sunk off
Malaya. Japan invades the Philippines. General Douglas MacArthur
withdraws from Manila on 23 December and leaves the Philippines on
22 February.

December 12: The Japanese occupy Kowloon.

December 16: Japan invades British Borneo.

December 24: The Japanese begin the Third Battle of Changsha, but
their offensive is defeated on 15 January.

December 25: The British surrender Hong Kong.

December 22–January 14: The Arcadia Conference in Washington, DC.
Roosevelt and Churchill decide on a "Europe-first" strategy.

1942

January 1: Britain, China, the United States, the Soviet Union, and twenty-two other countries sign the United Nations Declaration. Sir Archibald Wavell is appointed supreme commander of American-British-Dutch-Australian (ABDA) forces in Southeast Asia.

January 3: Chiang Kai-shek is appointed supreme allied commander of the China Theater, which includes French Indochina and Thailand.

January 11: Japan invades the Dutch East Indies and Dutch Borneo.

January 16: The Japanese begin the invasion of Burma.

January 26: Japanese forces begin their offensive toward Singapore from Malaya. With Allied forces, including British Indian Army units, deployed in the Middle East and North Africa and without air or naval cover, the defense of Fortress Singapore is doomed to fail. The British surrender on 15 February.

February 1: Mao Zedong begins his "Rectification Movement" in Yan'an.

February 2: The Japanese invade Java.

February 6: The AVG engages Japanese air units over Rangoon.

February 7: Britain accepts the assistance of the Chinese Expeditionary Force in Burma.

February 9: The Japanese Fifteenth Army is ordered to seize strategic places in Burma. Following the occupation of Moulmein, their forces seize Rangoon on 8 March and begin an immediate offensive toward Tounggoo, which they seize on 29 April. The Allied command is in disarray. Wavell resigns as ABDA supreme commander on 24 February and dissolves the ABDA Command. Churchill dispatches Sir Harold Alexander to take overall charge in Burma of British Indian Army and the Burma Corps under General William Slim. Mutual suspicion between the British and the Chinese undermines effective Allied cooperation.

February 16: Japanese forces land at Leizhou, Guangxi Province.

February 27–March 1: The Japanese are victorious at the Battle of the Java Sea.

March 4: General Joseph Stilwell arrives in Chongqing and accepts appointment as chief of staff of the Chinese army.

March 10: Stilwell is appointed commander of the Chinese Expeditionary Force. Chennault's AVG is incorporated into the U.S. Air Force as the Fourteenth Air Force.

March 15: Following initial British rejection of Chinese support, the Chinese Expeditionary Force under General Wei Lihuang enters Burma.

March 23: The Chinese 200th Division under Stilwell is encircled at Tounggoo. Attempts to halt the Japanese advance in Burma fail as Japanese undertake rapid advance toward Lashio.

March 23: Japan invades the Andaman Islands in the Bengal Sea.

April 18: The Doolittle Raid. B-25s drop bombs on Japan and then land on the China coast.

April 29–May 1: Lashio and Mandalay fall to Japanese forces.

May 20: Japan completes its invasion of Burma.

May 14: The Japanese begin a large offensive in Zhejiang to clear Nationalist air bases from which raids might be made on Japan. The offensive will continue through June.

June 4–5: The Battle of Midway. Japan loses four carriers; the United States loses one. On 9 June, Japan abandons its attempt to occupy Midway.

June 20–25: The second Washington Conference. In an acrimonious debate, Churchill criticizes the plan of U.S. chief of staff General Marshall for an immediate cross-channel invasion and secures Roosevelt's assent to the participation of U.S. forces in North Africa (Operation Torch), partly to demonstrate to Stalin that Britain and the United States are fighting the Germans and partly to safeguard the Mediterranean and the Suez Canal. Churchill and Roosevelt agree to participate as equal partners in development of the atom bomb.

June 29: Stilwell is appointed supreme commander of the Chinese Expeditionary Army in India (Ramgarh), and Luo Zhuoying is appointed deputy supreme commander.

August 8–9: The Battle of Guadalcanal begins. It will end on 1 February 1943 with a Japanese withdrawal.

September 27: The Japanese begin "autumn mopping-up operations" against the Jin-Cha-Ji Communist base area in north China.

September: The British offensive into the Akyab Mountains along the Arakan Coast, Burma, ends in a debacle.

October 10: Britain and the United States declare the end of extraterritoriality and announce the abrogation of their unequal treaties in Asia.

October 13: At Xi'an, Shaanxi Province, Chiang Kai-shek meets a Communist general, Lin Biao, to discuss improved military cooperation.

October 21: The Japanese attack Communist bases in the Taihang Mountains.

December 19: Japanese operations drive Nationalist forces from the southern Taihang Mountains.

December 20: Japanese air units raid Calcutta.

June–December: The Americans begin flying supplies from India over "the Hump" (Tibet) to China.

1943

January 14–24: At the Casablanca Conference, the Allies adopt unconditional surrender as war aim. Again, after much debate, the United States and Great Britain agree on an early invasion of Sicily to stretch the Wehrmacht and so support Stalin, on a limited operation on the French coast, and on a British invasion of the Arakan mountains in Burma in support of efforts to reopen a link through north Burma to China. Their aim is to establish U.S. bomber bases in China from which to attack Japan.

January 31: Japanese and Thai forces attack Yunnan, occupying several border towns.

February: Stilwell directs construction of the Ledo Road toward the Burma-India border.

February 21: The Japanese occupy Guangzhouwan, Guangdong Province.

March 23: Japanese forces begin a westward offensive from Yichang, Hubei Province.

April 10: The Soviet Union withdraws forces from Hami, Xinjiang Province, which it has occupied to secure strategic ores, including tungsten.

April 24: The Fourteenth Air Force attacks Japanese units in Burma.

April 20: Japanese mopping-up operations take place against Communists in the Jin-Cha-Ji base area and Nationalist forces in southern Hebei and northern Henan.

April 25: Japanese forces surround headquarters of the Nationalist Twenty-fourth Army Group in the Taihang Mountains.

May 2: The Fourteenth Air Force attacks the Japanese over northern Hunan.

May 5: The Japanese begin substantial operations in western Hubei and northern Hunan. In mid-June, they retreat to their original positions.

May 11–25: Trident: the third Washington Conference. Roosevelt agrees to further postponement, for a year, of a cross-channel invasion of France. With respect to China, Roosevelt and Marshall favor

Chennault's air strategy against Stilwell's advocacy of building up China's armies supplied through the Burma Road to take on the Japanese in China. Trident nonetheless supports the reinvasion of Burma. Chiang Kai-shek agrees on condition of substantial Allied air and naval support and the participation of U.S. infantry forces.

May 9: The Fourteenth Air Force attacks Japanese air units over Guangzhou.

May 22: The Communist International is disbanded.

May 31: The Fourteenth Air Force supports Chinese army operations at Yichang.

June 1: The United States begins submarine warfare against Japanese shipping.

June 6: Nationalist general Hu Zongnan transfers the Yellow River Defense Force north to blockade Shaan-Gan-Ning Communist base area (Yan'an). The third stage of CCP-KMT friction begins.

July 23–24: The Fourteenth Air Force engages Japanese air units in Hunan and Guangxi.

July 28: The Fourteenth Air Force attacks Hong Kong and Kowloon.

August 2: In Yan'an, Mao Zedong states that the third anticommunist high tide has ended.

August 21–25: The Fourteenth Air Force raids Wuhan.

August 17–24: Quadrant: Allied conference in Quebec. Foreign Minister Song Ziwen of China is present informally. Quadrant sets a target date for Overlord, the invasion of France from Britain, for 1 June 1944; approves the invasion of Italy; postpones the reinvasion of Burma; decides to step up the bombing campaign against Germany; and sets the aim to defeat Japan within one year of the German surrender. Following the disastrous British attack on the Akyab coast, Churchill decides to create Southeast Asia Command, of which Lord Louis Mountbatten will be supreme Allied commander, separate from the India Command and China. Stilwell will be deputy supreme commander.

September 6–13: At the eleventh plenum of the fifth KMT Central Committee, Chiang Kai-shek states that CCP is a political issue and that military actions against it will be halted.

September 8: Italy surrenders to the Allies.

September 16: Japanese forces begin mopping-up operations against Communist Jin-Cha-Ji base area.

September 20: The Fourteenth Air Force engages Japanese air units over Kunming.

September: Japanese mass forces for autumn mopping-up campaign against Ji-Lu-Yu Communist base area in north China.

November 2: Battle of Changde in Hunan Province begins. The Japanese reach the outskirts of the city on 18 November and seize the city on 3 December, but are dislodged by Chinese forces on 8 December.

November 8: The Fourteenth Air Force attacks Xiamen.

November 17: The Fourteenth Air Force attacks Hong Kong.

November 22: The Fourteenth Air Force attacks Japanese positions in western Hunan.

November 23–26: Chiang Kai-shek attends the Cairo Conference with Churchill and Roosevelt. Several plans for operations in Southeast Asia, including the reinvasion of Burma (Operation Tarzan), are discussed, but neither British nor U.S. war planners press hard for their acceptance. Tarzan is nonetheless approved. When Chiang continues to demand significant U.S. and British participation, Roosevelt promises significant amphibious operations in the Bay of Bengal. The conference declares that Manchuria will be returned to China.

November 25: The Fourteenth Air Force attacks Japanese airfields on Taiwan.

November 18–December 1: The Tehran Conference. Roosevelt and Churchill agree to an early invasion of France in return for a Russian promise to step up operations against Germany and participate in the war against Japan three months after the German surrender.

December 1–3: Second Cairo Conference. Churchill and Roosevelt agree on scaling down operations in Southeast Asia and reducing naval and air assistance. Chiang Kai-shek is not present. Roosevelt and Churchill decide that landings in Europe prevent deployment of amphibious forces in Southeast Asia, and Roosevelt informs Chiang accordingly.

1944

January 9: The British Indian Army recaptures Maungdaw, Burma.

January 10: The Chinese Expeditionary Force reenters the Hukawng Valley.

January 16: The Nationalists invite Zhou Enlai to return to Chongqing.

February 10: The fourth Nanyue Military Conference opens. Chiang orders war zones along the Yangtze River to prepare for the beginning of a general counteroffensive within three months but indicates that he recognizes the need for foreign assistance, especially of airpower and heavy artillery.

February 11: The Fourteenth Air Force conducts a raid on Hong Kong and Kowloon.

February 23: U.S. carrier-based forces attack the Marianas. American amphibious forces complete the occupation of the islands on 8 August, providing a base for B-29 Superfortress bombers to attack Japan and thus rendering U.S. heavy bomber bases in China less significant.

March 3: A seriously ill Wang Jingwei travels for medical care to Nagoya, where he will die.

March 4: The Fourteenth Air Force raids Hainan.

April 17: The Japanese begin the Ichigō offensive to establish overland link through China to Southeast Asia. Initial operations focus on clearing Chinese armies from Henan and Hubei.

April 21: Large-scale Japanese offensives begin in Henan to clear the Peking–Wuhan Railway. Chinese defenses collapse rapidly. The Japanese occupy Zhengzhou on 22 April, followed by Xinzheng and Mixian the next day.

April 29: Nationalist air units bomb Yellow River bridges.

May 6: Chinese and Nationalist air units attack Hankou, but the Japanese Ichigō offensive reaches Xiangyang, Hubei Province.

May 9: The Japanese clear the Peking–Wuhan Railway.

May 10: Japanese forces advancing west along Longhai Railway approach Luoyang, Shanxi Province.

May 14: Japanese air forces attack Kunming.

May 17: The Chinese Expeditionary Force, supported by Wingate's Chindits and Merrill's Marauders, takes Japanese airfield at Myitkyina. The siege of the city itself lasts until 4 August.

May 25: The Japanese take Luoyang and succeed in clearing the Longhai Railway.

May 26: Japanese Ichigō forces enter Hunan along three different routes, beginning the battle for Changsha and Hengyang.

May–June: Stilwell leads Chinese divisions down Mogaung Valley, Burma, against skillful Japanese resistance.

May 11–September 30: The Chinese Y-Force begins operations in Yunnan.

June 6: Normandy landings open a second front in Europe.

June 8: The Japanese completely encircle Changsha.

June 15: U.S. B-25 bombers attack Japan from China.

June 17: The Japanese begin a general offensive against Changsha and take the city the next day.

June 25: The Allies complete their advance through Mogaung Valley.

June 29: The Japanese begin the Battle of Hengyang and seize the airfield on 30 June.

July 7: Roosevelt demands the appointment of Stilwell as commander in chief of all Chinese forces.

July 28: Chinese and U.S. air units attack Yuezhou, Hunan Province.

July 31: Japanese air units raid Liuzhou and Guilin, Guangxi Province.

August 1: The U.S. Air Force strike Japanese industries in Manchuria.

August 8: The Japanese occupy Hengyang.

August 9: The Fourteenth Air Force attacks Shanghai.

August 16: Chinese armies attack Yichang. U.S. bombers attack the Japanese at Hengyang.

September 1: The battle for Guangxi and Guizhou begins with a massive Japanese offensive toward Guilin.

September 3: Japanese forces advance southwest along Hunan–Guilin Railway.

September 5: The Japanese occupy Qiyang, Hunan Province.

September 9: In Guangdong, Japanese forces occupy Huaiji and Xindu. In Fujian, they take Wenzhou.

September: The Japanese launch the Guangxi-Guizhou campaign of their Ichigō offensive.

September 14: The Chinese Expeditionary Force recovers Tengchong, Yunnan Province. Japanese forces occupy Quanxian, Guangxi Province.

September 16: Japanese forces in Guangdong seize Gaoyao.

September 19: Roosevelt cables Chiang Kai-shek that he must not withdraw Chinese Expeditionary Force from Burma and must place Stilwell in unrestricted command of all Chinese forces.

September 20: Japanese forces occupy Wuzhou, Guangxi Province. Over the next few days, they also occupy Rongxian and Guanyang.

September 25: Chiang Kai-shek asks Roosevelt to withdraw Stilwell and appoint another U.S. officer to take charge of Chinese forces.

September 28: Japanese forces based on the Leizhou Peninsula advance toward and surround Guilin, Guangxi Province.

October 1: Japanese forces occupy Changning, Hunan Province.

October 12: Japanese forces take Guiping, Guangxi Province. Massive Allied air bombardment of Taiwan takes place.

October 13: Japanese forces along the Hunan–Guilin Railway open an offensive toward the Darong River.

October 18: Stilwell is relieved of command and replaced by General Wedemeyer.

October 23–26: Battle of Leyte Gulf. Japanese kamikaze attacks begin.

October 24: Japanese forces begin a flanking attack on Nanning, Guangxi Province.

October 27: The Japanese launch air strikes against Chengdu and Enshi.

October 29: Following Stilwell's withdrawal, Chiang Kai-shek appoints General Wedemeyer chief of staff of the China theater.

November 8: Japanese forces occupy Luzhai, Xiangxian, and Liucheng, Guangxi Province.

November 11: Guilin falls into Japanese hands. The Japanese also occupy Liuzhou.

November–December: Due to disasters caused by Ichigō offensive, Chiang Kai-shek orders withdrawal of two Chinese divisions from Burma to help stop the Japanese drive into south China.

November 15: The Chinese Expeditionary Force in Burma takes Bhamo.

November 18: Japanese occupy Huaiyuan, Guangxi Province.

November 28: Japanese forces enter Guizhou Province along the Guangxi–Guizhou Railroad.

December 2: Japanese forces occupy Dushan, Guizhou Province, closing in on the Sichuan border.

December 24: Japanese forces seize Nanning.

December 18: The Fourteenth Air Force bombs Wuhan and Yueyang.

December 28: The Chinese Expeditionary Force makes rapid advances in Burma.

December: The Guangxi-Guizhou campaign of the Ichigō offensive finally grinds to a halt because of severe logistic problems.

1945

January 4: The British occupy Akyab, Burma.

January 9: The United States begins the invasion of the Philippines.

January 20: The Chinese Expeditionary Force seizes Wanding.

January 22: A large U.S. air offensive begins against Taiwan.

January 25: The Fourteenth Air Force attacks Japanese airfields near

Peking. The Japanese take Lufeng, Guangdong Province. The Fourteenth Air Force bombs Nanjing.

January 26: The Japanese seize Shaoguan, Guangdong Province.

January 31: The Japanese succeed in clearing the Wuhan–Guangzhou Railroad.

February 4–11: At the Yalta Conference, Stalin, Churchill, and Roosevelt meet. Stalin agrees to establish the United Nations; Roosevelt accepts Soviet influence in Eastern Europe. Stalin agrees to join the war against Japan. A secret agreement internationalizes Dairen (Dalian), a Russian naval base at Port Arthur, and joint Sino-Soviet control of Manchurian railroads.

February 19: The United States begins its invasion of Iwo Jima.

February 22: Chinese forces retake Mengshan, Guangxi Province.

February 25: A massive U.S. bombing of Tokyo takes place.

March 3: The United States takes Manila.

March 7: The Chinese Expeditionary Force takes Lashio, Burma. Chinese forces retake Liucheng, Guangxi Province.

March 20: The British Indian Army takes Mandalay.

March 30: The Chinese Expeditionary Force links up with the British Indian Army.

April 5: The Soviet Union abrogates the neutrality agreement with Japan.

April 9: The Battle of Hunan begins.

April 16: Chinese forces reoccupy Xiangyang and Zizhong in Hunan Province.

April 23: Soviet forces occupy Berlin.

May 8: Chinese forces begin general counteroffensive in western Hunan.

May 8: Victory in Europe.

May 11: Chinese forces occupy Fuzhou, Fujian Province.

May 27: Chinese forces retake Nanning, Guangxi Province.

June 18: Chinese forces take Yongjia, Zhejiang Province.

June 28: Japanese forces withdraw from Liuzhou, Guangxi Province.

June 28: General MacArthur announces victory in the Philippines.

July 5: Chinese forces take Zhennan, and Japanese forces retreat into French Indochina.

July 10: Massive U.S. bombing of Japan begins.

July 17: Chinese forces liberate Ganzhou, Jiangxi Province.

July 17–2 August: The Potsdam Conference takes place.

July 23: Chinese forces take Nanxiong, Guangdong Province.

July 25: U.S. air forces attack Shanghai.

July 27: Chinese forces occupy Guilin.

July 31: Chinese forces move into western Jiangxi. They take Xinning and Shanggao the next day.

August 6: United States drops an atom bomb on Hiroshima.

August 8: The Soviet Union declares war on Japan.

August 9: The United States drops an atom bomb on Nagasaki. Soviet forces begin a rapid offensive in Manchuria.

August 15: Japan surrenders unconditionally and accepts the Potsdam Declaration.

September 2: Formal Japanese surrender takes place on the USS *Missouri* in Tokyo Bay.

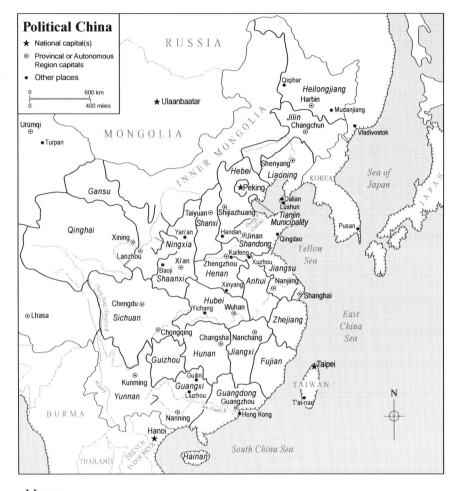

Map 1

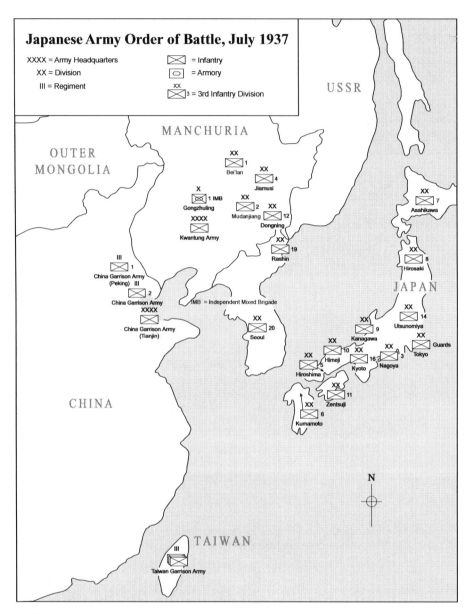

Japanese Army Order of Battle, July 1937

XXXX = Army Headquarters   ⊠ = Infantry

   XX = Division   ▭ = Armory

    III = Regiment   ⊠3 = 3rd Infantry Division

USSR

MANCHURIA

OUTER
MONGOLIA

XX
⊠1
Bei'lan

XX
⊠4
Jiamusi

X
⊠ 1 IMB
Gongzhuling

XX
⊠2
Mudanjiang

XX
⊠ 12
Dongning

XXXX
⊠
Kwantung Army

XX
⊠ 19
Rashin

XX
⊠7
Asahikawa

III
⊠ 1
China Garrison Army
(Peking) III

⊠ 2
China Garrison Army

XXXX
⊠
China Garrison Army
(Tianjin)

IMB = Independent Mixed Brigade

XX
⊠ 8
Hirosaki

JAPAN

XX
⊠ 20
Seoul

XX
⊠ 9
Kanagawa

XX
⊠ 14
Utsunomiya

XX
⊠ 10

XX
⊠ 5
Himeji

XX
⊠ 16
Kyoto

XX
⊠ 3
Nagoya

XX
⊠ Guards
Tokyo

XX
⊠ 11
Zentsuji

XX
⊠ 6
Kumamoto

XX
⊠
Hiroshima

CHINA

N

TAIWAN

III
▭
Taiwan Garrison Army

Map 2

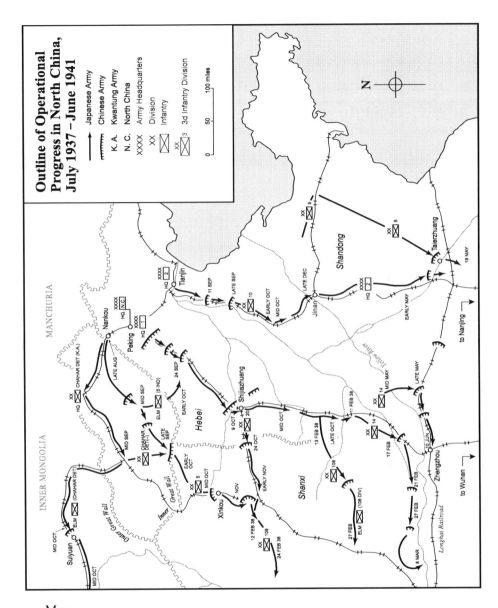

Map 3

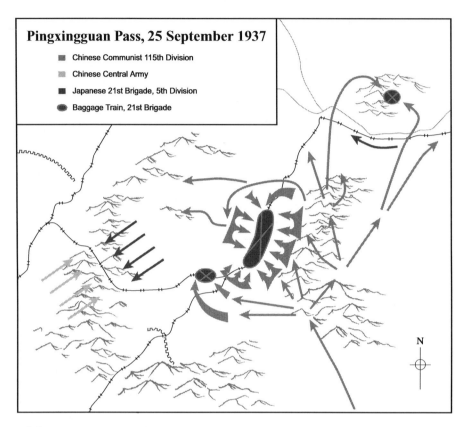

Map 4

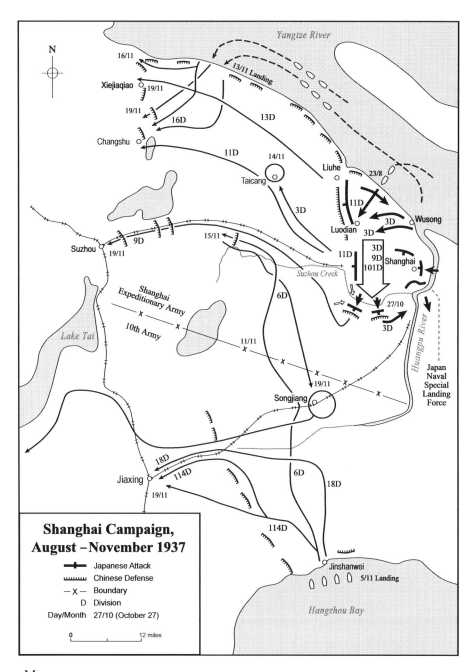

N

16/11

13/11 Landing

Xiejiaqiao   19/11

19/11   16D

13D

Changshu

11D   14/11

Taicang

Liuhe   23/8

11D

3D   Wusong

Luodian   3D

3D

3D
9D
101D   Shanghai

11D

Yangtze River

15/11

9D
Suzhou   19/11

Shanghai
Expeditionary Army

X

10th Army   X

Lake Tai

Suzhou Creek

6D

11/11
X

X

19/11
X

Songjiang   X

27/10

3D

Huangpu River

Japan
Naval
Special
Landing
Force

18D

Jiaxing   114D

19/11   6D

18D

114D

Jinshanwei

5/11 Landing

Hangzhou Bay

**Shanghai Campaign,
August – November 1937**

━┿━ Japanese Attack
ᴟᴟᴟᴟ Chinese Defense
— X — Boundary
D   Division
Day/Month 27/10 (October 27)

0   12 miles

Map 5

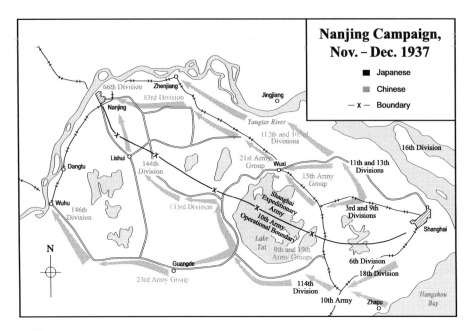

Nanjing Campaign, Nov. – Dec. 1937

- Japanese
- Chinese
- — x — Boundary

66th Division
Zhenjiang
Jingjiang
83rd Division
Nanjing
Yangtze River
112th and 103rd Divisions
16th Division
Dangtu
Lishui
144th Division
21st Army Group
Wuxi
11th and 13th Divisions
15th Army Group
Wuhu
146th Division
133rd Division
Shanghai Expeditionary Army
10th Army Operational Boundary
3rd and 9th Divisions
Shanghai
N
Lake Tai
9th and 19th Army Groups
6th Division
Guangde
18th Division
23rd Army Group
114th Division
10th Army
Zhapu
Hangzhou Bay

Map 6

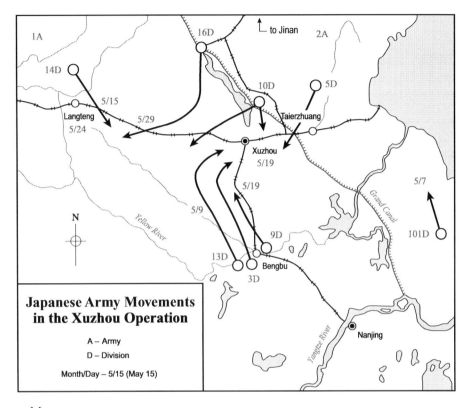

1A

16D

to Jinan

2A

14D

10D

5D

5/15

Langteng

5/29

Taierzhuang

5/24

Xuzhou

5/19

5/7

5/19

N

Yellow River

5/9

9D

101D

13D

Bengbu

3D

Grand Canal

Japanese Army Movements in the Xuzhou Operation

A – Army

D – Division

Month/Day – 5/15 (May 15)

Yangtze River

Nanjing

Map 7

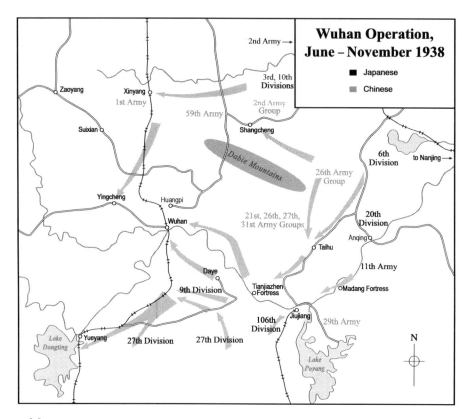

Map 8

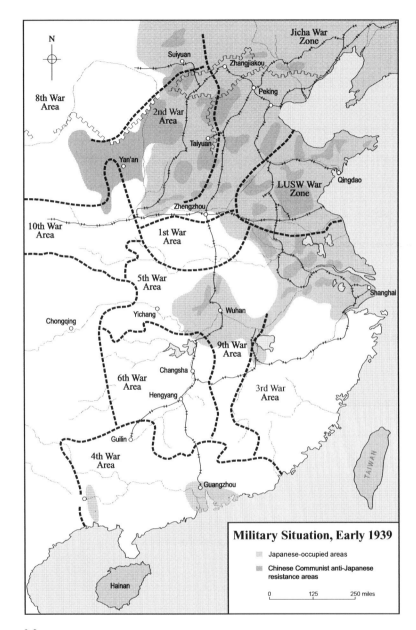

N

Jicha War
Zone

8th War
Area

Suiyuan

Zhangjiakou

Peking

2nd War
Area

Taiyuan

Yan'an

LUSW War
Zone

Qingdao

Zhengzhou

10th War
Area

1st War
Area

5th War
Area

Shanghai

Chongqing

Yichang

Wuhan

9th War
Area

6th War
Area

Changsha

3rd War
Area

Hengyang

TAIWAN

Guilin

4th War
Area

Guangzhou

Military Situation, Early 1939

Japanese-occupied areas

Chinese Communist anti-Japanese
resistance areas

0   125   250 miles

Hainan

Map 9

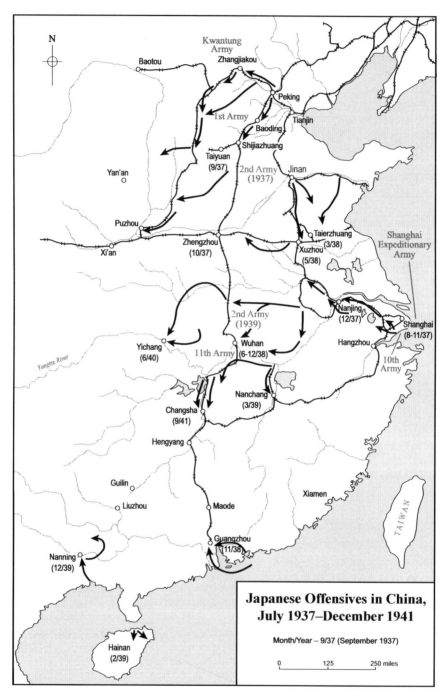

N

Baotou

Kwantung
Army
Zhangjiakou

Peking

Tianjin

1st Army

Baoding

Shijiazhuang

Taiyuan
(9/37)

Yan'an

2nd Army
(1937)

Jinan

Taierzhuang
(3/38)

Shanghai
Expeditionary
Army

Puzhou

Zhengzhou
(10/37)

Xuzhou
(5/38)

Xi'an

Yangtze River

Yichang
(6/40)

2nd Army
(1939)

Wuhan
(6-12/38)

Nanjing
(12/37)

Shanghai
(8-11/37)

Hangzhou

11th Army

10th
Army

Changsha
(9/41)

Nanchang
(3/39)

Hengyang

Guilin

Liuzhou

Maode

Xiamen

TAIWAN

Nanning
(12/39)

Guangzhou
(11/38)

Hainan
(2/39)

**Japanese Offensives in China,
July 1937–December 1941**

Month/Year – 9/37 (September 1937)

0   125   250 miles

Map 10

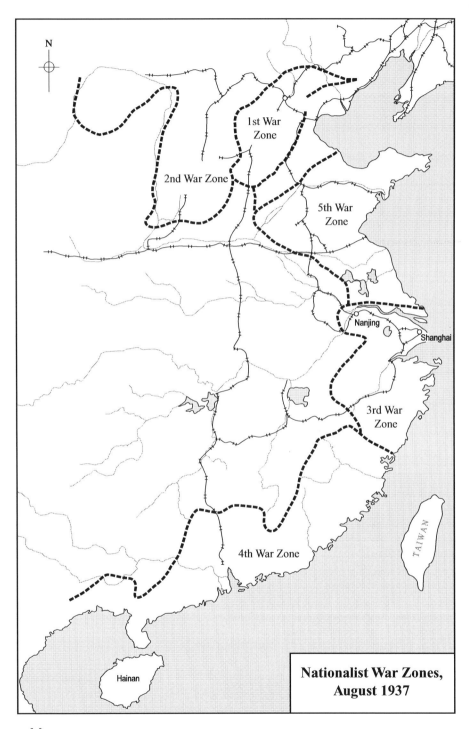

N

1st War
Zone

2nd War Zone

5th War
Zone

Nanjing

Shanghai

3rd War
Zone

TAIWAN

4th War Zone

Hainan

**Nationalist War Zones,
August 1937**

Map 11

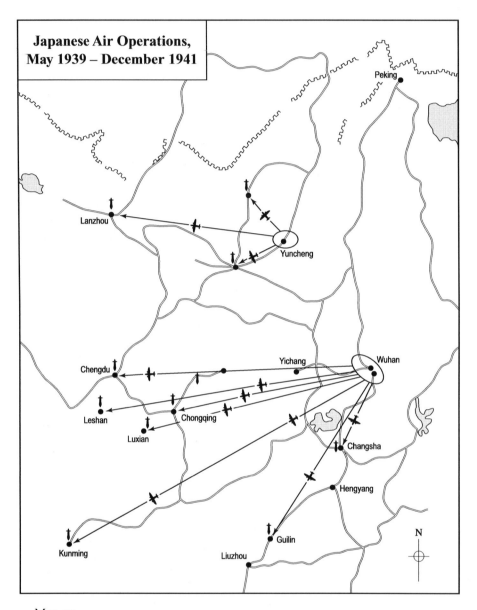

Japanese Air Operations, May 1939 – December 1941

Peking

Lanzhou

Yuncheng

Chengdu

Yichang

Wuhan

Leshan

Chongqing

Luxian

Changsha

Hengyang

Kunming

Guilin

Liuzhou

N

Map 12

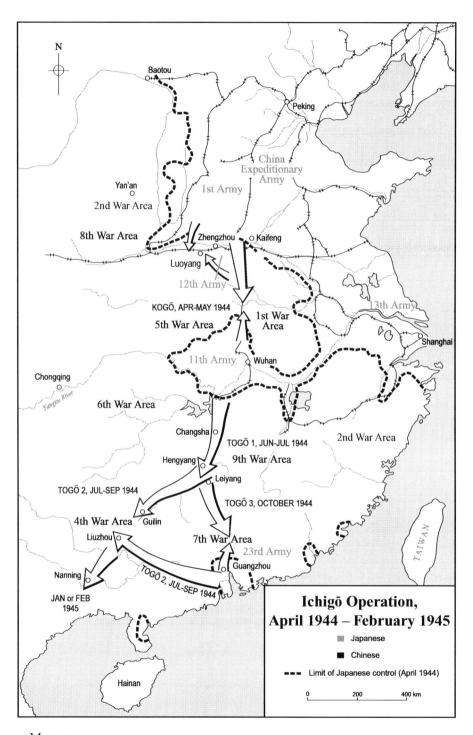

N

Baotou

Peking

China
Expeditionary
Army

1st Army

Yan'an
2nd War Area

8th War Area

Zhengzhou   Kaifeng

Luoyang

12th Army

KOGŌ, APR–MAY 1944

5th War Area

1st War
Area

13th Army

Shanghai

11th Army   Wuhan

Chongqing

Yangtze River

6th War Area

Changsha

TOGŌ 1, JUN–JUL 1944

Hengyang

9th War Area

Leiyang

2nd War Area

TOGŌ 2, JUL–SEP 1944

TOGŌ 3, OCTOBER 1944

4th War Area   Guilin

Liuzhou

7th War Area

23rd Army

TAIWAN

Nanning

TOGŌ 2, JUL–SEP 1944

Guangzhou

JAN or FEB
1945

**Ichigō Operation,
April 1944 – February 1945**

    Japanese

    Chinese

- - -   Limit of Japanese control (April 1944)

0   200   400 km

Hainan

Map 13

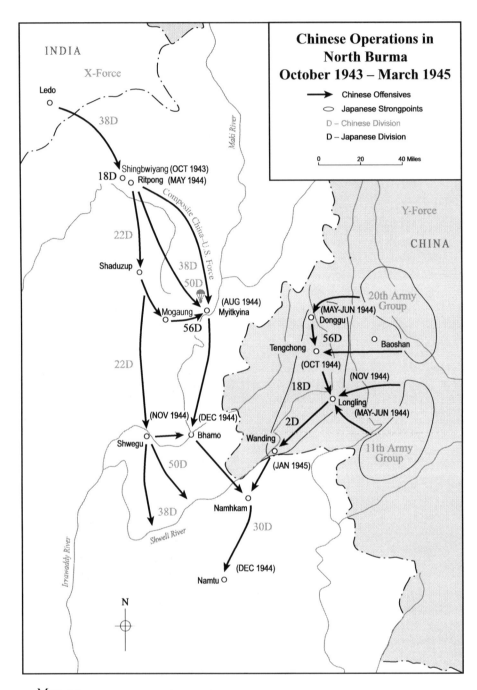

INDIA

X-Force

Ledo

Maki River

38D

Shingbwiyang (OCT 1943)
18D Ritpong (MAY 1944)

22D

Composite China–U.S. Force

Shaduzup

38D
50D

Mogaung (AUG 1944)
Myitkyina

56D

22D

Y-Force

CHINA

(MAY-JUN 1944)
Donggu

20th Army
Group

56D Baoshan

Tengchong

(OCT 1944)

(NOV 1944)

18D

Longling
(MAY-JUN 1944)

(NOV 1944) (DEC 1944)

Shwegu Bhamo

50D

2D

Wanding

11th Army
Group

(JAN 1945)

38D

Shweli River

Namhkam

30D

Irrawaddy River

N

Namtu (DEC 1944)

Chinese Operations in North Burma October 1943 – March 1945

➤ Chinese Offensives
⬭ Japanese Strongpoints
D – Chinese Division
D – Japanese Division

0   20   40 Miles

Map 14

1 An Overview of Major Military Campaigns during the Sino-Japanese War, 1937–1945

EDWARD J. DREA AND HANS VAN DE VEN

Following the Marco Polo Bridge Incident of 7 July 1937, neither the Chinese nor the Japanese high command anticipated the outbreak of a total war that would ultimately spread throughout China and beyond, and would last eight long years. The Japanese high command initially believed that they could contain the fighting while gaining Chinese acquiescence to their demands. The Chinese Nationalists, having decided not to give in to further Japanese demands curtailing their sovereignty in north China, also sought ways to avoid the spread of the fighting, fearful of the unpredictable consequences and devastation of a war against a superior enemy. Both armies had recently commenced programs of military reform and rearmament, the Japanese in 1936 and the Nationalists in 1934 after they had eliminated Communist bases from central and south China. Although these circumstances militated against a wider war with neither side willing to back down, clashes quickly escalated into multidivision engagements.

The Japanese army reinforced its China Garrison Army and soon mobilized reserves to bring three divisions to wartime strength. By the end of July, Chinese forces had been driven from Peking and Tianjin while the general staff in Tokyo had ordered more than 200,000 additional Japanese troops to north China. These developments convinced Generalissimo Chiang Kai-shek, leader of the Kuomintang Party (KMT) and commander in chief of the Central Army, that he had to fight Japan even though his forces were not fully prepared.

The Japanese hoped to wrap up the campaign quickly through the encirclement and destruction of Chinese field armies in north China, but they lacked an overarching military strategy. Japanese military operations in China evolved in an ad hoc fashion from campaign to campaign with little if any linkage toward a strategic military goal. It still remains difficult to assess the Chinese Nationalists' strategic thinking in 1937, which adjusted to meet actual wartime contingencies. In general, to resist Japan the Nationalists hoped to play on Japanese fears of a war with the Soviet Union that would drive Japan to seek a quick solution to any conflict in China. They were willing to trade space for time and fight a war of attrition, but they were also determined to seize the initiative when possible and force the Japanese to fight at times and places of China's choosing.[1]

Following the Marco Polo Bridge Incident, Chiang sent his German-armed and trained divisions of the Central Army north to back up local warlord forces, including those of Song Zheyuan, who faced the Japanese during the incident. Moreover, Chiang had long prepared for the opening of a second front at Shanghai and had also concentrated Nationalist forces between the two fronts around Xuzhou. There the Nationalists had fortified and prepared the battlefield to engage the Japanese, who would be operating at some distance from their supply bases in terrain that would reduce their advantages in mobility as well as naval and air power. Available Nationalist war plans make clear that withdrawal from the coast and retreat inland, even as far as Chongqing, had been contemplated for some time.

This does not mean that Chiang had correctly anticipated the course the fighting took during the first year of the war, nor does it mean that events went according to plan, let alone aspiration. Chiang was repeatedly disappointed with the performance of his armies. It was only when forces in north China crumbled in the face of the Japanese onslaught that he decided to escalate the war, apparently in the belief that the Japanese, concerned about the Soviet Union, would negotiate an agreement favorable to him rather than risk further escalation. But even if Chiang had prepared for a worst-case scenario, he lacked the strategy and military power to evict the Japanese armies from China. The Japanese were likewise without ideas and resources to make him surrender.

The Japanese axis of attack to secure north China followed the two parallel main rail lines—the Tianjin–Pukou route on the east and the Peking–Wuhan route on the west. The First Army drove south from Peking while the Second Army was to move south, then swing west to trap Chinese forces between the two armies north of the Huto River. To control and coordinate the operations of both armies in late August, Tokyo activated the North China Area Army (NCAA).

China's geography both helped and hindered Japanese plans. The theater eventually covered an area equivalent to the United States east of the Mississippi River. Placing Peking just north of Michigan's Upper Peninsula puts Shanghai at Washington, DC, and Guangzhou (Canton) at New Orleans. Wuhan would correspond to St. Louis and Chongqing would be in southwestern Kansas. The vastness of the Chinese countryside rendered a contiguous defensive line impossible, enabling Japanese units to sweep swiftly around or outflank Chinese strong points. Disunion, not just between the Nationalists and the Communists, but also between the Nationalists and various warlord armies in the north, south, and west of China, added to the difficulties of fighting effectively according to a unified military strategy. The Japanese, while often outmaneuvering their divided foes, never had sufficient manpower to seal their envelopments, and the Chinese repeatedly took advantage of gaps to escape encirclement. Thus, Japanese field commanders constantly pressured the army general staff and subsequently Imperial General Headquarters (IGHQ), established in November 1937, for authority to extend the area of operations ever deeper into China.

From the beginning, the conflict would be essentially a struggle between ground forces on the continent. This being so, except for a naval blockade of Chinese coastal cities and support for the Japanese army's landing operations, the principal contribution of the Japanese navy would have to come from its air units, both carrier- and land-based. Indeed, Japanese naval air power was to play a major, though not decisive, role in the first three years of the war.[2]

Responsibilities for operational theaters had been determined between the two services at the outset of the war: the army air force assigned to north China and the navy to central and south China. Since the Japanese army had few air units based in Manchuria or China proper at the outset of the war, with the outbreak of fighting in Shanghai Japanese naval aircraft operating from carriers stationed in the East China Sea and medium bombers flown from bases in western Japan, Taiwan, and the Kwantung Leased Territory effectively opened the air war in China. Their initial targets were Chinese coastal cities and air bases close to the coast. The navy's first long-range, transoceanic strikes by its twin-engined Mitsubishi G3M medium bombers flying from Kyushu and Taiwan took both China and the Western world by surprise. But Japanese inexperience in strategic bombing, faulty organization and tactics, the lack of fighter escort, and the incendiary vulnerability of these unarmored aircraft sustained losses out of proportion to the modest damage they initially inflicted on their targets.

As Japanese ground forces pushed southward, a third major offensive by units of the Kwantung Army and the North China Area Army's strategic reserve, the Fifth Division, occupied Chahar Province to the north and west of Peking. Operations at first went smoothly as Japanese mechanized forces and aircraft opened the way for mobile infantry columns moving along the Peking–Suiyuan Railroad. In mid-September, however, the Fifth Division suffered a tactical setback in the mountainous terrain at Pingxingguan, where China's Central Army forces and the Chinese Communist 115th Division bloodied the Japanese before being forced to withdraw.

Meanwhile, in mid-August, heavy fighting had erupted in Shanghai when Chiang opened a second front on 14 August, hoping to overwhelm

the Japanese units stationed near the city with a massive blow.[3] Nationalist forces split the Japanese naval infantry and penetrated to the Japanese
wharves along Shanghai's waterfront, but then their offensive stalled. The
subsequent major fighting in the Battle of Shanghai occurred north of the
city after Japan landed reinforcements and the Chinese occupied prepared
fortified positions. Both sides avoided combat in Shanghai itself because
the great powers had commercial, financial, and administrative interests in
the city, including the International Settlement and the French Concession.
Japan wanted to avoid a clash with the Western powers at this point, and
China could not afford to alienate those powers.[4]

Japan's general staff sent the Shanghai Expeditionary Force (two divisions) to the scene, and Chiang also poured in more reinforcements (eventually seventy divisions) for a showdown. Unable to dislodge the determined Chinese defenders and suffering severe losses, by mid-September
Tokyo dispatched three more divisions to Shanghai in hopes of achieving a
decisive victory. A combination of natural obstacles and military fortifications turned the Japanese offensive into a meat grinder as both sides fought
desperately to advance across a few hundred yards. During October the
Japanese lost about 25,000 men in their attacks against prepared Chinese
defenses, but Chiang's casualties were also severe. Both sides committed
reserves, but neither could break the cycle of attrition warfare. Chiang,
however, had successfully dragged Japan into a protracted battle of attrition at Shanghai to relieve pressure on his north China front.

In early October, the general staff in Tokyo ordered the NCAA to
destroy Chinese forces throughout Shanxi Province, from where they
could harass Japanese flanks and shield Nationalist and Communist bases
in northwestern China. The Japanese general staff also commandeered
two divisions from the NCAA for Shanghai service as it activated the
Tenth Army on 20 October for an amphibious envelopment southwest of
Shanghai, to be executed in early November. On 30 October, the staff
created the Central China Area Army to oversee the campaign. By early
November, repeated Japanese assaults had broken through China's last
line of defense along Suzhou Creek west of Shanghai, and Japanese forces
had landed south of the city, threatening a broad encirclement of Chiang's
forces at Shanghai. Chiang withdrew the remnants of his badly battered
armies. Total losses for the Shanghai fighting were astronomical, with
more than 40,000 Japanese and perhaps 200,000 Chinese casualties.

Although the fighting did not match the ferocity of the Shanghai combat, Japanese columns entering Shanxi from Hebei Province to assault the
provincial capital of Taiyuan met stiff resistance around Xinkou in battles
that raged from mid-October into November. Simultaneous attempts to
the east by the First and Second armies to envelop Chinese field armies
near Shijiazhuang on the Peking–Wuhan Railway were again forced to

withdraw, but they avoided encirclement, preserved their strength, and left the Japanese overextended with still more territory to occupy. The general staff in Tokyo had repeatedly attempted to limit such operations, but the field commanders insisted that bolder offensives were necessary to annihilate the Chinese armies. By late November, a substantial part of China north of the Yellow River was in Japanese hands, but KMT forces had neither capitulated nor disintegrated. Something else was needed.

Tenth Army's solution was to seize the KMT capital at Nanjing in expectation that this would force Chiang to negotiate. The 170-mile march upriver from Shanghai to Nanjing began in mid-November and moved rapidly as Japanese forces either outflanked or bypassed Chinese troops holding high ground or relied on superior air, naval, armor, and artillery firepower to batter isolated and retreating units and open the way for the fast-moving infantry. The lightning campaign convinced IGHQ that the capture of Nanjing would cause the KMT to crumble, and it gave its approval ex post facto for the attack on the capital. By 10 December Japanese forces were at the walls of Nanjing.

The Nationalists realized that they could not hold Nanjing, but as a symbolic action Chiang ordered his forces to defend to the death the city that was China's capital and the place where the grave of Sun Yat-sen, the Father of the Country, was located. For domestic and international reasons, Chiang needed to demonstrate that he still had the will to resist Japan and that this resistance had national support. One of his erstwhile enemies, General Tang Shengzhi, was willing to take command of the doomed Nanjing garrison, suggesting that past differences were forgotten when the survival of the nation was at stake. Unfortunately, the Central Army's planned staged withdrawal from Shanghai disintegrated when discipline broke down, leaving the defense of Nanjing dependent on unruly warlord troops or raw recruits. Fighting continued in the city for the next three days as Chiang repeatedly changed his mind about the defense of the capital, which was not formally surrendered, and the indecisiveness added to the chaos that overtook the city.[5] Finally, the Chinese defenders retreated in confusion. Japanese troops then perpetrated one of the most horrendous war crimes of the twentieth century: the mass slaughter of Chinese civilians and surrendered Chinese military personnel.[6]

By the end of 1937, Japan had seized the Peking–Tianjin corridor, Shanxi, the lower Yangtze region, and sections of the main railroad lines through these territories. Furthermore, improvements in bombing tactics and formations and the capture of inland air bases, along with the addition of fighter escorts, eliminated most of the defects in Japan's early air campaign by the autumn of 1937 and allowed the air forces to take the fight to the enemy. Taking advantage of these innovations, the navy's air campaign focused on three missions: interdiction of China's communication and supply routes, support of the army's ground operations through the destruction of enemy bases and military units, and terror bombing of China's cities and civilian populations to force the Nationalist regime to capitulate, or at least bring it to the bargaining table. In cooperation with army air units, the first two of these missions were carried out by Japanese naval air forces with relative effectiveness. Land-based bombers from both services relentlessly attacked the road and rail communications in north China that were the avenues for desperately needed Soviet aid. Navy carrier aircraft repeatedly bombed Chinese coastal shipping and road and rail traffic in the southern China interior as well as along the coast.

Despite Japanese conquests, the terror at Nanjing, and the sustained bombing offensive, the Chinese did not submit. The KMT made Wuhan on the Yangtze River in central China its new center of national resistance. The Central Army adopted Fabian tactics as it withdrew deeper into the vast hinterland beyond the immediate reach of Japanese military might and continued the fight. Contrary to the Japanese army's expectations, the fall of Nanjing had not brought an end to the China war. Instead, the news of widespread Japanese atrocities seemingly hardened Chinese resistance.

After reaching an agreement with General Li Zongren, the leader of the Guangxi Clique, whose forces ranked second only to those of the Central Army, Chiang appointed him commander in chief of the Fifth War Zone headquartered at Xuzhou. As the fighting raged at Shanghai and elsewhere, large numbers of troops were concentrated under Li's command. The hope was to use the Tianjin–Pukou, Peking–Wuhan, and Longhai railways to supply Fifth War Zone forces as they maneuvered to frustrate Japanese efforts to link up their scattered armies in north China and the lower Yangtze. The Xuzhou area was a good location for the Chinese to make a stand. It was beyond the range of Japan's naval and air units, Japan's field armies would be at the end of their supply lines, and major rivers and large lakes near the city would hamper Japanese mobility. Thus, the Chinese had set the scene for what would become the decisive battle of the first phase of the Sino-Japanese War.[7]

As for the Japanese, by the end of 1937 the equivalent of Japan's peacetime army establishment of sixteen divisions and 600,000 men was committed to China operations, which had no end in sight.[8] Moreover, imperial army forces in central China were exhausted: they had been worn down by heavy casualties, insufficient ammunition stocks, and inadequate logistic support. IGHQ stood down major operations in central China in order to reconstitute its forces, refit them, and restore discipline. It also sought time to mobilize ten new divisions in the home islands by mid-1938 and to convert essential industries to a wartime production schedule. But as the fighting expanded and the casualty lists lengthened, the Japanese home front's expectations of the rewards of the war grew accordingly.[9]

Japanese forces under the command of the North China Area Army, however, pushed for continuing operations. With their forces relatively intact after six months of campaigning, aggressive field commanders demanded greater latitude in conducting offensive operations southward. The NCAA's Second Army launched its offensive from Shandong Province in March 1938, intending to clear the area north of the Yellow River in anticipation of future operations against Xuzhou or Wuhan. Two widely separated Japanese columns moved from the north and the east against Taierzhuang, on a spur of the Tianjin–Pukou railways and transportation hub on the Grand Canal. Both pincers encountered sharp Chinese resistance when they ran headlong into crack KMT troops of Twentieth and Second army groups. Although Japanese Fifth Division units temporarily occupied a portion of Taierzhuang, they soon found themselves threatened with encirclement and withdrew. Thereafter, in two weeks of close combat between 24 March and 7 April, the Japanese Fifth and Tenth divisions lost several thousand men breaking out of the encirclement. Reinforcements later returned to drive the seriously weakened Chinese forces into retreat. The Japanese setback was celebrated across China as a major victory and greatly enhanced Chinese morale. It was also of great political significance because it coincided with major national and KMT conferences being held in Wuhan to rally the country. For the Japanese, these Chinese claims of victory and heavy Japanese losses further reduced the chances for scaling down field operations.[10]

On 7 April, just as the fighting at Taierzhuang was drawing to a close, IGHQ ordered a massive encirclement campaign to destroy the Kuomintang's field armies. Conducted from the north by the NCAA and from the south by the Central China Expeditionary Army (CCEA), activated 14 February 1938, the operation involved seven Japanese divisions (200,000 troops).[11] Their north-south envelopment would close at Xuzhou and trap at least fifty KMT divisions. Although the two-month operation during April and May captured Xuzhou, once again the Japanese were unable to trap the Chinese armies, most of which escaped the encirclement with their formations and equipment under cover of a heavy fog and mist that blanketed the area. During the campaign, Japanese field logistics became dangerously overextended, and frontline units suffered from insufficient munitions and rations.

Having failed to achieve a settlement by seizing the KMT capital and being unable to eliminate the KMT's main armies, the Japanese army switched strategies, forgoing a decisive engagement in exchange for occupying strategic points. This time, the objective was Wuhan, which was an administrative center, a staging and logistic base for Chinese forces defending the central Yangtze region, and a rallying point for the defense of China in the summer of 1938.

By mid-May, Japanese forces crossed the Yellow River and then turned westward along the Longhai Railway toward its junction with the north–south Peking–Wuhan rail line at Zhengzhou. Control of Zhengzhou would secure rail transportation for an offensive against Wuhan. In early June, as China's forces withdrew from Xuzhou and the Japanese threatened a rapid assault on Wuhan, Chiang ordered the breaching of the Yellow River dikes at Huayuankou (in Henan Province) to check the enemy's westward offensive.[12] Massive flooding isolated parts of two Japanese divisions and halted their thrust about sixty miles east of Zhengzhou. Chiang's actions stopped an immediate attack on Wuhan and allowed Chinese troops to retreat and regroup. But the Japanese did not abandon their plans to take Wuhan. They waited until summer when the Yangtze River's high water levels enabled the Japanese navy to support Japanese infantry pushing west along both banks of the great river. Time and again, naval gunboats would thrust ahead, attack Chinese fortifications from the rear, and clear a path for the advance.

Tragically, almost 900,000 Chinese civilians perished in three badly flooded provinces and another 3.9 million became refugees.[13] Moreover, as the Japanese drove scattered Central Army troops out of the region and flooding disrupted enormous swaths of territory, local control and authority collapsed.

Approach operations east of Wuhan along both banks of the Yangtze River and in the mountains to the north during July and August pushed back Chinese defenses, beginning a campaign that eventually involved 300,000 Japanese and 1 million Chinese troops. Poor roads and rugged mountainous terrain bedeviled Japanese logistics, which collapsed under the strain of overextended lines of communication. Operating along the banks of the Yangtze in stifling midsummer heat, both sides were exposed to epidemic malaria and amoebic dysentery. Thirsty soldiers drank any available water, and an outbreak of cholera ravaged Eleventh Army as its ill-supplied units fought and maneuvered in central China's summer heat.

Chiang was certain the Japanese could be stopped and Wuhan held. He threw many of his best remaining units into the protracted fighting. To break especially strong Chinese resistance, Japanese troops selectively used poison gas, euphemistically known as "special smoke."[14] Aside from the hardships of the campaign, IGHQ was disquieted by the outbreak of regimental-size fighting in July and early August between Japanese and Soviet forces at Changkuofeng (Zhanggufeng) on the Korean-Soviet border. Uncertain whether the Soviets intended to enter the war in China or were merely probing Japan's defenses, army leaders placed the Wuhan operation on hold until they resolved the border dispute in mid-August.

Finally, on 22 August, IGHQ ordered Eleventh Army to seize Wuhan in conjunction with Twenty-first Army's amphibious offensive directed against Guangzhou. Capture of these strategic locations would deny the KMT its military and administrative base in central China and a major port and supply base in southern China. These losses and sealing the coast would, the Japanese hoped, cause the Chinese to lose their will to fight. Guangzhou fell to the Japanese on 21 October, followed by Wuhan five days later, the culmination of a ten-month campaign that cost Chiang his best officers and seriously weakened the Central Army forces.[15] To avoid a repetition of the Nanjing massacres, Chiang ordered a general withdrawal before the Japanese reached the city, and relocated his capital at faraway Chongqing in the remote interior of Sichuan Province.

After the fall of Wuhan, the Nationalists also reoriented their military strategy. The first year of warfare had illustrated the futility and costliness of large-scale, set-piece battles, which thereafter the Chinese avoided. Believing the Japanese would not risk a major confrontation with the European powers or the United States, they estimated that the Japanese would not conduct extensive operations in south China. The Nationalists made Sichuan Province, densely populated, agriculturally self-sufficient, and well shielded by mountains, into their base of resistance. Simultaneously, the Nationalists tried to take advantage of Soviet-Japanese tensions in north China by extending the conflict northward. They established war zones across China to protect vital lines of communication to the Soviet Union as well as to the southern coast, French Indochina, and Burma; to defend important strategic or supply bases; and to cut off Japanese routes of advance in northwest or central China. These war zones presented a multiplicity of threats that forced the Japanese to disperse their forces across China's vastness, leaving them unable to concentrate for a single decisive blow. The strategy also allowed the Nationalists to harass the enemy and prevent him from consolidating occupied areas. As part of this plan, the Nationalists created guerrilla zones in the Japanese-occupied rear areas of north China. Finally, the Nationalists reduced their operational field forces by one-third and instituted an intensive retraining program, to reconstitute their armies for a long war.[16]

As for the Japanese, after the Wuhan battles they had reached the limits of their offensive potential and lost the flexibility to conduct large-scale operations.[17] They were also concerned about the imminent possibility of facing far more powerful forces along the Soviet-Manchurian border. After the fall of Wuhan, the Japanese aimed at bottling up the Nationalists in Sichuan and rendering them irrelevant. They would consolidate their grip on the occupied areas and gradually reduce their force structure in China from 800,00 to 400,000 troops. Great effort went into promoting collaborator regimes to serve as alternatives to Chiang Kai-shek.

In March 1939, IGHQ directed the capture of Nanchang in Jiangxi Province, which Japanese forces had earlier bypassed. Located along Lake

Poyang, Nanchang was a major transshipment point for supplies bound for war zones in central and south China as well as the new capital at Chongqing. The Eleventh Army opened its offensive on 20 March and a week later was in Nanchang. Fierce Chinese counterattacks to retake the city continued over the next two months, but without success. In May, Chinese troops from the Fifth War Area under General Li Zongren moved into mountainous north of Hubei Province to establish bases and threaten the Peking–Wuhan rail line. This touched off Japanese preemptive operations that were more typical of this period, designed to disrupt concentrations of KMT armies by rapid envelopments followed by equally quick withdrawals. Just as these operations commenced, however, large-scale fighting again erupted between Japanese and Soviet forces, this time at Nomonhan, a tiny village on the ill-defined Manchuria–Outer Mongolia border. These multidivision battles involving armor and aircraft raged from May through early September, forcing IGHQ to suspend major ground activity in China.

With the land war stalled, the Tokyo high command turned to the skies, concluding that the only way to force the Nationalist regime at Chongqing to surrender was by subjecting the Chinese civilian population, particularly those in the wartime capital, to hardship and terror through aerial bombardment. Once again, the navy's air arm was to be the main instrument of such a campaign. In September 1939, the navy, in cooperation with the army air service, launched Operation 100, the first of a series of long-range air strikes against Chinese bases in northern China.

The Nazi-Soviet nonaggression pact signed in late August and the subsequent German invasion of Poland on 1 September 1939 convinced Japan's field armies that the dramatic change in the international situation offered Tokyo a window of opportunity to resolve the China Incident by force of arms. IGHQ directives for limited operations to secure the occupied zones greatly dissatisfied field commanders. Thus, Eleventh Army commander Lieutenant General Okamura Yasuji's objective during the September–October offensive was to encircle and destroy about thirty Chinese divisions between the Yangtze River and Changsha. Lacking sufficient troops to seal the encirclement, Eleventh Army still inflicted great damage on KMT forces but could not cut off their retreat. A Chinese counteroffensive forced three Japanese divisions to withdraw from the area by early October. Once again the war drifted into stalemate. By November 1939, Okamura saw no way to accomplish IGHQ goals outside of offensive operations.[18]

In mid-December, however, Chiang stunned the Japanese with a nationwide winter offensive employing seventy divisions. Heartened by Japanese defeats at Nomonhan and Changsha, in the fall of 1939 the Nationalists had developed a plan for war zones along the Yangtze, the north China railroads, and near Guangzhou to harass Japanese lines of communication and isolate Japanese units at Wuhan.[19] Even if the winter offensive came as a shock to the Japanese, it nonetheless never developed into the major action its designers hoped. Tensions between the Communists and the Nationalists had escalated in the fall of 1939 while Shanxi warlord Yan Xishan reached an accommodation with Japan.

Japanese divisions subordinate to the Eleventh Army were widely dispersed on 80- to 120-mile frontages that lacked defenses constructed in any depth. Regrouping the widely separated small units into larger echelons for counterattacks was difficult because Chinese forces destroyed railroads and bridges that the Japanese road-bound army depended on for its mobility. Moreover, the imperial army was configured for offensive operations, disdained defense preparations, and suffered correspondingly high casualties. Without a strategic reserve, the Japanese found themselves hard pressed, but logistic and command difficulties hampered the KMT's ability to exploit its initial successes.

By mid-January 1940, the high command had regrouped Japanese armies and struck back at KMT forces. Chiang, besides having to send his one mobile division to assist in the defense of Nanning, also had to divert reinforcements to relieve pressure by advancing Japanese southwest of Hangzhou. In addition, the Japanese invasion of Guangxi Province in south China, which threatened Sichuan from the south, caught the Nationalists by surprise. The winter offensive turned into a hard-fought series of battles between Chinese and Japanese troops in south China, rather than a Chinese counteroffensive along the Yangtze and in north China. By mid-February, Chiang's offensive had collapsed, with heavy losses of men and material. Japanese counterattacks drove the Chinese back to their base areas and restored the original zones of control. If nothing else, however, the offensive convinced the Japanese high command that the enemy was still full of fight.[20] Demonstrating this at one of the most critical times of the war was perhaps Chiang's principal objective in launching the winter offensive.

Meanwhile, from late 1938 into 1940 the Japanese army in north China had undertaken a series of pacification and counterguerrilla sweeps. Tokyo needed to secure rear areas in China to prop up Wang Jingwei's puppet regime, established on 30 March 1940 in Nanjing,[21] and thus emphasized control of the occupied areas over continuing offensives.[22] In early 1940, the NCAA announced its plan to make the region a model of enforcement of local order for all of China, mainly through a series of suppression campaigns throughout Shanxi Province. To isolate Chinese Communist guerrilla units and other anti-Japanese formations, the Japanese constructed a series of strong points along major roads and railroads. Many were manned by puppet troops while Japanese garrison divisions conducted sweeps in the more dangerous areas. This "point and line" strategy was effective against traditional hit-and-run guerrilla tactics.

Less successfully, the naval air force continued its attacks against Chongqing and nearby bases by launching Operation 101. The lack of Japanese fighter escort initially enabled Chinese interceptors to shoot down large numbers of Japanese bombers. Only in the late summer of 1940 did the appearance of the superb Mitsubishi A6M "Zero" fighter completely change the tactical situation in the skies over Chinese cities. First-line Japanese naval pilots swept Chinese aircraft from the sky, but to no lasting advantage. Even though, by the end of Operation 101, Japanese bombers had dropped 2,000 tons of bombs on Chongqing, reducing the city to rubble, killing thousands of civilians, and forcing the government and civilian population to burrow into the limestone hillsides to survive, the campaign accomplished little else. Certainly, the Nationalist government had given no sign of willingness to surrender or even negotiate. It was a sign of the bankruptcy of Japanese strategy against China that the Japanese air forces could think of nothing else than to undertake Operation 102, simply another round of the bomber offensive against Chongqing. It too failed to achieve anything more than further destruction.

The failure of strategic Japanese air operations in China to bring about victory or even to create a significant operational advantage for Japan prefigured the problems faced by all strategic bombing campaigns in World War II. Western military establishments, however, wrote off the Japanese experience in China because of Eurocentrism in Western thinking, a vested professional interest in validating strategic bombing doctrine, and the conflicting and inflated intelligence reports coming from the China theater.

On 1 May 1940, the Japanese Eleventh Army commenced the Yichang operation, an attempt to dislodge Fifth War Zone forces in north and central Hubei Province, break open the doorway to Chongqing, and secure an operational air base to stage raids against the KMT capital. IGHQ, however, refused to authorize any reinforcements and only approved the plan contingent upon a two-month operation against Yichang, after which the units would return to their original locations.[23] A combination of heavy artillery, tank regiments, and extensive air power support pushed aside Chinese resistance, and by 12 June Yichang had fallen. Five days later, as ordered, Japanese troops were marching out of the city to return to their bases. During this interval, the German triumph in the West caused IGHQ to change its thinking. The fall of France and the Low Countries, together with the anticipated collapse of Great Britain, isolated China from Western support and offered the Japanese army fresh hope to settle the China war. IGHQ ordered the troops to turn around, retake Yichang, and develop it into a major air base to conduct intensified strategic bombing of Chinese cities to break the will to resist. Yichang could also serve as a springboard for movement south and could restore the freedom of maneuver the field commanders sought. A further expression of Japanese inclinations to use force to end the China fighting appeared in September 1940 when the army occupied northern French Indochina in an attempt to seal Chinese borders from outside sources of resupply. Later that month, Tokyo signed a nonaggression pact with Berlin and Rome, placing itself squarely in the Axis camp.

Earlier, in the summer of 1939, the Japanese general staff and war ministry had proposed major reductions to troop strength in China, from 850,000 to 400,000 by 1941. The China Expeditionary Army objected strenuously and finally agreed to reduce its forces to 750,000 by the end of 1939. In March 1940, however, the staff and ministry concluded that if Japan could not defeat China militarily during 1940, it had to make the CEA self-sufficient in order to rearm, modernize, and prepare the army for the anticipated war with the Soviet Union. The only means to accomplish this was through troop withdrawals to begin in 1941 and a corresponding reduction of occupied territory. By 1943, the Japanese would occupy the Shanghai delta and a triangular area in north China. Although some withdrawals occurred, the projected levels were never remotely achieved, and in January 1941 a revised plan called for the reduction of fewer troops over a longer period.[24]

China, however, refused to go away. In a dramatic shift from guerrilla to conventional warfare, Chinese Communist forces in north China launched the Hundred Regiments Offensive in August 1940. Designed to sever Japanese road and rail communications, inflict casualties, and destroy Japanese-controlled factories and mines, the wide-ranging, well-coordinated attacks caught the Japanese and their puppet troops by complete surprise. By mid-September the Japanese had regained their footing and slugged it out with Chinese Communist forces in set-piece battles where superior Japanese firepower and equipment turned the tide. By November, the Communists were in retreat, and the Japanese in murderous pursuit.[25] The scope of intensity of the Communist offensive occasioned a rethinking of counterinsurgency policy in the Japanese army.

In north China during midsummer 1941, General Okamura, now commanding the North China Area Army, moved from a passive strategy of blockade to an active and comprehensive counterguerrilla strategy based on terror, forced relocation, and plunder. The Chinese nicknamed it the "Three-All Policy," "kill all, burn all, loot all," an accurate description of the hundreds of small punitive campaigns that brought destruction and misery to north China well into 1943. Between late January 1941 and March 1945, the NCAA launched at least thirty suppression campaigns of multidivision scale that lasted from a few weeks to three or four months in an effort to stamp out Communist guerrillas, disrupt KMT forces, and secure occupied north China.[26]

IGHQ also sought to cut off all supply lines to Chongqing. In July 1940, under Japanese pressure, Britain agreed to close the Burma Road,

China's overland southern line of communication to the outside world. In mid-September, Japanese forces moved into northern French Indochina to close the Hanoi–Yunnan Railroad. In January 1941, Tokyo mobilized four infantry divisions, one air division, and the Second Expeditionary Fleet to strike major ports from Fujian (opposite Taiwan) to Guangzhou during the first half of the year. In February and March alone, Japanese units executed eight separate regimental-size amphibious assaults against ports all along the Guangzhou–Hong Kong coastline as they tried to disrupt coastal traffic and cut overland supply routes for Chiang's armies.

In keeping with its designs for troop withdrawals and stabilization of the occupied zones, IGHQ tried to tamp down major operations after January 1941. Henceforth, the Japanese navy used a naval blockade and aerial bombing of China's cities to break the Chinese will to resist. Chongqing, Kunming, and other major cities were subjected to relentless bombing campaigns that drove their populations into underground shelters and wrecked Nationalist efforts to construct an industrial base and arms industry. By the summer of 1941, with its strategic focus shifting to preparations for a Pacific war, the navy began withdrawing its bomber force from China, giving respite to Chongqing and other cities.

Tokyo also sanctioned limited but bloody ground campaigns. Without sufficient manpower, however, the Japanese punitive campaigns could not hope to achieve much more than preempting Chinese plans and disrupting their troop concentrations. Attempts to destroy Thirty-first Army Group in late January and early February 1941 along the Peking–Wuhan rail line failed when the Chinese traded space for lives. Indecisive campaigns from mid-March to early April against Jiujiang, south of the Yangtze, produced heavy Japanese casualties with no substantive gains.

The Nakahara operation of May–June 1941, for example, involved six divisions and two independent mixed brigades enveloping twenty-six KMT divisions in the rugged mountains west of the Shandong Peninsula between the Yellow River and the Grand Canal. Five weeks of fighting left 42,000 Chinese dead and 35,000 captured at a price of about 3,000 Japanese killed and wounded. The Japanese then withdrew, gaining only an ephemeral tactical success.

These large-scale raids might temporarily scatter Chinese defenders, but once the Japanese departed, as they always did, Chinese forces moved back into the area. Terrain worked in favor of the Chinese as the absence of roads and railroads impeded Japanese progress and stymied logistic support. Major Chinese forces usually concentrated behind natural obstacles like major rivers or mountains, making the Japanese come to them and withdrawing if the odds were too unfavorable. Japanese troops repeatedly reconquered the same places only to withdraw after a few days, knowing that they would soon be back.

This pattern of warfare characterized the major campaigns of 1941. On 25 January Japanese forces opened operations to clear the southern section of the Peking–Hankou Railroad. Chinese forces in the Fifth War Zone gradually withdrew until the Japanese outran their supply lines. Then the Chinese counterattacked the ill-supplied Japanese, cut off their rear and attacked simultaneously from the flanks, and forced the Japanese to fight their way out of the encirclement back to their original positions. In mid-March, another Japanese offensive aimed at Shanggao in Jiangxi Province, where a major base in the Ninth War Zone under General Luo Zhuoying threatened the Yangtze River route and blocked Japanese approaches from the east toward Changsha. Although Japanese forces broke through three defensive lines and entered Shanggao, they too became surrounded, and relief forces from Wuhan had to extricate them. Once again, the Japanese retreated with severe losses.[27] A later campaign did seize the Zhongtiao Mountains in southern Shanxi commanded by General Wei Lihuang of the First War Zone. This was a major shock for the Nationalists because the region blocked communications between Yan'an and Communist bases elsewhere and denied the Nationalists a base from which to pressure the Shanxi warlord Yan Xishan.

In April 1941, the new commander of Eleventh Army, Lieutenant General Anami Korechika, decided these back-and-forth forays were counterproductive and recommended a major campaign against Changsha to destroy the 300,000-strong KMT armies and to seize China's granary. Anami believed that these twin blows would end the war once and for all, but the Nazi invasion of the Soviet Union on 22 June 1941 caused IGHQ to shelve Anami's proposal until the Japanese government made its momentous decision in July 1941 not to attack the Soviets but to move south against the Asian colonial possessions of the Netherlands, Great Britain, and the United States. In the same month, Japanese troops occupied southern French Indochina, both to exert more pressure on Chongqing to surrender and to acquire advance air and staging bases for future southern operations. In late August, IGHQ gave Anami the go-ahead to attack Changsha.

On 18 September, Anami sent four divisions southward against Changsha. Backed by artillery, armor, and air power, they took the city ten days later but withdrew afterward to their original positions. In early October, General Chen Cheng launched a Chinese counteroffensive against Yichang that threatened Anami's western flank. Chen siphoned troops from the Changsha operations to relieve the surrounded and badly outnumbered Thirteenth Division that had defended the beleaguered city for ten days. A second Changsha offensive by the Japanese, kicked off on 24 December, entered the city a week later only to meet fierce counterattacks from the Chinese Tenth Army Group, whose forces surrounded two Japanese divisions in early January 1942. Outnumbered and outmaneuvered, the

Japanese finally retreated northward by mid-January. The campaign left Japan no closer to a military solution to the China fighting than it had been in July 1937.[28]

Anami, however, was not the type of commander to give up. In September 1941, Eleventh Army proposed to IGHQ the capture of Chongqing, an operation of unquestioned boldness but limited practicality. The KMT capital was about 270 miles upriver from the westernmost Japanese outpost on the Yangtze and sheltered by narrow gorges and mountains that made any attack a daunting prospect. Those difficulties did not deter the planners, who set to work on a scheme to take the Chinese capital.

At a cabinet meeting on 14 October 1941 War Minister General Tōjō Hideki emotionally rejected U.S. demands that Japan withdraw its troops from China, citing the domino effect it would have on the security of Manchukuo and Korea. He invoked the spirits of Japan's war dead to reject what he termed the diplomacy of surrender.[29] Four days later, Prime Minister Konoe Fumimaro's third cabinet collapsed, and Tōjō became the new prime minister. By that time, four and one-half years of constant warfare had cost Japan more than 180,000 dead (including 48,344 who died of sickness) and over 323,700 wounded (including 36,470 permanently disabled).[30] Nevertheless, Japan opted to expand the war into Southeast Asia and the Pacific rather than forsake its China policy.

Japan's attack on the U.S. fleet in Hawaii on 7 December 1941, and its invasion of Malaya the same day, opened the Pacific phase of the Asia-Pacific war. Japanese units in southern China quickly overran the British colony of Hong Kong in December, conquered Malaya by 15 February 1942, and invaded Burma in March. Despite initial, and for China deeply humiliating, British objections, Chiang sent Chinese troops, including his only mechanized division, to assist in Burma, partly in order to fight alongside his new allies and also to defend China's one remaining connection with the outside world.[31] They, along with their new British and American allies, were routed. The defeat resulted mainly from insufficient air and naval power and from an ill-equipped infantry. Trucks and tanks left the Allied armies dependent on roads while the lightly armed Japanese troops took to the jungle, quickly outflanking and enveloping the defenders. Profound disagreements over strategy, including whether to defend Mandalay in northern Burma or counterattack toward Rangoon, did lasting harm to Allied relations.

The aerial attack on Tokyo and several other Japanese cities led by Lieutenant Colonel James Doolittle's U.S. carrier-based medium bombers in mid-April 1942 lifted U.S. morale but had a dramatically different effect on China. To prevent future air raids on the homeland, IGHQ ordered the occupation of airfields in eastern China's Zhejiang and Jiangxi provinces that lay within striking range of Japan. The Thirteenth Army in Shanghai commanded five divisions and three independent mixed brigades. These struck southwestward and, by mid-May, had pushed out from Hangzhou to link up with two divisions from the Eleventh Army at Nanchang. By September, the Japanese had destroyed Chinese air bases, some recently constructed, and laid waste to surrounding areas while clearing the 180-mile-long Hangzhou–Nanchang rail corridor.[32] A neglect of logistic planning marred the operation. Shortages of food, ammunition, and transportation left hungry Japanese soldiers mired in the mud during the heaviest rainy season in sixty years. Sickness, especially from malnutrition, accounted for three times the number of the 4,000 battle casualties. Thereafter, the Eleventh Army at Nanchang became responsible for securing the vast area running along the north and south banks of the Yangtze River.

In north China, the NCAA tried to work out a regional truce, offering warlords weapons and money for their puppet regimes in an effort to link them to the Wang Jingwei government. The initiative failed because of the demands of the Pacific theater on Japan's resources.[33] In central China, planning for the Chongqing operation to deliver the knockout punch to Chinese field armies and destroy the enemy's logistic base areas gained momentum in the spring and summer of 1942 while Japan was near her military apex. By the spring of 1942, the army had assembled sixteen divisions for a five-month campaign to seize Chongqing. In September, the general staff ordered CEA to complete preparations for its offensive, but the U.S. landing on Guadalcanal in August and subsequent fighting in the Solomon Islands forced Anami to abandon the Chongqing plan because Tokyo needed reinforcements for the new theater. By 1943, IGHQ was routinely transferring first-line divisions to shore up hard-pressed Japanese forces in the Pacific and southwest Asia theaters. To replace these units, the army upgraded brigades to division status, although they lacked mobility and artillery support. These ersatz divisions took responsibility for securing occupied zones while the remaining first- and second-line divisions conducted limited campaigns during February, May, and November of 1943.

From mid-February to the end of March 1943, the Eleventh Army, using Japanese and Chinese troops loyal to Wang Jingwei, launched a clearing operation against the Communist New Fourth Army and the weakened KMT Twenty-fourth Army Group on the mountainous plateau along the northern Hebei-Shanxi border. At the cost of a few hundred Japanese dead, counterguerrilla operations killed or detained more than 30,000 Chinese and drove KMT forces south of the Yellow River. The Eleventh Army followed up with a three-division campaign in Henan Province during May and June in western Hubei. Aligning six divisions along a broad 120-mile front running north from Yichang along the Yangtze River to Lake Dongting, the Japanese advanced in converging columns and penetrated to a depth of one hundred miles into the Sixth War Zone. The Chinese held the northern shoulder of the Japanese salient at the Shipai fortress, but the overall fighting from early May to mid-June inflicted heavy losses on understrength and poorly equipped KMT forces.

The final major operation of 1943 against Changde was the most ambitious, involving six Japanese divisions between early November and mid-December. Four Japanese divisions crossed the Yellow River between Shashi and Lake Dongting and pushed sixty miles west in four columns on an eighty-mile front that converged on the city. Two more divisions attacked from the north, crossing the Li River and advancing through mountainous terrain before swinging south on Changde. The newly established Chinese-American Composite Wing and U.S. Army Air Force units delivered effective air support that forced the Japanese to move and assemble only at night.

Since 1942, the Japanese Army Air Force had taken up the responsibility for air operations on the continent. With the appearance of American air power in China, those operations became largely defensive. But the army air arm responded in mid-December 1943 to the Allied air threat by bombing Chinese airfields along the Xiang River south of Changsha and air bases in southwestern China. Neither Japanese ground nor air efforts, however, could redeem the situation. Chinese forces recaptured Changde on 9 December as reinforcements converged on the city. Despite severe losses, and more than 40,000 Chinese killed or captured, by late December KMT forces had restored their original front lines, ejected the Japanese, and inflicted proportionately high casualties on the enemy, killing 1,274 Japanese in the fighting.

The commonality of the 1943 operations was that the Japanese conducted their offensives along wide frontages, employing converging columns to seize their objectives. In north China, their intent was to wreak as much havoc as possible with military and civilian affairs. Unable to garrison more conquered territory, they invariably withdrew, and the Chinese Communist or central government troops slowly reclaimed the devastated region. At Changde, the objective was to capture the administrative and economic center to disrupt the lines of communication to Chongqing. Unable to occupy Changde for any length of time, the Japanese operation was a failure.

In 1944, U.S.-trained and equipped Chinese divisions in Burma—designated the X-Force—and smaller American units tried to reopen the Burma Road leading into China as part of a general, albeit limited, Allied counteroffensive in north Burma. Chinese success in the Hukawng Valley pushed the Japanese back, and the combined forces reached Myitkyina in mid-May. Although this victory caused the Japanese Thirty-third Army to abandon north Burma, a stubborn Japanese garrison at Myitkyina held out until early August against three Chinese divisions, giving the Japanese time to prepare another defensive line farther south. At the same time, a desperate but bold Japanese campaign had encircled units of the British Fourteenth Army at Imphal and Kohima along the India-Burma border, threatening the Allied supply line in Assam, including that of X-Force. Meanwhile, in early May, Chinese Twentieth Army Group (sixteen divisions) in Yunnan—known as the Y-Force—crossed the Salween River on a broad front about a hundred miles east of Myitkyina in an attempt to open the Burma route from the northeast by ejecting the Japanese Fifty-sixth Division from Longling and ultimately linking up with X-Force at Bhamo, Burma.

On 1 June, Eleventh Army Group joined the fighting on the southern flank that was threatening to isolate the Japanese mountain strongholds. Because the Japanese still held Myitkyina, Chiang could not reinforce Y-Force, and Japanese counterattacks against Chinese river-crossing points, use of the jungle-covered mountain ranges to slow the Chinese drive, the onset of the monsoon season, and a successful Japanese counter-stroke against the southern Chinese pincer, halted the Chinese advance in late June. Further counterattacks to drive the Chinese west of the Salween ended in failure in mid-September. By this time, the catastrophic defeat of the Japanese Fifteenth Army along the Burma-India border relegated the Japanese Thirty-third Army to the strategic defensive. Simultaneously, the growing Chinese awareness of the scope of the Ichigō campaign diverted their attention from north Burma.

The Ichigō offensive undertaken by the Japanese China Expeditionary Army along the Peking–Wuhan, Wuhan–Guangzhou, and Hunan–Guangxi railways between mid-April 1944 and early February 1945 was the largest military operation in the history of the Japanese army, using approximately 500,000 troops (twenty divisions), about 80 percent of the China Expeditionary Army's 620,000 troops. Its objectives were to destroy American air bases in China, which threatened the Japanese mainland with air raids, and open an overland route from Pusan, Korea, to French Indochina. Beginning around April 1944 replacements for Ichigō were brought from Korea and Manchuria to the Wuhan sector. Many units had no equipment and only one weapon for several soldiers. Individual items, such as bamboo canteens, were substandard. Soldiers were ordered to arm themselves with discarded enemy weapons.[34]

The first phase of Ichigō (mid-April to late May 1944) witnessed the North China Area Army moving south to clear the southern portion of the Peking–Wuhan Railway and occupy Loyang. The CEA's Eleventh Army simultaneously advanced north along the rail line to link up with NCAA forces to secure the critical line of communication. The Chinese Central Army was slow to react to these opening gambits, being uncertain of Japanese ambitions. Furthermore, the Henan famine had severely degraded its forces, and the starving local population had turned hostile toward the Nationalist army.[35] Japanese aims, which became clear during the second phase (May to December 1944), consisted of massive sequenced offensives as the Eleventh Army captured Changsha and Hengyang (which was desperately defended), combined with the Twenty-third Army to capture American airbases at Guilin, Liuzhou, and Nanning. Chiang's forces, being dispersed over broad frontages, were poorly positioned to concentrate against the attackers. The Japanese Twenty-first Army then moved from northern Indochina to meet these forces, thus opening an overland line of communication running the length of China. By this time, however, the Asia-Pacific war had turned decisively against Japan.

In Burma, the Chinese had made good progress since mid-October, threatening the Japanese Thirty-third Army's left flank by advancing south from Myitkyina.[36] Three divisions linked up at Bhamo and then struck southwest, pushing back the weakened Japanese Thirty-third Army. The Japanese fought doggedly, but by December they had retreated to the east side of the Shwell River.[37] Although the continuing Ichigō operation and the threat posed to U.S. airfields in southwest China forced Chiang to divert troops from Burma operations to protect the airfields, Chinese forces continued their two-pronged offensive in northern Burma. In late January 1945, X- and Y-forces linked up, reopened the Burma Road in February, and reached Lashio in mid-March, thus breaking the five-year-long Japanese blockade of China and culminating a decisive land campaign.

In January and February 1945, Japanese armies in south China again lashed out at American air bases. U.S. aircraft persistently struck Japanese columns, reducing their mobility while supporting Chinese defenders. Subsequent Chinese counterattacks by modern, well-equipped KMT forces inflicted serious losses on the Japanese, who by May 1945 had suffered 15,000 killed and 50,000 wounded.[38] In late June, the Chinese recaptured Guilin, and the Japanese fell back to Guangzhou. Although large Japanese forces still held most Chinese cities and huge swaths of territory, they no longer had the ability to conduct offensive operations and were bottled up in enclaves when the Asia-Pacific war officially ended in September 1945.

All told, in eight years of war in China, Japan suffered 410,000 killed (230,000 after December 1941) and 920,000 wounded.[39] Although no reliable figures are available for Chinese losses, perhaps as many as 10 million Chinese soldiers died during the fighting, and civilian casualties certainly were as high if not double that figure. The protracted fighting also dislocated tens of millions of Chinese who took to the roads in search of survival.[40]

The dry recitation of military campaigns in these general terms renders them equivalent to the blue and red arrows that adorn military campaign maps. It must always be remembered that between July 1937 and September 1945 China endured enormous suffering on a scale so great that no one has yet captured its totality. Even without Japanese reprisals or endemic brutality, the fighting itself shattered China's political and administrative institutions, destroyed the civilian economy, dislocated hundreds of millions of Chinese, and inflicted tremendous collateral damage the length and breadth of the nation. Coupled with an invading army that initially had no long-term occupation policy, Chinese civil administration disintegrated as Japanese troops watched. Japan's inability to supply its far-flung armies led IGHQ to order them in December 1942 to live off the land, in effect institutionalizing plunder. While a general overview of the military operations can place the war in context, it cannot hope to describe the misery and suffering wrought by the continental conflict. Who can describe the panic and horror in a Chinese village as an armed Japanese foraging party approached? The Chinese people lived with that terror for more than eight years as their nation was torn asunder.

2 *The Dragon's Seed*

ORIGINS OF THE WAR

MARK R. PEATTIE

The seeds of the conflict can be found as early as the nineteenth century,[1] rooted in the soil of imperial China, an agrarian bureaucratic empire whose institutional inadequacies at a time of gathering economic, demographic, and technological change complicated its efforts to preserve domestic tranquility within the country and made difficult China's resistance to foreign encroachment from without.[2] Lacking strong allies and firm control over its border regions and peoples, and suspicious as to the nature and intentions of foreign powers standing on its frontiers and approaching its coasts, China was unable to halt the pace and scale of the incursions on its sovereignty and territory in the last three decades of the nineteenth century: Japan's invasion of Taiwan, 1870–1871; Russia's occupation of the Ili Valley in Xinjiang Province in 1879; the loss of Annam to France in 1885; and, most painful and serious, the calamitous war with Japan over Korea, 1894–1895, in which Chinese forces were defeated on land and sea and after which Korea was stripped from China as a tributary, and Taiwan, the Liaodong Peninsula, and the Pescadores were ceded to Japan. After that, further humiliations followed one after another: French demands to adjust the Sino-Annamite border; Germany's seizure of Jiaozhou Bay on the southern coast of the Shandong Peninsula; British demands for an offsetting port at Weihaiwei on the northern coast of the same peninsula; French demands for a leasehold at Guangzhou on the southern China coast, demands that provoked a British expansion into the Kowloon "New Territories" opposite Hong Kong. Most of these new foreign enclaves were surrounded by zones and spheres where each foreign controlling power held exclusive rights for extractive industries and modern communications.

Then with the opening of the new century had come the disastrous decision of the Qing court to encourage and support the spasm of antiforeign violence led by the Boxers, an initiative explicable by the depth of popular resentment at thirty years of foreign humiliation of China. At all events, the utter defeat of the court and the Boxers by coordinated foreign military expeditions ended in the Boxer Protocols, which, among other punitive stipulations, authorized foreign troops, including the Japanese, to be stationed at key points from Peking to the sea.

It has been customary in Western literature to view the Boxer upheaval in terms of a traditional émeute and China's punishment under the Boxer Protocols as the nadir of China's fortunes in its modern history. Yet, stirring the ashes of China's defeat, historians have come to see the Boxer upheaval as less a rebellion than a serious episode in China's military history—a war between China and the West, one that gave voice to a new Chinese patriotism, the beginnings of a nationalism essential to the resistance to the Japanese invader forty years on. In the meantime, however, it cannot be denied that control over China's borderlands had been further weakened; its ports, rivers, and economic resources had fallen under foreign control; and a legacy of national resentment had accumulated that would bear bitter fruit in the new century.

Japan's Encroachments in China, 1894–1915

The encroachments by Western powers on Chinese sovereignty had been undertaken by nations half a globe away whose full strategic reach was checked by time and distance. Japan, on the other hand, had been a fellow Asian neighbor. But Japan's own modern transformation in the latter half of the nineteenth century had brought with it a new and aggressive attitude toward national expansion, an outlook framed by the tigerish demands of Japanese self-interest. Convinced that Japan's national security depended on an outer cordon of satellite territory on the Asian continent, Japan's political and military leadership had sought to control events on the Asian mainland, beginning with the Korean peninsula.[3] Once Japan's strategic priorities shifted in the late 1880s from passive defense of the Japanese coastline to an active political and military presence on the continent, it acquired a lethal potential. By the last decade of the century, Japan had been on a collision course with a belated Chinese determination to defend its position in Korea. The disasters that had overtaken China's armed forces during the Sino-Japanese War of 1894–1895 had not only led to the loss of territories mentioned above but emboldened Japanese policies on the continent and strengthened Japanese contempt for China's capacities.[4] Yet by the decade that followed the punitive humiliations of the Boxer Protocols, Japan came to play a significant role in the Qing Dynasty's effort to save itself through reform while at the same time maneuvering to gain a dominant position on the China mainland.

While the Qing had suffered a string of humiliations that had demonstrated how inadequate were many of its institutions, particularly its armed forces, these defeats had led not to a collapse of the monarchy but to a rally of sorts in the last decade of its existence, 1901–1911. And it was the empress dowager, arch symbol of Chinese conservatism, who now gave her approval to a program of radical reform that progressive Chinese intellectuals had advocated without success for nearly twenty years.

Among the many reform projects was the reorganization, reconstruction, and modernization of the nation's armed forces. For the most part, the archaic structures of the traditional Manchu military forces were abandoned and new, more modern armies were raised by local power holders but officered by young men with a greater sensitivity to the nation and to foreign threats. Of these "New Armies"[5]—more efficiently organized, better trained, armed with more modern weapons, and given a more professional command structure—undoubtedly the best was the Beiyang Army of Yuan Shikai, governor of metropolitan Zhili Province. Established as part of the reform program of the imperial government, the Beiyang Army was perhaps the most important military development between the suppression of the Taiping Rebellion in the mid-nineteenth century and the formation of the Nationalist Army by Chiang Kai-shek in the third decade of the twentieth century. In relation to the archaic Manchu military formations of the past, the Beiyang Army was an admirably modern force.[6]

But what provides particular interest in this survey of Sino-Japanese interactions in the first decades of the twentieth century is the fact that in training, discipline, and organization the Beiyang Army was modeled on the Japanese military. Japanese influence was particularly pronounced in the development of the Beiyang Officers Training Academy, which Yuan Shikai established at Baoding. In addition to dispatch of military students to Japan for advanced training, Yuan brought Japanese instructors to Baoding to teach at the academy.[7] Given the fact that, in these years, the Japanese army represented the cutting edge of military professionalism in East Asia, Yuan's use of Japanese expertise was a logical outcome of the dynasty's belated program of modernization. For its part, the Japanese military had an obvious interest in shaping and guiding the most powerful land force in China, the nearest thing to the existence of a Chinese national army. This pattern of Japanese penetration of Chinese military institutions was to continue through the subsequent warlord period and well into the 1930s.

During the first decade of the twentieth century Japan came to exert a major influence—for good and ill—on the course of events in China. Japan also came to serve as a model for Qing reforms in education, administration, and military professionalism and, at the same time, as an incubator of anti-Qing revolutionary sentiment among the thousands of Chinese students who had been sent to Japan to study in Japanese universities. Japan thus played the role of earnest instructor in the practice of modernity while at the same time harboring chauvinists and adventurers who saw China only as a field for personal ambition and national expansion. It was on this uncertain foreign terrain that Sun Yat-sen, the exiled anti-Manchu radical, took up the cause of revolution, trying to building a revolutionary organization, working out a revolutionary ideology, and gathering funds from overseas Chinese for his revolutionary cause. In these years, Sun worked with a circle of Japanese friends—idealists as well as ultranationalists—whose main appeal to Sun was their pan-Asianist vision of Asian friendship and cooperation against a common enemy, Western imperialism.[8]

As we know, Sun's plans for the overthrow of the monarchy were overtaken by events. Weakened by foreign interventions and even more by the fraying of political legitimacy and cohesion, the Chinese imperial system collapsed in 1911, in part through Sun's active agency. Although Sun, upon his return to China, was elected to the provisional presidency of the republic established at Nanjing, the new power holders were those former Qing army officers who set themselves up as provincial military governors. Under these conditions, Sun soon relinquished his position to Yuan Shikai, the one leader with sufficient power, skill, and experience to quell civil war and avoid foreign intervention. In these unstable conditions, Japan perceived new opportunities for expansion in China, especially in Manchuria. Indeed, Japanese military projects to separate Manchuria from mainland China began as early as 1912. Although these initiatives were blocked by the civilian government in Tokyo, belligerent elements, both within and without the Japanese government, continued to agitate for bold and aggressive policies in China.[9]

Until the outbreak of World War I, the Japanese government kept these elements in check because it recognized that adventurism might clash with Western interests in China. Looked at another way, under the nineteenth-century treaty system, China had been able to limit the rapacity of any single treaty power by the rivalry and the antagonism of all the others. But with Western attention focused on the war in Europe, Japan took advantage of China without such an impediment. In 1914 Japanese troops occupied the Shandong Peninsula as part of an Anglo-Japanese expedition to eliminate German interests in East Asia and the Pacific, following which Japan's dominant position on the peninsula was confirmed in later Sino-Japanese negotiations. Then, early in 1915, Japan presented its notorious Twenty-one Demands, brazen in their attempt to provide Japan with hegemony in China as a whole and devious in the manner in which they were delivered to the government of Yuan Shikai.[10] Exposed to international scrutiny and blocked by international pressure, the demands and their aftermath nevertheless illuminated the scale of Japanese aspirations in China. Although those aspirations may have been largely economic—a

bid for exclusive access to China's resources—their political consequence
was titanic, for they provoked the first great tremors of Chinese nationalism, setting off mass rallies, anti-Japanese boycotts, and impassioned protests to the world by Chinese students, intellectuals, and political leaders.
Even those Chinese who had reason to hope for Japanese amity and assistance now saw such hope betrayed. Yuan Shikai, for example, had begun
his attempt to reestablish the monarchy with the not unfounded expectation that Japan would supply material support for his quixotic effort. But
Japan's withholding of both funds and recognition played a significant
part in the collapse of his schemes.[11] For his part, Sun Yat-sen, desperate
for outside support for his embattled republican effort, compromised Chinese integrity on more than one occasion in his dealings with the Japanese.
He was, however, to be repeatedly disappointed in his efforts to gain their
support, though to the end he never resigned himself to the harsh fact of
Japanese intentions in China.[12]

To Japanese advocates of a "forward policy" on the continent, the fragmentation of China after the fall of Yuan Shikai appeared to provide fertile soil for political and military maneuvering to achieve more gradually
what the Twenty-one Demands had failed to do at one stroke. For Chinese
patriots everywhere, Japan was now clearly seen as China's single greatest
foreign menace, a view that would last through the next three decades of
civil war and invasion. Where in the nineteenth century China had been
an arena of European imperial competition, it now became the battlefield
between two contending regional forces: an emerging Chinese nationalism
and an explosive Japanese expansionism.[13]

The Institutional Dysfunctions
of Japanese China Policy

It would be a mistake, however, to see Japanese policy in China
working as a smoothly running juggernaut, guided by a single, clearly
fixed plan devised over the decades. On the contrary, there were simply
too many Japanese actors and would-be actors on the China stage to effect
such a coherent policy. As Marius Jansen has observed, "The scene was
full of busy figures. China adventurers, professional patriots, agents of the
military and economic establishments, all known to each other, and all
contacting the same Chinese, and yet each seeing his purpose in a different
way."[14] Thus, buffeted by contending interest groups, Japan's China policies tended to lurch from one objective to another.

To begin with, structural and political weaknesses within Japan confused the development of a clear-cut policy. First among these debilities
was a lethal flaw in the modern Japanese constitutional system. It centered

on a link between a theoretically supreme imperial throne, supposedly the source of all political legitimacy and authority, and an ill-defined locus of political responsibility. It meant that any institution in the Japanese state could, if it had sufficient practical power, pretend to act in the name of an inviolable emperor and thus assume a supreme decision-making role. With one critical exception, however, no institution could claim an actual constitutional right to do so. The exception was the armed services' "right of supreme command," which made the services directly responsible to the emperor and not to civil authority. It thus gave the army and navy the legal authority to act and speak in the name of the imperial throne. As the throne was not constitutionally responsible to any other institution within the Japanese state, the services could theoretically act as they pleased, without check or interference from civil government.[15]

Early in the history of modern Japan, when civil and military authority in Japan were informally combined in the persons of the *genro*—the senior military and civilian leaders who, as young samurai activists, had founded the modern Japanese state and who went on to become its elder statesmen—the malevolent consequences of this flaw were not apparent. As the *genro* gradually disappeared from the Japanese political stage because of age, infirmity, and death in the first decades of the twentieth century, their functions were split between other institutions—the political parties, business, the civil bureaucracy, and the military—and the possibilities for chaos, particularly in Japanese military and foreign policies, became obvious and ominous. Of those institutions contending for power on the new political landscape, the armed services, by virtue of their claim to the delegation of imperial authority, held the strongest position.

In the immediate postwar years, the political parties capitalized on the declining political muscle of the civil bureaucracy and acquired a measure of political legitimacy and authority. Yet the political parties were soon riven by factionalism; tainted by corruption, greed, and an innate selfishness; and hampered by a failure to cultivate a mass constituency. Without mass support and unable to present the Japanese people with any vision of public good, and incapable of dealing with the principal crises of the 1920s, both foreign and domestic, they found that their fortunes rested on political sand. Japanese public support shifted to the one-shot solutions of right-wing nationalists and the increasingly strident demands of the Japanese armed services.

The Japanese military was also often incapable of planning and acting as a smoothly integrated machine because of factionalism and interservice rivalry. The army and the navy had different strategic priorities, different institutional cultures, and different claims for public and budgetary support, disputes that prevented them from shaping a coherent Japanese strategic vision. First and foremost, fundamental disagreements divided the two services over long-range strategic priorities. The army was focused on Russia and the navy on south China and Southeast Asia. The attempt to rationalize these differences and to develop a joint military/foreign policy had begun in 1907 with the drafting of the first Imperial Defense Policy. This policy was a three-part document prepared by the armed services and formally sanctioned by the emperor, but neither this first policy statement nor its subsequent revisions (in 1918, in 1923, and 1936) ever resolved the basic difference in strategic priorities between the two services.

In the 1907 policy statement, the army set forth its basic strategy of not allowing an enemy to violate Japanese soil and its corollary,[16] an outward-radiating definition of Japan's territorial security from which the army drew up plans for forward offensive operations on the Asian mainland. Military operations called for quick, decisive victories in the opening battles of any war in order to guarantee Japan's negotiating position at the end of the conflict. This doctrine of "rapid war, rapid decision" (sokusen sokketsu) was an essential element of the first Imperial Defense Policy of 1907.[17]

Within each service, rival factions and fiercely contending bureaucracies hampered coordination. In the army, the factions were regional, generational, ideological, and personal. The oldest rift went back to the feudal origins of the army and the tensions between its three most powerful domains—Chōshū, Satsuma, and Hizen—which had overthrown the old feudal order in the mid-nineteenth century. Over time, with the dominance of the Chōshū Clique in the upper ranks of the army, the bureaucratic tensions became generational as younger outsiders entered the officer corps. These men were contemptuous of the lingering influence of the aging Chōshū Clique. More familiar with the new military technology that emerged from World War I, they were impatient with the unwillingness or inability of their superiors to prepare the army for modern warfare, and they fumed at the apparent incompetence of political party governments to deal with the problems of social and economic inequity in Japan.[18] Some younger staff officers pressed for a thorough modernization of the army and the nation's preparation for total war, by the 1930s seen largely as against the Soviet Union. Others, believing that Japan could not win a technological race against any of the great powers, turned to a restoration of the Japanese fighting spirit and the indoctrination of all ranks in the inevitable victory of a Japanese "Imperial Way" (Kōdō).

Adding to policy and organizational dysfunctions was the considerable autonomy of Japanese field armies on the Asian mainland, especially the Kwantung Army, headquartered at Port Arthur in the Kwantung Leased Territory. Established in 1906 for the defense of the territory and for the protection of Japanese lives and property in Manchuria, which in practice largely meant defending Japan's South Manchuria Railway, the Kwantung "Army" was originally little more than one division in strength (10,000 men plus six battalions of an independent railway garrison). In 1919, it had been divested of its administrative role in order to concentrate on its defensive responsibilities. By the 1920s, however, its ambitious staff officers espoused an aggressive expansion of Japanese interests in Manchuria. Emboldened by a military command system that allowed the army—and its field units—to be accountable only to the Japanese emperor, the Kwantung Army exhibited increasing operational independence from civilian control and even from the directives of central army headquarters in Tokyo.[19]

To only a slightly lesser degree the same stance was taken by the army's other field force in China: the China Garrison Army.[20] Originally composed of about 900 men and termed the Tianjin Garrison, the China Garrison Army was stationed in north China as a result of the diplomatic protocols following the Boxer Rebellion.[21] Over time, with each new political and military upheaval in China, the Japanese army strengthened its protocol force in Tianjin, until, by the mid-1930s it had grown to 4,000 men. Its staff adopted the same activist coloration as their colleagues to the north in Manchuria and became far more involved in intelligence operations and in plans for offensive preparations in north China than with the mere protection of Japanese life and property there.[22]

Finally, there was the Japanese Naval Landing Party in Shanghai. Its origins lay in the placement of the navy's gunboats on the Yangtze River beginning in the late nineteenth century. Over the next two or three decades, the Japanese navy had drawn from this small river flotilla a number of naval landing parties (*rikusentai*)—naval infantry—which could be put ashore when Japanese communities and businesses appeared to be threatened by violence in times of Chinese upheaval. In 1932, the largest of these riverine infantry forces, that in Shanghai, was given a permanent presence ashore, adjacent to the Japanese quarter in that city. It developed close ties with the Japanese community, particularly with Japanese paramilitary groups in the city, and in so doing became the fist for an emerging Japanese belligerence in Shanghai.[23]

The autonomy of these field forces on the Asian continent also benefited from a commander's prerogative to move a subordinate unit within his own theater of operations in the interests of security. This privilege was the right of "field initiative" (*dokudan senkō*). While the emperor's approval was required for the transfer of units from one field command to another (say from the Kwantung Army to the Tianjin Garrison), none of these commands needed to obtain imperial approval for the shifting of units within its own jurisdiction. Indeed, the potential for abuse of this privilege by aggressive officers in the field was manifest.[24] Japanese garrisons on the Asian mainland thus provided flashpoints for potential Sino-Japanese conflict and thus contributed significantly to the fractured nature of Japanese policy in China.[25]

Japanese Military Attitudes toward China

China's abject military defeat in 1894–1895 had accelerated Japanese contempt for things Chinese. Japan's general understanding and sympathy toward China had reached its nadir by World War I, when China's cultural reputation survived only among specialists in Japanese academic institutions and among small numbers of Japan's intellectual elite. China was now seen as a stage for the personal ambitions of various Japanese radical idealists and expansionists, as a resource base for Japanese industry, as a lucrative field for the profit of Japanese capital, and as territory for the ever-expanding requirements of Japanese national security. But in none of these perspectives did the need for specialized knowledge of China appear to be pronounced. The Foreign Ministry and the army's field commanders in China had the greatest contact with China, and while each developed a core of China specialists, with only rare exceptions did China hands reach high rank in the army and the foreign service. The highest echelons in both services were essentially occupied by generalists whose expertise was focused on the institutions of the modern West rather than on the "backward" countries of Asia.

Japanese businessmen believed an expanding economy required dependable markets and sources of raw materials abroad, and these in turn were originally seen as best secured by Japan's full participation in a liberal, capitalist, international system. But Japanese policies during World War I and the postwar trend to autarky badly hurt Japan's international export trade. Thus Prime Minister Shidehara Kijurō's, "whole China policy," according to Akira Iriye, "can be characterized as an attempt to reduce obstacles in the way of selling more goods to China."[26] Shidehara (a generalist, not a China specialist) and his allies in the Foreign Ministry offered an alternative to the bludgeoning approach of the Japanese military in China but still sought Japanese domination, not partnership. But even China sympathizers and experts in the Foreign Ministry found their efforts to halt the tide of Japanese belligerence overridden by Japanese military field commanders.[27]

An assessment of the Japanese army's understanding of China presents a picture of sharp contrasts. On the tactical level, it is clear that both the Tokyo high command and the two field armies in China had detailed information on Chinese units and their movements. This was in large part due to the effectiveness of Japanese signals intelligence in China. A codes and ciphers office (*angohan*) was established within the Intelligence Bureau of the Army General Staff in Tokyo in 1927 and for a critical period, 1930–1936, was part of its China Section. By the early 1930s, branch signal intelligence offices were set up at various places in Manchuria and later elsewhere in China. Because of the ease with which these field units broke Chinese military code systems, the China Garrison Army was able to learn the composition, strength, and activities of Chiang Kai-shek's forces. For its part, the Kwantung Army was able to read 70 percent of the secret communications between the major warlords in north China, a fact that gave the two Japanese field armies a tremendous advantage and almost always enabled the Japanese military to take the initiative against Chinese military forces.[28]

No doubt some useful political intelligence was also gathered by Japanese field units in China.[29] Yet, by and large, in the decade before the outbreak of the war, incredibly, the Japanese armies in the field and the high command in Tokyo failed to appreciate the one critical strategic development in China: the gathering pressure of national hostility to the belligerent Japanese presence on the continent. It was a myopic blunder of stunning proportions, one that was fundamental to the origins of the war.

There were several reasons why this blunder should have occurred. First, as in the case of the Foreign Ministry, the generalist in the Japanese army, not the specialist, and certainly not the China specialist, was the one who had the decisive voice in the making of Japanese military policy in China. Second, although it has been customary to write of the implacable nature of the army's interests in China, recent scholarship has made it clear that the outlook and activities of army officers active in China policy were often shaped by their individual bureaucratic interests.[30] The officers assigned to legations, the General Staff, or the Kwantung Army served up a disparate range of perspectives and opinions, views usually shaped by their parochial concerns. In the early 1920s, for example, when the army's approach to China was comparatively passive, playing one Chinese warlord off against the other, the Japanese military adviser to each warlord was intent on presenting to the army high command only the interests of that warlord, as it affected the career interests of the adviser himself.

In consequence, the Japanese army failed to develop a comprehensive expertise on China, even though certain officers had served lengthy tours in China and even though some of those officers gathered accurate intelligence during the 1920s and '30s. Indeed, early in the 1920s, a number of military attachés in Peking developed realistic perspectives on the rise of Chinese nationalism. But too often such opinions were rejected or ignored by their superiors, who were generalists with little interest in China matters. Moreover, most Japanese military men serving in China who regularly associated with Chinese—those appointed as military advisers to various Chinese warlords and those who were attached to the army's Special Service organs in China[31]—were usually exposed to the most venal and corrupt elements in China. They remained blinded by their own attitudes and prejudices, which were, in turn, shaped by what they saw around them. Too often, they saw the Chinese as greedy individuals, unable or unwilling to care about the welfare of their nation. In this view, China's would-be leaders were luxury loving, corrupt, and uninterested in anything other than advancing their own positions and their private concerns.[32] The rough state of the Chinese countryside confirmed Japanese prejudices that the Chinese were a poor, ignorant, superstitious, and dirt-ridden lot, oppressed by greedy and rapacious landlords, lacking any aspects of advanced civilization, and incapable of anything more than a brutish existence. Only a few officers—like Major Ishiwara Kanji, who served in central China in the 1920s—were perceptive enough to realize the possibilities of Chinese progress and the ominous danger of eventual Chinese retaliation to Japanese bullying. The vast majority of officers, even those in the China Section of the General Staff's Intelligence Bureau, smugly spoke of *chankoro* (Chinks), and their knowledge of China, even of its military geography, was stunningly limited.[33]

The Rise of Chinese Warlordism

If the structure of Japanese institutions involved in the making of Japan's China policy can be termed dysfunctional, the nature of Chinese institutions in the post-imperial contest for power in China was chaotic.[34] Those military figures like Yuan Shikai held power by the force of their armies but could claim no legitimacy to rule. They were men trapped in a period in Chinese history when the traditional sources of political legitimacy had collapsed with the monarchy and had not yet been replaced by the legitimacy of popular will based on ideals of public welfare and patriotic principles. For their part, the civilian politicians who had emerged with the republic may have held various visions of a new political order but had no military power with which to realize them. Such conditions explain the collapse of Yuan Shikai's quixotic attempt to assert his control by claiming a throne for himself. They also illuminate the difficulties of Sun Yat-sen in trying to forge a republic based on his famous "Three Principles." After the failure of the Second Revolution of 1913, aimed at reestablishing republicanism, Sun fled once more to Japan and there tried to reorganize his political party, the Kuomintang, into a tighter political structure dedicated to fighting Yuan Shikai's betrayal of the republic. But over the next few years, in his new obsession with "democratic centralism," Sun himself failed to grasp the significance of the rising tide of anti-Japanese sentiment in China. Upon his return to China in 1917, Sun threw himself into the emerging warlord-parliamentarian struggles and endeavored to set up his own military government at Guangzhou. But the weakness of his position at Guangzhou in relation to the warlord power holders there led him to take positions that compromised his revolutionary ideals. Desperate for material support for his faltering cause, he offered

Japan access to Chinese resources far beyond anything that Japan had as yet demanded. Such accommodations may have been impelled by Sun's attachment to the pan-Asian visions of his Japanese contacts as much as by the difficulties of his position,[35] but, critically for China, they undoubtedly helped to deepen the interference of Japan in Chinese affairs.

That interference had continued unabated even after the failure of the Twenty-one Demands, largely through the agency of Japanese finance. With a booming trade free of international competition during World War I, and with a large capital surplus, Japan was in a position to use that capital as wedge to accomplish in China much of what the demands themselves had failed to achieve. Premier and former marshal Terauchi Masatake saw money as the avenue to an alliance with the group of warlords who had entrenched themselves in Peking—and through them to control the course of events in north China. His willing tool was Premier Duan Qirui, who entered into a military alliance with Japan, imported Japanese military instructors, and accepted a huge loan, largely for military assistance to the northern militarists arranged by Terauchi's secret agent, Nishihara Kamezō. On the surface these schemes seem to have provided Japan with the freedom of action in China that had been envisioned in the Twenty-one Demands and to have lessened official Chinese opposition to the Japanese occupation of the Shandong Peninsula at the opening of World War I. Indeed, Marius Jansen has called them "the most ambitious, coordinated and expensive plans Japan yet had for China."[36]

But they ultimately came to naught. The outburst of Chinese popular anger in May of 1919 over the failure of the Versailles Peace Conference to repudiate the secret treaties confirming Japan in its wartime gains in Shandong shook the government to its core and ultimately led to the abandonment of Japanese claims to the peninsula. The loans, moreover, did Japan little good. Japan had wasted its accumulated surplus on warlord allies who were little more than "elaborately decorated and plumed political birds of passage"[37] and in the process inherited a renewed Chinese resentment toward Japanese efforts to collect interest on their loan.

For China the Nishihara loan, by supplying money to the militarist groupings in Peking, helped to perpetuate a pattern of warlord satrapies and thus delay the country's unity and stability. The identification of the complex and shifting alliances of the various militarist groupings that evolved in China during the 1920s and the marches and countermarches against each other can be of interest in this chapter only insofar as any of them significantly affected Sino-Japanese relations at the time. Essentially, by the middle of the decade, north and central China were left divided under contending warlord factions. The Peking-Tianjin area and Shandong had fallen under the control of the Fengtien Clique of Zhang Zuolin, "the Warlord of Manchuria," quondam bandit and military governor of Mukden (Shenyang), who came to be known as the "Old Marshal." Although Manchuria was his home territory, Zhang had given every indication that his ambitions were national in scope. Principally opposed to the Fengtien Clique was the Chihli Clique, which held Hubei and Henan provinces under Wu Peifu, a former Beiyang Army commander. Some have seen the collision between the Fengtien and Chihli cliques and their factional allies in 1924 as a critical process in China's eventual unification since, by their very destructiveness, they opened the way for the emergence of Chinese nationalism. Arthur Waldron, specifically, has seen the "destruction and disruption caused by the wars of 1924" as "indispensable pre-conditions" to the Nationalist revolution that followed.[38]

Be that as it may, these were conflicts that led to increasing involvement in Chinese affairs by the Japanese military. Against the background of the shifting fortunes of warlord conflict it is possible to discern an emerging Japanese strategy to achieve a dominant position in the country. Ever since Yuan Shikai and the Twenty-one Demands, the conviction of Japanese leaders, civilian and military, had been that the nation's interests in China generally, and in Manchuria specifically, were best served by the establishment of an informal hegemony over the country rather than through an attempt to establish direct imperial rule,[39] which after World War I was, in any event, now excluded by the Washington treaties. To achieve such indirect control, Tokyo concluded that it was necessary to identify a power holder (or military faction) best positioned to unify the country and then to influence that power holder through his increasing dependence on Japan for material and political support. Arthur Waldron probably gets it right when he asserts that "Tokyo hoped for . . . a Chinese government at once strong enough to keep order, abide by the treaties, and unify the country, yet weak enough to conform to Japanese wishes."[40] Waldron might have added that Tokyo's minimum requirement, short of indirect control over greater China, was a leader in Manchuria through whom Japan could work to protect its interests in the region. Initially, Tokyo believed it had found such a power holder in the person of Zhang Zuolin. For that reason, in the second Chihli-Fengtien War of 1924, Japan had backed Zhang against his Chihli rivals with money, weapons, intelligence, and advisers, support that was critical in Zhang's eventual victory.[41] But Waldron asserts that the Chihli defeat and the collapse of the central government at Peking, brought about through assiduous Japanese support for Zhang and his Fengtien Clique, produced widespread disorder and subsequently a firestorm of antiforeign anger—hardly the pliable situation for which Japan had schemed.[42] What Japan should have learned after the fiasco of the Twenty-one Demands, and had to learn repeatedly, was that Japan's formula for a dominant position in China—a united China submissive to Japanese dictates—was impossibly self-contradictory.[43]

In the south, meanwhile, from 1921 to 1924, Sun Yat-sen at Guangzhou had begun to reorganize his increasingly radical political forces. As part of the process, Sun had begun to establish ties with the Comintern, the one foreign element that seemed favorable to his cause at a time when his repeated proposals for Western assistance to China's reform and reconstruction had been ignored. Worse, his hopes for the mobilization of a northward military expedition to unify China had foundered amid a rupture with local warlords, and he was once more forced to flee to Shanghai. Returning to Guangzhou in 1923, he had renewed and strengthened his ties with the Chinese Communist Party while strengthening his ideological and political control over his own party apparatus, the Kuomintang.

Looking beyond his tightened management of the Kuomintang, Sun continued to cherish the vision of a united China under his revolutionary government, an objective that he concluded was attainable only with the establishment of an indoctrinated party army that could march northward to defeat the warlord cliques in Peking and unite the country. The forge for such an instrument was to be the Whampoa Military Academy. Opened in 1924, with Chiang Kai-shek as superintendent, the academy was to be staffed with Soviet advisers, and the faculty was to be composed largely of Japanese-trained officers.[44]

The establishment of the military academy, with its emphasis on ideological training and the inculcation of military discipline, was Sun's last major accomplishment before his death the next year. He was succeeded in the leadership of the party and the party army by Chiang Kai-shek, graduate of Yuan Shikai's military academy, a member of Sun Yat-sen's party, and "a figure of some importance in the shadowy area between Shanghai business and revolutionary politics."[45] Chiang had inherited Sun's vision of a military campaign to bring the northern military warlord cliques under control and to unify China. What is more, he commanded the National Revolutionary Army, which could undertake such an effort.[46]

Out of the chaos and confusion of political and military factionalism in southern China, Chiang Kai-shek, by skill, ruthlessness, and political acumen, had emerged to seize the leadership of the national revolution aiming to rid China of the evils of warlord factionalism and imperialist exploitation. Its spearhead was the Northern Expedition, begun in 1926 to unify China. The Kuomintang armies marched north and east to the great cities of the Yangtze River Valley, at first with the active participation of the Communists and the left wing of the Kuomintang. Once his armies had arrived in Shanghai, Chiang turned on the Communists and, in a bloody campaign of suppression, eliminated them as a political force in urban China for two decades. Held up briefly in late 1927 in Shandong by a clash with a Japanese field force there, the Northern Expedition surged on to Peking, which Chiang occupied in 1928, though he made Nanjing his capital.

In this review of the origins of the Sino-Japanese conflict, the complex narrative of the events surrounding the Northern Expedition of 1926–1928—the explosive force of the antiforeign May 30th Movement, the emerging split between the left and right wings of the Kuomintang, the ineffective efforts of Stalin and the Comintern to control the tumultuous developments provoked by the campaign, and the abortive efforts of Mao Zedong to stimulate peasant uprisings and urban rebellions—can be bypassed since they have been so expertly treated elsewhere.[47]

At all events, the character and import of the Northern Expedition has been best encapsulated by Hans van de Ven, who has seen the campaign and those who opposed it as fostering a culture of violence, as bringing about military fragmentation, and as fostering bitter personal rivalries. In this light, van de Ven has argued, the "unity" that the expedition had supposedly achieved at Nanjing by 1928 was in fact illusory. Chiang Kai-shek had ridden to power through his control of the most effective military forces in China, and in the combat that led up to his occupation of Nanjing he had demonstrated both uncanny political acumen and bold decision on the battlefield that had kept his rivals and opponents off balance. But maintenance of his position depended as much on the networks of support that he had cultivated among his warlord allies, business allies, and even allies in underworld circles.[48]

Factions and Regionalism in China at the Outset of the "Nanjing Decade"

Thus began the "Nanjing Decade" of 1927–1937, ten years of administrative organization, economic growth, political factionalism and infighting, and the grueling task of holding the country together at a time of warlord rivalry, Communist insurgency in the interior, and the rapacious inroads of Japanese field armies on China's borders. While there was indeed a central government with a central army during these years, Chiang's practical authority rested on his skill in balancing and manipulating the interests of an uncertain coalition of warlords and factions within the government and the army. Although a number of the regional military figures held nominal positions in the central army, they were bound to the central government only by what they regarded as their own personal interests at any given moment. Having been in the thick of the warlord fighting of the 1920s and, having contended with Chiang Kai-shek for power in those conflicts, most regarded themselves as equals, and many still harbored national ambitions. By no means were they willing to submit automatically or permanently to the will of a central government. The tenuous nature of Chiang's relations with these individuals and factions was to be an ongoing drag in his efforts to contend with an increasingly belligerent Japanese presence in China.

The most prominent of the warlord figures may be briefly identified as they were positioned in China at the outset of the Nanjing Decade. In Manchuria, there was Zhang Zuolin, bandit chief and battle-scarred veteran of the 1920s. Waiting in the wings was his son Zhang Xueliang, known as the "Young Marshal," who was to take over his father's control in Manchuria after Zhang Zuolin's assassination in 1928. Feng Yuxian, the famed "Christian General" consolidated his control of northern Henan Province in 1927, though he publicly declared his support for Chiang Kai-shek's Kuomintang that year.[49] Yan Xishan, a veteran of the warlord struggles of the 1920s, had entrenched himself in Shanxi Province by the end of the decade.[50] Song Zheyuan had been given an army command by his patron, Feng Yuxian, but eventually allied himself with Chiang Kai-shek and was given command of the Twenty-ninth Army in Chahar. Although most of these military men had been rivals of Chiang Kai-shek at various times in the 1920s, since Chiang controlled the largest military force in China, none contemplated a major and open military challenge to his authority.

Also complicating the political scene at the outset of the Nanjing Decade was a shifting collection of party alliances, bureaucratic factions, and economic groupings, some closely allied with Chiang Kai-shek, some working to thwart him, others moving in between these polarities, and all taking his time and energy to balance, mollify, or intimidate. There was the "C. C. Clique," which held powerful positions in the government; there were members of the Shanghai banking and financial community; and there were a number of powerful members within the Kuomintang. Among the last, the leading figure was Wang Jingwei, intimate associate of Sun Yat-sen, the most important figure in the party after Chiang Kai-shek himself, and, at various times, ally and rival of Chiang. An eloquent and mercurial advocate of civilian leadership for China, he was not averse to enlisting support of regional military figures to achieve it. His efforts included attempts to found a rival national government in Peking in 1930 and the creation of an active opposition to Chiang in 1931. Both failed, but they made it clear to Chiang that Wang was an opposition figure to be reckoned with. This led to an uneasy collaboration at the outset of the 1930s whereby Wang held the presidency of the Republic while Chiang remained supreme military commander and thus had a free hand to deal militarily with the Chinese Communists, now entrenched deep in the mountain fastnesses of Jiangxi Province.

To Chiang Kai-shek, the Communists—eventually and particularly Mao Zedong—were the greatest threat to China and Chiang's dominant position in China. Undoubtedly, Chiang held this view because he saw that both their ideology and their objectives were not only radically different from his own but also total in scope. Thus, they would not compromise and could not be compromised. They could only be exterminated, an objective that Chiang Kai-shek in Nanjing would pursue with single-minded determination during the 1930s, even as Japanese field armies battered at China's doors.

But more than anything else in the Nanjing Decade, Japan and Nanjing's policy toward Japan were the chief determinants of the tortured course of Chinese politics in the 1930s. On the one hand, the general aim of the Japanese field armies in China was to try to forestall the sort of national unity Chiang Kai-shek was trying to forge. It was an effort that exploited the fissures of Chinese regionalism and, through bribery, subversion, and intimidation, attempted to pull suitably pliable Chinese regional leaders out of the orbit of Nanjing's authority. On the other hand, it was the decade-long effort by Chiang Kai-shek to delay, circumvent, and compromise by every means short of war these Japanese efforts to dismember China piecemeal. To undertake this task, Chiang concluded that it was essential first to achieve domestic peace and stability, a condition that called for the extermination of the Communist insurgency. Only then could a final stand be made against the Japanese aggressor. But this very policy of "pacification first, then resistance"—fighting fellow Chinese while negotiating with the foreign invader—was to so arouse public indignation during the decade that it threatened to pull China apart. To that extent, Chiang Kai-shek's troubled mission was to find himself in a race with the progress of voracious Japanese military ambitions in China on the one hand and an emerging confrontation with an enraged Chinese public on the other.

Japan's Seizure of Manchuria and Its Consequences, 1931–1932

In the late 1920s a series of economic crises in Japan led to social and political unrest, which seriously distorted the direction of Japanese foreign policy. In the first half of that decade, the nation's economy had been stimulated by the government's public investment following the Kantō earthquake of 1923. By 1927, however, Japanese financial crises, including a series of spectacular bank failures and the impoverishment of rural communities due to the collapse of rice prices, later exacerbated by the onset of the world depression, dealt a sequence of blows to Japanese domestic markets and to the export trade that, in turn, led to widespread unemployment in Japan. By the beginning of the 1930s, the Japanese public had lost confidence in the nation's industrial leaders, in the fairness of the international global economy, and in the ability of the established political parties to rescue the nation from economic disaster.[51] To many at the reins of government, overseas expansion offered the solution to overpopulation, unemployment, economic depression, and security concerns. On the continent, the Japanese military ambition enjoyed its greatest freedom from interference by the civil and military authorities in Tokyo. The consequent belligerent expansionism of Japanese field armies challenged the wave of resurgent Chinese nationalism in the late 1920s.

As Chiang Kai-shek's military expedition to unify China had moved north in 1927, fighting a continuing struggle against Communist efforts to derail it, the Japanese field units in northern China and Manchuria had taken alarm at the potential threat to Japanese interests on the mainland. In the spring of 1928, the civil government had dispatched 5,000 troops to protect Japanese nationals in Shandong Province, which lay directly in the path of the northward-sweeping Nationalist forces. In this volatile environment any spark could set off a conflagration between the two sides. Indeed, the belligerent actions of the Japanese commander at Qingdao had ignited just such an explosion at Jinan in a firefight with Nationalist forces outside the city. Japanese units had then occupied Jinan, which they held until 1929, when a settlement was negotiated.[52]

Behind such aggressive initiatives of the Japanese army to block or deflect Chiang's Northern Expedition was Japan's overriding concern for the preservation of its special strategic and economic position in Manchuria. The three institutions that shared power in the region—the army, the Foreign Office, and the South Manchuria Railway—all parleyed with warlord coalitions in Peking to secure formal recognition of Japanese interests in the region, but they had little success by the late 1920s.

For the army, particularly for its field force in Manchuria, the Kwantung Army, the preservation and expansion of those interests could only be guaranteed by the separation of Manchuria from Chinese control. In the latter half of the 1920s, the army began to work with the Manchurian bandit leader Zhang Zuolin to check the Northern Expedition's advance toward Manchuria. But to the younger activist staff officers in the Kwantung Army, Zhang's national ambitions made him unsuitable as an acquiescent Manchurian puppet. The officers came to believe that only violence could remove him as an obstacle to Japanese designs on the region. They assassinated Zhang by blowing up his private train in Manchuria in June 1928, hoping to create a chaotic situation that would force the high command in Tokyo to authorize the Kwantung Army to occupy the region. Zhang's murder, however, failed to create the pretext for direct military intervention, and thus the schemes of the plotters were temporarily blunted. The conspiracy was the most dramatic attempt to date by Japanese field armies to hijack Japanese foreign policy on the continent.[53] Its failure did not inhibit others whose intrigues drew motivation from growing friction between the two nations over the status of Manchuria, over Chinese boycotts of Japanese goods, especially in the Shanghai area, and over recurring minor but violent incidents in China.

The Japanese Foreign Ministry vainly attempted to minimize the discord. But a rising tide of national sentiment in Japan, propelled by right-wing agitation in the Diet, the press, and the public, subverted efforts for a peaceful resolution. In Manchuria the Kwantung Army, beginning in 1929, actively worked to destabilize the situation. These machinations for a Japanese takeover in Manchuria were set in motion by the brilliant, visionary, and charismatic chief of the Kwantung Army's Operations Section, Colonel Ishiwara Kanji, who believed that outright occupation of Manchuria was essential to Japan's existence and was a vital strategic barrier blocking the southward expansion of Soviet influence.[54]

Though the Japanese high command in Tokyo was not privy to the details of the Ishiwara's conspiracy, it was certainly aware of his general intent and that of his Kwantung Army staff colleagues.[55] Although opposed to any extreme and violent initiative by the Kwantung Army, Tokyo did little to clarify its policy because it too had drawn up contingency plans to seize Manchuria at some point. The differences between the headquarters in Tokyo and Port Arthur were largely over timing and scope. Concerned that army headquarters in Tokyo might restrain or postpone the execution of its plans, in September 1931 the Kwantung Army staged an incident involving an explosion on the South Manchuria Railway tracks just north of Mukden, and used this Chinese "atrocity" to justify the seizure of the Mukden barracks and arsenal. Two years of meticulous tactical planning enabled the Kwantung Army (outnumbered twenty to one) to rapidly expand its operations despite belated efforts by Tokyo headquarters to rein them in. Justifying its actions on the grounds of operational security and the principle of "field initiative," the Kwantung Army quickly overran most of Manchuria. The "Manchurian Incident"—as the army called it—also led to a consensus within the Japanese military that insubordination by the Kwantung Army—while not total—had generally succeeded, because it had provided the Japanese military with a proconsular position in Manchuria from which it could not be easily dislodged by any Japanese government.

But military conquest of Manchuria by such a relatively modest force did not ensure that Japan could keep or manage it. Facing the heavy administrative demands of holding a vast new territory, the conquerors therefore created the Japanese client state of Manchukuo, nominally ruled by Henry Puyi, the last of the Manchu emperors. A bizarre attempt to give the whole scheme some legitimacy in the eyes of the Chinese, the takeover utterly failed to achieve such status. Yet, in its general outline, this method of working through pliable local leaders of an ostensibly autonomous state came to characterize Japanese administrative policy in conquered China for the next decade.

The Japanese takeover of Manchuria soon created more adverse comment in Western capitals than Tokyo had anticipated. To distract international attention from Manchuria, the Japanese Special Service organ in Shanghai now began to stir up anti-Japanese protests in Shanghai. The subsequent disturbances soon lurched out of control, and in January 1932 the commander of Japanese naval forces in the city called out the local Naval Landing Force, joined by vigilante elements from the Japanese community, to "maintain order." These forces met unexpectedly fierce Chinese resistance, forcing the navy to call for reinforcements in the form of two army divisions. During the two months of combat that followed, the Chinese Nineteenth Route Army and Fifth Army fought on without reinforcements and without the backing of any national mobilization by Nanjing for a general struggle against the Japanese aggressor. For its part, Japan became increasingly uncomfortable with the close foreign scrutiny of the massive destruction its forces were inflicting on this international city. At the personal insistence of Emperor Hirohito, the Japanese theater commander undertook to limit his operations in Shanghai. A cease-fire in May established a demilitarized zone, and all Japanese units, except the Naval Landing Force, withdrew.[56]

As Marius Jansen recounted years ago, Japan's Manchurian adventure drew international opprobrium in the form of the critical report of the Lytton Commission of the League of Nations, which called upon Japan to withdraw from Manchuria. This condemnation of Japan by the Western powers in turn led to Japan's stormy withdrawal from the League in 1933 and to a wave of popular support in Japan for overseas adventures as an antidote to the economic and social crises at home.[57]

For Nationalist China, the loss of Manchuria was disastrous. Worse than the loss of Manchurian customs and tariffs was the fact that China's long northern border with the Japanese puppet state of Manchukuo became a porous divide across which Japanese goods flowed into China without hindrance. But the most pernicious effect on the Chiang Kai-shek government was the damage done to Chiang's great effort to achieve national unity, seen by Chiang as the indispensable requirement to all reform and national progress. Chiang's unwillingness or inability to commit what forces he had to confront the Japanese conqueror in Manchuria and Shanghai created violent pressures within China—outraged public opinion and the suspicion and hostility of his rivals in China both within and without the Nationalist party—that threatened to topple his regime.

Further Incursions: Japanese Designs on North China

With twenty-twenty hindsight one can see that the latest round of Japanese bullying of China also potentially provided Chiang's Kuomintang regime with a symbol for rallying Chinese public support. Ominously, moreover, the Japanese "pacification" of Manchuria and the end of the fighting in Shanghai did not extinguish the flash points for Sino-Japanese hostility. In the fall of 1932 several of these burst into flame. Skirmishes took place at Shanhaiguan, an historic Chinese coastal town at the eastern terminus of the Great Wall where, under the terms of the Boxer Protocols, the Japanese maintained a small garrison. There a series of clashes broke out between the garrison and the forces of a local Chinese warlord. The first two clashes were settled locally and peacefully, but the third, on New Year's Day 1933 and apparently instigated by the Japanese garrison commander, led to fierce fighting and eventually drew in a Japanese infantry division and significant Japanese naval forces. Under such pressure the Chinese withdrew south of the Great Wall, and the Japanese took possession of the south gate of Shanhaiguan. China protested the affair to the League of Nations but failed to convince the powers to intervene, and thus the crisis ended, but not before Japan had added this humiliation to the growing list of injuries inflicted on China.[58]

Ignoring the danger of possible escalation, the Japanese army insisted that the security of Manchuria, now described as Japan's lifeline, required the creation of a buffer zone to the southwest of Manchuria to deflect assertive and irredentist Chinese nationalism. Furthermore, Manchuria was not the treasure house the staffs of the Kwantung and Tianjin Garrison armies expected. Hence, the officers began to covet the resources of north China—its coal and iron in particular—to make up the difference. Assessing the chances for the success of another incursion, these officers rationalized that north China was still a collection of contending warlord fiefdoms and thus vulnerable to Japanese intimidation, subversion, and bribery.

Misguided assumptions about territorial security, material ambition, and political opportunism all combined to impel Japan forward into north China and Inner Mongolia after the conquest of Manchuria, heedless of any Chinese response. As in the case of Manchuria, the basic objective was the creation of a Japanese-dominated buffer zone from which Nationalist influence was to be driven out. The basic strategy would be to instigate and then work behind movements for regional autonomy, a process supplemented by the activities of the army's notorious Special Service organs: agitation, subversion, and constant political warfare to further fragment Chinese authority in the region.

The first of Japan's fatal steps to move beyond Manchuria's western borders was the decision of the Kwantung Army to "round out" its possession of Manchuria by occupying neighboring Jehol Province. The prospect of this new Japanese incursion had been widely rumored in China on the eve of the Japanese attack. Zhang Xueliang, in command of the largest

Chinese forces in Jehol, had sought Chiang Kai-shek's commitment of central army units in repelling the imminent Japanese assault. But Chiang, in the midst of an anticommunist campaign in Jiangxi, had demurred, limiting his support to the public rhetoric of resistance. Zhang himself committed only his weakest troops to the defense of Jehol. The result was another Chinese disaster when two Japanese divisions invaded the province in February 1933 and routed Zhang's units, which fled in panic and disorder. The Japanese conquest of Jehol appeared to leave Peking and Tianjin open to Japanese assault and, in so doing, created a firestorm of popular protest against Chiang's policy of "pacification first, then resistance." Yet Chiang held firm to his course in the face of maneuvering by his rivals and fierce criticism from the public.[59]

Although Chiang Kai-shek may have held to his policy of dealing with his domestic enemies first, the appetite of Kwantung Army extremists for further gains in north China was unabated. The result was a series of sharp battles along the Great Wall as Kwantung Army units sought to seize and hold certain passes critical to the Chinese defense. In this fighting the intermittent efforts of moderates in Tokyo headquarters were sporadically more effective in restraining the belligerent operations of the Japanese field army than the fierce but poorly coordinated resistance of Chinese regional and central army units. As part of an emerging pattern in the Japanese army's strategy in China, the army's Special Service branch in Tianjin attempted to support the Kwantung Army's ground operations by efforts to provoke popular unrest in Hebei against the Nanjing regime, but without great success.[60]

Then, in May 1933, the Kwantung Army broke through Chinese defenses on a broad front and, spilling over the Great Wall at various points, once more threatened Peking and Tianjin. Chiang Kai-shek, faced with a military debacle and aware of a looming political crisis, sought a truce that would stave off both outcomes. He appointed subordinates to carry out the negotiations in order to make it appear that any agreement with the Japanese invader would be local and temporary. For their part, officers of the Kwantung Army, who were once more acting on their own or at least in advance of Tokyo headquarters, carried out the negotiations, not Japanese consular representatives in China. The subsequent Tanggu Truce of May 1933 was in every important way a major humiliation for China in that it created a 5,000-square-mile demilitarized zone over a large portion of Hebei Province south of the Great Wall from which Nationalist military units were to be immediately excluded. Under the agreement Japanese forces would "voluntarily" withdraw to the Great Wall on a timetable of their own choosing.[61]

The Tanggu Truce marked the first surge of Japanese military power into north China. It also opened the way for massive Japanese political and economic inroads into the region. Worse, the Japanese penetration of Hebei Province followed and confirmed a divide-and-rule strategy that the Japanese had pursued in Manchuria: the separation of large areas of Chinese territory from Nationalist control by fostering puppet regimes in that territory obedient to Japanese dictates. It can be argued, of course, that Chiang Kai-shek had staved off worse disaster. Peking and Tianjin had not fallen. The negotiations had been localized, Chiang Kai-shek's name had been kept clear of the agreement, and its most sensitive terms had been kept secret. Most important to Chiang's policy of dealing first with his internal enemies then with the external aggressor, the temporary cessation of combat in north China allowed him to turn back to his extermination efforts against the Communists.[62] But the damage to his cause was profound, and the precedent it established was ominous.

Japanese Aggression and Nanjing's Defensive Strategy, 1933–1937

The narrative of Sino-Japanese relations from the Tanggu Truce of 1933 through the spring of 1937 is dominated on the one hand by the efforts of Japan's field armies to detach north China from Nationalist control though violence, agitation of anti-KMT unrest, and subversion. Yet, on the other hand, it is marked by Chiang Kai-shek's endeavors to keep the Japanese field armies at bay through compromise, delay, and defensive operations while he directed the energies and forces of his Nationalist government in a series of campaigns against the Communist enclaves within China's borders.

Throughout these four years, the Japanese Foreign Ministry played an ambiguous role. Intermittently, Japanese diplomats tried to step in to settle differences between the two countries through talks with Nationalist representatives in Nanjing, raising hopes in both capitals when they did so that a lasting Sino-Japanese rapprochement might be possible. But the Japanese field armies, at once impatient with the pace of such negotiations and alarmed that they would result in a strengthening of Nationalist authority in the very provinces that they were trying to detach, repeatedly blocked prospects for a real settlement. At other times, the Foreign Ministry seemed to fall in step with the designs of the Japanese military, a tendency notably epitomized by the infamous Amau (Amō) Statement of 1934, which attempted to set forth a Japanese "Monroe Doctrine" arrogating Asian affairs to Japan and warning Western nations that Japan would not tolerate any Western material or moral support for the Nanjing regime.[63]

Alarmed that negotiations with the Nationalists would strengthen Nanjing's authority in north China, the Kwantung Army provoked a number of violent incidents in Hebei and Chahar provinces in late 1934 and early 1935 designed to embarrass both Nanjing and Tokyo. For its part, the Nanjing government, in dealing with these events, was hampered by the virulently anti-Chiang faction in Guangzhou, which continued to snipe at Chiang's efforts to find an accord with Japan. Chiang, distracted by his efforts to crush the Communist forces retreating on what became famous as the "Long March" in June 1935, authorized his minister of war, General He Yingqin, to enter into negotiations with the commander of the Tianjin Garrison, Lieutenant General Umezu Yoshijirō. The final agreement, on June 10, represented a capitulation of the Nationalists to Japanese demands on a grand scale: the withdrawal of all Kuomintang Party organs and all Nationalist military forces from Hebei Province entirely, not just from the demilitarized zone.

Although the He-Umezu accord provided the Tianjin Garrison Army with a freer hand in Hebei, the Kwantung Army, not to be outdone, now pressed for increased control in Chahar Province. This was part of a scheme promoted by Colonel Doihara Kenji of the Mukden Special Service organ to accelerate Japanese penetration of neighboring Inner Mongolia, which was to be organized into an "independent" puppet state to be called Mengukuo (Mengjian). Less than two weeks after the He-Umezu arrangement, Doihara made his move, presenting the new provincial governor, Qin Dechun, with a whole range of demands designed to put an end to Nanjing's military and political presence in Chahar. With Kwantung army units on his border and without any sign of rescue from Nanjing, Qin folded and signed the agreement with Doihara.

These two "agreements" of 1935 drastically undermined the prestige of the Nationalist government and, worse, weakened its government in north China.[64] Conversely, their divide-and-rule arrangements had given Japan a dominant position in north China, particularly in Hebei and Chahar provinces.[65] Encouraged by the ease with which they had forced the agreements on a nonresisting Nationalist regime, the Japanese field armies kept pushing along their provincial frontiers to pry them totally out of Nanjing's control. The various Japanese incursions after the humiliating accords of 1935 demonstrated to a widening circle of Chinese people that even acceptance of Manchukuo as an accomplished fact would not halt Japan's southward assault on China's borders. Such a realization contributed to the growing and ultimately explosive pressure for a change in Nanjing's policy toward Japan.

Aiding and abetting Japanese subversion and intimidation of Chinese officials in north China was a campaign of economic warfare carried out by the Japanese field armies in those provinces as part of a program to dominate the region economically as well as politically. One of the most injurious elements of this effort was the smuggling of cheap goods into north China, particularly along the coast, in order to evade Chinese tariffs. Because the Nationalist government simply had too few men to staff its customs stations, this activity, which the Japanese euphemistically termed a "special trade," often flourished openly and brazenly. In Hebei Province, such smuggling was carried out with the tacit approval of the Kwantung Army. Not to be outdone in this shadowy enterprise, the Japanese navy gave protection to smuggling operations based in Taiwan and carried out on the south coast.[66]

This "special trade" had a number of serious consequences for China. It badly undermined the authority of the Nationalist government in those provinces where it was carried out. Just as serious, it substantially weakened Chinese customs revenues, which in previous years had provided the central government with almost half of its income.

Further, the smuggling trade injured legitimate business in north China. As a consequence, in a number of cases, failed Chinese businesses were quickly bought up by the Japanese, thus tightening Japan's economic grip on the region. With the weakening of Chinese economic institutions in north China, the Japanese military, particularly the North China Garrison Army, advanced schemes for the exploitation of the resources and markets of the region.[67]

Inevitably, these Japanese economic inroads added to the rising tide of anti-Japanese feeling in the country, heralded by a wave of protest in the Chinese press. In this popular crisis, Wang Jingwei, as foreign minister and chief of the Executive Yuan, took the brunt of public criticism, while Chiang Kai-shek endeavored to stay out of the spotlight. Only by threatening to resign, along with a number of other Kuomintang leaders, was Wang able to compel Chiang to share the burden of public anger at the current policy of appeasement. Then, in October 1935 after an attempt on his life, Wang was hospitalized and obliged to relinquish his governmental and party posts.

In this new situation Chiang was obliged to assume all public responsibility for the government's relations with Japan. Stubbornly, however, he clung to his policy of pacification before resistance.

For the time being, Chiang's ability to sustain this policy continued to rest on a careful balance of political interests in China, particularly with those lesser but powerful military figures, the regional warlords like Feng Yuxian and Yan Xishan. But among these Zhang Xueliang, still smarting over Chiang's decision not to contest the Japanese invasions of Manchuria and Jehol, was a potentially disruptive military figure. Recognizing this and seeking to forestall any rash move by Zhang to strike at the Japanese and create a conflict that Chiang could not control, Chiang appointed Zhang as chief of the anticommunist headquarters at Xi'an,

Henan Province. Chiang obviously believed that this assignment would both isolate Zhang and compel him to participate in Chiang's campaign against the Communists. It was to be a fateful and mistaken decision for Chiang Kai-shek, one that would make Zhang Xueliang a pivotal figure in the dramatic redirection of Chinese policy.

Throughout 1935 the two Japanese field armies in China continued their machinations, interference, and intimidation for the purpose of destabilizing Nationalist authority in north China and pressuring Chinese officials and regional warlords like Song Zheyuan to join in a Japanese-dominated autonomy movement. The chief instigator of these activities was Colonel Doihara of the Mukden Special Service organ. The range and audacity of the provocations of Doihara and his associates in the Kwantung Army were remarkable: the arrest of Kuomintang officials on Chinese territory (particularly in Peking and Tianjin) by Japanese military police; the Japanese demands that Nanjing suppress all anti-Japanese sentiments in the press throughout the country; unannounced, provocative flights by Japanese military aircraft over Peking and Tianjin; marshaling of large numbers of Japanese troops along the borders of Hebei Province; and a host of other lesser provocations. In these endeavors, the two Japanese field armies were blind to the realities and consequences of their actions. Convinced that they were themselves fighting Communism and corruption in China, they were, in fact, arousing hatred by the Chinese masses.[68]

If Doihara and his superiors had believed that these measures would soon bring about the collapse of Chinese resistance to Japanese efforts to dominate north China, they were soon disabused of that notion. By the end of 1935 their outrages had ignited a powder keg of public anger, the "National Salvation Movement," which found its voice in the burgeoning student demonstrations and massive protests calling for an end to China's civil war and for nationwide resistance to Japanese aggression. The scale and intensity of this national outburst had several important consequences. To begin with, although Chiang Kai-shek had drawn into his own hands unprecedented military and political power in the past half decade, his room for maneuver and accommodation in pursuit of his Fabian policy of delay toward Japan was now all but eliminated. Similarly, the regional warlords on China's northern borders fronting Japanese occupied territory no longer had the option of further concessions toward Japan, lest their own military forces rebel or defect.

For the Japanese, the spasm of Chinese national hostility came as a rude shock. The hard-line extremists in the Kwantung and North China Area armies were now confronted with the failure of their policy of manipulation and intimidation of regional Chinese military leaders to achieve Japanese domination of north China. Faced with the prospect of enormous street protests and newly obdurate Chinese regional leadership resisting both threats and blandishments, Japanese field commanders now had to choose between abandoning their dreams of controlling north China through pliable Chinese clients or simply resorting to violence and crushing all Chinese resistance by force.

At this juncture—late November 1935—moderates in the Tokyo high command belatedly intervened to rein in the strong-arm strategies of Colonel Doihara and his colleagues in the field. Recognizing that his schemes and the provocative activities of the field armies had failed to achieve their purpose, the Army General Staff ordered them halted and recalled Doihara in semidisgrace. Taking advantage of this pause in Japanese pressure, Nanjing, after an intense round of negotiations with Japanese field commanders, worked out an arrangement that established a semiautonomous Hebei-Chahar Political Council, to be headed by Song Zheyuan; the council would retain a significant degree of Nationalist authority in the two provinces.

There were, as well, other developments that delayed the progress of Japanese belligerence in China. The first of these was the humiliating collapse of the Kwantung Army's territorial schemes. Throughout 1936, Japan had been able to exploit a string of minor but recurrent Chinese provocations for short-term tactical advantage, but to Japan's long-term strategic detriment.[69] Then, in November of that year, Kwantung Army adventurism in Inner Mongolia backfired. Trying once again to gain secure borders for Manchukuo, the Kwantung Army staff backed an anti-Chinese Inner Mongolian separatist movement. The Kwantung Army supplied a Mongolian prince with weapons, equipment, and Japanese advisers, expecting to carve out still another "autonomous region." Within a week, however, Nationalist forces smashed the invasion and drove the Japanese and their puppet forces ignominiously from Suiyuan. The Japanese government, humiliated by the reckless initiative of its field army, attempted to cover it up by denying any official Japanese involvement in the debacle.[70]

The Young Officers' Rebellion of 1936 and the Return to a Tokyo-Directed China Policy

Setbacks on the Asian continent were not the only elements altering the direction and pace of Japanese policy in China. Even more important was a sudden shift in early 1936 in the pattern of political and military power in Tokyo away from civilian and military extremists and back into the hands of less ideological and more cautious officers and officials. It is true that right-wing elements and disaffected company-grade officers in Japan staged a series of assassinations and attempted coups d'etat between 1931 and 1936. There is absolutely no evidence, however, that

such extremists were ever in any position of direct influence in the making
of Japanese China policy by either the civilian government or the armed
services during these tumultuous years. The established conservative order
was too firmly established for that. But there were high-ranking officials,
particularly in the army, who were known to bear sympathy toward their
ideologically zealous subordinates and who, in order to advance their own
careers and agendas, were ready to make their support overt should some
dramatic occasion arise.

The denouement of this military radicalism was the 26 February 1936
Incident, a mutiny by radicalized officers of the army's First Division who
occupied strategically located buildings near the Imperial Palace. Within
a few days their hopes crumbled before the angry denunciations by the
emperor and the obdurate hostility of the mainstream army leaders who
suppressed the rebellion.[71] There followed a sweeping purge of the rebels'
supporters and sympathizers within the army, particularly from among
its higher echelons, opening the way for a takeover of key General Staff
positions by officers committed to innovation, modernization, and renovation in the army. Henceforth, responsible officers and civilian officials—
not wild-eyed ideologues, hot-headed junior officers, or the members of a
single political party dictatorship—made major Japanese policy decisions
regarding China from 1937 to 1945.[72] Nor, indeed, was Japanese military
policy in China initiated by Japanese field armies, now kept under careful
watch by the high command in Tokyo, though the Army Ministry and the
Army General Staff were still rent by dissension and conflicting viewpoints
about the China situation. In short, the suppression of the Young Officers'
revolt did not steer Japan onto a collision course for war with China.

The Spring of 1937: The Redirection of Japan's
China Policy and China's Turn to War

In the spring of 1937 a sudden and surprising shift came about in
the strategic priorities of the Japanese army. The origins of the shift lay
in the emergence in the mid-1930s of a powerful Soviet military presence
in northeast Asia. This new development rapidly altered Japanese army
perspectives on China. Some officers in the Tokyo high command, like
Colonel Ishiwara, now argued for Japanese policies that encouraged, not
thwarted, Chinese unity. In this new outlook, the former policy of divide
and rule in north China was to be discarded and all sordid and selfish
maneuverings and other acts of "imperialist aggression" in China avoided.
Only by bringing China into a cooperative relationship through a policy
of "benevolence" (jinai), Ishiwara argued, could Japan really prepare for a
confrontation with the Soviet Union.[73]

Others disagreed, of course. The army's senior leadership remained seriously divided over its China policy. Under Ishiwara's influence, the General Staff was persuaded of the need to avoid a full-scale war with China and to concentrate instead on a massive rearmament and modernization program as part of Japan's preparations against the Soviet Union. But there was a formidable group of hard-liners—on the General Staff (some located, ironically, in Ishiwara's Operations Division), in the Army Ministry, and in the Kwantung and China Garrison armies—that constituted a powerful and intransigent voice in the shaping of the army's China policy. These "hawks" had no compunction about using force against China and thought any "coddling" of China would be injurious to Japanese military prestige and would only encourage Chinese intransigence. Besides, they argued, if past experience was any guide, the Chinese would quickly collapse once actual fighting began.[74] Theirs was still a powerful and intransigent voice in the shaping of Japan's China policy.

Drafted principally by the General Staff, the army's latest war plans under the 1936 revision to national defense policy now viewed north China as a strategic rear area in the event of operations against the Soviet Union. It was assumed that as long as the Kuomintang remained weak and China divided, the prospects for full-scale war with the Nationalists were unlikely. To maintain that situation, it was critical that frictions and incidents with China be avoided if possible. If anti-Japanese outbreaks in north China did occur, the Tokyo high command wanted them contained. In early 1937, the General Staff had formally declared that its China policy was to be one of "promoting mutual assistance and co-prosperity" and of the abandonment of plans to separate north China from Nationalist control. For its part, the Army Ministry now called for the dissolution of the Japanese puppet regime in East Hebei.[75] Already, in March of the previous year, the cabinet of Prime Minister Hirota Kōki had adopted a conciliatory policy in its recognition of a unified China and its opposition to diplomatic coercion under the threat of military force.

One does not need to endow Hirota, Ishiwara, and other like-minded Japanese figures of influence and authority with an aura of overnight clairvoyance or benevolence to recognize that the new course they proposed was the only China policy—short of a sudden and complete abandonment of the Japanese presence in China—that retained even a shred of common sense in July of 1937. Whether the army's new obsession with the Soviet "threat" was also rational must be the subject of a different study. At all events, as Edward J. Drea makes clear in chapter 4, the Japanese Army's de-emphasis on preparations for the possibility of military operations in China was matched by a significant increase in Japanese troop strength along the Manchurian-Soviet border.

Even Japanese units in north China were instructed to undertake training programs directed toward a mastery of tactics deemed necessary to deal with the imminent possibility of operations against a Russian enemy. In this new perspective, to many in the Tokyo high command, a possible war with China was regarded as an irritating distraction, to be dealt with summarily since the Chinese were without military capability, but to be avoided if possible.

But in China, the pace of growing national fury at Japanese aggression had at last overtaken these belated Japanese steps to halt the slide to war. To a great extent, developments in China in 1936–1937 caused that nation's Japan policy to spin out of the hands of Chiang Kai-shek. True, Chiang still held as his central priority the consolidation of his power and the elimination of the Communists, the last overt challenge to his authority. From Chiang's perspective the National Salvation campaign and the demands for a frontal assault against the Japanese presence in China were dangerously premature. Though he was in no position to make further concessions affecting China's sovereignty, he could and did strike at those heading the national protest movement, arresting some and threatening others. Such repressive tactics only increased the fires of public anger. Ominously for Chiang, Zhang Xueliang and Yang Hucheng, appointed by Chiang as commanders of the anticommunist headquarters at Xi'an, now publicly voiced their support for the National Salvation Movement. Alarmed, Chiang Kai-shek flew to Xi'an in December 1936 to demand that Zhang and Yang support him in his final drive to wipe out the Communists in their remote base in Shanxi Province. But his two commanders had had enough. Their earlier efforts against the Communist enclave had failed, and they had less to fear from Chiang Kai-shek than they had from the furnace of national indignation.

Misjudging the situation, Chiang thus walked into a hornet's nest. Arriving in Xi'an, he was suddenly arrested by his two hosts, who presented him with a number of demands before he could be set free. Chief among these was Chiang's public support for the National Salvation Movement, an end to the civil war against the Communists, and the redirection of Nanjing's Japan policy toward national resistance. With little choice, Chiang agreed to these terms. Zhang Xueliang set Chiang free, released news of the agreement, and accompanied Chiang back to Nanjing to the tumultuous acclaim of cheering crowds. For its part, the National Salvation Association welcomed Chiang's return to power and joined with the Communist Party in calling for a united front against the Japanese occupier.

The die was now cast, though the Japanese may have been slow to realize it. The tug-of-war between Tokyo and Nanjing over north China appeared no longer amenable to negotiation or compromise. It is hard to see how war could have been avoided in 1937, or at least within the next several years. In this there is great and tragic irony. The tragedy in the drift to war in China and Japan in the spring of 1937 is that of an incongruence in the perceptions and timing of the policies of the two countries. While Japan, for reasons that may have been entirely self-interested and delusional, was prepared now to moderate its near half century of aggression in China, its change of attitude was a half century too late. The Nationalist regime, understandably endowed with fifty years of indignation, now began to assume an increasingly adamantine, vengeful, and uncompromising stand against Japan.[76] The spark set off outside Peking on the night of 7 July 1937 was much like those numerous minor military frictions in the Sino-Japanese relationship in the past that had been quickly extinguished through negotiation. But this time it could not be doused through compromise, and, fanned by the national determination of an aroused people, it burst into flame.

Part II

THE TWO ARMIES ON THE EVE OF THE WAR

It is a commonplace belief that the Japanese and Chinese armies were mismatched. Japan possessed a modern industrial base, a strong military institution, and popular support for its army. China had none of these advantages. Nevertheless, Chinese forces under Chiang Kai-shek managed to force the Japanese army into a protracted war of attrition. The reasons for this seeming paradox may be found in Chang Jui-te's and Edward J. Drea's respective essays on the state of the Japanese and Nationalist armies in 1937.

In chapter 3 Chang Jui-te demonstrates that influential Chinese military thinkers had been considering the notion of protracted war since the 1920s. Under German tutelage from the 1920s into the mid-1930s, the Kuomintang army slowly but steadily prepared to defend China against what leaders regarded as certain aggression from Japan. This defensive orientation gave rise to a Fabian strategy; strong positional defenses, especially around Shanghai; and an attempt to build an army sadly lacking in popular support and money. Nonstandardization of weaponry plagued the Kuomintang army, as did shortages of artillery weapons and transport. Logistics were weak and bedeviled the army throughout its existence. More significant, perhaps, was the lack of coordination between regional forces and the national army, between Chiang Kai-shek and his lieutenants, and between politicians and intellectuals and the military. Chang discusses at length the army's training system, noting its shortfalls in recruiting, its unevenness because of regional strengths or weaknesses, and its inability to produce sufficiently trained staff officers. Chiang was in the process of reforming and rebuilding a woefully unprepared Kuomintang army, but in July 1937 time ran out.

In Edward J. Drea's account in chapter 4 the Japanese army is a mirror image of its Chinese counterpart. Drea concentrates more on strategic and operational planning, tactics, and doctrinal development. He presents a picture of a highly trained, toughly disciplined, confident military organization that was well equipped by 1937 standards. Japan's military leaders thought in terms of rapidly moving offensive operations designed to force decisive battles and gain quick victories in short-term wars. Following the Manchurian Incident of 1931, the army devoted its attention more to the resurgent Soviet Union than to China. Just as Chinese military leaders regarded war with Japan as inevitable, Japanese generals presumed the same about a war with the Soviet Union. Thus, the Japanese army crafted a doctrine, operational plan, and force structure to fight the Soviets. Planners assumed contingency operations against China, should they occur because of local friction, and assumed a regional conflict with a brief and decisive result for Japan. By 1937 the army was in the midst of a process of reorganization and modernization it expected to complete in the early 1940s. Until then, the army wished to avoid a major war on the Asian continent. But for the Japanese army, too, time ran out.

3 *The Nationalist Army on the Eve of the War*

CHANG JUI-TE

Introduction

Noon, 7 July 1937: Xu Yongchang, director of the Nationalist government's Military Affairs Commission, said to a friend, "Young people from rich families and students are not willing to become soldiers nowadays. Only the poor join up. In fact, once their living conditions improve, the poor also don't want to serve. If we implement a conscription system, people will join against their will and will lack ardor. This being so, to defeat Japanese aggression, we must reform the education system to change people's attitudes or our country will perish." Chiang Kai-shek then sent a letter today that discussed educational reform in detail. But that night the Marco Polo Bridge Incident occurred.[1]

On 2 August 1937, Chiang sent a telegram to provincial military and civil officials, declaring that the government was committed to fight the Japanese. The telegram invited officials to Nanjing to discuss strategy. Bai Chongxi, the number two man of the Guangxi Clique and a widely admired strategist, discussed the telegram with senior Guangxi officials as well as with Li Zongren, the clique's leader. The consensus was that Li and Bai should decline the invitation, as their rival Chiang Kai-shek might imprison them. Chiang Kai-shek and Li Zongren had competed for national leadership ever since the Northern Expedition of 1926–1928.

Bai, on the other hand, held that Guangdong and Guangxi had consistently advocated resisting Japan and that the Chinese people supported that policy. He also believed that if he did not go to Nanjing, not only would he be casting doubt on Chiang's sincerity, he would also fail to live up to his own public promises, for which the Chinese people would condemn him. Bai won the argument and convinced Li Zongren to promise Chiang the Guangxi Clique's support for war. Bai immediately departed, while Li Zongren stayed in Guilin to organize the mobilization of the province, ready to follow Bai if necessary.[2]

The exchange of telegrams between Guangxi and the Nationalist government was brought to the attention of Liu Xiang, provincial chairman of Sichuan, and Long Yun, provincial chairman of Yunnan. Both appealed to Bai to reconsider. Liu and Long noted that although they too had heard that the Nationalist government was prepared to send its armies into the field to fight Japan, doubts remained about its real commitments. They warned that in case Chiang did not go to war and Bai and Li lost their freedom, the Nationalist government would be able to establish control over Guangxi Province, after which they would be next. In his answer, Li Zongren urged Liu and Long to support the Nationalist government and mobilize their provinces as well, stating that otherwise their inactivity would constitute a concession to the Japanese invaders.[3]

On the evening of 7 August 1937, Chiang summoned the Supreme Defense Council and the Central Committee of the Nationalist Party (KMT) to discuss military strategy. In attendance were provincial level military and civil officers in Nanjing, as well as regional military leaders such as Yan Xishan, Bai Chongxi, Yu Hanmou, He Jian, and Liu Xiang. The discussion ended with Chiang declaring that "when faced with war, we must resolve to be determined and implement our decision unreservedly, for our survival depends on it. We must stick to our plan. We must entrust the Nationalist government to make the necessary preparations for war, as it is left to it to decide to proceed or retreat. Local governments must obey and follow the Nationalist government without hesitation." All participants stood up to signify their unanimous agreement.[4] Railroad Minister Zhang Jia'ao (Chang Kai-ngau), who attended the meeting, stated, "The conference united the entire nation—[a thing] unseen for centuries."[5] It was rumored that Yan Xishan and Liu Xiang attended the conference because of Bai Chongxi's decision to travel to Nanjing.[6] However, upon his return to Sichuan, when Liu discussed with his aides the dispatch of Sichuan forces to the front, one suggested that he need not personally lead them, as he suffered from a gastric ulcer. Liu responded that "in the past, I have fought bitter civil wars, but now we have the opportunity to join in the war against Japan. We must do our best for the nation so that history may record our positive contributions to its welfare."[7]

China began the Sino-Japanese War against this background of internal division. This chapter discusses the development of the Nationalist army during the years before the beginning of war. I discuss military strategy and tactics, equipment and logistics, the construction of national defense projects and bases in China's hinterland, military education and training, the staff system of the army, the military hierarchy, and reorganization of armies and divisions as well as their combat effectiveness. This chapter excludes the navy and the air force, which remained seriously underdeveloped. The chapter suggests that despite real progress in many areas, the Nationalist army was no match for Japan in 1937, largely because its rapid modernization was thwarted by these domestic political and military divisions.

Strategy, National Defense Planning, and Tactics

Beginning in the decade 1910–1920, some Chinese intellectuals began to consider a full-scale conflict between Japan and China as inevitable. In the ensuing discussions about China's strategic options, Jiang Fangzhen, also known as Jiang Baili, was the first to advocate protracted warfare as China's military strategy, thus anticipating China's approach to the Sino-Japanese War. In his youth, Jiang had studied in Japan and developed a deep understanding of Japan's government and military. As early as 1917, Jiang predicted that China and Japan would become involved in a drawn-out war and that the combat zone would be west of the Peking–Wuhan and Guangzhou–Wuhan railways.[8] Later, in *Guofang lun* (On National Defense), Jiang again argued that China should use protracted warfare to frustrate Japan's desire for a quick victory.[9] He argued that China should exploit its huge population and vast territory to prolong the war so as to erode Japan's strength over time and gradually turn the situation to China's favor. He continued to argue that China should not defend coastal areas but confront the enemy west of the Peking–Wuhan Railway.

Chiang Kai-shek came to agree that "the longer the war drags on, the more advantageous for China."[10] Despite much popular criticism, both the Nationalist government and General Zhang Xueliang, the ruler of Manchuria, had decided not to resist Japan by force when it attacked Manchuria in September 1931 and Shanghai in 1932. Chiang Kai-shek was especially reluctant to confront Japan, as he still faced a Communist insurgency in his heartland and because he believed that Chinese troops would suffer a rapid defeat. He predicted that, within three days, Japan could seize the key areas along the Chinese coast and the Yangtze River and cripple China by destroying its military, transport, and financial lifelines.

After the North China Incident in May 1935, Japan became increasingly aggressive in north China, and Chiang gradually toughened his stance. The Nationalist government proposed a twin strategy of seeking peace and security but also preparing for war. If peace became impossible, China would mobilize its national resources to seek ultimate victory in prolonged war.[11] China formally adopted protracted warfare as its basic strategy in its National Defense Plan. After the Sino-Japanese clash at Shanghai of 28 January 1932, to prevent the conflict in Shanghai from escalating further, the Military Affairs Commission drew up a plan, which divided China into four defense areas and one preparation area. While some troops were to maintain local security, commanders of these areas were to concentrate their remaining forces to prepare for a confrontation with Japan. This was the earliest National Defense Plan primarily aimed to defeat Japanese aggression. Several other national defense plans were drawn up subsequently.[12] Although detailed, they were not implemented until 1935.

In that year, the Military Affairs Commission promulgated a General Defense Guideline. It contained two alternative approaches toward a Japanese invasion. The first, conservative in nature, stipulated that Nationalist troops should hold predetermined key positions and use protracted warfare to thwart the enemy. The second plan proposed that "in order to stop the enemy's ambition to invade China and to protect the integrity of our territory, China will concentrate its best forces and carry out decisive battles in appropriate regions to defeat the enemy. Our priority is to defeat enemy units stationed along the Yangtze River and along the seacoast."[13]

In August 1935, German military adviser General Alexander von Falkenhausen submitted a recommendation to Chiang Kai-shek. He predicted that Japan would follow three routes of advance into China. One ran from north Hebei to Zhengzhou city, the second from Shandong toward Xuzhou, and the third across the Yangtze River to the capital, Nanjing, and then along the Yangtze to Wuhan. He believed that Japan would send its strongest forces along this third route. Von Falkenhausen therefore suggested that China should regard the Yangtze River as the main combat area. He also proposed that Sichuan should be regarded as a final place of retreat.[14] In 1936, a preliminary draft for a new National Defense Plan divided China into four zones: a war zone, a defense zone, an internal security zone, and a preparation area. The war zones included ten provinces: Chahar, Suiyuan, Hebei, Shanxi, Shandong, Henan, Jiangsu, Zhejiang, Fujian, and Guangdong. The General Defense Guideline stated that "if the situation was unfavorable, the troops in the war zone should ultimately retreat to their predetermined resistance lines." The draft plan adopted Sichuan as the general base for the war. It also indicated that Nanjing, Nanchang, and Wuchang would serve as bases for resistance south of the Yangtze River and that Taiyuan, Zhengzhou, Luoyang, Xi'an, and Hankou would serve as such north of the Yangtze River.

In January 1937, in issuing its annual War Plan, the Chinese General Staff Department suggested three possible regions for military conflict between China and Japan. The plan contained two proposals: Proposal A emphasized long-term combat. "If the situation is unfavorable, China should carry out its plan of protracted warfare and gradually force the enemy to expand their strength while seizing any opportunity to take to the offensive." This proposal focused on the Peking–Wuhan Railway and stated that China should concentrate its forces and seek to defeat Japan immediately. If this failed, Chinese forces should fall back to predetermined defensive positions, regain strength, and then prepare to shift to the offensive in an effort to destroy the Japanese invaders. In Proposal B, China's forces would attempt to prevent the enemy from invading China. "The aim is to exhaust the enemy's strength in China within a certain period. Along the coast from Shandong Peninsula to the lower Yangtze south of the Hangzhou Bay, China should resolutely halt the enemy's attempts to land its forces. In north China, we should attack the enemy's units from north of the Great Wall and seize the opportunity to enter Manchuria with our main forces." The basic goal of proposals A and B was for China to stop the enemy north of the Great Wall on the northern front, stop enemy advances east of Peking and Tianjin, and prevent Japanese landings along the eastern coast.[13]

Before the Marco Polo Bridge Incident, the Nationalist government completed some of the major projects provided for in the plan. It established six military supply depots at Nanjing, Bengbu, Xinyang, Huayin, Nanchang, and Wuchang. These depots were to handle all supplies stored in the Peking-Pukou, Peking-Shanghai, Tianjin-Pukou, Peking-Wuhan, Lianyungang-Lanzhou, Fujian, and Zhejiang areas. Under these six depots were twenty-nine small storehouses and sixteen larger storehouses to be used for field combat. Nanchang and Wuchang would serve as the national core depots. The depots were to house (1) 60 million rounds of small-arms ammunition at various sites north of the Yangtze River, 40 million at Wuchang, and 100 million at Nanjing, sufficient for twenty divisions for three months; (2) grain for 500,000 persons and fodder for 100,000 horses for one month; and (3) 3 million gallons of automotive gasoline and 2.5 million gallons of aviation gasoline. Ten rear hospitals were to be established to accommodate 10,000 casualties and twenty temporary hospitals, to treat 10,000 wounded near the front. Medical supplies sufficient to sustain one hundred divisions for a duration of six months were also to be available. Construction of antiaircraft facilities in major cities such as Nanjing and Wuhan was also begun. However, when the war began in July 1937, not all projects were completed.[14]

Unlike the Japanese army, Chinese forces focused on defensive strategies. In July 1934, Chiang Kai-shek addressed the Mount Lushan Military Officer Training Camp. He stated that four possible strategies existed to deal with Japan. The preferred option was to rely on defense as offense. The second option was to build fortresses in several places. The third option was to defend positions tenaciously. The final strategy was to focus on guerrilla warfare and use irregulars (such as guerrilla and volunteer forces) to tie down the enemy's major forces. Chiang stressed that China should mobilize its people so that the entire nation would participate in the war.[15] In a speech delivered in January 1938, Chiang stated that guerrilla warfare was one kind of formal warfare and should be conducted by regular units with a high level of combat efficiency.[16] Guided by Chiang's idea, the Nationalist military regarded positional warfare as a major strategy, complemented by mobile warfare and guerrilla warfare.

When confronted by Japanese units with formidable firepower and mobility, Nationalist troops suffered great losses after putting this military strategy into practice. As the war progressed, the Nationalist military learned from their previous battles and adjusted their tactics. They began to value guerrilla warfare, and by the end of 1939, while preparing for the second stage of the war, Chiang Kai-shek adopted the concept that "guerrilla warfare should be more important than regular warfare." Several guerrilla warfare cadre training classes were organized to train middle and senior military officers. In combat, the Nationalist military deployed guerrilla units throughout the battlefield, to wear down the enemy. The Nationalist troops destroyed roads to reduce the enemy's mobility, shifted toward the enemy's rear and exterior lines, and attacked the enemy's supply lines. In consequence, Japanese forces could not make their superiority tell, and, once exhausted after an initial push, became vulnerable to Chinese counteroffensives. The most famous example of this strategy was the Chinese victory in the Third Battle of Changsha in 1942.[17]

Organization, Weapons, and Logistics

There was a significant inequality between the Japanese and Chinese armies in terms of equipment. Table 3.1 compares a Nationalist and a Japanese division.

In addition to the materiel listed above, each Japanese division also had one mechanized "group" with thirty-nine light military vehicles and twenty-one light armored cars, 6,000–7,000 horses, 200–300 automobiles, and special troops, including poison gas teams. Nationalist divisions did not have any of these. Although, in theory, a Nationalist division had an armored regiment, that unit had fewer than seventy-two armored vehicles.[18]

A major weakness was a lack of artillery. In 1936, a division officially had one artillery battalion divided into three artillery batteries with twelve guns total. It also had one mechanized cannon company with four direct-fire weapons. A Japanese division had four infantry regiments and one mountain artillery or field artillery regiment. Each artillery regiment had three field artillery battalions and a howitzer battalion, and the infantry regiment itself had one mountain artillery section (four weapons). The infantry battalion had one Type 70 mountain gun section (two guns). In total, a Japanese division had sixty-four artillery pieces of various calibers,

TABLE 3.1

The organization and equipment of a Nationalist and a Japanese division

Organization	Japanese division	Chinese division
Infantry	2 brigades (4 regiments)	2 brigades (4 regiments)
Artillery	1 regiment	1 battalion
Cavalry	1 regiment	1 battalion
Engineering unit	1 regiment	1 battalion
Transport unit	1 regiment	1 battalion
Other	Special troops	Special troops

Equipment	Japanese division	Chinese division
Personnel	24,400–28,200	10,923
Rifles	9,586	3,821
Light machine guns	292	274
Heavy machine guns	96	54
Grenade launchers	304	243
Mountain/field artillery	48	16
Regiment/battalion artillery	56	30

four times as many as a Chinese division, and of far higher quality. In reality, in 1936, twelve of the twenty elite Chinese "reformed divisions" still lacked artillery battalions. The ordnance in the "reformed divisions" was composed mostly of the old Type 60 mountain gun. In the entire country, few of the 200 divisions had any artillery at all. If they did have it, the guns were mostly those that had fallen into disuse by field artillery regiments, or mountain or field artillery pieces that had been provided to local forces. Some units even used trench mortars to serve as a stopgap measure. Artillery weapons came from various countries, but they often lacked observation and signal components and were short of ammunition. Most mountain guns and field artillery were the Type 75; although they could deliver fire support, their range was limited, and they inflicted little damage.

In 1937, for example, in the fighting in Shanghai, the mountain artillery of the Guangxi Twenty-first Army Group had a range of only 1,200 yards, while the Japanese field artillery could hit targets at 8,000 yards. Domestically made mountain artillery suffered from inferior steel-making technology in China. The gun shields were of poor-quality steel, and the gun barrels turned red after firing several rounds and were at risk of exploding.[19]

The Nationalist ordnance and equipment listed in the tables above were only for "reformed divisions," and not all of those met the necessary specifications and standards. Moreover, the equipment of local forces varied greatly in quality. Some local units actually had better equipment than that of Nationalist units. For instance, before the Sino-Japanese War, Yunnan units had French antitank guns and heavy machine guns. The air-cooled French machine guns proved better than the German water-cooled machine guns of Nationalist government units.[20] But most local troops had inferior equipment. The forces under Wang Mingzhang of the 122nd Division from Sichuan, which bravely defended Tengxian County during the Xuzhou Battle, had light and heavy machine guns made in Sichuan, which often broke down. Their Type 79 rifles were also made in Sichuan. Some arms dated from the Qing Dynasty. Their range was limited, and they sometimes broke down after firing fewer than one hundred rounds.

Prior to the war, Nationalist and local forces had weaponry from various foreign and domestic sources. Even domestically made weapons did not conform to one standard. Those made in Hanyang and Manchuria differed in design and specifications. German, French, Russian, Japanese, and Italian products also were not uniform. The arms of even a single unit did not conform to a single standard, let alone that for all China's armed forces, thus creating enormous logistic problems, with consequent effects on combat effectiveness, especially in the initial stage of the war.[21] Nationalist ordnance factories produced more than 3 million rounds of small-arms ammunition a day, potentially ensuring a sufficient supply,[22] but this incompatibility of ammunition and weapons reduced the usable quantity of small-arms ammunition.

Chinese communications facilities were poor. In the Nationalist army, signal units were not independent but were part of engineer units. Radio was of low quality, and in cases of emergencies, telegrams often could not be sent out for days. Orders often had to be dispatched by post.[23] In 1937, the entire country had only 3,000 military vehicles,[24] necessitating reliance on horses and mules for transport. Twenty Nationalist divisions needed 10,647 horses and 20,688 mules. Yet at the end of 1935, they had only 6,206 horses and 4,351 mules.[25] According to one statistic, in 1936, the mortality rate of the Nationalist military's horses was a high 5 percent. The number even reached 10 percent for some units.[26]

The distribution of weaponry was a source of dispute during army reorganization programs after the Northern Expedition. Although Chiang's own forces belonged to the regular army, the quality of the equipment they received varied widely. At the time, domestic production of weaponry was limited, and imports could not make up the difference. Priority was given to small arms. Chiang Kai-shek used army reorganization to weaken forces uncommitted to his rule. Staff officers of the Nationalist army noted that forces loyal to Chiang received the best weapons. Because the northwestern and northeastern forces nurtured good relations with KMT, they received relatively better weapons, while Shanxi troops received inferior ones. Troops in the Guangxi faction received even poorer weapons because Guangxi leaders had stronger political ambitions. The forces of Shi Yousan, Li Hongchang, and Sun Dianying, regarded as bandit troops, understandably received poor weapons. While the distribution of arms increased the propensity of some local forces to side with the KMT, it alienated others, inadvertently causing additional years of turmoil after the Northern Expedition.[27]

Logistic accounting was poor in the Nationalist military. Military expenditure constituted a large element of all government spending—65.48 percent in 1937.[28] Personnel costs were the most important item, but accounting by army units was less concerned with accuracy than with improving the resources of a given unit. Surpluses were not returned but were used to award military officers and soldiers for merit in battle, to care for the wounded, or to build up a reserve. If there was a deficit, troops turned to "living off vacancies." That is, if soldiers deserted, their units did not promptly report this information. If new soldiers were expected, the units reported that the soldiers had arrived before they had done so. Military commanders generally selected their most trusted subordinates to serve as accountants and logistic officers.[29] After the war began, the harm became obvious. During the Battle of Shanghai in 1937, some soldiers on the front line were not provided food for days and were not paid for months. Wounded soldiers and civilians often had to travel around searching for medical treatment. When the main forces relocated, they often left grain, ammunition, weapons, and petroleum en route. General Chen Cheng, commander in chief during the Battle of Shanghai, noted that "this phenomenon fully revealed that we do not have the ability to supply our frontline troops. It showed that China is still a backward country with poor management."[30] Many shortcomings in logistics seriously hurt the morale and combat effectiveness of the troops. In a speech given in 1933, Chiang Kai-shek pointed out that many soldiers deserted because of the poor food and inadequate clothing brought about by poor logistics. Soldiers were also demoralized because their salaries were reduced or embezzled.[31] A shortage of professional staff and equipment hampered medical care.[32] Disease and mortality rates were high. According to official statistics from 1936, approximately 10 percent of the soldiers became sick each year, and the mortality rate was as high as 5 percent.[33] According to Japanese military authorities, one in every three wounded Japanese soldiers died. Conversely, a Dutch military officer who was in China during the initial stage of the Sino-Japanese War noted that one in every two wounded Nationalist soldiers died.[34]

Because Nationalist forces had poor equipment and limited transport capacity, they were forced to recruit farmers and rent vehicles. Because they also lacked the necessary facilities such as tents, they had to rent houses. Not surprisingly, clashes between the military and civilians were frequent.[35]

Construction of Defense Projects and Rear Bases

China is a large country with a long coastline. Important fortresses built in modern times included Wusong, Jiangyin, Zhenjiang, Jiangning, and Wuhan along the Yangtze River, and Zhenhai, Humen, and Changzhou along the seacoast. With the exception of the Wuhan fortress, constructed in 1929 and 1930, all others were built during the late Qing Dynasty and still had uncovered cannon batteries. They suffered from poor maintenance, and many components had become obsolete and could not be replaced. Their military value was negligible.

After the January 1932 Shanghai Incident, the Japanese military destroyed the Wusong forts, thus leaving the entrance to the Yangtze River wide open. The coastline from Jiangsu to Shandong had no defenses at all, so the Japanese could land at will. In December 1932, the Military Affairs Commission formed a fortress group, responsible for constructing fortresses and defensive installations. The commission asked for the assistance of German military advisers. Following the 1935 North China Incident, the Nationalist government sped up the construction of defensive installations in accordance with national war planning. Much construction focused on Nanjing, as it was the capital. The Nationalists further planned to build fortresses first along the seacoast and the Yellow River and then in key regions north of the Yellow River. The government also ordered a large amount of heavy artillery from Germany, of which the first batch arrived before the Marco Polo Bridge Incident. The artillery included several dozen pieces of flat-fire antiaircraft, dual-purpose heavy artillery. These were installed at the Jiangyin, Zhenjiang, Nanjing, and Wuhan fortresses. By the summer of 1937, the construction of nine fortresses was complete: Nanjing, Zhenjiang, Jiangyin, Ningbo, Humen, Mawei, Xiamen (Amoy), Nantong, and Lianyungang. China had a total of 41 forts and 273 fortress cannon.[36]

Some defensive installations were badly managed. Many units posted on their defensive perimeters had not received training, nor did they have appropriate maps. Barbettes in fortresses were not well hidden and could store few shells. Fortress troops had little training. Once war broke out, the result of these conditions was obvious. Along the Suzhou–Fushan and Wuxi–Jiangyin defense lines, the Japanese held command of the air. Nationalist troops retreated chaotically. The fortresses were locked, and keys had gone missing as units had been transferred frequently, or as county magistrates, who sometimes had keys, had fled when the war erupted. When Nationalist forces needed the fortresses, they sometimes could not locate them, and when they did, they were not always able to enter them.[37] Nevertheless, the fortresses and fortifications were not entirely useless. They strengthened Chinese positions at the defense line from Cangxian County to Baoding, from Dexian County to Shijiazhuang, and in southern

Shandong. They also played a role in resisting Japanese troops advancing along the Peking–Wuhan and northern Tianjin–Pukou railways and during the Battle of Taierzhuang.

Prior to the war, China's political and economic center lay in the regions along the seacoast and the Yangtze River. As Japanese encroachment expanded, the Nationalist government was forced to construct bases in China's hinterland. The Japanese attack on Shanghai in 1932 drove the Nationalists to move the capital to Luoyang. On 5 March, the Second Plenum of the KMT's Fourth Congress set up the Western Capital Preparation Committee to prepare for the relocation of all government organs to Xi'an in case all-out war erupted. In February 1933, the Central Political Conference passed the Northwest Development Bill. In February 1934, the National Economic Commission established a northwestern branch to take charge of development projects in the area.[38] On 18 October 1934, Chiang Kai-shek flew to Lanzhou, noting in his diary: "Northwest China has abundant resources. Japan and Russia are ready to bully us severely. Yet if we can strengthen ourselves and develop northwest China to the fullest possible extent, we can turn northwest China into the base of China's revival."[39]

It was not the northwest but Sichuan that became China's hinterland base during the Sino-Japanese War. In October 1934, the Communist army evacuated its soviet in south China, beginning the Long March that would end in the northwest. Chiang Kai-shek had by this time decided to make Sichuan China's base of last resort. In January 1935, the Nanchang Field Headquarters of the Military Affairs Commission, which had been in charge of fighting the Communists and was the supreme military and political authority of most provinces along the Yangtze River and the central China coast, dispatched a special advisory group to Chongqing. Thereafter, the Nationalist army entered Sichuan. On 10 February, the Nationalists appointed a new provincial government in Sichuan, thus bringing Sichuan's long-standing regionalism to an end. On 2 March, Chiang flew to Chongqing, and two days later, he gave a speech emphasizing that "Sichuan should be the base for China's revival." He stated that he came to Sichuan to monitor the suppression of the Communist army and to unify the provincial administration. On the seventh, Chiang instructed Minister of Finance Kong Xiangxi (H. H. Kung) to dispatch officials to improve provincial finances in Sichuan, beginning with the standardization of the currency and fixing exchange rates between Sichuan and the rest of Nationalist China. Thereafter, Chiang surveyed Guizhou, Yunnan, and other regions in the southwest, staying until early October. In November 1935, he established a Chongqing branch of the Military Affairs Commission with wide powers, including supreme military authority.

In June 1937, Chiang sent He Yingqin, minister of Military Affairs, to Sichuan to convene the Sichuan Military Reorganization Conference.

Chiang incorporated reorganized Sichuan troops into the Nationalist order of battle. Under Chiang's direct supervision, the incorporation of Sichuan into the Nationalist order was rapid. Sichuan's garrison area system, which had divided the province into autonomous military zones, was abolished, and all garrison forces were subordinated to the provincial government, which issued pay. Independent revenue gathering by these forces, on which they had depended in the past, was proscribed. The Central Bank set up branches in Sichuan, including branches at Chongqing, Chengdu, and Wanxian. It issued bonds to pay for military and construction expenses. The New Life Movement was vigorously promoted and opium smoking banned.[40] Such policies were also carried out in Guizhou and Yunnan. In this way, the southwest was prepared as rear-area base for the Nationalist government during the war. The future would illustrate the enormous significance of this project for the fate of China.

Recruitment and the National Military System

The Republic of China had continued to use the Qing Dynasty's conscription system after the 1911 revolution. But after it came to power, the Nationalist government sought to implement national military service. It promulgated a military service law in 1933 and began to implement this law in 1936. According to this law, military service was divided into service in the Nationalist army and territorial citizen army units. Men between the ages of eighteen and forty-five were expected to serve in the territorial units if they did not serve in the Nationalist army. There were three stages for the territorial units: active service, usually two to three years; first reserves, normally six years; and second reserves, until the age of forty-five. The Ministry of Military Affairs divided China into sixty divisional conscription headquarters. Divisional and regimental conscription headquarters were first established in the six provinces of Jiangsu, Zhejiang, Anhui, Jiangxi, Henan, and Hubei. By December 1936, around 50,000 new soldiers had been drafted.[41]

This military service law was advantageous to the middle and upper classes. Government staff were not required to enlist, so privileged families registered their children with an agency of the government bureaucracy. Students in middle schools and universities were also exempted. Children from poor family backgrounds chose to take on military service because they did not have money to go to school.[42] Leaders of towns and villages were in charge of carrying out recruitment, often conspiring with army recruitment personnel. One recruitment principle stipulated that they were "to draft one person if there were three sons, two persons if there were five sons, and not to draft anyone if there was only one son." But the wealthy and the privileged could gain exemptions for all their sons. In contrast, poor families might see their only son conscripted if they did not pay the appropriate bribe.[43] The heads of towns and villages exercised great power in the recruitment process. Prior to the war, a saying in southern Anhui ran "In the past, county magistrates could exterminate an entire family but now village heads can annihilate an entire household."

The new recruitment system provided various money-making opportunities. Military personnel who were to accompany draftees to the units in which they were to serve would allow draftees to escape for a fee. Draftees themselves could also make money by agreeing to serve as a substitute for someone else. To be a draftee could become an occupation. In 1936, 600 people were drafted in the Wuhu area of Anhui province. According to the recollection of the administrators of this area, every draftee had been traded, replaced, or seized.[44]

A few regions handled recruitment successfully. For instance, Guangxi implemented a recruitment process from 1933. Less than 40 percent of the draftees came forward voluntarily.[45] Nevertheless, due to successful training, by July 1937 Guangxi had gone through four annual cycles of recruitment, training, and demobilization into the reserves. After the Sino-Japanese War erupted, the Guangxi government made plans to send forty regiments to the front. As soon as the order was given, farmers from various counties rushed to the county government to enlist. Because too many people enlisted, the government drew lots to determine whom to take. In less than a month, four armies (forty regiments) were formed.[46]

Beginning in 1929, the Nationalist government also implemented military training for high school students and older. Each week students had one theoretical and one practical class for a total of three hours. From 1934, students had to go through a military training program for three months before they could graduate.[47] Graduates of military academies served as military instructors.[48] By the end of 1936, more than 237,000 high school students had received military training.[49] Student military training was directed by the Society for the Implementation of the Three People's Principles of Sun Yat-sen, which also provided political instruction and sometimes collected information on students' political views.[50] During the Battle of Shanghai, discussed by Yang Tianshi in chapter 5, students in Shanghai formed three battlefield service groups of 1,000 students to carry the wounded and assist with transport. Many were killed or wounded, but others became junior officers. Thus, student military training appears to have been reasonably effective.[51]

Military Education and Training

Although the Nationalists worked hard to improve military training of both officers and troops, they had inherited deep-seated problems that they were not able to overcome completely. A paucity of facilities, outmoded training manuals, low regard for military instructors, and the persistence of regionalism and warlordism hampered progress. The Japanese would mercilessly expose these shortcomings of the Nationalist army.

The Central Military Academy, with origins in the Whampoa Military Academy, established in 1923 in Guangzhou to train officers for the Northern Expedition, became the premier training base of junior military officers. It offered a preliminary or basic course, followed by a cadet course. The basic course, lasting for eighteen months, included general education, special education in various subjects, and field practice. Cadet training taught students the skills that junior military offices required and took two years. The academy admitted seventeen classes before the outbreak of war.[52] Admission was competitive, as military officers were paid well. In 1935, 10,000 applications were received to enroll in the twelfth class, but only 7 percent were admitted.[53] Upon graduation, cadets were usually assigned to those divisions in the Nationalist army loyal to Chiang Kai-shek. As they had received instruction from German advisers, the quality of these cadets was high.[54]

The Nationalists had less then a decade to improve China's military training institutions. The Ministry of Military Education was established in 1928. The National Revolutionary Army, which had fought in the Northern Expedition, consisted of independent warlord forces that did not necessarily implement the ministry's reform measures. Its influence was also restricted by Chiang Kai-shek, who served as the principal of most academies and had a habit of bypassing the ministry. For Chiang, the ministry was one place to give a high position with little actual power to those whose loyalty was doubtful but whom he wanted to bind to his regime. General He Yingqin, close to the Guangxi Clique; General Li Jishen, who engaged in power struggles with Chiang; and General Tang Shengzhi, from Hunan—all of whom served as inspector generals of the ministry—were examples of this category of officer.[55]

In modern China, mostly veterans served as sergeants. Some units trained sergeants, but because they lacked formal education, they lacked standing. Truly qualified sergeants were rare. While serving as minister of Military Training, General Bai Chongxi suggested setting up a sergeant school and establishing a professional noncommissioned officer system. But the Ministry of Military Affairs objected on financial grounds. Although commanding officers enjoyed rapid promotion, military instructors did not. Nor was there a system by which instructors were transferred to commands in the field or commanders were assigned for a period to a military academy.

With minor changes to cover, for instance, tank warfare or machine guns, Qing Dynasty military manuals continued to be used at the Central Military Academy until the beginning of the war. After the Ministry of Military Training was established, a bureau for military translation was set up. It evaluated existing course materials and translated military manuals, but its contributions were limited.[56] A further shortcoming of instruction at military academies was the stress on theory and the neglect of field practice. After the start of the Sino-Japanese War, military education began to focus on case studies and stress practical application.[57]

In order to raise the quality of military officers, from 1931 the Nationalist army instituted schools for artillery, infantry, transport, engineering, and signals. The administrators and facilities of these schools were thought to be of high quality. For instance, Wang Jun headed the school for infantry, Zou Zuohua was in charge of the artillery school, and Lin Bosen was responsible for the engineering school. All were highly regarded and served as special advisers at the headquarters of He Yingqin. They attended important meetings dealing with fortification projects and combat plans for major battles.[58]

The Nationalists adopted German models of military training instead of the Japanese ones previously used. They appointed German advisers to take charge of training cadres at military academies. They also trained three instructional divisions. Prior to the Sino-Japanese War, 15,000 students graduated with a German military education. About fifty combat divisions emerged from the three instructional divisions.[59]

The progress of other Nationalist army forces was more limited because their training was inappropriate for contemporary battlefield realities. Before World War I, troops fought in close formation, as firepower was limited. After World War I and the widespread introduction of machine guns, dispersed formations became the norm. In 1935, a new drill manual issued by the Ministry of Military Training introduced small-group tactics.[60] But few forces adopted these. In consequence, during the Battle of Taierzhuang, Lu Han's forces from south China suffered a high casualty rate.[61]

As General Chen Cheng pointed out in 1938, an outmoded stress on parade ground drill and formal military manners was a further problem. He wrote that "we have paid too much attention to stereotypical formality and procedure of no practical use. Sometimes even though soldiers could not get a haircut or take a bath for several months, their camps had to be in order. They had intensive training in close-order drill but did not learn much about gun handling, marksmanship, or maneuvering. Even in peacetime this was wrong, but after the Sino-Japanese War began, we still continued in this way, even using it for highly educated youth."[62] In contrast, the Communist army had simplified training, focusing on two key skills: firing with live ammunition and running, to enhance the troops' physical strength and mobility. This training greatly increased their combat effectiveness in the harsh terrain without roads in which the Sino-Japanese War would be fought.[63]

Finally, the Nationalist army's training did not reach all soldiers. Only half of all combat soldiers were properly trained, and the rest were neglected.[64] According to one statistic, there were 5 million military personnel during the Sino-Japanese War. Three million worked in logistic services. Few of these had received much training, with disastrous consequences for overall combat effectiveness.[65]

Staff System

Highly trained staff officers have become increasingly important as warfare has become more complex. Napoleon drew up operational plans close to the front line and sent orders to the front by courier. During World War I, military commanders collected information in their headquarters and used telephones and automobiles to send orders to the front. In World War II, as the battlefield expanded from land to include the sea and the air, senior commanders made decisions in headquarters far from the battlefield and depended on large numbers of staff officers with specialized skills to keep them informed.

In China, the staff officer system was underdeveloped. Only 2,000 commanders and staff officers had been trained by 1937.[66] Prior to the Sino-Japanese War, commanders handled most staff work themselves. In that period, staff officers functioned as military secretaries and merely drafted orders, reports, and maps. Some staff officers had no military training, and as a whole staff officers were not respected, so that the most talented officers eschewed service in this branch.[67] Staff officer departments of local forces were in even worse shape. In March 1937, Liu Ziqing, a Whampoa graduate, served as director of political instruction in the Forty-fourth Army, a force of Sichuan warlord Liu Xiang, whose headquarters were at Chengdu. Liu Ziqing provides an extreme example:

The commander in chief was not supposed to manage the army and even did not know its whereabouts . . . But he could appoint relatives and former subordinates (who were officials and businessmen as well) to the army. Each month they received a bit of money. At headquarters, there was a long table and two rows of chairs. At around ten o'clock in the morning, senior officers signed in to signify their presence. Those with other business left, while the remaining ones sat down to engage in the leisurely discussion of star actresses, fortune telling, business projects, mah-jongg, and opium. Occasionally they talked about national affairs. They also chatted about news in the papers and local gossip. In the afternoon, they mostly played some rounds of mah-jongg, held banquets, and visited madams . . . Most mornings the commander usually attended as chairman, so initially I also reported for duty, but afterward I realized it was a waste of time and went very rarely. At headquarters, most of the staff wore long gowns or Western-style suits. Military uniforms were rare.

In brief, the senior, middle, and junior staff officers in the Nationalist army were inferior in knowledge as well as skill to their counterparts in advanced nations.[68] Most commanders during the Sino-Japanese War based their actions on the experiences they had gained during China's civil wars. Unsupported by skilled staff officers, they were not capable of thorough planning, nor had they developed the kind of flexibility and responsiveness to rapidly changing battlefield conditions that were critical to success during World War II.

Personnel in the Military Hierarchy

In modern warfare, quality of troops is at least as important as quantity. Below, I divide army personnel at the initial stage of the war into three categories: senior military personnel, consisting of commanders in chief, army commanders, and division commanders; middle and junior officers; and finally enlisted ranks. I discuss the educational background of each.

Senior military personnel were mostly trained at the Baoding Military Academy of the early republic. Two-thirds of commanders in chief, 37 percent of army commanders, and 20 percent of division commanders were trained there. The higher his position, the more likely it was that an officer had begun his career at Baoding. Only 10 percent of division commanders, a few army commanders, and no commanders in chief were Whampoa graduates. Commanders who were trained in local military schools and had practical experience in combat accounted for one-third of all commanders (see table 3.2).

While the prevalence of civil war offered opportunities for rapid promotion, it also made it impossible for officers to update their training at military academies or to gain experience in different branches of the military. German advisers repeatedly expressed their concern about this to Chiang Kai-shek. They argued that officers should first serve in junior capacities before assuming command.[69] During one 1938 battle, Chiang Kai-shek pointed out that "our commanders in chief equal only our enemy's regiment commanders; our army and division commanders are only as competent as our enemy's battalion and company commanders."[70] Nationalist officers on the whole did not regard high-ranking Japanese officers as great strategists but respected them as highly competent, diligent, and professional commanders who rarely made serious mistakes.[71]

Regarding middle and junior officers, on 28 January 1936, American military attachés in China issued a statistical report concerning the edu-

TABLE 3.2

Educational background of ranking officers before 1937

Education	Chief commander		Army commander		Division commander	
Whampoa Military Academy	0	(0%)	7	(10%)	20	(11%)
Baoding Military Academy	4	(67%)	25	(35%)	36	(20%)
Abroad	0	(0%)	1	(1%)	6	(3%)
Army academy	0	(0%)	2	(3%)	9	(5%)
Local military academy and promoted from ranks	2	(33%)	35	(49%)	63	(36%)
Unclear	0	(0%)	1	(1%)	43	(24%)
Total	6	(100%)	71	(100%)	177	(100%)

SOURCE: Chang Jui-te, *Kangzhan shiqi de Guojun renshi* [Anatomy of the Nationalist army, 1937–45] (Institute of Modern History, Academia Sinica, 1993), 7.

cational background of Chinese officers (see table 3.3). According to the report, prior to the war, 70.9 percent of army officers had been trained in military academies, among whom 31.6 percent were trained at the Whampoa Military Academy. After the establishment of the Central Military Academy, most graduates were assigned to core Nationalist government forces. In Chen Cheng's Eighteenth Army, 80 percent of officers (from platoon and company commander up to division commander) were trained in the Whampoa Military Academy.[72] The report estimated that only 10,731 cadets had been trained at the military academy before the war.[73] After the Sino-Japanese War began, and as the demand for military officers rose sharply, training courses were shortened, so that quality declined. Although some military officers did not receive formal military training but learned about warfare on the battlefield, they were often highly respected by the troops.[74]

Table 3.3 shows that 29.1 percent of Nationalist military officers were lacking a formal military education. Although soldiers promoted to officer excelled in combat, they lacked leadership skills,[75] they rarely made good instructors,[76] and they had received little formal education. According to a 1935 estimate, more than half of them were completely illiterate.[77] Other officers looked down on them, and they were not promoted rapidly.[78]

The infantry was the major component of the Nationalist army. Middle and junior officers of the infantry accounted for more than 80 percent of the army's officers. A registry of military officers in the army, navy, and air force published in 1936 contained the profiles of 1,105 colonels and 2,159 lieutenant colonels in the infantry. Their educational backgrounds are shown in table 3.4.

The table makes clear that Whampoa graduates had begun to move up

TABLE 3.3

Educational background of military officers in
the Nationalist army (1936)

Background	Number	Percentage
Whampoa Military Academy	43,018	31.6%
Army junior school	20,033	14.7%
Army middle school	11,493	8.4%
Baoding Military Academy	6,575	4.8%
Various military officer camps	5,621	4.1%
Engineering soldier school	2,175	1.6%
Military supply school	2,175	1.6%
Foreign military academies	1,922	1.4%
Military medical school	1,414	1.0%
Special troops school	1,075	0.8%
Army academy	992	0.7%
Ordnance school	237	0.2%
From the ranks	39,744	29.1%
Total	136,474	100.0%

SOURCE: "Report: Statement on Commissioned Personnel Strength and Classification as to Training," *U.S. Military Intelligence Reports: China, 1911–1941*, 28 January 1936, Reel V, 521–524.

TABLE 3.4

Educational background of colonels and lieutenant colonels (1936)

Rank	Whampoa Military Academy	Baoding Military Academy	Promotion from the ranks	Others	Sample
Infantry colonel	160 (14.48%)	294 (26.61%)	53 (4.79%)	598 (54.12%)	1,105 (100%)
Infantry lieutenant colonel	475 (22.00%)	406 (18.81%)	135 (6.25%)	1,143 (52.94)	2,159 (100%)

SOURCE: Military Committee Bureau for Examining the Qualifications of Officials in Making Appointments, comp., Directory of officers and assistants in the army, navy and air force. Nanjing: Military Committee Bureau for the examination of the qualifications of officials in making appointments, 1936, vol. 1, 143–259, and 317–544, from Chang Jui-te, *Kangzhan shiqi de Guojun renshi*, 27.

the military hierarchy, outnumbering Baoding graduates at levels below that of lieutenant colonel. During the Sino-Japanese War, the quality of middle and junior infantry officers declined. In 1944, 27.3 percent of middle and junior infantry officers were from formal military academies. Officers promoted from the ranks increased to 28.1 percent. In 1937, in an ordinary infantry battalion, 80 percent of military officers were military academy graduates. This proportion fell to 20 percent during the war.[79]

The educational level of soldiers before the war remains unclear. The general impression is that most soldiers were illiterate. Sociologist Tao Menghe surveyed 946 soldiers from a Shanxi garrison brigade in 1929. He found that 13 percent of soldiers were able to compose a letter on their own, while the rest had never learned to read or could not write a letter.[80] In contrast, in August 1938, General Feng Yuxian found that 80 percent of a regiment in Hunan were literate.[81] During the Sino-Japanese War, the quality of recruits declined steadily. More than 90 percent of soldiers were illiterate, and few had any basic scientific knowledge,[82] making it difficult for them to master their weapons. On the battlefield, they were heavily reliant on middle and junior officers for direction. During the Battle of Shanghai in 1937, combat was seriously affected by the large number of casualties among junior officers.[83]

Because soldiers were of low social status, recruits were mostly from poor families,[84] who were stigmatized. Many young people did not inform their families before they enlisted. Families were reluctant to marry their daughters to army men.[85] Draftees were mostly poor, uneducated, and in poor physical shape. According to a survey of the family occupation of soldiers of one Shanxi unit in 1930, 79.8 percent of soldiers came from peasant families. This percentage is similar to the share of farmers in the entire society.[86]

Military officers believed that soldiers from peasant families held many virtues: they were simple, brave, obedient, steadfast, and could endure great hardship.[87] A U.S. military observer noted that Chinese soldiers were cheap to maintain: their cost was only 2 percent that of a Japanese soldier.[88] This American argued that if properly trained, equipped, fed, clothed, and paid, Chinese would make great soldiers.[89]

Unfortunately, during the Sino-Japanese War, living standards in the army fell rapidly. Physical standards declined accordingly. In 1943, the Nationalist military sent 1,800 recruits to Ramgarh in India for training. Of those, 68 percent were rejected on physical grounds.

Prewar Reorganization and Combat Effectiveness

In autumn 1933, General Hans von Seeckt, the father of the post–World War I German army, visited China on Chiang Kai-shek's personal invitation. In his recommendations for military reform, he pointed out that China's greatest problem was that its forces were far too numerous and came from diverse backgrounds. He wrote, "At present the most pressing goal is to . . . establish a small, well-equipped army with high morale and combat effectiveness to replace the numerous badly armed and trained forces."[90] He suggested an army of sixty divisions and also proposed that a training regiment should be formed for military officers to instill in them the skills needed for modern warfare. Chiang accepted von Seeckt's suggestions. On 26 January 1935, Chiang convened a National Military Reorganization Conference in Nanjing. On 1 March, the Army Reorganization Bureau was set up in Wuchang under the leadership of General Chen Cheng. In the same month, General Alexander von Falkenhausen became the head of the German Military Advisers Group. Prior to the Sino-Japanese War, around nineteen divisions (about 300,000 soldiers) received training from German advisers and were equipped with German-style weapons.

Troop reduction was difficult for both political and military reasons. In 1936, the Nationalist government decided first to equip and bring up to strength ten "reformed divisions," which were assigned positions in accordance with the National Defense Plan. Surplus materiel was used to equip ten more "reformed divisions." The plan was that from 1936 to 1938, sixty divisions should be established to form the backbone of the Nationalist army. Prior to the Sino-Japanese War, only half of this plan was achieved.[91]

At the outbreak of the Sino-Japanese War, forces originating in the First Army of the National Revolutionary Army and the Whampoa cadets who had fought the Northern Expedition had the highest reputation. The Japanese called these "core central forces." The Guangxi Army, the Northwestern Army, and the Northeastern Army were also highly rated, as were some Uighur army units, the Guangdong Army, and the Shanxi Army. Provincial forces such as the Yunnan Army and the Sichuan Army were not highly regarded.[92]

Actual combat effectiveness did not always coincide with a force's reputation or its training levels. In the early stages of the Sino-Japanese War, the core central forces excelled in the Battle of Shanghai, but less so in other campaigns, although some units behaved heroically. During the latter stages of the Sino-Japanese War, the Chinese Expeditionary Army, dispatched to Burma, was equipped with the most modern arms, was well trained and highly disciplined, and performed well in combat. The Guangxi Army and some of the Northwestern Army did well in the battles of Linyi, Taierzhuang, and Xuzhou. Sometimes even badly equipped and trained forces performed impressively, demonstrating that there was more to combat effectiveness than weaponry and training. Troop morale and patriotic motivation, as well as the competence and resolve of commanders, were just as important.[93]

Conclusions

Nationalist forces were generally far inferior to those of the Japanese enemy. In 1937, General He Yingqin pointed out that in 1932 and

1933, Nationalist forces had not been able to prevail even when they out-numbered Japanese forces by four to one.[94] In the 1940s, a noted American journalist stationed in China, Theodore H. White, thought that Chinese forces usually could not win even if they outnumbered the Japanese enemy by five to one. Chiang Kai-shek pointed out in 1938 that three Chinese divisions were needed to counter one Japanese division.[95] Even if we take into account that Chinese divisions had between one-half and one-third of the strength of a Japanese division, such statements nonetheless illustrate the weakness of China's military.

This essay has suggested that Nationalist military reform did not deliver the elite force that the Nationalists hoped for or needed to confront Japan effectively on the battlefield. Nationalist troops received poor training, their military officers were ignorant, their tactics were obsolete, the sup-ply system was outdated, and their combat effectiveness was low.[96] These conditions were the result of serious financial shortages,[97] weak industrial development, and as a result of continued civil war after 1928, a late start in preparing for war with Japan.

In November 1937, Chiang Kai-shek stated, during a national defense conference, "In recent years we have worked hard, prepared actively, and achieved national unification. By the time of the Marco Polo Bridge Inci-dent, we were in a better domestic situation and achieved a better state of military preparedness that we had before then. Since 1935, our strength has doubled. It increased by more than two or three times since Janu-ary 1932 or September 1931 [when Japan attacked Shanghai and Mukden respectively] . . . If peace had been possible, we should have delayed the war for two or three years. With an additional three years, our defense capability would certainly have been drastically different . . . Now, if we merely compare the military strength of China and Japan, we are certainly inferior."[98] Even this assessment was too optimistic. Chiang failed to con-sider that Japan's military strength would not have remained stagnant.[99] Nevertheless, had both Nationalist government and provincial militarists concentrated on preparing for war against Japan, Japanese warmongers confronted with a China that was united and prosperous might have abandoned their aggressive ambitions. The catastrophe that was the Sino-Japanese war might then have been avoided to the benefit of both countries.

TRANSLATED BY SHUXI YIN

4 The Japanese Army on the Eve of the War

EDWARD J. DREA

Introduction

Bamboo branches decorated with multicolored strips of bright paper, tiny ornaments, and charms bounced through the fields and lanes as Japanese celebrated the 7 July Tanabata festival. According to popular custom, the colored paper tied to a bamboo branch would float away in a stream or river and bring good luck back to its sender. But no good luck would return to Japan that summer night in 1937. Thirteen hundred miles west of Tokyo other Japanese were in the fields that night. Captain Shimizu Setsurō's Eighth Company, Third Battalion, First Infantry Regiment, China Garrison Army—the designation for Japanese army forces stationed in north China under terms of the Boxer Protocol of 1901—was conducting night maneuvers near the Marco Polo Bridge about three miles southwest of Peking. Orders of the day had exhorted the soldiers to do their best to show respect for their loved ones at home on Tanabata.[1]

Shimizu's infantrymen, along with the rest of the Third Battalion, were stationed at Fengtai in Peking's southwest suburbs. The presence of a regular battalion of the Japanese army in north China during July 1937, its force structure, mission, and training requirements exemplified the culmination of Japan's revised China policy and the advent of a far more hazardous turn in Sino-Japanese relations. Officers and men checked their weapons carefully because they used live ammunition during training exercises, a precaution recently ordered by Colonel Mutaguchi Renya, commander, First Infantry Regiment, in response to an upsurge in Chinese popular reaction to the Japanese military presence in north China.[2]

Their company-level training completed, Mutaguchi was putting his troops through a tough, realistic battalion-level training regimen regardless of the stifling 90-degree-plus July heat. As a concession to the grueling and relentless exercises that had worn down his infantry company, Shimizu ordered his men to lighten their loads by leaving behind their heavy steel helmets and carrying half-full field packs for that night's exercise.[3] Still, the infantrymen were loaded with bulky equipment—partial field pack, canteen, ammunition pouches, emergency rations, weapons, and so forth—as they marched from their barracks through Chinese-controlled territory to their live-fire maneuver ground, a desolate area near the Marco Polo Bridge. Exactly how and why the Japanese infantrymen, entangled among Chinese military units, were training near the bridge that evening requires an understanding of the Japanese army's military policy toward China in the 1930s.

National Security Policy and North China

It is not necessary to replicate the several excellent English-language studies that recount the Japanese army's attempt to subvert the authority of the Nationalist government and promote regional autonomy movements in north China,[4] but it is worth noting that the army played a central role in orchestrating changes to Japan's national policy toward China between 1932 and mid-1937. At least since 1933, Japanese field armies had promoted a series of autonomous zones in north China as officers assigned to the Kwantung (Guandong) Army, dubious about China's ability to become a modern nation, considered it inevitable that the vast geographic area would fragment into regionalism. The policy, of course, preserved the status quo of a weak and divided China that was beneficial to Japan's strategic interests in Manchukuo.[5]

Japanese army officers were also always quick to cite the danger created by the Kuomintang's five-year plan, inaugurated in 1933 with the help of German military advisers, to modernize and expand the government army,[6] and the growing anti-Japanese sentiment spreading throughout north China. In March 1936, for instance, Major General Itagaki Seishirō—Kwantung Army chief of staff and, along with Colonel Ishiwara Kanji, chief, Operations Section, General Staff since August 1935, a mastermind of the Manchurian Incident—was certain that in the event of a war with the Soviet Union, a united China would ally itself with the Union of Soviet Socialist Republics (USSR).[7] Distrustful of China, he was likewise convinced that the Kuomintang was the stumbling block to improved relations with Japan.[8] The field armies' solution to the Chinese threat was to launch a preemptive war to destroy the Chiang Kai-shek regime.

Any attempt by Tokyo to reverse the military's China policy risked determined opposition from the Kwantung Army, which, in February 1937, called for even more forceful covert action to expel the Kuomintang from north China and endorsed a preemptive war against China to secure strategic rear areas for future operations against the Soviet Union.[9] At a March meeting in Tokyo, staff officers from the China Garrison and Kwantung armies insisted that any concessions to the Chinese would be a terrible mistake and even in the best case would achieve only "temporary results."[10] Arguing that the timing was inauspicious for any concessions to China, the Kwantung Army forcefully disagreed with any dramatic policy shift, and in June Lieutenant General Tōjō Hideki, recently appointed chief of staff, Kwantung Army, remarked that preparing for war against the Soviet Union without crushing the Nanjing government "to remove the menace to our rear" was "asking for trouble" (ke o fukute, itai o moto-meru).[11] In early spring 1937, Prince Konoe Fumimaro inherited a China policy riven by disagreements, although all agreed that China could not be allowed to divert the empire from its preparations against the USSR. The end was clear; the means were not.

War Plans

Cabinet approval of the Fundamentals of National Policy in August 1936 implied that the army and navy needed a period of stability while they retooled Japan's war machine. The trick was to reconcile long-term strategic goals with short-range practical interests in north China without upsetting the status quo. Expanding requirements drove the army's contingency planning. Its traditional mission in north China was to protect Japanese interests and the approximately 13,000 Japanese citizens residing there. Tokyo's usual response to serious incidents was to deploy troops from homeland garrisons to China, deal with the localized emergency, and then withdraw the forces. By the mid-1930s, the growing Soviet threat to Manchukuo (Manzhouguo) rendered that doctrine obsolete. Incidents in north China took on strategic implications because they diverted the Kwantung Army's buildup against the Soviet Union. Turmoil in north China disrupted free access to the strategic raw materials the army needed for its modernization and rearmament. Hostile Chinese forces adjacent to the Kwantung Army threatened its strategic left flank should war erupt with the Soviets. With these contingencies in mind, the army rewrote its operational war plans on the assumption that north China was Japan's strategic rear area for operations against the USSR.

Since 1913 the army and navy had annually submitted to the throne specific operational war plans based on the general guidance found in part II of the imperial defense policy outlining the operational use of forces.[12] Plans originally spanned the period from 1 April through 31 March of the following year, but from 1927 the coverage shifted from September to September.[13] The 1937 operational plan, for example, was effective from September 1936 to September 1937. The services customarily submitted

their respective operational plans to the throne in April and received imperial sanction in June.

Naturally, force requirements for China operations fluctuated depend-
ing on circumstances. The 1911 operations plan for general war called for
thirteen divisions to occupy southern Manchuria, capture Peking, then
occupy Zhejiang and Fujian. Limited contingency operations in north
China required two divisions to secure the rail line of communication from
Peking to the sea.[14] A few weeks after the 1931 Manchurian Incident, the
General Staff in Tokyo drafted plans to counter a Sino-Soviet alliance.
Their scenario for a two-month campaign required fifteen to sixteen divisions, most of them engaged against the Soviet Red Army. Two divisions
would secure north China, while smaller units screened the Inner Mongolian front protecting the Japanese western flank in Manchuria.[15] After
further refinement, in early 1932, the General Staff posited three contingencies in China. The traditional mission of protecting Japanese interests
and citizens required a standard two-division force. Another established
mission was maintaining a line of communication between the Chinese
capital and the sea. The China Garrison Army, at the time about 1,700
officers and men and reinforced by one division, had that assignment. In
the unlikely event of all-out warfare, Tokyo would deploy three divisions
to reinforce the Kwantung Army plus seven other divisions and three cavalry brigades to subdue resistance in north China and the Shandong Peninsula. Two additional divisions would secure key areas of central China.[16]

Between 1932 and 1936, China received less attention as the General
Staff was preoccupied with the Soviet military buildup in the Far East.
So long as the Kuomintang remained weak and China divided, chances
of a full-scale war were minimal, and the General Staff's basic policy was
to avoid escalating incidents or expanding field operations in China.[17] If
anti-Japanese outbreaks did occur, central headquarters assumed that
relatively small-scale, limited operations with limited objectives, involving
at most four divisions, would quickly restore order in the Peking–Tianjin
corridor.[18] The 1935 operational plan (effective September 1934–September 1935) accordingly reduced the force structure for operations in China
from twelve to nine divisions. In north China, the China Garrison Army
and a brigade of the Kwantung Army, reinforced by three divisions, would
occupy strategic locations around Peking and Tianjin. Two more divisions,
working jointly with the navy, would land on the Shandong Peninsula,
then fan out to seize and occupy strategic points there. In central China,
three divisions, also conducting joint operations, would land near Shanghai and occupy that area. Depending on the military situation, they could
also drive into the Chinese interior and seize Wuhan, thereby assisting
Japanese forces advancing southward out of north China. A single division
would occupy key points in south China. The 1936 revised operational

plan was similar except for the elimination of the Wuhan phase, dropped by staff planners because not enough troops were available for such an operation and because of apprehension over recent Soviet actions.[19]

This uneasiness centered on the alarming Soviet military buildup in the Far East, and permeated the 21 May 1936 draft rearmament plan presented to the throne as part of the national budget formulation process.[20] The army proposed to counter the Soviet buildup by improving Japanese strategic mobility in Manchukuo. Renovation and expansion of airfields, ports, roads, and railroads, plus construction of army air force arsenals, storage depots, and medical facilities highlighted the infrastructure improvements that the army anticipated would speed deployments from Japan to the operational areas of Manchukuo.[21] The disposition of the Japanese divisions in eastern Manchuria (see map) within striking distance of Vladivostok or Blagovechensk indicates their wartime objectives. The Kwantung Army relied on a mobile independent mixed brigade, composed of armored car and mounted cavalry units stationed at Gongzhuling in central Manchuria, as its reaction force to meet contingencies in north China. Major units were not massed in western Manchuria, where they would be expected to deploy before any planned invasion of north China.

Nevertheless, General Staff planners were always looking over their shoulders at China, and what they saw disturbed them. Resurgent Chinese nationalism, the Chinese Communist move north of the Yellow River in February 1936 and subsequent occupation of much of Shanxi Province, as well as the spread of anti-Japanese agitation throughout north China, posed the danger that limited military operations might spin out of control into full-scale warfare. China's improving military forces would likely make it more difficult for Japanese forces to achieve their assigned objectives. Around Shanghai, for example, the Chinese had reinforced their defensive network by constructing extensive, in-depth, and permanent fortified positions.[22]

The August 1936 war plan of the Second Section of the General Staff recognized the geopolitical importance of avoiding war with China, but for planning purposes assumed that China might enter a Japanese-Soviet war on the side of the Russians. In that scenario, army planners expected a small expeditionary force to destroy anti-Japanese forces in north China with a single, rapidly delivered knockout blow that would limit the scope of fighting and the involvement of Japanese forces. Prolonged occupation of key Chinese locations, however, might prove necessary to ensure access to strategic raw materials.[23] These concepts found their way into the revised operational plan of 1937.

Although no copy of that document exists, the plan, as reconstructed by former staff officers, expanded the army's objectives to include the occupation of north China's five provinces and added new missions in central

China. To accomplish these more ambitious goals, the General Staff reinforced the existing nine-division contingency force to fourteen divisions.[24] As necessary, three additional divisions would reinforce the five already earmarked for north China operations. In central China, three divisions would seize the Shanghai area, but because of the recent Chinese military preparations around the city and the operational and tactical disadvantages of fighting in a restricted urban terrain, two more would land at Hangzhou Bay south of the congested metropolis. From there, they would advance inland, capitalizing on freedom to maneuver in the expanded area of operations. After destroying resistance around Shanghai, Japanese forces would converge to advance on Nanjing, ultimately occupying the Shanghai–Nanjing–Hangzhou line. Unlike previous operational plans, but consistent with Imperial Defense Policy, the army would settle in for long-term occupation to secure strategic rear-area locations in China in order to support operations against the USSR.[25] The administrative plan accompanying the revised operational guidance detailed the scope of the occupation of north China.

The China Garrison Army premised its 15 September 1936 administrative plan for the occupation of north China on hostilities either against China or a Sino-Soviet alliance.[26] For "Case A" (general military operations in north China), Japanese army units would advance southward along rail lines from Peking to occupy the area between the Great Wall and the Yellow River, that is, north China's five provinces.[27] One division would then remain in the area to maintain order in the occupied zones. "Case B" (operations against a Sino-Soviet alliance) relied on smaller Japanese forces to establish a defensive line from Zhangjiakou via Peking to Tianjin and to occupy the territory behind that line. These screening units would conduct a holding action to impede any approaching Soviet forces. The occupation would secure Japan's strategic rear area, ensure Japanese access to strategic materials, and protect the army's open strategic flank while it conducted its main operations against the Soviets. Case B reduced the area to be occupied in north China, but only because the demands of fighting the Soviets left fewer units available for operations against the Chinese.[28] In either scenario, the army relied on economy-of-force operations, followed by a prolonged occupation of north China.

Meanwhile, in mid-September 1936, the General Staff in Tokyo issued instructions to preempt major outbreaks in north China by moving a division in Manchukuo closer to the north China boundary. Should fighting break out, the China Garrison Army, with support from Kwantung Army units, would, as necessary, launch punitive operations against Chinese forces. Higher headquarters expected local commanders to act quickly and decisively and rely on rapid maneuver and shock action to settle outbreaks locally and with the minimum force necessary. As no other countermeasures were considered, Japanese operational planning for north China, even to deal with minor incidents, was based on an all-or-nothing approach to the use of force.[29]

Yet the army's senior leadership remained badly divided over its China policy. Under Ishiwara's influence, the General Staff wanted to avoid military action that might lead to a full-scale war with China and to concentrate instead on the army's massive rearmament and modernization program. A majority of high-ranking officers in the Army Ministry and General Staff, especially the General Staff's Second (Operations) Section as well as those in the Kwantung Army, favored using force against China, believing it necessary to quell rising anti-Japanese sentiment. Besides, if past experience was any guide, these officers believed the Chinese would quickly collapse once the actual fighting began.[30]

Just as the services lacked a unified military strategy, the army's senior leaders lacked a uniform concept for China operations. On the one hand, operational planning called for permanent occupation of large swaths of north and central China, while on the other, the General Staff wanted to contain any outbreaks in order to focus its efforts against the Soviet Union. Nor was there any long-term operational planning. Instead, by focusing on the initial battles, the army relegated planning for protracted combat operations to be "contingent upon circumstances."[31] In sum, the Japanese army preferred to avoid military force to resolve Chinese issues if possible,[32] but it was also unwilling to back down in the face of Chinese demands.

Doctrine

Since 1914, *Tōsui kōryō* (*Principles of Command*) was the doctrinal bible for senior Japanese army commanders and staff officers responsible for combined arms warfare at the corps- (*gun*) or army- (*hōmen gun*) echelon. New weapons, new tactics, and new organizations of World War I forced all major armies to reconsider their existing military doctrine at strategic, operational, and tactical levels, and the Japanese responded by modifying the *Principles of Command* to combine its traditional post–Russo-Japanese War emphasis on the intangible forces in battle with the latest concepts of modern, total war. The 1918 revision of the *Principles* acknowledged the implications of "recent great advances in materiel" for total war, but insisted that victory in battle ultimately depended on devotion to duty, patriotism, and self-sacrificing service.[33]

It was during the 1920s, however, that the General Staff's Operations Section, under the direction of Major General Araki Sadao, produced the most far-reaching and influential revision of *Principles*. A fervent anti-communist and an ideologue who believed in the intangibles of combat,

Araki selected Lieutenant Colonel Obata Toshishirō and Captain Suzuki Yorimichi as the principal authors to rewrite the manual. Obata, a Soviet expert, was heavily influenced by German General Count Alfred von Schiefflen's classic theories of a "war of annihilation," while Suzuki, the top graduate in the thirtieth Staff College class, shared Araki's emphasis on the role of "spiritual" or intangible advantages in warfare. Brilliant but arrogant, aloof, and indifferent to opposing opinions, the two worked in secrecy to devise a doctrine based on what Leonard Humphreys terms "intense spiritual training" and bayonet-led breakthroughs to compensate for the opponent's materiel superiority.[34] The 1928 edition of the *Principles of Command* embedded the dogma that élan and morale were the "primary causes of victory or defeat," a condition unchanged "from time immemorial."[35] In short, the intangible aspects of warfare became the linchpin of the army's modern heritage and ideology.

The latest iteration of the *Principles of Command* retained the operational concept of fast-moving Japanese mobile offensive operations forcing a decisive battle (*kaisen*) early in the campaign. Thus, it reaffirmed the *sokusen sokketsu* principle of rapid war.[36] The sole means to achieve these objectives was the offensive, and the army expected commanders at every echelon to press home attacks, annihilate the opposing enemy units, and seize key territory. The rank and file were indoctrinated with this spirit of the offensive and drilled to expect sure victory. The emphasis on offensive spirit was so extreme that Araki struck the words for *surrender, retreat,* and *defense* from the manual because of their negative psychological connotations for troop morale.[37]

The spirit of the offensive similarly permeated the *Sentō kōryō* (Principles of Operations), first issued in 1929 as the handbook for combined arms warfare for division and regimental commanders. It also regarded hand-to-hand infantry combat as the culminating point of battle, described as an unchanging tenet of Japanese military doctrine since 1910.[38] Senior field commanders were expected to display initiative (*dokudan*) in skillfully maneuvering their units to encircle the enemy in order to make possible the climactic assault with cold steel. Infantry was the primary maneuver arm, and artillery supported the infantry assaults. To keep pace with a fast-moving infantry advance, the army designed light and mobile artillery. At the operational level, encirclement and night attacks were the ingredients of victory, and even outnumbered units were expected to envelop enemy flanks aggressively. Against fixed positions, units would advance under cover of darkness, avoiding enemy artillery fire and positioning themselves for a dawn attack that combined firepower and shock action to overrun enemy positions. In a meeting engagement, commanders would maneuver to turn the opponent's flanks, surround the enemy units, and then destroy them. If forced on the defensive, commanders had to seek opportunities to deliver a decisive counterattack to smash the enemy and regain the initiative.[39]

These higher-level operational doctrines were distilled into tactical form in the January 1928 edition of the Infantry Manual (*Hohei sōten*), provisionally revised in May 1937 (*Hohei sōten sōan*). The introduction to both editions was identical and stressed the need to achieve a rapid victory (*sokusen sokketsu*) by overpowering and destroying enemy forces. Infantry was the primary arm in combined arms warfare, and the infantryman depended on cold steel as the basis of the spirit of the attack. The 1928 Infantry Manual stressed the commander's responsibility to inculcate his troops with a "faith in certain victory" (*hisshō shinnen*) in the glorious tradition of Japanese arms.[40]

Although adapting certain lessons of World War I, the 1928 and 1937 revisions perpetuated bedrock principles of a Japanese style of warfare derived from the Russo-Japanese War. Tactics and doctrine, for instance, evolved from national, racial, and geographic characteristics of an army. Military education and training endowed material and technical expertise with the intangibles of morale and combat élan. Regulations were limited to those necessary for combat, and training was kept as simple as possible. These fundamentals remained unchanged between 1909 and 1941.[41]

According to both manuals, victory depended on a combination of tangible and intangible qualities found in the "magnificent tradition of Japanese arms" and patriotic spirit. Both stressed night attacks, close combat, and shock action to break enemy positions. Major changes between the two manuals involved wording more appropriate to the modified division structure, discussed below, and the new tactical formations then being organized. The 1928 edition, for instance, emphasized infantry tactics to the detriment of combined arms and mutual supporting capabilities and made no mention of antiarmor tactics. The 1937 draft integrated the infantry company, machine gun unit, organic artillery, armor, field artillery, and combat engineers into the basic combined arms formation for small unit and battalion training.[42]

Infantry tactics of 1928 employed an extended skirmish line with an interval of four paces per soldier. Individual combat initiative was discouraged, except in unusual circumstances, since success depended on concentrating firepower and manpower on narrow frontages to overwhelm the defenders. Two light machine gun squads and four rifle squads per platoon enabled the infantry company's skirmish line to build up concentrated small-arms fire in preparation for a bayonet-driven breakthrough of enemy positions. For the final assault, an infantry company concentrated itself along a 150-yard-wide front and might expect 50 percent casualties in carrying the main enemy defensive line. But historical perspective illuminates the flaw in these tactics. During World War I, armies constructed

TABLE 4.1
Development of the firepower of the Japanese squad over time

Year	1923	1928	1940
Weapons	Light machine gun in squad Heavy machine gun at battalion Assault artillery at regiment	Same	Same; grenade discharger in platoon heavy machine gun and assault guns in company; battalion artillery and rapid-fire antitank guns
Firepower	Important role	Same	Less emphasis
Assault	Decisive role	Same	Assault to extreme
Dispersion	Linear by platoon Support to rear	Same	Column with light machine gun in front and flank with grenade discharger in between
Interval	4 paces	Same	6 paces
Rush	Under 50 yards as squad—if necessary as half-squad	If necessary by individual	30 yards by half squads or by individual
Fire Direction	Platoon leader directs Squad leader controls direct fire	Platoon leader indicates opening fire; squad leaders order firing; if necessary, individual fire	Squad leader orders grenade discharger fire; after opening fire, individual firing

SOURCE: Xu Yong, *The Conqueror's Dream: Japan's Strategy of Invading China* (Guilin: Guangxi Normal University Press, 1993), 28.

defenses in depth, that is in several lines of trenches, pillboxes, and strong points, each independent of the other and all covered by artillery fire. If the attacking infantry suffered heavy losses overcoming the first line of resistance, how could it press its assault against multiple lines of defense?[43]

The 1937 revision described in depth new tactics to overcome fixed Soviet defenses. Drafted in anticipation of arms and equipment either under development or in production and as yet unavailable to field units, it became official doctrine in 1940. In the summer of 1937, however, units of the China Garrison Army were already field testing the new tactics. The provisional manual adopted combat team tactics as squads formed an umbrella-like skirmish formation. The tactical formation had a light machine gun team at the point with two ammunition bearers to its rear on either flank. In back of the light machine gun team were riflemen in column formation at an interval of six paces. The light machine gun provided firepower to cover the formation as it closed with the enemy in hand-to-hand combat. Increased firepower expanded the assault frontage to 200 yards, and the combination of greater dispersion and night movement would reduce losses from enemy artillery fire as the infantry advanced through successive lines of resistance. The platoon leader became responsible for the final assault into the enemy lines, and as tactical responsibility devolved from platoon to squad leaders, greater individual initiative was expected from junior officers and noncommissioned officers (NCOs). Wider dispersal on a fluid battlefield also meant the frontline infantry had to display aggressiveness and initiative.[44] The development of firepower in the squad over time is shown in table 4.1.

Yet contrary to popular impressions, the Japanese did not rely solely on the bayonet or the spirit of the offensive when fighting the Chinese. They brought to bear superior firepower and modern equipment in combined arms warfare, relying on regimental heavy weapons and artillery to soften enemy positions before infantry assaults. Without such firepower, unsupported infantry attacks could not have succeeded in taking objectives.[45] Although the Japanese army of 1937 emphasized the intangible aspects of combat, it also improved mobility and concentrated greater firepower in its tactical maneuver units. The result, from squad through regiment, was a hard-hitting, compact force tailored specifically for fast-moving offensive operations. Increased firepower and more and more emphasis on *attaque à l'outrance* produced tactical and operational doctrine that complemented national strategy, imperial defense policy, and war plans. At every level—down to the lowliest infantrymen—the premium was on aggressive offensive action, rapid decision, and annihilation of opposing forces.

Force Structure and Personnel

In January 1937 the imperial army numbered approximately 247,000 officers and men arrayed in an order of battle of seventeen standing infantry divisions, four tank regiments, and fifty-four air squadrons with 549 aircraft. The China Garrison Army and Taiwan Garrison Army each had two infantry regiments, and there was a separate independent mixed brigade in Manchuria.[46] Two divisions were permanently stationed in Korea, and four others were assigned on a rotating basis to the Kwantung Army in Manchukuo. The balance was in the home islands. A large pool of reservists and partially trained replacements were available upon mobilization to fill out the peacetime Table of Organization and Equipment (TO&E) units to their wartime strength.

Conscription was the army's source of enlisted manpower, although a few young men did volunteer for active duty. For purposes of conscription, Japan was divided into divisional areas that were, in turn, subdivided into regimental districts, the administrative units responsible for conscription, mobilization, individual activations, and the handling of veterans' affairs in their respective jurisdictions. Conscripts normally served with the regiment affiliated with their region or prefecture. Regiments of the Imperial Guards in Tokyo, however, selected conscripts nationwide, as did the Seventh Infantry Division in sparsely populated Hokkaido and regular army units permanently stationed in Korea, China, and Taiwan. Draftees from Okinawa Prefecture normally served in Kyushu-based regiments.[47]

All males reaching their twentieth year underwent an army-conducted preinduction physical between 1 December and 30 January of the following year. The results sorted potential conscripts into three categories: A, B1, and B2 were suitable for active duty, while various others were deemed unsuitable for the rigors of army life. In 1935, 29.7 percent of those examined received A classifications, and 41.2 percent were graded B1 or B2.[48] Among the 742,422 eligibles in the 1937 cohort, the army conscripted approximately 170,000, or 22.9 percent, a percentage more or less constant since the post–Russo-Japanese War years.[49] Among the draftees were 153,000 men from the A category and 17,000 more from the B. Conscripts served two years on active service, with variations depending on military specialty and previous military training as civilians, and upon discharge had a lengthy reserve obligation.

Altogether 470,635 were B category: otherwise fit for active duty, but with the exception of those actually drafted, excess to the army's normal active duty personnel requirements. The army instead assigned these men to the First Replacement Pool, where they received about 120 days of basic military training, mainly basic instruction in the use of small arms and elementary tactics. Regular officers and NCOs formed the cadre that trained the replacements in their respective regimental districts.[50] Thereafter, the army annually called the replacements and reservists to active duty for several days of training.

Army leaders regarded discipline as the lifeblood of the institution. Basic training hammered into conscripts the absolute nature of unquestioning obedience to orders throughout the ranks. Subsequent training promoted field craft, such as skillful use of terrain to surprise an enemy or encircle an opponent. Training exercise plans, however, lacked variety, suffering from the restricted size of maneuver areas in Japan and from predictable solutions to field problems.[51] Training was severe, combining strict formal discipline and regulated corporal punishment with harsh informal sanctions and unregulated violence inflicted by the platoon to instill unquestioning obedience to orders.[52] As the notion of the "imperial army" and emperor cult became more pronounced, appeals to imperial symbols and imperial authority reinforced unquestioning obedience to superiors, who were transmitters of the imperial will. It was around this time that the term *kōgun* (imperial army) gained currency over *kokugun* (national army) in a conscious attempt by army authorities to link the military directly with the throne.[53]

Beginning in 1925, the army posted regular officers as instructors in military training at middle and technical schools throughout Japan. The Young Men's Military Training Corps (*seinen kunrensho*), a voluntary organization established by the army in 1926, offered civics education and military training conducted by members of the Reservists Association to youths aged sixteen to twenty who had completed their schooling. The major benefit of both programs was that qualified graduates who were subsequently conscripted could reduce their term of active service by six months.[54] In exchange, the army inculcated military values and virtues in large numbers of impressionistic youngsters.

Officers came from three sources: the imperial military academy (slightly more than 300 per year since 1932), volunteers who met educational and medical standards and who had served first in the ranks and then attended the officer cadet school, and selected enlisted men chosen to attend the officer cadet school. Following reforms in 1927, a reserve officer system (*kanbu kōhosei seidō*) opened the way for commissions to middle school graduates who had completed the school military training program. After four months on active service, the army tested the volunteers and accordingly divided them into A (officer cadets) and B (NCO cadets). Officer cadets attended an eleven-month course offered at regional officer cadet schools, after which as cadet aspirants they served four months with a regular unit. Upon successful completion of service they received commissions as reserve officers.[55] In 1929, qualified graduates of the military training courses also became eligible to volunteer for a reserve officer program. They entered the army at higher enlisted grade and, if they passed comprehensive tests after one year of service, they matriculated to the officer cadet school for further training, after which they were commissioned as reserve second lieutenants. The officer cadet schools produced about 4,000 reserve officers annually in peacetime.[56]

The army selected its NCOs from conscripts it allowed to reenlist and from men who had volunteered for active duty before being drafted and passed the qualifying exams. The Army NCO Preparatory School, established in 1927, trained the NCO candidates.[57] In 1936, more than 14,000 young men volunteered for NCO training, a national rate of 31.4 applicants per 1,000 inductees. Regional variances of 81 per 1,000 in rural Miyazaki Prefecture to 8.2 per 1,000 in urban Osaka highlighted the tendency of most NCO candidates to come from rural Japan. As a rule, these soldiers were the second and third sons of farming or peasant families with little prospect of employment at home but who found a secure home and job in the army.[58] Volunteers spent a year training with their parent unit and a second year at the preparatory school. Upon graduation they assumed their NCO duties.[59]

Organization

The 1937 Japanese infantry division was a square formation; the peacetime strength was established at about 12,000 officers and men organized in two brigades (about 4,000 men each) of two infantry regiments (2,000 men each). A field artillery regiment, an engineer regiment, and a transport battalion were organic to the division. An infantry regiment had three battalions (about 600 men each) composed of three rifle companies (160 men each) and a weapons platoon. A rifle company had three rifle platoons and one light machine gun platoon. Regiments also had infantry assault gun platoons, and battalions, a heavy machine gun company.[60]

Upon mobilization, a fourth infantry company[61] augmented each battalion and, together with reserve fillers (almost 5,000 of them as transport and service troops), brought the authorized wartime strength for an infantry division to more than 25,000 officers and men. Wartime infantry companies numbered 194 officers and men; machine gun companies, 139; and a battalion assault gun platoon, 56. The wartime infantry company had 3 rifle platoons and a grenadier platoon (144 officers and men). Each rifle platoon had 1 light machine gun and 11 riflemen per squad and 3 grenade dischargers and 9 riflemen in the fourth squad. In 1937 a platoon had only 2 light machine guns and 2 grenade dischargers, but the 1937 rearmament plan would rectify this shortcoming by 1940. The machine gun company was organized into 4 platoons, a total of 8 Type 92 heavy machine guns divided in 2 sections per platoon. The battalion assault gun platoon had 2 sections each equipped with 2 Type 41 infantry assault guns.[62]

Although the size of the expanded wartime infantry battalion (in excess of 1,100 officers and men) hindered mobility and made it more difficult to control and maneuver, the Japanese army retained a large four-company organization to ensure that the battalion echelon had sufficient organic manpower to sustain its combat effectiveness in the opening battles. The integration of crew-served infantry weapons into battalions and companies provided the infantry with greater organic firepower, allowed for increased dispersion, and accommodated tactical innovations and new formations.

Weapons and Equipment

Reforms undertaken in 1922 had reduced personnel in favor of new or improved weapons and equipment. An advanced 75 mm Type 90 field artillery piece boasting increased range and a more accurate projectile entered the forces in 1930 and with the 105 mm Type 10 howitzer and 75 mm pack mountain artillery (disassembled for transport on pack animals) became the standard division's artillery complement.[63] Field artillery was light, mobile, and small caliber to keep pace with fast-moving meeting engagements. Unencumbered by a lengthy baggage train, infantry and artillery units could deploy quickly off the march formation and maneuver swiftly around enemy flanks. Army leaders further compressed road march formations by eliminating the fourth artillery battery of each artillery regiment, sacrificing firepower for speed and mobility. Heavier guns were of course also employed, but usually in set-piece battles where mobility was not at a premium.

Tactical considerations were not the sole reasons for weapons procurement decisions. Japan's industrial base was incapable of manufacturing large quantities of heavy artillery. It took, for example, eight months to manufacture one 150 mm Type 15 cannon and eighteen months to produce a 240 mm Type 24 howitzer.[64] Standard artillery and armor in army inventories are listed in table 4.2.

A 1936 division's field artillery regiment with Type 90 field artillery (or lighter Type 94 mountain artillery) had thirty-six guns. Training stressed quality rather than quantity, as suggested by the conservative "one-round-one-hit" (*ippatsu-ichimei*) firing doctrine. Live-fire training was rare because artillery firing ranges in Japan were lacking.[65] Artillery ammunition stockpiles fell far short of projected operational requirements. Government-run arsenals produced more than 111,000 artillery shells in 1936, or less than one-tenth of the number prescribed in wartime consumption tables.[66] Similar industrial and manufacturing backwardness affected motorization and armor.

Motorization was costly, dependent on foreign supply, and of dubious value on the inferior road networks of Manchuria, north China, and the Soviet Far East. Military estimates of 250,000 trucks to put the army on wheels were beyond the capacity of the fledgling Japanese automobile industry, which until 1933 annually manufactured fewer than 1,000 automobiles. Japanese tanks, "handcrafted, beautifully polished, and hoarded" in Alvin Coox's felicitous phrase, were, like heavy artillery and artillery shells, in short supply.[67] The army opted for light (ten tons or less) and medium tanks (sixteen tons or less) because units would have to deploy armor overseas, making size and weight vital considerations when loading or off-loading transport ships. Smaller tanks were also better suited to the north China and Manchurian terrain, being light enough to cross unbridged rivers on pontoons or ferries. As with motor vehicles and heavy artillery, the Japanese industrial base could not mass-produce tanks. As late as 1939, factories were manufacturing an average of twenty-eight tanks (all models) per month.[68] Foot soldiers in 1937 were as reliant on animal transport for mobility as their grandfathers had been during the Russo-Japanese War. Against hodgepodge Chinese armies, the Japanese

TABLE 4.2

Standard artillery and armor in Japanese army inventories

Year	Weapon	Caliber/Range	Weight/Speed	Remarks
1929	Type 89 15 cannon	150 mm/11.2 miles		Siege artillery
	Type 89 medium tank	57 mm gun	14 tons/15 mph Four-man crew	
1930	Type 90 field artillery gun	75 mm/6.6 miles		Standard division gun
1931	Type 91 10 howitzer	105 mm/6.7 miles		Field artillery
1932	Type 92 infantry assault gun	70 mm/1.7 miles		Battalion gun
	Type 92 10 cannon	105 mm/11.3 miles		Heavy field artillery
1934	Type 94 mountain gun	75 mm/5.2 miles		Light pack artillery
1935	Type 95 artillery gun	75 mm/6.6 miles		Field artillery
	Type 95 light tank	37 mm gun	8.1 tons/24 mph Four-man crew	
1936	Type 96 15 howitzer	150 mm/7.4 miles		Heavy field artillery
	Type 96 24 howitzer	240 mm/10.3 miles		Siege artillery
	Type 96 15 cannon	150 mm/16.5 miles		Siege artillery
1937	Type 97 medium tank	57 mm gun	15, 8 tons/24 mph Four-man crew	

army enjoyed technological and material superiority, but against first-rate opponents, these deficiencies in heavy artillery, armor, and vehicles were to have catastrophic consequences.

Still another factor limiting Japanese industry in the production of tanks, trucks, and artillery was the decision in 1936 to expand the army's air arm and homeland air defense network, a policy that shifted resources, capital, and technology away from the army's ground forces.[69] The mission of the nascent Japanese Army Air Force (JAAF) was to support ground operations by conducting reconnaissance, bombing enemy bases, and attaining air superiority (*chijō zettai kōkū yusen*). Direct support of ground operations was minimal, and Japanese staff officers did not foresee aerial bombing as a supplement to, much less a replacement for, artillery bombardment. The expanded air arm's strategic mission was to execute preemptive air strikes against Soviet air bases in the Far East to prevent air attacks on the homeland. In the mid-1930s, the army possessed about 650 aircraft, roughly 450 of which were operational. The JAAF demanded rigorous training stressing quality over quantity, and, up to December 1941, turned out only about 750 pilots annually. Training developed basic flight skills, and specialized tactical instruction was left to the new pilot's unit.[70] Total military aircraft production rose from 445 planes in 1930 to 4,768 in 1940 as the Japanese civilian aviation industry adapted foreign technology to meet requirements. The army made only one large foreign purchase— 82 Italian Fiat heavy bombers in 1937–1938—and the planes proved to be clumsy firetraps in the skies over China.

New Formations

Following World War I, major armies pondered the role of firepower, mobility, and dispersion in future conflict. Modern warfare demanded new weapons and formations to achieve operational and tactical success. In Japan's case, the geography and terrain of northeast Asia and the empire's industrial capability influenced decisions on forces, equipment, and weapons. Planners, doctrine writers, and strategists agreed that Manchuria was the future battleground, but there was less unanimity about the proper force structure for Manchurian operations.

Although there were calls for a triangular division from the early 1920s, Japanese planners expected a single division to conduct independent, sustained operations on extended frontages, a role normally assigned in European and American armies to a corps echelon (two or more divisions). Traditionalists in the Operations Section favored the square infantry division because its additional manpower, weaponry, and equipment enabled it to sustain losses yet continue to function effectively on the battlefield.

The larger square division's advantages in firepower and manpower, they reasoned, would also overwhelm smaller triangular formations, which, in any case, were unsuitable for operations on extended frontages because they lacked the sustaining power to fight a prolonged decisive engagement. Thus, the Japanese army retained the huge, cumbersome square division, despite the World War I trend in Europe to smaller, more mobile triangular formations.[71]

In the mid-1930s reformers countered that square divisions were difficult to control and maneuver, occupied too much road space during the march to be brought to bear rapidly against the enemy, and were especially vulnerable to the concentrated firepower of modern weapons because of their dense ranks. In 1936, the Army Ministry announced plans to convert the force structure to a triangular configuration by eliminating one brigade headquarters, one infantry regiment, and one artillery battery from the division. The new configuration, one brigade with three subordinate regiments, stiffened with new, modern weaponry, would streamline formations by reducing personnel while strengthening the units by increasing their organic firepower and strategic mobility.[72]

The resulting division design was an infantry brigade headquarters with three infantry regiments, an enlarged artillery brigade, an engineer regiment, and expanded signals and transport units. The seventeen infantry regiments that were excess to the square divisions (one from each regular division) became the cadre to form six new triangular divisions. This reorganization enabled the army to achieve its goal of twenty-three active divisions by 1940, the year Tokyo expected the outbreak of general international war.[73] The conversion and modernization of units and equipment would, however, require several years.

As reported to the throne in May 1936, the First Replenishment Plan, scheduled to begin the following year, was an ambitious five-year effort to completely refit the army's weaponry, enhance its firepower, and improve its signals communications to facilitate mobility by allowing commanders to coordinate and direct their widely dispersed subordinate units.[74] With the exception of the Nineteenth Division in Korea, each division would establish a machine gun company in its infantry battalions while each field artillery regiment added one battery of Type 10 howitzers. Newly organized artillery assault gun units echeloned at infantry regiments would provide direct artillery fire support to tactical units.

Logistics

According to logistics doctrine, Japanese maneuver units normally operated within a 120- to 180-mile radius of a railhead for purposes of resupply and reinforcement.[75] A field train transport (*daikōri*) unit moved supplies daily from the railhead to a division control point for distribution. The division established a field depot (*yasen sōkō*) to move supplies from field transport to company and lower-echelon units. At the depot, transport troops (*shichōhei*) transferred supplies to a combat train (*shōkōri*) that hauled the ammunition, rations, and equipment to the frontline units. Horse-drawn wagons and pack animals were the usual means of transportation.

Each wartime division had a transport battalion, which varied in size from about 2,200 to 3,700 men depending on the type of division the unit supported. The division carried one day of supplies.[76] Mobilization added an ordnance unit, a field hospital, and a sanitation unit, as well as additional field and combat trains to the logistic lifeline. The size of the transport regiment increased from about 1,500 officers and men with more than 300 horses to almost 3,500 troops and more than 2,600 animals. One company of the battalion usually carried small-arms ammunition, two companies carried artillery shells, and two carried rations, although this arrangement was flexible depending on the operation. Pack horses or dray horses were echeloned to company and carried or pulled infantry assault artillery guns, mortars, artillery ammunition, and rations.[77]

The infantry carried minimal rations—about two and one-half pounds, mainly rice, with tinned condiments and salt, so the field train packed a field kitchen whose provisions included fresh vegetables, rice or bread, soy sauce, and pickles. Each evening a forward echelon train (*zempō kōri*) distributed supplies it had received from the field transport unit in the combat unit's bivouac area. When combat seemed imminent, a section of the transport battalion (*senshin shichō*) moved forward bringing essential combat stores—ordnance, equipment, medical supplies—directly to the frontline units. These units also provided resupply, medical evacuation, and repair of ordnance and equipment once fighting started. An innovation of the 1937 draft Infantry Manual was the *taizōku*, or ammunitions section, which the China Garrison Army was field testing during its unit training in the early summer of 1937.[78]

Overall, however, the army neglected logistics, with the Staff College favoring instruction in the more glamorous concepts of strategy and tactics rather than the mundane subjects of resupply and maintenance.[79] The infantry scorned men in transport units as second-class troops because many of these fillers had not even completed their basic reserve training and were ineligible for promotion. Promising officer cadets at the military academy ridiculed the supply services, and the army assigned officers who were graduates of middle schools, not the military academy, to such postings. Officers commanding logistic units were openly regarded as second rate and indeed their designation as special-duty transport troops stamped them as separate and unequal.[80]

The China Garrison Army

The China Garrison Army, established by the Boxer Protocol of September 1901, was charged with the protection of Japanese consular and diplomatic missions in China as well as the defense of the line of communication between Peking and Tianjin. In October 1901, the army formally activated the Japan–Imperial China (*Nisshin*) Garrison Army, but, two years after the 1911 Chinese Revolution, redesignated it the China (*Shina*) Garrison Army. In size, the China Garrison Army was not really an army as the designation is normally used and was not even a regular TO&E unit (*kensei butai*), that is, a unit whose troop basis was fixed by imperial decree.[81] As a provisional unit, it had no affiliation with any regular army force but instead drew on several regular divisions for company- and platoon-size units assigned on a temporary one-year rotating basis. By 1922 this "army" consisted of three infantry companies, about 600 officers and men,[82] but its troop strength varied depending on conditions in China. In response to Chiang Kai-shek's 1927 Northern Expedition, Tokyo strengthened the garrison to five infantry companies—one at Peking and four at Tianjin—along with the headquarters unit, the latter commonly referred to as the Tianjin Garrison.

Following the Manchurian Incident, the Japanese army's repeated attempts to destabilize north China, create puppet regimes, impose Japanese control over the region, and support and encourage extensive smuggling in north China to undermine the economy fueled Chinese resentment and a revived anti-Japanese movement. By early 1935 the army saw north China seething with Communist-provoked sedition and anti-Japanese sentiment, leading the Army Ministry on 16 May 1935 to double the size of the China Garrison Army to 1,771 officers and men.[83] Two infantry companies deployed in Peking and the bulk of the force—eight infantry companies, an artillery company, and engineer platoon—was stationed in Tianjin. That decision touched off widespread student-led anti-Japanese demonstrations throughout China.[84]

Besides its realization that it needed to react to the deteriorating situation, Tokyo reinforced the China Garrison Army to counterbalance the ambitions of the Kwantung Army. In late September 1935, the newly appointed China Garrison commander, Major General Tada Hayao, emphasized this new independence by expressing his resentment over the Kwantung Army's meddling in his operational area of responsibility.[85] The Army Ministry backed Tada, and in November 1935 it ordered the China Garrison Army to coordinate closely with central headquarters, not the Kwantung Army, when handling local incidents, thereby keeping the Kwantung Army's hands out of north China.[86] Although the reinforced China Garrison Army's mission was then clear, specific restraints concerning its operational scope were not.

With conditions in China worsening and the Japanese cabinet revising policy for north China, a December 1935 conference in Tianjin served as the venue for Colonel Kita Sei'ichi, China section chief, General Staff, to propose further reinforcement of the China Garrison Army. Later that month staff officers inspected potential sites for barracks to house the anticipated reinforcements.[87] The army's January 1936 revised China policy charged the China Garrison Army with handling north China affairs and restricted the Kwantung Army to areas north of the Great Wall.

Informed by the army of the proposed reorganization and reinforcement in mid-January 1936, the emperor approved the plan but cautioned the army not to make the action overly conspicuous.[88] The Army Ministry and General Staff then worked out the details of reinforcements, and, on 17 April, the Hirota cabinet approved their recommendations. The next day General Staff orders designated the commander of the reinforced China Garrison Army an imperial appointee directly subordinate to the emperor, elevated his rank to lieutenant general, and converted the command to a permanent TO&E unit with its own regimental colors. Henceforth, the China force was an independent unit.[89] General Staff and Army Ministry orders concurrently made the headquarters, China Garrison Army an independent TO&E unit whose chain of command for operational matters ran to the General Staff and for administrative matters to the Army Ministry. As Lieutenant General Nishio Toshizo, vice chief of staff, explained in May to the China Garrison Army's new commander, Lieutenant General Tashirō Kan'ichirō, reinforcing the unit to wartime strength would enable it to play a more prominent role in north China in accordance with forthcoming revised operational directives.[90] On 15 May 1936 the Army Ministry publicly announced the dispatch of "some reinforcements" to the China Garrison Army because of the recent dramatic increase in acts of violence against Japanese residents there and the menace of anti-Japanese Communist bands.[91]

At its wartime establishment, the China Garrison Army tripled its personnel to 5,774 officers and men and added even greater firepower by organizing its two newly activated independent infantry regiments on the triangular model with a heavy machine gun company, more signals units, and an attached infantry assault gun unit. In short, the General Staff had created the equivalent of a wartime brigade capable of conducting independent, self-sustained combat operations.[92]

Troops from units of various infantry divisions were transferred to form the new brigade. At an 18 June 1936 ceremony held at the Imperial Palace, the emperor activated the new First Independent Infantry Regiment, China Garrison Army, by investing Colonel Mutaguchi with the regimental colors. The colors were uncased nine days later in Peking, headquarters of the new regiment.[93] The size of the reinforcement and the unit's conversion to a permanent overseas garrison naturally alarmed the Chinese, who viewed these developments as still another Japanese attempt to detach north China.[94]

Reinforcements

The reinforced China Garrison Army retained its traditional missions of guaranteeing access to Peking from the sea and protecting imperial officials and subjects residing in the area, as well as monitoring Chinese fulfillment of the May 1933 agreement between the Kwantung Army and Chinese representatives.[95] The accompanying army directive of 6 May 1936 further assigned it responsibility for matters not directly related to the defense of Manchukuo and encouraged the liberal use of force to maintain law and order in north China.[96] In case fighting broke out, the 1937 annual operational plan apparently directed the unit to seize various strategic points such as Tianjin, Peking, Zhangjiakou, and Jinan (Shandong Province) during the initial stage of combat operations.[97] But historians should be cautious in assessing these developments. The reinforcements and revised operational plan do not add up to a conspiracy to wage war. Only a few months later, in September 1936, army authorities rejected the Navy General Staff's requests to dispatch troops to central and south China because the army did not want to fight a general war in China and would employ only the minimum necessary force there.[98]

Regardless of such intentions, the high command lacked a coherent operational policy for China. The General Staff, reflecting Ishiwara's views, acknowledged on 1 September 1936 that "it would be exceedingly disadvantageous to both sides to start a war."[99] Yet two weeks later the General Staff approved the China Garrison Army "decisively punishing" any incident in north China that might damage the "prestige of the imperial army."[100] The General Staff was skittish about sending troops to north China, preferring to let the on-scene commander settle incidents locally, while the Army Ministry believed striking at Nanjing in central China would cause the collapse of the Kuomintang and the demise of Chiang Kai-shek.[101] In similarly contradictory fashion, the Kwantung Army took a hard-line military approach to north China while the China Garrison Army pushed economic development free from covert operations.

Settling In

Tripling military strength almost overnight created a pressing need for barracks and cantonment areas to house the additional soldiers, whom the indignant Chinese sarcastically referred to as "uninvited guests."[102]

Land in the international settlement at Peking was unavailable, being already taken by two companies of Japanese infantry and other foreign garrisons. The General Staff initially favored stationing reinforcements at Baoding, Peking, and Tianjin, but Lieutenant General Umezu Yoshijirō, vice army minister, rejected the Baoding location because it lay outside the established boundaries of the 1901 protocol. Rather than risk an international incident by deploying forces beyond treaty limits, the staff opted to station the Third Battalion, First Infantry Regiment, at Fengtai in Peking's southwestern suburbs.[103]

Although Fengtai had housed a British army garrison several years earlier, it was a poor choice for the Japanese barracks. It was too small to house the Third Battalion at a single location, forcing the army to construct barracks at three separate sites, which fragmented the unit into smaller dispersed elements that made overall command and control difficult for the regimental headquarters. Chinese Twenty-ninth Army units were garrisoned at several points between the Japanese barracks, leaving units of both armies entangled with one another and increasing the chances of accidental encounters and provocations. Tokyo's decision also touched off a wave of anti-Japanese sentiment as Chinese student-led demonstrations erupted throughout major Chinese cities, fed by wild rumors that Japan was constructing an airfield or an enormous barracks complex to house a vast army.[104] Ishiwara later admitted that Tokyo's initial bad judgment left the battalion isolated at Fengtai, surrounded by Chinese forces, and prominent as a magnet for anti-Japanese sentiments.[105]

Tensions

On the evening of 18 September 1936, the fifth anniversary of the Manchurian Incident, Chinese troops of the Twenty-ninth Army at Fengtai scuffled with Japanese soldiers from the Seventh Company, the Third Battalion's rear-guard medical unit. When a Japanese officer arrived on horseback at the scene, Chinese struck his horse and then fled into their barracks area. The battalion commander, Major Ichiki Kiyonao, ordered an emergency assembly, surrounded the Chinese bivouac, and demanded the Chinese authorities hand over the agitators at once. As a face-saving gesture, Major General Kawabe Masakazu, the brigade commander and Ichiki's superior, ordered the regimental commander, Mutaguchi, to settle the incident quickly.[106] Mutaguchi concluded an agreement calling for the Chinese to apologize, punish those responsible, withdraw from the immediate vicinity of the Japanese barracks, and remain two miles away. Although Mutaguchi and Ichiki also wanted to disarm the Chinese, to comply with Kawabe's wishes and "in the spirit of Bushido," they agreed to allow the withdrawing Chinese to keep their weapons.[107]

Later, the Chinese claimed the Japanese had not disarmed them because they feared the power and influence of Twenty-ninth Army. Mutaguchi was furious at the insult to Japanese arms, vowed he would make no further concessions, and promised if another incident occurred, to eliminate the anti-Japanese perpetrators at a single stroke.[108] Mutaguchi warned his regimental officers against allowing "our overly tolerant attitude toward the Chinese to damage the prestige of the imperial army" and instructed his subordinates to strike hard and quickly in the future in order to nip such incidents in the bud.[109]

· An irritant to the Chinese was the Japanese field exercise conducted from late October into early November. The maneuvers were the largest ever conducted by Japanese forces stationed in China and mobilized about 6,700 active duty and reserve troops for a series of complex battle drills, night maneuvers, and tactical field problems. During the exercises, the army quartered troops in Chinese homes, and although the local Chinese were compensated for any damage resulting from maneuvers, the net result was more tension between the two sides.[110] Superimposing the Suiyuan fiasco of December 1936 on a summer and fall of discontent brought anti-Japanese sentiment to a boiling point and led Tokyo to caution the Kawabe brigade not to do anything that might worsen the dangerous situation.[111]

High Command and Field Officers

In March 1937 the annual personnel assignments saw Ishiwara promoted to major general and assigned concurrently as chief, First Department (Operations) General Staff. However, Army Vice Minister Umezu, another hard-liner on China and a bitter rival of Ishiwara, maneuvered the Hayashi cabinet into approving the services' choices for army and navy ministers, not those whom Ishiwara proposed.[112] General Sugiyama Hajime, another China hawk, replaced the terminally ill General Nakamura Kōtarō as army minister within days of Nakamura's appointment and remained in that post until June 1938. Lieutenant General Imai Kiyoshi, army vice chief of staff and an Ishiwara supporter, was also suffering from a terminal illness that rendered him ineffective for much of his brief five-month tenure between March and August 1937.[113] Imai had been expected to play a key role in the high command because the army chief of staff, Prince Kan'in, was a figurehead, appointed in 1931 only because the army was so faction ridden it could not agree on a candidate.[114] Ishiwara hurt his conciliatory policy by picking Colonel Mutō Akira, a known hard-liner on China who believed that only force would resolve the Japan-China impasse, to assume the important post of chief, Operations Section, General Staff.

From Kwantung Army headquarters, Commanding General Ueda

Kenkichi, another China hawk, and his chief of staff, Lieutenant General Tōjō Hideki, advocated a preemptive war against China as the best way to advance the Kwantung Army's interests. The China Garrison Army was more moderate, because Lieutenant General Tashirō and his chief of staff agreed with central headquarters' policy of restraint.[115]

The operational commanders, Major General Kawabe Masakazu, commander of the China Garrison Army's infantry brigade, and Colonel Mutaguchi Renya, the First Infantry's commander, were physical and psychological opposites. Kawabe, a small man whose serious demeanor only highlighted a frail appearance, was a thoughtful and reflective personality with an extensive background in staff assignments. Mutaguchi, the hot-tempered, ambitious field soldier, was a big man of prodigious carnal appetites whose drunken carousing was legendary. Kawabe's passive personality led him to seek compromises and choose the path of least resistance. Mutaguchi was arbitrary, self-confident, and a risk taker, everything Kawabe was not. Yet the two got along. Mutaguchi admired Kawabe's propriety,[116] and Kawabe, whose preference was to assign tasks and then let subordinates do them without further meddling, respected his activist subordinate so long as the rambunctious colonel did not disrupt the chain of command.[117]

Other line officers with tactical units, like the China Garrison Army's artillery regiment commander, Colonel Suzuki Yorimichi, author of the *Principles of Command* and an Araki protégé, and Lieutenant Colonel Morita Tetsuo, attached to Mutaguchi's regiment and a veteran of the Shanghai fighting of 1932 and complicit in the 26 February Rebellion, were hard-liners to the degree that they, like many other Japanese officers, were unwilling to back down from perceived Chinese provocations. Although some historians see the presence of these hotheads transforming the character of the China Garrison Army from a passive to an active role,[118] the two were absorbed in training their troops, not in plotting conspiracies.

On the Eve

After the war, Emperor Hirohito recalled that around the beginning of the summer of 1937 Sino-Japanese relations had reached an explosive level,[119] a widespread feeling at the time. Following his mid-May 1937 staff inspection visit to north China, Captain Imoto Kumao, assigned to the General Staff Operations Section, wrote of the overwhelming feeling among Japanese of all sorts in north China that the Chinese only understood force and without military force nothing could be resolved. He also remarked on the increasing Chinese hostility and growing bellicosity directed against Japanese control of Fengtai, where several of Mutaguchi's units were stationed and which had become a powder keg.[120] Certain that his force could quickly handle any trouble, Mutaguchi dismissed Chinese military capabilities and related problems in north China out of hand.[121] Mutaguchi was more intent on shaping up his new command, which was a showcase for Tokyo's new personnel policies and revised tactical doctrine.

Rumors, however, persisted that Japanese officers were scheming to start a war, and during May China hand Colonel Shibayama Kenjirō, of the War Ministry's Military Affairs Section, and Seventh (China) Branch chief, General Staff, Colonel Nagatsu Sahishige, conducted liaison visits to Manchuria and north China. Their reports, submitted in early June, described a Communist-inspired anti-Japanese campaign aimed at university students that the Kuomintang was unable to control, and the general sense in north China was that it was just a matter of time before something happened.[122] After receiving their estimates, in mid-June Ishiwara ordered his trusted agent, Lieutenant Colonel Okamoto Kiyotomi, to the China Garrison Army to investigate these allegations, a decision indicative of Ishiwara's and the Operations Section's lack of confidence in the army's China experts. Okamoto found no evidence of any incipient conspiracy and reported back that, despite the worsening anti-Japanese feeling and the dangerous situation around Fengtai, unit discipline was strict as troops conducted intensive training in anti-Soviet tactics.[123]

On the Line

Standard practice in the Japanese Army was to train recruits with their parent units before shipping them overseas. On an experimental basis, the Army Ministry sent raw conscripts directly to the China Garrison Army for training and unit integration.[124] The result was a not altogether happy mix of second-year soldiers, who were on loan from other units and were mostly peasants hailing from northeast Japan, and the newcomer conscripts who were city boys unused to roughing it outdoors. Mutaguchi had to meld these veterans and green conscripts into a fighting unit and do so to overcome doubts in army headquarters about the soldiers' ability to function well as a unit because of their different dialects, customs, and living habits.[125] He relied on tough, relentless field training centered around repeated night exercises conducted under wartime conditions.

Mutaguchi filled the training table with night combat and dawn attack exercises to habituate his forces to night movement and improve their terrain recognition skills.[126] Training emphasized the tactics in the draft Infantry Manual, with constant inspections and tactical drills to develop proficiency in night fighting among all officers and men of the regiment. Each officer familiarized himself with the unit defense plan to repel surprise Chinese attack in his assigned sector and exercised his troops with unscheduled emergency assemblies (*shutsudō*).[127] Mutaguchi demanded that his troops and units not simply go through the motions during field training. Junior officers and NCOs were on notice to report the slightest infractions, and Mutaguchi continually emphasized to his men that they were a frontline unit expected to deal rapidly, violently, and decisively with any incident. His order of the day distilled the army's operational and tactical doctrine of fighting outnumbered by capitalizing on mobility, speed, and the offensive. "A frontline unit has great responsibilities so action must be at lightning speed. Because our numbers are inferior, the premium is on night combat."[128]

The basic training cycle concluded in May, and, beginning in June, the soldiers at Fengtai entered their unit training phase (June to October), practicing company and battalion echelon battle drills and field maneuvers, including a minimum of two night exercises per week. June 1937 found Lieutenant General Kazuki Kiyoshi, director of General Affairs, and Colonel Senda Sadaō, inspector general of Military Education and the head of the Infantry School Tactics Department, at Fengtai for a firsthand look at the progress of the new training program. Kazuki endorsed the priority for tactical training to fight the Russians and approved the need for supplementary training to fight the Chinese. The greatest deficiency in training, in Kazuki's opinion, was the lack of suitable drill and maneuver areas in north China. From the end of June to the beginning of July, Senda inspected units at Peking and Fengtai to observe training conducted according to the revised draft Infantry Manual.[129]

From a narrow military perspective, Mutaguchi was merely whipping a new unit into fighting trim, but to the Chinese all this unusual activity—constant patrolling, unconcealed reconnaissance of suitable exercise areas, altered drill and tactical training, VIP visits to oversee field exercises—was easy to misconstrue as something more sinister and a new stage in Japanese belligerence.[130] Surely the Japanese soldiery were psychologically on edge and ready for action. By July 1937, mutual hostility predisposed both sides to assume the worst about the other.

Intelligence

A combination of facts, stereotypes, assumptions, and opinions fashioned the Japanese army's divergent appreciations of the situation in north China. The Second Department's China Section was responsible for intelligence assessments and relied on a network of military attachés, officers assigned to Japanese garrisons in China, Special Service Office (*tōkumu kikan*) personnel, and Japanese military advisers serving with

Chinese units to gather raw data. The field armies interpreted the pro-Japanese attitude of Chiang Kai-shek's regime as mere camouflage to buy time for a growing anti-Japanese movement.[131] The same was true of the autonomous governments, which were superficially pro-Japanese, anti-Kuomintang, or anti-Communist, but their secret contacts with the Nan-jing government revealed their anti-Japanese attitudes, especially in the Twenty-ninth Army, whose officers allowed agitators to drum up morale with anti-Japanese propaganda.[132]

The new breed of China experts, or *Shinatsu*, who appeared in the late 1920s appreciated the rise of Chinese nationalism but felt the Kuomintang had lost its revolutionary zeal and slipped into corruption, nepotism, and factionalism. This analysis equated the anti-Japanese sentiment among Chinese not with a popular reaction to an oppressive Japanese presence but to the Kuomintang's machinations that stirred up popular resentment to maintain Chiang's authority. Thus, Japan had to drive the KMT from north China.[133]

At the operational level, intelligence analysis was marked by a tendency among Japanese commanders to ignore unpleasant assessments and select data that supported their operational plans. In sum, the *Shinatsu* evolved into regional specialists who possessed broad, in-depth knowledge of military, economic, political, and social trends in their respective regions but tended to emphasize the defects of the new China, not its positive aspects. Moreover, the China hands exerted little influence on army policy because the direction of that policy was determined by officers who were not China specialists and were focused on the Soviet Union. Furthermore, few Japanese officers aspired to a career in intelligence, and those who did would rarely reach senior rank.[134] Still, tactical intelligence collection was quite good, a testimony to Japanese field craft, but it was improperly analyzed and not fitted into a larger strategic context. Thus, Japanese intelligence about Chinese military forces was detailed and accurate, but analysis based on the data was flawed by preconceptions about the fighting ability of the Chinese soldier, views shared by the China experts.

Special intelligence—that is cryptanalysis, signal intercept, and radio traffic analysis—targeted Chinese wireless communications. In July 1930, the Codes and Ciphers Office was assigned to the China Section, where it remained until July 1936. The Japanese apparently had success against various Chinese military and diplomatic cipher systems, and in 1935 the China Garrison Army established its own special intelligence office. Intercept operators gathered extensive order of battle intelligence on the strength, disposition, and organization of KMT and warlord armies, but had less success against KMT aviation units. Like the *Shinatsu*, Japan's code breakers shared a disdain for the Chinese and ignored the Chinese Communists as bandit gangs.[135]

The China Garrison Army credited the Chinese Twenty-ninth Army with 15,000–16,000 troops with its main strength around Peking (four division equivalents) and another 10,000 or so troops in the immediate vicinity. Beginning in the spring of 1937, Japanese units began picking up tactical signs that convinced them the Chinese were preparing for war. Indicators included reinforcing guards at Peking gates in June, strengthening units near the Marco Polo Bridge to more than two battalions, preparing new fighting positions, digging trenches and constructing concrete pillboxes near the Marco Polo Bridge, infiltrating agents into Japanese maneuver areas to gather intelligence on night tactical exercises, and increasing strictness among Chinese railroad guards evident since late June.[136] They did not, however, evaluate China as a serious opponent. They believed that the Chinese armies would crumble quickly because they lacked fighting spirit and suffered under poor leadership. Chinese soldiers, according to the Japanese, fought as individuals in a military system of nonstandardized TO&Es that lacked effective command and control. Thus, fighting strength and equipment varied from unit to unit with little coordination.

In 1933, the Infantry School distilled the army's analysis of combat experience gained fighting the Chinese into a classified report. Some observations were straightforward tactical evaluations. The Chinese army was seen, for example, as tenacious on defense but not necessarily strong on offense because it suffered from poor junior officer leadership, lack of fire discipline, and generally inferior military discipline. Other assessments were based on alleged national characteristics. China's subsistence-level lifestyle, for example, supposedly inured its troops to field hardships. Chinese were seen as being easily deceived by propaganda, fighting for personal gain so easily bought off, and quickly losing their will to fight if their leaders disappeared. "Against the weak, they are strong; against the strong, weak. That is the innate Chinese personality. So strike hard and never appear weak."[137] Such interpretations reinforced standard Japanese tactical doctrine for commanders at all levels to press home night bayonet attacks against the Chinese no matter what the odds. In sum, the how-to-fight report complemented tactical infantry doctrine and echoed the shibboleths about faith in inevitable victory found in *Principles of Command*.

More ominously, however, firsthand combat experience in Manchuria, north China, and Shanghai since 1931 had taught the Japanese soldier to expect Chinese guerrilla units to pass themselves off in mufti as farmers, students, or coolies in order to infiltrate rear areas. In city fighting entire units of Chinese uniformed soldiers switched to civilian clothing, making it difficult to distinguish them among the larger population. Chinese duplicity and feigned surrenders made prisoners of war a real threat to Japanese troops. It required little imagination for tired, angry, and suspicious Japanese soldiers to view Chinese civilians and prisoners as still highly dangerous and thus free game.[138]

Conclusion

Soldiers and, by extension, armies fight according to their training and doctrine. Force structure, weapons, and equipment complement tactical drills and operational concepts. When fighting broke out in north China in July 1937, the Japanese army responded according to ingrained doctrine premised on rapid, hard-hitting tactics designed to win a short war. The ability of Japanese forces to react quickly, maneuver rapidly, and fight skillfully, just as they had been trained, equipped, and indoctrinated to do, proved initially advantageous, but without a long-range strategy, ultimately futile.

The strength of the Japanese army in July 1937 was its first-class system for training and indoctrination of recruits, professional schools producing capable NCOs and junior officers, well-trained company and field-grade officers, improved weapons and equipment, a coherent and integrated doctrine at all echelons of command, and, compared to the Chinese, superior weaponry and firepower, better command and control, better communications, and in almost all cases superior morale and unit esprit de corps. Moreover, ample personnel reserves were available for mobilization to support operations.

These advantages initially concealed serious structural weaknesses. The Japanese army had no integrated strategic plan for a protracted war against China, and existing operational plans assumed a quick end to any fighting. Without clear objectives, the Japanese army resorted to ad hoc expedients in lieu of a comprehensive plan of operations. Logistic problems exacerbated planning deficiencies. Because the Japanese army did not anticipate a full-scale war with China in 1937, it had not stockpiled ammunition and equipment for such an eventuality. Artillery shells, in particular, were in woefully short supply and would be exhausted after several weeks of heavy, sustained fighting. The same was true of other equipment. Japanese industry was manufacturing crew-served weapons, tanks, trucks, aircraft, and so forth on a peacetime timetable. Units were poorly deployed for a lightning campaign in China and unready for protracted operations. Intelligence confirmed rather than challenged existing stereotypes of the Chinese military. Finally, July 1937 found the Japanese army in the midst of a turbulent and controversial long-term process to convert its divisional structure, revamp its doctrine, and modernize its equipment while engaged in sporadic combat operations, occupation duties, a forward defense role, covert operations, and murderous internal factional rivalry. The army also had to guarantee the availability not only of Manchuria's strategic raw materials but also of those of the five provinces of north China to retool its war machine.

To accommodate this transitional period, national policy was evolving from the persistent and aggressive efforts of the field armies to disestablish Chinese political authority in north China to a more conciliatory stand. One result was to increase tension between the field armies and the General Staff in Tokyo and to create substantial cleavages among senior officers over the "solution" to their so-called China problem. Reactions in Tokyo to initial reports of the Marco Polo Bridge fighting illustrate the point. In the Army Ministry, Colonel Shibayama, recently returned from his inspection tour of north China, felt "something troubling has occurred" (*yakkai na*), while Mutō Akira of the General Staff rejoiced that "something wonderful has happened" (*yukai na*).[139] No one, of course, expected a protracted war of attrition with China to follow. It was simply another case of a little trouble erupting in China, and a single gunshot would show the imperial army meant business.[140]

China Garrison Army chief of staff Major General Hashimoto Gun later remarked that "The Marco Polo Bridge Incident probably could have been avoided, but a second or third such incident would have come along. Unless the fundamental problems were solved, the slightest incident invariably would touch off the fuse."[141] At the macro level, by mid-July 1937, Japanese expansionism and Chinese irredentism made solution of those "fundamental problems" impossible. At the micro level, the officers and men of the Third Battalion embodied the evolution of Japan's national and military strategies as well as the army's operational planning, force structure, and tactical doctrine. That these soldiers stationed on the frontier responded aggressively to a local emergency as they had been trained and indoctrinated to do should not come as a surprise.

Photo 1. Chinese antiaircraft battery at
Nanjing, 1937

Photo 2. Battle of Changsha, 1939

Photo 3.   Chinese trenches during the Battle of Taierzhuang, 1938

Photo 4.   Chongqing bombed

Photo 5. Victory celebration in Chongqing, 1945

Part III

FROM THE FIGHTING AT THE MARCO POLO BRIDGE,
JULY 1937, TO THE FALL OF WUHAN, OCTOBER 1938

Escalation and response characterized the opening stage of the Sino-Japanese War, and the essays in this section revolve around that theme. Hattori Satoshi and Edward J. Drea deal with the issue in the context of the Japanese field armies' incessant demands on Tokyo for greater latitude to expand operations, more reinforcements, and a paramount role in military decision making. Yang Tianshi adopts a different approach, describing Chinese military operations through the initiatives of Chiang Kai-shek. Yang devotes little space to the north China campaigns in order to focus his narrative on the complexities driving Chiang's decision to fight at Shanghai and the consequences that flowed from that decision. He argues persuasively that Chiang took the initiative at Shanghai to expand the war, to open a second front to relieve Japanese pressure on north China, and to demonstrate to the world Chinese determination to resist the invader. Where Yang does write of operational matters, he underlines the terrible cost in casualties the Chinese paid to stand in Shanghai and suggests that greater flexibility on Chiang's part may have produced a better result.

Hattori and Drea give more attention to operational and even tactical considerations affecting the Japanese army's war against China. Campaigns in north China are discussed in detail because the Japanese expected to conclude the war quickly and to reap the spoils in that region. They make plain that army authorities in Tokyo were not anxious to extend the fighting to Shanghai. But with insubordinate field commanders in north China chafing at the bit and naval special landing forces in peril at Shanghai, they gave in to the navy's demands and dispatched major reinforcements to the city. Yang notes that once Chiang determined to fight, he threw his best troops into battle. The reader will see the havoc and casualties that resulted.

These first two essays stress the lack of command and control exercised by higher headquarters. The General Staff in Tokyo usually appears about one step behind the aggressive field commanders. Likewise, Chiang had great difficulty enforcing his operational orders. Some Chinese commanders ignored him, others disobeyed him, and even those who followed him required careful handling. This deficiency greatly impeded China's war effort and recurs frequently throughout this volume.

Both chapters treat Chiang's vacillation over the fate of Nanjing—to surrender the city or not. His procrastination led to the worst of all possible outcomes: Chinese defenders uncertain of overall strategy for the capital and Japanese troops incensed by die-hard Chinese resistance in a hopeless defense. Taken together the narratives compel a reassessment of the early days of the struggle. Further study is needed to illuminate the peculiar command and control policies of the opposing forces, the tactics and operational concepts of each side as the fighting expanded, and the military's dominant role in overall decision making.

The central China campaigns of 1938 fundamentally altered the nature and direction of the war in China. Stephen MacKinnon describes the campaigns as a watershed for Chiang Kai-shek and for the Chinese armies. Slowly, painfully, and often brutally, Chiang and his oligarchy of commanders fashioned a political-military strategy to stave off Japanese victory. MacKinnon attributes much of this success to the development of Chinese leadership capabilities and personal ties among Chinese senior officers who coalesced around their willingness to resist Japanese aggression. His account of the major operations of 1938 focuses on the desperate defense of Wuhan during the summer of 1938 that caught the world's imagination. But, more important, the determined defense and orderly withdrawal validated the Chinese strategy of a protracted war of attrition and sowed newfound confidence among the Chinese military.

This new spirit of resistance appeared throughout 1939 in the ebb-and-flow battles for Nanchang and Changsha, where the Chinese displayed a new aggressiveness, together with an ability to coordinate operations on multiple fronts. These fiercely fought campaigns weeded out incompetent senior commanders and promoted those willing to take on the Japanese. Nonetheless, the Chinese army still lacked the necessary equipment, logistic support, and military infrastructure to defeat Japan. Thus, the Yichang operation of May–June 1940 was a terrible setback for Chiang, but the Japanese too were exhausted. Henceforth, only limited operations would occur until 1944. As an aside, MacKinnon raises the question of whether the defense of central China might presage later anticolonial struggles where the colonizer won on the battlefield because of superior firepower, organization, and equipment but could not translate military success into a political solution to the war. This question surely deserves further attention.

Tobe Ryōichi discusses the major campaigns in central China between 1938 and 1941 through the lens of Japan's Eleventh Army, which was in overall command of the operations. Unlike the slowly coalescing Chinese forces, the Japanese army continued to be riven with factionalism and to be unable to work out a military strategy after the seizure of Nanjing. At the beginning of 1938, the General Staff sought a military victory to end the war by force of arms and believed the destruction of China's field armies around Xuzhou would achieve that goal. Unable to trap the Chinese armies at Xuzhou, the high command estimated that the capture of

Wuhan would break the Chinese will to resist, a strategic shift in emphasis. But Tobe notes that the scope of campaigns and the vastness of the theater of operations ended Japanese army hopes of securing a military victory. Even the capture of Wuhan left the Japanese facing a determined foe and forced them to adopt a political-military strategic approach that involved a long-term occupation coupled with attempts to create puppet regimes in China. Moreover, Japan's bloody defeat at Nomonhan on the Manchurian-Mongolian border at the hands of the Soviet army in the summer of 1939 and the outbreak of war in Europe that September changed the strategic equation for Tokyo. Yet in order to capitalize on the new situation, Japan somehow had to bring the war with China to an end.

The Japanese Eleventh Army pressed for a massive offensive to knock China out of the war and to provide the military basis for the puppet regimes. But the Chinese struck first in the winter offensive of 1939–1940, which caught the Japanese off guard. Even hard-bitten Japanese commanders were impressed with this newfound Chinese offensive spirit. If the Eleventh Army wanted a military solution, the General Staff in Tokyo would settle for a political settlement and, as a preparation for that resolution, attempted to consolidate Japanese positions in China, to reduce troop levels there, and to prepare for the inevitable war with the Soviet Union. Again, field commanders resisted Tokyo's approach, insisting that military force was the answer. But, in fact, Japan was having great difficulty sustaining its field forces in China. Equipment and ammunition shortages plagued operations. Makeshift logistic arrangements broke down with crippling regularity. In short, with a strategy for a short-term war in 1937, the army tried ad hoc strategic initiatives but never put together a comprehensive strategic-military approach to the China war. Thus, by 1941, the Eleventh Army was overseeing punitive raids, foraging expeditions, and an occupation in the context of limited operations designed to conserve resources, equipment, and manpower. It was a strategy of stalemate, as Tobe notes, and one that left the Japanese winning the battles but unable to defeat the Chinese armies. Tobe's chapter makes plain the need for further exploration of the command relationships between Tokyo and the field as a means to understand what the Japanese thought they were achieving in China.

5 *Chiang Kai-shek and the Battles of Shanghai and Nanjing*

YANG TIANSHI

On 7 July 1937, Japanese forces stationed at Lugouqiao (Marco Polo Bridge) south of Peking (now Beijing) were conducting nighttime exercises. One soldier lost his way; when his commanding officer demanded entrance to the town of Wanping, near the bridge, he was refused. The soldier found his way back to his unit, but Japanese forces attacked, and the Chinese garrison resisted. This was the first act of the bitter eight-year war between China and Japan.

At first, the Chinese army saw north China as the main battleground. Chiang Kai-shek took personal command and sent his German military adviser, General Alexander von Falkenhausen, to the front. But on 13 August, Chiang decided to clear the Japanese forces from the Shanghai area. China was now fighting on two fronts, but Shanghai soon became the main battleground. The Chinese committed about 750,000 soldiers, the Japanese, 250,000. The fighting lasted three months and resulted in one of the largest battles of the war.

Chiang Kai-shek's Decision for War

After the Mukden Incident (18 September 1931) Generalissimo Chiang Kai-shek pursued a policy of appeasement toward Japan for a long time. After the Marco Polo Bridge Incident, Japan's intentions seemed obscure to Chiang. Writing in his diary, Chiang asked himself, "Is Japan using a moment when our war preparations are not complete to force us into an international settlement? . . . Is this the time for us to launch a counteroffensive?"[1] The next day, he dispatched his troops to reinforce the Twenty-ninth Army "to defend the country against aggression." He cabled Qin Dechun, the mayor of Peking: "First, we must resolve to fight and to sacrifice. We must actively prepare for war. Then, with our sovereignty intact, we can negotiate with the Japanese."[2]

At the time, China was no match for Japan in national power and in military strength. Given this weakness, some people both inside and outside the national government actively argued for appeasement, or at least for delaying the start of war. Inside the government, Xu Yongchang, a member of the Standing Committee of the Military Affairs Commission, claimed that China would need at least six months to prepare for war with Japan, given that the Japanese air arm was far larger than the Chinese one. On 14 July 1937, Xu cabled He Yingqin, the minister of Military Administration, saying, "We should still actively pursue peace."[3] On 18 July, Xu had a message passed to Wang Chonghui, the minister of Foreign Affairs, that said, "As long as we can bear it, we should continue to plan for the path of peace."[4] He Yingqin agreed with Xu and suggested that he talk with Chiang Kai-shek, who was then at Lushan, his summer retreat near Jiujiang.[5] On 21 July, Xu wrote to Chiang, "As long as we can endure the Japanese, we must do so. Once war breaks out, no matter whether a third country intervenes, Japan and China will suffer tremendous losses. Japan is an industrialized nation and will recover easily. We are the opposite. The outcome for China would be horrible; nobody could then save China."[6]

Among the intelligentsia, Jiang Menglin, president of Peking University, Professor Hu Shi, and others advocated enduring hardship and seeking peace. They believed that it would be worse to seek peace after defeat and that now was the time to negotiate. On 6 August, Hu made the following proposals to Chiang:

1. China should use any opportunity to negotiate with the Konoe cabinet.
2. Since Japan has fundamental financial problems, there is hope for peace.
3. At the moment, the Chinese state will collapse without our modern armed forces. We should not risk their destruction.[7]

Hu Shi hoped that if China's efforts were successful, China and Japan could have peace for fifty years.

A country's destiny often depends on a choice between peace and war, and Chiang Kai-shek faced a major dilemma. But within days, Chiang decided to throw down the gauntlet and confront Japan. On 12 July, Chiang decided to make a stand on the Yongding River and the Cangzhou–Baoding line, and ordered that there would be no initiatives to seek a compromise with Japan.

On 16 July, Chiang gathered over 150 leading Chinese at Lushan to discuss the decision for war. The subsequent statement asserted that "if war breaks out, whether you are from the north or the south, whether you are young or old, no matter who you are, you have the duty to defend our country."[8] The leaders reached no consensus on whether to make the declaration public. Chiang himself could not make up his mind. In his diary on 16 July, he wrote: "Is it right to make this declaration public?"[9] The next day, he wrote, "It is obvious that the Japanese bandits are playing their standard trick to force us to comply without fighting. We must resolve to fight. Then perhaps we can resist their aggression and avoid the devastating consequences of all-out war. Perhaps now is the time to make public the declaration to demonstrate our determination to fight." On 19 July, Chiang determined to override any opposition to his decision and to make the statement public. He wrote in his diary, "I believe that this is the only way to bring a peaceful outcome to the present crisis."

Yet Chiang did not close the door on peaceful resolution: "Until the last ray of hope is extinguished, we seek to resolve the Marco Polo Bridge Incident in a peaceful manner." As Japan continued its military operations, Chiang made up his mind to fight. On 27 July, Japanese troops attacked Tongzhou and other places near Peking. In his diary, Chiang wrote, "War is inevitable. We must fight . . . Being leader of the nation, I must not do anything to cause people to be ashamed of me."[10]

On 28 July, Chinese forces withdrew from Peking, and the next day, troops defending Tianjin attacked local Japanese units, but the Chinese suffered such heavy casualties that they withdrew two days later. The loss of Peking and Tianjin, the two largest cities in north China, convinced Chiang that he would lose popular support unless he fought. Chiang believed that China had many weaknesses—a lack of national cohesion, faulty infrastructure, and incomplete military preparations. For China to go to war was risky. On the other hand, Japan could be seen as "apparently strong" but "internally weak." "If we focus on the morale of our nation, if we can boost national spirit, we may be able to turn the danger around, and even find benefits from the current turmoil."

On 7 August, Chiang convened the National Defense Council. He Yingqin reported on military preparations, proposing to mobilize 1 million men. He listed many difficulties: the growth of fiscal expenditure; the shortage of weapons and ammunition, barely enough for six months; defense projects that were incomplete; and an air force that was substandard. At the meeting, resistance was formally established as national policy.[11]

China Strikes First

Shanghai lies on the coast of the East China Sea, no more than 180 miles from Nanjing, then the capital of China. The Shanghai ceasefire agreement of 1932 stipulated that China could use only Peace Preservation Forces to maintain order in Shanghai, while Japan could station troops and build strongholds in the Japanese defense sector of the International

Settlement in Shanghai and areas north. In response, in 1934 the Nationalist government issued a secret order to construct a series of defensive lines
around Shanghai, as recommended by General von Falkenhausen.[12] The
government also devised operational plans to seize Japanese fortified positions in Shanghai.[13]

After the Marco Polo Bridge Incident, Chiang Kai-shek ordered General Zhang Zhizhong, garrison commander of Nanjing and Shanghai, to
strengthen Shanghai's defenses. Zhang ordered some of his men to disguise
themselves as Peace Preservation Forces and enter Shanghai to take up
stations at Hongqiao Airport and elsewhere. On 30 July, Zhang proposed
that the Nationalist government approve a preemptive strike if the situation in Shanghai deteriorated. Chiang replied, "We must make the first
strike against our enemy, but you must await orders on the timing."[14]

The Japanese navy pressed for expansion into central China. On 16 July,
Rear Admiral Hasegawa Kiyoshi, commander of the Third Fleet, reported
to the Navy General Staff that "limiting the fighting would benefit Chinese forces . . . To finish China off, we must focus on taking Shanghai and
Nanjing."[15] On 7 August, the navy minister, Admiral Yonai Mitsumasa,
suggested to the army minister, General Sugiyama Hajime, that he dispatch army troops to Shanghai at once.[16] The next day, Hasegawa received
an order that new forces were to be deployed to deal with the worsening
situation.

On 9 August, members of Zhang Zhizhong's Peace Preservation Forces,
guarding Hongqiao Airport, exchanged fire with a Lieutenant Oyama Isao,
a member of the naval landing party, killing him and his sailor driver.[17] The
Japanese used this incident as a pretext to bring more warships to Shanghai and to increase the size of the naval landing forces. Japan demanded
that the Chinese Peace Preservation Forces withdraw and that the defense
works be dismantled. The central command of the Japanese navy notified
the Japanese Third Fleet that force was the only way to resolve the current
conflict, and that Japan should attack twenty days after the army had been
mobilized. On 10 August, the Japanese cabinet agreed, and two days later
the army ministry ordered the mobilization of 300,000 troops, to be sent
to Shanghai and Qingdao.

The Peace Preservation Forces were the only troops that China had in
the Shanghai region. Chiang Kai-shek thought that if these forces withdrew, Shanghai, like Peking, would be occupied by the Japanese. He
rejected Japan's demand and ordered Chinese troops to prepare to fight.
On 11 July, Chiang learned that Japanese warships were concentrating
off Shanghai. He decided to put barriers across the river at the mouth of
the Wusong. On the same day, he ordered Zhang Zhizhong to move the
Eighty-seventh and the Eighty-eighth divisions to take up offensive positions in Shanghai. They were to eliminate Japanese troops in Wusong and

Shanghai.[18] The Japanese naval landing forces numbered no more than 5,000.[19] On 12 August, the Central Committee of the Kuomintang (KMT) secretly decided that a state of war existed.[20]

Zhang Zhizhong had planned to attack before dawn on 13 August. Chiang Kai-shek ordered him to "await further instructions and not provoke a small-scale engagement,"[21] because diplomats from four countries (Britain, the United States, France, and Italy) were still mediating. That morning, skirmishing broke out and quickly escalated. Japanese warships continuously bombarded the center of the Chinese part of Shanghai.[22] At dawn on 14 August, Zhang Zhizhong received orders from Chiang Kai-shek to launch a general offensive. The Chinese National Air Force bombed and strafed the *Izumo*, flagship of the Third Fleet, anchored in front of the Japanese consulate general headquarters of the Japanese naval landing forces. The Battle of Shanghai had begun, and a second front had been opened. At the beginning of the battle, the Chinese massed elite troops to attack Japanese strongholds in Shanghai. Street fighting took place at Hongkou, Yangshupu, and many other parts of Shanghai. On the seventeenth, Zhang Zhizhong reported to Chiang that "Our initial goal was to take advantage of Japan's weak points and advance, not to conquer strongholds. But every street was blocked by the enemy, and they were using armored cars as mobile strongholds. So, in the end, we had to attack every target." On the night of the twentieth, the Chinese pushed Japanese units into a narrow zone on the left bank of the Whampoa River. They surrounded the naval landing party command post and other strongholds built with reinforced steel and concrete. The Chinese needed heavy weapons to succeed in this attack, but they had only three howitzers, which quickly malfunctioned.

Is it really true that the Chinese lacked sufficient heavy weapons? Chiang Kai-shek himself wrote on 20 November, "We did not use our full strength against the enemy in Shanghai. Minister He Yingqin did not deploy weapons for close combat. I called urgently for armored cars and cannon, but it was too late because Japan's main force had already landed."[23]

Chiang was not pleased with Zhang Zhizhong's command. On 20 August, General Chen Cheng told Chiang that expansion of the fighting in north China was inevitable. If the enemy gained the upper hand there, it could send its mobile units south toward Wuhan. China should escalate military operations in Shanghai to draw off the Japanese army and prevent a major offensive in north China.[24] On the same day, the Military Affairs Commission concentrated troops in east China to rapidly clear Japanese naval and army bases in the Shanghai area and to interdict or destroy Japanese reinforcements. The committee designated Zhejiang and southern Jiangsu as the Third War Zone. Chiang was appointed commander of this zone, General Gu Zhutong deputy commander, General Chen Cheng front commander, and General Zhang Zhizhong commander of the Ninth

Army Group in the zone surrounding Shanghai. General Zhang Fakui was appointed commander of the Eighth Army Group, in the zone on the northern shore of Hangzhou Bay, to cover Shanghai's left flank.

These measures demonstrated that Chiang gave priority to the Shanghai front, but he was still not planning a protracted battle. In his diary on 20 August, he wrote, "We have made progress in the Battle of Shanghai. Japanese troops are panic-stricken. The Japanese army and navy are at odds. Inside the Japanese government, there is no consensus. Japan is on the horns of a dilemma. Britain proposes to mediate. We must seize this opportunity. Perhaps a face-saving means can be found to get Japan to leave Shanghai."[25] The next day, Japan rejected Britain's mediation. Chiang was concerned about Japanese escalation,[26] and on 22 August he ordered the establishment of the Fifteenth Army Group, with General Chen Cheng as commander, stationed on the south bank of the Yangtze River, to guard Shanghai's right flank.

The Failure to Stop Japanese Landings

Japan's forces in Shanghai were limited. To continue operations, Japan had to dispatch reinforcements by sea. The Chinese navy was extremely weak and could not prevent the landings despite efforts to blockade the Yangtze channel. The Chinese National Air Force had only about 180 operational aircraft, too few to interdict Japanese troop shipments.[27]

On the night of 13 August, the Japanese cabinet ordered the dispatch of reinforcements. Two days later, the Japanese government declared: "To counter China's cruel and ruthless behavior, and to make the Nanjing government reflect on its mistakes, we have to take decisive measures now."[28] On the same day, the Japanese government appointed Lieutenant General Matsui Iwane as commander of the Shanghai Expeditionary Force, composed of the Third and Eleventh divisions. His army was to support the Japanese naval landing party in eliminating Chinese troops around Shanghai and occupying the city. On 17 August, the Japanese cabinet decided to "abandon the previous nonescalation policy, and take any measures necessary under wartime conditions."[29] On 23 August, supported by naval gunfire, Japan's Eleventh Division forced a landing at Chuanshakou on the southern bank of the Yangtze River. The Third Division landed at the Wusong Railway dock. Shi Shuo (of the Ninth Army Group) later recalled, "After dawn on 23 August, the Japanese naval air units launched a fierce bombardment. Our reinforcements could not enter the battle. The Japanese navy shelled heavily to cover the Japanese landings. The Fifty-sixth Division was stationed along the Yangtze and the Peace Preservation Forces were too weak to repel the Japanese landing.[30]

China tried to stop the enemy from advancing farther inland. Under heavy shelling, General Zhang Zhizhong rode a bicycle to the front line. He made Wang Jingjiu frontline commander in Shanghai and ordered him to hold current positions. Zhang sent the Eleventh and the Ninety-eighth divisions north to block advancing Japanese troops. Despite their fierce attacks at Luodian and other places, they were unable to prevent the landings. On 28 August, after more than half of the Chinese defenders had been killed or wounded, Japan's Eleventh Division took Luodian, and three days later Japan's Third Division occupied Wusong.

On 1 September, Japan's elite Twelfth Division, from Kurume, and two other divisions reached Shanghai. Japan launched an all-out offensive on 5 September, consisting of a concerted military, naval, and aerial attack. During the fighting along the Yunzaobin River "both sides suffered tremendous losses. The water in the river turned red; the fabled 'blood flowing like rivers' became a reality."[31] Chen Cheng reported that five divisions had suffered over 9,000 casualties. More than half of the Sixth Division was killed or wounded in the fighting for Wusong.

Because the topography of the riverine area was favorable for a concerted attack by Japanese army, navy, and air forces, and because Japan kept pouring in reinforcements, Chinese troops had to retreat to avoid further losses. As Shi Shuo later recalled, "The Japanese troops landed continuously along the Yangtze and Huangpu rivers. They fought with our troops for every stronghold. Very often the Japanese took a strongpoint in daylight, which we then recovered at night . . . Under heavy fire from Japanese warships, we suffered heavy casualties. It was very common that a unit was reduced to a few members and had to be replaced only a few days after it went into combat. I witnessed a regiment of the Central Training Unit go into combat at full strength. When it came back, only a few orderlies were left."[32] On 10 September, the right flank of the field of the Fifteenth Army Group was broken. The next day, the Ninth Army Group was ordered to move to Beizhan, Jiangwan, and other places.

After China failed to stop these landings, Japanese reinforcements poured in. On 11 September, a Japanese unit redeployed from Qingdao and took Yuepu. The following day, ten infantry battalions, also detached from the North China Army, entered the Shanghai battlefield. On 14 September, a detachment from Taiwan landed in Shanghai. The tide of the fighting had turned against the Chinese.

Sino-Soviet Communications and the Decision to Hold Shanghai

After 11 September, Chinese troops embarked on a stubborn defense. As supreme commander, Chiang Kai-shek quickly realized China's precarious situation. After Luodian fell, Chiang wrote in his diary:

"The situation on the battlefield has deteriorated and turned against us. Our morale has been shaken." After Wusong was lost, Chiang expressed his anxiety in his diary: "Conditions have turned against our troops." Chiang now had to work out how to pursue the war. On 2 September, he wrote, "The enemy's weakness is that they are turning a minor front into their major front. Their tactics are reactive; they are being pushed into action. Our strategy must be to focus on making it difficult for our enemy to advance farther. He will then face the dilemma of whether to advance or retreat. We can use our capacities of endurance to achieve our goal in a protracted battle." This entry shows that although the battlefield situation in Shanghai was bad, Chiang was determined to "stay focused" and to drag Japan into protracted fighting in Shanghai. Later, the deputy chief of staff, General Bai Chongxi; the head of the Operations Office, General Liu Fei; and others proposed that the Battle of Shanghai "be ended when the initial goals are achieved," and troops be transferred to defensive positions outside Shanghai. Chiang initially accepted this idea and ordered its execution, but the next day, he countermanded the order.[33] On 14 September, he asked himself in his diary, "Should we mass troops to fight in Shanghai? Or should we withdraw inland and gather strength for protracted resistance?" The former would mean that the decisive engagement would be in Shanghai; the latter would mean that China would retreat to defensive positions outside the city. Despite private anxiety, Chiang ordered Chinese troops to move to Shanghai. He wrote: "Many units have suffered more than 50 percent casualties. But if we do not stand firm, how can we deter our enemy?"[34]

On 16 and 17 September, Japan launched another general offensive north of Shanghai. Chinese troops were shaken, and frontline commanders asked permission to withdraw. Chiang ordered them to stand firm and went to the front lines to stiffen morale.[35] On 21 September, he redeployed his forces for the coming battle.

Why Shanghai?

Why did Chiang Kai-shek decide to concentrate on Shanghai? On the one hand, he wanted to relieve the pressure on the north China front and to keep supply lines from the Soviet Union open. There were two routes, which both ran through Shanxi, but on 11 September the Japanese took Datong (in Shanxi). In his diary entry for 14 September, Chiang Kai-shek bitterly criticized General Yan Xishan, commander of the Second War Zone, for not holding Datong. He wrote, "This loss has made communications with the Soviet Union very difficult. Yan bears even greater blame for it than Song Zheyuan for losing Peking and Tianjin. It is dreadful!"[36] On 26 September, Chiang learned that Chinese troops along the Peking–Wuhan Railway had been defeated and forced to retreat. The second supply line between China and the Soviet Union was at risk. He decided to strengthen the Shanghai front to draw off Japan's main forces from the Peking–Hankou corridor.

On 8 October, Chiang decided to send Guangxi troops, known as brave and capable fighters, to Shanghai. A week later, he wrote, "By the time the war has lasted six months, next March at the latest, Japan will be facing either internal turmoil or external threat. We will hold out." On 17 October, Chiang went to Suzhou to take direct command. The next day, Chinese troops launched a general counteroffensive on the Shanghai front.

Chiang hoped to use military means to bolster China's diplomatic struggle, especially to influence an impending international conference in Brussels. After the Marco Polo Bridge Incident, the Nationalist government had appealed to the League of Nations to censure Japan as an aggressor. The League proposed a meeting of the signatories of the 1922 Nine-Power Treaty negotiated in Washington, of which Japan was a signatory, as was China. It had reaffirmed the Open Door policy and had accepted China's right to self-determination. Japan had withdrawn from the League itself after its occupation of Manchuria. The meeting convened in Brussels on 30 October. On 22 October, Chiang notified all troops of the impending conference and exhorted them to "make extra efforts . . . to demonstrate our morale and strength, improve our international status, and win sympathy and support from friendly nations."[37] To strengthen his position, Chiang brought in reinforcements from all over China. On 24 October, he cabled General Long Yun in Yunnan, asking where his promised troops were. Chiang ordered Long to have his troops "move as fast as they can and try to reach Shanghai and join the fighting before the start of the Brussels meeting."[38]

The Japanese government took countermeasures. It continued to transfer troops from north China, Manchukuo, and Japan to the Shanghai front. On 1 October, Prime Minister Konoe, Army Minister Sugiyama, Navy Minister Yonai, and Foreign Minister Hirota Kōki agreed on an Outline for Dealing with the Sino-Japanese War. They decided to launch a new offensive in October, escalate the war in north China and central China, and drive Chinese troops out Shanghai. Japan wanted to force the Nationalist government to negotiate an end to the war. Japan now had nine divisions and more than 200,000 troops on the Shanghai front, more than in north China. On 17 October, the Army Ministry ordered its troops to seize strategic points in Shanghai before the Brussels meeting.[39]

Meanwhile, on 21 October, the Chinese Twenty-first Army Group, led by General Liao Lei, a member of the Guangxi clique, arrived in Shanghai with reinforcements from Guangxi. These troops launched an immediate counteroffensive along the Yunzaobin River. The troops fought bravely, but their weapons were obsolete, and they lacked experience in fighting a well-equipped enemy. They could not reverse the situation. On 22 October, Chiang Kai-shek wrote in his diary: "I had hoped that after the troops from Guangxi entered the fighting, we could hold out. But against our expectations they were defeated and we had to retreat. The military situation is shaky. It is very discouraging."[40] The next day, due to heavy casualties, the Guangxi force retreated to recover.[41] Other units also suffered heavy casualties. Only one soldier in ten of the Thirty-third Division survived. The division commander was wounded, and a brigade commander was missing.[42] On 25 October, Japanese troops turned the positions of the Eighteenth Division, Seventy-eighth Army, forcing the abandonment of this strategic stronghold in northwestern Shanghai. Chiang Kai-shek realized that he had to redeploy and ordered a strategic withdrawal to the south bank of Suzhou Creek.

To give the impression that China still held the north bank of the creek, he decided that "to impress people in China and abroad, we will leave one battalion in Zhabei."[43] The 524th Battalion, Eighty-eighth Division, the famous "Lone Battalion," received the assignment and held the Sihang godown in the midst of the Japanese positions on the north side of the creek. This was the moving and tragic story of 800 gallant warriors defending the besieged warehouse alone. (Actually, only 400 solders were there.) After securing a major propaganda coup, on 31 October they retreated with British assistance to the International Settlement, where the British interned them.

Chiang Kai-shek was now fully aware that the Sino-Japanese War would not end quickly. The strategic principle he adopted was to fight a protracted war of resistance. On 18 August, he had issued the Second Letter to Our Troops Resisting Japan: "When the enemy attacks, we resist. When our enemy is exhausted, we seize the initiative and strike." "We must hold our ground and not retreat. We must use trenches, fortresses, and walls to frustrate the enemy's offensive."[44] On 13 September, Chiang issued a Letter to Our Troops in All War Zones, emphasizing the need to defend and resist. "Even if we have only one soldier and one bullet left, we must fight to the end."[45] On 28 October, Chiang held a military conference. He reiterated his commitment to "building up our defense facilities and strengthening our positions . . . We must not fear the destruction of our positions or fear that we will lose everything . . . We have already retreated to the last defensive line for Shanghai. Everyone must resolve to . . . stand firm, and defend [the city] to the death. We must live or die with Shanghai."[46]

This spirit of sacrifice was essential to defend the country and defeat the enemy. But the enemy held sea and air supremacy and was well equipped with heavy weapons. A protracted war of resistance could only bring enormous casualties and still lead to the loss of territory. The Japanese had

1,500 aircraft, while China had only 300 fighters and bombers.[47] On 24 August, General Zhang Zhizhong had sent a secret telegram to Chiang Kai-shek and Minister He Yingqin, stating, "These days, Japanese airplanes are very active. They bomb all day without interruption. During the day, our troops are pinned down. The enemy's planes pose a great threat to us."[48] General Bai Chongxi held the same opinion: "There is no way that we can fight without control of the air. In daytime, our troops cannot fight because of Japanese aircraft. At night, our troops cannot fight either because of the enemy's searchlights. If we want to wage a protracted war of resistance, we must work out some other plan."[49] During the Battle of Shanghai, Chinese troop morale was high, and the soldiers fought bravely. But Chiang relied only on protracted warfare. He concentrated several hundred thousand elite troops along a long, narrow strip along the southern bank of the Yangtze. They set up several lines of defense and fought stubbornly but without flexibility. They suffered tremendous losses. This was a misguided strategy. The next year, Chiang reflected on the Battle of Shanghai and criticized himself for not ordering troops to retreat before the Brussels meeting. "Instead, while we were exhausted, I reinforced Shanghai and stuck to resistance. We were totally defeated. It was my fault."[50]

Chiang Kai-shek's Neglect
of the Defense of Hangzhou Bay

Japan's initial strategy for the offensive against Shanghai was to land troops southwest of Shanghai and to take the Shanghai-Yangtze delta. Japan had been gathering intelligence and local information around Hangzhou Bay for a long time.[51] The northern shore of the bay was deep enough for warships, and had sandy beaches suitable for landings.

On 20 August, Chiang Kai-shek learned that Japanese naval landing forces were ashore on a reconnaissance mission. Chiang ordered the tightening of the defenses.[52] On 18 October, the Military Affairs Commission received intelligence that the Japanese were planning to land in Hangzhou Bay but assumed this was a secondary operation involving at most one division.[53] General Zhang Fakui, however, was alarmed and redeployed his Sixty-second and Sixty-third Divisions to Hangzhou Bay. On 26 October, Nationalist government forces retreated to the southern bank of Suzhou Creek. Zhang Fakui sent the Sixty-second Division to Pudong, weakening the defense of the bay.[54]

On 5 November, Lieutenant General Yanagawa Heisuke, commander of Japan's Tenth Army, put three and a half divisions ashore with the support of naval gunfire. The Chinese were rapidly overwhelmed. Zhang ordered the Sixty-second Division from Pudong and the newly arrived Seventy-ninth

Division to counterattack. Chiang Kai-shek also transferred the Sixty-seventh Division from Henan to push toward Songjiang. On 6 November, Chiang wrote in his diary, "If our troops hold the current positions, in three days the danger will be past."[55] Heavy rains, muddy roads, and relentless bombing by Japanese aircraft slowed the Chinese reinforcements. Moreover, Japan kept landing more reinforcements. The Sixty-seventh Division was beaten before it had a chance to regroup, and on 8 November the Chinese right flank collapsed. Japanese units simultaneously breached the Suzhou Creek defenses, and the Chinese troops, now faced with the enemy on their flank and at their rear, risked being surrounded and exterminated.

To avoid encirclement, General Bai Chongxi suggested to Chiang Kai-shek again that the Chinese withdraw to the outer defenses. On 7 November, Generals Zhu Shaoliang and He Yingqin proposed withdrawal.[56] Chiang weighed the costs and benefits, and wrote in his diary: "One choice is to maintain our strength and fight a protracted war. The second choice is to save face but exhaust our strength. The former is more important." The same day, Chiang ordered a general retreat from the south bank of Suzhou Creek,[57] but was deeply concerned that this measure would have a negative impact on the Brussels conference.[58] Later, Chiang Kai-shek acknowledged in his diary that the neglect of the defense of Hangzhou Bay "was our biggest strategic mistake."[59]

A good strategist must be able to organize both offense and retreat. Chiang Kai-shek ordered the withdrawal from the south bank of Suzhou Creek, but the retreat soon degenerated into chaos. One Chinese solider recalled, "Throughout the Battle of Shanghai, I was at the front. After three months of fierce fighting, the casualties were very high, but our soldiers maintained high morale and discipline. After soldiers came back from the front, they needed only some rest and replenishment; then they could continue fighting. But with the general retreat our troops lost morale and discipline. If we had made an organized retreat from Dachang, we would not have seen the collapse of an army of several hundred thousand men, precipitated by this one mistake."[60] On 11 November, the mayor of Shanghai announced the fall of the city.

Japanese losses to 8 November were 9,115 killed and 31,257 wounded, a total of 40,372 casualties.[61] Chinese losses were far greater. He Yingqin on 5 November reported officially 187,200 killed or wounded, four and a half times the Japanese number.[62] The retreating Chinese had lost their weapons, ammunition, and rations, and their morale had collapsed.

To Defend or Abandon Nanjing?

After Japan occupied Shanghai, two opinions divided the Japanese military. One was that the Japanese troops needed rest. The other held that although the troops were tired, they should push on to Nanjing. On 7 November, the Japanese military formed the Central China Field Army, at the time commanded by Lieutenant General Matsui Iwane. The next day, the Japanese split their forces. The Shanghai Expeditionary Army headed west along the Shanghai–Nanjing Railway. The Tenth Army and Kunisaki Brigade, commanded by Major General Kunisaki Noboru, advanced on the southern shore of Lake Tai. On 13 November, the Japanese landed in Baimaokou on the Yangtze River and attacked aggressively. Two days later, the Tenth Army concluded that Chinese troops were close to collapse, and if it attacked aggressively it could occupy Nanjing in twenty days. The Central China Area Army (Provisional; on 1 December 1937, it became the Central China Expeditionary Army) agreed that a unique opportunity existed to defeat the Chinese comprehensively and end the war.[63]

The Japanese moved west along the north and south shores of Lake Tai and threatened Nanjing. On 13 November, Chiang Kai-shek moved the capital and continue a protracted war of resistance. Opinions diverged over whether to defend Nanjing. The majority of senior commanders opposed defending Nanjing to the last man. As Minister of Foreign Affairs Wang Shijie recalled, China should not make "a sacrifice which is unnecessary, meaningless, and without strategic benefit" for the Republic. Bai Chongxi advocated guerrilla war. General Liu Fei recommended symbolic resistance.[64] Chiang vacillated. On 17 November, he wrote, "Should we defend Nanjing or abandon it? It is hard to decide."[65] Both Chiang and Tang Shengzhi believed that China should make great sacrifices to defend the capital and the mausoleum of former president Sun Yat-sen, to defend Nanjing. Chiang proposed that he take the responsibility to defend Nanjing himself, but senior commanders were opposed. Tang, who was ill at that time, volunteered to lead the defense.[66] On 19 November Chiang appointed him commander of the Nanjing garrison.[67] Chiang was well aware that Nanjing was almost indefensible. On 27 November he inspected the defenses and wrote, "It is hard to defend Nanjing, but we must do it."[68]

The debate over appeasement or resistance had continued since the start of the Battle of Shanghai. On 8 September, Chiang Kai-shek wrote in his diary, "Now, we have no choice but to fight to the end. We must silence those people arguing for appeasement."[69] His diary on the next day stated, "There is no way out other than to sacrifice and resist. The people arguing for peace are impractical pedants. How can we have peace now!"[70]

Yet after China's defeat in Shanghai, the voices of appeasement grew louder. Ju Zheng, minister of justice, had opposed appeasement and had called for the arrest of Hu Shi. But after Shanghai, he argued for negotiations. "If no one else dares make international settlements and sign a peace treaty, I will."[71] On 21 November, after Chiang had finished organizing the defense of Nanjing, he sighed, "The men of letters (*wenren*) are old and impractical. They ask for appeasement after military defeat. Some senior military commanders have also lost their guts and argue for peace. Alas! These people have no revolutionary spirit. Why on earth did they talk about resistance before?"[72]

Central command's existing plan was to defend Nanjing with a minimum number of troops along the Nanjing–Shanghai Railway. These troops were to use existing defense facilities and conduct a staged withdrawal. Some forces would be transferred to the Shanghai–Hangzhou Railway to oppose Japanese troops advancing along the southern shore of the Lake Tai. Others were to be transferred to Nanjing to strengthen the city's defenses. When reinforcements arrived, they would assemble at Guangde (southern Anhui) and attack the enemy at the Qiantang River.[73] By mid-November, the Chinese had already retreated to the last line of defense between Shanghai and Nanjing, sometimes referred to China's Hindenburg Line.

A Chinese proverb says, "A military debacle is like the collapse of mountains." The retreating troops had no adequate maps, found the fortifications locked, and had no officers to give them orders.[74] On 19 November, Japanese troops occupied Suzhou, breaking the so-called Hindenburg Line. The Chinese troops continued their disorderly retreat. Chiang believed that Nanjing's outer defenses, along the Xicheng Line, could be defended because it had "favorable terrain and strong fortifications." But China's defense along this line also failed. On 20 November, Chiang ordered five divisions and two independent brigades from Sichuan, but these weak and undisciplined warlord troops fled when the Japanese approached.[75] On 23 November, Chiang went to Changzhou to hector his frontline commanders, but the calamitous situation did not improve.

Chiang's diary records the chaos. "There was no sense of doing things by stages. All the troops retreated in a rush. There was no order or control."[76] By 30 November, Japanese troops were poised to encircle Nanjing from the southeast and southwest. On the next day, Jiangyin Fortress, which had blocked Japanese naval operations from reaching Nanjing on the Yangtze, fell. On the same day, an imperial command directed "the commander of the Central China Expeditionary Army of Japan to cooperate with the Japanese navy to attack China's capital, Nanjing."[77] Japanese troops attacked Nanjing from three directions.

Chiang Kai-shek was opposed to truce negotiations, but he did not reject international mediation. When Japanese troops landed in Hangchou Bay, Oskar Trautmann, Germany's ambassador to China, was entrusted by Tokyo to pass on Japan's preconditions to Chiang Kai-shek. Chiang assumed that the preconditions were still based on the Anti-Comintern Pact and rejected them.[78] On 24 November, the Brussels meeting concluded. Chiang had placed great hope on this meeting, which encouraged international support for China but no direct intervention. On 2

December, Chiang met Trautmann and agreed to Japan's conditions, but he demanded a ceasefire before negotiations. However, on 7 December, Chiang left Nanjing by plane, and his diary recorded: "We have no choice but to fight. I have to stand firm myself."[79]

On 5 December, the Japanese attacked Nanjing's outer defenses, breaking through three days later. On 9 December, Japanese troops approached the city walls and gates, where fierce fighting erupted. General Matsui demanded Nanjing's surrender before noon on 10 December. The Chinese refused, and the following day Matsui ordered a general offensive.

During the Battle of Shanghai, Chinese troops had suffered great losses. After the battle, there were major shortages of arms, ammunition, and food. Chiang Kai-shek tried all measures to regroup the troops, but found only twelve depleted divisions to defend Nanjing. Morale was low, units lacked cohesion, and thousands of the defenders were raw recruits rushed into battle.

Chiang had decided to defend Nanjing for two reasons. One was to save face. The other was that Chiang had some expectation that the Soviet Union, the only power that had given the impression that it might support China, would intervene. On 21 August, China and the Soviet Union had signed a nonaggression treaty. The Soviet Union guaranteed that China could obtain Soviet munitions. On 1 September Chiang had predicted that ultimately the Soviet Union would participate in the war against Japan.[80] On 28 September, Soviet Ambassador Bogomolov was recalled to Moscow. Before he left he talked with Wang Chonghui, the Chinese foreign minister, about the preconditions of Soviet entry into the war with Japan.[81] On 22 October, Chiang asked Yang Jie, head of the Chinese military delegation in Moscow if and when the Soviet Union would go to war with Japan. At a 10 November farewell banquet, Marshall K. Y. Voroshilov asked a member of the military delegation to pass on a message that the Soviet Union would not stand idly by if the situation became critical in China. On 30 November, Chiang Kai-shek cabled his thanks to Voroshilov and Stalin. "China has made its last and largest efforts for national survival. We have to retreat from Nanjing. We are looking forward to the powerful support from our ally the Soviet Union. We sincerely hope that you will send troops."[82] On 5 December, Stalin and Voroshilov replied that the Soviet Union would send troops only if all or the majority of the signatories of the Nine-Power Treaty agreed "to deal jointly with Japanese aggression." Moreover, permission from the Supreme Soviet, which would not convene for six to eight weeks, was needed.[83]

This telegram differed from the reports of Yang Jie. Although Chiang realized there was "no hope that the Soviet Union would enter the war,"[84] he continued to refer to that possibility to "encourage his senior commanders."[85] On 6 December, Chiang cabled Li Zongren and Yan Xishan, whose troops were astride the supply lines to the Soviet Union: "We must defend Nanjing. In one month, the international situation may change dramatically. China may avoid disaster."[86] The phrase "the international situation may change dramatically" refers to the possibility of the Soviet Union entering the war.

On 11 December, Chiang Kai-shek ordered Tang Shengzhi to "retreat when the conditions are untenable. Thus, we can regroup for a future counteroffensive."[87] The next day, he changed his mind and cabled Tang, "After such fierce fighting, the enemy may not dare pursue the attack. We must stay in Nanjing and defend it for the duration—so long as there is no trouble inside the city. We must make any sacrifice to boost the status and prestige of our nation and army. This is the only point at which we can turn the current defeat into victory for our revolutionary cause . . . If we can hold on for one more day, we can add greater honor to our nation. If we can hold for more than two weeks, the situation inside and outside our country may change dramatically. Our field armies will reinforce Nanjing. We should have no fear that the enemy will encircle us."[88]

After the Japanese had penetrated the city's gates, the main Nanjing garrison decided to break out of the encirclement, while the remaining forces would cross the Yangtze. However, panic soon overcame the retreat. Only a few units managed to break out. Most massed along the Yangtze, confused, demoralized, and in chaos. Outside the Yijiang Gate, "the bodies of people who had been trampled to death were piled up in a mountain."[89] Terror was everywhere. "There were only a few boats. Everybody fought to get on one. People opened fire recklessly. Boats that had put out to midstream were fired on by troops on the bank who could not get a boat. Some sank; some were overloaded and foundered."[90] On 13 December, the Japanese took Nanjing, and began a massacre.

6 *Japanese Operations from July to December 1937*

HATTORI SATOSHI WITH EDWARD J. DREA

Military Developments from the Marco Polo Bridge
Incident to the Fall of Nanjing

Who fired the first shots near the Marco Polo Bridge on the night of 7–8 July 1937 remains an open question to Japanese historians.[1] It is clear, though, that the spasm of fighting between units of Japan's China Garrison Army and China's Twenty-Ninth Army sparked a conflagration that eventually engulfed East Asia. Japan's protracted total war with China would exhaust its national strength, but in mid-1937 the Japanese military overlooked such a possibility for two reasons. The first was political. The objective for using military force was ambiguous. By deploying military force on a large scale, Japan aimed to punish the Nanjing government and force it to change its policies regarding Japan. Tokyo expected to resolve the Marco Polo Incident quickly by force, following a pattern of previous incidents. Because Japan was unable to gauge correctly the fundamental changes occurring in China, the premise of using force proved invalid, but, lacking other alternatives, Japan drifted into a full-scale conflict on the Asian continent.

The second reason was military. Japan was confident of a decisive battlefield victory within a few weeks of operations. There was, of course, concern and division within the Japanese military about large-scale operations in China, but the dominant view dismissed the possibility of serious Chinese resistance. Furthermore, the strategy of rapid, decisive battle (*sokusen sokketsu*, literally, "rapid combat, quick decision") would avoid a protracted war with China. The essence of the military strategy involved decisive battlefield engagements to destroy the central government's main field armies by rapid maneuver, encirclement, and annihilation. By 1939, Japan occupied most major Chinese cities, but Tokyo's initial objective was not to occupy territory but to destroy China's Central Army.

As the fighting expanded, Japan deployed large numbers of aircraft in battle to gain an asymmetrical advantage over China. The army and navy each had a separate air arm. As of 1937, the army had fifty-four air squadrons while the navy had 200 carrier-based and 390 land-based aircraft.[2] Both services introduced a new generation of domestically produced aircraft in the late 1930s. In July 1937, the army air force relied chiefly on twin-engine Type 93 heavy bombers (capable of carrying a 2,200-pound bomb load), twin-engine Type 93 light bombers (650-pound load), and biplane Type 95 fighters (with two machine guns). The navy possessed twin-engine Type 96 attack aircraft (capable of a 2,200-pound load), equivalent to the army's heavy bombers; biplane Type 96 carrier-based bombers (550-pound load), biplane Type 95 carrier-based fighters (armed with two machine guns), and monoplane Type 96 carrier-based fighters (armed with two machine guns). The army's Type 95 and navy's Type 96 carrier fighters were exceptionally good. By the end of 1937, new Type 96 medium bombers and Type 97 carrier-based attack planes were deployed to the China theater, greatly enhancing Japanese air power.

Although the two-year-old Chinese central air force had seven land-based and seven water-based squadrons, approximately only one hundred aircraft were operational. Chinese pilots also lacked experience. Claire Chennault, a retired U.S. Army officer who inspected the Chinese air force between May and June of 1937 at the request of Chiang Kai-shek, found it far inferior to Japan's air units.[3] Japan's air forces were superior in both quantity and quality, and it easily obtained command of the air over China. By providing aerial reconnaissance, support to ground operations, and strategic bombing, Japan made efficient use of its air power advantage.

Japan also deployed small numbers of tanks and armored vehicles in China and made effective use of heavy artillery and naval gunfire. In July 1937, the army had two tank brigades and one tank battalion, with Type 89 medium tanks (57 mm gun, 12 tons), Type 92 heavy armored vehicles (one machine gun, 3.5 tons), Type 94 light armored vehicles (one machine gun, 3.2 tons), Type 95 light tank (37 mm gun, 7.5 tons). In June of the same year, Japan fielded the new Type 97 medium tank (57 mm gun, 15.3 tons). Japan thus possessed overwhelming technological superiority over China.[4]

The entire Chinese navy consisted of eight small cruisers, forty gunboats, and four torpedo boats, compared to four light cruisers, thirteen frigates, and twelve gunboats in Japan's Third Fleet, which was responsible for China. Behind this force was the powerful Combined Fleet (First and Second Fleets) that included five battleships and three aircraft carriers. The Japanese navy controlled the China coast and made maximum use of naval gunfire as well as carrier aircraft to support ground operations. In sum, Japan's superior weaponry gave it an advantage over China that more than offset Japan's numerical inferiority.

The early phases of the Sino-Japanese War unfolded on three fronts: in north China, Chahar, and Shanghai. Japanese army operations on these radically different battlegrounds and their overall importance until the fall of Nanjing are the subjects of this chapter.

Escalation of Armed Conflict

Following the Marco Polo Bridge Incident, armed clashes broke out in the Peking vicinity. The Japanese China Garrison Army, made up of a brigade (5,600 troops), faced the Chinese Twenty-ninth Army, boasting five divisions and four brigades (75,000 men). As the situation in north China worsened, the cabinet dispatched two brigades from the Kwantung Army and one division from the Korea Army to Peking and Tianjin to reinforce the China Garrison Army. It also mobilized three divisions in Japan in response to intelligence reports that China's Central Area Army was moving north toward Peking. Reinforcement of the China Garrison Army was completed by 18 July. During this time, the situation seemed to stabilize and ceasefire talks were under way in Peking. New fighting in Langfang and Guang'anmen on the twenty-fifth and twenty-sixth, however, convinced the Japanese cabinet to send three divisions (the Fifth, Sixth, and Tenth), for a total of 210,000 men in north China.

Japanese military leaders remained optimistic about resolving the crisis, despite additional mobilizations on 21 August. The conflict had not yet led to all-out war between Japan and China and, believing it would not become one, the four ministers meeting on the twenty-fifth decided against a formal declaration of war.

The North China Campaign

On 31 August the Japanese General Staff established a new North China Area Army under General Terauchi Hisaichi that incorporated the China Garrison Army and recently arrived reinforcements into its order of battle. The North China Area Army was organized into the First Army (commander, Lieutenant General Katsuki Kiyoshi) and Second Army (commander, Lieutenant General Nishio Toshizō), each with three divisions. The First Army consisted of the Sixth, Fourteenth, and Twentieth divisions; the Second Army consisted of the Tenth, Sixteenth, and 106th divisions. The 109th Division, then en route from Japan, as well as the Fifth Division, involved in the Chahar campaign (discussed below), were directly under headquarters, North China Area Army. Auxiliary forces included two tank battalions and two heavy artillery brigades augmenting the First Army, a heavy artillery brigade assigned to the Second Army, and two heavy artillery battalions echeloned directly to North China Area Army headquarters. The overstrength tank battalions had seventy-eight Type 89 medium tanks and forty-one Type 94 light armored vehicles. Counting the tank battalions deployed in the Chahar campaign, the army thus committed almost all its armor force to the China front.

To support the massive ground operations, the General Staff assigned air groups for each field army, First Air Group for the First Army and Fourth Air Group for the Second Army. The First Air Group consisted of one fighter and one light bomber regiment plus a heavy bomber squadron. The Fourth Air Group had a fighter and a light bomber regiment as well as a reconnaissance and a bomber squadron. The First Air Group was a more powerful attack force while the Fourth Air Group specialized in reconnaissance. The North China Area Army had two air reconnaissance regiments, one heavy bomber regiment, and one fighter squadron. Aerial reconnaissance also supplemented the weak communications capability of the Japanese army.[5]

The First Army's main axis of attack was south along the Peking–Hankou Railway toward Baoding. The Second Army advanced along the Tianjin–Pukou rail line, moving parallel to the First Army's left flank, supporting its attack, and swinging west from Dexian to cut the Chinese line of retreat.[6] The operational goal was to encircle and annihilate the Chinese field forces in accordance with guidelines of the Japanese government and the General Staff, which sought to subdue the Chinese government by destroying the Chinese forces. Occupying territory was not a priority.

Katsuki's army advanced rapidly, thanks to bribes paid to Chinese commanders south of Peking to retreat without fighting. In mid-September, Feng Zhanhai (Feng Chan-hai), commander Ninety-first Division, withdrew his troops opposing the Japanese Fourteenth Division. A few days later Wan Fulin's corps pulled out from the Sixth Division's front. The remaining three divisions spread themselves thinly to defend a forty-mile-long front on relatively level terrain.[7] The Japanese First Army easily outflanked or bypassed them and rapidly rushed south. By 18 September, Katsuki had split the Central China Area Army in two but had not been able to destroy it.[8]

After failing to encircle the Chinese forces, Katsuki decided to force the decisive battle at Baoding. Army bombers struck important rear areas such as Shijiazhuang and Baoding, as well as bridges and railways, to cut off the Chinese line of retreat.[9] On 19 September, Chiang ordered his forces to stand at Baoding, and a decisive battle seemed imminent. The Central China Area Army's Second Corps commander, however, had already ordered a withdrawal, and the neighboring Third Corps reported heavy losses, rendering it ineffective. This left the Second Army to hold a forty-mile-wide front against the approaching Japanese.[10]

Japanese initial operational guidance set a stop line between Baoding and Tuliuchen (Duliuzhen), but the North China Area Army was already proposing deeper thrusts into north China. On 20 September, General Terauchi had indicated his intentions, remarking, "The officers and men shouldn't return without filling their canteens with water from the Yellow River as a souvenir."[11] Two days later Katsuki sent his Fourteenth and Twentieth divisions wheeling around Baoding from the southwest and ordered the Sixth Division to take the city. Despite the lack of coordination among Chinese defenders, Baoding was a strong position and, if properly defended, capable of withstanding Japanese assaults. A great brick wall sixty feet high and fifteen feet thick encased the city. An inner moat ran outside the city walls, separated by as much as 600 yards from a deep outer moat. Between the moats lay pillboxes, barbed wire entanglements, fortifications, and fighting positions, all cleverly camouflaged by soybean vegetation. The deception completely fooled Japanese reconnaissance pilots, who reported only cultivated fields near the city walls.

On 24 September, Japanese artillery battered the north walls of Baoding, and an infantry brigade steeled itself to assault the breach. Shortly after the artillery lifted, however, Chinese commanders ordered a general retreat, abandoning the well-prepared defenses. Some 90,000 troops from First and Second armies occupied Baoding and Dexian respectively, wrapping up the campaign at the cost to the Japanese of about 1,500 killed and 4,000 wounded. Once again, the main Chinese forces had escaped the slowly developing encirclement, in part because of unexpectedly heavy fighting in the Chahar campaign.

The Chahar Campaign

Elements of the Chinese Twenty-ninth Army (143rd Division, Fortieth Independent Brigade, and Thirteenth Independent Cavalry Brigade) were stationed in Chahar Province, while the main force of the Shanxi Army and Suiyuan Army (five divisions and three cavalry divisions) were in north Shanxi and Suiyuan along with the Central Army (Eighty-fourth and Eighty-ninth divisions). In early August, the Eighty-ninth Division advanced south of the Great Wall to Nankou, threatening the China Garrison Army in Peking. The First Cavalry Army (three cavalry divisions and two infantry divisions) simultaneously forced the Mongolian Army (eleven divisions) of Prince De to withdraw from border areas. In mid-August, the Japanese China Garrison Army attacked the Eighty-ninth Division from the south while elements of the Kwantung Army moving through Inner Mongolia struck Chinese forces from the north.

The Kwantung Army wanted to seize Chahar and, after receiving the Japanese General Staff's approval, on 14 August activated an expeditionary headquarters commanded by its chief of staff, Lieutenant General Tōjō Hideki. Tokyo's objective was to secure the strategic flank of Manchukuo, while the

Kwantung Army's goal was to establish puppet regimes in north China and incorporate the occupied area into a Japanese sphere of influence.[12]

The Chahar Expeditionary Force consisted of three mixed brigades, including the only Japanese full-fledged mechanized unit, equipped with medium tanks, heavy and light armored vehicles, and light tanks. On 30 August, the army high command ordered the task force and the China Garrison Army to occupy Chahar Province. The North China Area Army deployed Lieutenant General Itagaki Seishirō's Fifth Division, the theater's strategic reserve, for the operation. Relying on armor units to penetrate Chinese lines, the fast-moving Japanese also used rail lines to move troops and supplies to strategic locations throughout Chahar. Despite the proficiency of the tanks and armored cars of the First Independent Mixed Brigade, the Kwantung Army's "lessons-learned" assessment criticized the armored units for lacking shock effect and for frequent breakdowns. Vehicles also required large quantities of supplies and much maintenance, so the army declared them dysfunctional in combat. Accordingly, the brigade was disbanded in 1938, a development that greatly slowed the formation of mechanized units in the Japanese army.

The Second Air Group supported the ground offensive in Chahar. From mid-August, the air group, based in Chengde and Jingzhou, bombed enemy positions and transportation, flew reconnaissance missions, and even air-dropped supplies to encircled Japanese forces. Air units were sent forward to advanced airfields to keep pace with the rapid ground advance spearheaded by the mechanized forces. After bombing Taiyuan in late August, certain units returned to their home bases, leaving two fighter and two heavy bomber squadrons as a provisional air regiment (*rinji hikōdan*).

Mid-September found the Fifth Division and the Chahar Expeditionary Force advancing southwest through the rugged mountains of Shanxi Province. They captured Datong on 13 September. Five days later, Lieutenant General Katsuki, anticipating his decisive battle, ordered the Fifth Division to swing southeast toward Baoding to encircle retreating Chinese forces.[13] Shortly after repositioning his forces, Itagaki learned from aerial reconnaissance that Chinese units were concentrating near Pingxingguan (Dayingzhen) Pass. Concerned these forces might move east through the pass and threaten his rear, on 21 September Itagaki dispatched a regimental-size task force under Twenty-first Brigade commander Major General Miura Keiji to disperse the enemy troops and control the road on either side of the pass.

Pingxingguan

Miura's task force departed by truck in midafternoon the next day, but the overland move was much slower and more difficult than expected.

Driving along a single rutted dirt track winding through the steep mountains, the forty-nine trucks carrying his infantry and heavy weapons (crew-served machine guns and organic battalion artillery) managed a speed of only seven miles an hour.[14] By late afternoon, lead elements were still about five miles east of the pass when they encountered a few hundred Chinese troops who had retreated after a brief firefight. With night falling, the Japanese moved slowly forward until they reached a village about a mile from the pass, where they met stiff resistance, including mortar and automatic weapons fire. After beating back a counterattack by the Chinese Seventy-third Division, Miura launched a night attack. Supported by pack artillery and heavy machine guns, the two Japanese companies pushed through the pass and by early morning had seized the high ground on the west side of Pingxingguan. Chinese reinforcements soon appeared and tried to retake the lost ground. Fighting for the heights continued throughout 24 September.

Meanwhile, the Chinese Communist 115th Division (685, 686, and 687 regiments), the Eighth Route Army, about 6,000 effectives, commanded by twenty-nine-year-old Lin Biao, had maneuvered south around the Japanese rear and by 24 September interdicted the road east of the pass between Miura's task force and his supply base. The same day, the Central Army's Seventy-first Division launched several sharp counterattacks against Miura's outnumbered forces west of the pass, threatening to overrun the Japanese.

Central Army and Communist forces planned to attack both Japanese flanks at dawn on 25 September, but drenching rains delayed the advance of Central Army reserves. The downpour also muffled the sound of an approaching Japanese night attack. Assault parties also took advantage of poor Chinese night security to surprise the Seventy-first and Eighty-fourth divisions and drive them from their positions west of the pass. Miura believed that he controlled both sides of the pass and assumed that the Chinese, as usual, were in full retreat. Unaware Lin Biao's forces blocked the eastern entrance to the pass, he ordered his resupply column (*taikyori*), waiting about fifteen miles east of the pass, forward with rations and ammunition to replenish his badly depleted task force.

The supply train of seventy horse-drawn wagons and eighty trucks made slow progress along the single dirt track, sections of which heavy rains had turned into muddy bogs. Most of the hundred-plus soldiers handling the horses and wagons were untrained and unarmed. The handful of regular service corps (*shichōhei*) troops carried only ten cavalry carbines, and a single infantry platoon of thirty men provided security. The eighty trucks carried another 176 men, few of them infantry. The resupply column was not expecting trouble and was woefully unprepared to defend itself.

Following a sunken road worn down by centuries of passing caravans, the column approached the pass through the man-made defile whose sides rose as much as thirty-five feet above the track. Around midmorning, about four miles east of the pass at a point where the track narrowed, the Chinese Communist 115th Division struck from ambush. Communist troops rained hand grenades and small-arms fire from the high ground overlooking the road onto the trapped convoy. Although the Japanese fought back in desperation, the combination of surprise, command of the high ground, and overwhelming numbers turned the road into a killing ground.

Communist troops killed almost all the teamsters as well as the infantrymen protecting the wagons. At his field headquarters, Miura heard the heavy gunfire and sounds of explosions from the fighting and promptly ordered a battalion-size rescue force to the convoy's aid. The Chinese 685th Regiment, blocking the only road to the trapped baggage train, stopped the Japanese battalion in its tracks while elements of the 685th and 686th regiments finished off the motorized convoy. Only five trucks at the rear of the column escaped. After looting weapons, equipment, and clothing, the Communists burned the vehicles and withdrew southwest into the rugged mountains. Although the Communists claimed that they had killed 3,000 Japanese troops, a more realistic number is 200. But there was no question that Lin Biao's guerrillas had achieved a significant tactical success.

While the 115th Division destroyed the Japanese resupply column east of the pass, the Central Army's Sixth and Seventh Army Groups, including the Seventy-first Division, attacked Miura's dispersed units west of the pass in a series of day and night assaults. Losses were heavy on both sides, and the Japanese barely managed to hold the high ground as the Chinese spread out through the valleys and hit them from all directions. Isolated; under heavy attack; low on ammunition, food, and water; without proper heavy clothing in the cold mountains; and greatly outnumbered, Japanese soldiers were reduced to scavenging ammunition and weapons from Chinese corpses.

Itagaki promptly ordered his Forty-first and Twenty-first infantry regiments, supported by an infantry regiment of the Kwantung Army, then about fifty miles northeast of the pass, to rescue the beleaguered task force. They moved along a single narrow road through the mountains during heavy rains, which slowed their progress. The relief force split up about forty miles north of Pingxingguan, the Twenty-first Regiment swinging westward to outflank the Chinese and the two other regiments continuing to the pass. To the northwest, the Fifteenth Brigade, Chahar Expeditionary Force drove southeastward from Datong to encircle the Chinese. Central Army forces defending positions along the inner Great Wall about fifty miles northwest of Pingxingguan inflicted heavy casualties on the Japanese. The Japanese Forty-first Regiment finally reached Miura on 28 September, and the same day the Twenty-first Regiment dislodged the stubborn defenders along the Inner Great Wall about forty miles northwest of the pass, unhinging the entire Chinese defense and threatening to surround the besiegers. Nonetheless, fighting continued through the twenty-ninth, when the Second Brigade broke through the Chinese Central Army's defenses and advanced west. Facing encirclement and certain destruction, the Japanese Sixth Army Group withdrew southwestward the next day. Japanese accounts do not give overall losses, but Chinese accounts claim almost 3,000 Japanese casualties, while acknowledging they suffered ten times that number.

After five days of tough fighting in rugged terrain, Miura's forces held the ground, but their heavy losses and casualties suffered by relief columns made it a Pyrrhic victory. Chinese forces, Communist and Nationalist, had retreated southwest, surviving to fight another day. The determination of the Chinese Central Army forces on offense and defense and the skillful hit-and-run tactics of the 115th Division punished the Japanese and became a staple of Chinese propaganda.

Further Operations in North China

On 1 October, the Japanese General Staff ordered the North China Area Army to destroy Chinese forces in Shanxi Province, then estimated at more than twenty divisions (of either the Shanxi Army or the Central Army) that were fortifying Taiyuan, Yangquan, and Yuanpingzhen. The Japanese Fifth and Twentieth divisions moved on Taiyuan while the Fifteenth Division, reinforced by a mixed brigade, attacked southward from Yuanpingzhen on 13 October. The Fifteenth Division immediately encountered strong Chinese resistance from prepared defenses that halted its advance. From 19 to 26 October, the Twentieth Division fought thirteen Chinese divisions dug in near Jiuguan, driving off numerous fierce counterattacks but unable to break Chinese lines. One regiment maneuvered to the rear of the Chinese defenses, forcing a Chinese withdrawal. The reconstituted Fifth Division joined the pursuit of the retreating Chinese on 3 November, reaching Taiyuan five days later. The Twentieth Division, moving to the west, inflicted heavy losses on Chinese units withdrawing from Taiyuan. Because the offensive aimed to secure territory, it may be regarded as a tactical and operational success. Shortly thereafter, all Japanese forces except the Twentieth Division withdrew from Shanxi Province.[15]

The Chahar campaign concluded with the Kwantung Army in control of Chahar and Suiyuan, as well as the northern half of Shanxi, provinces. The Japanese quickly established puppet regimes. While the operation had secured the strategic western flank of Manchuria and advanced Japanese interests in Inner Mongolia, it had not only failed to destroy Chinese field forces but had also encouraged Chinese resistance after the embarrassing setback at Pingxingguan.

Japanese intelligence estimated that twenty-three Chinese divisions were fortifying positions near Shijiazhuang, and on 6 October Terauchi ordered the Japanese First Army to destroy them. The Second Army would again support the encirclement, but despite several fierce engagements the First Army moved too slowly to trap the Chinese field armies.[16] Second Army troops could not close the gap and merely gained more territory that they were ill prepared to control.[17] The North China Area Army retained six divisions to guard the Peking–Hankou and Tianjin–Pukou railways as well as northern Shanxi.

Not only the complexity of military operations caused the General Staff to have difficultly controlling the field armies. For example, on 25 September the Japanese General Staff ordered the North China Area Army to limit operations north of a line between Dezhou and Shijiazhuang. But Terauchi repeatedly ordered the First Army to drive farther south, and by December, Second Army units moved south of the Yellow River into Shandong Province and seized Shinan, a key railroad junction. Unilateral decisions by field commanders subsequently approved by the General Staff became commonplace because of the guideline on offensive warfare for the purpose of annihilating Chinese forces. Operational commanders justified their insubordination on the basis of the prerogative of field command, insisting that the officer on the scene was better able to assess and act on the situation than his faraway superiors in Tokyo. Violations of General Staff orders were repeated in later campaigns.

By late October, the North China Area Army had largely conquered all targeted areas with its swift southward thrust. Yet it had failed to achieve the strategic objective of destroying Chinese military forces or their will to fight, as the Chinese skillfully avoided being lured into decisive battles. The Chinese refused to capitulate, contrary to initial Japanese predictions.[18] To achieve its strategic goal of a decisive battle, in early October, the Japanese General Staff opted to expand the fighting in Shanghai.

The Shanghai Campaign

Although the Japanese General Staff had initially sought to limit the fighting to north China, since July tensions had been building in Shanghai, long a flash point in Sino-Japanese relations. On the night of 9 August, Chinese troops killed a Japanese junior naval officer and an enlisted man on patrol near a Chinese air base.[19] Clashes between naval landing forces and Chinese troops erupted on 13 August, and the next day Chinese aircraft bombed Japanese positions in the city.

Beginning on the fifteenth, Japan launched its first strategic bombing campaign. Navy land-based squadrons of about twenty aircraft each, staging from Taipei or Ōmura, bombed Chinese air bases near Nanjing, Nanchang, and Shanghai in an effort to destroy the Chinese air force. Because of the great distances to the targets, the bombers flew without fighter escorts and suffered heavy losses from Chinese fighter aircraft.[20] Meantime, the navy rushed reinforcements to Shanghai, but the 4,000 naval infantrymen found themselves heavily outnumbered and hard pressed by the highly motivated Central Army forces.

The army reluctantly agreed to navy calls for reinforcements at Shanghai, and, after cabinet approval, on 17 August mobilized three divisions (the Third, Eleventh, and Fourteenth) to form the Shanghai Expeditionary Army. Lieutenant General Matsui Iwane, recalled from the reserve list to take command of this force, was summoned to Tokyo for an imperial audience. Despite misgivings that Japan might be dragged into a lengthy war, Emperor Hirohito instructed Matsui to defend Japanese interests in Shanghai and its northern environs and protect Japanese nationals residing there.[21]

On 18 August, Hirohito questioned both service chiefs about the possibility of concentrating their forces to deliver a knockout blow to the Chinese military that would quickly end the fighting.[22] Two days later, the chiefs responded that a bombing campaign was the most effective way to break the Chinese will to resist. The campaign would be accompanied by Japanese occupation of strategic locations in north China, destruction of the Chinese Central Army, and, at an appropriate time, a blockade of the China coast. The next day, the army requested permission to mobilize three reserve divisions, the 101st, 108th, and 109th (100-series divisions were triangular formations composed of reservists in their thirties and regarded as inferior to regular divisions), two more than allotted in prewar planning for China operations. Meanwhile, on 18 August three more battalions of naval infantry had arrived in Shanghai.

Four days later, the Shanghai Expeditionary Army's Third Division, under cover of naval gunfire, went ashore at Wusong to reinforce naval landing forces holding positions in the eastern sector of the International Settlement. The Third was to cut the Shanghai–Wusong Railway, occupy the nearby airfield, and destroy the Wusong fortress batteries to allow the navy unimpeded access to the Yangtze. It would then link up north of Shanghai with the Eleventh Division,[23] which had landed about twenty miles northwest near Chuansha. The Eleventh's orders were to drive southwest, seize Luodian (about twelve miles inland), and, joining the Third Division, push westward to isolate Chinese forces defending Shanghai.[24]

The Eleventh Division moved over a landscape cluttered with natural and man-made obstacles. Cultivated fields, dry rice paddies enclosed by steep 5-foot embankments, poor roads, swampy terrain, and a maze of canals and creeks that were 3 to 7 feet deep and anywhere from 10 to 200 feet wide fragmented tactical formations. Thick, reinforced brick walls encircled most built-up areas, transforming them into natural defensive strongpoints. Small complexes of farms, towns, and villages bristled with interlocking fields of fire, and Japanese infantrymen soon realized that each factory and warehouse was a likely center of resistance. The heaviest fighting erupted near Luodian, where the division had to breach the thick whitewashed brick walls of the Chinese barracks and then fight hand to hand to evict the determined defenders.

The Third Division initially fought mostly in built-up urban areas of the Chinese city east of the International Settlement. Fighting raged for control of warehouses, factories, and municipal buildings. The brick-constructed compounds, narrow lanes, and twisting alleyways restricted infantry maneuvers and fields of fire. Bunched-up troops become easy targets for Chinese mortar fire, machine gun teams, and snipers. The Japanese infantrymen needed heavy artillery to blast defenders from buildings, but based on earlier terrain studies, the General Staff had declared the soil too spongy to support heavy artillery or tanks. Thus, both divisions had deployed without their heavy artillery or armor support.[25] Reduced firepower forced the Japanese to rely on smaller-caliber infantry support weapons to breach the sturdy brick walls that sheltered defenders in compounds and buildings. Without artillery to blast through the defenses, the advance proved slow and unexpectedly costly to the Japanese.

Nevertheless, the opening operations proceeded according to the Japanese timetable. The main force of the Eleventh Division captured Luodian on 28 August. Meanwhile, an infantry regiment of the Third Division moved north along the coastal road while a task force detached from the Eleventh Division advanced southward, trapping the defenders. Units of the Third Division took the Wusong coastal batteries on 31 August, and by 8 September the road was open to Japanese military traffic, providing a secure logistic base.[26]

By early September, the General Staff anticipated a decisive battle likely to occur around Shanghai in early October. The Operations Section, anxious because of estimates that the Soviet Union would enter the conflict in November, wanted a quick end to the fighting.[27] On 5 September, the General Staff instructed the North China Area Army to stand down new operations and transfer two divisions to Shanghai. Terauchi reluctantly transferred the divisions, but ignoring the guidance went ahead with his plan to encircle Chinese forces near Suzhou.

Meanwhile, the main force of the Third Division pushed through the eastern part of the Chinese section of Shanghai, crossed the Shanghai–

Wusong rail line, and formed an arc-shaped lodgment about one mile inland.[28] House-to-house fighting raged as the Chinese fought from the typical thick gray-walled brick homes and factories. Neighborhoods became minifortresses and changed hands several times a day. Even after destroying the houses and breaching the walls, the Japanese infantry confronted defenders who fought on from the rubble.

As of 9 September the Third had suffered more than 2,100 casualties, while the Eleventh had lost 1,600, most of them in the fighting around Luodian. The General Staff mobilized another ten reserve infantry battalions to replace battle casualties.[29] By 13 September, the Third Division had pushed to within a half mile of the Shanghai racecourse, an advance of five miles in a week. Repeated strong but poorly coordinated Chinese counterattacks over the next several days failed to dislodge the Japanese defenders, although the attacks inflicted more losses.

Japanese observers from General Staff reported that rushing the divisions to Shanghai without proper combat service support left them unprepared for sustained operations against an estimated 190,000 Chinese troops. Chinese soldiers fought well, used cover and concealment effectively, and did not surrender even when surrounded. Their example had rallied the Chinese people to Chiang and incited strong anti-Japanese sentiment.

Chinese commanders designed their tactics to negate superior Japanese firepower. Chinese infantrymen, fighting from prepared defensive strongholds, relied on small arms, hand grenades, mortars, and hand-to-hand combat weapons to pin down advancing Japanese infantry. With the two sides often separated by a few yards, Japanese gunners could not bring their artillery to bear without endangering their own troops. Japanese units had to rely on their organic infantry weapons, small arms, and ultimately their bayonets to rout out the stubborn, well-concealed defenders. The forces fighting near Shanghai needed more and heavier field artillery to smash enemy fortifications before they advanced, and more machine guns as well as hand grenades to sustain their push into heavily defended built-up zones.[30]

The Japanese General Staff originally had expected a quick, decisive campaign, similar to that of early 1932, and believed two divisions would suffice for the operation. As the fighting worsened and Japanese losses in September rose to more than 2,500 killed and 9,800 wounded,[31] on 23 September the General Staff mobilized three more divisions, dispatching the Ninth and Thirteenth along with the 101st to Shanghai. The following day, imperial approval was given to mobilize four divisions, including the Sixteenth, 108th, and 109th. At this time, however, thirteen regular divisions were overseas, either fighting in China (eight) or stationed in Manchuria (four) and Korea (one). Two reserve divisions were also in north China. With the Eighth Division already under orders to reinforce Manchuria, only three regular divisions remained in Japan (the Seventh [Hokkaido], Ninth [Kanazawa], and Guards [Tokyo]). The General Staff selected the Ninth Division for Shanghai even though it had just returned home in May 1937 after two years' overseas service in Manchuria. The reserve 101st Division, filled with recalled overage reservists, many in their thirties with wives and families, was also deployed, ostensibly for garrison duty in Shanghai.[32] Both divisions arrived in Shanghai in late September, but without their logistic and medical units that were still awaiting transport.

With fresh reinforcements, Matsui created a 29 September operational plan that envisaged four divisions (the Eleventh, Ninth, Third, and 101st) advancing west in converging parallel columns to Dachang, a suburb of 30,000 that commanded a key road junction about seven miles northwest of Shanghai's Zhabei district. From Dachang the forces would pivot south and reach Suzhou Creek by 8 October, thus trapping the defenders along a line north and parallel to the International Settlement and French Concession. To reach Dachang, however, the Japanese would have to fight their way through a heavily fortified zone constructed in great depth between the Suzhou and Zoumatang creeks. Matsui expected the offensive to take about a week.[33]

On 1 October, the Third Division breached enemy defenses along the Shanghai highway only to encounter the Chinese main line of resistance along Suzhou Creek, a misnomer because in places the unfordable crossing was between 100 and 300 feet wide. The Japanese had to fight their way across the creek under unrelenting Chinese fire, then make a frontal assault against a network of mutually supporting fortifications. Lacking sufficient artillery or logistic support for such an operation, Matsui concentrated his units on a narrow front to overwhelm the defenses by sheer force of numbers.

The Ninth Division deployed in the center of a three-mile front, with the Third Division on its right and the Eleventh Division on its left.[34] Using organic battalion artillery to destroy Chinese forward machine gun emplacements, the division pushed Chinese outposts back to Suzhou Creek, but only after heavy fighting all along the line. By 5 October, expeditionary headquarters and naval aerial observers reported the Chinese in general retreat on the division's right flank.[35] The same day, Matsui ordered units of the Thirteenth Division (originally deployed as a theater reserve) to protect the Ninth's right flank and be ready to exploit the imminent breakthrough. He also instructed the Eleventh Division to plug the gap created between the Ninth and Thirteenth divisions in order to check any enemy counterattack from the west on the Ninth's exposed flank. Finally, he threw the 101st Division into the fighting.[36] Far from retreating, however, the Chinese were consolidating at their main defensive line. Fighting from mutually supporting fixed fortifications interlaced between walled villages and natural obstacles, the defenders stopped the Japanese, inflicting enormous casualties. Enfilade fire from fortified towns was especially lethal, and repeated fierce Chinese counterattacks, as many as ten a night, regained lost ground as fighting seesawed along Suzhou Creek for three days.[37]

The 101st launched its main assault on 7 October.[38] Fighting resembled the trench warfare so familiar from World War I. Infantrymen and engineers dug approach trenches parallel to Suzhou Creek. Saps dug off the trenches to the north bank of Suzhou Creek allowed assault troops and engineers hauling flat-bottomed assault craft and bridging equipment to move through this trench network shielded from Chinese artillery and small-arms fire. Japanese artillery tried to suppress Chinese fire while shock troops and engineers carried small twenty-man steel boats over the bank and into the creek. Volunteer swimmers guided and helped pull the small boats across the broad creek. When they reached the far bank, assault troops climbed bamboo ladders to scale a steep six-foot-high bank crowned by barbed wire. Once over that obstacle, they were exposed to interlocking small-arms and preregistered mortar fire from Chinese defenders, in short, a well-designed killing zone. All the while, the boats shuttled reinforcements forward into the fighting and carried back the wounded and dying.[39] After a series of repulses along Suzhou Creek, on 10 October Matsui shifted the 101st from the front line into a rear echelon role to protect the Third Division's left flank. The loss of upward of 3,000 reservists in the role of assault troops within ten days sent shock waves through the Japanese home front.[40] Henceforth, the two regular divisions, the Third and Ninth,· carried the offensive, and after heavy fighting succeeded in crossing Wusong Creek.

After gaining a foothold on the south bank, the Japanese still had to fight their way through a one-mile-deep series of pillboxes, bunkers, fighting positions, and obstacles between Wusong and Zoumatang creeks. Small farmhouses and individual strongpoints changed hands several times a day in fierce thrusts and counterattacks. Upward of 60,000 Japanese troops were thrown into the cauldron. Four divisions attacked along a narrow six-to-eight-mile frontage to destroy the seven Chinese divisions that field intelligence estimated defended the confined area. Japanese commanders adopted new tactics to concentrate firepower from artillery, air, and infantry weapons against limited objectives. After a punishing barrage, small infantry units assaulted the battered position along narrow fronts, trying to encircle and isolate strongpoints. Dependence on firepower quickly exhausted Japanese artillery stocks, and guns were restricted to 20 percent of their authorized daily ammunition quotas.[41]

Heavy rains from 7 to 13 October made flying impossible, giving the Chinese time to reinforce and strengthen their second line of defense unimpeded by bombardments. Downpours left swollen creeks impassable, turned dirt roads into muddy bogs, flooded trenches and foxholes, ruined food, and soaked the already weary infantrymen. Smoke from cooking fires immediately attracted deadly Chinese mortar fire. A hastily constructed light-rail system enabled the Japanese to move rations and ammunition forward to resupply points, but from there supply trains bogged down in the viscous mud. Individual transport unit soldiers ended up carrying supplies forward to the front lines on their backs.[42] Nevertheless, the Japanese also took advantage of the brief lull to replenish and restock ammunition and supplies as well as to bring up new drafts of replacements.

To move supplies, ammunition, and fresh troops forward across the maze of creeks, engineers jury-rigged bridges by placing planks over the rungs of hastily constructed bamboo ladders. They then carried the ladders into the creek and, depending on the water's depth, stood naked in the creek as human supports for the "bridges" as porters or infantrymen crossed single file.[43] Afterward, narrow pontoon bridges might be erected. Small junks and sampans were used to cross wider, deeper channels, but here too engineers constructed their bamboo bridges and, when available, light pontoon footbridges.

Between 13 and 23 October, in heavy fighting, the Ninth Division broke through Chinese defenses in built-up factory areas straddling Wusong Creek. As long as the Chinese held this key defensive terrain along the division's right flank, they could sweep the flanks of Japanese units maneuvering south between Wusong and Zoumatang creeks with murderous enfilade fire. Infantrymen first captured a corner of the factory compound, then combat engineers methodically destroyed barbed wire entanglements and other obstacles. Navy aircraft and heavy artillery bombarded Chinese positions, preventing Chinese reinforcements from moving forward and disrupting counterattacks. Machine gunners covered infantry flame-thrower-armed assault parties that moved forward to burn out defenders room by room.[44]

Meanwhile, two regiments of the Ninth Division together with the Third Division fought their way through three lines of defensive works, slowly wearing down the Chinese between Wusong and Zoumatang creeks. Heavy-caliber artillery, recently arrived from Japan, pounded fortifications. Naval aircraft bombed them, and Japanese infantry massed fire on individual targets. The advance was a brutal battle of attrition, but firepower and numbers eventually prevailed.

On 25 October, the Ninth Division finally reached Zoumatang Creek and that night used bamboo bridges to cross the barrier. After being repulsed three times, one battalion finally gained a lodgment on the south

TABLE 6.1

Japanese losses during the Shanghai campaign

Division	Prewar Strength	Killed	Wounded	Total Casualties
Third	14,624	3,013	8,578	11,591
Ninth	13,182	3,883	8,527	12,410
Eleventh	12,795	2,293	6,084	8,377
Thirteenth	13,614	1,010	4,140	5,150
101st		873	3,801	4,674
Total		11,072	31,130	42,202

SOURCE: Hata Ikuhiko, *Nankyō jihen* [The Nanking incident] (Chūō kōronsha, 1986), 93.

bank and broke into the Chinese main defenses by daybreak.[45] The Third Division followed and expanded the foothold the next day as the Chinese defenders, exhausted and having suffered terrible losses, finally began to retreat. The Japanese were little better off. Corporals were leading devastated infantry companies with fewer than twenty men left standing. In twenty days of heavy fighting, most of it concentrated in the narrow belt between Suzhou and Zoumatang creeks, the Japanese lost about 25,000 men, including nearly 8,000 killed in action.[46] The three regular divisions, the Third, Ninth, and Eleventh, suffered about 70 percent of the losses. To advance about eight miles to Suzhou Creek cost the Ninth Division alone 2,872 killed and 6,684 wounded.[47] Only the infusion of more than a dozen drafts of replacements, almost all recalled reservists, had enabled the unit to sustain combat operations while suffering appalling losses.[48]

Supported by division and army artillery, on 29 October, the Ninth Division crossed Suzhou Creek in daylight under enemy fire. Machine gun teams aboard junks and sampans crossed first, gained a lodgment, and spread out. Then engineers threw a temporary bridge across the creek and reinforcements poured across, expanding the bridgehead. Later crossings were made at several points, and reinforcements continued to move across hastily constructed bridges during the night. Matsui belittled the difficulty of the crossing, but veterans remembered the six days of tough house-to-house battles that followed as they pushed through several fortified towns south of the creek.[49]

All told, the Suzhou crossing and aftermath cost the Ninth Division another 961 killed and double that number wounded.[50] Matsui reinforced the division with the 101st Division in order to pursue the retreating Chinese. After the Tenth Army's successful landing at Hangzhou Bay south of Shanghai on 9 November to cut off the Chinese escape route, he called off the pursuit.[51] The Shanghai campaign ended on that inconclusive note. Overall Japanese losses were more than 40,000.[52] (See table 6.1.)

To Nanjing

On 20 October Lieutenant General Yanagawa Heisuke assumed command of the newly activated Tenth Army, composed of the Eighteenth and 114th divisions sent from Japan and the Sixth and Sixteenth divisions transferred from north China. His order of the day warned his men that because mufti-clad Chinese soldiers might infiltrate their lines, they had to deal firmly with all Chinese civilians suspected of aiding the enemy.[53] It was thus open season on all civilians. Yanagawa's mission was to destroy Chinese forces in decisive engagement near Shanghai, although he had grander notions. On the early morning of 5 November, supported by navy units, the Sixth and Eighteenth Divisions made a surprise landing in the Jinshanwei area on Hangzhou Bay. Two Chinese divisions nearby melted away, and the Japanese force moved quickly inland. Facing encirclement and loss of an escape route, two days later Chiang ordered a general retreat from Shanghai in order to preserve what remained of his fighting strength and continue the resistance.

With two field armies near Shanghai, on 7 November, Japanese Imperial General Headquarters (IGHQ) organized the Central China Area Army (Provisional) with Matsui Iwane as commander in chief to coordinate the operations of the Japanese Shanghai Expeditionary Army and Tenth Army. Their announced mission was the destruction of Chinese forces in the vicinity of Shanghai, and Japanese units were prohibited from advancing beyond a line from Jiaxing to Suzhou, about sixty miles west of Shanghai. Matsui harbored hopes of seizing Nanjing, but because of the tremendous losses suffered by his forces, he supported Tokyo's decision not to expand the fighting for the time being.[54]

Yanagawa's Tenth Army forces, however, were fresh, and on 15 November he demanded an all-out offensive to capture the Chinese capital, the Kuomintang government already having fled. If the Chinese tried to turn Nanjing into another Shanghai, Yanagawa would avoid a costly frontal attack by laying siege to the city. Japanese aircraft would then rain mustard gas and incendiaries on the besieged city for a week to break the defenders' will.[55]

Yanagawa's unilateral pursuit began on 19 November. Three days later, Matsui ordered him to hold the Tenth Army in place while allowing advance elements to proceed to Lake Tai. The chaotic Chinese retreat and weakness of the secondary defenses west of Shanghai convinced Matsui that Nanjing was ripe for the taking, and on 22 November his chief of staff requested Tokyo's approval for the operation. The General Staff was divided. Two days later it abolished the stop line, but it remained silent about Nanjing.[56]

At the first imperial conference held at recently established Imperial

General Headquarters the same day, participants signaled their displeasure upon hearing that the army was considering an attack on Nanjing. The vice chief of staff promptly ordered the Central China Area Army to restrain the Tenth Army. The next day, however, Central China Area Army special intelligence reported to Tokyo that the Chinese Central Army had lost half of its eighty-three divisions, and the remainder suffered from low morale for lack of food and ammunition. Matsui was certain the capture of Nanjing would cause the collapse of the Chinese forces.[57]

On 1 December, the General Staff approved an attack on Nanjing. Concurrently, the provisional Central China Area Army became the China Expeditionary Army. Matsui stayed on as commander, while Prince Asaka, a member of the imperial family, took command of the Shanghai Expeditionary Army. Two days later, Matsui ordered a deliberate, cautious advance to secure strategic points, roads, and waterways and to fight a decisive battle west of the Ningzhen mountain range and Nanjing.[58] Tenth Army wanted a more rapid thrust. Supported by aircraft and armored units, the Japanese forces rapidly moved toward Nanjing, averaging nearly twenty miles a day, which was near the physical limit of the infantry. The speed of the pursuit caused Matsui on 5 December to amend his orders. Japanese forces would now attack the city.

During the pursuit upriver toward Nanjing, Japanese soldiers routinely torched homes and buildings along their route of march to deny Chinese troops convenient ambush positions.[59] But the widespread arson exceeded any tactical value. When a newly arrived replacement regimental commander cautioned his officers about arson, a battalion commander asked, was he aware that army headquarters said to burn everything in central China? The Tenth Army chief of staff finally had to caution troops not to burn homes and entire villages indiscriminately because they would need them as shelters during the winter months.[60]

Artillery and aircraft pounded the retreating Chinese, and Japanese infantry units, free again to maneuver, outflanked strongpoints or brought firepower to demolish resistance. If frontal attacks became necessary, tanks and armored cars spearheaded the penetration that accompanying infantry exploited. The Japanese China Expeditionary Fleet sent minesweepers and gunboats up the Yangtze River to bombard Nanjing. Army and navy aircraft supplied intelligence about retreating Chinese and attacked the disorganized columns. The bombing of Nanjing continued as the navy's carrier- and land-based pilots dominated the skies.[61] Chinese commanders unintentionally assisted the Japanese by clinging to high ground, regardless of its tactical value. Especially along the southern route where the Tenth Army ground remorselessly forward, there was little high ground, and stubbornly perching on it only isolated Chinese units as Japanese swept around the strongpoints.[62]

One junior officer in the Ninth Division recalled that the pursuit was like a training exercise, but without proper logistic support.[63] The lack of support was because the Tenth Army ordered only essential combat stores and medical supplies to accompany the combat units. Rations were not included, and units were encouraged to be self-sufficient and not depend on rear-area support, which would not be forthcoming anyway.[64] Widespread looting and pillaging resulted.

On 8 December Japanese units swiftly punched through or easily outflanked Nanjing's overextended outer defenses (a fifty-mile-long arc-shaped perimeter between twenty and thirty miles east of the city walls). Two days later, they smashed the second line, five to ten miles outside the main gates, and then hit the third and final defensive line protecting the city. Heavy fighting ensued for possession of a city already suffering under heavy bombing.

The Japanese launched an all-out night attack along the entire front on 10 December. Artillery support lit up the skies, creating a "nightless city" as the Sixth and 114th divisions assaulted the heights protecting the southern gates of the city. Barbed wire entanglements, antitank ditches, reinforced concrete pillboxes, and mutually supporting defensive positions slowed them, and Chinese counterattacks to retake lost ground caused casualties to soar on both sides. Ultimately, the Japanese prevailed. Meanwhile, their Sixteenth Division took most of the high ground dominating the northeast sector of the city, and the Ninth and Third divisions converged on the center gates of the city. The Japanese controlled the heights, but they looked down on a wide, water-filled moat that protected the thirty-foot-high city walls.

On 11 December, the Sixth Division concentrated its artillery to cover a single brigade's thrust at a southwest gate. Thick morning fog disrupted an attempt to breach the wall with explosives, but the assault under cover of supporting artillery drove the Chinese defenders back into the city. Around the same time, the Ninth Division units secured a foothold across the moat at the central gate. The next morning the Sixth Division's attacks stalled, and assaults by Ninth Division against the east wall and Sixteenth Division to seize the remaining high ground to the north met fierce resistance. By early afternoon, however, artillery fire had destroyed part of the southwest wall, enabling a few small units of the Sixth Division to break into the city. They crossed the moat on sampans, burned houses at the base of the wall to create a smokescreen, and then scaled the rubble on bamboo ladders. By late afternoon engineers had rigged a wooden bridge across the moat, substituting themselves as human posts to hold the flimsy structure in place.[65]

With the city under incessant artillery fire and with Japanese troops in the city, at around 7 a.m. on 13 December the Chinese commander ordered a general retreat. The retreat quickly degenerated into panic when a Japanese pincer movement by the Forty-fifth Infantry from the south and the Thirty-third Infantry from the north sealed off the city. Some Chinese tried to break out of the Japanese encirclement; others abandoned their weapons, exchanged their uniforms for civilian clothing, and fled into the recesses of the city. Street fighting broke out, bringing orders from the chief of staff, 114th Infantry Division in the southeast sector of the city to burn two-story buildings to eliminate enemy resistance.[66]

Matsui had previously ordered the Tenth Army and Shanghai Expeditionary Army to each select two or three infantry battalions and military police units to enter Nanjing.[67] With street fighting raging in the eastern and northwestern neighborhoods, on the evening of 13 December Yanagawa ordered the Tenth Army to crush all resistance and rescinded Matsui's order. Japanese forces rushed into the city, tripling the number of armed troops inside the city's walls to 70,000. The troops were to eliminate all pockets of resistance, using artillery and anything else available, including arson. They were also warned to beware of Chinese "stragglers," meaning everyone from prisoners of war to suspicious-looking civilians.[68]

The Ninth Division, which suffered another 460 killed and 1,156 wounded in the fighting for Nanjing, reported that during mop-up operations in the capital the unit annihilated (*senmetsu*) about 7,000 "stragglers."[69] Lieutenant General Nakajima Kesago, commander of the Sixteenth Division, was even more direct. His 13 December diary entry noted that army policy was not to take prisoners but to kill them upon capture. Later, he learned that one unit handled 15,000 prisoners and a company, 1,300. He also wrote that disposing of several thousand people required dividing them into small groups of 100 or 200 each, then later having mass burials in large trenches.[70]

As Yang Daqing, a distinguished chronicler of the Nanjing horrors, and others have suggested, the breakdown of Japanese logistics, the unexpectedly determined Chinese resistance, and the equally unanticipated overnight disintegration of the defenders caught the Japanese unprepared to deal with large numbers of prisoners and civilians in Nanjing. Units had suffered heavy casualties, and revenge, lack of discipline, and junior officer insubordination, combined with Japanese attitudes about surrender and contempt for Chinese, led to mass killing by the rank and file. But senior officers' abdication of command and control allowed subordinates to issue orders regarding treatment of prisoners. High-ranking officers looked the other way at mass executions and in some cases even encouraged the killing.[71] In military terms, the indiscriminate killing, arson, pillaging, and rape at Nanjing were counterproductive, for these actions compelled the Kuomintang and Central Army to continue to resist Japanese aggression. China did not lose its will to fight, negotiations to end the fighting through German Ambassador Oskar Trautmann collapsed, and Chiang Kai-shek refused to capitulate to Japan.

For the Japanese army, the military operations from the Marco Polo Bridge Incident to the fall of Nanjing were their first integrated air-land operations making great use of their air power advantage. They misread their experience with armored forces in Chahar. Mobilization, though effective, revealed shortcomings. Units deployed without their full equipment or personnel. Ammunition shortages, especially of artillery shells, plagued operations around Shanghai. Logistic difficulties hampered operations in north China and Shanghai because Japan's industrial base was not geared for a full-scale war. The same was true of personnel. Replacements and reservists were often not sufficiently trained, and their units suffered heavy losses as a consequence. In general, the army underestimated the Chinese military and seemed nonplussed when they met determined Chinese resistance. Japanese senior commanders responded by throwing more troops into the fighting at Pingxingguan in late September and during the terrible struggle for Shanghai throughout October. Matsui's unimaginative tactics of frontal assault and attrition resulted only in Japanese units battering themselves to pieces against the solid Chinese defenses. True, the Chinese suffered far worse losses and were starting to crack, but it took the Tenth Army's landing on their flank to turn a retreat into a rout.

Seen from a strategic perspective, failure of *sokusen sokketsu* in campaigns across north China and from Shanghai to Nanjing left the exhausted Japanese army mired in a stalemate that persisted throughout the Sino-Japanese War.

TRANSLATED BY YANG DAQING

7 The Defense of the Central Yangtze

STEPHEN MACKINNON

At 7 a.m. on the damp cold morning of 26 January 1938, a single shot rang out in the third-story sanctuary of Changchun (Forever Spring) Temple, a quiet Taoist retreat nestled inconspicuously on the southern side of Shuangfeng Hill near the railway station just outside the eastern gate of Wuchang. General Hu Zongnan had put a bullet through the head of a kneeling middle-aged figure, General Han Fuju, whose army had just surrendered control of Shandong, north China's most populous province. To this day General Han has the distinction of being the highest-ranking officer in the modern history of the Chinese military to be executed for malfeasance and cowardly performance as a commander.

Since at least 1930, General Han Fuju had exercised independent military and political control over Shandong as its governor. With the outbreak of the Sino-Japanese War in the summer of 1937, although nominally beholden to Chiang Kai-shek as head of the Nationalist government's Military Affairs Commission (*Junshi weiyuan hui*), General Han continued to govern and organize without much consultation the defense of this strategically important province and its capital of Jinan. After his attempts to negotiate a separate deal broke down, the Japanese launched an offensive, bombing Jinan and moving ground troops rapidly south from positions in the Peking, Baoding, and Tianjin areas. Chiang Kai-shek ordered General Han and his Third Army Group to resist to the last man. Accustomed as he was to following Chiang's orders only when it suited him, General Han vacillated at first. Finally, rather than risk the destruction of a personal army of 80,000 men, he decided to retreat, leaving Jinan basically defenseless. The result was little fighting and much panic on the part of the civilian population in and around Jinan throughout the month of December.[1] This was happening at the same time that the Nationalist government's capital at Nanjing was under siege. To Chiang Kai-shek and his colleagues, the quick and effortless way with which the Japanese occupied Jinan, and then the port city of Qingdao on 27 and 28 December, respectively, would permit the Japanese northern army to push rapidly south down the Jinpu (Tianjin–Pukou) railway at nearly full strength. By the end of January they would pose the threat of joining forces with the large army under General Matsui Iwane, which had just captured Nanjing. Adding to this threat, as a result of the losses of Jinan and Nanjing, was an atmosphere of pandemonium: the spectacle of large numbers of troops and civilians fleeing in all directions, especially to the south and west toward Wuhan.[2]

As for General Han's fate, the specifics are as follows: On 5 January 1938, the general left his army in the field in southern Shandong and flew to Kaifeng with much of the Jinan treasury and a silver coffin. On 6 January, he was arrested and brought to Wuchang. The decision to execute General Han Fuju was taken collectively on 16 January, at a special military tribunal and meeting of the military leadership called by Chiang Kaishek. It was the first concrete act of unity taken in almost a decade by independently powerful regional militarists like Li Zongren, Bai Chongxi, and Feng Yuxiang. They were willing now to work in concert with Chiang and loyalists like Chen Cheng and Whampoa graduate Hu Zongnan. There was much collective anger. General Han's cowardly refusal to stand and fight the Japanese was seen as having contributed directly to the failure to organize an adequate defense of the capital, Nanjing, and its humiliating loss at a terrible price in terms of civilian casualties. During the tribunal General Han remained silent, apparently in a state of utter disbelief. Finally, at the end, as he was being led off, Han defiantly cried out, "I take responsibility for losing Shandong. But who takes responsibility for losing Nanjing???"[3]

General Han had a point, but he had badly misjudged the changing political climate and the willingness of fellow militarists to fall in behind Chiang Kai-shek against the Japanese despite Chiang's erratic recent performance as a battlefield commander. The Japanese Imperial Army, the generals agreed, was implacable, merciless, and perhaps unbeatable. Only by combining was there a chance for survival. Divided they would fall.

For the resistance forces, General Han's trial and execution was a symbolic military and political turning point. Wuhan became the de facto capital of republican China, around which the next line of defense of the central Yangtze region was to be organized before a final retreat west, if necessary, to Chongqing in mountainous Sichuan Province. For the first time in two decades, Chinese military leadership seemed willing to adopt a common overall approach to strategic planning within a unified command structure headed by Chiang Kai-shek as chair of the Military Affairs Commission and field commander Chen Cheng as vice chair.

From all sides of the political spectrum, the Wuhan press hailed General Han Fuju's trial and execution and expressed support for Chiang's military leadership. This included statements of support in a new daily, the *Xinhua ribao*, under the Communist leadership team of Zhou Enlai and Wang Ming, who had just arrived in Wuhan from Yan'an.[4] Of more immediate significance in military terms was the commitment of over a half million troops to the defense of central China from Chiang's former rivals, powerful regional militarists like Li Zongren and Bai Chongxi, whose Guangxi troops were arriving fresh from the south. More understandable perhaps was the commitment of what remained of northern regional armies like units loyal to the once powerful Feng Yuxiang—although most of Han Fuju's Shandong army deserted after his execution, either joining the Japanese as puppet troops or turning to banditry or guerrilla warfare or both.

It is often said that Chinese military leadership had no coherent strategy for the Anti-Japanese War. The rapid military collapse of resistance forces defending coastal China and then the fall in December of the capital, Nanjing, followed by Jinan and Qingdao, certainly supports this view. But, in fact, with the advantage of hindsight and newly released documents from both Japanese and Chinese sides, the reverse seems true. On the Chinese side, serious planning for the war, especially the defense of the central Yangtze Valley, went back at least until the early 1930s.[5] In late January 1938, there was consensus among the commanders who gathered for a war council in Wuchang around the idea of forcing a protracted or prolonged war (*chijiu zhan*) that would last for years. In other words the plan was to bog down the Japanese in the vast real estate of central China.[6]

The Japanese, on the other hand, were on the surface much better prepared in terms of training, armament, and supporting industrial infrastructure (including the routing of supplies from Manchuria). Their leaders—civilian and military—embraced a liberating, modernizing agenda for China. The Japanese saw themselves as fighting to save China from itself, to bring modernity—economic, social, and political—and global integration to a China that by itself was hopelessly mired in the past.[7] They exercised nearly total air superiority with devastating effect: a seemingly endless capacity for bombing and strafing by navy planes before and during a campaign as well as strategic bombing behind the lines against Chinese cities.[8] Yet in retrospect it has become apparent that the Japanese leadership had done little strategic planning for a prolonged war (meaning a war that would last over a year). Chiang Kai-shek's China was expected to fragment and collapse quickly under pressure of the Japanese blitzkrieg and terror tactics, followed up by application of maximum firepower from fast-moving, well-armed mechanized ground troops. The war in China, they thought, would be short and decisive. The Japanese neither expected nor were prepared to fight a "protracted war" of attrition.[9]

By the winter of 1937–1938 the international press as well as foreign military observers and diplomats certainly thought the Japanese were on schedule, and many were impressed by their modernizing agenda as well.[10]

The record is clear on this point. It shows a strong consensus of foreign expert opinion predicting the collapse of unified resistance to the Japanese after the fall of Nanjing, with the surrender of Wuhan coming within a month or two. Chiang Kai-shek was known to be carrying on talks with the Japanese through intermediaries—including German diplomats. Besides the advantages of overwhelming firepower, Japanese generals were seen as superior to the Chinese in training and in ability to coordinate troops. The survival of a single military command structure on the Chinese side that could hold a unified strategic vision, let alone coordinate tactically, was seen as highly unlikely given China's fractious regional political history. And, finally, the troops that were expected to face the Japanese in defense of Wuhan were considered inferior and untried.[11]

Moreover, between generals in the field and between the generals and Chiang Kai-shek there was little loyalty or love lost. His own regional commanders had kidnapped Chiang in December 1936. In addition, there was the conflict between Chiang and the Communists to the northwest. "The Communists are a disease of the heart—the Japanese a disease of the skin" was a well-known Chiang quotation. Finally, many, like *New York Times* bureau chief Hallett Abend, saw Japanese domination of China as a positive development that would lead ultimately to the modernization of the country and a more stable political environment for foreign investment.[12]

It is within this international and strategic context that the defense of the Yangtze in 1938–1939 took place. The military outcome of the defense of central China was more than just a surprise for both Japanese and foreign observers. It represents a key turning point in the history of the war. The net effect of the defense of Wuhan and follow-up battles in 1939 for Nanchang and Changsha was stalemate and prolonged war. By 1940, at great cost, the Chinese grand strategy of *chijiu zhan* (war of attrition) was working.

The defense of Wuhan is a story with a late-twentieth-century twist, anticipating the ironic outcomes of anticolonial wars of the middle and late twentieth century. In central China in 1938 and 1939, the Chinese lost almost all of the battles but in the end won the war by gaining political strength as the fighting continued. On the battlefield, the costs to the enemy were great enough to produce stalemate and prolong the war until outside events finally ended it.[13]

*Location, Condition, and Disposition
of Chinese Armies on the Eve of the Campaign*

China began the war in 1937 with an estimated regular force of 1.7 to 2.2 million men. These troops can be divided into six categories based on the degree of their political loyalty to their commander in chief, Chiang Kai-shek. First, there were the troops controlled directly by Chiang. Second, there were troops who had been loyal to Chiang in the past but were less directly controlled by him. Third, there were provincial troops over whom Chiang could exercise command in ordinary times. Fourth, there were a different set of provincial troops over which Chiang had little direct influence. Fifth, there were the Communist forces: the Eighth Route Army in the caves of the northwest and the New Fourth Army taking shape in 1938–1939 in the hill country of the central Yangtze region between Wuhan and Nanjing. Finally, there were the northeastern or Manchurian units that had been defeated and displaced by the Japanese in 1931. The first two categories included roughly 900,000 men, who were the better armed and trained. There were a million at least in the relatively independent provincial armies—poorly armed but more experienced and fiercely loyal to their commanders in the field. About another 300,000 were split between the Communist and Manchurian forces.[14]

Geographically, most of the troops loyal to Chiang Kai-shek in the first two categories had been dispatched to the central coastal areas and heavily involved in the defense of Shanghai and Nanjing, where they suffered tremendous losses. Most devastating in military terms was the loss of 70 percent of the young officer corps, whom Chiang had spent precious resources to train in the 1930s.[15] Although overall command was split between generals Chen Cheng and Hu Zongnan—both strong Chiang loyalists—the surviving units, which totaled about 400,000 men, had retreated in disorganized and often leaderless fashion up the Yangtze toward Wuhan in the winter of 1937–1938.

The independent, regional armies of the north, like units under General Han Fuju in Shandong province, had taken big hits—with many units going over to the Japanese and later serving as puppet troops, turning to banditry, or continuing to resist as loose guerrilla units. This meant that after the first six months of the war, the Chinese units that remained intact were the relatively autonomous, sizable armies located in either the southwest or northwest under the command of leading regional militarists like General Li Zongren and Bai Chongxi (in Guangxi), Long Yun (in Yunnan), Yang Sen (in Sichuan), Zhang Fakui and Xue Yue (in Guangdong), or Yan Xishan (in the Shanxi-Suiyuan region). The Communist forces numbered about 100,000 and were relatively unscathed in bases to the north and east of Xi'an, but were roped off as it were by Yan Xishan's regional army and the deployment of over a dozen divisions under General Hu Zongnan. Thus, despite considerable attention by scholars, the Communist-led units of the Eighth Route Army have been seen as having little or no part in the battle for the central Yangtze Valley in 1938.[16] The bulk of the 700,000 men who made up the forces who were the heart of the Chinese defense in 1938 were from Guangxi, Sichuan, Guangdong, and elsewhere and had been together as units under the command of generals like Li and Bai or Zhang Fakui and Xue Yue since the 1920s.[17]

Early in 1938, as retreating troops regrouped around Wuhan and fresh units came north from Guangxi and east from Sichuan, the positioning of divisions and command structure for the defense of the central Yangtze was reorganized by war zones. The Fifth War Zone was redefined geographically as the area north of the Yangtze (Anhui, Hubei, and Henan provinces) and put under the command of General Li Zongren. His army included a mix of Li's own Guangxi units and those loyal to General Bai Chongxi with troops that were loyal to Chiang Kai-shek. The latter were commanded either by untested young commanders like Tang Enbo or by recently disgraced figures like Zhang Zizhong, a former Feng Yuxiang associate to whom Li Zongren decided to give a second chance (despite his role in the humiliating surrender of Peking in 1937). Altogether about fifty divisions (roughly 9,000 men to a division), or 450,000, fought on the Chinese side in the Fifth War Zone.[18] Initially, the headquarters was at Xuzhou in northern Jiangsu, a strategically important border city situated at the north–south and east–west juncture of the Longhai and Jinpu railway lines.[19]

To the south of the Yangtze, and put directly under General Chen Cheng, was the Ninth War Zone, encompassing Hunan, Jiangxi, and Hubei provinces, with the tri-cities of Wuhan as the command center. Altogether, Chen Cheng commanded a larger force, seventy-eight divisions, or 702,000 men, in the Ninth War Zone. These were a mixture of units with strong provincial loyalties, like those of the Guangzhou general Zhang Fakui. They were expected to work closely with units that were more directly tied to Chiang Kai-shek and commanded by graduates of the Whampoa Military Academy (where Chiang had been the commandant in the 1920s). Added to the mix were displaced provincial troops of questionable loyalty who had served formerly under regional militarists like Feng Yuxiang and Zhang Xueliang. There was also the newly formed New Fourth Army, which in 1938 was in its infancy as a guerrilla force operating under General Ye Ting.[20]

The Fifth and Ninth War Zone armies, as reassembled in January, represented the approach the Chinese military leadership took to the organization and positioning of forces. As a field organization, the Chinese forces were reorganized using German models, with large armies grouped together as field armies (i.e., the Fifth and Ninth War Zones). At the same time, Russian influences were increasingly evident in the strategic positioning of Chinese units along communication lines. This approach was apparent in the adoption of battle formations, that is, the use of front and route armies as well as rear-area service units. Overall, these different approaches meant there was a lack of coherence in the deployment of forces facing the Japanese.

When more rational and aggressive plans were drawn up, they were rarely followed in practice. Moreover, military intelligence about Japanese movements was poor. Prisoners were usually shot on the spot, with interrogation a rare occurrence. Thus, with little reconnaissance being carried out, rumors replaced intelligence, sometimes with disastrous results (like the unnecessary preemptive burning of Changsha by Chinese generals in November 1938).[21]

In short, the Chinese overemphasized positional warfare in their strategic deployments and remained too fixed in position—except to retreat. The large, layered units just mentioned were positioned for holding on to communication routes (such as the Peking–Hankou or Longhai railway lines), probably for reasons of good transport and logistics. But the net effect was to tie down the main fighting forces, around which the Japanese could then more easily outmaneuver or outflank. Chinese mobility was further limited by a lack of commitment to guerrilla warfare as a widespread tactic. And, finally, in the name of a "protracted war" strategy, Chinese commanders too often avoided decisive confrontation with the Japanese, even when they were at a tactical advantage, so as to reduce the possibility of meeting irreversible defeat. Avoiding defeat was understandable, considering the devastating losses absorbed in the defense of Shanghai and Nanjing as well as the background of many generals as provincial militarists who were expert at political and military survival. At critical moments in a battle, the timidity of division commanders would outrage Chen Cheng, Li Zongren, Bai Chongxi, and Chiang Kai-shek.

At the beginning of the central Yangtze campaign, by March of 1938, the Chinese enjoyed a six to one numerical advantage over the Japanese, throwing 1.1 million men (or 120 divisions) against a Japanese force of 200,000 (20 divisions). But the advantage of numbers dissolved in the face of the massive superiority of the Japanese in equipment, mobility, and firepower. According to one calculation by an American military observer, the combat effectiveness (defined as numbers times firepower) of a Chinese division ranged from one-third to one-twelfth that of its Japanese counterpart.[22] Not only was Chinese weaponry inferior but also little replenishment of men and arms took place or was even possible. Leaving aside bravery and esprit de corps, these disadvantages meant that at the front one hundred Chinese divisions were often no better than twelve Japanese divisions in terms of fighting effectiveness.

The Chinese for the most part fought with small arms, machine guns, and hand grenades. Effective use of artillery was limited. A Chinese air force existed, but it was defensive and not employable in a tactical sense. Chinese forces were most effective fighting at night and in hand-to-hand combat, when their generals could take better advantage of the numerical superiority and organize mass wave counterattack tactics.[23]

Finally, there was the problem of the complex and overly politicized command structure built up by Chiang Kai-shek in the 1930s. Orders from Chiang Kai-shek had to pass down through six tiers of commanders before an operation was possible. Moreover, after the debacles at Shanghai and Nanjing, Chiang was prone to try to micromanage the battlefield himself by circumventing normal communication channels and sending direct personal orders to commanders in the field—sometimes contradicting previous directives of just a few days earlier.[24] Not surprisingly, moreover, in the distribution of equipment, Chiang favored central army units over which he had direct control and which had loyal commanders like Tang Enbo and Hu Zongnan who belonged to the Whampoa Clique. Needless to say, Chiang's favoritism bred discord and insubordination at all levels of the Chinese command hierarchy.[25]

Given these problems—the confusion of command, lack of firepower, overemphasis on positional warfare, and the demoralizing debacles at Shanghai and Nanjing—how does one explain the Chinese success in 1938 at organizing a prolonged, spirited defense that tied up the Japanese Imperial Army in the central Yangtze Valley for ten months? Or, more specifically, how could the Chinese bog down the Japanese on the battlefield around Xuzhou during the spring of 1938 (including a victory at Taierzhuang) and then follow up with a spirited defense of Wuhan that lasted into late October?

Surely the answers lie in part with the nature of the leadership and personalities who were in command on the Chinese side. Despite Chiang Kai-shek's attempts to interfere, Chen Cheng, the overall field commander, ran the defense of the central Yangtze in an informal but disciplined manner. Overcoming old rivalries and conflicting provincial loyalties, Chen and his associate commanders performed in 1938 as a surprisingly cohesive group. One reason, I believe, was a generational bond of experience that the generals shared in terms of educational background and military experience during the turbulent decade of the 1920s. Most, including the senior commander Chen Cheng himself, were graduates of the Baoding Military Academy.

The Baoding Factor

Founded in 1912, the Baoding Military Academy (Baoding junguan xuexiao) had functioned as China's West Point or Sandhurst into the 1920s. It was the place where the elite of China's new professional officer corps were trained, before the establishment of the Whampoa Central Military Academy in 1924. Baoding emphasized discipline, German- and Japanese-based technological expertise, and esprit de corps among graduates. At Baoding professionalism was more important than political indoctrination.[26] Embodying the Baoding spirit at Wuhan was Jiang Baili, republican

China's most important military intellectual and the academy's first com-mandant. In 1938 Jiang was made the new head, with rank of general, of the Army War College that had just been relocated to the Wuhan area. Undoubtedly responsible for the promotion and new position were Bao-ding alumni (now generals) who over the years had proven fiercely loyal to the academy and Jiang Baili (whom Chiang Kai-shek had imprisoned between 1929 and 1931).[27]

In retrospect, it was the Baoding generals, like Chen Cheng, Bai Chongxi, Luo Zhuoying, Tang Shengzhi, Ye Ting, and Xue Yue, who were key planners in the defense of Wuhan. Li Zongren, the commander of the Fifth War Zone, was a graduate of the Yunnan Military Academy (modeled after Baoding) but otherwise shared a background similar to the others (the same can be said for Zhang Fakui, who attended the academy in Wuchang). Few of these figures had studied overseas (as would be true for a later generation like Tang Enbo and Sun Liren). Most had struggled since the 1920s with Chiang Kai-shek over his efforts to marginalize and separate them from their armies. By 1938, however, with the exception of Han Fuju (not a Baoding man), they understood the seriousness of the Japanese threat and the need to rally around Chiang's leadership.

In other words, the generals defending Wuhan were members of the Baoding generation. They were seasoned regional commanders who had survived the internecine struggles of the 1920s and early 1930s. For them, a kind of epiphany occurred around the decision to execute Han Fuju. They had agreed, and this brought them together in a new way. For the time being, the Baoding generals exhibited an esprit de corps and mutual respect for one another's professionalism that surprised foreign observers. They found that they were able to work together on the battlefield and to agree, politely, to circumvent Chiang Kai-shek's directives when necessary.

A related factor was the character of the troops these gentlemen com-manded. The troops were a mixture of conscripts and soldiers of fortune, some of whom had served for over a decade in units organized by their commanders. As mercenaries or professional soldiers operating essentially in alien territory (for troops from Guangxi, Guangzhou, Sichuan, and Shandong, the central Yangtze was certainly alien), they were fiercely loyal to their commanders. But also cutting across units was a shared sense of outrage over the Japanese invasion. The soldiers understood the threat to their home provinces. This meant that desertions were relatively infrequent and discipline within units was relatively high—by comparison to the forced conscription and high desertion rate that later characterized many of the units more directly under the command of Chiang Kai-shek loyalists and Whampoa Military Academy graduates. All of the above was espe-cially true for the Guangxi divisions under Li Zongren and Bai Chongxi, whom foreign observers came to regard by the end of 1938 as among the best fighting units on the Chinese side.[28]

Thus, I believe it was the improved chemistry of the moment, in terms of communication and the prowess of certain commanders, that helps to explain the ability of the Chinese to hold out for ten months and inflict unacceptable losses on the Japanese. The division commanders of the Fifth and Ninth War Zones were drawn together by the will to resist the Japanese, not by loyalty to Chiang Kai-shek. The troops in both war zones were a mélange of regional forces with different levels of armament and experience. Although poorly armed and trained, most remained intensely loyal and followed orders.

High casualty figures, not high desertion rates, characterized the Chinese side during the battle for control of the central Yangtze Valley. Add to this the fact that the ability of the commander in chief, Chiang Kai-shek, to effectively meddle in or micromanage the battlefield (as he did in Shanghai) was reduced or neutralized by the loss of crack units and his best officers earlier in the war. At the same time, the relative political independence of many commanders limited their ability to coordinate operations and come to one another's aid as the tide of battle turned in a particular place. And so in the end, relentless bombing and the exercise of superior mobility and firepower did carry the day, and the Japanese took Xuzhou and then Wuhan by the end of 1938.

At times, historians have treated the Xuzhou and Wuhan campaigns as separate events. To the Chinese and Japanese commanders on both sides at the time, however, the Xuzhou and Wuhan campaigns were intimately connected. Commanders on both sides saw the connection in terms of a pincer move by the Japanese that was intended to bring the north China and central China wings of the Imperial Army together south of Xuzhou for the delivery of a speedy coup de grace to Wuhan by midspring. To block this move, the Chinese high command decided a major stand had to be made at Xuzhou.[29]

The resulting battles for Xuzhou and Wuhan turned out to be much slower and more costly for the Japanese compared to the ease with which the Imperial Army sliced off East China coastal provinces during the first six months of 1937. It is the long, drawn-out nature of the struggle in 1938 that gives the battle for control of the central Yangtze region central place as a turning point in the military history of the war.

The Battle for Xuzhou

The battle for control of the central Yangtze region lasted ten months, from January to October 1938. In terms of geography and order of battle, the initiative lay with the Japanese because of their superior firepower as well as their mechanized maneuverability on land and in the air. Foreign observers at the time and historians in retrospect have often faulted the Chinese leadership for being too defensive and unwilling to take the offensive in pursuit of the enemy, especially on those occasions when the Japanese became overextended, tied down, or in retreat.[30] But before accepting such views, one should consider the facts on the ground at the time and the difficulties the Chinese forces would have had in taking the offensive, given that mobility was limited to forced marches or the use of railway lines. Likewise, given the lack of heavy firepower, softening up the enemy before an attack was not possible. Much of the time the Chinese had little or no artillery and, of course, little ability to bomb and strafe the enemy from the air.

In January 1938, the Japanese plan was to connect large units from the North China Area Army (under Generals Itagaki Seishirō, Nishio Toshizō, and Isogai Rensuke) with the Central China Expeditionary Force (or Eleventh Army) under General Hata Shunroku that was headquartered in Nanjing. Units of the North China Area Army began moving south along the Jinpu Railway from Jinan, and units under General Hata began moving north up the Jinpu Railway from Nanjing. Once united at Xuzhou, the two armies would launch a coordinated attack in a pincer movement from the north and east on central Yangtze Valley strongholds, taking Jiujiang first and then Wuhan. Success by the end of March seemed assured—a success that seemed certain to break the back of united front resistance under Chiang Kai-shek.[31]

At this point, the war council that Chiang convened at the end of January in Wuchang made an important decision—go all out in the commitment of troops to the defense of Xuzhou, the key strategic city to both Chinese and Japanese planners at the junction of the Longhai and Jinpu railroads.[32] In retrospect, the determination to defend Xuzhou was perhaps the most important decision of the war because the effectiveness of the Chinese resistance around Xuzhou tied down and embarrassed the Japanese, forcing them to rush reinforcements from Manchuria (under General Doihara Kenji) and from Nanjing. Both deployments seriously delayed previously planned campaigns to the west and north from Taiyuan and up the Yangtze from Nanjing. It also forced a major rethinking of troop allocations and a change in personnel, as well as Tokyo's mechanism for handling the China theater from Tokyo.[33] The prolonged, bloody struggle for Xuzhou pushed the Japanese to give high priority to the central Chinese theater.

The Chinese military leadership recognized the strategic importance of holding on to Xuzhou and began in January to prepare for its defense. From a core of 80,000 troops, which Li Zongren commanded at headquarters in the city, about 300,000 more troops were added from scattered units positioned along the Jinpu and Longhai railway lines. The idea was to trap the much smaller Japanese units as they came by rail and road from the north, south, and east. Once drawn in and overextended, the Japanese could be tied up and perhaps even stopped at positions to the north and east of Xuzhou. For five months the battle for Xuzhou raged—with both sides taking heavy casualties and claiming victories.

In mid-May, the Japanese finally took Xuzhou, marching into an empty city defended by only a few thousand soldiers. But earlier there had been costly setbacks. At the end of March, the Japanese had been lured into a major engagement at Taierzhuang, about thirteen miles to the northeast of Xuzhou, where three divisions were beaten back and forced to retreat, with casualties running from 15,000 to 20,000 killed (about the same on the Chinese side). Eventually, the Japanese reconquered Taierzhuang, but in this battle and the effort to take Xuzhou the Japanese lost valuable time, and their morale was shaken. On the Chinese side, the reverse was the case. Despite the defeat, Xuzhou was a morale booster. Li Zongren, Bai Chongxi, Zhang Zizhong, Sun Lianzhong, and Tang Enbo became national heroes. Retreating Chinese troops were approaching the defense of Wuhan with new confidence and determination.[34]

Needless to say, the history of the five-month battle for control of the Xuzhou railway junction is complicated, both chronologically and geographically. This is especially true for the Chinese side because of the variety of units deployed—with an ever-changing cast of division commanders—at any one time or place, with some fighting and some not. As the Japanese closed in on Xuzhou from the north, east, and south, what pattern there was to the thrust and retreats from myriad clashes, large and small, was a zigzagging motion, with action swinging first to the north, then to the east, then to the south, and then back and forth again.

In early February, mechanized Japanese armored units with strong air support simultaneously attacked Chinese divisions protecting the Jinpu Railway. The pincer movement first engaged Chinese troops about a hundred miles to the north and south of Xuzhou. To repeat, the Japanese plan was for units of the North China Area Army to push south toward Xuzhou, and units of the Eleventh Army, or Central China Expeditionary Army, to push north up the railway line from the Nanjing area, meeting triumphally in Xuzhou. Then, after a short pause to regroup, the large force would proceed west along the Longhai Railway to Zhengzhou. From Zhengzhou, the combined units could then proceed south, down the Pinghan (Peking–Hankou) Railway to lay siege to Wuhan. But by the end of the month, a large Chinese force of about 300,000 had successfully blocked the Japanese advances. This position forced major battles to the south around Bengbu on the Huai River and to the north on the railway line at Tengxian.

The standoff at Tengxian, a railway stop about seventy-five miles north of Xuzhou, was particularly important and bloody. The defenders were relatively untested and poorly armed troops from Sichuan. Their commander was Wang Mingzhang, an old comrade and close associate of theater commander Li Zongren. Heroically, the Sichuanese held out until mid-March, when heavy artillery barrages and the growing size of the Japanese force finally overwhelmed them. General Wang lost his life in defense of Tengxian.[35] At the same time (mid-February), the Japanese began moving a large force inland from the port of Qingdao, working their way across country southwest toward Xuzhou. At Linyi, about thirty miles northeast of Xuzhou, they were confronted by large deployments of entrenched Chinese forces. The commanders were Generals Pang Bingxun and Zhang Zizhong. The latter, a northerner and former associate of Feng Yuxiang, had been held in contempt by Chiang Kai-shek and in the press since July 1937 for surrendering Peking without a fight. Li Zongren decided to give Zhang a second chance and in January 1938 gave him a command in the Fifth War Zone. Zhang would redeem his reputation in the battle for Linyi.

In March and early April Chinese resistance in the Xuzhou area was at its most effective. Chinese units fought major engagements to the north, south, and east of the city, significantly slowing Japanese advances. It even looked, to surprised foreign observers, as if the Japanese might be stopped.[36] Chinese units led by Generals Pang and Zhang took a terrific pounding but stopped the Japanese divisions under Itagaki Seishirō in a three-week battle at Linyi. Overnight, Zhang Zizhong became a national hero and international celebrity.[37]

In mid-March, both forces paused and regrouped for an even greater battle at Taierzhuang—on a railway spur line along the Grand Canal about thirteen miles northeast of Xuzhou. There, General Zhang was joined by units commanded by a northerner, Sun Lianzhong (also a former associate of Feng Yuxiang), and a young officer, Tang Enbo, whose units included artillery pieces. But General Tang was inexperienced and reluctant to commit his units to the battle. He was a graduate of the elite Japanese military academy Shikan Gakkō and was a protégé of Chiang Kai-shek's chief of staff and military alter ego, General He Yingqin. Tang's relations with theater commander Li Zongren were not good. To get General Tang to close in and risk his artillery at Taierzhuang, Li reportedly threatened court-martial and execution.

The small town of Taierzhuang was obliterated in the battle that raged from 22 March to 7 April 1938. Finally, Japanese troops under General Isogai Rensuke ran out of ammunition and were forced to retire. Much of the combat was at night and hand-to-hand. Both sides lost roughly 20,000 men before the Japanese withdrew.[38] By mid-April, another pause and a stalemate of sorts prevailed. The Chinese units under Zhang and Sun were battered and exhausted. But, initially, they made an attempt to pursue the

Japanese as they retreated north and east into Shandong from the charred remains of Taierzhuang.

By the end of April, the tide had began to turn in the favor of the Japanese as reinforcements of men and supplies arrived. Japanese strength in the Xuzhou neighborhood reached 400,000 men as fresh troops and materiel poured in from Tianjin and Nanjing. New Japanese commanders (the infamous Doihara Kenji among them) ordered a series of counterattacks. Xuzhou was to be approached from the southwest, east, and north. The intent was to surround the city, lay siege, and destroy the large number of Chinese troops deployed in its defense. Reinforcements were also deployed on the Chinese side, bringing total strength in the region up to 600,000. By the end of April, the fighting on three fronts around Xuzhou was fierce, with much bloodshed on both sides. But slowly Japanese firepower on the ground and bombing from the air prevailed. On 9 May the Japanese captured Mengcheng, well to the north of the Huai River. From there, the southern flank force split into two parts: half went west and then north to cut off the Longhai Railway escape route from Xuzhou, and the other divisions moved straight north up the railway line to Suxian, which is just outside Xuzhou. At the same time, to the north, the Japanese units from north China massed at Jining and began moving south beyond Tengxian. Along the coast an amphibious landing was made at Lianyungang to reinforce troops attacking from the east. What remained of Taierzhuang was captured in May—an event that was symbolically important to Tokyo.

On 17 May, the noose around Xuzhou tightened appreciably as Japanese artillery hit targets inside the city. What followed was probably the most important and skillful Chinese maneuver of the Xuzhou campaign: a brilliantly executed strategic retreat to the south and west across the Jinpu railway line. On 15 May, Li Zongren, in consultation with Chiang Kai-shek, had decided to pull back from Xuzhou and to focus on an escape plan. On that day, the evacuation of the civilian and military population of the city began. Li ordered troops to melt into the countryside and then move south and west at night, crossing the Jinpu Railway and splitting into four groups that would head west. The idea was eventually to regroup in the rugged Dabie Mountains region to the south and prepare for the defense of Wuhan. Li's generals left reluctantly, having held out for so long. Tang Enbo was said to have wept.

Marching by night and hiding in the wheat fields by day, forty divisions, or over 200,000 men, quietly slipped out of Japanese reach in less than a week. At a critical point on 18 May fog and a sandstorm covered the tracks of the retreating troops as they crossed the Jinpu Railway. On 21 May Li wired Chiang Kai-shek that the withdrawal was complete. Two days earlier, on 19 May, Japanese units under General Hata Shunroku had marched into the abandoned ruins of Xuzhou, taking 30,000 prisoners.

What happened next was remarkable and highly controversial—at the time and ever since. The Japanese (units of the North China Area Army) were advancing east down the Longhai Railway, taking Kaifeng on 6 June. They were poised to cross the Yellow River and threaten the railway junction with the (north–south) Pinghan line at Zhengzhou. Chiang Kai-shek flew to Zhengzhou at the end of May and decided to order General Wei Rulin to blow up the dikes of the Yellow River at Huayuankou so that the river would change course and flow south into Anhui Province, joining the Huai and then heading east toward the sea. Chiang's purpose was to stop the Japanese advance by flooding their path to the west and south. The dikes were blown on 5 June and again on 7 June 1938. The devastation and cost in civilian suffering that resulted was almost incalculable.[39]

The move did force a change in Japanese war plans for the Wuhan campaign. Units of the North China Area Army did not reach Zhengzhou; they were forced to retrace their steps and head south, down the Jinpu Railway to join General Hata's forces near Nanjing. Thus the attack on Wuhan was redirected but not overly delayed. It began a few weeks after the blowing of the dikes at Huayuankou as a two-pronged drive upriver from Nanjing.[40]

The blowing of the dikes at Huayuankou brought to a dramatic and tragic end the five-month Xuzhou campaign. For the Chinese side, the outcome was bittersweet. Initially, there was jubilation, especially in the refugee-swollen de facto capital of Wuhan, because of the initial victories at Linyi and Taierzhuang.[41] The loss of Xuzhou was a blow, yet the strength of the defense and the escape of Li's troops seemed to demonstrate that the Japanese were becoming bogged down in central China. Chances seemed improved for Wuhan; the tri-cities might be able to hold out. The Japanese commanders were angry. Having reorganized and reinforced in June, they were doggedly determined to end the "China Incident" at Wuhan.

Historians, and observers at the time, have differed widely on who on the Chinese side was making the key decisions and should be given credit for the impressive stand in and around Xuzhou. Chinese historians on Taiwan in the 1950s, and recently on the mainland, favor crediting Chiang Kai-shek for sagely micromanaging defensive strategy from Wuchang.[42] Certainly Chiang bombarded field commanders with private communications and instructions via telephone and telegrams. Diana Lary credits the effectiveness of the Chinese defense to the Guangxi generals Li Zongren and Bai Chongxi, especially the former.[43] Foreign military attachés, like Evans Carlson, and journalists, like Israel Epstein, pointed to midlevel commanders like Tang Enbo, Zhang Zizhong, and Sun Lianzhong as the true heroes of the campaign, who persevered despite incompetent meddling by Chiang Kai-shek, Li, and Bai.[44]

It also has been charged that the Chinese generals were insufficiently aggressive in their strategic moves. Advisers like von Falkenhausen and the Russian Kalyagin, along with American military attachés Evans Carlson, Joseph Stilwell, and Frank Dorn, point to the failure to effectively pursue retreating Japanese divisions after they were stopped at Linyi and Taierzhuang, thus giving them time to regroup and counterattack. In retrospect, the charge seems unrealistic, given the inadequacy of equipment, absence of airpower, and the badly battered state of Chinese troops at the time. The Japanese were stopped but not beaten. The high morale of the Chinese troops alone could not have driven the Japanese into the sea.[45]

What has gone relatively unrecognized by historians and foreign observers alike was the skillful and important retreat of the 200,000 to 300,000 Chinese troops that General Hata thought he had trapped at Xuzhou in late May 1938. Badly battered, but with about half his troops intact, General Li and the divisions of the Fifth War Zone survived the Xuzhou campaign and were able to regroup in the Dabie Mountains. This retreat was important because it delayed the attack on Wuhan and forced General Hata to employ a more difficult and costly stratagem of fighting his way up the heavily fortified Yangtze River—capturing river communities town by town until he could lay siege to Wuhan.

Still, on the Chinese side, the human cost of the battle for Xuzhou had been great, deeply shaking the confidence of the man in charge, Li Zongren. In June, he returned to Wuhan to a hero's welcome. Apparently haunted by the ghosts of those lost in the defense of Xuzhou, Li was hospitalized for mysterious reasons—for depression as much as for physical ailments (the official explanation was that an old bullet wound had flared up). Bai Chongxi took over the Fifth War Zone duties and command of the 400,000 or so troops bivouacked in the Dabie Mountains area, waiting for the Japanese to attack from the east.[46]

Defending Wuhan

In June 1938, the Japanese amassed 400,000 men for the assault on Wuhan. The attack was planned initially as a two-pronged offensive to the north and south of the Yangtze under the overall command of General Hata. One column, made up of North China Area Army units, moved across country southwest from Hefei along the Jinpu Railway. The other thrust, by a larger force of combined Eleventh Army and naval units, would push a steady assault moving upstream and west from Nanjing along the southern bank of the Yangtze.[47]

The Chinese marshaled at least 800,000 men for the defense of Wuhan and the central Yangtze Valley. Grand strategy and deployment of troops was worked out in practice as much by Chen Cheng, the overall theater commander, and the generals under him as it was by Chiang Kai-shek.

Basically, their approach involved the placement of troops in the most defensible or important places along the path of the advancing Japanese. Fifth War Zone troops under General Bai Chongxi defended the region north of the river, and Ninth War Zone troops were deployed along the southern bank of the Yangtze. In the north, the idea was to tie up the Japanese in the rough terrain to the south and north of the Dabie Mountains and prevent them from cutting off the Pinghan Railway north of Wuhan. And to the south (Ninth War Zone) the Chinese worked furiously on constructing riverine defenses in order to block the main assault below Jiujiang and push the Japanese farther south into the Poyang Lake district.[48]

The Chinese side was favored by the terrain (although many of the troops and commanders were from elsewhere) and support from the local populace, as well as by sufficient time to dig in and erect earthen defenses. The summer of 1938 was hot, steamy, and disease ridden. Foot soldiers on both sides were crippled that summer by dysentery and malaria. Besides the obvious superiority in firepower and mobility on the ground and in the air, the Japanese enjoyed one natural advantage, that during the summer of 1938 the Yangtze was near its high-water mark. The water level facilitated effective shelling of Chinese defense positions by Japanese gunboats throughout the campaign as well as helping a flotilla of supply ships to arrive in support of advancing troops.

Japan opened with a resounding victory. On 15 June the first defensive stronghold on the Yangtze at Anqing (over a hundred miles east of Nanjing) fell after only one day of fighting. The two divisions of Sichuan soldiers under General Yang Sen (the militarist who dominated Chengdu in the 1920s) were outmaneuvered by an amphibious landing behind their defenses and quickly overwhelmed. General Yang fled in disgrace, not to be heard from again.[49] From Anqing, which had an airfield, the Japanese were able to coordinate a combined army/navy assault on Jiujiang, the major riverine port and railway junction one hundred miles upstream (by rail Jiujiang was the northern terminus for traffic to Hangzhou, Nanchang, and Guangzhou). To thwart the capture of Jiujiang, Chinese engineers and a thousand coolies had been working at night since May on the construction of impressive defensive installations with artillery emplacements at Madang, which was located midway on the route to Jiujiang, at a place where the banks of the Yangtze formed a natural boom.[50]

Tragically, the defense of Madang turned into a debacle and major setback for the Chinese. The Japanese caught the Chinese by surprise on 24 June by landing upstream from Madang, cutting off major defensive units at the county seat of Pengze. Pengze's local commanders were off on a training junket at the time, so Pengze fell quickly, almost without a struggle. Suddenly, Madang was surrounded, and with the Japanese use of poison gas, the defenders panicked. The elaborate earthen defenses at Madang fell without the frontal assault they were built to defend against.

The end came as Japanese gunboats crashed through river barriers on 29 June. The loss of Madang was a major embarrassment and left the way to Jiujiang almost undefended. Chiang Kai-shek court-martialed the officers in charge of Madang, executing the divisional commander for Pengze, General Xie Weiying (Whampoa graduate) who had ignored telephone calls (from Bai Chongxi and others) to reinforce Madang at the time of the surprise attack.[51]

Guangzhou Generals Zhang Fakui and Xue Yue, with a force of over 200,000 men, were in charge of the defense of the Jiujiang-Ruichang area. Their mission was to meet the Japanese and push them south into the Poyang Lake district. Both were seasoned commanders and players in the militarist politics of the 1920s who had served under Chiang Kai-shek during the Northern Expedition of 1926–1927. Xue Yue was a Baoding graduate with closer ties to Chen Cheng than Chiang Kai-shek, and Zhang Fakui (educated at the Wuchang Military Academy) was accustomed to operating independently from bases in Guangzhou. For the defense of Jiujiang Xue Yue commanded about 80,000 troops. At first, the Chinese units stood their ground at Hukou, to the north of Poyang Lake, losing the city on 8 July after a brutal five-day battle. The battle for Jiujiang, the province of Jiangxi's major port city, began on 23 July. It was over by 28 July. The evidence is inconclusive, but the Japanese may have used poison gas again in their attack. In any event, the defense led by Xue Yue was haphazard and disorganized. Moreover, the call for retreat came early and suddenly, leaving the civilian population at the mercy of their conquerors. Japanese troops were merciless in their treatment of the remaining civilian and military population, repeating a mini-Nanjing massacre at Jiujiang.[52]

If the massacre and destruction at Jiujiang was meant to terrorize the populations and armies upstream into submission, it failed. Chinese resistance at the next major target, the commercial center of Ruichang, ten miles inland from Jiujiang, on the road west toward the Wuhan–Guangzhou railway line, went much better. It lasted for a month, drawing the Japanese into a major seesaw battle. General Zhang Fakui's large force made the Japanese pay heavily for every kilometer advanced. At about the same time Japanese units thrust south toward Nanchang and became quickly bogged down in the Lushan Mountain area. Overextended and cut off from supplies, they turned back and rejoined the battle around Ruichang.[53]

To the north in the Fifth War Zone, Chinese resistance was better organized and more effective, slowing down the Japanese advance earlier in the campaign. The commanders were familiar names from the Xuzhou campaign—Sun Lianzhong, Zhang Zizhong, Tang Enbo, and others. To the south of the Dabie Mountains, they managed to tie up the Japanese for three weeks at Taihu (more or less directly north of Madang), with the enemy not taking this position until 25 July. It then took all of August for the Japanese to push west to Guangji, where they met stiff resistance that lasted until 9 September.

The battle at Guangji (which is just north of the Yangtze) was a prelude to a major encounter at Matouzhen on the river. There Xue Yue and his Guangzhou divisions redeemed their reputations. At one point in the see-saw battle over a critical position at Shahe, General Xue Yue threatened the life of a young division commander (Yu Jishi, a Whampoa graduate) in order to force him to refrain from retreating and leave the remaining units to the mercy of the Japanese.[54]

Thus, the Japanese found in September that they needed three weeks to advance ten miles up the Yangtze. In part the slowness was because the Chinese counterattacked effectively at the end of August at Huang-mei, ten miles to the south of the river, which forced the Japanese commander, Imamura Katsuji, to bring in emergency reinforcements from other positions.

The final big battle on the Yangtze occurred at the river fortress of Tianjiazhen, where Chinese engineers, with Russian advisers and thousands of coolies, had erected massive battlements. The resulting struggle was one of the bloodiest of the campaign, raging until 29 September, when the Japanese (after using gas) finally captured an uninhabited smoldering ruin. The way had now been pretty much cleared for the final army-navy assault upriver on Wuchang.[55]

At about the same time (August–September), to the north of the Dabie Mountains the Japanese units of the North China Area Army launched an end run from Hefei to the west aimed at capturing control of the Peking–Hankou Railway at Xinyang. Li Zongren resumed his command in the Fifth War Zone and seemed to be in charge of the defensive maneuvers against this Japanese foray to the north. Initially, the Japanese were slowed for weeks as they attempted to cross the Pi River at Lu'an. But once across the river, resistance withered and the Japanese moved rapidly through Shangcheng. They met significant resistance again at Huangchuan, where the hero of Taierzhuang, General Zhang Zizhong, managed to pin them down for over a week.[56]

The Japanese finally reached Xinyang on the Pinghan Railway on 30 September. A significant defense of the city by the divisions commanded by General Hu Zongnan was expected, in part to cover the retreat of Li Zongren's battered and exhausted Guangxi divisions into the mountains to the West. Instead, Hu Zongnan and his army disappeared to the north, and the Japanese took Xinyang without a fight. Li Zongren, the theater commander, was furious. But Hu Zongnan was the closest of the Whampoa generals to Chiang Kai-shek, and too senior for Li to threaten with disciplinary action.[57]

Losing control of the Pinghan Railway sealed the fate of the Wuhan tri-cities complex (made up of Hankou/Hanyang/Wuchang). It meant that the Japanese could now swiftly move troops and equipment directly south and attack the tri-cities from the north of Hankou at the same time as amphibious landings from General Hata's flotilla were conducted to the south, on the edge of Wuchang. With the noose tightening rapidly, Wuhan was about to be encircled.

The orderly evacuation of troops and equipment—as well as Chiang's military headquarters at Hankou (Chiang Kai-shek's quarters at Wuchang had been destroyed by bombing)—began in late September and was well under way by early October. Chiang and Chen Cheng were determined not to repeat the mistakes made at Shanghai and Nanjing, nor to risk the narrow escape Li Zongren engineered at Xuzhou. Earlier, as is well known, a Herculean effort had begun in August to remove and transport upriver Wuhan's industrial capacity, especially munitions production. By the end of October, thousands of tons of equipment were stockpiled on wharves upriver at Yichang, waiting to be shipped up the gorges to Chongqing for the duration of the war.[58]

Wuhan capitulated to attacks from the north, east, and south on 25 October. Guangzhou had fallen quickly four days earlier, made more vulnerable perhaps by the absence of the seasoned Guangzhou units that were fighting under Generals Zhang Fakui and Xue Yue in the defense of Wuhan.

Finally, the capture of Wuhan left Changsha defenseless, or so it appeared to Chiang Kai-shek. In a terrible mistake in judgment, Changsha, the capital of Hunan Province and one hundred miles south of Wuhan, was torched without reason. On 12 November 1938, the city was burned to the ground on Chiang Kai-shek's orders as a preemptive scorched-earth tactic invoked to frustrate a Japanese attack from the east (an assessment based on poor intelligence). In a state of panic, Chiang had ordered the burning of Changsha over the strenuous objections of Chen Cheng. Once the magnitude of the mistake—and the suffering of the civilian population—was apparent (the Japanese did not try to take Changsha until a year later), Chiang ordered a military tribunal and execution of the three top leaders of the police who had actually set the blaze. Zhang Zhizhong, the general in charge—who was also the governor of Hunan, a Whampoa graduate, and a trusted associate of Chiang—escaped explicit blame.[59]

In military terms, it had been an extraordinary ten months. The Chinese military had begun the year 1938 panicky from the loss of Nanjing and Jinan. Ten months later, the mood was different. Yes, the sacrifice and destruction had been tremendous. But the retreat from Wuhan was orderly. The Japanese were clearly bruised and overextended—with little stomach left for pursuing the Chinese to the west in the near future. The new policy of strategic retreat in the context of a "protracted" war of attrition seemed vindicated.

In November a major military conference was called at Hengyang (south of Changsha). Perhaps Chiang Kai-shek was somewhat humbled by the tragic torching of Changsha. Muted self-criticism of the conduct of the war to date was permitted. Greater attention to guerrilla warfare was endorsed. At the end, Chiang called for a strategic defense of the Nanyue region that included elaborate recruitment, deployment, and training plans. The blueprint was impressive and detailed.[60] But more important was what Chiang did not say. Chiang, Chen Cheng, and General Bai had learned the need to be more aggressive, to counterattack. They also had a better idea of who their most reliable generals were. Overall, the Whampoa graduates had not performed well (Japanese-educated Tang Enbo, who was close to Chiang, was an exception). For the key engagements that lay ahead in 1939 in defense of the Nanyue region, it was agreed that senior "Baoding generation" generals Chen Cheng, Xue Yue, and Luo Zhuoying would be in charge.

Nanchang and Changsha

In the spring and fall of 1939, after a four-month lull, the Chinese and Japanese armies met again in major battles over control of the important southern Yangtze Valley and railway terminus cities of Nanchang and Changsha.[61] The Chinese were no longer playing a defensive game. Both sides were aggressive, making the battles quite different from those of Xuzhou and Wuhan. The battles were characterized by seesawing attacks and counterattacks—with heavy casualties taken by both sides.

The commander of the Nanchang campaign was the Guangzhou general and Baoding graduate Xue Yue. In charge of operations in the field was General Luo Zhuoying, also a Baoding graduate and a close associate of Chen Cheng. Chinese forces, numbering about 230,000 (including guerrillas), were positioned along the southern banks of the Xiu River, north of Nanchang. The battle began on 20 March 1939 with a Japanese assault across the river under General Okamura Yasuji, an attack that opened with the use of heavy cannon, poison gas, and massive firepower from four air wings, followed by ground troops. Resistance was strong, but Nanchang, the capital of Jiangxi Province, fell on 27 March after fierce house-to-house combat and destruction of most of the city. Out of the chaos hundreds of thousands refugees fled south.[62]

This time, however, the Chinese leadership, although humiliated, did not concede defeat. A well-organized counterattack began in early April, with the Chinese aiming to recover Nanchang from the southwest. At this point, Luo Zhuoying, more than Xue Yue, seemed to be in charge. By 26 April the Chinese occupied the Nanchang airport (a key strategic point).

The stunned Japanese then brought in reinforcements, plus air strikes and the use of gas units. The Chinese counterattacks continued with human wave tactics and high casualties. Then the Chinese began to falter. Chiang Kai-shek's order on 1 May was "Capture Nanchang! If this goal is not accomplished, all commanders above the rank of brigadier will be punished." The counterattack resumed, producing heavy house-to-house fighting. At the point when the Chinese seemed to be on the verge of prevailing, tragedy struck. On 8 May two generals fell—both division commanders— one dead (Chen Anbao) and the other (Liu Yujing) seriously wounded. This event seemed suddenly to have broken the spirit of the Chinese troops who stopped dead in their tracks and began retreating. On the next day, 9 May, a doubtless much chagrined Chiang consented to the withdrawal of the badly battered but nearly victorious Chinese army.[63] What exactly happened on 8–9 May and why the Chinese withdrew when so close to victory remains a mystery. Nanchang stayed in Japanese hands the rest of the war, and its occupation cut the province of Jiangxi in half. Still, the counterattacks by the Chinese had been a costly and unpleasant surprise. The Japanese would not venture south again until the Ichigō campaign of 1944.

In early August 1939, the Japanese launched an attack on Changsha, an important city of a half million, the capital of Hunan province, and the gateway to the Nanyue region to the west. In the end, General Okamura Yasuji's force of 120,000 faced the full force of the Ninth War Zone army of 365,000 men under General Chen Cheng. As it unfolded, the battle was on a larger scale than the Nanchang encounter. The height of the fighting was from mid-September to mid-October, when the Japanese finally retreated to their starting positions to the north and east. The Chinese turned back the Japanese with well-timed human wave attacks and expert tactical moves executed by General Chen Cheng. Battles were fought simultaneously on three fronts: (1) to the east, one hundred miles from Changsha along the upper reaches of the Xiu River in northern Jiangsu; (2) in the rough no-man's-land of northeastern Hunan; and (3) due north up and down the Changsha–Yizhou portion of the Changsha–Wuhan rail line. The victory on the last front was the most satisfying and decisive. Chen Cheng masterfully lured Japanese divisions south to the outskirts of Changsha and then suddenly struck from all sides with a large body of troops. The Japanese escaped the trap, but not before taking large losses in men and equipment.[64]

Yichang

Heady, perhaps, from the defense of Changsha, at a second Hengyang conference the Chinese began planning a summer 1940 offensive using the combined Fifth and Ninth War Zone armies to counterattack in the Wuhan area. Anticipating such a move, the leadership of the Japanese Central China Expeditionary Army (Eleventh Army) in Nanjing, with the consent of Tokyo and the promise of reinforcements, decided to launch a preemptive strike in May 1940, which was aimed at the capture of the riverine port of Yichang. Control of Yichang would cut communications and supplies between Sichuan and the wartime capital of Chongqing, provide a forward air base for bombing, and separate the Chinese Fifth and Ninth War Zone armies. As Tobe Ryōichi in chapter 8 ably recounts the essential facts of the campaign and its two phases, those facts need not be repeated here. In the battle for Yichang, the Japanese Eleventh Army under Sonobe Waichirō faced divisions of the Fifth War Zone army under Li Zongren, probably 300,000 men in total. The heaviest fighting, and the most painful for the Chinese side, occurred in the first phase, from 1 May to 21 May, in the Dahong mountain range between Suixian and Zaoyang (see map). General Zhang Zizhong, hero of Taierzhuang, refused to retreat. On 16 May he was surrounded while personally commanding two regiments in the foothills of the Dahong mountains. After an eight-hour battle, he died in a hail of machine gun fire—in the history of the war, the only senior Chinese commander to die in combat.[65]

The Japanese launched the second phase of the campaign on 31 May with a surprise crossing of the Han River and quick thrusts directly west toward Yichang. By 6 June Jingmen had fallen and the fate of Yichang was a forgone conclusion, despite desperate calls for its defense to the last man by Chen Cheng and Chiang Kai-shek. Yichang was captured initially on 12 June. There was confusion among Japanese commanders as to whether they had orders to stay or not. The strategically important city was reoccupied on 16 June and remained in Japanese hands for most of the rest of the war.

The loss of Yichang proved a devastating blow to Chongqing, as the high command around Chiang Kai-shek recognized at the time. Besides the tremendous losses in men and equipment, the campaign had seriously weakened the Fifth War Zone army and isolated it from the Ninth War Zone army, which remained bivouacked and rebuilding in the Changsha area (and out of action from 1939 to 1941). But the Japanese were likewise exhausted. Defeat at Nomonhan in Mongolia and the rapid pace of events in Europe (Paris fell 12 June) turned Tokyo toward a less aggressive stance in China and guarded optimism about secret negotiations with Chiang Kai-shek (the capture of Yichang was thought to pressure him in this direction). The net beneficiaries were probably the Communist-led guerrilla units in the central Yangtze hinterland. The occupation of Wuhan and Yichang isolated Chongqing and overextended Japanese forces (which were also reduced in number by late 1940). In the foothills, from

Shanghai to Yichang, pockets of guerrilla resistance activity were left free to fester and expand. This concerned both the Japanese and Chiang Kai-shek (hence the New Fourth Army Incident of 1941, described in chapter 12). Clearly the fall of Yichang signaled that the war in China had reached an entirely new stage.[66]

Conclusion

Over ten months in 1938, and again at Nanchang and Changsha in 1939, the Chinese army won the grudging respect of surprised foreign observers as well as their Japanese adversaries. Until then leadership and the will to stand and fight had been haphazard. But there was enough of it—especially at Xuzhou in April and near Wuhan in August and September of 1938—to slow down the Japanese onslaught that a year earlier seemed unstoppable. Foreign military advisers and observers pointed repeatedly to the lack of a disciplined, simple chain of command that seems almost a prerequisite for conduct of a modern war. Given the political context and immediate history of the Chinese military, the chain of command was admittedly loose, but also there was much more willingness to compromise and coordinate deployment of troops. Chiang Kai-shek issued elaborate plans and almost daily instructions to commanders, but his control of what was going on in the field was inconsistent. When Chiang did intervene and was listened to, the results were often disastrous. A classic example was the unnecessary, premature torching of Changsha in late November 1938 by the Chiang loyalist (Whampoa graduate) and governor of Hunan, Zhang Zhizhong. In a different way, the decision in June 1938 to blow the dikes on the Yellow River at Huayuankou was also a case in point.

After the fall of Wuhan there was a four-month complete lull in the fighting. Then, in the spring and fall of 1939, the inconclusive battles over Nanchang and Changsha were fought. With the disappointing fall of Yichang and the tremendous sacrifice of men and arms its defense entailed, the counterattacking tactics adopted at Hengyang in November 1938 were tabled. With the capture of Yichang the Japanese had cut off the supply route to Chongqing from the east and separated the Ninth and Fifth War Zone armies. Thereafter, until the Ichigō campaign of 1944, reduced levels of combat in the central and western Yangtze Valley continued for most of the rest of the war. In terms of the history of the war as a whole, after Wuhan, the struggle clearly entered a new "war of attrition" phase.

This takes us back to the question asked at the outset: why was Wuhan, and later Changsha, able to hold out for so long? The often-overlooked factor lay with the generals in the field and their success in continuing to motivate their men and maintain a semicoordinated defense. Surprisingly, this coordination was the result of successful communication between divisional commanders who were either strangers or former rivals of one another in the warlord politics of the 1920s. There were cliques among generals: Whampoa, Guangzhou, Sichuan, Guangxi, Feng Yuxiang associates, and so on. Strong personal enmities continued, between Chen Cheng and He Yingqin or Li Zongren and Hu Zongnan, for example. Nevertheless, the decision to execute Han Fuju seemed to have clarified the minds of these ex-militarists, and it brought them together. Overcoming distrust and enmity from the past, they recognized the seriousness of the common threat. The generals were stirred patriotically, as they had been during the Northern Expedition of 1925–1927, and were willing to unite again behind Chiang Kai-shek.

The chemistry behind the 1938 alliance of generals around Chiang Kai-shek, however, was different from 1926–1927 in the sense that Chiang functioned more as a symbolic leader of the defense of Xuzhou and Wuhan than as a field commander. Personal loyalty to Chiang Kai-shek was not what brought the generals together. For many of the senior commanders, the Baoding connection was important—their shared training and camaraderie of experience. This connection was one of the reasons Ye Ting was acceptable as commander of the Communist-dominated New Fourth Army that was being created as a guerrilla force during the summer of 1938 and would number 30,000 men by 1940. The big dividing line between generals was Whampoa versus Baoding, a difference that was both professional and generational. At Whampoa political education and party discipline along Leninist lines were stressed, whereas at Baoding the training was professionally focused (around German and Japanese models), nonpolitical, and Confucian in the sense that personal loyalty was stressed. Conflict between generations of commanders surfaced in the heat of battle and reached the point at times where senior Baoding generation officers like Li Zongren and Xue Yue threatened the life of younger Whampoa era graduates such as Tang Enbo or Yu Jishi to get them to fight and not retreat prematurely. Yet the personal loyalty to field commanders of the common soldier remained high—especially after the victories at Taierzhuang and Linyi, and later the defense of Changsha in 1939. Despite the heaviest casualties of the war, the Chinese army had a desertion rate in 1938–1939 among ordinary soldiers that was surprisingly low.

Finally, there was the political fallout from the losing battle for Wuhan and the central Yangtze Valley: the defection in late 1938 of prominent civilian politicians, Wang Jingwei, Zhou Fohai, Tao Xisheng, Chen Gongbo, and others. The bombing and loss of Wuhan, Guangzhou, and later Yichang, plus the tremendous carnage and destruction that went with it, produced, on the one hand, an attitude favoring accommodation with the Japanese by civilian political figures. On the other hand, among professional military leaders, confidence was building in the ability to resist the Japanese on the battlefield and in the ultimate success of a war of attrition strategy. It is significant that no military figures of note joined Wang Jingwei's government—although the Japanese certainly tried to contact those Chinese leaders with Japanese educational backgrounds (like Tang Enbo, Zhang Zizhong, Jiang Baili, He Yingqin, and others).

What controlled the defense of the central Yangtze in 1938–1940 in a political sense was a two-headed military oligarchy under Chiang Kaishek. One group consisted of able commanders, Baoding-generation figures like Zhang Fakui, Xue Yue, Bai Chongxi, Li Zongren, Chen Cheng, and Ye Ting, who were treated as heroes in the streets of Wuhan and later Chongqing. The other wing were those with less field experience who were intensely loyal to Chiang Kai-shek. Many, like Hu Zongnan, He Yingqin, Yu Jishi, and Zhang Zhizhong, were Whampoa graduates. Their performance or ability as battlefield commanders was less impressive. A workable alliance of this hydra-headed military oligarchy of senior commanders who lined up behind Chiang Kai-shek seemed to last at least through 1940.

As for Chiang himself, although his judgments as a field commander were questionable, he did prove himself in the Xuzhou, Wuhan, Nanchang, and Changsha campaigns by injecting himself directly into every twist and turn of the battles. He showed personal courage by flying to Xuzhou, Zhengzhou, Madang, Xinyang, and Changsha on the eve of a battle to appear to take command. In the end, he was the last to fly out of Wuhan on 24 October, just before the Japanese arrived. Chiang understood that his continuing physical presence was symbolically important, and his colleagues appreciated this. As for tactics, he issued contradictory orders, and therefore they were sometimes selectively disregarded. But in strategic terms, he negotiated with the oligarchs of the senior command structure the careful placement of division commanders and their troops in ways that made political and military sense. In short, the central Yangtze campaigns turned Chiang into a more determined and effective leader. His leadership was further enhanced by the defection of Wang Jingwei and others at the end of 1938. The key to Chiang's effectiveness over the 1938–1940 period was his skillful role as the symbolic leader of the diverse military oligarchy of senior commanders that was rallying around him.

8 The Japanese Eleventh Army in Central China, 1938–1941

TOBE RYŌICHI

Introduction

The Eleventh Army of the Imperial Japanese Army (IJA) was organized in July 1938. Stationed in central China, this unit participated, immediately after its formation, as the main force in the Battle of Wuhan during the summer and fall of 1938. Later, it was designated as an "operational force" with the mission to "frustrate the enemy's intention to resist Japan by attacking their swarming forces at opportune moments."[1] This paper focuses on the Eleventh Army to analyze the IJA's operations in central China.

A study of the Eleventh Army and its actions is a particularly good way to come to grips with the Imperial Japanese Army's operations. First, when viewed from the perspective of military strategy, the Battle of Wuhan was a key turning point in the Sino-Japanese War.[2] The Eleventh Army was organized specifically for this operation and saw the bulk of the fighting throughout the campaign. The Second Army also participated in the *Bukan sakusen*, as the drive on Wuhan is known in Japan, but its role was secondary. It was absorbed into Eleventh Army after the end of the operation.

Second, after the Battle of Wuhan the Eleventh Army became Japan's only army-echelon-size formation in China tasked with breaking Nationalist resistance. The Eleventh Army usually consisted of more than seven divisions with around 200,000 men. It was the only strategic corps-size force with the capability of making deep penetrations into Nationalist territories.

Third, the Eleventh Army was the link between military strategy in the field in China and Tokyo's grand strategy. After the autumn of 1938, Japan turned to political and diplomatic measures as the principal means to conclude the war. The task of the Eleventh Army was to undertake military operations in support of these measures. A good example was the Yichang operation of early summer 1940, which I will examine below.

In the following sections, focus is on the Eleventh Army during several key stages in the conflict with China: the Battle of Wuhan, the Imperial Japanese Army's three operations in 1939, the Chinese winter offensive in 1939, the Yichang operation, and, finally, the Eleventh Army's operations on the eve of the Pacific War.[3] My conclusion argues that the Eleventh Army was not able to achieve its principal aim of compelling the Chinese Nationalists to submit because Tokyo never made sufficient force available, and therefore the unit's operations had to be limited in scope.

The Battle of Wuhan

The IJA captured Nanjing in December 1937. The fall of the enemy's capital did not result in China's collapse, so the Japanese were compelled to continue with a war they had hoped to bring to an end quickly. To make matters worse, Japan was pressed for military resources and had its hands full just supplying weapons and ammunition both to the existing divisions and to the new divisions mobilized for the China war. Faced with these circumstances, Imperial General Headquarters (IGHQ) adopted a policy of nonexpansion in February 1938. This implied that the IJA would not undertake any new offensives until the summer, when newly mobilized divisions were expected to be combat ready. It was decided that, until then, Japan should concentrate its efforts on securing the occupied areas and forming a new central government in China. Major General Hashimoto Gun, director of the Operations Section of the Army General Staff from March 1938 to mid-September 1939, thought that the IJA would have to devote all its efforts to consolidating its strength in 1938 and would not be ready for new major operations until 1939.[4]

But the nonexpansion policy was soon withdrawn, as the North China Area Army (NCAA) continued its pursuit of the Chinese forces threatening the occupied areas in central China and insisted on expanding its area of operations. Colonel Inada Masazumi was appointed chief of the Operations Section of the Army General Staff in March 1938, though Hashimoto's subordinate approved the expansion. Inada sought to bypass IGHQ and Hashimoto by following NCAA policy to take appropriate measures if the local situation warranted it. He was not willing to halt all action while awaiting future developments.[5]

Taierzhuang and Chinese Claims of Victory

The Second Army of the NCAA moved southward along the Tianjin–Pukou Railway to pursue Chinese forces in China's Fifth War Zone in north China. By late that month, a portion of the Tenth Division, the Setani Detachment, advanced to Taierzhuang, northeast of Xuzhou.[6] The Chinese Second Army Group defended Taierzhuang and, reinforced by the Twentieth Corps, counterattacked. The Setani Detachment was soon involved in a bitter fight, so the Sakamoto Detachment was dispatched from the Fifth Division to reinforce the beleagured unit. During the fierce combat, communications between the two Japanese forces broke down. The Setani Detachment mistook its counterpart's movements as a retreat and withdrew from the battlefield. The Sakamoto Detachment then decided to retreat as well.

Even if the Japanese withdrawal was the result of a communications failure rather than enemy pressure, it nonetheless was Japan's first major retreat in the war. Although the Japanese soldiers did not feel that they were defeated at Taierzhuang,[7] their casualties were high, and the battle was a definite setback. The Chinese took full advantage of this event and proclaimed the Japanese withdrawal a great victory. Chinese propaganda asserted that the Japanese forces were annihilated. Although the Chinese exaggerated the damage inflicted on the Japanese, it is true that this "victory" greatly enhanced Chinese morale.[8]

Xuzhou and the Yellow River Dikes

A further result of the battle was to make clear to the IJA that large Chinese forces had concentrated at Xuzhou, a strategically important junction of the Tianjin–Pukou and the Longhai railways. In early April IGHQ ordered both the NCAA and the Central China Expeditionary Army (CCEA) to "destroy the enemy around Xuzhou." The Japanese captured Xuzhou in mid-May but could not achieve the objective of "destroying the enemy." The eight Japanese divisions committed to the operation tried to envelop the fifty Chinese divisions at Xuzhou, but they lacked sufficient force. Most Chinese units were able to retreat through the many gaps in the Japanese encirclement. The NCAA pursued the Chinese forces westward toward Zhengzhou, the junction of the Longhai and Peking–Hankou railways, in violation of IGHQ policy set forth earlier in the year. At this point, Chinese Generalissimo Chiang Kai-shek brought the Japanese to a halt by breaking the dikes of the Yellow River and flooding the countryside.

The Xuzhou operation did not contribute to a settlement of the war. It was less the "Battle of Xuzhou" than an advance toward Zhengzhou, threatening an immediate advance south toward Wuhan, that led Chiang Kai-shek to take the drastic action of breaking the dikes of the Yellow River. Chiang claimed that he had concentrated forces at Xuzhou and sought to engage the Japanese there in order to allow the defenses of Hankou to be put in readiness.[9] It was after the quick collapse of the Xuzhou front and the equally rapid Japanese advance toward Zhengzhou that Chiang decided to flood the north China plain, which did indeed delay the Japanese advance toward Wuhan, although it also spelled misery for a large number of Chinese civilians.

Wuhan Becomes the Next Objective

Hankou was the last major city in north China along the Yangtze River that remained under Chinese control. It was the largest of the tri-cities of Wuhan at the junction of the Han and Yangtze rivers. The other cities were Wuchang, where Chiang's general headquarters were located at that time, and Hanyang, an industrial city. Hankou was a political, economic, and military center, as well as a key railway and river junction. IGHQ had studied operations against Wuhan and Guangzhou since the fall of Nanjing. The Intelligence Division of the Army General Staff estimated that the capture of Wuhan, especially if combined with the seizure of Guangzhou in south China, would leave Japan in control of the major parts of China and enable it to conclude the fighting.

The principal objective of the Wuhan operation was to capture strategic points; the secondary goal was to destroy the enemy's forces. According to Japanese plans, Wuhan would not be taken until early September, and military and political pressures would be brought to bear on China in the hope of ending the war. At the same time, because the Yangtze River was a key supply line, it was not believed that an operation against Wuhan could be postponed for long, because the river was navigable for the Japanese navy only during the summer and early fall when its water levels were high.

The Eleventh Army Reorganized

For the attack on Wuhan the Second Army was transferred from the NCAA to the CCEA, and the Eleventh Army was organized under the CCEA. Lieutenant General Okamura Yasuji, a highly regarded China expert, was appointed commander in chief. The army consisted of the Sixth, Ninth, Twenty-seventh, 101st, and 106th divisions and the Namita Detachment (a portion of the Taiwan Composite Brigade). The Sixth and Ninth were standing divisions from the prewar army. As square divisions, each had four infantry regiments and a total numerical strength of about 25,000. The 101st and 106th were reserve divisions organized in wartime. Only the commanders of regiments and battalions in these divisions were on the active list. The rest, both officers and men, were reservists. While the strength of the reserve division was numerically equivalent to that of the standing division, they were inferior in terms of fighting capacity. The Twenty-seventh was a triangular division with three infantry regiments. It grew out of the army expansion and modernization program begun in 1936. While it had fewer troops, it had stronger artillery units and mechanized supply trains, and so had greater mobility. The Twenty-seventh Division was different from the triangular divisions organized after 1939, the so-called guard (garrison or security) divisions, which had poor maneuverability, although they too had fewer troops, in this case about 14,000 in number.

The artillery strength of a reserve division, a guard division, and a Chinese division respectively has been calculated as 62 percent, 44 percent, and 16 percent of the artillery of a standing division.[10] According to one estimate, a single Japanese regiment could match one Chinese division loyal to Chiang Kai-shek (nominally having 12,000 troops but often far fewer, sometimes even less than half that number), and one Japanese battalion could oppose one Chinese division of local warlords.[11] Lieutenant General Sawada Shigeru estimated that one Japanese company could take the offensive against one Chinese division, and one Japanese battalion could defend against an assault by one Chinese division.[12] Another veteran of the China front suggests two Japanese infantry battalions (average strength of 700–800 men each) could take on a Chinese division, and cases where a single battalion did so, usually three battalions (the equivalent of one regiment) were needed to attack and destroy a Chinese division.[13]

The Eleventh and Second armies were tasked to execute the attack on Wuhan. The Eleventh Army, as the main force, was to advance along both banks of the Yangtze River. Its Sixth Division was to go through marshland dotted with lakes along the northern bank. The Namita Detachment and the 106th and 101st divisions were to move over relatively hilly terrain along the southern bank. The Eleventh Army was to engage the Chinese Fifth War Zone forces north of the Yangtze and the Ninth War Zone forces south of the river. The bursting of the Yellow River dikes had rendered the initial plan, in which the Second Army would have advanced along the Huai River, impossible. Instead, it had to advance on a more southerly route along the Dabie Mountains.

Eleventh Army's Initial Moves against Wuhan

In early June, the Sixth Division moved to Luzhou and advanced westward on roads made muddy by rainfall. The division captured Jianshan on 17 June, but then was brought to a halt by the summer heat, which brought flies and mosquitoes: malaria soon took hold among the troops, and 2,000 men were hospitalized. The Namita Detachment moved up the Yangtze River with support of the navy, capturing Anqing in Anhui Province, 180 miles downriver from Wuhan, on 12 June. The Naval Air Force made use of Anqing's air base to support the advance. Following a hard but short fight, the detachment captured the fortress at Matouzhen, thirty miles upriver from Anqing, which had been thought able to block the Japanese for a long period.

After a standstill of more than a month, the Sixth Division finally recovered from malaria and resumed its offensive. It encountered stubborn Chinese resistance west of Taihu, eighteen miles southwest of Qianshan, but captured Huangmei on 2 August. The Chinese leadership, surprised that Huangmei fell sooner than expected, concentrated its forces near Guangji and broke the left dike of the Yangtze. Meanwhile, the Namita Detachment again started its westward movement, advanced under a burning sun, and occupied Jiujiang on 26 July. Just one hundred miles downriver from Wuhan, Jiujiang was the most important river port between Wuhan and Nanjing. Once in control of the city, the Namita Detachment suffered from cholera and could not move for a while.

The 106th Division, following the detachment, pushed into the Lushan area, southwest of Jiujiang, intending to go along the Nanxun (Nansin) Railway toward Nanchang. However, it encountered unexpectedly strong Chinese resistance and suffered a high number of casualties. The division had left Japan without training. The Lushan area was mountainous and without roads, forcing the division to abandon trucks and rely on pack-horses to move supplies. Soldiers had to disassemble their heavy crew-served weapons and carry them on their backs. Logistics were poor, as was medical care. By 9 August one regimental and three battalion commanders had been killed, while one regimental and two battalion commanders had been wounded. More than half of the company and platoon commanders had become casualties. In one extreme case, all the officers of a company were killed, so a noncommissioned officer had to take over command. When active-list officers were killed in a reserve division, its fighting capacity was reduced by half. Some companies lost two-thirds of their troops. "Special smoke" (a euphemism for poison gas) was employed to avoid annihilation. The 101st Division, sent into the Lushan area, found itself in similar circumstances.

While both divisions engaged in severe fighting, IGHQ gave the order for the CCEA to attack Wuhan on 22 August. The military clash with the Soviet Union along the border at Zhanggufeng, which had broken out in late July 1938, had been brought to a conclusion, ending IGHQ fears of Soviet intervention.

The Namita Detachment, still recuperating from cholera, began to move forward and captured Ruichang on 24 August. The Ninth and Twenty-seventh divisions then joined in the westward movement along the southern bank of the Yangtze. The Chinese stoutly resisted the Japanese offensive from strong positions west of Ruichang. The Namita Detachment attacked these positions, but short of ammunition, especially artillery shells, it suffered great damage. The Ninth Division, going south of the detachment, also faced a hard fight against the Chinese in strongholds that used the natural fastness of the terrain and deployed in such a manner that they could counterattack the advancing Japanese from every quarter.

Meanwhile, the Sixth Division, which had stayed in Huangmei for almost a month, left for Guangji. Between Huangmei and Guangji the Dabie Mountains are closest to the Yangtze, creating a defile that the Chinese had fortified to a depth of fifty miles. Guangji fell on 6 September after several days intense fighting. The Sixth Division then faced the task of capturing Tianjiazhen, a fortress, like Matouzhen, dominating the Yangtze. Unless in Japanese hands, the Yangtze could not be used for transport, and the occupation of Wuhan would be impossible without that vital line of supply. Therefore, a detachment was sent south from the Sixth Division over the intervening and roadless hills to assault Tianjiazhen, twelve miles southwest of Guangji. The Imamura Detachment had great difficulty capturing the enemy's positions. It ran short of ammunition and had to resort to assaults with grenades, swords, and bayonets to finally capture the fortress on 29 September. Casualties among the Thirteenth Infantry Regiment, the main force of the Imamura Detachment, numbered more than 1,000, about a third of its strength, including four-fifths of its platoon commanders and two-thirds of its company commanders.[14] Meanwhile, the main elements of the Sixth Division at Guangji also found themselves under heavy Chinese counterattacks.

Japanese Operations Supporting
the Main Assault Damage Chinese Morale

While the Eleventh Army in central China battered its way westward, the Twenty-first Army landed at Bias Bay near Guangzhou on 12 October. The Guangzhou operation was carried out simultaneously with the assault on Wuhan. Guangzhou fell on 21 October, earlier than Hankou. Chiang Kai-shek was shocked by the Japanese success of the Bias Bay landing.[15] On the same day, the Second Army occupied Xinyang, a strategic point on the Peking–Hankou Railway one hundred miles to the north of Wuhan. The defending Chinese Fifth War Zone forces undertook a sudden withdrawal. It would seem that the success of the landing near Guangzhou and the fall of Xinyang turned the tide of the campaign. The Chinese will to fight appeared to weaken as they began withdrawing from Wuhan.[16] If anything sapped morale on the Chinese side, it would have been the early surrender of Matouzhen and then the fall of Tianjiazhen. It appears that the fall of Guangzhou was long expected. That Chinese forces withdrew from Wuhan rather than defend it to the death was justified as averting another calamity and preserving forces.

On 25 October, the Sixth Division entered Wuhan. The Namita Detachment reached Wuchang on 26 October and captured Hanyang the next day. On 3 November, the birthday of the Meiji emperor, a triumphal entry ceremony was held in Hankou. The CCEA tried to avoid repetition of "unlawful acts" that had taken place in Nanjing, and it exercised strict control over the Japanese soldiers so as not to offend Chinese and foreign residents. The Battle of Wuhan came to an end when Yueyang, at the northern exit of Dongting Lake, eighty-five miles north of Changsha, was captured and the Yuehan (Wuhan–Guangzhou) Railway was cut on 11 November.

The Eleventh Army had won a major victory, but Japan was unable to attain its strategic purpose of forcing the Chinese to surrender. Military historian Kojima Noboru has written that the Eleventh Army could have attained a strategically more significant result had priority been given to the annihilation of enemy forces rather than the capture of Wuhan. He has implied that the Japanese main forces should have pursued the Chinese forces withdrawing toward Changsha from Wuhan.[17] However, such a course would not have allowed the Eleventh Army to make use of the Yangtze River as a supply line.[18] The primary objective of the operation, as set by IGHQ, was the capture of Wuhan, and this goal was achieved.

General Okamura observed after the war that the Japanese forces during the Battle of Wuhan had to fight three strong enemies: the Chinese forces, the terrain, and the heat.[19] The Chinese forces were numerically superior, not only overall but also in each battle. The Chinese Fifth and Ninth War Zones deployed 120 divisions with between 500,000 and 1 million troops. On many battlefields, the Chinese were often more than ten times as numerous as the Japanese forces.

The terrain was unsuitable for the IJA, and Chinese actions such as the flooding of wide swaths of land and the destruction of the roads diminished Japanese advantages in mobile warfare. The Chinese forced Japanese units to engage in battles in mountains with no roads. Japanese troops had to adapt to the situation on the spot, sometimes exchanging modern wagon transportation for horse carts or pack animals. Even these had to be abandoned at times. The summer heat in the Yangtze Valley was severe. Temperatures could reach as high as 105 degrees Fahrenheit. The blazing sun and the high humidity exhausted marching Japanese soldiers and accelerated the spread of diseases such as malaria and cholera.

The Japanese losses during the Battle of Wuhan were unexpectedly high. For example, in the case of the Ninth Division, 1,102 men (including

48 officers) were killed in battle and 2,895 men (including 145 officers) wounded. The division reported that it counted 36,895 Chinese abandoned corpses and took 1,487 prisoners of war (POWs).[20] The Ninth Division, facing a relatively less difficult situation, nonetheless also suffered severe losses. The Namita Detachment's casualties were 733 killed and 2,322 wounded, a third of its original strength. As for the Eleventh Army as whole, 4,567 were killed (including 172 officers), and 17,380 wounded (including 526 officers), compared to the Chinese reported loss of 143,493 abandoned corpses and 9,581 POWs.[21]

Why were the Eleventh Army's casualties so high? To the reasons advanced by General Okamura, one more may be added: high Chinese morale. The Chinese forces fought with far greater determination than expected, though at the end of the campaign they decided to retreat rather defend Wuhan to the last man.

The Policy of Peace and Order First

After Wuhan, Japan attempted to end the war by political rather than military means. IGHQ estimated that neither further offensives nor the capture of other strategic points would inflict enough serious damage to force China to surrender, and such undertakings were not worth the huge effort that would be required. IGHQ concluded that the best way forward was to nurture a new central government for China and thus isolate Chiang Kai-shek politically.[22] An IJA policy document stated,

One stage of the war ended with the Hankou and Guangzhou operations. We should now give priority to restoring peace and order in occupied areas. Efforts to destroy remaining anti-Japanese forces will be continued, but mainly by political means. The expansion of occupied area should be avoided unless imperative for security reasons. Existing occupied areas will be divided into "areas of peace and order," where we aim at maintaining stability, and "areas of operation," where we intend to destroy enemy forces. Only Wuhan and Guangzhou are "areas of operation." We will use these areas as bases for destroying the anti-Japanese forces at opportune moments if Chinese forces are concentrated or preparing for an offensive. However, we have to avoid the unnecessary expansion of battlefields. So the forces deployed there should be kept at minimum.[23]

Based on this policy, IGHQ intended to bring China to its knees by "long-term siege." The CCEA was to operate within a line from Anqing to Xinyang north of the Yangtze River and Yueyang and Nanchang to the south. IGHQ abolished the Second Army, transferring its Third, Thirteenth, and Sixteenth divisions to the Eleventh Army, whose headquarters were relocated to Wuhan. In January 1939, the strength of the Eleventh Army was seven divisions and one independent composite brigade.

The Nanchang Operation

The immediate task of this newly reconstituted Eleventh Army was to carry out limited offensive operations with the objective of preventing the recovery of Chinese forces damaged by the offensive against Wuhan. Eleventh Army planners believed that an operation against the city of Nanchang was well suited to this task. Nanchang, at the mouth of Poyang Lake, was the capital of Jiangxi Province and a critical position for any Chinese counteroffensive. The Chinese air force maintained an air base there. One of the supply lines for foreign materiel to the Nationalists ran from the south China coast through the Nanchang area.

The objective of the Nanchang operation was to cut this line of communication, especially the Chekan Railway leading to Yichang. Originally, the operation had been planned as a part of the Wuhan operation, but it could not be carried out owing to the difficulties encountered by the 106th and 101st divisions in the Lushan area. General Okamura assigned both divisions as the spearhead of the operation, giving them a chance to restore their lost honor and to raise their morale.

At dusk on 20 March 1939, the operation began as the 106th and 101st divisions crossed the Xiu River, which flowed from west to east into Poyang Lake. The largest artillery barrage of the Sino-Japanese War pounded the Chinese on the other side of the river. The 106th Division broke through the Chinese fortified positions and, moving rapidly southward, crossed the Gan River and finally severed the Chekan Railway south of Nanchang on the afternoon of 27 March. The 101st Division, advancing straight toward Nanchang, occupied it on the evening of the same day. Meanwhile, the Sixth Division made a diversionary movement toward Wuning, seventy miles northwest of Nanchang, capturing it on 29 March after tough fighting in the mountains.

In the Nanchang operation the Eleventh Army engaged the Chinese First, Nineteenth, Thirtieth, and Thirty-second army groups, which had a total strength of about 170,000. Japanese killed in action numbered about 500, and those wounded, almost 1,700. The Chinese losses were reported as nearly 24,000 killed and about 8,600 captured. The tactical objective of the operation was achieved, and the 106th and 101st divisions restored their reputations by making rapid assaults against the enemy. But the operation's strategic significance was not great. Rather than forestalling further Chinese action, from late April until early May, the Chinese Thirty-second and Nineteenth army groups attacked the Japanese at Nanchang as a part of their spring offensive, but were driven back.

After the Nanchang operation, the Eleventh Army intended to undertake the east bank of the Xiang River operation, having received intelligence from the CCEA that the Chinese Fifth War Zone command was concentrating huge forces—about thirty divisions—northwest of its front, apparently preparing for an offensive. The Japanese thus planned to carry out a preemptive strike against the Chinese.

The Third Division began a feint near Xinyang on 1 May, and four days later the Sixteenth and Thirteenth divisions moved northward from Anlu, sixty miles northwest of Wuhan, and then turned to the right to drive the Chinese Eighty-fourth and Thirteenth corps to the east of Zaoyang, forty miles northwest of Anlu, seeking to envelop them. Two divisions tightened the encirclement and attacked the Chinese on 10 May. Almost all Chinese forces were driven out of the area east of the Xiang River by the end of the month. The Japanese did not pursue because they withdrew into a region designated as lying beyond the IJA's area of operation. Eleventh Army's casualties in this operation were about 650 killed and almost 1,800 wounded. It counted some 15,000 Chinese killed and took nearly 1,600 prisoners. The Eleventh Army had succeeded in giving the Chinese a severe shock.[24] Yet the final defeat of the Chinese was no closer, and, in fact, Chinese forces soon filtered back into the region.

Changes in Grand Strategic Priorities

At this point, the international strategic situation, as it affected the Sino-Japanese War, changed radically. The Nomonhan Incident, between Japanese and Soviet forces, which occurred in the border area between Manchukuo and Mongolia just after the start of the East of the Xiang River operation, had escalated into a major Russo-Japanese encounter. The Japanese political and military leaders paid more attention to it than to the war with China. But that September the incident ended with a humiliating cease-fire. By that time, World War II had broken out in Europe. IJA leaders sought to end the fighting in China so as to be able to take advantage of these changed circumstances.

One of the means to settle the war seemed to be the establishment of a new central government. The Central China Expeditionary Army was abolished, and the China Expeditionary Army was organized in Nanjing to support the new central government headed by Wang Jingwei and to direct operations as a whole. In Central China, the Thirteenth Army was organized in Shanghai with the task of maintaining peace in the Nanjing-Shanghai area. The Thirty-third and Thirty-fourth divisions were transferred to the Eleventh Army, while the veteran regular Ninth and Sixteenth divisions were removed from its command.

The first mission after these changes was what the IJA called the Gan-Xiang (or Gan and Xiang rivers) operation. The Japanese navy referred to it as the Xiangjiang or Xiang River operation, while Chinese named it the

First Battle of Changsha. The operation was intended to weaken Chinese Ninth War Zone forces south of the Yangtze by putting military and political pressures on Chiang's government, and to frustrate Chongqing's will to continue the war. The Eleventh Army intended to finish the operation quickly and then have its forces return to their barracks. The operation was planned to be carried out in the area between the Gan River in Jiangxi and the Xiang River in Hunan, beyond a line marked out by the IGHQ. The mountainous terrain compelled Japanese forces to use horse-drawn carts and wagons for transportation.

On 15 September the 106th Division marched southward from Fengxin, fifty-five miles west of Nanchang, toward Gao'an, where it enveloped Chinese units. An element of the division went north to Wuning and then southwest to Sandu. Its main force pushed westward into the Jiuling Mountains, where the Chinese took advantage of the hilly terrain and offered stiff resistance. The division returned to its jumping-off point on 9 October.

In the west, the Sixth, Thirty-third, and a part of the Thirteenth divisions started their offensive on 23 September. The Sixth Division, moving from south of Yueyang, crossed the Xinjiang River, seventy-five miles north of Changsha, broke through the Chinese positions on the opposite side of the river, went southward along the Yuehan railway, and finally crossed the Milo River, forty-five miles north of Changsha. The Thirty-third Division also went southward. A part then turned left, moved to Sandu, and linked up with the 106th Division. All forces began their withdrawal in early October. Although the main forces could have captured Changsha, the Eleventh Army had to adhere to the limits IGHQ had placed on its actions.[25]

In the Gan-Xiang operation the Eleventh Army engaged thirty Chinese divisions. About 850 Japanese soldiers were killed in combat, and some 2,700 were wounded. It counted nearly 44,000 Chinese killed and took almost 4,000 prisoners. Although the offensive could claim to have accomplished its intended objectives, it appears not to have achieved any strategic results. The Chinese were able to claim that they had driven back the Japanese forces, and it really mattered little to Chinese propaganda whether the Japanese intended to occupy the points they captured.

The Eleventh Army's Assessments

The Eleventh Army's report on the three operations observed that the Chinese fighting capacity had clearly declined. Chinese forces were usually "routed and dispersed" when the Japanese launched raids and pursued them over flat terrain. This tendency was attributed to poor Chinese generalship, the declining quality of Chinese soldiers, and insufficient weapons and ammunitions. But the Chinese will to resist remained as high as before. The fighting capacity of the forces loyal to Chiang Kai-shek was formidable when they were entrenched in fortified positions utilizing advantageous terrain.[26]

After the war, Colonel Miyazaki Shūichi, a staff officer of the Eleventh Army, summarized the situation: "The three operations were not casual ad hoc actions. After the Wuhan campaign, the Chinese forces recovered. The Eleventh Army worried that it might not be able to deal with them in the future if it did not take preemptive action. As mosquito larvae hatch in stagnant puddles, troops become demoralized if they don't fight. Troops have to rest after an operation and work hard in training, but then they must fight again. It was necessary to keep to this cycle after the Hankou operation." According to Miyazaki, the Eleventh Army understood fully that returning to the original positions was tantamount to abandoning the places captured with much effort and sacrifice, and that it might give the Chinese material for propaganda. However, the Eleventh Army would be short of troops if its forces did not return to their original positions.[27] While Miyazaki's observations have much to recommend them, nonetheless a repetitive series of offensives and victories could not bring an end to the war. An end to the war could be achieved only if Chinese forces outside areas of Japanese occupation were destroyed because they supported resistance within these areas. Therefore, according to General Okamura, "Irrespective of the existing policy of 'peace and order first,' we should carry out a major offensive operation on the scale of the Battle of Wuhan with the whole strength of the CEA. We should inflict a devastating blow against Chinese regular forces, above all against the forces loyal to Chiang Kai-shek, and crush their will to resist."[28] Such thinking led the Eleventh Army to contemplate an operation to capture Changsha and Hengyang, to take Yichang, or to seize the whole Peking–Hankou Railway.[29] But Okamura's proposal was not endorsed by the CEA. Indeed, the Chinese struck first, launching their winter offensive in 1939.

The Yichang Operation

In mid-December 1939, the Chinese began a counteroffensive on almost all fronts in north, central, and south China. Nanning, in south China, which the Japanese had just captured, was subjected to a Chinese counteroffensive as well. The Japanese barely held it and were able to beat back the enemy only after having incurred heavy casualties. The Third, Fifth, and Ninth war zones forces—a total of seventy-one divisions, which comprised 80 percent of the whole Chinese army—attacked the Eleventh Army. At that time Eleventh Army had just seven divisions and two independent composite brigades. The Thirty-ninth and Fortieth divisions had come under its command only in October, while the 101st and 106th Divisions had been transferred back to Japan.

Although the Eleventh Army had information about Chinese preparations for a counteroffensive, it had not been overly concerned because the "spring offensive" of the previous year had been a limited operation. General Okamura shared this optimistic assessment.[30] In reality, this time the winter offensive was a major operation that continued for about forty days.

The area occupied by the Eleventh Army was so vast that its units were widely dispersed and could not be deployed in great depth.[31] No forces were held in reserve, and fortifications were poor. Finally, the Eleventh Army had originally been organized for offensive operations and not for defensive duties.

Lieutenant General Sawada Shigeru, vice chief of Army General Staff, was in China from late December until early January on an inspection tour of the central and south China fronts. He reported that the Chinese attacked simultaneously and along entire fronts, thus making it impossible for the Japanese to send forces in relief from places that the Chinese did not attack, as had been possible previously. The Chinese held the initiative during the winter offensive. When it became possible for the Japanese to begin counterattacks, they were not effective.[32] Some military experts argue that the Eleventh Army's defense might have been broken if Chiang Kai-shek had thrown into the attack the large forces in Hunan Province that he had transferred to south China to retake Nanning from the Japanese.[33]

The winter offensive began on 12 December and ended on about 20 January. The Eleventh Army counted some 51,000 Chinese killed and took 987 POWs. Its casualties were 2,141 (including 109 officers) killed and 6,126 (including 225 officers) wounded. These were among its severest losses in the war so far, second only to those it incurred during the Battle of Wuhan. The relatively small number of Chinese prisoners shows that the Chinese held the initiative on the battlefield and that their morale was high. General Okamura Yasuji was shocked: "We have never seen the Chinese army undertake such a large-scale and determined attack." The greatest surprise was that Chinese corps started major attacks simultaneously and continued them for a considerable time. According to the Eleventh Army, this effectiveness showed that the authority of Chiang Kai-shek reached down to the smallest units. Japanese headquarters admitted that "the enemy is still going strong."[34] The Chinese fighting capacity had been restored more quickly than expected. General Sawada was surprised by the new weapons the Chinese had at this time.[35] In view of the winter offensive, the policy of "peace and order first" was considered a failure. At the same time, the CEA could not carry out General Okamura's major strategic offensive, as it lacked the necessary forces.

The Army Rethinks Operations

The IJA had drawn up an expansion and modernization program in 1936 at a time when Soviet Russia was considered the main enemy. In 1938, a new program had been developed, based on the assumption that Japan would engage in a war with Russia while continuing the Sino-Japanese War. The IJA's China operations were so costly that the program could be carried out only if the scale of the fighting in China was reduced. The Military Affairs Bureau of the Army Ministry therefore decided in 1938 to reduce the 850,000 troops in China to 700,000 by the end of 1939, and to 500,000 by the end of 1940.

The plan had two further aims. Rapid mobilization after the outbreak of the war had resulted in a decline in troop quality. In August 1938, almost 90 percent of Japanese soldiers in China were from the IJA's reserves. Hence, force reduction also aimed at improving quality. Some officers in the Army General Staff believed that a partial withdrawal from China and concentration on the consolidation of Japanese control in north China might lead to an end to the war. Fewer troops would be needed if this course of action was adopted.

When the IJA lost the Battle of Nomonhan, IGHQ became even more convinced of the need to implement the new expansion and modernization program. The outbreak of the war in Europe strengthened that conviction further. Although at the IJA leadership level there was a broad consensus in favor of force reduction in China, the CEA itself not only objected to such a reduction but in fact wanted an increase for an operation to crush Chinese resistance. General Sawada, learning about the winter offensive in the course of his inspection of the front, seemed to support the CEA's position.[36]

On 3 May 1940, the IJA leaders decided on a compromise. They allowed a temporary increase of two divisions but insisted that 100,000 troops would be withdrawn from China by the end of 1940. At the end of May, the staffs of the IGHQ visited the headquarters of the CEA in Nanjing. They requested the CEA's consent to this compromise and obtained it on 6 June, just when the Yichang operation was at a critical point. Let me first describe the operations leading up to the initial capture of Yichang and then discuss how divergent opinions in Tokyo and China among Japanese military decision makers led to conflicting orders concerning the occupation of Yichang.

On to Yichang

Yichang, 110 miles upriver from Hankou, is a point of strategic importance. There, the Yangtze flows out of the high mountains on the eastern Sichuan border onto a plain. Large ships could sail upriver to Yichang, where cargo was transshipped to small ships for Chongqing. The capture of Yichang would break this supply line. The question was whether Yichang should be permanently occupied after it was captured. General Okamura favored this course, but the CEA did not in fact have the required forces, nor did it fit into the IJA's policy of force reduction over time. The navy also favored occupation, as it hoped to use the air base at Yichang to bomb Chongqing.

In early March, Lt. Gen. Sonobe Waichirō had replaced Lieutenant General Okamura as commander of the Eleventh Army. An operational plan was decided on a month later. The Eleventh Army would destroy the Chinese Fifth War Zone main forces north of Xiangyang and Suixian east of the Han River, then envelop the Chinese west of the river around Yichang and destroy them. The areas where the offensive would be undertaken were beyond the line set by IGHQ demarking the area of operations. Thus, IGHQ issued new orders that enabled the Eleventh Army to go beyond the line "for a time," which meant capturing Yichang but not occupying it for any length of time.

Meanwhile, it has been alleged that the emperor specifically told the army not to move against Yichang if it could be avoided.[37] The emperor's remark was conveyed to the CEA in late April. Even if true, we do not know what he really meant or how his remark influenced the CEA. Moreover, according to General Sawada, the emperor actually once suggested the capture of Yichang, but his military aide reminded him that the occupation of the city would impose an unbearable burden on the IJA. This same officer has guessed that the navy, hoping to occupy Yichang, influenced the emperor in his suggestion.[38]

The Yichang operation kicked off on 1 May. The Third Division advanced westward from Xinyang, the Thirteenth Division moved northward from Anlu, and the Thirty-ninth Division moved northward from Suixian. The forces' aim was to envelop the Chinese Thirty-first Army Group (commanded by General Tang Enbo) at the bank of the Bai River, which the three Japanese divisions reached on 10 May. But the Chinese escaped from the trap, withdrawing in the belief that, as usual, Japanese forces would retreat once they had achieved their objectives. At this time, the Chinese Thirty-third Army Group, commanded by General Zhang Zizhong, crossed the Han River from west to east. The Japanese Thirteenth and Thirty-ninth divisions began to go southward seeking out General Zhang's forces. General Tang assessed this movement to be the usual Japanese withdrawal and launched an assault on the remaining Third Division. Enveloped by a large force, the Third Division soon exhausted its supplies. The three divisions were able to concentrate near Zaoyang, drawing the Chinese to that location, and attacked them simultaneously on 19 May. The Chinese were routed instantly. The Japanese, considering the limit of their logistics, stopped their pursuit on 21 May.

This action brought the first stage of the operation to an end. The Eleventh Army had fought with forty-seven Chinese divisions. It counted almost 22,000 enemy killed and took some 1,000 POWs. Its casualties were substantial: about 850 killed and nearly 3,000 wounded. General Zhang Zizhong, a graduate of the Japanese Military Academy and a hero of many battles, was killed in a battle with the Thirty-ninth Division. Japanese soldiers buried him with respect.[39]

At this point, a controversy erupted in the Eleventh Army about whether to continue the operation. Some argued for ending it, insisting that the large-scale destruction of enemy forces should be seen as a real success while further campaigning in midsummer heat would exhaust the army's soldiers. Others maintained that the Eleventh Army would lose the confidence of the IGHQ, the CEA, and others if the second stage of the operation and the capture of Yichang was not carried out, and carried out without delay. The expansionists prevailed in the end.[40]

The second stage began on the night of 31 May, when the Third and Thirty-ninth divisions crossed the Han River again. The Third Division captured Xiangyang and moved southward. The Thirty-ninth Division advanced straight to the south. Meanwhile, the Thirteenth Division made a surprise crossing of the river at Shayangzhen, one hundred miles upriver from Hankou. It quickly swept westward, routing the Chinese confronting it. The division captured Yichang on 12 June. But five days later, an order from the Eleventh Army compelled it to begin its withdrawal. The next day, it would once again turn around.

As mentioned earlier, conflicting opinions at different levels of the military command led to these contradictory orders. The German attack on Western Europe beginning on 10 May convinced some, such as General Sawada, that an opportunity now existed to break the deadlock in China by delivering a serious blow against the Nationalists.[41] A complicating factor was that secret negotiations between the Nationalists and the Japanese convinced some Japanese that a major attack now, especially when Germany was defeating all before it, would convince Chiang that any further resistance was hopeless. Within the Eleventh Army, however, many worried that not enough forces were available for a durable occupation. Only on 16 June did IGHQ reach the decision that Yichang should be occupied. It was then that the Thirteenth Division was ordered to turn around once more and occupy Yichang.

During the Yichang operation, the Eleventh Army's casualties were 1,403 (including 106 officers) killed and 4,639 (including 203 officers) wounded. It counted 63,127 Chinese killed and took 4,797 POWs. Although the operation weakened the Chinese Fifth War Zone, its scale and effects were not so different from the three operations in 1939. It was not the strategic offensive that General Okamura had proposed, and it had little effect on frustrating the Chinese will to resist.

It is said that the occupation of Yichang put the heaviest pressure of the war on Chongqing.[42] The occupation and the intensified bombing of Chongqing, it is also said, rendered Chinese resistance more difficult.[43] However, the political objective of the occupation was not achieved. When the Eleventh Army was ordered to occupy Yichang, it obeyed, concluding that "In view of the drastic changes in the international situation, it is of vital importance to secure the area west of the Han River permanently and maintain a firm basis for promoting our political strategy of consolidating the Wang Jingwei government."[44] The Eleventh Army understood that it occupied Yichang for political purposes. But its hope that, combined with the altered conditions in Europe, the occupation of Yichang would force the Nationalists to submit proved too optimistic.

"Cut Short" Operations

The permanent occupation of Yichang would prove only a short change in policy. Afterward, IJA policy returned to the policy of "peace and order first." Because of the German victories over France and the Netherlands, and because Britain had to concentrate on its own defense, European colonies in Asia became vulnerable as Japan turned its attention to Southeast Asia. The IJA moved into northern French Indochina. Major Imoto, transferred in October from the CEA to the Operations Section of the Army General Staff, found only one map of China on the wall of the staff room. All others were maps of Southeast Asia.[45] A Japanese offensive in Southeast Asia meant that the IJA's efforts in China would have to be drastically curtailed. In January 1941, it decided that the primary aim in China was to maintain peace and order in occupied areas. No more large-scale offensives were to be carried out. Instead, it would carry out "cut short" operations, as occasion demanded.[46] Blockades, consolidation, air offensives, and enemy attrition were the main ingredients of the new strategy.[47]

The Eleventh Army's first major action after the Yichang operation was the Han River operation. When Chiang Kai-shek ordered the Communist New Fourth Army to move to north China, General Tang Enbo's Thirty-first Army Group went north to put pressure on it. Misunderstanding, the Eleventh Army interpreted the move as part of preparation for a general counteroffensive and decided to forestall it. At that time, the Fourth Division (guard division) had been transferred from Manchuria to the Eleventh Army, and the Seventeenth Division (reserve division) was temporarily transferred to it from the Thirteenth Army.

The Han River operation began on 24 November 1940. The Third and Fourth divisions to the east of the Han River and the Seventeenth and Thirty-ninth divisions to the west of the river intended to catch and destroy opposing Chinese forces. But the Chinese, adopting their usual strategy of retreat, withdrew. So the Japanese soon reached their objectives, and also as usual, began to withdraw to march back to their original positions. The operation ended on 2 December. The Eleventh Army engaged with a portion of the Chinese Fifth War Zone forces and counted 6,349 abandoned corpses, and took 474 POWs. Its losses were 132 killed and 445 wounded. The operation lasted for only one week. Some soldiers welcomed this operation, as after Yichang they had suffered from a lack of supplies and had been harassed by guerrillas.[48] By putting soldiers back into action, the operation was useful for lifting morale.

Then the Eleventh Army began the Yunan operation. The objective was to destroy the Chinese Thirty-first Army Group, which was located in the Yunan plains north of Xinyang. The operation began during the night of 24 January 1941 when the Fortieth Division on the right, the Seventeenth Division in the center, and the Third Division on the left advanced north along the Peking–Hankou Railway. The forces campaigned in the depth of winter. The Chinese again simply withdrew before the Japanese advance. The Chinese Second Army Group advanced from Xiangyang to rescue the Thirty-first Army Group but was driven away by the Third and Seventeenth Divisions. In early February, the Japanese decided that they had achieved the objective and once more pulled back. The operation ended on 12 February. According to Japanese military sources at the time, the Chinese suffered 16,000 casualties, while Japanese losses were slight.[49]

In this stage of the war, even the Eleventh Army as the "operational force" had to guard wide areas and disperse its units. Therefore, when it carried out an operation, it had difficulties in deploying a standard division or regiment. The operation's Fortieth Division consisted of four of its own battalions, one from the Thirteenth Division, one from the Thirty-ninth Division, and two from the Thirty-fourth Division.[50]

In March, the Eleventh Army carried out the Jin River operation south of the Yangtze. At this time, the Thirty-third Division was to be transferred to the NCAA. So the Eleventh Army planned to deliver a blow against the opposing Nineteenth Army Group of the Ninth War Zone to ensure a safe removal. The operation began before dawn on 15 March. The Thirty-third Division started from Anyi, twenty-five miles northwest of Nanchang, moved south, and after two weeks turned around. The Thirty-fourth Division moved from the south of the Thirty-third Division to the west, captured Gao'an, and then advanced toward Shanggao, sixty-five miles south of Nanchang, where the Nineteenth Army Group's headquarters were located. This operation was not so much a "cut short" offensive as a common procedure at the time, an attack in order to prepare for a troop transfer. When it approached Shanggao, the Thirty-fourth Division encountered a strong Chinese counterattack and was confronted with a critical situation. The Thirty-third Division was sent to rescue it and help it withdraw. Both divisions retreated but encountered other Chinese forces and found themselves encircled. After intense fighting, they broke through and managed to return to safety on 2 April. The Chinese Nationalists naturally exploited the opportunity to proclaim that they had scored a major victory. The Japanese casualties were almost 15,000.[51]

In May, the Eleventh Army started the North of the Yangtze (Jiangbei) operation. Its objective was to act in concert with the NCAA's Central Plains (Zhongyuan) operation to destroy the Chinese Twenty-second Army Group in an action that was planned to last seven to ten days.

On 6 May, the Third Division moved northward from Yingshan, thirty miles south of Xinyang, pursued the Chinese retreating to Zaoyang, fiercely attacked hard, and then broke off the engagement, returning to their barracks on 22 May. The Fourth and Thirty-ninth divisions began to move on 8 May, advanced respectively to the north of Anlu and Jingmen, fifty miles northeast of Yichang, and returned to base on 15 May. Once Japanese forces withdrew, the Chinese returned, so no substantial change occurred in the situation.[52] The losses the Eleventh Army suffered were 115 killed and 375 wounded.

The Changsha Operation

At this time the Eleventh Army had seven divisions and three independent composite brigades. Its total strength was about 230,000. About 36 percent of its officers and 49 percent of its rank and file were on the active list.[53] In April 1941 Lieutenant General Anami Korechika, former vice minister of the army, replaced Lieutenant General Sonobe as commander of the Eleventh Army. General Anami was a believer in the idea that a knockout blow was necessary to force Chiang Kai-shek to surrender. He sought to deliver the knockout by attacking Changsha, where the Ninth War Zone's headquarters were located. The German attack on the Soviet Union led the IJA to concentrate forces in Manchuria in anticipation that Japan would join Germany in its attack. Although the IJA decided against that course of action, the cabinet decision to move into Southeast Asia and begin preparations to enter French Indochina in July strained Japanese military sources. Some staff officers in fact advocated the abandonment of the Changsha operation. They insisted that the IJA had to provide for the war against the United States, Britain, and the Netherlands. In the end, IGHQ did give its blessing to the Changsha campaign, but with the proviso that it be kept to a minimum duration. Rather than the hoped for knockout blow, the Changsha operation became nothing more than another "cut short" operation.

On 18 September, the Fourth, Third, Sixth, and Fortieth divisions began a rapid southerly advance from Yueyang. They crushed the crack Seventy-fourth Army and captured Changsha on 28 September, while several units then advanced to Zhuzhou further south. On 1 October, less than two weeks after the beginning of the action, the forces began to withdraw.

Meanwhile, fifteen Chinese divisions of the Sixth War Zone advanced in a great mass to retake Yichang, where Japanese defenses had been weakened because troops had been transferred to the Changsha operation. The units of the Thirteenth Division defending the Yichang area were facing enemy forces twenty or thirty times as large as themselves. When the Chinese attacked in full force on 10 October, the division's situation was so desperate that the staff prepared to burn regimental flags, destroy secret papers, and commit suicide. The Thirty-ninth Division, itself under heavy attack by the Chinese, sent reinforcements to relieve the Thirteenth Division. These combined forces narrowly managed to hold Yichang. The Japanese finished clearing Chinese forces from the Yichang area by 26 October. At Changsha, the Chinese returned once Japanese forces had withdrawn. As before, no significant change in the situation had been brought about.

The Eleventh Army had fought with nearly 500,000 Chinese, counted about 54,000 killed, and took almost 4,300 POWs in this operation. Its losses were 1,670 (including 122 officers) killed and 5,184 (including 272 officers) wounded. It destroyed a main force of the Ninth War Zone and captured Changsha, but higher military authorities did not permit it to occupy the city. Once again, the Chinese could claim in their propaganda that they had scored great successes by preventing the occupation of Changsha and almost evicting the Japanese from Yichang.

From this time on, the coming Pacific War occupied most of the Japanese attention. The IJA leadership thought, as General Sawada had stated before, that the war with China could not be settled by battles there but required war with the Western powers. In September 1941, Lieutenant General Ushiroku Jun, chief of staff of the CEA, went from Nanjing to Tokyo to argue that it would be easier to overthrow Chiang Kai-shek's regime than to defeat the United States and Great Britain, and that the operation to capture Chongqing should be considered more seriously than advances toward Southeast Asia. However, everyone in Army General Staff turned a deaf ear to his argument.

Conclusion

At a military conference at Liuzhou (Guangxi) convened by Chiang Kai-shek in February 1940, China's wartime leader analyzed the Japanese military. He argued that its strong points were surprise attacks on poorly defended places, firm defense of occupied positions, aggressive offensive, and disguise of intended movements. Japan's weakness, according to Chiang, was that it did not deploy enough forces and did not sustain its operations for long enough. Japanese operations also suffered from the fact that they did not have sufficient reserves.[54]

Remarkably, all the Japanese weak points analyzed by Chiang were related to the limits imposed on force deployment. It has often been pointed out that the Japanese forces were constrained by the limited area they controlled in China. They "controlled only points and lines." The lack of forces also constrained Japanese offensive operations, as is illustrated by the size of the Eleventh Army.

The Eleventh Army did not carry out any operations proportionate to its mission of crushing the Chinese will to resist. The Hankou operation was never repeated. A large-scale strategic advance, as proposed by General Okamura, was not realized. The Yichang operation was not executed as an operation. Indeed, most operations of the Eleventh Army were constrained by its limited troop strength and therefore had no greater aim than preempting Chinese counteroffensives or nipping them in the bud. Even when it captured important points, the Eleventh Army usually had to abandon them and return to its original positions. The Eleventh Army's strength was insufficient both in human and material resources. This deficiency was a major feature of Japanese operations in central China.

A second deficiency was insufficient consideration of strategic objectives. As noted above, the Eleventh Army did not carry out operations capable of accomplishing the objective of crushing the Chinese will to resist. However, limited numerical strength was not the only reason for this. Japan could not bring the war to an end by military means alone. But it does not seem that the Eleventh Army's operations were planned or executed in close coordination with political strategy. When the Yichang operation began, for example, Japanese leaders were conscious that the strategic environment had been altered by the European war and by Nationalist-Japanese negotiations. But the operation was not launched with consideration of such linkages beforehand. In the midst of the operation, its commanders did ponder these developments, but discussions did not go beyond the issue of whether the Eleventh Army should occupy Yichang.

The operations of the Eleventh Army, the only "operational force" in central China, were never sufficiently informed by broader strategic considerations. Most were executed to forestall the enemy's counteroffensives or to keep up army morale. Again and again the operations repeated the pattern of advance followed by retreat after a limited objective had been reached. This pattern was effective neither militarily nor psychologically. When the Eleventh Army's operations had something to do with strategy, ironically they were influenced and constrained by the IJA's strategic concern with areas other than China, namely the USSR or Southeast Asia.

A further point is that the IJA was designed to fight on the battlefields of China. Terrain and climate in central China were very different from those of the war theater where the IJA was supposed to fight, namely the expanses of Manchuria and Siberia. The heat in central China tortured the IJA in the Hankou operation. Diseases such as malaria and cholera inflicted serious losses. General Okamura reported that about 150,000 out of 400,000 troops engaged in the Hankou operation suffered from malaria.[55] Most roads in the war theater were bad, while frequent rainfall turned them into quagmires. The Chinese destroyed the roads repeatedly to obstruct Japanese advances. The IJA had to change modern transport to a long out-of-date one based on packhorses. Mountain guns were more effective than field guns.

Part IV

THE MIDDLE YEARS AND
THE SEARCH FOR MILITARY SOLUTIONS

By the end of 1938, Japanese and Chinese military forces, like two exhausted wrestlers, held each other in check, each seeking some alternative thrust or technique to dislodge the opponent or to weaken his death grip. For the Nationalist Chinese, after the fall of Wuhan in October, it meant avoiding direct confrontation with the advance of the materially superior Japanese army, abandoning the great river valleys of central China, and withdrawing into the mountain fastnesses of Sichuan Province to Chongqing on the Yangtze River. There, in haste, in turmoil, and crowded among a huge number of refugees, the government built up its new capital, remote in distance and circumstance from the polished commercial and industrial treaty port enclaves along the coast where it had emerged and from which it had drawn its strength. From Chongqing, the Nationalist regime would attempt to regroup and carry on the struggle.

The Chinese exodus presented the Japanese armed forces with a new and difficult strategic situation. The Nationalist government, driven from the field but not crushed, was now out of reach of Japanese ground forces, which could no longer force a political settlement, let alone achieve outright victory. The continued existence of a Chinese national government and military meant that the Nationalist cause still remained a focal point for popular support and for foreign military and economic assistance. As Edna Tow's chapter asserts, this new situation radically reshaped the China combat theater from conventional ground campaigns to new means and environments for waging war. The chapters in this section all speak to this reality.

Hagiwara Mitsuru's essay in chapter 9 is focused on the Japanese extended campaign of strategic aerial bombardment to terrorize the civilian populations of the cities in the Chinese interior, most specifically including Chongqing, in order to pressure the Nationalist government into negotiations to end the war. Carried out largely by Japanese land-based bombers, the campaign caused massive damage and huge casualties in the cities but failed to bring about the political outcome that its planners intended—the first of a number of strategic bombing failures that became more familiar in the West during World War II

Edna Tow's essay is the first serious, comprehensive, and analytical English language treatment of China's response to the Japanese aerial campaign, particularly as it concerned the defense of Chongqing. That response, she relates, was manifested in two ways: an active air defense against Japanese

aircraft—air patrols by Chinese fighter aircraft and mobile antiaircraft batteries—and passive civil defense to protect the civilian population: construction of air raid shelters, institution of a host of regulations and procedures to
prepare the populace for impending aerial attacks, public education in civil
defense, and continuous refinement of all these systems. While unable to
prevent horrific losses inflicted on the city, the measures succeeded in keeping the capital's inhabitants in the war and in support of the government.

Outside assistance is often a critical means of survival for a nation
locked in a death struggle with a materially superior enemy. In his essay,
Zhang Baijia traces the three stages of foreign military assistance to China:
German unofficial and commercial assistance from the mid-1930s to the
end of the decade, Soviet aid from 1939 to 1942, and American support
from 1942 to the end of the war.

Of course, foreign military assistance is invariably embedded in the
hard strategic interests of the donor nation more than in nobler motives
of national sympathy and humanitarianism. But in Zhang's perspective,
German aid to China was, while it lasted, important not only in the reconstruction of the Nationalist army prior to the war but in the involvement
of the most disinterested of the three donor nations. Yet, ultimately, it fell
victim to shifting German strategic interests, which deemed Japan a more
valuable ally than China, and thus in 1939, Germany acceded to Japanese
demands that German aid to China be terminated.

As the Germans walked away from China, the Soviets moved in, reestablishing links broken in 1927. If the Russian motives were obvious—bol-
stering China as a means of keeping Japan occupied and away from Russia's eastern borders—Zhang presents a favorable view of the importance,
scale, quality, and reasonable terms of the Soviet aid to China. Remarkably, Zhang informs us, little of this aid made its way into Communist
hands. But, in 1942, with the USSR locked in a life-and-death struggle
with Germany, Soviet strategic interests eventually shifted, and significant
Russian aid came to an end that year.

Some American military assistance had found its way to China even
before the outbreak of the Pacific War, but the Roosevelt administration
greatly increased this aid after 1942, largely, as Zhang sees it, to keep
China in the war and thus to be a drain on Japanese capacities. In taking
up American military assistance to China Zhang enters a subject more
familiar yet poorly understood by Americans. He criticizes the Stilwell
mission as beset by "misunderstandings, insufficient preparations, and
divergent objectives and priorities," but he does so no more severely than
many Western scholars in the decades since. Most Americans will be surprised, however, at Zhang's assertion that "the United States provided
little aid to China" and that that meager amount was supplied under
"procedures that seemed calculated to affront China." Still, Zhang Baijia's

controversial judgments are a useful antidote to the comic strip simplicities and exaggerations that have pervaded the popular imagination about the American wartime role in China.

Chapter 12, by Yang Kuisong, provides an analysis of still another response for a nation overpowered and overrun by a militarily superior enemy: irregular or guerrilla warfare. The Chinese, both Nationalists and Communists, adopted that option early in the conflict. Yang's concerns focus on the question of why, in north China at least, Communist guerilla warfare was classically successful while that of the national government was not. His explanation centers on his assertion that the difference in outcome hinged on the differing relations between insurgent militia and Chinese civilians. He notes that, as north China was largely a rural and agricultural region, to have any prospects for success an insurgency would have to be fully grounded on a peasant base. For their part, Communist militias were indeed largely composed of rural villagers who lived in the locales where Communist units operated. To this extent the countryside provided an almost endless source of recruits.

In contrast, Nationalist guerrilla units were too often a mixed bag of personnel of widely different origins and livelihoods. Many of their officers were former members of the regular army who often had little affinity with the local publics they were supposed to protect. Without close rapport with the local populace, they were unable to replace their losses suffered in the face of superior Japanese firepower and in campaigns of attrition were unable to remain in the field. Yang also notes the Nationalist guerrilla cadres' mind-set, which was too often shaped by their former training and experience with regular army units. Where Communist guerrillas shaped their tactics and techniques to objective conditions on the ground, government-backed insurgents, in contradiction to their roles as guerrilla fighters, too often tended to undertake large-scale assaults, frontal battles, and fixed positions. Against the firepower, organization, and discipline of the Japanese army, these tactics were usually fatal.

But Yang is too thoughtful a historian to trace the evolution of Communist insurgency uncritically. Not only does he recount the Japanese rout of the Communist "Hundred Regiments Offensive" in 1940, he also remarks on the disaster that overtook the Communist New Fourth Army at the hands of the Nationalists in 1941. These were sobering setbacks, and the lessons of defeat had as much to do with the shaping of victorious Communist guerrilla warfare as did their stunning successes.

Chapter 13, the last essay in this section, turns for alternatives to conventional ground warfare—in the air and behind the lines—back to the gritty, bloody ground combat of the common foot soldier. The World War II Japanese soldier's reputation for suicidal "banzai attacks," atrocities, and suicidal kamikaze tactics remains an enduring and powerful image to this day. Kawano Hitoshi's examination of combat motivation among soldiers on the China front contrasts the popular image with the experience of army veterans. Based on a small sample of veterans of the Thirty-seventh Division, a unit whose operations ranged throughout China, Kawano's tentative conclusions offer a different perspective on the Japanese army, at least in the China theater.

Far from fighting and dying only for a sacred emperor or a mythical ideal of Bushido (the way of the warrior), Japanese soldiers, like those in any armed force, forged close personal bonds within their units and sub-units that sustained them in combat and in their army experience. Soldiers adopted various methods to confront the possibility of being killed—resignation, fatalism, indifference, and denial—but Kawano also observes that the army doctrine that death in combat was preferable to the dishonor of surrender reinforced a streak of fatalism in the soldiers' psyches.

The individual accounts of military life and combat service that Kawano narrates offer a variety of reasons for becoming a soldier, from simply resigning oneself to be drafted to upholding a family tradition of military service in the Russo-Japanese War (1904–1905). Peer pressure came not only from fellow soldiers in the unit but also from the conscript's family, neighborhood, and local authorities who joined in rituals and ceremonies, formal and informal, to support and ultimately compel military service. This process of socialization of future soldiers began at an early age and received official emphasis in the school system.

In their recollections, Kawano tells us, veterans stressed the importance of solid training, good weapons, and competent, even caring, leadership by junior officers as essential for their morale. But a number of accounts cited by Kawano point to the foundation of a soldier's morale: the notion of family or village honor. What also becomes clear is a penchant for casual brutality, specifically including the use of Chinese prisoners for live bayonet drills.

From one perspective these responses to shared danger in combat can be seen as universal, a Japanese version of Stephen Ambrose's "band of brothers." But in other ways Kawano's account, in its discussion of peer pressures, treatment of prisoners, and the devotion to death before dishonor, is very Japanese. It is, in any event, a fresh look at soldiers too long stereotyped as mindless robots or insects.

9 The Japanese Air Campaigns in China, 1937–1945

HAGIWARA MITSURU

The Sino-Japanese War of 1937–1945 was the first major conflict in which airpower played a significant role from the beginning of hostilities. It also saw the initiation of long-range over-water strategic bombardment by one side against major urban centers of its enemy.

Despite these radical departures in the use of airpower, there have been few studies in Japan of the Japanese air campaign against China during the war and very little attention to the subject in the West.[1] A number of reasons explain this neglect. First, since there was no independent air force in Japan at the time, accounts of the air campaigns over China have tended to be fragmented between the air services of the Japanese army and navy. Second, since the far greater number of air operations over China were undertaken by the navy, the contributions of the army air force have been slighted. Finally, at the time, any air operations in East Asia seemed irrelevant to the strategic situation in the West, and few Western language translations of Japanese accounts of the air war in China have appeared in the more than half century since.

Force Structures and Doctrines of the Combatants

World War I provided Japan with an opportunity to develop its military aviation capabilities. At the time of the Japanese siege of Qingdao in 1914, the Japanese army deployed a newly formed air unit, and the Japanese navy dispatched a number of seaplanes aboard its seaplane carrier, the *Wakamiya*. The following year the army formed a permanent air squadron, and, in 1916, the navy established its first land-based air group at Yokosuka.

Both services also formed administrative bureaucracies to oversee the development of their arms. In 1919, the army established a special air branch specialty that took charge of its doctrinal and aviation training. In 1925, the branch formed its first air regiments, and the army air arm became a separate branch of the service. In 1936, the Army Aviation Department became a bureau of the Army Ministry, with responsibility for drafting and recommending military aviation doctrine. Until 1936, air regiments came under the nearest ground division, but that year they were placed under the direct control of the newly established Aviation Department. In 1927, the navy created its own Aviation Department, which was placed under the Navy Ministry and made responsible for aviation procurement and training.

As aviation gained a degree of autonomy within the army and the navy, there was agitation within the army to establish an air ministry that would control an independent air force. Although a certain degree of similar sentiment existed within the navy, the impetus was blocked by the navy's high command, which feared that an independent air arm would be dominated by the army. Thus, each service developed its own air arm without the slightest coordination or cooperation with its sister service.

Initially, both the army and navy viewed aviation largely in terms of its contribution to reconnaissance, but both services soon began to conceive of other uses for their airpower. By the late 1920s, the army air service was tasked to support the army's ground operations. After the Manchurian Incident of 1931, the army expanded its doctrinal concerns beyond fighter combat to include operations by both fighters and bombers to destroy both the enemy's air bases and its air force.

The navy's air service, for its part, had as its mission the support of the navy's capital surface units. By the 1930s, the navy had begun to shape its air doctrine to conform to the requirements of the long-anticipated decisive surface engagement with the American battle fleet somewhere in the central or western Pacific. As part of its concept of attrition operations to reduce the size of the American battle line before the decisive surface encounter, Japanese plans began to envisage preemptive aerial strikes against the enemy battle fleet. To this end, Japanese aircraft carriers began to deploy fewer fighter aircraft for fleet air defense and more offensive aircraft—dive-bombers and torpedo bombers—to strengthen such preemptive attacks. To add to the long reach needed for such operations, the navy also developed twin-engine land-based bombers and long-range flying boats.[2] Against this background of the navy's obsession with offensive airpower, a view arose within the navy that both battleships and fighter aircraft should be abolished.

In the Japanese army, China was viewed as a strategically vital theater, particularly in relation to Japan's long-range preparations against the Soviet Union. After the Manchurian Incident, the Kwantung Army strengthened its air arm and identified targets in north China to be attacked in case of hostilities. As part of Japanese plans for the dismemberment of north China and the separation of Inner Mongolia from Chinese control, the Kwantung Army deployed its aircraft throughout north China.

Though the Japanese navy continued to regard the U.S. Navy as its chief hypothetical enemy and saw its main theater of operations as the central and western Pacific, it nevertheless believed that maintenance of naval supremacy in East Asian waters, including the seas off China, was essential. To this extent, it saw the Nationalist Chinese air force as a threat to the navy's ability to patrol the Chinese coasts and river systems, particularly the Yangtze. As a countermeasure, the navy decided to downgrade its surface patrol operations and to strengthen its air strike capabilities against various land targets in China.[3]

Japanese Aircraft and Personnel on the Eve of War

In 1937, the Japanese army's air arm had a total of more than 1,000 aircraft organized in fifteen air regiments (of which five belonged to the Kwantung Army) composed of fifty-two air squadrons of ten aircraft each, for a total of 520 operational aircraft.[4] The naval air service consisted of thirteen land-based air groups and thirty-two carrier based air groups for a total of 600 aircraft. Including reserve aircraft, the navy possessed some 800 planes on the eve of the Sino-Japanese War. The navy's ocean flight platforms included the carriers Hōsho, Akagi (being renovated at the beginning of the war), Kaga, and Ryūjō, as well as the seaplane carriers Notoro and Kamoi.

Although Japan's nearly 2,000 military aircraft dwarfed the 300 planes China was able to put in the air, the number fell far short of the aircraft possessed not only by the United States and the Soviet Union, said to possess 4,000–5,000 planes, but also by France and Germany, which probably maintained 2,000–3,000.[5]

Until the 1920s, Japan was limited in its capacity to design military aircraft and relied on the import of foreign designs that were manufactured under license agreements. By the 1930s, however, Japan had improved its technological competence and, by the eve of the war with China in 1937, had achieved aircraft design and manufacturing independence. Under the government's "prototypes system" aircraft manufacturing firms were paired to compete for orders of various aircraft that were to be designed and manufactured according to specifications set forth by the army or the navy. The firm that won the competitive bidding was awarded the government contract, with the losing firm expected to be a second-source supplier,[6] producing its competitor's design under license.

Under this arrangement, the Japanese military services, particularly the navy, produced some of the finest military aircraft of the day. Among these were the navy's Mitsubishi A5M4 Type 96 carrier fighter with a top speed of 280 miles per hour at 10,000 feet, and the twin-engine Mitsubishi G3M2 Type 96 land-based medium bomber with a range of well over 2,000 nautical miles. In 1935, the army deployed the Kawasaki Ki-10 Type 95 fighter with a top speed of 248 miles per hour (at nearly 10,000 feet) and a service ceiling of over 32,000 feet, one of the finest biplane aircraft of its day. But only a comparatively small number of these high-performance aircraft had been introduced by the outbreak of Japan's war with China; half of the army's bomber force was still composed of obsolete Type 93 attack bombers. Even though the navy's aircraft were superior to those of the army, most of the navy's carrier fighters were still outdated Nakajima A2N1 Type 90 or A4N1 Type 95 biplanes, and the carrier-based attack aircraft were the obsolete Mitsubishi B2M1 Type 89, Yokosuka B3Y1 Type 92, and Aichi D1A2 Type 96 biplanes.

For its part, though it depended entirely on joint ventures with foreign firms for the manufacture of military aircraft, China produced only a few dozen planes a year, relying largely on the assembly of imported models, many of which were of American or Italian design. One of the best of these imports was the famed Curtiss Hawk III fighter plane, which outperformed its older Japanese counterparts.

The Japanese army trained its air crews both at the army flight schools and in its operational units. Most army flight schools provided specialized flight training for field grade and noncommissioned officers, but the flight school at Tokorozawa provided basic flight training. The Japanese naval air service conducted most of its flight training within its operational air groups. Basic flight training in the navy enrolled volunteers with either an elementary school or four-year junior high school education. There was also a reserve system for civilian pilots as well as for university and technical high school graduates. Altogether, these training programs increased the number of Japanese air crews from 5,000 at the beginning of the 1930s to 10,000 on the eve of the war with China. This figure was still far behind flight-training numbers in the United States and the major European countries, but far ahead of China, which had only 700 air personnel in 1937.

In sum, Japan's airpower rose rapidly in the 1930s, but on the eve of full-scale hostilities with China it was still inadequate to meet the challenge of all-out war, though both services were implementing large-scale expansion plans when the war broke out. Both services embarked on their expansion plans in 1937, but the army had already implemented its long-range strategy to deploy thirty-five air regiments and 142 air companies by 1942, while the navy had begun a planned expansion of its air strength to fifty-three land-based air groups of 2,000 aircraft by 1940.

Air Mobilization and Operational Plans
at the Outset of the War

When the war started in north China in July 1937, Japan's military services immediately mobilized their operational units. Assuming that combat would soon expand to central and south China, the two services quickly came to an agreement that north China would be the army's theater of operations, and the navy would be responsible for central and south China. The army quickly reorganized eighteen of its air squadrons based in southern Manchuria into a provisional air brigade, which was then redeployed to north China. The squadrons of the Kwantung Army were dispatched to Tientsin. The 200 aircraft thus mobilized constituted half of the army's combat-ready aircraft at the time.

For its part, the Japanese navy had already (in November 1936) arranged for the organization of special combined air groups composed of two or more air groups in order to provide greater air strength under a single command. The first of these were the First Special Combined Air Group (consisting of the Kisarazu and Kanoya air groups and organized 11 July 1937) and the Second Special Combined Air Group (consisting of the Twelfth and Thirteenth air groups). In addition, the navy briefly organized two air groups of seaplane reconnaissance aircraft, the Twenty-first and Twenty-second, which were sent to patrol the north China coast, along with three of the navy's aircraft carriers. All told, these forces comprised eleven units of 128 aircraft, increased to fourteen units in September.[7] Significantly, the navy mobilized the majority of its fighter, dive-bomber, and medium land-based bomber units. The size of this aerial deployment clearly indicates that, from the beginning of hostilities, both Japanese military services were anticipating large-scale air operations against China.

The directives issued to the China Garrison Army—Japan's field army in China proper at the time—make it clear that the role of the army air units in China was to strike at China's military bases so as to weaken its resistance and to support Japanese army ground operations.[8] The orders limited the army air brigade's targets in China to those within the army's area of operations rather than deep preemptive strikes against the Chinese Nationalist air force.[9] The navy, on the other hand, issued much more aggressive orders to eliminate Chinese air capabilities in the event that the war spread to central China. In late July, the Japanese Third Fleet's operational plan stated that, on the first day of all-out combat, it would employ all available operational units to attack enemy air bases in order to destroy the Chinese air force.

Various reasons account for the two services' different air missions at the start of the China conflict. To begin with, since Chinese airpower in north China, controlled by the Chinese Twenty-ninth Army, was weak and geographically distant from the main Chinese air bases in central China, the Japanese army saw little need to undertake operations against it. Moreover, there were few targets in north China whose destruction would have made a strategic difference. Certainly, with the exception of some air combat around Taiyuan in Shanxi Province, there was little Chinese air resistance in north China, and by January 1938 Japan had occupied the region stretching from north Chahar Province to Shandong Province.

In central China, however, Chinese Nationalist air bases were located in or near major cities—Hangzhou, Nanjing, Jurong, and Guangde—all within striking distance of the general Shanghai area. From these bases Chinese airpower could threaten Japanese naval units operating off the central China coast or on the lower Yangtze River. Thus, the Japanese navy saw the need for preemptive attacks against the Chinese air force in the event of war.

Initial Air Battles, Summer 1937

When fighting broke out in Shanghai on 13 August 1937, the Japanese navy had in hand a plan for a surprise air attack the following day, but the attack was aborted due to bad weather. While the navy was waiting for a break in the weather, Chinese aircraft bombed the Japanese Naval Landing Force Headquarters in Shanghai, along with the old armored cruiser *Izumo* (anchored off the Japanese Consulate General in Shanghai), which served as Japanese fleet headquarters in central China. This attack prompted a Japanese retaliation that quickly led to a series of air clashes over Shanghai.

In the first few days of the greater war, Japanese naval aircraft sortied from Japanese bases at Taipei and Ōmura, as well as from the carrier *Kaga*, to bomb Chinese air bases at Hangzhou, Guang'an, Nanjing, and Nanchang. These long-range transoceanic bombing missions, the first of their kind, took the world by surprise. They also provoked massive aerial dogfights over these targets, but the Japanese capture of the Chinese Gongda airfield outside Shanghai in early September eliminated the Chinese bomber threat. The Japanese then used the base to undertake repeated and indiscriminate bombing of Nanjing aimed at breaking Chinese civilian morale.

This initiative forced the Chinese air force to withdraw from the Shanghai area to the hinterland of Wuhan, and the Japanese were able to limit Chinese air operations to scattered night raids on Japanese advanced positions. By September 1937, Japanese naval air groups had gained air supremacy over Nanjing, and Japanese navy pilots could turn their attention to the support of Japanese ground forces in their siege of the city.

These successes demonstrated that, to a significant extent, Japanese air services had achieved their tactical missions by the early autumn of 1937. But as long as the Chinese were able to withdraw their air units to new bases in the interior, the Japanese were unable to achieve their original objective, the destruction of the Chinese air force. Moreover, indiscriminate bombing of Nanjing had not broken Chinese civilian morale, but it had drawn vehement international criticism of Japan.

· · ·

The air battles during the initial month of the war, moreover, had also highlighted certain weaknesses in Japanese airpower, of which the most important was the loss of, or damage to, Japanese aircraft in these encounters. As of late August 1937, the Japanese had lost thirty-two aircraft (twenty in combat and twelve in operational losses).[10] For the three months from the middle of September to the fall of Nanjing, Japanese naval aircraft losses climbed to 117 aircraft (51 carrier fighters, 27 carrier dive-bombers, 21 carrier attack bombers, and 18 land-based medium bombers).[11]

In seeking the cause of these losses, particularly by the navy, in the initial stage of the China war, several problems can be identified. The first was the mediocre performance of Japanese aircraft, since most of those deployed at the start of the war were nearing obsolescence, and the new aircraft had yet to come on line. Japanese pilots were often at a technological disadvantage in those early dogfights. The Curtiss Hawk III, China's principal interceptor fighter, exceeded its Japanese counterparts in power, cruising speed (aided by retractable landing gear), and diving speed. Moreover, its 12.7 mm machine guns were greatly superior to the 7.7 mm machine guns of its Japanese opponents.[12] Certainly, the Nakajima A2N1 Type 90 carrier fighters deployed on the *Kaga* were inferior to the Curtiss Hawk III in every way. Many Japanese Mitsubishi B2M1 Type 89 carrier attack bombers were destroyed in the fierce air battle over Hangzhou of 21 September because they were too slow to compete with the Chinese Curtiss Hawks. Even the brilliant Japanese Type 96 carrier fighter suffered from the inherent vulnerability of its fuel tanks.[13]

The Kanoya and Kisarazu land-based air groups possessed the latest models of the navy's bombing aircraft—the land-based Mitsubishi G3M Type 96 medium bomber—but nevertheless lost half their operational aircraft in the early series of air battles. The Japanese bombers initially operated without fighter escort and thus were vulnerable to Chinese interceptor attacks. This, in turn, was due to the navy's excessive reliance on the Type 96, because a significant portion of navy airmen believed that fighter escort was unnecessary for bomber operations. This mistaken view would be rapidly overturned, but until the Japanese were able to establish a fighter base in the Shanghai area, only a modest number of fighters were available for escort. Even when fighter numbers were increased, most of them were carrier fighters with a comparatively short range, so they could not protect the bombers throughout their missions.

A final problem was tactical. In those early days, the principal bombing formation was a flight of six aircraft. Once the flight reached the target, it normally divided into two sections, which reunited after completion of their bombing run. The Chinese quickly learned to attack them just as they were recombining and were thus able to knock them down one by one.[14]

The Chinese air force, of course, was not free from its own defects. One major problem was tactical competence, particularly bombing accuracy. Chinese aircraft, particularly their Curtiss A 12 "Shrike" attack aircraft, concentrated heavily on attacking Japanese warships and transports to prevent Japanese troops from landing ashore, but these operations had little effect, in large part because of their fixed frontal machine guns, which were of small caliber.

Moreover, Chinese bombing tactics were largely horizontal, conducted in a gradual descent rather than in a steep dive. Thus, they rarely hit an enemy vessel and, on the contrary, in level flight were quite vulnerable to ship-borne antiaircraft fire.[15] Later on in the war, the Chinese used the Curtiss Hawk as a bomber, but given the tactics used, this resulted only in serious losses in these aircraft.

Thus, although the Chinese air force slugged it out with the Japanese during the initial stage of the war, it rapidly lost its edge because of faulty tactics, combat losses, and a lack of logistic support. Thus, despite several problems of their own, the Japanese soon gained air supremacy over any region where Japanese aircraft flew. After the Chinese air force lost most of its prewar aircraft, it received aid from the Soviet Union in the form of aircraft and Soviet combat air crews. With its withdrawal to Wuhan, the Chinese air force began to rebuild its capabilities.

Air Battles over Wuhan, Summer 1938

After the fall of Nanjing, the Japanese army air units in China began to assist the ground operations around Xuzhou. The naval air service, on the other hand, repeatedly bombed Chinese air bases in Nanjing, Wuhu, Nanchang, and Wuhan. For attacks against Wuhan after August 1938, using the newly occupied air bases in Anqing and Jiujiang, both Japanese services provided support to ground operations. In southern China, in order to shut down China's communications and supply routes, Japanese naval aircraft bombed roads, bridges, and railways, particularly in Guang-zhou. In the subsequent air battles over Wuhan, the Chinese were able to deploy some 500 Soviet-made aircraft, flown by some 150 Soviet volunteer pilots. Once Japanese ground forces occupied Anqing in June 1938, Japanese pilots flying from airfields closer to Wuhan were able to gain total air control over the Wuhan area. In August, the Chinese air force had evacuated Wuhan and had withdrawn to Hengyang and Liangshan. By October, it had ceased all offensive operations, while attempting to reconstitute its forces.

By October 1938, Japan had won the air battle over central and south China. The reasons for the Japanese victory are readily apparent. First, a significant change in navy air group force structure was put in place, designed to achieve greater command and control and combat efficiency. The size of each air group was increased from twelve to eighteen aircraft. Second, for major strategic bombardment operations bombers were provided with fighter escort. For such operations, carrier attack bombers were used either as decoy aircraft to draw enemy fighters away from the medium bombers or were employed to make preemptive strikes against the selected enemy target before the land-based medium bombers launched their own bombing runs.[16] Third, since more of the latest models—like the navy's Mitsubishi A5M Type 96 carrier fighter—were being allocated to the navy's frontline air groups, the Japanese were finally able to gain a decisive edge over the Chinese.

It is clear, as well, that the Chinese air force had debilitating problems. First, there was the problem of Chinese equipment. By 1938, the principal Chinese fighter aircraft was the Soviet-made Polikarpov I-15. The I-15 surpassed the Japanese Type 96 in acceleration, but it couldn't turn as sharply and thus was less maneuverable in a dogfight than the Curtiss Hawk III. Moreover, the new aircraft and consequent change in equipment required considerable retraining of Chinese air crews. Second, the addition of Soviet volunteer pilots to China's air defense was not without its difficulties. Although the Soviet pilots had a great deal of cockpit time, they were replaced every three months, so they had little time to profit from their combat experience in China. Moreover, they frequently proved troublesome, particularly in their relations with the chain of command in the Chinese air force.[17]

Finally, Chinese offensive air tactics were flawed. Pilots continued to concentrate on the bombing of Japanese warships and transports and on quixotic attempts to demonstrate temporary claims to air supremacy.[18] Among examples of the latter was the surprise attack on Taiwan in February 1938 and the flight over Kyushu in May of that year, neither of which achieved anything of military value, though they had considerable symbolic and propaganda value for the Chinese cause. True, on occasion, the Chinese were able to overcome the Japanese, simply by massing greater numbers of aircraft, as in the fierce air battle over Wuhan on 29

April 1938,[19] but these aggressive tactics quickly wore down Chinese air defenses.[20] Considering that by 1939 the Chinese air force possessed fewer than one hundred aircraft, we can assume that most of the planes obtained from the Soviet Union the previous year had been shot from the sky.[21]

The outcome of the air battles over Wuhan in the summer of 1938 marks the achievement of general Japanese air supremacy over China. But neither the outcome of these aerial contests nor the Japanese occupation of Wuhan itself brought Japan's China war any closer to an end, since the Nationalist government simply withdrew farther into the Chinese interior and carried on the national war of resistance.

Air Battles Following the Ground Stalemate, 1938–1941

With the fall of Wuhan and Guangdong the war became stalemated. The new national capital at Chongqing, deep in the mountainous interior of Sichuan Province, was too far in rugged terrain for the Japanese army to reach it. Thus, for the time being, the army abandoned all major offensives and used its ground forces largely in an attempt to provide security within its occupied zones.

With the war on the ground stalemated, the Tokyo high command came to see airpower as the most practical means of striking at the Nationalist regime and bringing it to the negotiating table. In this circumstance, the Japanese air services stepped up their bombing raids against Chinese targets in the interior, striking at Chinese military bases, including airfields. In central China, the Japanese navy repeatedly bombed Chinese air bases in Sichuan Province, raids that triggered fierce dogfights with Chinese interceptors over these cities.

The Japanese air services also attempted to sever China's communication and supply links with the outside world. In north China, the Japanese army concentrated on bombing Lanzhou, a major supply base and transshipment point for weapons and supplies coming into China from the Soviet Union. After the fall of Guangdong, other than the supply lines in the northwest from the Soviet Union, the great majority of foreign assistance entered China along routes from Indochina, Burma, and the southern Chinese coast. In order to interdict these coastal supply routes, Japan seized such major supply sites as Nanning, Shantou, and Hainan Island, as well as bombing bridges in China along the terminus of the Burma Road.

Yet these attacks failed to achieve the results the Tokyo high command had hoped for. Repeated bombing attacks in the interior failed to completely destroy China's air force. Attacking land routes into China did not completely cut off China from the outside world. Mountainous terrain and bad weather made it difficult to locate, let alone bomb, the bridges along the Burma Road. Even if roads and railroads were bombed and coastal cities occupied, supplies still entered China along alternate routes. To interdict all supplies entering China would have required Japan to expand the war beyond China's borders and to blockade entry ports like Rangoon, Haiphong, and Hong Kong. Such a course of action would have brought World War II to Asia before December of 1941.

More importantly, all these tactics increased the wear and tear on Japanese air units, particularly those of the navy. Adding to the inherent problems in Japan's strategic air campaign was the increasing effectiveness of Chinese air defenses on the ground. (For a detailed discussion of Chinese air defenses see chapter 3 by Chang Jui-te.) Toward the end of the war, for example, Chinese antiaircraft fire around Chongqing could reach 23,000 feet and was inflicting damage on a significant number of Japanese aircraft on missions over the city.[22] The Chinese also developed an effective early-warning system against Japanese air raids that enabled the Chinese to track Japanese missions almost from the moment they left Japanese advanced air bases. Nor were those Japanese air bases in China themselves immune from occasional Chinese air attacks, since neither of the two Japanese air services made any substantive efforts at base defense, a fact demonstrated by the extensive damage inflicted on the navy's major air base at Wuhan.

In 1939, both Japanese services once more began bombing Chinese cities without fighter escort, in large part because the urban targets in the Chinese interior, like Chongqing and Chengdu, were well beyond the operational radius of Japanese fighter aircraft. It was 500 miles from the Japanese air base at Wuhan to Chongqing and 600 miles to Chengdu. Yet the navy's Type 96 carrier fighter, which had been the principal escort aircraft, had an operational radius of only 375 miles. There was, moreover, the problem of inadequate defensive armament of Japanese medium bombers used on these long-range missions. The Mitsubishi G3M Type 96 medium bomber was armed with only three machine guns, one in a dorsal turret on top of the fuselage and two in turrets on each side of the aircraft, with no armament protecting the tail, the nose, or the underside of the aircraft.[23] The plane also shared a serious deficiency found in all Japanese aircraft, a defect particularly serious in the G3M bomber: highly inadequate armor protection, especially for aircraft fuel tanks. Such a deficiency repeatedly caused Japanese bombers to explode in flames when their fuel tanks were hit. As a result of these technological deficiencies of both fighter and bomber aircraft, Japanese bomber losses of both services once again began to mount—reaching twenty-six in 1939 alone—with the army losing bomber aircraft over Lanzhou, and the navy's losses suffered mostly over Chongqing.

Then, in August 1940, the Japanese introduced their Mitsubishi A6M Type 0 carrier fighter into the skies over China, and the aerial combat situation changed radically in Japan's favor. With excellent maneuverability and control, a top speed of over 330 miles per hour at 15,000 feet, a range of nearly 2,000 miles (three times that of the Type 96 carrier fighter), formidable armament comprising two sets of 7.7 mm machine guns and two 20 mm cannons, the "Zero" was one of the top-performing fighters in the world at the time.

The Zero soon became a multirole aircraft in the skies over China, knocking down Chinese interceptors and strafing targets on the ground. With the introduction of the Zero, Japan gained absolute superiority in air combat in China and in the control of the skies over Chinese cities, including Chongqing.

Conversely, China's aerial armory was slipping into obsolescence. Once it became clear that China could no longer compete in air combat, the Nationalist air force was faced with a painful choice: it could either see its operational units shot to pieces, or it could avoid combat in all but the most favorable situations so as to preserve the remainder of its strength. The air force chose the latter course and changed its overall air strategy to a long-term war of attrition in which Chinese interceptors usually withdrew upon the approach of Japanese bombing formations. Even when Chinese fighter aircraft were deployed, they generally used only delaying tactics against Japanese bombing formations. But while this strategy essentially abandoned to the Japanese the skies over Chinese cities, it meant that Japan was never able to utterly destroy Chinese air capability. In this situation, Japan was forced to continue the slogging infantry combat on the ground in a long-term war of attrition.

Strategic Bombardment of Chinese Cities, 1939–1941

In the three years following the onset of stalemate on the ground, the Japanese conducted repeated heavy and indiscriminate bombing of Chinese cities in an attempt to terrorize Chinese urban populations and thus break down the resistance of the Chinese population as a whole. One can argue that the first attempt to use a Chinese capital as such a target was the bombing of Nanjing in the autumn of 1937. But a full-scale, ongoing effort to break Chinese morale through this technique began with the first bombing of Chongqing in February 1938 and continued through 1941 in a series of operational stages. In May 1939, the navy launched a heavy incendiary attack against the capital, causing massive casualties. In the spring of 1940, it undertook Operation 101, the greatest aerial offensive of the war to date, followed in the spring and summer of 1941 by Operation 102, which employed both the navy's new Mitsubishi G4M Type 1 medium bomber and the army's counterpart, the Mitsubishi Ki-21 Type 97. In the three years from 1939 to 1941, at an average altitude of 16,000 feet, a total of over 6,000 Japanese aircraft bombarded Chongqing 141 times, dropping 15,000 bombs on the city[24] and causing great damage to government buildings and military installations and massive destruction of civilian life and property—some 10,000 homes destroyed and approximately 10,000 civilians killed. Soon, Chongqing, above ground, was simply rubble.[25]

And yet, despite these horrendous injuries inflicted on the city, the bombing did little to achieve Japan's objectives. In a strictly material sense, little was destroyed that had strategic value. In large part this was because Chongqing as a capital had so little of the infrastructure of a modern metropolis. Up until 1938, of course, it had been a rural city, with no industrial centers and with its municipal functions and institutions scattered in no particular order within its limits. Thus, despite the best work of the Japanese navy's photo-intelligence services, Japanese bombing units had a difficult time identifying any critical targets. Chongqing's rocky soil, moreover, facilitated the construction of deep underground shelters where government offices could be relocated and civilians could take refuge. And, finally, weather often limited Japanese bombing runs, particularly in the winter when the city was often shrouded in a blanket of fog, limiting Japanese operations over the city to the five months between May and October.

Most critically, the bombing strategy failed to bring China to its knees. The failure of the bombing campaign against Chongqing was merely the precedent for the inability of aerial bombardment in World War II to break civilian morale and force a government to capitulate.[26] Autocratic regimes such as Nationalist China, where civilian sentiment is limited in the governmental decision-making process, are particularly resistant to this sort of outside military pressure to bring about a change of government policy—a fact manifested later in the minimal weakening of civilian morale in Berlin and Tokyo. But even the population in a city like London in a democratic society does not easily break under the effects of prolonged aerial bombardment. Such bombing only serves to stoke the fires of civilian fury at the aerial aggressors and to redouble their support for their government. Thus, the ongoing aerial campaigns of the Japanese against Chinese cities only prolonged Japan's China war.

The American Entry into the China Air War, 1942–1943

With the outbreak of war between Japan and the Anglo-American Allies and Japan's invasion of Southeast Asia in late 1941, China became just one of several war fronts in Asia and the Pacific. The new strategic situation also dramatically changed the logistic realities and possibilities for China. Following the German invasion of the Soviet Union in June 1941, Soviet aid to China stopped. The Japanese conquest of most of Southeast Asia in the spring of 1942 cut the Burma Road, the principal land route into China from the south.

Offsetting this loss of material support for China was the initiation of substantial military assistance provided by the United States. The first manifestation of this support was the arrival of a group of American fighter pilot volunteers—the American Volunteer Group, later famously known as the Flying Tigers—who arrived in Burma for training in the summer of 1941 and who, by the winter and spring of 1942, were playing an active and aggressive role against Japanese airpower in southwest China. In addition, the United States began to train Chinese air crews. Far more important was the new equipment sent to China, including materiel for the Nationalist air force, by American air transport over the Himalayas, a route popularly known among American air crews as the Hump. In 1942 and 1943, the U.S. Army Air Force, using Chinese labor, built air bases for heavy bombers in Yunnan Province, from which the newly arrived Fourteenth Air Force could provide assistance to Chinese ground operations and could, potentially, strike at the Japanese homeland.

Between 1942 and 1944, the Japanese army air units in China countered these American initiatives. The first was a series of air strikes against the American air bases in China. As early as April 1942, following the Doolittle raid on Tokyo, the Japanese invaded Zhejiang Province in the mistaken belief that it had been the base for the raid. After the United States deployed B-24 bombers in Yunnan capable of reaching Japan, the Japanese army air service gave particular attention to the bases on which they were positioned. As the Americans developed advanced bases at Guilin and Hengyang in Guangxi Province, much closer to Japanese ground units, Japanese army bombers struck them. But from 1943, Japanese army air units in China were increasingly on the defensive, and Japanese aircraft losses mounted. Increasingly, Japanese bases in China and Japanese vessels on the Yangtze River were subject to Chinese as well as American air attacks.

The Changing Balance of Airpower
in the China Theater

By 1943, the Chinese air force was equipped with American-made aircraft of far better performance than the older aircraft from the Soviet Union. Even though the American Curtiss P-40 fighter was inferior to the Japanese army's Nakajima Ki-27 Type 97 fighter in turning radius, it excelled in firepower and speed at high altitude. As long as American fighter pilots stuck to hit-and-run tactics and avoided dogfights, they were more than a match for anything the Japanese could send against them. Conversely, serious deficiencies in Japanese aircraft design now became apparent in these contests. The army's medium bombers, like those of the navy, proved both flammable and vulnerable to fighter attack, and the army's newly introduced Nakajima Ki-43 Type 1 fighter could not fly fast enough to protect the bombers.[27]

By 1943, then, the relative air strength of the two original combatants had been reversed. Even before the Pacific War, the navy's withdrawal from the continent of all but a fraction of its air assets brought Japan's air strength in China down to about 300 operational planes, mostly army aircraft. By the beginning of 1944, the figure was down to 100. Conversely, with American-made aircraft flown in over the Hump, the number of Allied aircraft rose to 400 (300 operational) of which 170 belonged to the Nationalist air force and 230 to the U.S. Fourteenth Air Force. At this point in the war, therefore, Chinese aircraft outnumbered Japanese aircraft in China three to one.[28]

Given this radically changed numerical situation, it was now the Japanese army that sought to preserve what air assets in China it still possessed. The army essentially abandoned all daylight offensive operations as too costly and reverted to less-hazardous surprise attacks by fighters alone and to bombing missions at night or in bad weather. Clearly, the advantage in the air war in China had shifted dramatically to the Allied side.

· · ·

In February of 1944, the Japanese army launched its famed Ichigō offensive, a nearly year-long offensive into southeast China. The operation was intended to establish a supply route from Japanese-occupied Southeast Asia into Japanese-held China, particularly including the capture of the Peking–Wuhan, Guangzhou–Wuhan, and Hunan–Guangxi railroad lines, as well as the capture of the American air bases east of those rail lines in order to prevent their use by American bombers to strike at the Japanese home islands. (For a more detailed discussion of the Ichigō offensive, see chapter 16 by Hara Takeshi.) To facilitate the Japanese offensive the army temporarily increased its air strength in China, almost doubling the number of its operational aircraft.

To an extent, the Ichigō offensive seemed to have succeeded, at least in one of its objectives, driving American airpower from southeast China. By the end of 1944, the Japanese army had greatly expanded its control of territory along the rail lines and had captured the enemy air bases at Changsha, Hengyang, Guilin, and Liuzhou. But this temporary spasm of

Japanese power in China, as large as it was, was still too limited to reverse the general tide of the war, now running against Japan. On the contrary, as 1944 drew to a close and the Japanese offensive ran out of steam, Chinese and American forces in China prepared to go on the offensive. The Chinese Nationalist air force strengthened its base at Zhijiang in Hunan, and American B-29 long-range heavy bombers began operating out of the air base at Chengdu in Sichuan on bombing missions against Kyushu. By the time that Ichigō had ground to a halt in February 1945, it was clear that Japan had failed to achieve its main objective—the prevention of strategic air attacks on the Japanese homeland.

During 1944, moreover, Chinese airpower rapidly increased. Including American air assets in-country, the number of operational aircraft increased from approximately 300 in early 1944 to between 700 and 800 by the end of that year. For the Japanese, the situation was quite the reverse, since Japanese air assets decreased from 230 to 150 during the same year, worsening Japan's numerical disadvantage from three to one to five to one.[29]

But the Japanese airpower inferiority was not just quantitative; it was also qualitative. Where, four years before, leading-edge Japanese navy aircraft like the Zero fighter and the Nell bomber had blazed through China's skies sweeping all before them, the frontline aircraft on which the army depended in China were now badly outclassed by the enemy. The Type 1 Fighter and the twin-engine Kawasaki Ki-48 Type 99 medium bomber were no match for their American-made counterparts, the P-51 Mustang, one of the world's finest aircraft, with a top speed of over nearly 400 miles per hour, and the Boeing B-29 Superfortress heavy bomber with a range of 3,700 miles and a payload of nine tons. Even more serious was the deterioration of Japanese air crews. The army had long since exhausted its pool of experienced pilots in years of grinding combat, and their replacements were younger, inexperienced, and woefully inadequately trained. Inevitably, their badly inferior flight and combat skills only accelerated the combat losses in Japanese army air units in China.

In these conditions, through 1944, the Chinese gradually gained air supremacy over south and central China. At the same time, however, because of a calculated shift in American strategic priorities, including the decision to undertake the long-range aerial bombardment of Japan from captured Japanese islands in the western Pacific rather than from China, the United States Air Force began to scale down its presence in China. Nonetheless, the remaining Fourteenth Air Force squadrons in China continued to bomb Japanese shipping on the Yangtze and repeatedly bombed Taiwan. The Japanese army felt compelled to respond by carrying out attacks on American air bases in China, but such operations only further degraded Japanese air strength.

In 1945, with the advance of American airpower in the western Pacific coming ever closer to the Japanese homeland, the Japanese air presence in China was once more reduced to about one hundred operational aircraft. While both services moved much of their air assets to the defense of Okinawa, all plans for offensive air operations in China against enemy positions from bases captured during the Ichigō offensive were abandoned. The new mission of the air units left in China was to be the defense of the southeast Chinese coast so as to prevent American landings in Guangdong or the Shanghai area, which might establish stepping-stones for an invasion of Japan. In the event, of course, the United States set aside plans to use China as a jumping-off place for an invasion of Japan and instead stormed through the Ryukyu Islands. Thus, the remnant of the once proud Japanese air presence in China was left on its airfields without making any further contribution to Japan's war effort.

Concluding Remarks

Until the last six months of the China war, Japan had continued its deep penetration and had maintained its local air superiority in air combat over China. Nevertheless, Japan was never able to completely eliminate Chinese airpower. The reasons for the failure of Japanese airpower to achieve a fundamental strategic victory in China deserve some discussion as a conclusion to this essay.

There were, to begin with, basic problems in Japan's ability to mobilize effectively for the China war. In particular, one must note that Japan entered the conflict just as it was embarking on a major airpower expansion program, a fact that complicated plans for large-scale air operations in China. Prewar service priorities—the army's preparations for a full-scale war with the Soviet Union and the navy's planning for a maritime conflict with the United States—also limited full attention and commitment of Japanese airpower to the China theater. Within the context of these priorities Japan had to plan for potential combat theaters in Manchuria and the Pacific. Such plans also limited the material resources for the China theater, another reason for the relatively modest scale of Japanese air operations there. Indeed, after the Pacific War broke out, the largest share of all Japanese air forces was committed to Southeast Asia and the Pacific and, in consequence, Japanese air forces in China, specifically including air assets, were soon outnumbered by their opponents.

A further reason for the failure of Japanese airpower to deliver China a knockout blow was the inability of either the army or the navy air services to sever China's communications and supply routes with the outside world. True, by early 1942, Japan had managed to shut down most of the land routes through the interior and maritime routes along the Chinese coast. But the air supply route across the Himalayas remained open, and between 1942 and 1945 some 650,000 tons of supplies reached China from its Allies via the Hump. Much of this materiel supported Chinese and American air units in China.[30]

Finally, Japanese bombing operations in China consumed materiel that other more critical theaters could have used later. One notes here the navy's reliance on preemptive air strikes to destroy the Nationalist air force and its immediate targeting of Chinese air bases soon after the war broke out. But its excessive and mistaken belief in the preeminence of land-based twin-engine medium bombers, such as the Mitsubishi G3M and G4M, led to the relatively heavy losses of those aircraft. True, the introduction of the Mitsubishi A6M Zero did cut those losses, but the Zero was available as a fighter escort for only a year, from the summer of 1940 to the summer of 1941, when it was withdrawn from China along with the navy's other aircraft types. The Japanese army bombers that replaced the G3M and G4M were inferior in performance and thus suffered even greater losses. Indeed, when measured against such losses, the impact of the army's strategic bombing efforts seems quite small indeed, particularly since it failed to destroy the Nationalist air force or to bring the Nationalist government or Chinese population to their knees.

Of course, in judging the performance of Japanese airpower in China, one cannot ignore the circumstances of China itself. There is no denying that, for much of the war, the two Japanese air services were distinctly superior to the Nationalist air force. The Japanese services lacked a unified command, but the Chinese were militarily fragile and lagged behind the Japanese air services in logistic effectiveness. Yet China and Chinese airpower were able to survive because of the substantial infusions of foreign military aid and assistance, particularly after America entered the war. The Nationalist air force was able to carry on the fight even when the Nationalist army was forced to retreat in the face of the Japanese Ichigō Offensive of 1944. Moreover, because Chiang Kai-shek was a great believer in airpower and thus gave priority to strengthening China's air capabilities, the Nationalist air force was eventually able to develop into a modern fighting force under a unified command.[31] Despite ongoing operational problems, China was determined to be on a par with Japan in both weapons and the skills of its pilots. With American aid and assistance it was able to attain that goal.

The effect of Japan's involvement in the air war over China was critical to the performance of Japanese airpower, particularly that of the navy, in the Pacific War. The air combat experience gained by the navy's land-based air groups in China sharpened Japanese tactical skills in the first year of the Pacific War. The Zero, the best carrier fighter in the world at the time of its introduction into air combat in China, is an example of how the China war tested Japanese equipment and air crews. But air combat in China did not always translate later into effectiveness in the Pacific War. Except for air-to-air combat, few of the navy's air operations in China—support for army ground operations, bombardment of military bases, interdiction of land communication and supply routes—had much relevance for the navy's responsibilities in the Pacific War, which was, after all, a naval conflict, and more particularly a carrier war. Moreover, the China war revealed a stunning lack of cooperation between the two air services, neither of which shared equipment, doctrine, or training, a problem that made it all but impossible to conduct effective joint operations, even when the two air services did operate together.

Finally, in considering the meaning of the air war in China, I have written that Japanese air assets exhausted in China could have been deployed against the United States when the Pacific War broke out. But even after the two wars merged, the China theater required a certain level of commitment of Japanese airpower there, assets that were desperately needed elsewhere in Asia and the Pacific. To that extent, the air war over China, regardless of its outcome, contributed to the Allied victory over Japan.

10 The Great Bombing of Chongqing and the Anti-Japanese War, 1937–1945

EDNA TOW

The Sino-Japanese War (1937–1945) was a conflict of global dimensions and one that saw the first extensive and coordinated application of industrialized war technologies by the Japanese military against civilian populations and infrastructure in Asia. Japan's bombing campaigns in China targeted major urban centers, manufacturing facilities, and residential districts. Indeed, the strategic use of air power marked a critical stage in the struggle between the two nations, especially when ground operations became stalemated and a war of multiple fronts opened up in the wake of the Chinese government's relocation to the inland province of Sichuan. Recognizing that the conflict had shifted from a conventional battlefield of finite proportions to an open-ended protracted war, leaders on each side reassessed priorities and took steps to consolidate their position in a radically reshaped combat theater. It was against this background that Japan's high command turned to terror bombing in a calculated effort to wear down Chinese resistance and morale, a policy that was pursued with determined ferocity against the city of Chongqing, China's wartime capital and headquarters of the Nationalist regime of Chiang Kai-shek.[1]

Destination Chongqing

Although the bombing experiences of numerous European and Japanese cities during the Second World War are widely known and well-documented in studies of the period,[2] the "Great Bombing of Chongqing"—as it is termed in China—has received comparatively little attention and scrutiny by scholars in the West. This is remarkable considering that the city endured more than four years of direct and concentrated attack by Japanese bomber formations, during which the city was hit in excess of

200 times.[3] Extending from February 1938 to August 1943, Japan's campaign saw more than 9,500 aircraft drop approximately 21,600 bombs on the inland capital. According to internal reports compiled by the Chinese government immediately after the war, upward of 15,000 Chinese lost their lives as a result of these attacks, and over 20,000 people suffered injuries.[4] In addition to this human toll, Japan's bombardment of the city caused deprivation, disruption, and property losses of a magnitude that will likely never be known fully.

Although this aerial bombardment was by no means the first campaign of its kind, Chongqing's experience nevertheless marked a qualitative break from previous military confrontations in critical ways.[5] For one, Japan's air campaigns were much more extensive and sustained than anything that had occurred prior to this time, giving rise to a form of hostilities that no longer adhered to a strictly delimited time frame or a predefined theater of operations. In addition, the use of technologically advanced weaponry to target nonmilitary personnel and infrastructure transformed many ordinary Chinese into front-line combatants. The indiscriminate nature of mass bombing obliterated the line between the military and civilian sectors as the rules of modern total warfare provided few if any guarantees for the safety of civilian populations at large. Thus, in terms of scale, impact, and duration, the bombing was unprecedented.

Such observations were far from the minds of Chinese and Japanese military authorities as events unfolded in July 1937. Neither side anticipated how the conflict would escalate, and, because of this, both Japan's air campaign and China's air defense developed in response to what was a constantly changing political and military situation. Within this context, Chiang Kai-shek took the first steps in what was to be a major realignment of the Kuomintang's strategic policy: the transfer of all government ministries and personnel to the interior, a decision that would have immediate repercussions for the conduct of the war. In a speech given at the convening of the National Defense Council in October 1937, Chiang explained his rationale:

The most important point from a military perspective is that not only does victory need to have a predefined plan, one must have a predefined plan even with setbacks and defeats. Not only must victory be based on taking a definite stance, one must take a definite stance even with retreat. After a temporary defeat, there should be no cause for anxiety that this has been a wholesale defeat; instead final victory can be seized. Today, we take the initiative to retreat, and in the future, we will be able to take the initiative and advance; in other words, there is no cause for anxiety.[6]

Chiang recognized that the Nationalist armies were in no position to stem the Japanese advance into northern and coastal China, and with the national capital at Nanjing in danger of being overrun, his decision to retreat to the interior was a pragmatic move that would allow Nationalist forces to regroup and prepare themselves for a renewed offensive. To accomplish this, Chiang deemed it imperative to choose a well-fortified and defensible locale from which to carry on the struggle.

Chongqing possessed undeniable strategic benefits as the site for a new base of operations. The city was situated on a narrow peninsula that formed the confluence of the Jialing and Yangtze rivers, affording it a direct line of access to the coast via the river system. Built atop a rocky edifice, it was flanked on each side by sheer cliffs that provided strategic vantage points of the surrounding area and formed a natural defensive barrier against enemy ground incursions. These unique topographical features, combined with the city's advantageous position along a major transportation artery, entered into Chiang Kai-shek's tactical calculations when he issued the official relocation order in November 1937.

The mountain city filled a vital role in the ensuing struggle, first as a rallying point for the country, and second as a key axis in the new ideological and political front established by the Nationalists to wage a war of resistance. Almost immediately, the city was catapulted into the national limelight and became a center for decision making and ongoing debates over war strategy. Its newfound prominence attracted scores of downriver people and other populations seeking refuge from the fighting that had engulfed their own locales. However, with such visibility also came grim and unpleasant realities: as the provisional capital of China, the city became an obvious target for Japan's air campaigns. Chongqing, as it turned out, enjoyed only a modicum of safety because of the bombing raids, making life in the interior no less of a struggle for survival than it was in other parts of the country.

Japanese Terror Bombing of the Wartime Capital

From the very outset of the war, Japanese naval air units supported the army's ground operations, first in Shanghai and Nanjing and later on in attacks against other cities in central and south China. In this first phase, Chongqing was one among a handful of Chinese cities that were targeted for trial runs, as evidenced by a relatively modest bombing raid on the morning of 18 February 1938, when nine Japanese planes following a route along the Yangtze River emptied their payload of fourteen bombs in the vicinity of a military airfield, north of the city proper. Casualties and damage were minimal: three people were injured and three houses destroyed.[7] The small scale of this first air raid would seem to indicate that, as of early 1938, the Japanese navy had not yet planned a full-scale aerial campaign against the city, but at least six reconnaissance overflights and two more bombing missions against the city in the subsequent days and months suggest that the navy was considering such a possibility.

Chiang Kai-shek's defiant stance and his government's unexpected resiliency soon forced the Japanese high command to reconsider its war plan after initial offensives failed to secure China's immediate capitulation. By late 1938, faced with military stalemate and little prospect of a quick settlement of the China fighting, the Japanese Army Ministry and General Staff agreed that Japan had to shift to a protracted-war strategy. Evidence of this strategic reorientation came in the form of Imperial General Headquarters Order No. 241 (Tairikumei 241) of 2 December, issued by the high command and approved by Emperor Hirohito. This order acknowledged the changed situation and, among other matters, called for a strategic bombing campaign in central China. Accompanying Order No. 241 was Imperial General Headquarters Directive No. 345 (Tairikushi), dated the same day, to army commanders in China. It decreed that the air war would be given highest precedence and authorized attacks against strategic and political targets. Attached to the directive was a joint army-navy agreement that delineated respective areas of aerial operations and the air units involved. Heretofore, Japan's raids had not explicitly targeted nonmilitary facilities, though in practice, civilian populations and infrastructure would often fall victim to the collateral effects of aerial bombardment. The broad sanction granted by the directive left little doubt that ordinary citizens and commercial areas now fell within the scope of bombing objectives.[8] Following these orders, on 6 December, Imperial General Headquarters, Army Division, issued new guidelines that restricted further expansion of the ground war and sought to consolidate areas already under Japanese control. In order to achieve military objectives, the Japanese would rely on air attacks against vital bases in China and a naval blockade.[9]

Launching the air war was part of broader initiatives designed to force the Chinese government to the negotiating table, and the timing of these military decisions closely followed developments on the diplomatic front. In late December 1938, Prime Minister Konoe Fumimaro publicized a set of guiding principles for building a new order in East Asia. Roughly a week later, on 29 December, Wang Jingwei, a high-level Kuomintang official who had recently broken with Chiang Kai-shek over the conduct of the war, came out in support of a peace effort and endorsed Konoe's statement. In expressing public disagreement with Chiang, Wang emerged as an alternative, more conciliatory voice to the generalissimo, one that the Japanese political establishment, in turn, sought to leverage in order to weaken support for the Nationalist regime and exacerbate internal divisions on the Chinese side. Terror bombing was viewed as a critical complement to these political efforts, one that sought to destabilize Chiang Kai-shek's government and incite such widespread panic and fear among its population that the country would have no choice but to sue for peace. Systematic air attacks were thus part of a combined military and political offensive to wear down Chinese resistance through intimidation and attrition.

Japanese army and naval air forces previewed this new strategic orientation when they launched a coordinated bombing campaign that targeted the wartime capital in January 1939.[10] On three separate occasions that month, Japanese planes entered the airspace around Chongqing during daylight hours and bombarded different parts of the city and its outlying suburbs. Thick fog prevented the bombers from making a more targeted assault on the city proper. On the occasion of the third raid, however, the city was not so fortunate. Japanese bomber units descended on the capital around noon on 15 January and hit several sites in the central part of the city and on the north bank. Among the sites bombed were the densely built sections of the peninsula with no obvious military significance. More than a hundred people were killed in what amounted to the deadliest assault on Chongqing thus far, and it marked the first time that Japanese bombers struck what were predominantly civilian quarters of the city. This occasion also saw the first aerial engagement between both sides over Chongqing as twelve Chinese interceptors clashed with thirty-six enemy bombers in a fierce dogfight over the city.[11]

After these initial incursions by the Japanese, a several-month hiatus ensued because of the onset of the foggy season: heavy clouds blanketed the capital and made locating targets impossible. In addition, the few raids brought to bear on the city had already exposed some of the difficulties in executing long-range bombing runs into China's interior. Most notably, Japanese aerial assaults were often inaccurate and had little success against their intended targets. Unfamiliar terrain and bad weather were likely contributing factors, but Japanese air authorities viewed the lack of success as a symptom of more fundamental problems related to ineffective bombing formations and deployment techniques—issues that had vexed Japan's air services since the beginning of the war.[12] From February to April, therefore, they focused on supplementing training, making aircraft upgrades, and concentrating their forces approximately 850 miles downriver from the capital in Wuhan, which now served as a converted base for Japan's bomber units. Chongqing's residents, in the meantime, found themselves momentarily spared from air attacks.

When the bombing raids resumed on 3–4 May 1939, the stakes had clearly escalated. Over the course of back-to-back bombing days, Japanese air units deployed from Wuhan surprised the city and broke through Chinese aerial defenses to cut a swath of destruction, dropping lethal combinations of high explosives and incendiary ordnance. The bulk of these fell on commercial and residential sections located in the lower half of the Old

City. Official tallies put civilian losses in the range of 3,700 deaths, 2,650 injuries, and close to 4,900 structures destroyed.[13] Consulates belonging to Great Britain and Germany suffered severe damage, while the Chaotianmen market district and the Guotai Cinema complex were reduced to rubble. In their first application against the city, firebombs led to mass conflagrations all over Chongqing, which, for all of its stone edifices, was largely composed of wooden and bamboo structures.

The campaign continued through the summer and into the fall: between May and November, Japanese aircraft returned on at least twenty occasions, usually over a cluster of days, to terrorize the population and lay waste to large parts of the city. No apparent distinction was made between civilian or military targets—both fell victim to Japan's bombers. In many cases, enemy aircraft would alternate their flight path into the city to catch Chinese interceptors off guard. During this period, Japan honed many of the techniques and tactics that would define its campaign against Chongqing, including night bombing and the extensive use of incendiaries.

The scale of the bombing campaign underwent a dramatic expansion the following year when Japan launched its Operation 101. Starting in May 1940, a combined force of navy and army air units raided the provincial capital of Chengdu, in addition to Chongqing. Over a period of 110 days, Chongqing was hit over fifty times, with a peak in the month of June. Japan's bombers left few areas in the city untouched, as schools, civilian neighborhoods, and industrial and airport facilities alike came under bombardment. Suburban and residential areas in Jiangbei and Nan'an, situated on the northern and southern banks respectively, were not spared; neither were nearby townships. Estimates from the Japanese side noted that anywhere from fifty to one hundred tons of bombs were dropped in a given raid during this phase of Japan's aerial campaign.[14] By the time Operation 101 ended on 4 September, Chinese reports estimated that more than 2,600 Japanese sorties dropped almost 10,000 bombs, resulting in approximately 4,100 killed and 5,400 wounded.[15] The year 1940 marked the high point of Japan's aerial campaign against the city in terms of the aggregate number of aircraft dispatched, bombs dropped, days of attack, and total area affected.

Some general observations can be made about the timing, size, and pattern of Japan's bombing campaigns up to this point. The Japanese employed both day and night raids—and even these could be divided into early morning, midafternoon, and late evening attacks—meaning the city was never sure when or at what intervals raids would occur. The size of bomber contingents also varied according to perceived objectives; in the early stages of the campaign, a group of ten to forty aircraft might be dispatched on a given occasion for a concentrated attack. In later phases, this practice underwent modification as the Japanese air services experimented with different types of formations, including the dispatch of small groups of aircraft in continuous waves to harass the population and disrupt life in the city. This unremitting deployment kept the city on constant alert, giving little respite to residents and forcing authorities to maintain round-the-clock vigilance. The raids of 1940–1941 tended to follow this pattern, and it was not unusual for Chongqing's residents to be subjected to sustained bombardment by as many as 200 or more aircraft for many hours.

The Japanese air services proved themselves to be methodical and deadly. After several days of successive harassment, city residents enjoyed a brief break while the Japanese reconditioned their aircraft at Wuhan. Once completed, however, the cycle of bombing promptly resumed. During the later phases of the campaign, the Japanese navy adapted its tactics and sometimes employed smaller bomber formations, enabling it to launch more raids at shorter intervals and thus keep the city off balance. Of particular note also was the way in which Japan's air campaigns followed a seasonal tempo: local climatic conditions were such that dense fog shrouded the city from late fall to early spring. Before mounting large-scale raids, the Japanese army air force maintained a standard practice to dispatch weather reconnaissance missions to survey conditions; these patrols determined whether the fog and heavy cloud cover would impede the ability of Japanese air crews to identify visual reference points on the ground to guide them to their targets. Consequently, air raids tended to occur most frequently during the summer months, when the heavy fog that covered the peninsula lifted and the city was clearly visible from the air.

As 1941 began, Japan publicly reaffirmed its policy of strategic bombing in a New Year's Day announcement and resumed its campaign on a similar magnitude and scale. From January to September, the city was attacked nearly forty times, with the brunt of the attacks occurring in the summer months. Admittedly incomplete statistics compiled by the Municipal Police Bureau from June through August indicate the steady escalation of Japan's air attacks on the city. (See table 10.1.)

The campaign followed the pattern of previous years in its indiscriminate targeting of civilian and military quarters, leaving many sections of the city in flames and causing substantial disruption, property losses, and population displacement. The intensity of the campaign also did not let up, as the August raids proved. In that month, the Japanese air services used the occasion to apply some of the new techniques they had adopted: the deployment of multiple groups of aircraft, flying in smaller groups, and keeping to a tight formation. These techniques enabled the Japanese to maintain a steady bombardment of the city. The seven-day period between 8 and 14 August saw Japan dispatch a constant stream of bombers to attack the city roughly every six hours. During this time, the capital's air raid warning system was on high alert for an average of ten hours each day

TABLE 10.1
Japanese air raids on Chongqing, June to August 1941

	Raids	Japanese planes	Bombs dropped	Deaths	Injuries
June	9	353	1,385	1,249[a]	1,299
July	10	555	1,417	154	366
August	11	1,190	2,794	560	818

[a] This tally likely includes the dead from the 5 June tunnel tragedy, which accounted for roughly 80 percent of the deaths.
SOURCE: Compiled from Chongqing Municipal Government Statistics Office, "Loss figures from enemy air raids for Chongqing Municipality, June to August 1941."

and, at one point, sounded for ninety-six consecutive hours. To maximize firepower, the Japanese used a combined force of naval and army air units in the raids that took place over the final two weeks of the month.

In mid-1941, Japanese strategic priorities, particularly those of the navy, shifted toward the Pacific, and preparations began for war with the United States. As of September, Japan's air units were redeploying from China to other theaters, and Chongqing saw some indication of this reorientation: only two air raids were launched against the city that month, a significantly scaled-down number compared to the summer. By mid-October, Japanese army air units had 70 operational aircraft in China, 360 in Manchuria, and 670 planes assigned to Southeast Asia operations.[16] With fewer aircraft available, the frequency of air raids against the wartime capital accordingly decreased. After the Japanese attack on Pearl Harbor on 7 December, aerial operations against Chongqing virtually ceased: the whole of 1942 saw no raids directed against the city and only one in 1943. These last attacks never reached the intensity or scope of those launched during the three-year period from 1939 to 1941.

Chongqing's Air Defense System

The intense and sustained nature of Japan's bombardment led many contemporary observers to remark that the city was the "most bombed city in the world" at the time. Certainly, this description would not be far removed from what life in the city was like: Chongqing functioned under a perpetual state of alert and activity as Chiang Kai-shek's government worked tirelessly to deal with essential air defense tasks and prevent public panic. Under the direction of the Military Affairs Commission, Chongqing's municipal agencies oversaw a sweeping set of protocols and countermeasures to defend the city and protect the local population. These ranged from infrastructure projects, such as the construction of bomb shelters and air raid warning systems, to evacuation and refugee resettlement programs. Such operations were designed to minimize casualties and property losses caused by Japan's aerial onslaught and depended on the mass mobilization of the populace to be successful. Although the government developed many of these measures in direct response to the crisis at hand, air defense had been a real concern among Chinese military circles since the early 1930s.[17]

Broadly speaking, air defense—or *fangkong*—designated a comprehensive framework of institutions, infrastructure, and personnel charged with all matters related to civil and military defense against aerial attacks. Within this framework, air defense tasks and responsibilities were generally classified as belonging to one of two types: active (*jiji*) or passive (*xiaoji*). The former designation, as it might imply, referred to measures to engage and destroy enemy aircraft. Some of the key components of active air defense included routine air patrols and preemptive raids conducted by the Chinese air force, military operations and ground maneuvers carried out by mobile antiaircraft artillery units, and the installation of antiaircraft batteries and gunnery emplacements to form a defensive perimeter around likely targets. In contrast, passive measures referred to operations and programs intended to ensure air defense preparedness among the civilian population. Since active measures could go only so far to protect its citizens, the government developed a complementary set of rules, procedures, and instructions designed to educate and inform the public at large about air raid safety, proper behavior during emergencies, and other precautionary measures. Other tasks falling under this rubric included the organization of evacuation campaigns, disaster relief, and refugee assistance.

Compared to Japan, whose naval aviation sector had already made significant progress in bomber technology and deployment strategy,[18] China's air services were still inferior when hostilities broke out. In a military report to the Fifth Plenary Session of the Nationalist Party, General He Yingqin indicated publicly that as of June 1936 China's air force comprised some 600 aircraft of various types. In reality, the number was probably closer to half of that, and even then many of those planes were either training aircraft or were not operational.[19] The majority of this fleet was of foreign origin, with the United States supplying roughly 60 percent.[20] Heavy losses suffered during the initial fighting exacted a serious toll on these numbers, prompting the Chinese Aviation Commission, headed by Madame Chiang Kai-shek, to initiate the consolidation of existing aerial units and to seek help from abroad. From 1938 to 1940, while the United States imposed a partial arms embargo on China, the Soviet Union stepped in to supply the Nationalist air force with pilots and warplanes to close the gap. The result was an augmented Chinese national air force that was able to provide 160 aircraft to defend Chongqing and its environs by the end of 1940.[21] Overall, roughly 2,000 Soviet pilots contributed their services,[22] and Soviet advisers helped to establish a flight school. This infusion of Soviet manpower, equipment, and technical assistance contributed enormously to enabling the Chinese air force to counter Japan's claim to air supremacy in the first few years of the conflict.

Even though the U.S. embargo limited the formal transfer of munitions and armaments, it did not prevent individual or private-sector initiatives from aiding Chinese efforts to improve the country's air defense capacity.[23] One such effort occurred when Madame Chiang Kai-shek, in her capacity as the chair of the Chinese Aviation Commission, enlisted the help of retired air force major general Claire Chennault soon after the outbreak of war. Tasked with reorganizing China's air force, Chennault overhauled pilot training programs, updated Chinese aerial tactics, and coordinated air strategy. Under his supervision, aviation schools were reorganized to provide detailed instruction in specific aerial skills: pursuit, bombardment, and reconnaissance. Cadets logged valuable flight hours by participating in simulated combat drills and tactical maneuvers. In the period from July 1937 to December 1940, these programs trained approximately 900 students.[24]

Chiang Kai-shek also supported Chennault's plans to assemble a group of capable pilots from the United States who could compete with Japan's air units more directly.[25] Known as the American Volunteer Group (AVG)—or the Flying Tigers—this unit was originally anticipated as a defensive force for Chongqing.[26] However, because of strategic reassessments, the AVG never saw action in the skies over the wartime capital, and after Japan's bombing of Pearl Harbor in late 1941, its pilots were instead dispatched to the Burma theater. After the AVG was inactivated and its pilots merged into the China Air Task Force under the U.S. Tenth Air Force, Chennault continued to work closely with the Chinese Aviation Commission to modernize China's air services, proving himself to be a useful, if sometime contentious, liaison between Chiang Kai-shek's government and the Roosevelt administration. His high-profile efforts kept the spotlight on Chongqing's cause and publicized the importance of China's air war until American military aid resumed in 1941. With key American supporters like Chennault and others to facilitate negotiations, the United States soon regained its position as the main supplier of technical assistance and military armaments to China. This assistance would prove crucial because Japan's intensified air campaigns had seriously depleted China's air forces. By late 1941, however, additional purchases from the Soviet Union, the United States, and other countries raised aircraft totals to 364.[27]

Chongqing's aerial defense network derived direct benefits from these efforts. With a replenished supply of aircraft and pilots at their disposal, Chinese air units were stationed at nearby airfields such as Guangyangba and Baishiyi to intercept and destroy enemy aircraft. Air defense authorities also installed a network of communications and lookout posts along the flight route between Wuhan and Chongqing to monitor Japanese airfields and flight activity. In addition to charting the progress of Japanese flights from the moment they took to the air—relaying their number, composition, and estimated arrival time—this network also engaged in intelligence-gathering operations and reported on Japanese unit deployments. As described by Claire Chennault, the rough-and-ready system was akin to "a vast spider net of people, radios, telephones, and telegraph lines that covered all of Free China accessible to enemy aircraft. In addition to continuous intelligence of enemy attacks, the net served to locate and guide friendly planes, direct aid to friendly pilots who had crashed or bailed out, and helped to guide our technical intelligence experts to wrecks of crashed enemy aircraft."[28]

Besides the Chinese air force, Chongqing's active air defense infrastructure relied on a series of antiaircraft artillery emplacements strategically located at key sites around and downriver from the capital to form a ground-based defensive perimeter. These batteries were equipped with both large- and small-caliber antiaircraft weapons: in 1939, defending Chongqing were seventeen 75 mm antiaircraft guns, eight 37 mm rapid-fire cannons, and eight 20–25 mm cannons.[29] Later that year, in August, Chiang Kai-shek ordered the use of mobile antiaircraft artillery that could be moved to different locations to keep enemy bombers off balance.[30] To assist in night targeting and signaling, air defense authorities used an array of searchlight batteries and sound-ranging equipment imported from abroad to help pinpoint Japanese aircraft during night raids. Altogether, some twenty searchlight battery stations were spread around Chongqing, in the city proper, the South Bank and Jiangbei districts, as well as the airfields at Guangyangba and Baishiyi.[31]

The Chinese military command viewed these ground-to-air measures as vitally important for sending up defensive fire and distracting Japanese bombers. To improve their efficacy, the command ordered upgrades in training as well as the consolidation of artillery and searchlight units. Unit personnel were now expected to undergo a year-long training regimen divided into summer and winter terms. The command also expanded the instructional curriculum and mandated that recruits complete coursework in all aspects of antiaircraft gunnery and its uses. This coursework involved mastering such topics as "Principles of antiaircraft ordnance and gunnery" and "Daily tasks of heavy artillery units." Signal crews followed a similar course of study and learned the fundamentals of sound-ranging and lighting, searchlight technology, and signals communications systems.[32] Training in military observation techniques and other land-based air defense countermeasures rounded out the curriculum; essential texts consisted of Chinese translations of foreign military guides as well as drill manuals and technical specification primers produced by Chinese military affiliates. In all cases, recruits engaged in joint training exercises as well as individual physical drills to supplement their class instruction.

Chongqing's air defenses achieved mixed results. Both the Japanese and Chinese sides tended to inflate or minimize the results of their combat engagements when it was in their interest to do so, and in certain cases, the wrecks of downed Japanese aircraft were not always found until days after the fact.[33] Hit tallies and attrition rates posted by the Chinese indicate that Chongqing's air units, on the one hand, posed some deterrence to Japan's bombers, mostly in terms of disrupting attack formations and preventing Japanese aircraft from flying at lower elevations. Usually, this disruption caused Japanese bombers to drop their payloads prematurely and miss their intended targets. On the other hand, China's air defense forces were less adept in actual combat; in these cases, Chinese interceptors were only occasionally effective in warding off or downing Japanese bombers. Likewise, antiaircraft artillery units demonstrated sporadic success: according to internal reports compiled by the Chongqing Air Defense Command, from 1938 to 1941 Chinese antiaircraft units downed fifteen Japanese bombers and damaged eighty-five.[34] In view of this, China's military defenses complicated Japan's aerial operations but, ultimately, could not stop Japanese aircraft from bombing the city altogether.

The efficacy of these active air defense measures decreased as Japan expanded its air campaigns. One reason for this decline was that the Japanese air services deployed fighter escorts with their bombing missions, which tied up Chinese interceptors and prevented them from harassing or shooting down Japanese bombers. In addition, the Japanese naval authorities upgraded their fleets to faster and more agile aircraft capable of flying at higher altitudes and descending rapidly, which enabled them to evade Chinese warplanes and antiaircraft fire more easily. Finally, Japan's strategy of dispatching multiple groups of aircraft at timed intervals resulted in Chinese air units being stretched too thin to hold off a concentrated attack lasting several hours.[35] Oftentimes, they simply withdrew to avoid sustaining losses. The peak period of Japan's bombardment of Chongqing—the summer months of 1940–1941—reflected this pattern of engagement, and the Chinese air services stationed around the capital could provide only limited protection against Japan's aerial assaults, despite putting up spirited and tenacious resistance.

Fortunately, Chongqing's air- and ground-based defenses were not the only means on which the city relied for ensuring the safety of its citizens. In addition to these active measures, the Nationalist government marshaled manpower and resources to organize an extensive civil defense system. This system involved a multiagency effort at the national, regional, and local levels. As the Sino-Japanese struggle played out in the skies over the capital, the imperatives of air defense necessitated a corresponding reorganization of life on the ground and, not surprisingly, underground as well.

Air Raid Shelters and Daily Life in the City

Chongqing's "passive" air defense measures received high priority as air defense authorities formulated a crisis management plan for the city in late 1937. Among the first of these initiatives was the mass construction of air raid shelters. An integral part of the civil defense structure, these large-scale engineering projects dotted the capital's cityscape for the better part of the war years and were considered the most direct means of providing security to the capital's residents against air attacks. Preliminary discussion for underground construction began in response to a 1936 police census, which counted some 339,200 people in roughly 74,400 households within the municipal boundaries.[36] These data sparked concerns over a growing population that lacked space to expand. This trend was later confirmed by government-published figures, which recorded a steady annual increase in residential population numbers each year. (See table 10.2.)

Gu Zhutong, who would become commander of the Chongqing headquarters of the Military Affairs Commission, convened a meeting to discuss the possibility of constructing underground tunnels as a solution to overcrowding problems. Engineering consultant Zuo Yingshi, Chongqing mayor Li Hongkun, and the city's secretary general, Zhao Ziying, among others, offered recommendations, and it was decided that two tunnels would be built in sections near Linjiang Gate and Fuzichi in the north-central part of the Upper City and along the major east–west thoroughfare of Daliangzi in the southeastern part of the district.[37] A disaster management task force, one of the work groups that operated under the supervision of the city's civil defense corps, took charge of the project. With the approval of government authorities, a site was chosen, and construction began.

September 1937 saw further progress. In this month, the Air Defense Command, an agency under the direct supervision of the Military Affairs Commission, was established, and it was tasked with coordinating air defense efforts in the capital. In addition, Chiang Kai-shek's personal intervention gave air defense initiatives renewed importance. In a directive sent to the commission, he instructed all subordinate departments, work groups, and task forces to provide immediate direction and assistance to the people for building basic air raid shelters.[38] He listed general specifications as well as other relevant guidelines for compliance and concluded

TABLE 10.2

Population of Chongqing, 1937 to 1944

Year	Households	Total Population[a]
1937	107,682	475,968
1938	114,116	488,662
1939[b]	99,203	415,208
1940[b]	89,300	394,092
1941[c]	134,183	702,387
1942	165,293	830,918
1943	158,231	923,403
1944	185,505	1,037,630

[a] Actual totals were likely much higher because these totals do not account for the migrant population or boat people.
[b] The totals for the years 1939 and 1940 reflect population decreases arising from the evacuation of people to areas outside the city limits.
[c] The expansion of the municipality's boundaries in this year accounts for a portion of the increase in population numbers.
SOURCE: Chongqing Municipal Government, Chongqing yaolan (Chongqing, 1945).

with orders to construct a shelter in the area known as Central Park. Chiang's instructions underlined that air defense was not simply a technical endeavor in the service of a military objective but part of a larger effort that required the active participation of both government and citizens in order to succeed.

In the three months after Chiang's directive, roughly fifty air defense shelters with a capacity of over 7,000 people were built, including the experimental shelter at Central Park.[39] With nearly 500,000 people in the municipality and surrounding suburbs by the end of 1937, air defense authorities realized that they would have to adapt and refine Chiang's crude construction specifications to the actual conditions of the city. Larger-scale alternatives would have to be considered to keep up with the burgeoning population. Furthermore, concentrating manpower and resources on a few larger shelters would be more cost effective than dispersing those assets to build a multitude of smaller ones. After much discussion, a plan was drafted that envisioned a vast subterranean network of caves and tunnels, totaling two and a half miles in length, with multiple entry points accessible from different parts of the city. This layout, municipal officials believed, would maximize the number of neighborhoods that could be accommodated in shelters. In addition, the plan had a built-in safety precaution in the event that one entrance became obstructed or otherwise impassable, since there would be numerous alternative exits for residents to access.

Because the Old City was sorely lacking in civil defense facilities, it was a natural choice for the tunnel's proposed building site. Air defense authorities, working with municipal work units and the Chengdu–Chongqing Railway Bureau, surveyed the area in mid-December 1937. To coincide with a groundbreaking ceremony, city authorities established a project office in August of the following year. With an estimated cost of 468,000 yuan the entire project was to be completed in six months.[40] Excavating the air raid shelters, however, proved no easy task. Not only did it necessitate chiseling deep into the solid sandstone on which the Old City was built, but the pace of construction was impeded by a chronic lack of funding. A budget allocation of 200,000 yuan had been granted in February 1938 for air defense efforts, with requests for further funding subject to approval by the central government.[41] When additional money was not forthcoming— and faced with a revised project total of 710,000 yuan due to inflation and unanticipated construction costs—local authorities had no choice but to scale down the original project, opting instead to build a series of smaller caves and tunnel systems for shelters.

In the meantime, construction of air raid shelters in other parts of the city continued. In 1938, a total of 166 shelters were constructed, tripling the capacity of the previous year. The devastating air attacks of 3–4 May 1939 spurred the government to redouble its efforts and build roughly 800 more shelters, leading to a sevenfold increase in capacity by the end of the year.[42] This trend continued for the next several years: 1941 saw nearly 1,400 shelters built with a capacity of 370,000; in 1942, slightly over 1,600 shelters were excavated, accounting for a total capacity of 428,000; by 1944, several thousand shelters were counted, accommodating an estimated 450,000 people.[43]

Air raid shelters did not conform to one generic type. Besides the conventional dugout or cave configuration, shelters could range from fairly basic versions consisting of a dirt trench with a thin piece of wood used as an overhead covering, to elaborate privately run shelters charging admission fees and offering such amenities as chairs and tables, electric lamps and refrigerators, bathrooms, and reading material for those who could afford to pass the time in leisure. Indeed, private shelters had begun to appear almost immediately, and many were the exclusive retreats for high-level people from government and the military, publishing houses, larger factory and work units, and the well-to-do class.[44] Of the roughly 1,400 shelters in operation in mid-1941, approximately 470 were public bomb shelters, and 930 were privately managed.[45]

Besides air raid shelter construction, another major initiative was the government's annual evacuation campaigns. After the disastrous raids of

3–4 May 1939, air defense authorities spent the next several months preparing for a mass evacuation that would depopulate the city proper by some 250,000 people. Indeed, since February, plans for such an evacuation had already been in place. The Emergency Evacuation Committee formed that month adopted formal measures for mass relocation: it created fire lanes and drafted a timetable for evacuation. Voluntary evacuations would take place until 10 March. Thereafter, subject to necessity, local authorities would conduct forced evacuations in order to create firebreaks. Such campaigns became an annual event after 1939 and involved a large-scale effort by the government to relocate roughly 300,000 people on a temporary basis to the suburbs and surrounding countryside.

Exhortations and public announcements requesting volunteers usually began in late February, and actual relocation occurred during March and April. Military garrison personnel distributed registration cards to approved evacuees, identification that they had to show to guards in order to reenter the city.[46] As an added incentive, the government granted favorable terms and access to land and real estate to evacuees interested in opening up shops or businesses in outlying areas. As for suburbanites, if they took it upon themselves to set up "plain-use" dwellings for evacuees' use, they could receive up to 70 percent reimbursement from local authorities.[47] The bombing raids left countless people destitute and homeless, and they, along with other refugees, would often be among those evacuated. Based on government guidelines, certification of refugee status accrued certain benefits, including a resettlement package that included funds for food, upkeep, and travel to one's resettlement area as well as a four-month stipend.[48]

The establishment of an air raid alert system also contributed to the city's defense infrastructure. As already noted, this system relied on a network of observation towers, intelligence outposts, and ground and radio communications lines. Upon receiving notification that Japanese planes had been sighted leaving Wuhan, the city's civil defense corps would hang a red lantern from a vantage point visible to the rest of the city, a signal to inform residents of the possibility of an air raid. If observers sighted bombers at Yichang, located some 400 miles downriver from Chongqing in Hubei Province, authorities would elevate the city's alert status, stringing up a second red lantern and sounding a siren alarm, one long wail of twenty seconds followed by two short wails repeated six times.[49] At this point, roughly an hour's lag time remained before the aircraft would arrive over the city, and citizens were obliged to follow air defense procedures and head to their designated air raid shelters. As soon as bombers reached Fuling county on the outskirts of Chongqing, the urgent-warning alarm was sounded, consisting of a three-minute staccato wail that pierced the soundscape of the city. The lanterns were taken down, and there was nothing left to do but wait for the bombs to fall. Not until the sound of a single siren wail pierced the air, accompanied by the appearance of a green lantern, was it safe for the city's inhabitants to return to their homes and workplaces.

As early as 1938, municipal authorities issued a series of emergency regulations specifying air raid precautions, including mandatory citywide air raid drills to prepare citizens for such contingencies. Thereafter, as Japan's bombing campaigns escalated, these and other procedures were widely publicized through a variety of outlets: public notices, newspapers, and informational pamphlets spread the word about bomb shelter regulations, entry/exit protocols, street curfews, antigas protection, and enforced blackouts. Volunteer agencies supplied practical information on packing necessities and arranging daily schedules in case of air attacks. Neighborhood associations and work units held meetings to discuss safety measures, while fire prevention brigades, municipal police units, and civil defense forces mobilized personnel for training and exercises. School administrators also received guidance on how to prepare students for emergencies, and a youth corps was assembled to assist in air defense tasks. Commercial presses and government affiliates published a range of educational materials and specialized booklets instructing citizens on proper behavior before, during, and after air raids. In all cases, residents were expected to abide by air raid regulations, and gradually such procedures became a matter of routine for much of the population.

Japan's use of incendiary bombs against Chongqing proved highly effective in maximizing damage to the city's physical environment: if actual bombardment did not lay immediate waste to the area, then the ensuing fires most certainly did. In response, municipal authorities amended city building codes and construction guidelines to minimize the possibility of conflagrations such as those that had engulfed the city in the summer raids of 1939–1940. An emergency bulletin issued by the Municipal Bureau of Public Works in October 1940 stipulated that all new structures must be constructed with fire-resistant materials: wood, bamboo, and other materials would no longer be permissible; only bricks and stones could be used.[50] The following year, the bureau published a series of supplemental and revised guidelines that supplanted all existing temporary regulations and codified new standards to facilitate air defense tasks as well as fire prevention and rescue work. These standards took effect in 1941 and included provisions for expanding evacuation zones; widening thoroughfares to create improved fire lanes; fixing distances between structures; and specifying size, height, and space limits for city buildings. In addition, large-capacity buildings were required to build an attached air raid shelter for use by occupants.[51] Updating Chongqing's regulatory framework was a necessary step in strengthening the city's emergency response services, and it enabled municipal authorities to make corresponding upgrades in other areas of civil defense.

Both national and local authorities gave serious attention to the popular mood in the city, especially as Japan's bombing campaign continued unabated. Indeed, war weariness was a matter of utmost concern for the KMT administration from the beginning of the conflict, and government authorities were conscious of the potentially disastrous impact of air raids on popular morale. Chiang Kai-shek himself indicated as much when he gave a speech on 16 May 1939, entitled "Bombing of Civilians and Open Towns."[52] Moved by scenes of devastation and distress in Chongqing after the 3–4 May bombing raids, Chiang addressed the nation in his first extended public commentary on the subject. He condemned Japan's "ruthless and wanton bombings" of Chinese cities and noted that the purpose of such attacks was "to strike terror into the hearts of our people, forcing them into submission and surrender."[53] To the contrary, Chiang declared, the conduct of the people and official personnel were exemplary:

Since the recent massacres from the air at Chungking they have gone about their work as usual and have shown the same calm and steady courage. Such sterling qualities of character will render futile the nefarious schemes of the enemy. In addition, the Government has been working night and day to devise efficient and permanent measures for safeguarding the people against danger from the air. These measures are better and better each day, so that when raids occur in the future, they will cost the enemy dearly without accomplishing his main objective of terrorizing our people.[54]

Clearly, the psychological impact of the bombing raids was not lost on Chiang, and it prompted him to make a public statement not only to the people of Chongqing but to the rest of the nation. If China was to survive, he stated in no uncertain terms, the will of the people must remain resolute and unyielding, thereby rendering futile the enemy's plot to terrorize the populace into submission. Concurrently, to allay people's fears and prevent mass panic, the generalissimo reaffirmed the government's commitment to ensuring the people's safety and well-being. This awareness of the mental and emotional toll that aerial bombardment could exact on an unprepared population informed many of the government's wartime social programs and voluntary campaigns in the capital.

Public events, in particular, were one important vehicle used by the government to counter these stresses and encourage national unity. Sporting competitions, clothing drives, and music performances promoted Chongqing's collective spirit while also relieving some of the tedium and austerity of daily life. Citywide celebrations also helped foster a sense of communal identity forged through shared adversity. In 1940, for instance, to mark the occasion of China's first aerial engagement with Japan three years earlier, 14 August was proclaimed Air Forces Day.[55] Not long after, a second holiday—Air Defense Day—was established on 21 November to celebrate the first air raid drill conducted in Nanjing in 1934. On these days, prominent Nationalist officials, including Chiang Kai-shek and Madame Chiang, appeared at public rallies in Chongqing and reminded citizens of the importance of vigilance and perseverance against Japan's air raids. The Aviation Committee printed commemorative volumes days in advance to prepare for the events. Many military figures and well-known personalities were enlisted to write essays and reflections on air defense, not only to put an official stamp on the festivities but also to praise the joint efforts of citizens and soldiers in resisting Japan's terror campaign up to that point.[56] Throughout the war, in fact, such government-sponsored campaigns and mass rallies were a common sight in the wartime capital, prompting many foreign visitors to comment on the admirable resiliency of the population in the face of Japan's terror campaign.

From the perspective of the central government, these events could serve multiple purposes. In particular, they offered both encouragement and reassurance to Chongqing's residents that all measures were being taken to manage the crisis and to safeguard the population's well-being from Japanese air attacks. The presence of the generalissimo and his wife, often in the company of foreign dignitaries, was meant to assure citizens that China's leaders remained committed to the cause and stood united with Western allies to oppose Japanese aggression. In some cases, these gatherings provided an outlet for people and groups to come together in a collective display of unity: work units and newspaper agencies would often organize personnel to participate in marches and parades. The events served a practical function as well, since they drew attention to air defense as a joint responsibility of officials and citizens. All of these objectives were tied to the government's efforts to gauge and maintain popular morale in the city during the war.

Even as Nationalist authorities were mindful of the perils posed by air raids and took great pains to publicize them to the population, each successive cycle of Japan's campaign nevertheless exposed the ever-present dangers and myriad difficulties in defending a city against unpredictable attacks from the sky. While Chongqing's civil defense preparations as a whole became more efficient and routine every year, the system's essential effectiveness still depended on human judgment and execution. Unfortunately, authorities in the wartime capital learned this lesson the hard way, as evidenced by events that took place on the night of 5 June 1941, involving an air raid tunnel in the central district of Jiaochangkou. On this evening, large numbers of people had crowded into the shelter that served a busy downtown section. After more than three hours of continuous bombardment, crowded conditions and inadequate ventilation eventually combined to provoke mass panic. In the ensuing pandemonium to escape the tunnel, countless occupants were suffocated, crushed, or trampled to death.[57]

Known as the "6/5 Great Tunnel Tragedy," this incident and subsequent public outcry threw into vivid relief the enormous human stakes involved in air defense work. While the official government report counted 992 people dead and 151 people hospitalized for serious injuries, eyewitnesses contradicted these figures and claimed death tolls as high as 10,000. Although the actual tally may never be known for certain, the tragedy exposed a more problematic aspect of the government's air defense initiatives: namely, that despite the implementation of elaborate air raid procedures since mid-1939, such plans could not always fully account for—or preclude—the practical problems that arose from crowding people into shelters for extended periods under extreme stress. The 5 June tragedy vividly demonstrated that despite the government's concerted efforts, air defense imperatives did not always translate smoothly into people's daily lives and routines.

Assessing the Impact of Japan's Bombing Campaign
on China

Japan's terror bombing of Chongqing could not but leave a strong imprint on the city's administration and population. During the peak years of 1939–1941, the systematic and sustained air offensive undertaken by the Japanese air services leveled much of the city, disrupted essential services and operations, and displaced large numbers of Chinese. The air raids also exacted a substantial human and material toll and gave rise to a host of social welfare and public health issues.[58] Mass aerial bombardment affected individuals and groups from all walks of life—official and private, foreign and local, urban and rural—some more directly than others, to be sure. In carrying out their mission, the Japanese showed themselves to be determined and relentless, and Chongqing's population bore the brunt of this effort to terrorize Chinese citizens into submission. Yet Japan's strategic initiative did not achieve its main objective: China did not surrender, nor did Chiang Kai-shek's government concede to Japanese demands. There are many reasons for this outcome, and a brief review of some of the more decisive factors is needed to arrive at a final assessment of the air war and its significance for the Sino-Japanese conflict.

From the beginning, the Chinese government held to a steadfast and uncompromising stance in response to Japan's invasion, and this attitude carried over into its initiatives in the wartime capital. As early as 1936, Chiang Kai-shek instructed provincial and municipal authorities to consult and draw up plans to put Chongqing on a war footing. Air defense was among the areas identified as strategic priorities, and once outright hostilities erupted, local governments accelerated efforts to create a consolidated network and support structure that would enable the city to defend and safeguard its inhabitants. Municipal authorities, for example, engineered a simple but functional air raid warning system to alert the city of impending Japanese attack. They also undertook large-scale construction projects to provide shelter and security from bombardment. The government built hundreds of air raid dugouts and tunnels and sponsored campaigns to raise public awareness and educate the people in air defense preparedness. These efforts operated in tandem with systematic evacuation and resettlement programs that aimed to keep the population in the capital at manageable levels, thereby minimizing fatalities and injuries and preventing excessive strain on city services.

Similar attention was devoted to active military measures. Chinese air units and antiaircraft artillery detachments were deployed to Chongqing to provide an additional layer of defense. Chinese interceptor aircraft routinely deterred and harassed Japanese bombers. Although these aerial engagements did not prevent Japanese aircraft from dropping bombs, they disrupted Japan's air operations early in the campaign. Later, as the Japanese air services revised their strategy and dispatched larger bomber contingents with fighter escorts, the Nationalist air forces invariably found themselves outnumbered and outgunned. Hampered by both a lack of trained pilots and a fleet consisting largely of older planes, they could not compete with Japan's newer, more agile aircraft that easily outmaneuvered them. China's inability to secure aerial superiority over the skies of Chongqing, however, did not deter Madame Chiang Kai-shek and others in the administration from seeking overseas assistance to modernize key sectors in the Chinese military that were deemed essential to the war effort.

Central government involvement was also instrumental in the creation of the city's defensive infrastructure. In many cases, Chiang Kai-shek himself spurred action through his close attention to air defense tasks in the capital, and his personal intervention provided the institutional impetus for mobilizing national and local authorities to begin preparations for the air war. The generalissimo acted in consultation with the Military Affairs Commission and key personal advisers to set strategic priorities and formulate directives. An air defense bureaucracy was established. Senior officials holding positions elsewhere in the administration were appointed to serve as department and bureau heads. To facilitate implementation, the commission organized the Chongqing Air Defense Command to coordinate and oversee the city's air defense initiatives. As one of its principal responsibilities, the command issued emergency protocols for carrying out air defense operations in the city. It also worked closely with affiliate organizations, subordinate bureaus, and municipal agencies to ensure compliance and monitor progress at the local level. In this way, air defense—both as a military imperative and as a series of concrete measures—was integrated into the daily operations of city administration. By the end of 1939, the principal components of the civil defense system were in place, giving tangible expression to the government's policy of resisting Japanese aggression.

Given the extensive attention and resources allocated to air defense efforts, how well did these measures translate into practice and, more importantly, were they effective? While only a general assessment can be made at this point, municipal government files provide some glimpses into the day-to-day workings of Chongqing's air defense system. Internal memos indicate that the system underwent continuous refinement and that air defense work was hampered by endemic—though not wholly unexpected—difficulties. Initially, many problems stemmed from residents ignoring government warnings, or disorganization and inexperience on the part of local workers in carrying out tasks. However, as policies and programs became more established, problems of this sort were largely curtailed, only to be replaced by more chronic and persistent problems arising from insufficient funding, a lack of administrative oversight, and uneven implementation. Oftentimes, these conditions compounded one another, since budgeting constraints frequently led to drastically scaled-down projects and cutbacks in critical areas such as maintenance and personnel hiring. In some cases, these problems combined with troubling tendencies in the Nationalist bureaucracy itself to delay and hinder progress.

One sector that was especially vulnerable to such problems turned out to be air raid shelter management. Government regulations stipulated that all shelter facilities and equipment be certified before shelters could be opened to the public. As shelter construction proceeded and the number of public shelters increased, regular upkeep was needed to ensure continued compliance with government-mandated sanitation and use standards. However, since shelter authorities had only a limited number of qualified staff to oversee and handle such matters, inspections did not always take place, and repairs sometimes took weeks or months to be made. Residents commonly complained of shelters with stagnant pools of water, insufficient lighting, and ventilators that did not work. In addition, correspondence between different branches of the air defense bureaucracy reflected concerns over limited resources; administrative units made regular requests for supplementary budgetary allocations to fund construction projects and ancillary activities like routine maintenance and structural upgrades.

Nevertheless, despite these challenges in implementation, a review of the available data strongly points to the efficacy of these air defense measures. Specifically, even as Japan's air campaigns became more intense and the city's population numbers grew, death and injury totals did not appear to increase appreciably during the three peak years of bombardment. This result suggests that air defense preparations and countermeasures proved relatively effective in achieving their primary objectives: saving lives and containing damage. Accordingly, while air defense authorities in Chongqing encountered their share of criticism and controversy—the tunnel tragedy of 5 June 1941 being one of the more prominent examples—one finds that the system functioned as a vital safety net to reduce the severity of air raids and forestall wholesale despair and panic from taking hold of the city. In this respect, the role of air defense work in providing people with a sense of security and safety cannot be wholly ignored.

One might well wonder how Chongqing's population weathered the air raids and, what, after all, was life under bombardment like? Although people's individual experiences could vary according to a wide range of factors not limited to one's status, residence, and occupation, most agreed that coming under attack from the skies was a terrifying and disorienting event not easily forgotten. For the uninitiated and initiated alike, survivor Adet Lin recalls, a dull drone was the first indication of approaching bomber squadrons, and from a distance it invariably elicited a mixture of curiosity and unease. Many Chinese had read or heard about the bombing of other cities, but most had never seen a bombing, let alone experienced one firsthand, and there was little to prepare them for what was to come. The sight of Japanese aircraft on the horizon could hold an odd fascination, but such thoughts were immediately dispelled once the deafening roar of engines neared and the incessant pounding began. Indeed, it was the sound that unnerved people most, for it jarred the senses and "could never be rubbed out."[59] Subsequent encounters were not any less frightening, and no amount of preparation could erase the nagging uncertainty over where or when an attack might occur. Chongqing's populace, as we have seen, quickly learned that the bombs did not differentiate among its victims, and those who had come to the city to escape the fighting found little peace of mind.

The air raids of 3–4 May 1939 represented a turning point for the city, mainly because they shattered people's belief that Chongqing was somehow immune from attack. Though government officials had been preparing for such an eventuality, the reality of mass aerial bombardment was not fully comprehended until major sections of the city were set ablaze, buildings were reduced to rubble, and large numbers of the population were deprived of home and livelihood. As already noted, these scenes prompted air defense authorities to expedite plans to protect the capital from further conflagrations. In the popular realm, people altered their daily routines and took additional precautions so as not to be caught unprepared. Some heeded government advisories and took up temporary residence in the countryside where there was less likelihood of being targeted by Japanese bombers. Others made do by limiting their daily activities and traveling only when necessary. For those whose work or family obligations required them to go to different parts of the city, it was always advisable to be aware of nearby shelters in the event that the air raid warning siren sounded.

Because the government required citizens to clear the streets during alarms and seek out the nearest shelter, spending long hours underground became a regular part of people's lives. Factories and workplaces lacking their own shelters were usually assigned access to a nearby facility. Eventually, some publishing houses, production plants, and government offices moved their entire operations into protected facilities to forestall work stoppages. As for the general population, they could take cover in one of the many public shelters located around the city. However, conditions at these sites were not always ideal. Many of the tunnels had been created by drilling deep into the city's bedrock and were prone to water seepage. Poor air circulation added to the subpar conditions. In contrast to private shelters, public shelters had limited amenities: seating, when provided, often consisted of a few benches and stools, while buckets served the role of toilets. Han Suyin, who spent six hours in a public shelter on her first day in the city, summed them up as "wet, dark, and suffocating."[60] Indeed, when improvements were slow to be made, some people preferred to remain in their homes rather than have to endure uncomfortable waits in the public shelters.

Notwithstanding these and other hardships people faced on a regular basis, the government and local population were able to regain a measure of normalcy in their daily lives and operations in spite of the air raids. This normalcy was in part possible because Japan's bombing missions were carried out predominantly in the late spring to early fall, affording municipal authorities valuable time and breathing space the rest of the year to regroup and focus on reconstruction efforts. Residents, for their part, benefited from having a much-needed psychological respite. Indeed, throughout the war, people displayed a surprising adaptability to each turn of events, however traumatic. Israel Epstein, a Western journalist based in the city, observed that Chongqing's population seemed to bounce back in spite of the devastation inflicted upon them by Japanese bombers:

After the raid on May 3 this year [1941] the streets were a mess of smashed telephone poles, tangled wiring, the sinister sulphur dust of incendiary bombs, chunks of plaster and mortar, bits of clothing ripped from no longer existing cupboards, papers and personal letters blown out of somebody's desk drawers. But they did not stay like that for long. Everywhere the clean-up men were busy. Linesmen hitched up wires and had many circuits re-established by evening. Sweepers cleared away the debris and shopkeepers tidied up the sidewalks in front of their places of business. People bombed out of their homes collected what they could find of their belongings, built temporary shacks where enough material was available, cooked tea over little camp-fires, talked of whether the enemy would really bomb as much this year as he did last.[61]

These scenes were not unusual, and Japan's intimidation tactics did not make them any less commonplace. Such seemingly mundane sights offer some indication of the public attitude and reaction to the bombing raids: notably, Chongqing's population manifested a resolve that reflected a general acceptance of prevailing conditions. In many ways, they had already seen the worst and lived to tell about it. With little recourse but to adjust to the circumstances at hand, it is not surprising to find that citizens simply carried on with their lives as best as they could.

Finally, circumstances quite apart from Chongqing's air defenses—but nonetheless closely affiliated—also served to frustrate Japan's objectives. For all of the havoc that Japan's air raids caused, they were never able to cut off the wartime capital from the outside world, nor were they successful at interdicting China's supply and communication lines. Throughout the war, Chiang Kai-shek and Guomindang officials, private individuals and foreign visitors, were able to travel to and from Chongqing. From the wartime capital, it was possible to fly directly to Hong Kong and Rangoon before 1941, and from there, one could secure air passage to the United States. After these cities fell to Japanese forces, Kunming and Lanzhou served as the air transfer points. Correspondingly, the conflict as a whole disrupted the supply chains for basic commodities. While Japan's air campaign undoubtedly contributed to this state of affairs, it did not cause a wholesale breakdown of the flow of goods and foodstuffs to the city. This was largely because the Chinese government tended to view wartime shortages as a separate and distinct management problem and instituted specific measures to address the issue, among which were establishing a rationing system and forbidding war profiteering.[62]

On the political front, Japan's attempt to create internal divisions within the Chinese polity likewise failed to bear fruit. Despite its initial success in bringing the Kuomintang official Wang Jingwei on board in December 1938 and installing him as titular head of a reconstituted Nanjing regime two years later, the Japanese high command refused to give Wang much leeway to build a viable movement that would challenge the Nationalists. As a result, Wang's administration was never able to dissociate itself fully from either its puppet overseers or the stigma of collaboration, and his "peace initiative" found little appeal among the Chinese population. Wang himself did not live to see the end of the war,[63] and aside from his defection, no other serious challenge was mounted against Chiang Kai-shek's leadership from within the Kuomintang's ranks. Indeed, anyone who disagreed with Chiang or dared to voice differing opinions was quickly demoted. In certain cases, the Chinese secret police were dispatched to intimidate and set naysayers straight. With little tolerance for dissent, little impetus—oppositional or otherwise—existed to prompt a radical shift in war policy, let alone offer a compelling political vision that could undermine Chiang's authority.

The Japanese high command's assumption that concentrated air bombardment would destabilize the Chinese establishment accounted neither for China's continuing defiance nor for the thoroughgoing measures adopted by the Nationalist government to counter air attacks. Thus, the expected result of Japan's aerial campaign—China suing for peace—did not materialize. Both parties invested considerable amounts of manpower and resources to achieve their respective aims, a fact that testified to the seriousness with which each side viewed the air war. For the Chinese, air defense initiatives required coordination and cooperation among different branches of the bureaucracy, official personnel, and the population at large to be carried out. External factors such as foreign assistance and technical support, first from the Soviets and later from the Americans, gave Chiang Kai-shek's government valuable maneuver room in dealing with the Japanese threat while allowing it to conserve its resources. As for the Japanese side, naval air units had to be stationed at forward bases in Wuhan and Yichang in order to carry out their bombing missions into the interior. Because the Japanese navy dispatched air groups on a rotating basis, each cycle of the campaign necessitated a constant reinvestment of military resources into the China theater to carry out these bombing missions.

The "Great Bombing of Chongqing" represented a crucial juncture in the Sino-Japanese conflict, one that underscored both the expansive dimensions of the war as well as its destructive capacity. For many, air bombardment was not only a new and unfamiliar experience but also one that gave the war an unexpected immediacy. In this respect, it was not difficult for Chongqing's residents to imagine themselves as active participants in the war comparable to soldiers on the front lines. Indeed, far from breaking the will of the people, the air raids contributed to a heightened sense of shared purpose and hardship between state and society in the wartime capital, a sense that was conducive to building a unified consensus for resisting Japanese aggression. This opportunity did not go unnoticed by Chinese authorities, and their response was to formulate new strategies for preserving the established political and social order that was under siege. On a broader level, the experience of Chongqing shows how the air war, under the best of circumstances, still operated according to a certain logic, one that was constantly evolving in response to changing domestic and international circumstances, even as it was being shaped by internal and external constraints. Because of this process, the outcome of the air war was far from a foregone conclusion, and steps taken by each side had decisive implications for succeeding phases of the air war. In other words, the lesson, if one is to be sought, is perhaps that the strategic deployment of air power was insufficient by itself to effect the desired military outcome. Instead, one must take into account a range of factors—political, social, psychological, and technological—to understand how and why the conflict unfolded as it did. In this way, the air war as it was brought to bear in China serves as a valuable case study for illuminating the range of challenges, tensions, and dilemmas regarding total war and the limits of mass aerial bombardment to achieve total victory.

11 *China's Quest for Foreign Military Aid*

ZHANG BAIJIA

Introduction

From the outbreak of the Sino-Japanese War in 1937 to the end of the Second World War in 1945, Germany, the Soviet Union, and the United States of America in succession provided military aid and cooperation to China. This chapter investigates these historical experiences principally from the Chinese perspective. The two main themes are: (1) the Chinese background during each period of cooperation and the major military, diplomatic, and domestic political objectives of the Nationalist government in seeking foreign aid; and (2) the process of delivering aid, the amounts and kinds of aid, and the role of aid in the Sino-Japanese War. The conclusion compares China's different patterns of cooperation with each of these three countries.

German Advisers and German Munitions Exports to China

When the Sino-Japanese War broke out in the summer of 1937, the Nanjing Nationalist government's Central Army had been trained by German military advisers. The Model Forces, the most powerful part of the Central Army, were equipped solely with German weapons, China's main armaments factories relied on German machinery for producing weapons, and even China's defense plans had been prepared by German military advisers. So many German military advisers participated in the first major battle of the war, the Shanghai campaign beginning on 13 August 1937, that some Westerners and Japanese even called it the "German War." If we consider the close relations between Nazi Germany and Japan, this arrangement seems strange, but it had historical origins.

Traditionally, Germany had consistently been a major exporter to China of armaments technology, manufacturing machinery, warships, and munitions. In April 1927, Chiang Kai-shek established the Nationalist government in Nanjing, providing a new opportunity for Sino-German military and economic cooperation. Until then, Chiang had admired Germans unreservedly. He believed that the disciplined nature and the realistic spirit of the dedicated German nation could be a model for the education of China, that Germany's military could be a blueprint for the reconstruction of the Chinese armed forces, and that German financial institutions could participate in the work of restoring the Chinese economy. He still believed that Germany would support his establishment of a system of centralized authority and would support his anticommunism, but, unlike other powers, would have no desire to interfere in China's internal affairs.

Not long after Chiang Kai-shek took charge of the government, he began recruiting German advisers. All of the Germans who were recruited were directly employed as individuals by Chiang Kai-shek himself, so that the group of German advisers never obtained official recognition from the German government. The four men who served as the chief of the group of advisers from 1928 to 1938 were Major (Ret.) Max Bauer (November 1928 to May 1929), General Georg Wetzell (May 1930 to May 1934), General Hans von Seeckt (May 1934 to March 1935), and General Alexander von Falkenhausen (March 1935 to May 1938). During this period, 132 German military officers came to serve in China, the number peaking at 79 in 1933 and declining every year afterward until there were only 39 when the Sino-Japanese War broke out in 1937.[1] In addition to the military officers, significant numbers of engineering technical personnel and specialists in other areas were employed by Nationalist China.

The years 1928 to 1938 were a time in which the tensions between China and Japan grew sharper day by day, and the German advisory group performed an important role in the reconstruction of China's armed forces and national defense. The individual chiefs of the German advisory group made different contributions. Max Bauer established a "training unit" as a preliminary. Georg Wetzell expanded the "training unit" into three "model divisions" and also established ten artillery battalions, so that Generalissimo Chiang Kai-shek's Central Army had an elite force trained and equipped on the German model. He also improved China's military education system, and he pushed the Nationalist government to establish specialized troop branches, such as engineers, motorized troops, antiaircraft artillery, coast artillery, fortress troops, signal troops, and artillery observation units. Hans von Seeckt concentrated his energies on strengthening China's national defense capability, creating detailed logistic supply tables and a plan to develop the armament industry. On Chiang Kai-shek's request, he also designed a perimeter of national defense works between Shanghai and Nanjing in the Yangtze delta. This barrier was called China's Hindenburg Line and was an important construction project in China's national defense preparations against Japan. Falkenhausen proposed "protracted warfare to resist the enemy," suggesting the strategy of using Sichuan Province as the "final zone of resistance" against Japan. He also continued the three main projects initiated by his predecessors: training an elite mobile force, strengthening the defenses along the Yangtze River, and accelerating the development of China's defense industry. China's military-industrial authorities also relied on advanced German machinery in the reconstruction of old armaments factories and the establishment of a number of new ones.[2]

Under the leadership and assistance of the German military advisers, by the time of the outbreak of the Sino-Japanese War, the Central Army of the Nationalist government had been transformed from a force barely capable of fighting a civil war into a real army of national defense. As the work of the German advisers in China progressed, the Nanjing government's purchases of armaments and military material continuously increased. In the beginning, Sino-German trade basically followed the "cash-commodity" model. Because China had restricted foreign exchange reserves, the scale of the munitions trade was relatively limited. Most of the armaments purchased by the Nanjing government were artillery, light weapons, and ammunition, and the munitions imported from Germany were mostly used in Chinese civil wars. China purchased heavy weapons from Germany only in order to equip the German-style Model Forces. In May 1934, Chiang Kai-shek secretly informed Germany that from that time on China would purchase munitions only from Germany.[3] In August of the same year, Nationalist government finance minister Kong Xiangxi (H. H. Kung) secretly signed a Contract for the Exchange of Chinese Agricultural and Mineral Raw Materials for German Industrial Products with the German merchant Hans Klein. According to the terms of this contract, China could order munitions and armaments from Germany and pay for them with primary agricultural and mineral products.[4] In April 1936, the Chinese and German governments signed the Sino-German Credit Loan Contract. In fact, this agreement upgraded the previous contract signed by the Nanjing government and Hans Klein to a bilateral contract between the two governments. At the same time, the German government provided a loan of 100 million reichsmarks to the Nanjing government, which then used these funds to purchase commodities from Germany.[5] After the implementation of this barter agreement, the volume of China's purchases expanded rapidly, and they included weapons and munitions urgently needed for operations against Japan, as well as industrial machinery needed to begin China's planned national defense industry and to fulfill the export of mineral products to Germany.

The Sino-German barter trade was obviously mutually beneficial. China needed to purchase German munitions and military-industrial machinery to strengthen its national defense. At the same time, Nazi Germany was stepping up its efforts to strengthen its armed forces. The Wehrmacht needed to test its new weapons in China; Germany's defense-related economic agencies needed to obtain and store strategic minerals from China, particularly tungsten and antimony; and its industrial cartels and munitions merchants needed to expand their sales to China. These were the main pressures pushing the expansion of German trade with China, and they also made the Nazi government move to the forefront in this bilateral trade.

After the barter trade began, China ordered many kinds of munitions and weapons from Germany, from big-ticket items like aircraft and submarines for the navy to smaller items like pistols and electric switches. The exact amount of the Sino-German munitions trade during this period is difficult to determine. On the one hand, because of wartime necessities, China's orders often changed: for example, all of China's submarine orders were finally cancelled. On the other hand, because of the later change in Sino-German relations, Germany did not fulfill all of its contracts. In August 1938, China and Germany jointly examined the account of the Handelsgesellschaft für industrielle Produkte (abbreviated as HAPRO, called Hebulou in Chinese), which was in charge of the Sino-German barter trade. After the Sino-German barter contract was implemented in August 1934, China ordered 389 million reichsmarks' worth of weapons, ordnance, and machinery. As of the end of October 1937, munitions from Germany worth 50 million reichsmarks had actually arrived in China.[6] In November 1937, responding to China's urgent appeal, Germany allocated munitions worth 53 million reichsmarks from the Wehrmacht for sale to China. In December 1937, Germany shipped two batches of weapons (including more than ten dive-bombers) to China with a total value of 44 million reichsmarks.[7] Thus, in the initial stages of the Sino-Japanese War, at least 147 million reichsmarks' worth of munitions had been shipped from Germany to China, and these German weapons undoubtedly strengthened the combat capability of the Chinese forces.

When the Sino-Japanese War broke out in 1937, the German military advisers remained devoted to their duties, but the outcome of the German advisory group's decade of effort was soon to be jeopardized. After the Marco Polo Bridge Incident (7 July 1937) Falkenhausen was sent by Chiang Kai-shek to the front lines in north China to discuss operations plans with Chinese commanders. Then, ignoring the German government's prohibition, Falkenhausen rushed to Shanghai to command Chinese forces engaged in encircling and annihilating the Japanese troops. On 13 August the Nationalist government began its "preemptive containment" attack in the Shanghai theater, designating the Eighty-seventh and Eighty-eighth divisions, elite divisions trained by the German advisers, as the main attack force. From Falkenhausen's point of view, this was an invaluable opportunity to demonstrate the success of the German advisers in training Chinese troops. The Shanghai-Songjiang battle lasted for three months, during which time the German-trained Chinese troops demonstrated fairly impressive combat abilities in the face of the attacks of the Japanese forces. However, in early November, after additional Japanese forces made their amphibious landing at Hangzhou Bay, the war situation deteriorated sharply, and the defense of Shanghai collapsed. In the course of the Chinese retreat, the "Far Eastern Hindenburg Line," which had cost more than 1 million yuan, was abandoned without playing any part in the resistance. On 13 December, the Japanese forces occupied the Chinese capital at Nanjing. It has been estimated that, between the Battle of Shanghai and the loss of Nanjing, the Chinese Central Army lost from one-third to as much as 60 percent of its 300,000 personnel. Among all the Chinese combat troops, the newly formed elite forces suffered most, losing 10,000 junior officers and the ability to fight independently thereafter.[8] After the loss of Nanjing, most members of the German advisory team withdrew to Wuhan with the Nationalist government. After this, there was not much work left for them to do.

The Sino-Japanese War rapidly escalated and became a protracted war, which meant that one could foresee the end of the German advisory team's mission in China. When all-out war broke out, Germany announced its neutrality and assured China that the German-Japanese Anti-Comintern Pact had no relationship to the Sino-Japanese conflict. But, as the war escalated, Germany's neutrality in fact was hardly sustainable. From the end of October 1937 to the middle of January 1938, the German government attempted to mediate the Sino-Japanese conflict through Germany's ambassador to China, Oskar P. Trautmann. After this mediation failed, Germany adopted measures to accommodate Japan, and Sino-German relations deteriorated sharply. In March 1938, after the program had run for several years, Germany unilaterally halted the Sino-German cooperative program of training Chinese staff officers in Germany. In April 1938, Hermann Goering issued an order prohibiting German munitions exports to China, and the German foreign ministry informed China that it was recalling all German military advisers. At the end of June 1938, the German government ordered the advisers to leave China as quickly as possible; all who failed to comply with this order "would be regarded as traitors to their country, would be deprived of citizenship, and all of their assets within Germany would be confiscated."[9] Subsequently, on the pretext that China had not allowed all of the German advisers to leave China on time, Germany recalled ambassador Trautmann. Germany did not send any ambassador to China thereafter. On 5 July 1938, the German military advisory group headed by Falkenhausen left China for Germany.

From 1938 on, all the Nationalist government's diplomatic efforts to revive the Sino-German relationship failed, except that Germany allowed one last shipment of munitions to China. In July 1938, after repeated lobbying by concerned Chinese staff and German enterprises, the German government finally gave an implicit green light, allowing the munitions that China had ordered before the German embargo for shipment in July to be transferred to a Finnish company and shipped to China. Sino-German relations remained frigid for several years, until on 1 July 1941 Germany formally recognized Japan's Wang Jingwei puppet regime in Nanjing, and the Chongqing Nationalist government publicly severed relations.

Soviet Military Aid to China

In June 1938, as the German military advisers were about to leave, twenty-seven Soviet military advisers and experts arrived in China. Soviet advisers had worked in China previously but had been forcibly expelled in 1927, after Chiang Kai-shek put anti-Soviet and anti-Communist policies into effect. Eleven years later, Soviet advisers returned to China, but this time their mission was not to support the Chinese revolution but to help China resist Japanese expansion. Even before this, the Soviet Union had offered China large amounts of weapons and had sent volunteer aviators to participate clandestinely in China's air operations.

After the Mukden Incident on 18 September 1931, Japan occupied northeast China, threatening the security of the Soviet far eastern region. Facing a common enemy, the Soviet Union and China reapproached one another. On 12 December 1932, after a lapse of several years, China and the Soviet Union restored diplomatic relations. But since contradictions and mutual distrust still existed, the readjustment of Sino-Soviet relations did not go smoothly. After full-scale war broke out in 1937, the Nationalist government had no other options, and on 21 August China and the Soviet Union finally signed the Mutual Nonaggression Treaty, which laid the political foundation for the Soviet Union to provide assistance to resist Japanese aggression. After the Sino-Soviet nonaggression pact was signed, the Soviet Union immediately adopted active measures to aid China. Stalin had the clear strategic goal of making China's resistance sufficiently effective to contain Japan so that it would have little strength left to attack the Soviet far eastern region.

Shortly before signing the nonaggression pact, the Nationalist government asked the Soviet Union for help. On 14 August 1937, the day after the Shanghai campaign began, Nationalist Party central executive committee member Zhang Chong, on behalf of Chiang Kai-shek, submitted a draft munitions supply contract to the Soviet plenipotentiary representative in China, D. V. Bogomolov. In this contract, the Nationalist government asked the Soviet Union to provide 350 aircraft, 200 tanks, and 236 artillery pieces, and also requested that the Soviet Union dispatch Soviet pilots, aviation technicians, artillerymen, and tank crews to China to train Chinese military personnel.[10] After the nonaggression pact was signed, the Nationalist government immediately sent a military delegation to the Soviet Union to seek assistance. The delegation was publicly called the "Chinese delegation for investigating Soviet industry" and was headed by Deputy Chief of Staff Yang Jie of the Military Commission. Before the delegation departed, Chiang Kai-shek himself met with Yang Jie and gave him the assignment of seeking direct Soviet participation in the war against Japan. At a minimum, Chiang Kai-shek hoped that "the Soviet Union would supply munitions to China continuously."[11]

The Soviet Union responded promptly. On 8 September the Chinese delegation arrived in Moscow and was warmly received. Yang Jie wrote in his diary that the Soviet Union "tries to give all of the things that China asked for, and charges very low prices, which clearly demonstrates its good will in helping China gain victory." From October 1937 to February 1938, a steady stream of aircraft and munitions arrived in China from the Soviet Union. These included 297 military aircraft, 290 cannon of various types, 82 tanks, 400 motor vehicles, all kinds of spare parts, and a large amount of firearms and ammunition, in total worth $485,574,436.[12] In this first phase the Soviet Union had already shipped more heavy weapons (such as aircraft, cannons, and tanks) than Germany did in total, and some of these Soviet weapons were the best that the Soviet Union could provide.

During the war, China paid for most of the Soviet munitions assistance with Soviet loans. In all, the Soviet Union gave three loans to China. The first was for $50 million and was concluded in Moscow on 1 March 1938. The relevant articles stipulated that China was to use the loan to purchase armament industry products and industrial equipment from the Soviet Union, meaning in fact that China could purchase aircraft, cannons, and other munitions and goods urgently needed in the war; that China should pay back the loan, with interest, with commodities and raw materials that the Soviet Union needed, the most important of which were tea, tung oil, medicinal materials, leather, sheep's wool, silk, cotton, antimony, tin, zinc, nickel, tungsten, and red copper. The repayment period was to be five years, with an annual interest rate of 3 percent. The second loan was also for $50 million; it was concluded in Moscow on 1 July 1938, and it also had a repayment period of five years.[13] The third and last Soviet loan was for $150 million, signed on 13 June 1939 in Moscow, and the agreement stipulated that this loan should be repaid within ten years. The use, interest, and method of repayment of the last two Soviet loans were basically similar to those of the first. In total, the three Soviet loans to China were worth $250 million, and China used the loans on nine occasions. The first

and second loans, worth $100 million in all, were used up in five install-
ments by 1 September 1939. From 1 September 1939 to 1942, four more
installments used a little more than half of the third loan. Shortly after the
Soviet-German war broke out, the use of the third Soviet loan was halted.
Thus, China used about $173 million or 69.2 percent of the total amount
of the three Soviet loans.[14]

The Soviet Union not only gave China loans on favorable terms but also
provided ordnance and munitions at prices much lower than the international market prices at that time. According to the memoirs of Chinese
diplomat V. K. Wellington Koo (Gu Weijun or Vi Kyuin Koo), Sun Ke (Sun
K'o), head of the Legislative Yuan of the Nationalist government, said,
after returning from his second visit to the Soviet Union in 1939, that he
had obtained a new loan worth 160 million rubles from Moscow, and that,
compared to international market prices, this loan was equivalent to 400
million rubles because the Soviet Union charged low prices for the items
that China ordered. For example, the price of each aircraft was equivalent to only $30,000, so that in Chinese currency it took only 1.5 million
yuan to equip a Chinese division. Joseph Stalin and Military Commission
Chairman Chiang Kai-shek agreed to all of these favorable terms after
correspondence by telegram.[15] Prior to the German invasion of the Soviet
Union in June 1941, China used the Soviet loans to purchase the following
weapons and equipment: 904 aircraft of all types (including 318 light and
heavy bombers), 82 tanks, 1,526 motor vehicles, 24 tractors, 1,190 cannons of all types, 9,720 light and heavy machine guns, 50,000 rifles, more
than 167 million rifle bullets, more than 17 million machine gun rounds,
31,100 aircraft bombs, and more than 1.87 million rounds of artillery
ammunition, as well as airplane engines and full sets of replacement parts
for aircraft, aviation gasoline, and other munitions and equipment.[16]

One important aspect of Soviet assistance was the dispatch of volunteer
aviators. When full-scale war broke out in 1937, the Chinese air force
had about 300 combat aircraft. After the Shanghai-Songjiang campaign
started in mid-August 1937, the obviously inferior Chinese air force fought
bitterly and bravely, but by the end of November 1937, only about 30 aircraft survived, so the air force had completely lost its combat effectiveness.
After the Nationalist government's urgent appeal, the Soviet government
promptly took aircraft from the Soviet air force and sent them to China.
The first Soviet airplanes flew to China on 22 October 1937, accompanied
by the volunteer wing of the Soviet air force, composed of a fighter group
and a bomber group, in all 254 personnel. In early December 1937, the
Soviet volunteer wing entered battle at the critical moment of the defense
of Nanjing. Afterward, it carried out many combat missions in Shanghai, Nanjing, Wuhan, Lanzhou, Xi'an, Chongqing, Chengdu, and other
places. It also made a surprise attack on Taihoku (now Taipei) and struck
Japanese air, naval, and ground units. More than 700 Soviet air force vol-

unteers (including aviation technicians) came to China, and among them more than 200 gave their lives to the cause of the Chinese people's freedom and independence. Meanwhile, Soviet instructors trained more than 1,000 pilots and more than 8,000 aviation technicians. In the summer of 1939, the situation in Europe became increasingly tense, and the Soviet air force volunteers began to return to their country. Afterward, only a few advisers and instructors continued to devote themselves to training Chinese air force personnel in Lanzhou, Yining, and other places.[17]

Yet the scale of the Soviet aid to China continued to increase, and in June 1938, Chiang Kai-shek requested of Stalin, through Chinese ambassador Yang Jie, that the Soviet Union send high-level military advisers to China.[18] The Soviet Union responded promptly, sending advisers to China that month. During the war, the Soviet Union sent four successive chief military advisers to China. Military attaché M. I. Dratwin at the Soviet embassy came to China in November 1937 and served concurrently as the first chief adviser. Later, A. I. Cherepanov served from August 1938 to August 1939. K. M. Kachanov served from September 1939 to February 1941, and Vasilii I. Chuikov served from February 1941 to February 1942. The Soviet chief military adviser to China was directly under the Chinese supreme command, and beneath him advisory organs were established covering all the Chinese war zones and all branches of the Nationalist government's armed forces. The Soviet military advisers were talented officers; all had a high level of military education and were battle tested. They mostly did two kinds of work: training the Nationalist government's armed forces, and participating in the drafting and execution of plans for important operations.

Because of heavy losses in the initial stages of the war, Chinese forces urgently needed trained replacements as junior military officers and as technical specialists in the various service branches. The Soviet advisers adopted different training methods, based on combat realities, for personnel of different levels and different service branches, and tried energetically to raise the quality of the Chinese forces in the shortest possible time. They were irreplaceable in the training of the technology-intensive service branches, such as aviation, artillery, and armor. According to Soviet sources, 80 Soviet military advisers were in China in October 1939, and the number increased to 140 in early 1941. From 1937 to 1942, more than 300 Soviet military advisers came to work in China, and the total number of Soviet military advisers, experts, technicians, aviation volunteers, and others totaled about 5,000. Approximately 90,000 students in Chinese military schools were trained by Soviet advisers and experts.[19]

From 1938 to 1941, the Soviet military advisers participated in operational planning for several important campaigns on major Chinese fronts, such as the Wuhan campaign, the Yichang campaign, and the Second Changsha campaign. In this process, the chief Soviet advisers went to the front lines and made realistic recommendations, but their suggestions were seldom fully adopted by the Nationalist military authorities. The only exception was the Second Changsha campaign in the summer and autumn of 1941. In this campaign, the Chinese military authorities fully adopted the operations plan that the Soviet advisers had drafted, and, in consequence, the Japanese troops suffered heavy losses and were forced to retreat northward, temporarily abandoning their intention of advancing farther south.[20]

Overall, the Soviet military advisers maintained fairly good relations with the Nationalist military authorities, although they were never trusted by Chiang Kai-shek as fully as the German advisers had been. Because they were fairly experienced in working in China, the Soviet advisers paid full attention to proper working methods. An example of this occurred in the Second Changsha campaign. While they were drafting the operations plan, the Soviet advisers were fully aware that Chiang Kai-shek and his commanders lacked the courage to attack, but they did not criticize them openly, instead patiently working to win their support. After the victory at Changsha was announced, the Soviet advisers immediately lowered their profile, allowing Chiang and his commanders to take full credit for the victory. It was especially important that, in giving assistance to China, the Soviet Union avoid interfering in sensitive issues in China's internal affairs, insisting instead on giving all Soviet aid to the Nationalist government headed by Chiang Kai-shek. In this, Stalin's attitude was entirely pragmatic. Before Chuikov went to China, Stalin told him, "Logically, the Chinese Communist Party should be closer to us than Chiang Kai-shek. Logically, our main support should go to the Chinese Communist Party. However, if we did that, it would seem that we were exporting revolution to a country that has diplomatic relations with us. Chiang Kai-shek is receiving American and British aid. Mao Zedong (Mao Tse-tung) will never obtain support from these major powers. With Soviet aid and the aid from the Allies such as Great Britain and the United States, Chiang Kai-shek should at least be capable of containing Japanese aggression for a long time even if he cannot defeat it."[21]

Stalin's strategy was to let China pin down Japanese forces in order to avoid a Soviet-Japanese War, while the ultimate goal of Chiang Kai-shek's policy toward the Soviet Union was to make the Soviet Union participate in the war with Japan. To that end, the Nationalist government made continuous efforts. Chiang Kai-shek in person on two occasions urgently requested the Soviet Union to send troops to fight Japan. The first occasion was at the end of autumn 1937, when the Shanghai campaign was stalemated and the parties to the Nine-Power Treaty were about to convene in Brussels to discuss the Sino-Japanese conflict. The second instance occurred during the high summer of 1938. In July of that year, Soviet and Japanese forces clashed at Zhanggufeng on the Sino-Soviet border, and in August Chinese and Japanese armies fought a large-scale campaign around Wuhan. On both of these occasions when Chiang Kai-shek sought his assistance, Stalin responded that "now is not the right time for the Soviet Union to begin hostilities with Japan."[22] Afterward, the Soviets informed the Chinese that the Soviet Union would be able to participate in hostilities against Japan only in any of the following three cases: (1) if Japan attacked the Soviet Union, (2) if Great Britain and/or the United States went to war against Japan, or (3) if the League of Nations demanded that the countries in the Pacific Ocean area should wage war against Japan.[23] This reply was a clear refusal of Chiang Kai-shek's request. It is hard to say how much Chiang Kai-shek actually expected Soviet participation in the war against Japan, but in adversity, and fearing that this was his only possibility of help, he made a major effort to obtain it. Later, from May to September 1939, Soviet and Japanese forces clashed at Nomonhan on the Manchuria-Mongolia border. Once again, this raised Chiang Kai-shek's hope that the Soviet Union would go to war with Japan. This conflict was on an even larger scale than Zhanggufeng, but in the end it was also resolved peacefully.

In 1941, for a number of reasons, Sino-Soviet relations cooled rapidly. In January, Nationalist troops surrounded and exterminated the Chinese Communist Party's New Fourth Army in the Wannan (Southern Anhui) Incident. The Soviet Union intervened and put pressure on Chiang Kai-shek by threatening to halt aid. On 13 April the Soviet Union, seeing clearly that Japan had no intention of advancing northward, signed the neutrality treaty with Japan. On 22 June 1941 Germany invaded the Soviet Union, which afterward was too occupied to look eastward. In February 1942, the Soviet chief adviser, Chuikov, was recalled, a move that could be regarded as the signal that the Soviet policy of aiding China had come to an end. Since China had already concluded an alliance with the United States by then, Chiang Kai-shek no longer had any reason to invite Soviet advisers to come to China.[24] However, some Soviet advisers and experts remained until May 1944, when the Soviet government recalled them all because of the deterioration of Sino-Soviet relations after the Xinjiang (Sinkiang) Incident.[25] In August 1945, after the end of the war in Europe and according to the terms of the Yalta Agreement, the Soviet Union sent its armies into northeast China, thus hastening the end of the Second World War.

The Chinese-American Alliance and American Lend-Lease Aid to China

On 8 December 1941 (7 December in the United States) Japanese forces attacked Pearl Harbor, and the Pacific War began. On 9 December the Chinese Nationalist government formally declared war on Japan and announced that it was in a state of war with Germany and with Italy. On 1 January 1942, the United States, Great Britain, the Soviet Union, China, and others, twenty-six countries in all, jointly signed the United Nations Declaration, in which China was regarded as one of the four "Great Powers" of the world, as well as being formally allied with the United States. The Sino-American alliance aroused excessive expectations in both countries, and at the same time obscured the many kinds of difficulties that Chinese and Americans would have working together face to face.

Seen in hindsight, the road toward the Sino-American alliance was long and winding. When Japan occupied northeast China after the Mukden Incident on 18 September 1931, it could be said that in a certain sense Japan was openly challenging the Open Door Policy advocated by the United States, but the United States made only a moderate response. Secretary of State Henry Stimson put forward the Nonrecognition Policy, but the United States had no intention of taking substantive action. After Franklin Roosevelt was elected president, he confronted domestically both isolationist sentiment and the economic crisis of the Depression, and he basically adopted a policy of noninterference and nonintervention toward the Sino-Japanese conflict as he waited for the situation to develop.

As China was preparing to resist Japan, the United States helped to set up its civil aviation industry, the only aspect of Chinese defense construction in which the United States was then involved. In 1932, Colonel John H. Jouett of the U.S. Army Air Corps led a delegation to China and helped establish the Central Aviation Academy. The United States was China's most important aircraft supplier from 1933 to 1937. In the last half of 1937, a total of 279 American aircraft were shipped to China, but the number decreased sharply afterward.[26] Although cautious and low-key in helping China develop its aviation industry, the United States played an important role in the Chinese air force's embryonic stage.

The Nationalist government did not initially seek American assistance after the outbreak of full-scale war in 1937. Chiang Kai-shek believed that if China could hold out against Japan for a brief period, Great Britain, the United States, France, and the other Western countries would have to intervene to end the conflict as quickly as possible. At that time, China's diplomacy focused on Great Britain rather than on the United States. Only after both the Brussels meeting of the parties to the Nine-Power Treaty and the failed attempt at mediation by the German ambassador to China, Oskar Trautmann, did the Nationalist government begin to consider the question of wartime diplomatic policy seriously. The international situation eventually clarified in 1938, and the Nationalist government decided that its central wartime diplomatic goal should be to acquire American support. As Chiang Kai-shek concluded: "Great Britain is experienced and astute, and hard to lobby for help, and Russia has her own national policy, and our appeal to her for help has failed. But the United States is a democratic country in which public opinion matters, and it is relatively easy to activate her chivalrous spirit; moreover, President Roosevelt is ambitious to resolve the Far Eastern question thoroughly and comprehensively. If public opinion is sympathetic and Congress is supportive, then President Roosevelt will achieve his goals."[27]

During the first three years of the Sino-Japanese War, China could not obtain military assistance directly from the United States because of the country's Neutrality Act, so the Nationalist government made obtaining financial support and loan agreements the main objective. However, the United States government still permitted China to purchase a certain amount of small-caliber weapons and other materiel from the United States. After spring 1938, the Nationalist government used loan credits from the Sino-American Silver-Gold Exchange Agreement to purchase munitions worth $48 million.[28] In late 1938 and early 1939, China and the United States concluded the Tung Oil Loan Agreement, worth $25 million, their first loan agreement during the war. This loan was used mainly to purchase motor vehicles and improve the carrying capacity of the Yunnan–Burma road. The loan was the start of American aid to China and of wartime Sino-American cooperation. In March and September 1940 the $20 million Tin Loan Agreement and the $25 million Tungsten Ore Loan Agreement were concluded in similar fashion. According to the terms of these agreements, China still could not use these two loans to buy munitions that were forbidden by the Neutrality Act, but in reality the Nationalist government used the two loans to buy motor vehicles, armament industry machinery, aviation gasoline, and other munitions, and China also purchased 45,000 pistols and other items of military ordnance worth $2,684,700.[29] Motivated by the United States, Great Britain, from 1938 to the beginning of 1939, also extended two loans to China, amounting in all to £5.5 million.[30]

Germany, Italy, and Japan signed the Tripartite Pact in autumn 1940. Sino-American rapprochement accelerated rapidly as a result. On the one hand, as the international situation developed, the Roosevelt administration realized that China's power had to be strengthened in order to contain Japan; on the other hand, Chiang Kai-shek also seized this opportunity to put pressure on the United States. In mid-October, Chiang separately invited the British and American ambassadors to China for long conversations. When he talked with the British ambassador, he emphasized strongly that "in the Far East Great Britain and the United States rely solely on their navies and air forces, which were not enough to defeat Japan; they would also need the assistance of large ground armies in order to prevail." He warned that, if China ceased its war of resistance, Japan would then "be free to use all its human and material resources to implement its South-ward Advance policy."[31] When he talked with the American ambassador, he emphasized that the Nationalist government "was concerned only with the mad violence of the Chinese Communists" and "was not troubled any-more by the military aggression of the Japanese bandits." He stated that the Nationalist government's continued resistance "would not be possible unless it continued to receive substantial aid from the United States." He asked that the United States provide aircraft, send volunteers from its air forces to China, and at the same time give China a single large loan.[32] At the end of November 1940, Roosevelt, "fearing that there was some kind of activity going on between Chiang Kai-shek and Wang Jingwei," demanded that Secretary of the Treasury Henry Morgenthau promptly provide a large loan to China. On 30 November, the same day that Japan formally recognized the Wang Jingwei puppet regime in Nanjing, Roosevelt publicly announced a $100 million loan to China.[33] Afterward, Roosevelt ordered the U.S. departments of State, Treasury, War, and Navy to seek plausible channels to provide military assistance to China, and in February of the following year Roosevelt sent his administrative assistant, Lauchlin Cur-rie, to China to investigate the Chinese political and economic situation in preparation for the Lend-Lease Act, which was soon to be implemented.

Beginning in spring 1941, step by step, the United States put its China aid into the Lend-Lease Act assistance plan. On 17 April, after the conclu-sion of the Soviet-Japanese neutrality agreement, which had had a devas-tating impact on China's morale, the United States government decided to provide to China immediately $45 million worth of militarily useful com-modities.[34] This was the start of American Lend-Lease military assistance to China. On 6 May, Roosevelt formally announced that the munitions Lend-Lease Act applied to China, declaring that "defending China is the key to defending America."[35] In July 1941, Roosevelt sent Owen Latti-more to China to serve as political adviser to the Chinese government. In August the United States announced the appointment of John Magruder as military attaché and head of the American Military Mission to China (AMMISCA); Magruder's main responsibility was to oversee the delivery of Lend-Lease material to China.

After the Pacific War broke out, China and the United States immedi-ately formed an alliance. To strengthen Sino-American wartime coopera-tion, Roosevelt asked Chiang Kai-shek to serve as commander in chief of the Allied forces in the China theater, and sent Lieutenant General Joseph W. Stilwell, who had fifteen years' experience in China, to serve as the U.S. government's military representative in China, as chief of staff of the China Theater, and as commander in chief of the American forces in the China-Burma-India (CBI) theater.

However, because of the lack of mutual understanding and insufficient preparation, China and the United States were not able to establish a coordinated and effective joint command during the initial stages of their cooperation. After Stilwell took up his appointment, Chiang Kai-shek ordered him to go to Burma to command operations there. Because of many incompatibilities between the British and Chinese armies, coordinating them during the Burma campaign was difficult. Though eager for battle, Stilwell was not entirely familiar with the situation, and as a result he met with defeat. Stilwell abandoned the main body of his forces and withdrew into India, accompanied by an entourage of only about a hundred personnel. Chiang "as a result of this gradually lost respect for Stilwell's ability to command large troop formations, and gradually lost belief in his personal qualities."[36] Even worse than Stilwell's lack of success as an army commander was the total disagreement between the Chinese and the Americans in their conception and understanding of his official position. Chiang Kai-shek had agreed, in response to Roosevelt's demand, to have a lieutenant general of the United States Army come to China to serve as chief of staff, but Chiang expected to receive a chief of staff who did not understand the situation in China and would be willing both to obey his orders and to lobby for more aid from the United States. But, on the contrary, the person sent by the United States was a "China specialist" who also had multiple responsibilities. Stilwell's two most important responsibilities led to institutional confusion: as the American military representative in China, Stilwell had to follow the orders of the United States government and supervise and control all matters concerning American military aid to China, but as chief of staff, Stilwell was obliged to obey Chiang Kai-shek's directives.[37] From the beginning, China and the United States could not reach consensus on the definition of Stilwell's responsibilities, and this later became the focal point around which various kinds of contradictions turned.

Lend-Lease material occupied an important position in Sino-American wartime cooperation. On the eve of the Pacific War, China and the United States had reached agreement on three major points regarding military assistance to China: first, to provide training and technical support to assist China in establishing a modern air force; second, to provide training and equipment for a ground army of thirty divisions; third, to assist China in constructing railways and highways from Yunnan to Burma, along with the provision of rolling stock and vehicles.[38] However, while China waited for the flow of American aid to arrive, American plans to give assistance to China were thrown into disarray by the outbreak of the Pacific War. The "Europe first" strategy and the fact that China was at the end of the longest and narrowest supply line that the United States had maintained determined that the United States was unable to provide large amounts of modern military equipment to China, even after its entry into the war.

From the start, delivery of aid to China was greatly hindered by the problem of lines of communications, and plans for improving transportation over the Yunnan–Burma road were cut off in midcourse by the fall of Burma. The United States had intended to deliver to China commodities worth $45 million in 1941, as specified in the first Sino-American loan agreement. But, in fact, because of shipping shortages, only $26 million worth of commodities actually left the United States. The commodities were shipped to the transit port of Rangoon, where most of them had to remain because the Yunnan–Burma road, China's only passage to the outside, was jammed with heavy traffic. Because of mismanagement, those commodities that were shipped out of Burma suffered heavy losses in transit, and only one-third of them eventually arrived in Chongqing.[39] In April 1942, because of the Allies' defeat in the Burma campaign, the Yunnan–Burma road was cut. After the road was cut, in order to keep China in the war, the United States opened up an air transport route running from Assam Province in India across the Himalayas to Kunming in China and known as the Hump. This route was extremely dangerous. In all of 1942, only 1,571 tons (1,403 metric tons) of American aid arrived in China by this route. Although the amount was small, the aid shipped had a great psychological impact as a symbol of Allied assistance to China. In the years 1943–1944, the American Air Transport Command (ATC) and the Chinese National Aviation Corporation (CNAC) made the utmost effort, suffered great casualties, and shipped in 194,072 tons of commodities to China.[40] In May 1944, the Chinese forces led by Stilwell recovered northern Burma. After this, because of the much shorter air transport distance, the quantity of materials arriving by air in China increased visibly and significantly. In early 1945, the Stilwell Road was opened to traffic, and the transport situation improved one step further.

From mid-1941 to mid-1944, the shortage of materiel and the problems of allocation arising from this shortage made Sino-American cooperative relationships relatively tense. Almost from the very beginning, the United States War and Treasury departments demanded strict control and supervision of the American Lend-Lease aid. This was not only to decrease losses and enhance the effectiveness of the aid deliveries but was also because of the suspicions of General Magruder, who was responsible for the delivery of aid to China, that the Chongqing government intended to accumulate as much American goods as possible, not because they were needed for operations against Japan, but for use in civil war after Japan's defeat, in order to preserve the ruling position of the Kuomintang political authorities.[41] But from Chiang Kai-shek's perspective, the key cause of China's low priority in receiving Lend-Lease aid was that the power to allocate this aid was controlled by the Munitions Assignments Board of the British and American Combined Chiefs of Staff (CCS), on which China was unrepresented and was therefore treated unfairly, as "being nothing more than a kind of tool in this war game."[42] Chiang found it even more difficult to endure the change, decided on by the Munitions Assignments Board in May 1942, that Stilwell would be responsible for receiving Lend-Lease aid to China. Before this change, the ownership of the American aid was immediately transferred to China after the goods were loaded on ships and left the United States; but afterward, until Stilwell handed over the goods to China, authority over them still belonged to the United States.[43] The United States provided little material aid to China, it did so under difficult and complex procedures and harsh conditions, and moreover it often could not fulfill commitments that it had already made. These facts caused Chiang Kai-shek to become increasingly dissatisfied.

At the same time, Chiang Kai-shek's attitude toward the war of resistance became more minimalist every day, and this caused the American military circles represented by Stilwell to feel that they were being asked to endure what could not be endured. They demanded incessantly that Roosevelt put into effect the policy of "exchange" and "pressure" toward Chiang Kai-shek: that aid should be given conditionally and used as a lever to force Chiang Kai-shek to fight Japan and to reform the Chinese military.[44] Looking only at the requirements of the war against Japan, Stilwell and American military circles strongly demanded allocating Lend-Lease aid to outfit those Chinese Communist forces that were fighting the Japanese, and they got Roosevelt to approve the dispatch of a military observer group to Yan'an. Their intention in doing so was to ratchet up the pressure on Chiang Kai-shek. They exhausted their strength associating themselves with the efforts of the Chinese Communists to obtain American aid, and the Communists did begin to cooperate with the U.S. armed forces in the intelligence area, but in the end the Communists did not obtain one rifle or one bullet of Lend-Lease material.[45] As a result of Stilwell's striking the two sensitive nerves of Chinese politics called "authority over the military" and "Chinese Communists," a crisis in wartime Sino-American cooperation erupted. In October 1944, helped by Roosevelt's special envoy to China, Patrick Hurley, Chiang Kai-shek drove Stilwell out.

In fact, it was not only between the United States and China that contradictory opinions regarding the allocation of Lend-Lease aid existed; those differences were also present between the United States Army in China, represented by Stilwell, and the United States Army Air Force in China, represented by Claire Lee Chennault. Because Roosevelt was unable to aid China effectively, he settled this internal struggle by giving priority to air force operations, as advocated by Chennault and endorsed by Chiang Kai-shek.[46] Thus, for a time, Chennault's air forces had the priority allocation for delivery of the materiel coming over the Hump, and at the most difficult time in the war, they received 70 percent of the limited American material aid to China. At that same time, the Chinese forces received an allotment of only 500 tons or less of American Lend-Lease aid per month, and as of May 1944, they had obtained only a little more than 10,000 tons of weapons and equipment, most of which was used to resupply the Chinese expeditionary forces in western Yunnan, which had been trained by the American military.[47]

To help China establish a modern air force had been one of the major goals of the Lend-Lease law for military assistance to China. In the spring of 1940, Japanese air forces bombed Chinese air bases in Chongqing and elsewhere in Sichuan, putting the Chinese air force in difficulty. Before the Lend-Lease Act, the Chinese asked the Americans for 500 late-model aircraft by March 1941. After the Lend-Lease Act went into effect, the Chinese air force proposed a development plan whose goal was 1,000 combat aircraft.[48] But, in fact, China received only one hundred P-40 fighters before the start of the Pacific War. After the war began, China continued to negotiate with the United States concerning the aircraft, but the United States promised few aircraft, and moreover the aircraft that the United States promised often could not be delivered or were transferred to other theaters of war in midcourse; even the aircraft that were delivered were often seriously damaged in transit because the lines of communication to China were so long. For example, in 1942 out of 263 aircraft intended for China that were shipped from the United States to India, only 136, or about half, finally flew to China.[49]

After the outbreak of the Pacific War, the American Flying Tigers fought in China and wrote the most legendary chapter in Sino-American wartime cooperation. The official designation of this unit was the American Volunteer Group (AVG). The AVG was officially created on 1 August 1941, with American adviser Claire Lee Chennault as group commander, and the group had three pursuit plane squadrons under it with 125 planes in all, the majority being the 100 P-40 fighters that China had already received. The AVG fought the Japanese in Kunming, Rangoon, Guilin, and other places. It was disbanded on 4 July 1942, and its personnel were incorporated into the United States Army as the Twenty-third Pursuit Group of the Tenth U.S. Army Air Force, also designated the China Air Task Force (CATF), which conducted operations mainly in central and south China. In March 1943, this unit was expanded, becoming the Fourteenth U.S. Army Air Force. Afterward, a Chinese American Composite Wing (CACW) was created under the Fourteenth U.S. Army Air Force, in which Chinese aviation personnel who had been trained in the United States fought jointly with American aviation personnel stationed in China.[50]

Throughout the war, the United States provided far fewer aircraft to China than China needed, but by the end of the war the United States held first place in the total number of aircraft provided to China. According to statistics compiled in Taiwan, during the Sino-Japanese War China obtained a total of 2,351 aircraft from foreign countries. From the United States China purchased or rented a total of 1,394 aircraft—including 1,038 fighters, 244 bombers, 15 reconnaissance planes, and 97 transports—for 59.3 percent of the total. From the Soviet Union, China obtained 885 aircraft, including 563 fighters and 322 bombers, for 37.6 percent of the total. China obtained 36 aircraft from Britain, 24 from France, and 12 from Germany, a total of 72 aircraft from these three countries, for only 3.1 percent of the total. One point that deserves attention is that, of the aircraft that the United States provided to China, 552 or nearly 40 percent of the total did not arrive in China until the second half of 1944, and most of these were allocated to the Fourteenth U.S. Army Air Force. Only in 1946, after the end of the Sino-Japanese War, did the United States provide aircraft in numbers that met the Nationalist government's demands.[51]

Training and equipping the Chinese army was another major aspect of military assistance to China decided under the Lend-Lease law. China and the United States discussed this issue before the outbreak of the Pacific War, and from the beginning agreed on equipping thirty divisions. Afterward, during bilateral discussions, the number of Chinese troops to be equipped changed from time to time. During the Cairo conference, Stilwell drafted a preliminary plan for equipping ninety divisions; this was the highest number ever discussed, but it was never put into effect.[52] Around the time the war was winding up, planning had concluded with the decision that thirty-nine divisions of Chinese troops under the Nationalist government would be trained and equipped.

After being defeated in the Burma campaign, some of the survivors of the Chinese Expeditionary Force retreated to India, and the remainder retreated into Yunnan Province. Planning the counteroffensive in mid-1942, Stilwell first presented to the highest Chinese military authorities his proposal to train Chinese forces in India. The plan was that 100,000 Chinese soldiers were to be selected and sent to India in groups to be trained by American military officers, and they would be supplied and equipped with Lend-Lease aid allocated to China. Two corps would be organized with a total strength of six divisions, and the force would serve as a nucleus for later expansion that would create a new army of thirty divisions. These forces were created and used Ramgarh in Bihar Province in northeastern India as their training camp. They were designated the (Chinese) Army of India and also called X-Force (X-Ray Force); Stilwell served as training camp commander, with the Chinese general Luo Zhuo-ying as his deputy. The training began in September 1942 and was completed in January 1944. Later, the forces trained there were expanded into the New First Corps and the New Sixth Corps and were the main body of the army that would recover northern Burma.[53] Shortly after the training in Ramgarh started, Stilwell proposed a plan to train a second group of thirty divisions, a plan that received approval from the highest Chinese and American military authorities. On 1 February 1943, General Chen Cheng was appointed commander in chief of the Chinese expeditionary force. The training of the expeditionary force commenced immediately in Kunming and Dali in Yunnan Province, in Guilin, and in other places, officers and enlisted men being selected for training from the front lines and trained intensively in groups for six weeks. Because American models of weapons and equipment could not be delivered quickly enough, as of early 1944 only a force of three divisions, or one-tenth of the original plan, had received American weapons and equipment; it was designated Y-Force (Yoke Force).[54]

In both India and Yunnan, the training was provided by instructors from the United States Army, using methods appropriate to each branch. For the six-week infantry training course, two weeks were devoted to training in weapons care, two weeks to marksmanship training, and two weeks to tactical training. In the eight- to ten-week artillery training course, after two weeks of basic drill, firing with both practice ammunition and live ammunition was emphasized. Beginning, intermediate, and high-level commanders undertook exercises in their different courses. Although the training program was abbreviated, the force elements that received American-style training were visibly at a higher level, and their equipment was also greatly improved; not only did they have increased firepower, but they also had relatively efficient systems of signal communications, transportation, and rear-area security.[55]

After Stilwell left China, his successor, Albert Wedemeyer, decided to proceed with a plan of equipping thirty-nine Chinese divisions.[56] Although the relevant plans were made in the final stages of the war, the actual work of training and equipping the troops was completed only after the war had already ended. Of the forces that received American training and equipment, the six divisions of the New First Corps and the New Sixth Corps of X-Force and the sixteen Y-Force divisions of the Yunnan-based expeditionary force participated in the campaign to recover northern Burma. The remaining seventeen divisions seldom exchanged fire with the Japanese after receiving their equipment; they were later drawn into the civil war.[57]

Besides providing aid to the Chinese air force and army, the United States also helped the Nationalist government rebuild its navy. In January 1944, the Nationalist government submitted a plan to lease eight submarines from the United States. The United States originally agreed to lend four destroyers and four minesweepers to China, and it was decided that China would not have to return these warships after war. In February 1945, the Nationalist government sent 1,060 officers and enlisted men to the United States for training. In mid-1946, these officers and enlisted personnel completed their training and sailed their eight warships back to China.[58]

On 15 August 1945 Japan broadcast its surrender, and the Second World War ended. On 21 August President Harry S. Truman proclaimed that the Lend-Lease Act would cease to be implemented, but Lend-Lease aid to China continued until 1947, when its end was announced. During the entire Second World War, the United States provided materiel and service aid worth more than $50 billion to thirty-eight antifascist allies according to the terms of the Lend-Lease Act, of which, as a major ally, China received $1.602 billion (including the aid received after the war), amounting to 3.2 percent of America's total Lend-Lease aid to foreign countries.[59] Thus, China holds the fourth place as an aid recipient after Great Britain, the Soviet Union, and France, but it actually received little aid compared to the three other countries, especially Great Britain and the Soviet Union.[60]

A relatively large discrepancy exists between American and Chinese statistics concerning the Lend-Lease material that China obtained during the war. According to the statistics in the "China White Paper," from May 1941 to the end of the war, the Lend-Lease material and service aid that the United States gave to China was worth $846 million and included weapons and ammunition, aircraft, tanks, motor vehicles, warships, and various other kinds of military equipment, worth $517 million in all. The rest consisted basically of agricultural and industrial products and various kinds of services.[61] Based on the American-issued Shipment Invoice Commodity Notification Forms, the Nationalist government's Commodities Supply Committee in the United States estimated that the amount of aid to China was about $685 million. Based on the cumulative totals of Lend-Lease materials shipped overseas, the Ministry of Finance came up with a total of about $598 million.[62] The probable reason for the discrepancy between the American and the Chinese statistics is that some commodities were transferred directly from the American military to Chinese parties without going through the Nationalist government's Commodities Supply Committee; also, the Chinese statistics do not seem to have included service fees.

If we look at the development of military Lend-Lease aid to China, from 1941 to 1944, during the most difficult stage of the war when China most needed foreign assistance, the aid that China received was very little, only $280 million. The majority of the aid arrived near the end of the war, or even afterward. In the year 1945, China received aid worth $1.107 billion, about four times the cumulative total of the preceding four years.[63] However, by 1945, the goal and function of American aid had manifested an obvious change. As Patrick Hurley stated to Chiang Kai-shek in early 1945, "When the war comes to an end, your well equipped divisions will easily hold their ground and defeat the Communist army."[64] No consensus exists about how much Lend-Lease aid the Nationalist government received after the war, but the "China White Paper" reports a figure of $781 million.[65]

Conclusion

At different stages of China's war of resistance against Japan, the Chinese Nationalist government strove to obtain aid from Germany, the Soviet Union, and the United States, and cooperated militarily with these three countries. Aid from these countries constituted three distinct cases, and each had a background of different bilateral relations, confronted a distinct environment, and had a different cooperative model, so the outcomes were not the same. Here, I would like to compare and summarize the special features of these three individual cases.

Looked at from the bilateral relations background, China and Germany cooperated militarily on a relatively equal basis. The cooperative model was completely straightforward: Chiang Kai-shek hired Germans in his own name as a private person, and the German advisers were solely responsible to him. This model circumvented most of the difficulties that could arise in interstate cooperation. Although the two countries had different histories and cultural traditions, the close similarity in manner of thinking and class values of the cooperating parties basically filled the gap between them. In general, Chiang Kai-shek had confidence in his German advisers, and the work of the German advisory group in China promoted the improvement and development of Sino-German relations.

From the military viewpoint, the role of the German advisers was to infuse the Nationalist forces with a modern military perspective. The advisers helped to establish a relatively modern model contingent of the army and also improved China's armaments industry and logistic systems. Thus, the military forces that had been capable of only waging civil war began to be transformed into a real army of national defense. The importation of large quantities of German-model armaments and military industry equipment raised the combat effectiveness of the Chinese forces, as well as bringing huge commercial profits to Germany.

Looked at from the viewpoint of advancing the military cooperation of the two states, China and Germany did not cooperate because of any obvious common strategic interest but only in order to get what they needed from each other. This was an interesting and unusual but temporary phenomenon. Largely because of its nature, the bilateral cooperation became difficult to continue, and the Japanese invasion of China and the growing intimacy of German-Japanese relations determined that in the end China and Germany would have to go their separate ways. Sino-German military cooperation did not leave much of a legacy, in part because the Chinese elite forces, trained by the German advisers for a full decade, were destroyed in the first half year of the war of resistance, but more importantly because the fundamentally antifascist nature of the Second World War as a whole makes people unwilling to bring up this historical episode.

Cooperation between China and the Soviet Union was based on the common strategic interest of containing Japanese aggression and expansion, but cooperation was a short-term expedient for both sides. Reflecting on the lessons taught by their first cooperative occasion, the new cooperation had clear boundaries, and each side carefully protected its own fundamental interests against damage from the other side. Chiang Kai-shek feared that the Soviet Union would seize the opportunity to interfere in China's domestic affairs, while Stalin was concerned that China would drag the Soviet Union into war against Japan. Therefore, the Sino-Soviet cooperation model was relatively simple, being basically confined to the Soviet Union providing military assistance to China, and only when this assistance did not touch upon issues in other areas.

Considering the Soviet Union's limited national strength at that time, Joseph Stalin was quite generous, giving military aid to China that was both on time and in large volume. The Soviet Union provided large numbers of aircraft, helped China to rebuild its air force, and sent several hundred air force volunteers to participate in combat. The Soviet Union also provided large amounts of ordnance, including tanks, artillery, and other heavy weapons, to the Chinese army, and Soviet military advisers participated in the planning and command of several important campaigns. Taken together, the military aid that the Soviet Union gave China from 1938 to 1940 was roughly as much as that given by the United States from 1942 to 1944, if not more, and furthermore the Nationalist government obtained this aid with nothing resembling the expense and complications encountered later in receiving aid from the United States.

Stalin's astute nature was manifest in his holding on to his clear and well-measured goal in giving aid, which was that he wanted China to have the ability to contain Japan. Once the Soviet Union was relieved from the fear that Japan would attack it, Sino-Soviet cooperation virtually came to an end. During the several years that the Soviet Union aided China, Sino-Soviet relations improved visibly, and, in general, cooperation between the two countries was relatively smooth. With respect to this cooperation, it may be said that the Soviet Union fully achieved its expected goal, and it may equally be said that China obtained a great quantity of foreign aid at the stage of the war of resistance when it was most isolated and in the most danger.

The course of the Sino-American alliance clearly shows that the two countries had only a limited understanding of each other, that their relative strengths were different and their systems incompatible, and moreover each party had excessively high expectations of its ally, leading to difficulties during their period of cooperation. The Sino-American cooperation was comprehensive in principle, but the bilateral cooperation that actually developed in the majority of areas was inharmonious. Nevertheless, China and the United States made their alliance in order to defeat Japan, and in this sense one may still call it a success for both parties.

During the whole period of the war of resistance to Japan, the aid provided to China by the United States was the most comprehensive and the greatest in scale; however, few appreciate either American aid or Sino-American wartime cooperation. On the contrary, one hears many criticisms. Looking at the effects of the aid, both parties have reason to express dissatisfaction. From the American perspective, it is difficult to regard the aid to China as having been effective, since it amounted to no more than the minimum required for "keeping China in the war" and was never enough to enable China to attack Japan forcefully. From the Nationalist government's perspective, the American aid was for the most part "promised but not actually delivered" because, although that government controlled all of the American aid, what it received was much less than it had asked for and even less than the United States had promised. From the Chinese Communist Party's perspective, the American aid was the root cause that later enabled the Nationalist government to begin the anti-Communist civil war.

The solution of this problem lies in the fact that, although military matters were the main purpose of Sino-American wartime cooperation, they quickly became interwoven with complicated political questions. From the beginning, Chiang Kai-shek had hoped to hire American support to suppress the Chinese Communists, and in the later stages of the war, the United States government hoped that supporting Chiang Kai-shek would have the effect of digging a moat to defend against trouble from the Soviet Union. The nature of the Sino-American alliance underwent a transformation because of these considerations. American support for Chiang Kai-shek became an important contributing factor to the postwar outbreak of the Chinese civil war. Because various other considerations came up that were outside of the common goal of defeating Japan, the wartime alliance could only temporarily bridge the wide distance between Chinese and American purposes, and, in the end, these other considerations hardened into the long-lasting confrontation between the two countries.

Viewed overall, during the War of Resistance to Japan, China gained a relatively limited amount of assistance from foreign countries, which can be calculated as around $1.1 billion in total. China had to use worn-out weapons and exhaust its trifling resources to hold off a great enemy power, a situation not found in any other theater during of the Second World War. At the same time, as a divided and weak country, China had difficulty finding a firm ally, while other countries also found it difficult to regard China as a reliable partner. Thus, China's experience in seeking aid and cooperation from foreign countries was full of hardships.

TRANSLATED BY SHUXI YIN

12 Nationalist and Communist Guerrilla Warfare in North China

YANG KUISONG

During the war, both the Nationalist government and the Chinese Communist Party (CCP) adopted guerrilla tactics. The Kuomintang (KMT) began to do so in 1938; yet within two or three years its efforts failed. KMT forces behind enemy lines either surrendered to the Japanese, were eliminated by the CCP, or were forced to withdraw. By the end of the war, the KMT had no effective military capacity behind Japanese lines. In marked contrast, by 1945, the CCP's forces had grown from 20,000 to 30,000 men to nearly 1 million. The territory they occupied grew from a small piece of northern Shaanxi to encompass parts of eight other provinces. This enormous expansion made the CCP into a major military and political force, while in 1937 it had to accept junior status in a United Front with the KMT. The contrast between the success of the CCP's guerrilla warfare and the failure of the KMT's is obvious.

In 1937, China was still an agrarian nation, with a large majority of the population living in rural villages. For China to resist a highly industrialized Japan, the role of the peasantry was critical. Chinese military personnel came mostly from the villages, so the degree of coordination with and participation of the peasantry in the war effort had a direct effect on military effectiveness. Guerrilla warfare was possible only with the cooperation of rural populations.

This chapter analyses the reasons for the CCP's success and the KMT's failure in organizing guerrilla warfare. It rejects the argument that the CCP wanted to fight but the KMT did not. Apart from the CCP's adaptable strategy and tactics in guerrilla warfare, its success in mobilizing local populations behind Japanese lines was a key factor to its success. The KMT failure was a result of the fact that it never adapted fully to the demands of guerilla warfare as it continued to fight in large units and sought to defend large territorial positions. Nationalist guerrilla forces also seized large amounts of local supplies, thus alienating the local population. They were unable to withstand both Japanese and Communist pressure. A large number of Nationalist forces surrendered to the Japanese.

Beginnings

After the Marco Polo Bridge Incident, when Japan launched large-scale invasions of north and central China, the question of conducting guerrilla warfare became acute for both the KMT and the CCP. The main difference compared to the loss of Manchuria in 1932 was that in 1932 the armed forces and police units that remained behind could not have undertaken guerrilla warfare. Because the Japanese occupation of Manchuria went from south to north, such forces had no area into which they could have retreated. In China proper, however, the Japanese advanced across several fronts, so that the KMT's central armies and the regional forces could withdraw to rear areas to continue resistance against Japan. In China proper, guerrilla war behind enemy lines was basically a positive act, whether for the KMT or the CCP.

When the conflict began, the regular armed forces of the CCP numbered only 20,000 to 30,000 men, while those of the KMT were fully 1.7 million. After ten years of civil war, between 1927 and 1937, the CCP was forced by circumstances to recognize the KMT's legitimate authority when war with Japan broke out and the United Front was established. Yet the two parties were deeply suspicious of each other. Because of this and in view of the disparity in strength, the CCP naturally hoped to wage war in the enemy's rear to achieve independence and autonomy as well as to avoid friction and conflict with the KMT. Mao Zedong early on emphasized, "The Red Army is very good at mobile warfare, but defense is not its strength." He advocated that the CCP should "send a detachment deep into enemy territory and attack his rear."[1]

After the Nationalist government forces lost Peking and Tianjin (see chapter 5 by Yang Tianshi), CCP negotiators demanded from the KMT that the Communist forces should "carry out independent, autonomous, and dispersed guerrilla warfare."[2] On 20 August, Nationalist government headquarters issued its first systematic instruction to guide combat operations in the First War Zone, where the CCP's forces were located. It agreed to the CCP's demands and allowed the Eighth Route Army, as the rebaptized Communist forces were designated, to conduct guerrilla operations in the enemy's rear, but restricted its combat area to certain parts of Hebei and Chahar.[3]

Contrary to Nationalist government directives insisting that CCP forces mount guerrilla operations directly against Japanese units, Mao Zedong believed that they should disperse in the enemy's rear. Mao Zedong's suggestion came under strong criticism because domestic public opinion called for a fuller CCP participation in the defense of China. This criticism abated after the fall of Xuzhou (see chapter 7 by Stephen MacKinnon).[4] The broad expanse of China's interior was left open for guerrilla warfare because the Japanese could only occupy "points and lines," that is, strategic places and communication lines, and had to leave open the areas in between. As a result, doubts about the CCP's pursuit of rural warfare dissolved.

The earliest and most successful example of Eighth Route Army guerrilla warfare was at the Battle of Pingxingguan. In September 1937, the Chinese Communist 115th Division, under the command of Lin Biao, made flanking attacks on Japanese forces near Pingxingguan. Two regiments conducted an ambush, and Communist units overcame the entire Japanese supply train, putting two columns to flight and capturing a large amount of military materiel. After this victory, the Eighth Route Army broke off the engagement at night, battling Japanese reinforcements. CCP offensive operations were of this sort throughout the war, employing ambush and surprise, attacking the few with the many, and relying on quick attacks.

The CCP, building on its civil war experiences, stressed formation of base areas. They dispersed large numbers of troops to the countryside to establish a politico-military presence, organize production, and arm the population to develop opportunities to survive. In remote and hence fairly secure areas, they formed consolidated base areas, while close to the Japanese front lines they established guerrilla zones. In the early phase of the war, the main Japanese forces were occupied with large-scale battles with Nationalist government forces. Communist forces did not attack the Japanese rear but used all possible opportunities to expand rapidly in north China. By the end of 1938, the Eighth Route Army had grown from 30,000 men to over 200,000.

The Eighth Route Army set up four large strategic base areas, in Shanxi-Chahar-Hebei, southwest Shanxi, northwest Shanxi, and west Shanxi. It implemented Mao Zedong's directive to form guerrilla zones on the plains of Hebei and Shandong,[5] thereby exceeding the scope of operations imposed by the KMT. The 129th and 115th divisions moved units from the Taihang Mountains to the north Henan plains flanking the Peking–Wuhan Railway. Elements of the 120th Division moved into areas north of the Peking–Suining Railroad to set up the Chahar base area. Together with forces from the Shanxi-Chahar-Hebei military region, other units of the 120th Division advanced into eastern Hebei, establishing the east Hebei base area just west of Peking. Still other units entered the Daqing Mountains. By the fall of 1938, the Eighth Route Army had set up two tiers of base areas across north China.

These base areas were not fortified and were difficult to defend. With the exception of a few core mountain bases such as Taihang and Taiyue, where the terrain offered protection, these bases survived only because they were beyond the reach of the Japanese. As long as the Eighth Route Army did not threaten the Japanese, the Japanese could afford to ignore it. However, as the base areas expanded, they pressed closer upon Japanese areas, not only threatening Japanese transportation lines but also contending for resources, especially grains. After the fall of Wuhan in October 1938, as chapter 7 by Stephen MacKinnon shows, the Japanese halted large-scale battlefield operations and moved their forces north to consolidate occupied territories. The Japanese army carried out suppression campaigns, but these did not lead to decisive results. The Eighth Route Army continued to expand, reaching 500,000 men by 1940. This growth emboldened Mao Zedong to call for further expansion within a year to a total of 800,000 and an armed force of 2 million as a further goal.[6] The Eighth Route Army was able to repulse Japanese mopping-up operations thanks to its ability to gain the support of the population and its tactics of flexible maneuver.

The CCP's guerrilla war was conducted, in the main, by its regular forces. These forces were incorporated into the Nationalist order of battle as the 115th, 120th, and 129th divisions but continued to be commanded solely by the Eighth Route Army's leadership, itself subject to CCP control. The political structures in the base areas were created by Eighth Route Army detachments. They amalgamated military and political authority. The highest authority of the military region was often in actual fact the same as that of the political administration. They developed parallel political and military hierarchies reaching down into local society.

Militias formed the basis for the training of higher-level regular forces in the base areas. Teenagers under the age of eighteen formed youth regiments, which assisted in handling sentry and guard duty, inspecting travelers on the roads, and reporting on spies. Able-bodied men between roughly eighteen and fifty-five-years-old constituted the local militia, such as the Anti-Japanese Self-Defense Corps or the People's Self-Defense Corps. Each county had an Armed Forces Bureau in overall command of these militias. In each military region there was a regional corps office, with a corps commander, a political officer, and a civil affairs officer. Intermediate corps offices were set up in larger villages, while smaller villages had branch offices. Each had a branch commander and a political officer.[7] These carried out training, organized guerrilla small groups, and killed traitors. They also destroyed roads and transported ordnance, foodstuffs, and the wounded. At this early stage, local initiative still played a role in the formation of guerrilla units. Mobilization officers moved from village to village, explaining guerrilla warfare. With village leaders, they drew up lists of volunteers and determined the final rosters for guerrilla units.[8]

Popular slogans in the base areas were "If you have manpower, provide manpower; if you have money, provide money; if you have weapons, provide weapons" and "Defend hearth and home." Many people supported the resistance. The Nationalist government authorized favorable treatment to the families of soldiers, facilitating the enlistment of local young men into the guerrilla forces.[9] In areas where militia mobilization was popular, units might be integrated into local regular CCP forces in times of military necessity. Many had strong regional affiliations, as in the Shanxi-Chahar-Hebei base area, where the names of the Pingshan and Lingshan regiments indicated their local origins.

Militias played a major role in obstructing Japanese occupation policies. According to a report from the central Hebei base area, local forces had little capacity to resist the Japanese. They often fled with the villagers. Later, they began simple forms of resistance such as sniping, so that Japanese and puppet detachments no longer entered villages heedlessly. This success emboldened the villagers to contribute money and weapons, and to join militias. Under the leadership of a Peasant Salvation Society or a CCP cell, these small guerrilla groups began striking out at collaborators and engaging in so-called sparrow warfare with rifles and crude land mines.[10] They carried on dispersed attacks on small Japanese detachments and their fortified outposts. When the Japanese expanded their road network and built more fortified blockhouses, the guerrillas mobilized local people to wreck the road and harassed the Japanese by attacking them and setting off firecrackers. The Japanese would round up people by day to build roads, only to have the roads destroyed at night. When the Japanese and the puppets undertook larger-scale operations and a favorable opportunity presented itself, the guerrillas informed the Eighth Route Army, which took advantage of its knowledge of the local terrain to attack. Even when no regular forces were nearby, militias could still harass the enemy by planting land mines and using sparrow warfare, thus providing cover so that local populations could make a timely escape.[11]

When Japanese forces engaged in mopping-up operations, local militias several miles distant provided warnings by means of signal fires or single rifle shots, alerting forces and villages near occupied areas to make preparations. Regular forces redeployed away, and villagers hid grain and other valuable materials. By the time the Japanese arrived, no trace of the Eighth Route Army remained. If there was no time to redeploy, soldiers might be concealed in the homes of the local populace. The Japanese would often round up everyone in the village and force the children to identify the members of their families. The children called Eighth Route Army soldiers "uncle," "elder brother," "elder cousin," and so forth, allowing the soldiers to escape detection.[12]

During large-scale mopping-up operations, concealment in village homes became difficult. When possible, the Eighth Route Army counterattacked. For example, between May 1939 and April 1940, the Eighth Route Army on several occasions countered Japanese mopping-up activity with coordinated actions involving a number of regiments, exacting a high price from the Japanese. In one such action, Brigade Commander Abe Norihide was killed.

The Eighth Route Army also deployed other tactics such as "strengthen the walls and empty the countryside" (*jianbi qingye*) to avoid the main Japanese thrust. Even when troop strength permitted, it did not try to defend base area territory but instead held to the principle of conserving its own strength. Particularly in base areas among enemy-occupied areas, defense was impossible.[13] Here, the Eighth Route Army concealed itself until the Japanese withdrew, before returning to rebuild anew. These tactics caused the Japanese no end of frustration. Since the Japanese army knew well that its offensives had to be limited, they could not occupy the far reaches of the countryside indefinitely. Because they could not engage CCP armies in decisive battle, their only recourse was to thoroughly destroy the foundation on which CCP armies depended for their survival. Some Japanese forces—driven by frustration, rage, and lack of options— devised the Three-All Policy: kill all, burn all, loot all.

Rapid Expansion and Its Consequences

Chiang Kai-shek initially paid scant attention to guerrilla warfare. Because of the speed of the Japanese advance, several Nationalist army units were overtaken by the enemy advance. The Hebei Peace Preservation Force remained in southern Hebei. Wan Fulin's forces, formerly a part of the Zhang Xueliang's Fengtian, or Northeastern, Army and the northern Chahar Peace Preservation Force, commanded by Sun Dianying, remained in the southern reaches of the Taihang Mountains. After the fall of Taiyuan in Shanxi, thirty Nationalist government divisions moved into mountainous areas. General Yan Xishan, the ruler of Shanxi, divided the province into seven guerrilla districts. General Sun Tongxuan's Third Army Group was in southern Shandong, as was General Pang Bingxun's Fortieth Army. The KMT's provincial party chairman, Qin Qirong, organized guerrilla forces along the Shandong-Hebei border. Shen Honglie, the mayor of Qingdao on the Shandong coast, withdrew with marines to central Shandong. Behind Japanese lines in Jiangsu were the Eighty-ninth Army forces headed by provincial governor Han Deqin. At the end of 1938, the KMT had a total of 600,000 to 700,000 men behind enemy lines.[14]

At the end of 1937, General Bai Chongxi, vice chairman of the Nationalist government's Military Affairs Commission, proposed that "guerrilla war should be combined with conventional war, and guerrilla warfare should be strengthened." Chiang Kai-shek accepted his advice and gave the appropriate orders. On 11 January 1938, for instance, the Military Affairs Commission ordered the First War Zone to "mobilize the population to wreak destruction in the enemy's rear in cooperation with our armed forces."[15] The Fifty-third Army received orders to conduct guerrilla warfare in the Lingquan-Linxian area. The Fourth Cavalry Division received orders to move into strategic areas of the southwest Taihang Mountains and conduct guerrilla operations in concert with the Hebei People's Army, headed by Hebei Army commander Zhang Yinwu. The Twenty-fourth Army Group was ordered to carry on guerrilla warfare against the southern section of the Tianjin–Pukou Railroad. The Forty-eighth Army received orders to carry on guerrilla warfare against the eastern segment of the Longhai Railway, from Baotou in Shaanxi Province to Lianyungang in north Jiangsu, and the central segment of the Tianjin–Pukou Railroad, as were the Sixty-ninth and Fifty-seventh armies. The Military Affairs Commission also ordered eight divisions to establish a base area in the Dabie Mountains north of the Yangtze River for guerrilla warfare. In northern Jiangsu, guerrillas attacked communication lines. In 1938, during and after the Battle of Wuhan, the Third War Zone received orders to direct the Tenth, Eleventh, and Twenty-second army groups to conduct guerrilla operations in the Shanghai-Hangzhou, Nanjing-Hangzhou, and Jiangnan regions respectively. They were also directed to organize mortar and mining units along the Yangtze River to impede transport on the river. The Ninth War Zone was ordered to set up a base area in the Jin'gong Mountains with four divisions, in response to the needs of the Wuhan front.[16]

To strengthen control over forces behind enemy lines, the Nationalist government appointed generals Shen Honglie, Lu Zhongling, Liao Lei, and Han Deqin as provincial governors in occupied Shandong, Hebei, Anhui, and Jiangsu, respectively. It also set up in each war zone a party-government committee to coordinate party and government work. After the fall of Wuhan and Guangzhou, Chiang Kai-shek went a step further and proclaimed that "guerrilla warfare has become more important than conventional warfare. Turn the enemy's rear into the front. Use one-third of our strength in the enemy's rear."[17] Two additional guerrilla zones were set up, in Hebei-Chahar and Jiangsu-Shandong. The Fifty-first, Sixty-ninth, New Eighth, and Ninety-ninth armies were dispatched to Shandong and Hebei. The Nationalist government set up guerrilla cadre training classes, inviting CCP officers to serve as trainers. They also issued the manual *Essentials of Guerrilla Warfare* to each war zone and military academy.[18]

The KMT's dispatch of large numbers of troops into the Japanese rear culminated in the establishment of large base areas, such as those in the southwestern Taihang Mountains as well as the Zhongtiao, Lüliang, Wutai, and Dabie mountains in east Henan, Anhui, Hunan, Shanxi, west Zhejiang, south Shandong, and Hainan. The Nationalist government's Military Affairs Commission incorporated guerrilla forces into the command structure to maintain control and coordinate guerrilla and regular warfare. From 1938 to 1942, the Military Affairs Commission ordered guerrilla forces in the enemy rear to support major operations against the Japanese. For example, in March 1939, during the battle for Nanchang, Chiang Kai-shek ordered Ninth War Zone commander Xue Yue to deploy guerrillas to interdict enemy forces by attacking supply trains and the roads to Yangxin, Tongshan, and Chongyang.[19] Once the battle began, the Military Affairs Commission ordered the Second War Zone to launch a supporting offensive. During the winter offensive of late 1939 and early 1940, the KMT deployed main forces in the Second, Third, Fifth, and Ninth war zones. At the same time, it mobilized forces in the First, Fourth, and Eighth war zones as well as guerrillas from the Shandong-Jiangsu and Hebei-Chahar base areas. In spring 1940, when the Battle of Zaoyang-Yichang began, the Fifth War Zone ordered guerrilla forces to take part in the fighting, and for actual combat deployment brought both guerrilla and regular forces under a single unified command. In September 1941, when the second battle for Changsha began, the Military Affairs Commission ordered the Fifth War Zone to launch guerrilla warfare along both banks of the Yangtze River, the Peking–Wuhan Railway, and the main highways.[20]

In the above engagements, several important military leaders were lost. They included Fan Zhuxian (commissioner of Shandong's Sixth District), Tang Huaiyuan (commander of the Third Army), Wu Shimin (commander of the Ninety-eighth Army), Cun Xingqi (commander of the Twenty-fourth Division), Liu Zhandong (commander of the Xishui guerrillas), Tang Juwu (commander of the northeast guerrillas), and Lei Zhong (vice commander of the north Anhui guerrillas). These losses demonstrate that KMT guerrilla warfare in this period was serious and had not yet deteriorated as it would later.

However, the Nationalist government proved incapable of sustaining guerrilla warfare. By 1943, no KMT forces remained in Hebei, Shandong, or Chahar to wage guerrilla warfare. The KMT military leadership stuck to its belief that guerrilla warfare was but one form of conventional warfare. It did not comprehend the special nature and methods of guerrilla war.[21] KMT forces behind enemy lines carried out guerrilla war, relying as before on methods of conventional warfare. When on the offensive, they emphasized coordination with the main fighting at the front and preferred large-unit operations. When on the defensive, they tried to hold territory. Once the Japanese got hold of them, they suffered tremendous losses.

For example, in the Zhongtiao base area in Shanxi, the Nationalist government forces built fortifications and relied on terrain to protect it. In May 1941, the Japanese assembled six divisions, two mixed brigades, and a cavalry brigade to attack the base area from three sides. He Yingqin, chief of staff to the Military Affairs Commission, ordered seven armies to deploy themselves around a broad perimeter. They fought a pitched defensive battle relying on natural terrain and defensive works. But the Japanese crushed them. The defeats suffered by Pang Bingxun in the Taihang Mountains and Yu Xuezhong in the Shandong base area derived from the same causes. The Japanese military believed that "the political work and guerrilla warfare of the KMT military is far inferior to that of the CCP. It is inexperienced and inept."[22] Failing to adapt to conditions behind enemy lines, the KMT's guerrilla forces were driven from areas in the Japanese rear. Some troops threw in their lot with the Eighth Route Army, but many senior officers surrendered to the Japanese. Examples of those who surrendered are Sun Liangcheng (commander of the Thirty-ninth Army and concurrently director of the West Shandong Administrative Office), Wu Huawen (commander of the New Fourth Division), Yu Huai'an (commander of the New First Division), Rong Ziheng (commander of the 344th Brigade in the 112th Division and concurrently commander of the south Shandong guerrilla headquarters), Li Wenli (commander of the Forge Forward Second Column of the Shandong-Jiangsu War Zone), Pang Bingxun (commander of the Twenty-fourth Army Group and concurrently commander of the Taihang guerrilla headquarters), and Sun Dianying (commander of the New Fifth Army).

The KMT was unable to mobilize the population effectively. Local peasants often resented the presence of its forces. KMT guerrilla forces included central and local forces and were made up of soldiers from every background, including thugs and mercenaries. Officers often padded rosters to draw extra rations and secure more funding. Lax discipline and low morale provoked animosities and hatred among the peasants. Senior officers, needing resources to sustain their units, relied on local elites and landlords to squeeze the peasants or strong-arm the more prosperous peasants. Bad relations with the local peasantry were inevitable. KMT authorities were well aware of this reality. *Essentials of Guerrilla Warfare*, issued by the Military Affairs Commission, stressed concern for the welfare of the local population, but KMT guerrilla forces often did not comply with this exhortation. When the Nationalists and the Communists came into conflict behind Japanese lines, this led the majority of the peasants to side with the Communists. One old villager from Shanxi said,

We ordinary village folk all love the Eighth Route Army, and so does the village headman. When kids see the Eighth Route soldiers coming, they fight to walk their horses. When folks see soldiers approach, they ask, "What army?" "Eighth

Route" and everyone comes out to do chores for them. The Eighth Route always pays for its food and never abuses folks. In fighting against the Jap devils, they're better than the Shanxi Army and better than the First Cavalry. There wasn't even one traitor in the Eighth Route Army that came over from Shaanxi—the traitors all came from the Shanxi Army. A lot of guys from around here have joined the Eighth Route Army. In the villages they say, "If sooner or later you're gonna be a soldier, better join the Eighth Route Army now than wait to be drafted into the Shanxi Army."[23]

The fierce struggle between the Nationalists and Communists for control of territories behind the lines also had a major impact on their inability to maintain bases in Japanese-occupied areas. A major objective of the Nationalist government in recovering lost territory was to prevent CCP expansion. After the first year of the war, cooperation broke down. In 1939, the Eighth Route Army in Hebei undertook its first large-scale military action. First it wiped out several thousand troops belonging to Zhang Yinwu's Hebei People's Army. Then it crushed other major Nationalist government guerrilla forces, including those commanded by Qi Mingli (vice commander of the Hebei People's Army and concurrent commander of the Second Army), Jin Xianzhang (commander of the New Second Division), Xie Wenjiao (inspector of Shanxi's Eighth Subzone Special Office), Shi Yousan (vice commander of the Hebei-Chahar War Zone), and Zhu Huaibing (commander of the North Henan Peace Preservation Forces). In Shandong, the Eighth Route Army inflicted heavy casualties on the forces of Qi Zixiu (commander of the Shandong Security Forces' Fifth Division), Qin Qirong (commander of the Fifth Guerrilla Column), and Shen Honglie. In Shanxi, the Communists defeated Yan Xishan's plans to gain control of the Shanxi New Army by striking against the Shanxi Old Army. In all these conflicts, the troop strength on each side was usually more than 2,000 or 3,000, and in the largest-scale engagements each side might commit as many as ten to twenty regiments.

The success of the CCP in north China encouraged hopes that base areas could likewise be developed in central China. The Japanese rear in central China consisted of rich provinces along the lower reaches of the Yangtze River and in the Huai River watershed, where the Japanese occupied key cities and major transportation routes. The armies of the Guangxi Faction held the Dabie Mountains. Two army groups of General Gu Zhutong's Third War Zone were deployed along the Jiangxi-Anhui border and in southern Anhui and Jiangsu. Central and northern Jiangsu were the bailiwick of Han Deqin, vice commander of the Shandong-Jiangsu War Zone, and Li Mingyang, head of security of Dai Li's Loyal Salvation Army.

In the same period, the Communist New Fourth Army, organized from the Communists' southern guerrillas, merely occupied scattered areas in southern and central Anhui and southern Jiangsu. By April 1939, after the

New Fourth Army had been organized for only a half year, beginning with only three companies (*lian*) of about 300 men each, the force had already grown to twelve regiments and 10,000 men. Units headed by Li Xiannian and Chen Shaomin grew from a few hundred to several thousand within months. On 23 February 1939, the CCP leadership sent Zhou Enlai to the New Fourth Army headquarters to inform its members that their task was to consolidate in the south, fight in the east, and expand to the north. Shortly thereafter, two regiments of the New Fourth Army's First Column crossed the Yangtze River from southern Jiangsu to begin activities in the areas of Yangzhong, Daqiao, and Taishan. Six regiments moved east into the Suzhou, Taicang, Wuxi, and Jiangyin regions in the Yangtze delta. Four regiments of the Second Column moved from the Lake Tai region north across the Yangtze River and began operations in Yizheng, Liuhe, and Tianchang. They sent the Fourth and Fifth Columns to both sides of the Tianjin–Pukou Railroad.

Directed by the CCP Central Committee, the 115th Division in Shandong sent the Jiangsu-Shandong-Henan Column south to Lingbi, with one element entering northeast Anhui and the main force moving west of the Tianjin–Pukou Railroad. Peng Xuefeng's forces, also west of this rail line, began operations in the upper Huai region. The Shandong Longhai Southern Advance Column also received orders to move into the Peixian, Suining, and Tongshan regions to set up the northeast Anhui base area. The CCP leadership on 10 February 1940 set the goal of expanding Communist regular forces to 300,000 men, and self-defense forces to 3 million. The order commanded the Eighth Route and New Fourth armies "to form a single democratic anti-Japanese base area under the progressive government of the Communist Party."[24]

Chiang Kai-shek and the Nationalist leadership became deeply concerned with the rapid expansion of CCP military strength in north China and its growing presence in central China. They kept their forces on a high state of alert, fearing the challenge of the Communists and the warlords. In May 1939, the Military Affairs Commission promulgated Methods for Adjusting Guerrilla Forces, which contained orders concerning supply, training, reward, and discipline in the hope that unified organization, fixed command structures, and clear funding could make its guerrilla forces responsive to its authority. In July 1940, during the Seventh Plenum of the KMT's Fifth Congress, He Yingqin emphasized that no military forces could expand on their own initiative or acquire weapons by disarming straggling officers and men of local forces. In 1941, the Military Affairs Commission ordered the reduction by one-quarter, or 140,000 men, of Nationalist guerrilla units. Two years later, another 160,000 men were demobilized, and in 1944, a further reduction of 80,000 was ordered.[25]

At the same time, the Nationalist government tried to restrict CCP expansion. It required the CCP to gain KMT authorization before expanding its armed forces and enlarging its theater of operations. On 16 July 1941, despite CCP objections, the KMT stipulated that the Eighth Route Army be no larger than three armies with a total of six divisions. The New Fourth Army was limited to two divisions. All other detachments, columns, and guerrilla forces were ordered to disband. Their theaters of operation were restricted to the eighteen counties of the Shanxi-Gansu-Ningxia border region, the two provinces of Hebei and Chahar, and parts of northern Shandong and Shanxi. On 19 October 1941, Generals He Yingqin and Bai Chongxi, as chief of staff and vice chief of staff, issued a circular telegram ordering the Eighth Route and New Fourth armies to concentrate their operations within a month in Hebei, Chahar, northern Shandong, and northern Shanxi.[26]

Although the Nationalists ordered Communist forces to leave central China within one month, the CCP insisted on its operational independence and refused to accept restrictions. It agreed to move only the New Fourth Army in southern Anhui to the north of the Yangtze River. During the war of words that raged in the fall of 1941, neither side was willing to compromise. The subsequent New Fourth Army Incident sent shock waves through the nation and abroad. The incident happened when Nationalist government forces from the Third War Zone surrounded and attacked the headquarters detachment of the New Fourth Army, numbering some 9,000 officers and men. With the exception of about 1,000 men, including the commander, Ye Ting, the entire force was either killed in action or taken prisoner. The incident effectively ended cooperation between the Nationalists and Communists during the war.

The Communists under Pressure

Although the CCP worked hard to free itself from KMT efforts to restrict it, the expansion of Communist military forces encountered many difficulties after 1940. On 16 August 1940, the CCP politburo discussed prospects for military expansion. It saw two major problems. First, guns and ammunition were in exceedingly short supply. Many new units were unable to comply with the requirement that at least half of their troops have weapons. They were also short of ammunition. Despite substantial numerical growth, combat effectiveness declined.

Second, military expansion placed heavy burdens on the local people. In the Shanxi-Chahar-Hebei border region, party, government, and army personnel not engaged in production numbered 2.8 percent of the total population. In central Hebei, the figure was 2.9 percent, and in one county in the Shaanxi-Gansu-Ningxia base area, it reached 6 percent. Fiscal stability in Communist base areas required that personnel not engaged in production not exceed 3 percent of the population. The conclusion was that military expansion had already reached its limits in most base areas. The CCP leadership demanded that each base area plan military expansion accordingly. A directive stated that "to sustain the struggle over the long term, we must seize enemy territory . . . We must avoid concentrating our forces in our core areas and idly eating the storehouse empty."[27]

Excessive military expansion generated problems early on. To meet its expansion targets, the 359th Brigade of the 120th Division had, in late 1938, recruited middle-aged and even elderly men as well as secret society thugs, gangs of local toughs, deserters, and riffraff.[28] Due to desertion and losses, some units proved unviable.[29] The Eighth Route Army took corrective measures so that desertion declined.[30] However, a far more difficult task was to prevent army units from living off the local population and "eating the storehouse empty."

The policy of expanding into Japanese-held areas led to the 1940 Battle of the Hundred Regiments. In spring, the Japanese North China Area Army recognized the threat posed by the CCP's domination of north China. It turned to punitive strikes to counter the CCP, and ten of the fourteen divisions of the North China Area Army were assigned to pacification operations.[31] Already by the end of June, many Communist base areas were reduced to guerrilla zones. The result was that although CCP forces grew, the base areas necessary to sustain them diminished. The Eighth Route Army attempted to reverse this situation by ordering attacks into enemy areas. In July, it developed a plan to force the Japanese onto the defensive by large-scale, quick-strike operations against vital Japanese locations. Pushed on by the CCP Central Committee's policy of fighting the enemy for territorial influence, this plan developed into the Battle of the Hundred Regiments.

The Battle of the Hundred Regiments was the largest Communist operation of the entire war. It encompassed different kinds of combat operations. Apart from hit-and-run attacks,[32] the Eighth Route Army adopted large-scale mobile warfare,[33] assault operations,[34] and positional warfare.[35] The Eighth Route Army, although a serious threat, was insufficiently strong to inflict serious damage on the Japanese army. In the aftermath of the fighting, General Peng Dehuai, one of the top two or three Communist commanders, characterized the disparity in combat strength. He had personally led an attack on a Japanese-held village, surrounding it with seven times as many troops as the defenders. Although Peng's forces fought hard and absorbed large numbers of casualties, they were unable to defeat the Japanese, largely because of Japanese superiority in firepower. Although the Communists suffered 20,000 casualties in two months of fighting, they were unable to achieve their original objectives and had to withdraw.

Not only that, the Japanese revised their assessment of the Eighth Route Army. They assembled even larger military forces to pacify areas they had occupied and, against areas they could not hold, carried out the Three-All Policy of burn all, kill all, and loot all. Thus, the battle ended in a sharp reduction of area under Eighth Route Army's control. Virtually all of the base areas on the plains reverted to guerrilla zones, and Eighth Route Army operations in the enemy rear were more difficult than before. At the same time, the New Fourth Army Incident had wrecked relations between the Communists and the Nationalists.

Mao Zedong made a new assessment of the military situation. He pointed out the great disparity between the Communists and the Japanese in military technology and equipment. He noted that Communist forces faced increasing difficulties because of shortages in materiel and shrunken territory. He recognized that if the Chinese Communists continued to wage battles without regard for losses, the enemy would eventually crush them. The CCP leadership decided to restrict military operations once more to guerrilla warfare. They recognized that conventional battle against the Japanese was suicidal. At the present time, "our line is to wait for improvements in the situation. In the meantime, we preserve our strength while carrying out dispersed guerrilla operations employing every sort of tactic, from fierce skirmishing and nonviolent revolutionary duplicity to maneuvers against the enemy."[36]

Plans to enlarge the armed forces were abandoned. The Central Military Affairs Commission stated,

Armed forces should not expand during the course of the War of Resistance, except in unusual circumstances. Because of our high casualties, two regiments should now be combined into one, and so on down the line. The entire army should prepare, during the next two years, to be reduced by half. Prepare to reduce troops from 570,000 to around 200,000 . . . In mountainous base areas, the ratio of regular to local forces, not counting armed civilians, should not exceed two to one. In base areas on the plains, the ratio should be one to one. In difficult areas, such as east Hebei, the Daqing Mountains, and south Anhui, the distinction between the regular army and local forces should be erased entirely, and all forces are to be localized . . . In every base area, the total number of those not actively engaged in production (including those serving in party, government, army, popular organizations, and schools) should constitute no more than 3 percent of the total population . . . The ratio of army (including guerrilla forces) to those working in the party, government, and mass organizations should be 75 percent to 25 percent.[37]

The central Hebei base area lay close to key cities and communication lines in north China. It was surrounded and attacked frequently. By 1943, the Japanese had built 1,753 strongpoints and blockhouses, amounting to about one for every four and a half villages. Between the strongpoints and blockhouses, the Japanese had removed trees, buildings, and mounds obstructing lines of sight and direct fire. They also constructed over 500 miles of railroads and highways and dug over 2,500 miles of ditches. One-yard-deep moats divided county from county, district from district, and village from village, all to restrict Communist forces. The Japanese army imposed severe punitive measures. If a village concealed Communist soldiers or cadres, the Japanese torched the village or forced the populace to pay heavy compensation. The Japanese army frequently launched large-scale mopping-up campaigns. The most brutal was the 1 May mopping-up campaign against the central Hebei base area in 1942. The Japanese army pushed Communist forces into a narrow triangle to destroy them. During this campaign, Communist forces and the local population suffered severe losses. In one zone, the number of Communist soldiers was reduced from 4,500 to 2,000. In the entire military district, the Japanese inflicted 10,000 casualties. Civilian losses were several times higher.[38]

Nevertheless, limited Japanese troop strength meant that the Japanese could not bring all Communist resistance to an end. After a large-scale pacification campaign, they had to return to a defensive posture. The construction of blockhouses, the digging of moats, and the building of roads had the counterproductive effect of further dispersing their strength. After the summer of 1942, puppets and the Japanese had, on average, fewer than thirty men assigned to each blockhouse or fortification. Large fortifications had only a few hundred men, while smaller blockhouses might have only a dozen. Most were puppet soldiers; Japanese regulars made up only a quarter of the total. As a result, the combat effectiveness and firepower declined markedly.

Communist armed forces responded to this situation as follows: The Eighth Route Army dispatched from one-third to one-half of its forces to the enemy's flanks and rear. Local forces were reduced so that the company was the largest unit, and often it was platoons and squads that became the unit of combat. In central Hebei, Communist guerrillas sometimes concealed themselves in peasant houses to launch bayonet attacks against the Japanese or their puppets. Sometimes they charged head-on to drive the enemy back to its fortifications and blockhouses. At other times, they put pressure on the enemy along weakly defended communication lines to provoke terror among the Japanese. With larger Japanese and puppet detachments, they used the tactic of interlinked village defense, counterattacking in concert with one another. When a unit was surrounded, nearby village forces would send relief and surround the besieging enemy. In March 1943, three squads of central Hebei Communist forces were stationed in three villages. Two hundred Japanese surrounded them. But the three squads attacked the Japanese and puppets in coordinated pincer maneuvers, and after a day of fighting the forces were able to get away. In early June, a company of Communist guerrillas carried out a coordinated counterattack against Japanese forces in central Hebei, capturing enemy small arms before escaping. Finally, against large-scale enemy mopping-up campaigns, they adopted the tactic of dispersal, melting away by twos and threes or hiding in underground tunnels.[39]

Communist armed forces did not necessarily use the same combat methods in all areas. In the east Hebei base area, because guerrilla regiments had the mountains to rely on, they could preserve a relative degree of concentration. Their combat methods included making feints in all directions, avoiding enemy strongpoints while hitting weak formations, and undertaking hit-and-run attacks. Communists set ambushes, exploiting the "green curtain" of tall crops and the cover of darkness to attack small detachments of Japanese and puppets on the march. They would launch a brief but fierce attack with automatic rifles and hand grenades and then swarm forth like bees to engage in hand-to-hand combat.[40]

In the face of Japanese repression, the basic policy of the CCP was to bring the armed forces and the masses increasingly together in a single military organization. This concentration involved organizing guerrilla units from hardened locals and setting up Vanguards to Resist Japan, recruited from eighteen- to twenty-four-year-old youths. The CCP also organized Model Units, manned by twenty-five- to thirty-five-year-old males as well as self-defense units of thirty-five- to fifty-five-year-old males. Similar efforts were made to enlist women. The vast majority of peasants were organized by the Armed Forces Committee, an enlarged version of the Armed Forces Department. All levels of the administrative hierarchy contained a secretariat and a section to organize combat, training, logistics, and ammunition. Each was under the unified command of the Vanguards.[41] At the same time, squad-level units organized by the regular army penetrated market towns to assist the local population in carrying out armed resistance, practicing "just hit one" tactics, in which the worst traitors were killed to intimidate others. When necessary, main force elements were brought in to attack particularly active Japanese and puppet soldiers. They sometimes surrounded these soldiers' fortifications and ambushed exiting troops. At other times, they entered blockhouses when they were empty. Japanese punitive measures usually only provoked greater resistance.[42]

With the beginning of the Pacific War, the combat effectiveness of Japanese forces in north China fell sharply because of CCP policies described above. By 1944, the CCP's guerrilla war in north China had weathered its most difficult period. Troop strength had declined by only 100,000, far fewer than had been anticipated. As Mao noted late in that year, in 1940, the CCP had twenty base areas with a population of about 100 million and an army of 570,000 men. After the Battle of the Hundred Regiments, its strength had diminished. But, Mao argued, the party's line had been correct, so it lost only a few large base areas, the population under its control was reduced by less than half, and Communist armies had shrunk by only 100,000. By the latter half of 1943, Communist strength began to trend upward once again.

Communist Recovery

In the second half of 1943, the war situation changed significantly in ways advantageous to CCP forces engaged in guerrilla warfare in north China. The United States supported the KMT strongly, and the Americans were attacking the Japanese homeland from U.S. bases in China. The U.S. Navy threatened Japanese maritime lines of communication, leading them to plan for the opening of overland routes between China and Southeast Asia (see chapter 16 by Hara Takeshi). The Japanese were forced to redeploy units from north China to carry out the Ichigō offensive. Naturally, these circumstances lightened the pressure on CCP bases in north China, allowing the Eighth Route and New Fourth armies to operate more easily.

In early 1944, the Shanxi-Chahar-Hebei base area issued a directive to its regular forces to concentrate and, if circumstances allowed, attack puppet installations to force their withdrawal or annihilate them. However, carrying out this directive was easier said than done. Each base area faced different circumstances. A further problem was the continued rectification campaign aimed at routing out traitors within the CCP and enforcing Maoist ideology throughout the party ranks. It sharply criticized concentrated warfare and condemned the Battle of the Hundred Regiments for failing to have understood that the war against the Japanese required protracted guerrilla warfare. The call to shift back to fighting in larger units of concentration naturally led to anxiety as people feared that they might be accused of violating Maoist principles. As late as mid-April 1944, when the Japanese Ichigō offensive was already in full swing, Mao asserted that "our party is still not strong enough, still not unified enough, and still not consolidated enough. We cannot shoulder greater responsibilities than those we presently bear."[43]

During the summer of 1944, Nationalist government forces suffered defeat after defeat at the hands of the Japanese. The Americans increasingly took note of the Eighth Route Army in north China. They sent an observer mission to Yan'an and promised to provide military aid. The CCP leadership became eager to demonstrate Communist military strength. The Military Affairs Commission called for "heavy attacks on Japanese and puppets," advocating that armed forces located near large cities should strive to move from guerrilla warfare to encirclement of the cities, not only to threaten the Japanese but also to take them. To prepare for possible conflict with the KMT and to set up base areas in south China, the Military Affairs Commission ordered the Eighth Route Army to follow the Japanese as they advanced south and to set up a new base area in western Henan, south of the Yangtze. The Eighth Route Army established a detachment of 10,000 men that joined up with Communist guerrillas in northeast Guangdong. This move was the beginning of a significant CCP presence in south China with links to Communist forces in north and central China.

With the sanction of the CCP leadership, the Eighth Route Army again concentrated its forces for offensive operations. Yet years of dispersed guerrilla fighting meant that many forces had lost the capacity for coordinated large-scale operations. In August 1945 when the Soviet Army dispatched a column of the Russian-Mongol Joint Army into Chahar, it encountered Communist troops dressed as peasants with a hodgepodge of arms. Although they greeted the Soviets warmly and explained that they were Eighth Route Army, the mechanized Russian-Mongol column believed they were bandits and disarmed them at gunpoint.

The equipment of the Eighth Route Army was primitive. It had many sorts of weapons, and many soldiers had no weapons at all. The vast majority of units behind enemy lines had no heavy weapons. Gunpowder was produced locally and was of low quality. To confront Japanese forces in conventional combat was impossible because Communist forces had received no training in conventional warfare. Mao Zedong cautiously called for a limited policy of harassment, even though the overall strategic situation for the Allies had become promising, and in north China the Japanese menace had lessened. The CCP leadership had called for a "liberation army" modeled after the Greek Communists. Mao stated that "for now, our approach to the war should be to squeeze the enemy. While consolidating our current positions, we squeeze the enemy out step by step and prepare for a counterattack." CCP troops avoided major battles and attacked small enemy strongholds only when good opportunities presented themselves.[44]

After 1940, the dispersal of the Communist military among the civilian population had obviously worked. As the war neared its end, the CCP pushed large numbers of local and militia forces into its regular army structures. By late 1944 and early 1945, CCP regular armies had grown to 900,000 and local forces to as many as 2–3 million.

As it stepped up the concentration of its forces, in some areas the Eighth Route Army and the New Fourth Army increased offensive operations. At the end of 1944, the CCP leadership finally approved the shift from the defensive to the offensive and from guerrilla warfare to conventional warfare. Until the spring of 1945, the CCP's leadership estimate of when the Japanese would be defeated remained highly cautious. In early August, Mao Zedong continued to believe that the Japanese defeat was still a year away. He therefore emphasized guerrilla warfare, base area construction, and military buildup. Consequently, the overall disposition of forces on the eve of Japanese surrender still aimed just at preparations for a decisive battle and counteroffensive. Mao emphasized that the time for large-scale counterattacks had not yet arrived. Thus, the rate at which the CCP carried out its strategic shift of moving from guerrilla to conventional warfare naturally lagged behind actual events. On 9 August 1945, most CCP troops still engaged in guerrilla warfare.

Conclusion

Throughout the war, the KMT and the CCP waged guerrilla warfare. In comparing them, we can see that the KMT's guerrilla operations were primarily in support of regular warfare. The CCP's guerrilla warfare was conducted independently and had its own purpose. The tactical concept and combat methods of its forces differed from those of the KMT. The greatest difference lay in the relationship between soldiers and civilians. Because the KMT lost popular support, its guerrilla forces were unable to provide extended resistance against Japanese forces. Nor did they ultimately have sufficient strength to deny territory to the CCP. In the end, most KMT guerrilla forces would either pull out, surrender to the Japanese, or drift into the CCP armed forces.

The CCP's guerrilla warfare developed over time as lessons were learned from actual combat or the situation changed. The development occurred in three major stages. The first stage lasted from the beginning of the war through the Battle of the Hundred Regiments. From the day that Mao Zedong first set the policy of dispersed guerrilla warfare, the Eighth Route Army did not fight in large concentrations. The second stage, lasting from the beginning of 1941 until the end of 1943, was the most difficult period. The CCP disavowed concentrated warfare. It followed policies of dispersal and engaged in modes of combat later upheld as classic CCP methods. The third stage ran from the beginning of 1944 until the Japanese surrender in August 1945. The CCP sought to realize a shift in military strategy from guerrilla warfare to conventional warfare in preparation for a counteroffensive. Failing to anticipate the early Japanese surrender, the CCP leadership hesitated and delayed concentrating Communist forces. They tried a few dispersed offensive actions and gradually concentrated some of their forces in preparation for the formation of a centralized force with which to confront the KMT after the defeat of Japan.

The weakness of the CCP and its domestic political and military rivalries, especially with the KMT, determined the CCP's approach to the war. The Communists had to depend on their own strength and could not risk subordinating their efforts to those of the KMT. To be victorious, every strategic and tactical initiative was based on this fundamental reality. The approach made possible not only the CCP's survival but its enormous development through the course of eight years of bitter struggle.

13 *Japanese Combat Morale*

A CASE STUDY OF THE THIRTY-SEVENTH DIVISION

KAWANO HITOSHI

> They seemed to be fighting more *for* somebody rather than *against* somebody.
> —Roy Grinker and John Spiegel

> I hold it to be one of the simplest truths of war that the thing which enables an infantry soldier to keep going with his weapons is the near presence or the presumed presence of a comrade.
> —S. L. A. Marshall

> The best single predictor of combat behavior is the simple fact of institutionalized role: knowing that a man is a soldier rather than a civilian.
> —Samuel A. Stouffer

Introduction

Stereotypical portrayals of the Japanese soldiers emphasize ideological factors such as "fighting for the emperor," "for the sake of the nation," "the samurai spirit" (Bushido), or "the Japanese spirit" (*Yamato damashii*). Chiang Kai-shek believed the Japanese army was advantaged by the civil-military unity achieved with the ideology of *chūkun aikoku* (loyalty to the emperor and love of country) or *Yamato damashii*. He also thought that Japanese soldiers fought to the death because of strict military discipline and absolute obedience to orders.[1] A puzzling view of the Japanese soldiers as superbly skilled and disciplined combat soldiers who were at the same time savage, brutal, and cold-blooded killers, like a "Dr. Jekyll and Mr. Hyde" personality, dominates Western impressions of the Japanese military.[2] The *gyokusai* (death before dishonor) ideology and desperate and seemingly insane banzai and kamikaze tactics symbolize the mysterious and sometimes incomprehensible behavior of the Japanese soldiers in the Pacific theater, though these peculiarly Japanese phenomena were far less frequently observed in the China theater.[3]

A more balanced view discounts the idealized image of the Japanese soldiers while recognizing self-preservation, comradely ties, social peer pressure, and family honor as equally important factors in motivating them to fight.[4] In the following sections, I explore the issue of combat morale in the day-to-day lives of individual Japanese combat soldiers.[5] My focus is on the soldiers of the Thirty-seventh Division, Imperial Japanese Army (IJA), and relies on oral testimonies I obtained through interviews with more than forty veterans of the division.[6]

This chapter examines the combat experience of individual Japanese soldiers and their motivations to fight from their own perspective. It focuses on the so-called primary group tie,[7] or bonding experience, that promoted unit cohesion and the role of leadership as salient factors.[8] In other words, the description of combat behavior and the analyses of combat motivation are based on sociological and social-psychological theoretical frameworks.

The Unit History of the Thirty-seventh Infantry Division: An Overview

The Thirty-seventh Division was a provisional unit activated on 7 February 1939. Commanded by Lieutenant General Hirata Kenkichi, the Thirty-seventh Division traced its lineage to the Twelfth Division, which was headquartered in northern Kyushu. Its recruiting district included the industrial and coal-mining areas of northern Kyushu and Okinawa. The division's identity derived from its combat history and the characteristics of its geographic recruitment base.

Indicative of the army's shift from a strategy of a short, decisive war (*tanki-kessen*) to one of protracted warfare (*choki-jikyu*) in China, the Thirty-seventh was organized as a "security division" for occupation duty. It replaced the Twentieth Division in the First Army's order of battle in May 1939.[9] The Twentieth Division was a Type A, prewar, regular square division of two brigades of two infantry regiments each and an artillery regiment, with a total authorized strength of 28,959.[10] (See chapter 4 by Edward J. Drea.) In comparison, the Thirty-seventh Division was a Type C triangular division that had three infantry regiments and three artillery batteries, with a total authorized strength of 14,404, and about 44 percent of the firepower of a prewar division.[11] The Type C divisions also lacked logistic support and mobility,[12] and were typical of those stationed in China after 1939. The Thirty-seventh Division was one of ten divisions mobilized between February and June 1939, most of which were deployed to the China theater to relieve battle-weary Type A divisions such as the

Twentieth Division. The veteran divisions were reconstituted in anticipation of war with the Soviet Union along the Soviet-Manchurian border.[13]

The First Army's mission was to secure the southwest area of Shanxi Province. Subordinate to the newly organized China Expeditionary Army, headquartered in Nanjing, First Army consisted of the Thirty-sixth, Thirty-seventh, and Forty-first divisions and the Third, Fourth, and Ninth independent mixed brigades. Its total strength as of September 1939 was almost 133,000 personnel, about one-third of the overall strength of the North China Area Army.[14] The Thirty-seventh Division, with more than 200 "highly dispersed" positions, faced the Nationalist army's First, Second, and Tenth war zones, as well as the Eighth Route Army and local militia.[15] As of June 1939, the Chinese Central Army had 56,000 men organized in nine divisions. There was also the Shaanxi Army force of 31,800 (five divisions and two brigades), the Shanxi force of 6,000 (three brigades), and the local militia of around 3,300. A total of almost 100,000 enemy troops opposed the Thirty-seventh Division.[16] According to a July 1940 division report on the security situation, however, operations had reduced the enemy strength to around 60,000. The heavy losses rendered the enemy less aggressive and thus substantially lowered overall combat effectiveness.[17]

Military Operations

The Thirty-seventh Division engaged in numerous operations in north China in 1939–1944. Its infantrymen had their first taste of battle during the East Operation, a mop-up expedition east of Xiaxian toward the Zhongtiao Mountains in Shanxi conducted in December 1939. Facing 13,000 troops of the Third Army and the Chinese Nationalist army, the Thirty-seventh Division put almost 12,000 soldiers in the field and lost 163 men killed and another 529 wounded. Although the enemy suffered 2,745 killed and the Japanese estimated Chinese wounded at 5,000, the Thirty-seventh's first battle was indecisive because the unit withdrew as planned to its original positions. Thus, the unit's first engagement was an unpleasant memory.[18]

In an August 1940 report to the Imperial General Headquarters, Hirata summarized fifteen months of operations in Shanxi: "Since our assignment to the area, our division has engaged in combat almost daily. The total number of operations, including small- and large-scale engagements, was about 2,300, which meant we engaged in combat about 6.5 times a day on average. The division killed 2,000 of the enemy, and captured another 2,000 while losing 776 killed in action, 126 deaths because of disease, and 827 wounded and ill who were evacuated to Japan."[19] Between 1940 and

1943, the division participated in several other major campaigns.[20] As a result of the Battle of Zhongyuan of May–June 1941 in southern Shanxi, Chinese forces lost 42,000 killed and 35,000 captured, as opposed to Japanese casualties of 673 killed and 2,292 wounded.[21] Chiang Kai-shek termed the defeat "the greatest shame in the history of anti-Japanese war."[22]

The Thirty-seventh Division left north China to join the Ichigō offensive (see chapter 16 by Hara Takeshi and chapter 17 by Wang Qisheng), a massive campaign involving 500,000 Japanese troops under the command of the Twelfth Army.[23] The 12,943 troops moved 1,000 miles to Kaifeng by train by mid-April 1944 and played a key role in the forced crossing of the Yellow River at Zhongmou in the face of 3,000 Chinese defenders of the Provisional Twenty-seventh Division, First War Zone Army, and fought in various places including Xuchang and Lushi in Henan Province during the Peking–Hankou Railroad operation in April–June 1944.[24] One regiment covered 300 miles in twenty days, averaging 15 miles a day, while engaging in combat.[25] The division also participated in the Shōkei offensive, under the command of the Eleventh Army, from June 1944 to January 1945. During the six months of hard fighting, including the Baoqing and Guilin offensives, the division suffered more than 2,700 killed in addition to 400 killed in action during the previous operation in Hunan.[26]

The division crossed into French Indochina on 25 January 1945, where it participated in the Meigo offensive (March–April 1945) as the main force of the newly created Thirty-eighth Army, previously designated the Indochina Expedition Army.[27] The division's area of operations was in north Tonkin, where the French had built several strongholds. The Liangshan strongpoint,[28] for instance, was equipped with 80 cannons, more than 300 heavy and light machine guns, and 10 tanks, manned by 7,000 "elite" troops, including 300 French regulars.[29] Seizing these French strongholds cost the division an additional 991 soldiers killed.[30] The Thirty-seventh's casualties amounted to 4,673 killed during their last sixteen months of campaigning, or three times the number lost in five years of security operations in Shanxi.[31] Altogether, the Thirty-seventh Division suffered 7,338 battle deaths.

The Thirty-seventh Division was in Thailand at the end of the war, with its advance elements as far away as Singapore. It had moved from north China to Thailand by train, by ship, and on foot, a distance of more than 6,000 miles over 495 days.[32] The division fought hundreds of small skirmishes and dozens of large-scale battles. The soldiers believed that "Japan lost the war, but we never lost a battle." The battle-seasoned division's designated code name was "Winter,"[33] and the reputation of the "Winter Troops," symbolized by their blue-triangle insignia and esprit de corps, likely boosted morale.[34] A sergeant stated proudly that "when the Chinese soldiers saw our blue-triangle insignia, they just fled." In this sense, the Thirty-seventh Division had a different perspective than the numerous Japanese divisions that experienced devastating defeats and, in several cases, near extermination.

Much like the U.S. Army's notion that southerners make the best combat troops, the Thirty-seventh Division shared a perception that men from the Kyushu area excelled on the offensive,[35] while troops from northeastern Japan (Tōhoku) were best on defense, and the city boys from Osaka were most adept at regional control.[36] One episode illustrates the qualities of the combat-seasoned soldiers of the Thirty-seventh Division. When the officers and men of the Thirty-seventh Division entered French Indochina, Japanese soldiers already stationed there and local residents were surprised to see a ragtag bunch who looked like a defeated army. The Thirty-seventh's battle-hardened veterans were filthy, their uniforms were stinking and in tatters, few wore any insignia of rank, and many sported civilian shoes instead of military boots. Some marched along wearing forage caps; others did not. Many had long, uncut hair and heavy beards. Even in the eyes of the fellow Japanese soldiers of the Twenty-first Division, which consisted of mostly of northeasterners, the darkly tanned, unshaven faces looked alien. Nevertheless, once in combat, the seeming ragamuffins outperformed the Tōhoku troops and gained the reputation that they were superb fighters.[37]

Social Process of Mobilization
and Social Construction of a Japanese Soldier

"Many aspects of morale are linked with national characteristics and ways of life," claims N. Balchin, and thus a "full understanding of battle morale calls for a full understanding of national psychology."[38] My approach downplays the *ideological* aspect of the Japanese culture to focus on the *practices* of personal interactions to analyze combat motivation. The social interaction demonstrates how a Japanese soldier is *socially constructed* in a given sociocultural context. Thus, I describe several significant social processes of mobilization, how they interact at each stage of mobilization, and how the interaction affected combat motivation, recognizing of course that one's motivation to join the army can be quite different from one's frontline combat incentives.

According to Stanislav Andreski, Japan under Prime Minister Tōjō Hideki (1941–1944) was "a clear case of militarism."[39] Compared to a "volunteering society" like the United States or Great Britain in which a small peacetime standing army relied on volunteers, Japan displayed characteristics of a *mobilizing society*.[40] A mobilizing society maintains a universal conscription system and an active civil-military integration through a set of militaristic socialization systems involving public schooling, youth military training, and organized nationwide veterans' associations, as well as women's associations. Morris Janowitz underscores the importance of a "total social system" as a social imperative behind military effectiveness.[41]

Socialization as a future soldier began in childhood in prewar Japan. Born as a son of a local bus company owner in Kumamoto in 1918, Nemoto Kenji (a pseudonym, as are all the names of interviewees unless otherwise noted)[42] grew up in a family whose great-uncle was killed in action during naval operations at Port Arthur in the 1905 Russo-Japanese War and posthumously awarded the prestigious Order of the Golden Kite (*kinshi kunsho*).[43] Nemoto played war games with his peers every day as a child, and admits to being a "militaristic boy." It seemed natural to him to learn martial arts such as kendo (stick fighting) and judo, which were his favorite extracurricular activities at school.[44] He was conscripted in 1941, and he developed into a good combat soldier and was promoted to noncommissioned officer of engineers. Of course, not every Japanese boy wanted to be a soldier, but the militaristic sociocultural context in prewar Japan certainly influenced children's choices, and social values created enormous pressure to serve with honor. Nemoto, for instance, admits that one of his major combat motivations was to perform well in order "not to disgrace my family honor."[45]

Other cases of a veteran's influence on families include an uncle who discouraged his nephew from avoiding army service and encouraged the new conscript by giving him his lucky charm, the one-thousand-stitches (*sennin-bari*) the uncle carried during the Russo-Japanese War.[46] Sometimes, a nonveteran father who was qualified as a Class A soldier but was not conscripted would encourage his son to aspire to become an officer.[47] According to Roy Grinker and John Spiegel, having a veteran as a family member can be a strong motivating factor.[48] Nonetheless, not all fathers were so enthusiastic about their sons' inductions. Some were indifferent, and others made no particular effort to encourage their sons to join the military. The majority of the Japanese veterans whom I interviewed made no special mention of their family's influence over their enlistment.

Even when the family influence was absent, social pressures abounded. Neighbors, teachers, peers, and role models were powerful agents of conscription. Every grade school pupil learned the Japanese language with a textbook whose opening sentence was "Advance. Advance. Soldiers advance!"[49] As graduates of teachers colleges, which were considered as quasi-military academies, public school teachers also conveyed militaristic ideology. The social institution of conscription, which became embedded in the public school system that had developed since the 1870s, was further reinforced by the National Total Mobilization Law of 1938 that in theory established a highly structured educational and social system for the purpose of fighting a total war as an idealized "nation in arms."[50]

Upon graduation from a six-year primary school, or with two more years of advanced middle schooling, Japanese boys attended a youth school, a part-time educational and military training institution for working youth. Retired or former army officers familiarized the young men with basic military discipline and drill. The youth school system was formalized in 1935 in order to provide additional vocational and military training for teenage workers, and it became obligatory in 1939. Training at a youth school was held three or four days a week, usually for a couple of hours in the afternoon, with a retired veteran in charge of military training.[51] In the countryside, training would be held at a local primary school after ordinary schooling hours, though some factories offered their facilities for youth schooling in the urban areas.

Individual Testimonies
of Thirty-seventh Division Veterans

Goh Koji, born in Ohita Prefecture in 1922, enrolled in the Kashiwabara youth school, and since most training was on a part-time basis, he also helped out on his family's farm. He applied for the army's junior pilot training program, but he was rejected because of color blindness. At sixteen, he started work at Kokura Army Arsenal, Fukuoka. He passed his preinduction physical examination in 1942 as a Class A recruit. Among forty potential inductees in the district, only seven or eight graded Class A. Goh entered the army on 10 January 1943, joining the Sixth Engineer Regiment Replacement Unit in Kumamoto.

Once Goh knew that he would be drafted, he memorized the Imperial Rescript for the Soldiers and Sailors because new draftees were required to recite the lengthy and complicated ordinance as a matter of course during their basic training. His uncle and a cousin, who were veterans, as well as others, including a Nomonhan veteran at his factory, all told him that it would be too late to start studying the rescript after induction. Veterans were extremely influential during his conscription process.[52]

Goh's childhood was also filled with the trappings of a militaristic culture. Lieutenant Commander Hirose Takeo, a popular hero and deified as a "war god" during the Russo-Japanese War, was born in Goh's hometown and thus became a role model for the children in the region. War movies were regular fare at his primary school. Goh recalled, "Since my early childhood, I took it for granted that the way to preserve family honor, not to disgrace the family, and serve the country was to die in combat. It seemed natural growing up."[53] Social interaction with relatives and peers made him into a soldier *naturally*. His motivation to serve for the country was thus socially constructed.[54]

Once in the army, he began to see things differently. Two weeks after Private Second Class Goh joined the Thirty-seventh Division at Yuncheng, China, in January 1943, the harshness of the training made him consider desertion. Then he thought of his family. As the eldest son of six siblings, if he deserted it would reflect poorly on his two younger brothers and other family members and relatives. The need to preserve family honor inhibited him from deserting because serving his country was an extension of serving his family. Although it followed in the prewar Japanese social calculus that serving the emperor was only a logical extension of serving the country, Goh did not feel that way. Once in combat, he never even thought of dying for the emperor.

Goh's case demonstrates a typical pattern of motivation for induction and military service. Ideological thoughts of the emperor or even thoughts about his own family quickly disappeared from his mind when the fighting began. But the familial bond remained in his mind, at a deeper or subconscious level. After combat, thoughts of family and loved ones quickly resurfaced. As discussed below, "love and honor of the family and community" were in fact the most frequently mentioned combat motivators by the Japanese veterans.

In addition to socialization processes, symbolic interactions at various social ceremonies and rituals involving the military played important roles in motivating soldiers to fight. Japan had had a conscription system since 1873, and the army steadily expanded after the outbreak of the Sino-Japanese War in 1937 and the Pearl Harbor attack in 1941. Military service was institutionalized in society, and transition rituals and ceremonies for soldiers' induction and overseas deployment developed to a considerable degree. (However, during the Pacific War, large-scale public ceremonies for local units' deployment were avoided for counterintelligence reasons.)

The physical examination for induction, required of every twenty-year-old male citizen in prewar Japan, was an important life event or rite of passage for a young Japanese man. Many considered it an honor to be classified as Class A, fit for military service, although the classification did not necessarily mean that the candidate would be called for active duty in peacetime.[55] In 1937, the last year of peace, about 23 percent of the twenty-year-old cohort was inducted. As the war expanded, however, a Class A rating meant sure induction.

Induction rituals included a formal farewell party to celebrate the event. The conscript's family would invite relatives, neighbors, peers, members of the local youth and women's associations, family friends, schoolteachers, and the village mayor or local politicians, as well as Buddhist and Shinto priests.[56] Guests would bring small farewell presents for the inductee—

such as money (*senbetsu*), amulets (*omamori*), one-thousand-stitch towels (*sennin-bari*) with five-cent and ten-cent coins attached,[57] and a Japanese national flag with signatures (*yosegaki*, the so-called banzai flag)—tokens that symbolized that they wished him good luck in combat. A banner (*nobori*), which typically read "Mr. Tanaka Ichirō of the 227th Infantry Regiment, Congratulations on Your Induction!!" would be displayed in the front yard or at the house entrance. An induction party could cost as much as a wedding reception, which meant it was a significant life event for a man at that time.[58] (However, those who were drafted after the Pearl Harbor attack in 1941 tended to have an induction party on a smaller scale because of material and food shortages and rationing during the war.)

Besides induction and mobilization ceremonies, funerals for soldiers killed in action were symbolic interactions in terms of combat morale. When military funerals were held, they were important social events. For instance, Nomura Yasushi, an engineer noncommissioned officer (NCO) of the Thirty-seventh Division, attended military funerals a few times in 1937 and 1938. The ceremonies were normally held at a primary school's playground, where a memorial stage was erected. Distinguished visitors might include a representative from the army regiment, the mayor of the town, and some other important people in the town. Nomura was impressed by the largest and most solemn social functions he had witnessed in a small town in Kagoshima.

The social processes of induction constitute a subconscious basis of combat motivation, which can be called "latent ideology," that is, a soldier's love for family, the community, and, as a logical extension, his country.[59] On induction day, the townspeople would give the new recruits a send-off, accompanying the inductee from his home to the local train station. At the station, the new conscripts would line up on a stage and make a short speech on behalf of the group. Yamada Takeshi spoke in February 1942, exclaiming, "We shall die for the country." He figured that it would be the best thing to say because it was what the audience expected to hear.[60] His behavior was socially constructed as a role to represent the draftees who were supposed to serve the army, and thereby the nation. Social pressure did not allow him to say publicly that he would return alive, though the families of the soldiers held unspoken wishes for their sons to survive the war.[61]

Combat Organization
and Institutional Role of Soldier

The army's formal organization gave inductees a new institutional role as a common soldier with the rank of private second class. More than 600 officers and 1,500 NCOs from the Twelfth and Sixth divisions formed the Thirty-seventh Division's cadre. The 12,191 private soldiers were conscripts from the Northern Kyushu area and consisted of 8,000 active duty regulars and 4,000 reserve fillers.[62] The mixture was unusual because by August 1938 only 11 percent of the 650,000 enlisted men serving in the China theater were regulars, the rest being recalled reservists. With its large infusion of active duty soldiers, the Thirty-seventh ranked as a "fresh" division[63] with supposedly high morale. The organization table of the Thirty-seventh Division is shown in table 13.1, which also shows the organization table of the 225th Infantry Regiment. On paper the infantry regiment had three battalions of four companies each. A company had three rifle platoons each of four thirteen-man squads. In the field, however, the numbers varied. The Seventh Company, 226th Regiment, for instance, listed 118 officers and enlisted men present for duty on 13 April 1941. Sixteen days later, its reported strength was 109. About 77 men assigned to the company remained at its base camp, and others were detailed elsewhere.[64]

Imada Shinji, a new regular soldier, joined the army in January 1939.[65] Basic training lasted four months, though in wartime it was reduced to three months or less. It ended with the "first-term inspection." Imada's memory of the first three months of the barracks life is filled with nightmares of being beaten every day.[66] Hazing of new recruits was common in the barracks, as a formal organization operated during drill and training, but informal groups dominated daily life in the barracks. An American observer of the U.S. military organization observed, "Although in theory a formal, rational social organization governs every phase of the army life of enlisted men, in practice many army activities are controlled and carried on by informal social groups."[67] This observation seems to apply to the Japanese case, albeit with a much more violent fervor. In most cases, officers and NCOs did not intervene to control the informal aspect of the barracks life, so a culture of violence dominated the barracks, despite official regulations not to physically abuse new recruits.[68]

Although the violence repelled many inductees, some admitted that hazing served a purpose by making the green soldiers psychologically ready for the violence and senselessness of combat. Harsh punishment also cemented a sense of solidarity among the victims of the bullying, who shared an emotionally stressful but bonding experience.[69] The premodern traditional and informal regulation of barracks life, combined with a formal military organization and doctrine of a modern army, succeeded in forming close-knit primary group ties among the individual soldiers in small units.

After the first phase of basic training, the new recruits would begin advanced specialized training.[70] Civilian education made an initial difference because draftees with a secondary education or higher qualified for

TABLE 13.1

The organization of the Thirty-seventh Division

Unit/Subunit	Authorized Strength	Actual Strength	Authorized: Officers	Authorized: Enlisted men
37th Division	14,404	14,347	610	13,794
37th Division Headquarters	163	160	38	125
37th Division Infantry Brigade	9,329	9,323	338	8,991
37th Division Infantry Brigade HQ	14	14	5	9
225th Infantry Regiment	3,105	3,103	111	2,994
226th Infantry Regiment	3,105	3,103	111	2,994
227th Infantry Regiment	3,105	3,103	111	2,994
37th Cavalry Regiment	393	384	23	370
37th Artillery Regiment	2,067	2,037	101	1,956
37th Engineer (Pioneer) Regiment	592	588	21	571
37th Division Telecommunication Corps	201	201	7	194
37th Division Transportation Corps	657	652	32	625
37th Division Weapons Corps	121	121	2	119
37th Division Medical Corps	356	356	16	340
37th Division 1st Field Hospital	238	238	14	224
37th Division 2nd Field Hospital	238	238	14	224
37th Division Animal Hospital	49	49	4	45

SOURCE: Fujita Yutaka, ed., *Haru otozureshi daikoga* [Spring has come to the great Yellow River] (The Thirty-seventh Division History Publishing Committee, 1977), 48.

the officer candidate (OC) examination (see chapter 4 by Edward J. Drea). Those who passed the initial exam but failed its second phase were eligible to become NCOs. Those who passed both exams were called Type A Officer Candidates (A-OC),while those who passed only the first were called Type B Officer Candidates (B-OC).[71] Conscripts with a primary school education were eligible for the NCO qualifying exam but not the OC exam. This personnel selection policy determined by civilian education could be a demoralizing factor, especially for a highly skilled soldier who lacked formal education.

Another adverse factor among the new inductees in the Thirty-seventh Division was the Kyushu soldiers' discrimination against conscripts from Okinawa. Okinawa was the only prefecture that had no local regimental recruiting district, so the army apportioned draftees from Okinawa to various Kyushu regiments. Miscommunication was common because of the distinctly different local dialects, and it hindered unit cohesion. Discrimination also alienated Okinawans, who correctly did not feel they were full-fledged members of the regiment.[72]

The Thirty-seventh Division lacked sufficient transportation. It had about 2,600 draft horses, one-third of a regular division's allotment. Vehicles were also in short supply, only 89 being available of the 300 authorized. With transport limited, soldiers of the Thirty-seventh Division carried heavy crew-served weapons and supplies on their backs or used Chinese porters and the smaller Chinese horses whenever they could. The physically demanding long marches as well as chronic shortages of fresh food and clean water were major demoralizing factors in the field. Drinking impure water caused diarrhea, dysentery, and at least one major outbreak of cholera, in 1938. These endemic illnesses in the Chinese theater and poor sanitary discipline certainly affected troop morale.

Weapons effectiveness was a major concern of soldiers. Soldiers knew that the gas-operated Type 11 6.5 mm light machine gun, introduced in 1922, tended to jam easily because of carbon deposits when the cartridges were not sufficiently oiled. Despite the Type 11's superior accuracy, Japanese machine gunners favored the Czech light machine guns used by the Chinese troops because of their better operational effectiveness in the field. Japanese hand grenades during the early stage of the Sino-Japanese War were also a problem. The 7.5-second fuse was "too long" for actual combat.[73] Imada Shinji, a private who engaged in grenade-throwing combat in May 1939 in Shanxi, suggested a shorter 4-second fuse similar to the one the Chinese used. The Japanese army later made the change.[74] But the absolute superiority in heavy weapons, artillery, tanks, and armored cars of Japanese forces always improved the infantryman's morale.[75] (Table 13.2 summarizes the equipment and weapons possessed by the Thirty-seventh Division.)

TABLE 13.2

Equipment and weapons of the Thirty-seventh Division

Item	Authorized Number	Description
Horses	2,640 (2,040 actual)	592 horses needed to be procured in China
Hand grenades	36,000	
Carriage carts	137	
Rifles	9,062	
Light machine guns	230	194 Type 11s, 36 Type 96s
Heavy machine guns	76	
Heavy mortars	226	
Guns	76	24 75-mm field guns, 12 100-mm howitzers, 9 RiAs (75-mm gun), 18 BiAs (70-mm howitzer M92), 13 37-mm rapid-fire guns
Armored vehicles	5	1934 minitanks with 2 machine guns
Trucks	89	40 1941 Toyotas, 49 1934 6-wheelers

SOURCE: Fujita Yutaka, ed., *Haru otozureshi daikoga* [Spring has come to the great Yellow River] (The Thirty-seventh Division History Publishing Committee, 1977), 48.

As for logistics, it was left to individual units to solve chronic shortages of food and water supplies. "Improvised procurement" (*genchi chōhatsu*) was a major means to supplement minimal rations. The soldiers of the Thirty-seventh Division usually enjoyed more or less sufficient supplies when in garrison in Shanxi, but combat operations quickly consumed available stocks. When they entered French Indochina in 1945, rations were cut one-third.[76] In addition to food deprivation another problem was chronic sleep deprivation in combat. However, what mattered more in terms of combat morale is "relative deprivation," that is, a perceived difference in the amount of food and other supplies. As long as the soldiers perceived the delivery of supplies was equitable, the shortage of food was not detrimental to combat morale.

The Japanese Soldier in Combat

How did a green soldier become a skilled combat veteran? Could a new recruit become a mindless killing machine overnight? Informal norms shared by the members of a small unit, usually a squad or platoon, controlled the enlisted men's behavior.

"A soldier cannot do more on the battlefield than what he can do in training," said Japanese veterans. The Imperial Japanese Army's tactics during the Second World War stressed offensive operations, with a particular emphasis on the role of infantry and hand-to-hand combat as the decisive mode of combat in offensive operations.[77] Infantry assaults at night that culminated in a massed bayonet charge became a dominant paradigm in the offensive doctrine of the Japanese Army. The underlying assumption was that morale was more important than technology in modern warfare.[78] Therefore, bayonet training was an indispensable part of the Japanese infantry soldiers' preparation for combat.

The infantrymen of the Thirty-seventh Division, in particular those who were inducted after 1940, had to go through an inhumane bayonet exercise during the last stage of their basic training. This so-called baptism of blood involved driving their bayonets into live, helpless Chinese prisoners. Shimada Toshio, a private second class in the 226th Regiment in February 1942, recalls his bayonet training experience in China:

His hands and legs were tied to the two poles on his sides.

My emotion must have been paralyzed. I felt no mercy on him. He eventually started asking us, "Come on. Hurry up!" We couldn't stick the right spot. So, he said, "Hurry up!" which meant that he wanted to die quickly. It was quite hard to bayonet here [i.e., the heart]. However, it stuck like tofu because he didn't wear anything. If he wore winter clothing, it could be difficult. He must be one of those Chinese POWs brought for the purpose of bayonet training for the new recruits, I guess . . . There were forty-seven or forty-eight new recruits. All of us stuck him once or twice.[79]

Others did not want to kill an innocent POW. Shimada remembers a fellow recruit who refused on the grounds that he was a Buddhist priest. NCOs beat him severely. Another example is the case of an army veterinarian, Hita Isaji, who refused to kill a Chinese prisoner when ordered to do so. Hita told his small detail of five or six men that he was going to let the POW go: "We won't have to fight the enemy with bayonets. If we'd have to, then it would be the end of war. Killing just one Chinese POW won't help carry out our mission, nor will the killing experience benefit us. We'll let him go, while pretending that we have killed him. So keep your mouth shut. If you are ever questioned about him, tell them that he was killed."[80]

Obviously, the army kept no official record of how many Chinese POWs the Japanese executed in this fashion. It seemed a common practice among the infantry regiments of the Thirty-seventh Division to blood new recruits in order to prepare the green soldiers psychologically for killing at close quarters.[81] The "baptism of blood" was likely a widespread practice among the Japanese troops in China.[82]

Combat Tactics

The Japanese army favored night attacks.[83] For a night attack to succeed, the commander had to let his men know the objective clearly. Commanders selected highly motivated officers and enlisted men who were proven fighters and well disciplined to lead the assaults. They prepared for the operation well in advance, and the individual attackers would memorize the terrain and characteristics of the enemy position. An enveloping maneuver to hit the enemy position with a surprise attack from the rear was a key to quick success.[84]

Nemoto Kenji, inducted in 1941, fought for the first time in May 1941 during the Battle of Zhongyuan. He was a private first class in the Thirty-seventh Engineer Regiment, but he had passed the officer candidate exam a few days earlier. Nemoto's platoon was attached to the Second Battalion of the 226th Regiment, the left wing of the attacking force.[85]

On 7 May when they left the barracks, the platoon leader asked his men if they were ready for combat, and Nemoto replied, as expected, that he took it for granted that he could get killed in combat. Nemoto admired the military academy–graduate lieutenant leading his engineer platoon, which was attached to the infantry assault unit. The engineers were supposed to open lanes through enemy obstacles for the attacking infantry to pass through. Despite the darkness, Nemoto could see the enemy and hear bullets buzzing all over, and he spotted an infantryman moving toward the enemy position. Then, incoming bullets hit just behind the platoon commander. Nemoto believed the fire was from the rear, and shouted, "Enemy fire from behind!" Seasoned veterans screamed, "Who the hell said the bullets are coming from the back," "Our troops are behind us," and "Who said that? The stupid officer candidate?" In fact the Chinese had infiltrated behind the advancing Japanese and fired at them from the rear, hitting one soldier. This episode changed senior soldiers' perception about officer candidate Nemoto, whom they earlier had assumed useless in combat.

When I asked Nemoto if he was scared, he said, "I wasn't scared then. But when we were marching in silence without knowing when and how the enemy would shoot at us, I had the scariest feeling. When the bullets flew over my head, I'd duck. But once we started exchanging fire, we focused on our job. I left the fear somewhere else." Nemoto and his platoon carried only five days of rations, but the unit stayed in the field for forty days, generally living off the land. His physical condition deteriorated so badly during this time that he toyed with the notion of exposing his hand to Chinese fire in hopes a minor wound would get him evacuated. He was later evacuated because of pneumonia and hospitalized for six months. His convalescence cost him his status as an officer candidate.[86]

Hostility against the Chinese soldiers also seemed absent as a motivator among the veterans whom I interviewed. Only after some close friends had been killed did they harbor animosity against the Chinese. Racial prejudice may have played a role in cold-blooded killing of the POWs and local residents. During the actual fighting, racial prejudice and personal hatred against the Chinese soldiers did not seem to play a major role in motivation. In other words, in combat, impersonal professionalism and training prevailed during danger, whereas when the emergency passed, prejudices quickly resurfaced, making it easier to kill defenseless Chinese.

Several points can be made from Nemoto's case in terms of combat motivation. First, Nemoto had trust and respect for his platoon leader, who was later wounded in action. Second, he was scared before actual fighting started, but once in combat, he focused on his job and set aside his fears. Third, the precombat informal authority structure that assumed higher combat competence of senior soldiers changed after Nemoto proved his competence in actual combat. Fourth, even if he was one of the toughest and most motivated soldiers in the platoon, he considered getting evacuated by intentionally getting a minor wound. Because these thoughts occurred to him, many others must have had similar thoughts about self-inflicted or minor wounds, and some likely acted on them. This idea suggests that Japanese soldiers were not mindless automatons intent on dying for the emperor.

Imperialism versus Family and Community Honor

"Long live the emperor (*tenno heika banzai*)? No idiot says that!" That was Kayama Seiji's answer when asked if he had ever heard any soldier utter those words. Asked if he fought for the emperor, he said, "Hell, no. The emperor? I didn't give a damn."[87] Kayama may be an extreme case, but most of the Thirty-seventh Division veterans did not clearly state that they were fighting for the emperor. Almost none had personally witnessed anyone who called the emperor's name upon his death, although unit histories sometimes ascribe those last words to dying soldiers. When Kayama was inducted into the 226th Regiment in February 1942, he "just wanted to come back home early," and thought it fine to remain a private first class for the duration of the war. When a fellow soldier was mortally wounded by a direct shot to the head, the soldier mumbled, "Mom, mom . . ." As for Kayama, he fought through the war because of his mother. "My mother is waiting for me. I won't die." Upon his induction, his mother told him that she would prepare a meal for him every day while he was gone. This *kagezen* means that she wanted her son to come back alive eventually.

Born in the Ohita city as the third son of a farmer's family with eight children, Kayama was adopted by an uncle who owned a restaurant in Osaka where Kayama worked as a cook before induction. His weak physical constitution relegated him to a special training program for poorly conditioned soldiers. Still, as a new recruit in the regiment, he was forced to bayonet Chinese POWs. He felt sorry for them but did as he was told.[88]

As a cook at the battalion, regiment, and division headquarters, as well as a personal chef for the Thirty-seventh Division commander, Kayama's case was exceptional in a combat outfit. When the 226th Regiment was transferred for the Ichigō offensive in April 1944, Kayama was about to be left behind because of his poor health. He insisted that if he could not accompany the regiment, he would commit suicide, and so was allowed to join the others.[89] This episode suggests that solidarity among members of his unit was more important to him than personal safety.

Another type of motivation, honor of family and community, is likely to be mentioned by those who received a rousing send-off by their local neighborhood associations, and it was a more socially constructed loyalty than the personalized loyalty to the emperor. More than a hundred enthusiastic villagers gave Nagano Shin'ichi a rousing send-off when he was inducted into the 224th Regiment in Fukuoka in January 1937. "I wanted to live up to their expectations . . . because they had such a big ceremony to send us off," says the artillery warrant officer.[90] His combat motivation was socially constructed.

Kobayashi Saburō, a squad leader in the 226th Regiment, volunteered for the army in 1939. Born as the third son of an impoverished teamster, he worked for a small grocery shop after primary school. He joined the army not because of patriotism or imperialism but because of economic reasons, though he admits that he did not question the validity of prevailing imperialist ideology. Since the grocery shop business was not going well, he thought the army was the only option left for him during the tough economic times in the late 1930s. "It was a job for me, you know," says Kobayashi. He aspired to be a noncommissioned officer, that is, a professional soldier, and he was promoted to corporal in December 1941 and to sergeant a year later. Contrary to the public celebrations for conscripts, volunteers were rare in the Japanese army, and sometimes labeled as fools for volunteering for an institution that ordinary citizens were not particularly eager to join.

Kobayashi's first combat occurred in April–June 1944, during the Peking–Hankou Railroad clearance operation.[91] Just before the attack, his mind was "not fearful" but "just almost empty," focusing on the thoughts of death. Everyone kept quiet. He never thought about big issues like the emperor or personal ones like his family. Since he was a squad leader, he was absorbed in details to prepare for the coming battle and worried about how he would lead his men in combat.[92] His institutional role as a squad leader forced him to concentrate on the immediate and practical aspects of combat. In other words, a sense of duty and responsibility as a combat leader preoccupied him and motivated him to fight and lead effectively.

Role of Combat Leadership

The formal organization of the military in peacetime changes in combat. Some argued that it "shrinks" in combat, meaning that rigorous discipline becomes relaxed and the bureaucratic structure of the formal military organization gives way to a flexible association of groups of soldiers who face danger as equals. Simply pulling rank made no sense on the front line as pragmatism became the norm. The common wisdom among Japanese soldiers was "The number of years [in the army] matters in combat" or "the number of meals [in the army] is more important than the number of stars" (i.e., rank). A combat-seasoned corporal summed it up: "Even if you are an officer, your men would not necessarily follow your order on the front line."In the Japanese army, the role of leadership in combat was particularly important since it also constituted the vertical primary group tie. The characteristic of unit cohesion in the Japanese combat organization is this vertical mode of primary group formation compared to the horizontal mode dominant in U.S. military units.[93] The combat leaders, that is, squad, platoon, and company commanders, were at the core of unit cohesion.

Ogawa Tetsuo, a military academy graduate, was a platoon leader of the Thirty-seventh Engineer Regiment. Wounded in the right hand during the Zhongyuan fighting on 11 May, he was hospitalized for eleven days at the Yuncheng Army Hospital. He remained in the China theater for a year and later became a paratrooper, leading the famous airborne operation in Palembang, Sumatra, in 1942 that made him a war hero.[94]

Ogawa stated that he was fighting "not for the emperor" or because of patriotism, "but for my home town," and "for the honor of my family." He was critical of U.S. and European expansionism, but he also disapproved of decisions the emperor made regarding the Pacific War and believed that Hirohito bore responsibility for the consequences of the war.[95] Fighting in the Philippines late in the war, he found that his enthusiasm gradually waned and his morale declined. In combat, however, he was preoccupied with how he could effectively play the role of combat leader, though as an academy graduate, he was regarded as a bit of an overachiever in the eyes of senior NCOs.[96] In general, enlisted troops perceived military academy graduates as courageous but sometimes overeager and thus dangerous to follow.

For Imagawa Setsuo, a 1940 inductee, A-OC first lieutenant, and a company commander in the 226th Regiment, his combat incentive was "pride and responsibility as a commander."[97] While a platoon leader, he tried to gain the wholehearted trust of his men. Although a strict disciplinarian, he took good care of his platoon. He refused to show any fear in combat since his troops might lose their confidence in his leadership if he displayed weakness. When Imagawa tried to prove himself by rushing alone into an enemy position, a senior NCO scolded him about his recklessness under enemy fire. Imagawa remembered, "Usually, about three new academy graduates were assigned to our regiment. It seemed strange, but I found that always one of them got killed in action. I suppose it was because they charged into enemy fire since they were trained at the academy using blank cartridges.

Real bullets were not flying, so they did not know what actual combat was like. Once they experienced real fighting, they became good combat leaders. We knew real combat because we had gone through many battles since we were new recruits. We knew if the incoming rounds were too high or very close, and thus we could tell if it was dangerous to get out or not."[98] As a combat leader, he always tried to "lead by example." He assumed that otherwise his men would not follow him. "Leading by example" or "follow me" leadership seems to be a timeless, universal principle in all armies.[99]

Besides "leading by example," "protecting your men" was a commonly mentioned leadership principle among the Japanese combat leaders. Another A-OC officer, Yoneda Shingo, a platoon leader and company commander in the 226th Regiment, summarized his philosophy of leadership: "A company commander had to run in front of his men, or they would not follow. Standing up in front is all you need to raise your men's morale. What came most into my mind in combat was not to let my men get wounded or killed. These thoughts never left my mind in combat."[100] The leadership principle of not wasting your men seems to contradict the stereotypical view of the Japanese combat leaders who as "commanders did not mind sacrificing subordinates" or that "the Japanese were always willing to accept an exorbitant rate of casualties, causing their enemies to regard them as contemptuous of life."[101]

Fujita Akira, a Kyushu Imperial University graduate and A-OC first lieutenant in the 226th regiment, had been in the China theater since February 1941 when he was assigned to the First Company as a platoon leader. "You can't get your men wounded or killed in action. If your command or leadership is that bad," he remarked, "you'd quickly lose your men's trust. So a commander has to achieve the objective, but you should not compel your men to sacrifice themselves needlessly." He continued, "The reality is, if a man gets killed or wounded in a twelve- or thirteen-man squad, two or three men have to take care of him. Thus, our combat power would be reduced by half."[102]

Fujita remembered his bitter first engagement as a new platoon leader in fighting on 10 March 1941 against the Chinese Fifteenth Army. His platoon, three squads with thirty men total, was moving at night in mountainous terrain when enemy soldiers, silhouetted against the moonlight, fired at Fujita. He felt the shock of a bullet hit his left hand, but he nevertheless quickly returned fire with his pistol. He looked back, but no one was following him. He waited several minutes until his men caught up with him and then took his men's hand grenades, continued fighting, and forced the enemy to flee.[103] This first engagement made Fujita more cautious in later fighting so that he would not endanger his men's lives unnecessarily. At the same time, his leadership, even when wounded, earned his men's confidence.

Sometimes a combat leader needed to show his subordinates that he was not afraid of getting killed.[104] Once labeled a coward, a small unit leader lost his men's confidence and could no longer effectively lead them. Kobayashi Eiji, a squad leader in the 226th Regiment, asserted that "once your men see you as a coward, you cannot fight a war. Once they think their squad leader is no good in combat, they never follow his orders." Kobayashi always sought to show the best of his combat behavior by leading from the front to gain his unit's full trust and confidence in his combat leadership. He believed that if his men had confidence in him, they would not mind sacrificing their lives under his orders.[105] Since private soldiers never had a sense of the larger picture during any combat operation, they depended on their immediate superiors to a significant extent for direction and decision. This personal trust in a combat leader was an indispensable element of their motivation and unit cohesion.

Primary Group Tie and Unit Cohesion

"Taking good care of your men" is another leadership principle often mentioned by Japanese former combat leaders. A junior officer of NCO rank who would take night watch duty when his men were exhausted, or a superior who would not mind cutting his men's hair or shaving their beards was well liked by subordinates. As a platoon leader in the Thirty-seventh Engineer Regiment, Kihara Yoshio discovered that drinking moonshine alcohol with his men also boosted morale.[106] As Frederick Manning points out, "shared experiences" not only of combat but also of noncombat daily life, such as enduring the hardship of a long night march, tough training, or even drinking moonshine alcohol together, helped to form solidarity among unit members and promoted unit effectiveness.[107] Unlike European armies, the Japanese did not prohibit socializing among officers and enlisted men. The informal social activities shared by the officers and their men in the Japanese army enhanced the vertical mode of primary group formation and strengthened unit bonds.

Oyama Tarō was a sergeant in the artillery branch. His motivation was "mutual encouragement among comrades." As a squad leader, he always tried to encourage his men by telling them to help one another in combat. Mutual support and encouragement, as well as responsibility as a squad leader constituted a major part of his combat motivation.[108] Despite Oyama's assertion, paradoxically, most Japanese veterans did not mention comradeship as a major combat motivation. Does it mean that the horizontal mode of primary group tie was nonexistent? Japan's prewar sociocultural context took mutual help and group cohesion for granted. That these traits carried over into combat should not be surprising because they were common behavior acquired from civilian life. In other words,

348   THE SEARCH FOR MILITARY SOLUTIONS

mutual encouragement was so ingrained that it did not deserve comment. Another indicator of a strong sense of primary group tie, though again not consciously mentioned, concerned relationships among the soldiers. Veterans frequently remark that they were "more than brothers or family" or "brothers beyond blood."[109] Shimada Toshio stated: "It's more than that of family members. [We are] closer than parents and sons. Nothing comes in between us. We have nothing to hide."[110] No other words can describe the primary group tie more accurately.

Coping with Fear

Current literature on combat stress underscores the importance of "social support," that is, mutual reinforcement among unit members in successfully coping with stresses such as fear, anxiety, and physical exhaustion in combat.[111] In particular, coping with fear ensures combat effectiveness of an individual soldier and a unit. But coping with stress and fear exacts an emotional and psychological toll expressed in terms of neuropsychiatric casualties.[112]

According to U.S. Army statistics, there were about 100 psychiatric casualties, including about 3 from psychosis, per 1,000 men in 1942–1945 in all overseas combat theaters.[113] The corresponding official statistics for the Japanese psychiatric casualties are unavailable. But statistics on the number of psychiatric patients evacuated to Japan from overseas suggest that during the 1937–1941 phase of the Sino-Japanese War the percentage of psychiatric patients hospitalized at Kokura, Hiroshima, and Osaka army hospitals was between 1 and 5 percent. After the outbreak of the Pacific War, the ratio increased to about 10 percent in 1942, and it further rose to 23 percent in 1944.

More than 5,000 neuropsychiatric casualties were evacuated from the China theater in 1938–1940. In 1940, about 720,800 troops were in the China theater.[114] Some 1,287 psychiatric patients were evacuated in that year (2.9 percent of 44,393 total evacuations), and there were approximately 1.8 neuropsychiatric casualties per 1,000 men in China. Since they had serious mental disorders, that is, psychosis, this level was not radically different from that of the U.S. Army.[115] As for the Thirty-seventh Division, from May 1939 to July 1940, it evacuated 827 patients to Japan.[116] Among the army's 17,000-plus casualties in the same period, 339 were psychiatric patients.[117] This means that the Thirty-seventh Division had 23.5 psychiatric casualties per 1,000 men. In comparison, the U.S. Army's psychiatric casualties in the European theater during World War II (1942–1945) were 33.4 per 1,000 mean strength a year.[118]

Imada Shinji recalled an infantry company commander who suffered a nervous breakdown during a fierce night engagement at the end of

May 1939.[119] Another soldier in the Seventh Company, 226th Regiment, revealed that a second lieutenant recalled to active duty in 1944 shot himself because of neurosis.[120] These were extreme cases of failure to cope with fear or combat stress.

For most untested soldiers, their first engagement is usually a terrifying experience, and many find it difficult to effectively cope with fear in combat. Shimura Yasuo's first engagement occurred on 7 May 1941 during the Battle of Zhongyuan against the Twentieth Infantry Regiment of the Seventh Division, the Chinese Central Army. He remembered: "The incoming bullets sounded different than I expected. When I asked a senior soldier how far the Chinese were, he replied, 'Less than a hundred yards.' To tell the truth, I was so scared that I could not move. The platoon leader asked me why I didn't move. I just couldn't. When he hit me with the butt of his sword, I got up. Then I knew what it's like to 'lose your legs' from fear."[121] He was not the only one who "lost his legs." A senior private, who always hazed new recruits unmercifully, was also frozen by overwhelming fear in the intensive battle. The paralyzed private asked Shimura to carry him to the platoon leader. When Shimura did so, the lieutenant shouted the private's name, and he was then able to stand up. A frequently observed phenomenon was for soldiers to gather close to their combat leader when the battle got tough. "When you are scared, you want to seek somebody's help," says Shimura. This episode suggests the importance of leadership in combat motivation, as well as the importance of social support in coping with fear in combat.

"Losing your legs" was a common expression among Japanese soldiers to describe fear in combat. Other euphemisms include "samurai shakes" (trembling), "cold sweats," and "a prickling sensation of your scalp." According to a survey of an American division in the Pacific theater, 84 percent of the soldiers experienced "violent pounding of the heart," a "sinking feeling in the stomach" (69 percent), "shaking or trembling all over" (61 percent), "cold sweats" (56 percent), "feeling sick to the stomach" (55 percent)," "feeling weakness or feeling faint" (49 percent), "feeling stiffness" (45 percent), "vomiting" (27 percent), "losing control of bowels" (21 percent), and "urinating in pants" (10 percent).[122] Thus, physical symptoms related to fear were similar in both armies. Lieutenant Ogawa experienced the "samurai shakes" when he saw more than one hundred enemy soldiers approaching just before the shooting began on 11 May 1941. Once in combat, he found that his symptoms of fear disappeared, and he just focused on fighting with his sword. Concentrating on one's job was a means of coping with fear.

In general, soldiers used two modes of coping with fear: *active* and *passive*. Active coping strategies included concentrating on combat skills, taking advantage of the situation by actively seeking relevant intelligence about the enemy, and getting emotional or practical support from others. Distinguishing the sounds of incoming bullets, for instance, helped a soldier cope with fear. A bullet humming overhead was not life threatening, but a round making a sharp cracking or clipping sound was accurately aimed and dangerous. Moving quickly between bursts of enemy fire required skill. A soldier learned the split-second timing through his own combat experience while watching how experienced soldiers moved. He had to always dash out of the ditch or concealment up front because the enemy quickly adjusted fire on the position after they sighted the lead man. The ones behind tended to get hit. Frequently changing direction during assaults or moving your firing position avoided drawing concentrated enemy fire.

A typical coping strategy used by Japanese soldiers was *denial*, a defense mechanism to protect a soldier from anxiety and combat stress by selective forgetfulness of the stressful conditions. It involved a deliberate effort to redefine the combat situation to make it seem less dangerous and fearful.[123] Creating a personal myth of invulnerability and succumbing to resignation were commonly found modes of denial among the Japanese soldiers. Invulnerability assumed that "bullets never hit me," while resignation abandoned any hope of survival in combat. Fatalism was another mode of resignation.[124]

Because death in combat was assumed and seen as an honor, logically no one had reason to fear being killed. Of course, that "logic" runs counter to the natural instinct for self-preservation. Still, the presumption of death that derived from the formal doctrine had a latent function of making resignation or fatalism predominate in Japanese soldiers' minds. Fabricating the myth of an invincible Imperial Japanese Army also helped soldiers construct a myth of invulnerability, though the reality of defeats in battle toward the end of the Pacific War made this mode of denial less and less effective.

The Japanese army's field service regulations forbade capture. By encouraging soldiers to fight to the death, the doctrine may have helped Japanese soldiers to cope with fear. Japanese soldiers were, of course, taken prisoner in China. Some 7,000 soldiers who served in the Thirty-seventh Division were taken prisoner. The division also had deserters, usually classified as missing in action.[125] Although exact numbers remain unknown, more than 100 are believed to have joined the Eighth Route Army, and altogether around 750 deserted.[126]

Failed Leadership and Authority Conflict

While good leadership sustained high morale and unit cohesion, poor command demoralized a unit. Although the Thirty-seventh Division was one of the more successful divisions in the Japanese army, it too showed signs of wear and tear as the war dragged on. A platoon leader yielded command to a squad leader in combat with the excuse that he lacked sufficient combat experience.[127] Another platoon leader disappeared during combat. "Nobody knew his whereabouts," says Nomura Koji, a squad leader under his command.[128] In one case, troops respected a certain battalion commander's competence in battle but questioned his personality and integrity as a leader. Yoneda Shingo, a company commander in the 226th Regiment, commented: "He would take two or three Chinese female prisoners along with him at the battalion headquarters. The girls shaved their heads so that they looked like men. I had strong animosity against him because of that. Using prisoners for satisfying his own sexual desires is not what he was expected to do in the eyes of his men. A fellow company commander even asked me if I want to help kill the battalion commander. I told him not to because we would have been court-martialed for murder."[129] Chinese authorities executed the battalion commander as a war criminal after the war.

When a commander's combat competence is in question, a situation called "authority conflict" arises. Samuel Huntington termed this an "operational conflict" between military obedience and professional competence that concerns "the execution by a subordinate of a military order which in his judgment will result in military disaster."[130] Authority conflict is defined as a clash between formal organizational authority and informal authority based on the shared perception of members of the organization. For instance, when a platoon leader with no combat experience ordered a combat-seasoned squad leader to do something impractical, an authority conflict situation emerged. In theory, unquestioning obedience was always required in the Japanese army, and the disruption caused by disobedience to operational orders outweighed any benefits gained by individual initiative. In practice, however, the lives of the soldiers were at stake, and unthinking obedience was not necessarily the best solution. How did Japanese soldiers deal with such authority conflict situations?

Overt disobedience was rare, but Japanese soldiers disobeyed by various subterfuges. Direct confrontation included *opposing, suggesting,* and *holding.* The indirect approach involved *watching* or *neglecting.* Although directly opposing an order was impossible, soldiers would suggest changes to the commander. Sometimes they demonstrated their disobedience by silently "holding" the commander's legs when he tried to dash out of the trench to attack. A more common tactic was "watching": the men ordered to attack would not move and just watch the commander's combat performance. A squad leader of the 226th Regiment during the Battle of Zhongyuan suggested an attack on an enemy position, but the platoon leader did not support the idea. Nevertheless, the platoon leader chose five men and personally led them in an attack. He rushed forward deep into the enemy position only to discover that no one was following him. He shouted for his men to run forward and cover him but later learned that they had withdrawn without orders to remove the corpse of a soldier killed in the assault.[131] According to former Lance Corporal Yamada Yoichi, "Good company commanders at the beginning of the war didn't kill their men. No matter how brave a company commander was, if he killed his men, that's it. No respect for him. No matter how competent he was."[132]

One overly reckless company commander put his unit out of action. On 20 May 1944, during fighting against the Chinese 110th Division in the western suburbs of Zhengzhou, the infantry cannon company accompanied the 227th Infantry Regiment on a search-and-destroy mission after the regiment's First Battalion successfully occupied the city. Without knowing the exact enemy strength, the regimental commander, who later admitted that he tended to underestimate Chinese combat effectiveness, ordered his troops, including the cannon company, to advance toward the west to engage enemy forces. The cannon company had three platoons, each with one 37 mm direct-fire piece. That afternoon, the company commander discovered 400 enemy soldiers about 600 yards to the front and ordered an immediate attack. The Third Platoon's 35 men tried to destroy the enemy, but being unable to mount their weapon properly, their fire was ineffective. In a one-sided exchange, the Third Platoon eventually lost its gun as well as its platoon leader and a dozen men. About 15 survivors withdrew. The Chinese simultaneously counterattacked the First Platoon, overwhelmed it, and captured a second gun. Meanwhile, the men of Second Platoon withdrew to better defensive ground until a machine gun company reinforced them. They regrouped, pushed back the Chinese, and ultimately recovered the First Platoon's gun. Japanese casualties were 18 killed and 15 wounded, while the Chinese lost 405 killed and 40 prisoners.[133] But the heavy Japanese losses rendered the unit combat-ineffective for several weeks and was considered one of the worst operations in the division's history of battle in the China theater.

Conclusion

The individual Japanese soldier's combat motivation was complex, multidimensional, and socially constructed. Contrary to the stereotypical image of the Japanese soldiers fighting for the emperor, most soldiers in the Thirty-seventh Division fought for their families and local communities. Abstract notions of the country and the emperor, that is, the secondary symbols, only constituted the background of their combat motivation. A pure form of nationalism, such as love of one's hometown and the people around him, or "latent ideology," was much more significant than the imperialist ideology in motivating soldiers to fight. It was not the logic and ideas of state-sponsored ideology but the formal and informal social interactions involving the young Japanese conscripts that played an important role in their will to fight. Given the militaristic sociocultural context in prewar and wartime Japan, conscripts tried to live up to the public expectation, though sometimes they merely played the role of a good soldier in front of the audience.

Once in the army, the conscripts faced a harsh reality. Hazing and physical abuse dominated barracks life. The informal aspect of the military organization had a strong impact on the new recruits' lives. The seemingly irrational orders and excessively harsh punishments taught them how to cope with stress and fear of physical violence and thereby had a latent function of making them psychologically prepared for combat. Being subject to harsh discipline and enduring physical and mental hardship also developed solidarity among peers. Furthermore, the military socialization process compelled the men to conform to the enlisted men's informal social norms, which sometimes conflicted with the formal organizational norms and values. Nonetheless, the socialization process also played an important role in forming primary groups in the military organization.

Once in combat, the primary group tie, in particular the vertical solidarity between a combat leader and his subordinates, played the key role in motivating the Japanese soldiers to fight. Good leadership, that is, leading by example and taking good care of subordinates, boosted morale. Poor leadership sometimes led to authority conflicts with negative consequences. Even as good a division as the Thirty-seventh was not free from these demoralizing issues, a finding that suggests that other Japanese units in the China theater likely had greater morale difficulties. Nonetheless, the combination of tough training, solid leadership at the junior officer and NCO levels, comradeship, a willingness to endure hardship, and an ability to disassociate oneself from one's surroundings—be it battle or killing prisoners—enabled the Japanese army to retain its combat effectiveness throughout the protracted war in China.

While conclusions based on interviews with a few dozen veterans can only be tentative, the Thirty-seventh's experience was likely representative of the Japanese army in China. Assuming that the division enjoyed high morale because of its numerous successful operations, it might be somewhat atypical when compared to Japanese divisions defeated elsewhere in Asia and the Pacific. Even the successful Thirty-seventh, however, was not immune from demoralizing factors and troubles. My preliminary analysis of factors affecting morale of the Japanese soldiers in China presents a different prism through which to view the interpersonal dynamics of the Japanese army during this period.[134]

Part V

THE LATER JAPANESE OFFENSIVES

The Burma and Ichigō Campaigns

Military operations in northern Burma and China's western Yunnan Province during 1944 seldom receive attention in Western military literature, in part because the combatants were Asians, in part because of the complexity of maneuver, and in part because the ramifications for U.S.-China relations at the highest levels overshadowed the campaigns. While Western authors focus on the exploits of Brigadier General Orde Wingate's Chindits or Brigadier General Frank Merrill's "Marauders" in the fall of Myitkyina or the bitter Chiang-Stilwell controversy, few spend much time on the Sino-Japanese military campaigns along Burma's northern border regions. In chapter 14 Asano Toyomi's detailed operational assessment of changing Japanese strategies for the north Burma front highlights the shift from an offensive mind-set in support of the ill-fated Imphal operation to a strategic defensive outlook after the Fifteenth Army's defeat on the borders of India. The Imphal operation severely strained Japanese resources by drawing off troops from northern Burma, leaving the remaining Japanese defenders heavily outnumbered by fresh Chinese troops, trained and equipped by American advisers, the so-called Y-Force.

Forced onto the strategic defensive, only Japanese knowledge of local terrain, extensive fortifications constructed during their two-year occupation, and flexibility enabled them to repulse the initial Chinese drives from Yunnan across the Salween River into northern Burma. In 1944, the Japanese Thirty-third Army opened a series of limited counterattacks, the Dan operation, to block the reopening of the Ledo Road and draw Chinese forces away from the Ichigō offensive. By the time the campaign wrapped up in September 1944, Tokyo had relegated northern Burma to a secondary role, leaving the Thirty-third Army to block the Ledo Road as much as practicable. It played that role until Japan's surrender, holding out in the mountainous fastnesses.

In chapter 15 Zang Yunhu describes in depth the training of the Y-Force in Yunnan and notes that Chiang's endorsement of the Y-Force concept stemmed from his need for U.S. supplies and equipment. Zang links the Chinese high-level organizational planning for a campaign in Burma to Y-Force and the political and military influences on Y-Force's operations. Failure in the initial Chinese offensives in April 1944 led to widespread dismissals of senior officers and a commitment to drive the Japanese from northern Burma. Over the next several months, resources and manpower were spent on Y-Force despite the pressing demands to check the rampaging Ichigō offensive. Finally, in January 1945 Chinese determination paid off as Y-Force isolated the Thirty-third Army in its mountain strongholds, effectively knocking it out of the war and for the most part reopening the Ledo Road.

Ichigō was a massive campaign whose scale dwarfed the Normandy landings of June 1944 and rivaled Hitler's Operation Barbarossa, the Nazi invasion of the Soviet Union in June 1941. Hara Takeshi in chapter 16 and Wang Qisheng in chapter 17 examine the immensity of operations that began in April 1944 and by February 1945 had engulfed China from the Yellow River to the northern borders of French Indochina. Hara explores the strategic-level appreciation and planning process that moved contentious groups in the high command and imperial court to support Ichigō, a massive campaign, without any agreement on its proposed objectives. Japan was pressed by the Allies on the Pacific and Burma fronts and forced on the strategic defensive, but the belief that Ichigō offered Tokyo a chance to regain the strategic initiative resulted in Japanese field armies pushing the idea of a major southward operation to do that. Ichigō may have appeared a success, but by that stage of the war Japan lacked control of the air and could neither prevent long-range attacks against the home islands nor interdict tactical strikes against the newly opened overland route in China. In short, Tokyo was unable to capitalize on what its field armies had wrought. Hara concludes that, instead, Ichigō discredited Chiang's armies in the eyes of the United States, and the mobilization of Japanese troops garrisoning north China for the campaign created a power vacuum that the Chinese Communists quickly filled. This is worth greater consideration because it relates to Stephen MacKinnon's ideas about the nature of warfare in China.

Wang's analysis underlines previously identified deficiencies in the Kuomintang forces—problems of command and control, lack of trained staff officers, and uneven quality of fighting forces. Chiang Kai-shek and his Military Affairs Commission were divided over strategy to meet the Japanese offensive, at first underestimating its ambitious scope and later debating whether to withdraw before the onslaught or risk the Nationalist army by standing and fighting. Arguing contrary to conventional wisdom, however, Wang demonstrates that far from preserving his armies by not fighting, Chiang deployed far greater forces against the Japanese, including those from his strategic reserve holding the Chinese Communists in check. Furthermore, Chiang found himself reacting to foreign pressure, particularly that applied by the United States, to produce short-term success. This development circumscribed alternative strategies and forced him, with limited success, to coordinate theater-level operations such as the converging counterattacks against Hengyang. Chiang's armies fought, but too often inadequate training, endemic corruption, obsolete equipment, and inferior officers at all levels undermined their efforts against a determined, aggressive opponent.

Both armies experienced command-and-control difficulties; both suffered logistic shortcomings; both were in part reacting to foreign pressure; and both unintentionally laid much of China open to Communist control, Chiang by redeploying his forces aligned against the Chinese Communists to meet the Japanese threat and Japan by stripping its garrison units to participate in the grand offensive.

14 *Japanese Operations in Yunnan and North Burma*

ASANO TOYOMI

Introduction: The Yunnan–Northern Burma Theater in the Sino-Japanese War

A major purpose of this essay is to describe Japanese military operations in northern Burma and Yunnan within the context of the Sino-Japanese War and to analyze Japanese military strategy and tactics in these campaigns. Although the existing scholarship tends to focus on the Imphal operation,[1] discussion here will center on the military clashes between the Japanese and the British, American, and Chinese forces during the Allies' attempt to reopen the supply route from India to Chongqing in order to sustain Chiang Kai-shek's war effort against Japan.

The endeavor involved two distinct phases: (1) from the commencement of the Imphal operation in March 1944 to its termination on 2 July, and (2) the period thereafter until the reopening of the Ledo Road in late January of 1945. The phases reflect a drastic change in the nature of military campaigns in northern Burma, a strategic transition that I explore in this chapter.

Within the strategic context of the Sino-Japanese War, the Burma theater formed a contact point for multiple imperial powers. More specifically, the Yunnan–northern Burma theater was the arena where three emerging or existing world powers met: Japan, with its Great East Asia Co-prosperity Sphere; Great Britain, whose British Empire had been a modern global empire since the nineteenth century; and China, an emergent but divided state struggling with many elements of its dynastic past. The military campaigns in the Yunnan–northern Burma theater were not only an extension of the Sino-Japanese War but also a part of the World War II contest among these three powers that were trying to either maintain or establish their own hegemonies.

Geographically, the Yunnan–northern Burma area is sandwiched between the Gaoligong Mountains in Yunnan and the Arakan mountain range that branches out from the Himalayas and runs southward. Flowing alongside these mountains are large rivers such as the Chindwin, the Irrawaddy, and the Salween. Winters are cold because of the high altitude. The summer monsoon lasts from May to October. Northwestern Burma bordering India is a marshy area almost uninhabitable. The eastern part— the Yunnan–northern Burma area—is a food-rich region with its rice production. Accordingly, the Japanese and the Chinese wanted to control the logistically indispensable region as a supply base for operations in surrounding areas.

Although the Sino-Japanese War was limited to mainland China, Burma was regarded as a supply route for military materiel and personnel destined for China. The Western powers also supplied China via Guangzhou as well as through northern French Indochina, while Soviet aid was channeled by way of Xinjiang Province. The Japanese tried to close the southern routes by military force in an effort to strangle China economically and end the war. After the opening of the Pacific War, the Japanese army leadership sought to use Burma as a staging base for offensives against India—the original British supply base—and against the hinterland of China. Lieutenant General Mutaguchi Renya, commander of Fifteenth Army in Burma, became obsessed with the idea of invading India. Staff officers of the Fifty-sixth Division, stationed in Yunnan, and those attached to the Southern Army Group (SAG), however, contemplated a thrust from northern Burma toward Kunming and Yunnan in the Chinese hinterland.[2] In either scenario, northwestern Burma would serve as a crucial staging base.

In the first half of 1944, in conjunction with the Imphal operation, Japanese army operations against the Allies' Burma Road focused on the Hukawng area in western Burma. During the second half of the year, after the failure at Imphal, the army shifted eastward to Yunnan. This chapter concentrates on the Dan operation,[3] which started in late July of 1944 and aimed at breaking up Allied advances in northern Burma to reopen a supply route through north Burma from Assam to China. My treatment begins with a brief discussion of the Hukawng and Salween campaigns, which started in October 1943 as operations in support of the advance to Imphal.

Campaigns from the Occupation of Burma in 1942 to the Beginning of the Imphal Operation

Senior officers of the Burma Area Army (BAA), the Thirty-third Army, and two divisions—the Eighteenth and Fifty-sixth—took charge of campaign planning in this theater. The BAA commander, General Kawabe Shōzō, had been an infantry brigade commander of the China Garrison Army at the time of the Marco Polo Bridge Incident. Lieutenant General Tanaka Shin'ichi, chief of the Army Ministry's Military Affairs Commission in July 1937, then commanded the Eighteenth Division. Mutaguchi, the driving force behind the Imphal operation, had been a regimental commander stationed near the Marco Polo Bridge in 1937. Their strategies from the time of the Japanese occupation of Burma are summarized below.

OCCUPATION OF BURMA AND DEFENSIVE STRATEGY OF THE EIGHTEENTH AND FIFTY-SIXTH DIVISIONS

The Eighteenth and Fifty-sixth divisions, the main maneuver forces of Thirty-third Army, adopted an offense-oriented defensive strategy in Burma. Before its transfer to Burma, the Eighteenth Division under Mutaguchi had fought in the Malayan campaign and had captured Singapore. Once in Burma, the Eighteenth Division competed with the Fifty-sixth Division to be the first to reach their assigned objectives.[4] The divisions recruited soldiers from the same northern Kyushu district, which further intensified their competition.

Although the Allied troops in Burma outnumbered the Japanese by more than ten to one, they were divided and had been defeated in the face of swift advances of these two divisions and were forced to retreat to India. Myitkyina, which fell in the face of the Fifty-sixth Division's attack, was the northernmost point of the Japanese advance in Burma. The Eighteenth Division later took over that city and established its headquarters there. The Eighteenth also constructed an airfield for fighter and reconnaissance aircraft in the area and succeeded in substantially obstructing the Allies' supply activities to China not only on the ground but also from the air. As for the Fifty-sixth Division, it established its headquarters in Longling under the direct command of the BAA (until February 1944; thereafter, it came under the command of the Fifteenth Army) and faced the Chinese across the Salween River (called the Nujiang in Chinese and Thoulwin in Burmese) in Yunnan Province.

Both divisions had many physically fit miners from Kyushu's coal areas who were skilled in constructing fortifications. The units were seasoned combat veterans of military campaigns, and they were trained and equipped for motorized operations. Japanese motorized formations had demonstrated remarkable maneuverability, particularly in Burma, where they took advantage of the improved road infrastructure, including the transportation network that the British colonial rulers had developed. Later in 1944, however, the Japanese had to compete fiercely with the Allies for control of the vital transportation routes.

Over the two years of the occupation, the two divisions familiarized themselves with the geographic and climatic environments of the region. The Fifty-sixth Division settled into a garrison routine in the forested high plateaus of eastern Yunnan. Its soldiers cultivated fields to raise food, built their own food processing factories, constructed specially designed barracks as well as small stores selling food items produced in Japan, and introduced field brothels and "comfort women." Their barracks took on the appearance of a model immigrant village. Planning for the invasion of Yunnan was predicated on the construction of the fortifications manned by settlerlike soldiers as well as on the establishment of an economic and social self-sufficiency. The troops boasted that Yunnan was their training ground.

BOLSTERING OF DEFENSE IN BURMA BEFORE THE IMPHAL OPERATION AND MISSIONS ENTRUSTED TO THE BAA

Beginning on 27 March 1943, three Japanese armies—the Twenty-eighth Army in southern Burma, the Fifteenth Army in central Burma, and the Thirty-third Army in the north—were formed under the BAA, which was subordinated to the SAG, the Japanese army's umbrella command responsible for overall direction of the war effort in Southeast Asia and headquartered in Singapore at the time.[5] The BAA's initial mission was to defend Burma. Planning for the invasion of India was a secondary mission. Each army command operated with approximately three divisions. Full divisional order of battle and tables of organization for these three armies were not completed until April 1944—shortly after the Imphal operation commenced.

The Fifty-fourth and Fifty-fifth divisions, the first reinforcements transferred to Burma, were formed in Japan and assigned to the direct command of the BAA in May 1943. In late January 1944, the Second Division made its way to Burma. This division had been decimated in fighting on Guadalcanal in 1942–1943 and had to be reconstituted in Burma. Together with the Twenty-fourth Brigade, which had been activated in Burma, these units made up the Twenty-eighth Army.

These deployments reflected the Japanese offensive scheme to invade India. The Fifteenth Army had a personnel strength of 156,600—nearly 50 percent of the BAA's entire manpower of 316,700. The Fifteenth Army's size compared with 52,000 men of the Thirty-third Army, the 53,000 men of the Twenty-eighth Army deployed in the areas close to the sea, the 33,000 troops positioned in and around Rangoon, and the 15,500 men of the Fifth Air Division.[6] Concentration on the center resulted in the deployment of only 17 percent of the entire BAA force strength in the northern and southern areas of Burma. Thus, whereas the opening of the supply route running through northern Burma to China was given the top priority in the Allied strategy, the Imphal operation, which was to be launched from central

Burma, superceded everything else in Japanese strategic considerations in early 1944. Japanese planners believed that the capture of Imphal would complement the operation in the north against the Allies' supply route.[7]

The Thirty-third Army's Campaigns to the End of the Imphal Operation in July 1944

ACTIVATION OF THE THIRTY-THIRD ARMY: PROCESS OF ITS FORMATION AND ITS MISSION

Late in April 1944—about one month after the start of the Imphal campaign—IGHQ activated the Thirty-third Army to defend north Burma.[8] Incorporated into this newly created army were the Fifty-sixth Division; the Eighteenth Division, transferred from the Fifteenth Army; the Fifty-third Division, which had been deployed in the area earlier in the same year; and a part of the Forty-ninth Division.[9] The Thirty-third Army would protect the rear flank of Fifteenth Army during the Imphal fighting. On 30 April, the Thirty-third established its headquarters in Maymyo.[10] Lieutenant General Honda Masaki commanded Thirty-third Army and was a military academy classmate of Lieutenant General Matsuyama Yūzō, the commander of the Fifty-sixth Division.[11]

Mobile and intelligence warfare units operated under the direct command of the Thirty-third Army. Eight motorized companies within the Thirty-third Army command had 300 vehicles and provided rapid deployment for troops along the Burma Road—especially in the paved portion stretching from Lashio to Longling—in combination with the use of the railways connecting Rangoon, Mandalay, and Myitkyina. Mobile warfare proved effective because of the data provided by an intelligence unit, discussed below. According to Colonel Tsuji Masanobu, then a Thirty-third Army staff officer, at night when Allied planes were not active, traffic on the Burma Road was congested with vehicles bringing back wounded soldiers from the front and those transporting supplies and reinforcements in the opposite direction. The Fifty-sixth Division removed a considerable amount of ammunition stockpiled at the Lameng garrison to Myitkyina along this route prior to the beginning of the Dan operation.[12]

The Dan operation targeted transportation routes to deprive the enemy of their mobility. The big problem for the Japanese was how to safeguard the railway and road bridges from the Allies' aerial bombing. The Japanese positioned antiaircraft artillery along key railway lines as well as at the bridges while they secretly stockpiled three times as much material as needed to rebuild each of these bridges. In addition, as a precaution, they built pontoon bridges that they hid in the daytime.[13]

The Thirty-third Army's headquarters code-breaking team, which specialized in breaking Chinese army codes, supported these military operations. The unit was originally a branch of the SAG's special intelligence team.[14] (Prior to the creation of the Thirty-third Army, the unit was assigned to the Fifty-sixth Division, which was under BAA's direct command and was called the Mangshi unit.) When it began its activity, it had nineteen personnel and could read about one-third of the messages it intercepted. The turning point came in February 1944 when a Chinese codebook and a cipher table of the Chinese Yunnan Expeditionary Force inadvertently fell into Japanese hands after a Chinese military aircraft mistakenly landed at Tengyue (Momein in Burmese). Thereafter, the Thirty-third Army's intelligence team dramatically improved its performance with the aid of the captured ciphers, and the unit was augmented to fifty specialists who manned five radio signal receivers to intercept and then decipher Chinese messages transmitted from Kunming and Chongqing. These deciphered messages offered the Japanese advance notice of a full-scale offensive by the Chinese across the Salween River in May 1944. Then, in late July 1944, their code-breaking activity reportedly made another major breakthrough when IGHQ formally approved the Dan operation. By September the same year, code breakers had successfully broken almost all the secret codes of the Chinese. The team routinely decoded intercepted Chinese messages within two days of transmission and translated them into Japanese to make them available to the operational headquarters.[15] Such improvement in Japanese intelligence activity was a major factor behind the effective Japanese defense, despite being far outnumbered.

In late September 1944, the Thirty-third Army moved the intelligence units into its headquarters. Although an intelligence arm of the Thirty-third Army, the unit made a significant contribution to China-derived intelligence and rivaled similar organizations at higher echelons, such as IGHQ's special intelligence unit, the Guangzhou and Nanjing branches of the special intelligence team under the Chinese Expeditionary Army (CEA) general headquarters, and the SAG special information unit's headquarters in Saigon as well as its outstation in Singapore.[16] In recognition of its achievements, Thirty-third Army headquarters conferred a letter of commendation on the intelligence unit, along with the motorized companies, when its headquarters retreated to Lashio in January 1945—a rare instance of a citation awarded to a noncombat unit within the Japanese army.

FORCE STRENGTHS OF THE THIRTY-THIRD ARMY
AND THE ALLIES

Despite the accomplishments of these specialized units, the Thirty-third Army faced huge numerical odds against the Allied forces advancing from east and west: fifteen to one even at the beginning of the offensive. In the west, the newly formed X-Force, composed of the First and Sixth

Armies, each of which had three divisions, outnumbered the Japanese Eighteenth Division six to one. With the deployment of the Sixth Airborne Division and the Galahad Force—better known as "Merrill's Marauders" under American Brigadier General Frank Merrill—the odds rose thirteen to one. The prospect was equally bleak in the east as the Chinese Eleventh and Twentieth Army Groups—comprising fourteen divisions—plus the mechanized 200th Division based in Kunming were advancing on the Fifty-sixth Division at odds of fifteen to one.

This vast discrepancy in force ratios paradoxically compelled the Japanese army leadership to rely increasingly on the "offensive defense" strategy. Japanese troops certainly prepared strong defensive works, exemplified by the "model village" in Lameng. Yet the Japanese military leadership in Burma, acutely aware of its numerical inferiority, consistently planned for an advance beyond Burmese borders to preempt the Allies' counteroffensive by attacking Allied strongholds.[17]

Such an offense-oriented strategy disadvantaged Japanese preparations for garrison defense. For example, despite a serious effort to fortify Lameng, the Japanese had insufficient stockpiles of ammunition for its defense. Moreover, because the Fifty-sixth Division always considered Lameng as a staging base for its future offensive against Baoshan and Kunming, commanders failed to motivate their soldiers and junior officers to prepare adequate defensive fortifications.

HUKAWNG CAMPAIGN

The Allies' first priority was to reopen the supply route to China. The X-Force opened its advance into Hukawng in November 1943, that is, immediately after the Quebec Conference and at the end of the monsoon season of that year. At that time, preparations for the Imphal operation preoccupied Japanese planners, so units in northern Burma assumed a defensive posture to support the main campaign. IGHQ placed the Eighteenth Division, which undertook the Hukawng campaign, under the command of the Fifteenth Army. The Fifty-sixth Division had to scale down its original plan to occupy Baoshan and Kunming to a limited operation in the Salween region. The Hukawng campaign had multiple objectives: to cut the supply route connecting India and China, to provide flank protection for the Imphal operation, and to tie down a sizable number of the opponent's troops.[18]

The Hukawng operation in the early part of 1944 featured the Eighteenth Division's westward advance from the railway connecting Mandalay and Myitkyina toward Ledo, across the Hukawng Valley along a narrow road through a marshy area. Its objective was to forestall the Allies' offensive in the west of Kamaing and attract as many Chinese and American forces to it as possible. The division's orders stipulated, if practicable, an advance farther westward. Its commander, Tanaka Shin'ichi, had replaced Mutaguchi. Tanaka left behind the 144th Infantry Regiment under the command of Major General Maruyama Fusayasu in Myitkyina and led other units westward beyond Kamaing in late October 1943. Full-scale operations commenced in February 1944, after the monsoon season.

The Allies intended to open a new supply route to China by February 1944 to implement the decision reached the previous September at the Quebec Conference. This proposed new route stretched from Ledo to Baoshan and Kunming, running farther north of the old Burma Road. They also had a plan to improve existing tracks for mule transportation from Myitkyina to Baoshan through Tengyue.

In February 1944, the X-Force, composed of Chinese soldiers trained and equipped by American advisers, advanced into the Kamaing area across the Hukawng Valley. The newly formed First and Sixth armies under Lieutenant General Joseph W. Stilwell, as well as the U.S. Army's Galahad unit, gradually pushed the Eighteenth Division back. Two critical events accelerated the retreat. First, the airborne glider troops of British Brigadier General Orde Wingate landed behind the Japanese front lines on 5 March 1944 and cut the railway to Myitkyina. Second, in late May, the Allies occupied Mogaung, a strategic location at a debouchment from the Hukawng Valley, and attacked Kamaing from three directions.[19]

As the Imphal operation came to a virtual standstill in late May, Allied forces encircled the Eighteenth Division. The Japanese managed to break through the Allies' closing ring on 2 July and moved eastward. Although the Japanese command hoped that the restrictive terrain of the narrow Hukawng Valley would offset their numerical inferiority and allow them to outmaneuver the opponent, the Allies not only filled the valley with large numbers of troops but also sent contingents through rugged, hilly areas to menace the Japanese rear. Then airborne troops landed behind the Japanese positions to close the ring and leave the Japanese with no choice but to retreat and concentrate on the defense of their positions in the hilly rear areas.

This campaign provided valuable lessons for the Japanese which later fought a campaign in Yunnan. First, they learned that they had to disengage rapidly and retreat over a long distance, because a gradual withdrawal over a short distance allowed for successive encirclement by numerically superior opponents. Second, rather than favorable grounds for an outnumbered force to outmaneuver its opponent, valleys were potential traps where a more mobile opponent could easily encircle and even annihilate the Japanese forces.[20] In fact, the Eighteenth Division narrowly escaped such an encirclement, but only after destroying or abandoning almost all of its equipment, including field and mountain artillery pieces, and retreating under cover of the Fifty-third Division.[21]

The escape and retreat of the Eighteenth Division with the help of the Fifty-third Division diverted military efforts to defend Myitkyina and accelerated the process leading to its premature loss. In the end, the dispatch of the Eighteenth Division, including its headquarters, to the west to undertake a supportive campaign for the Imphal operation resulted in dividing already scarce forces into two groups and, in consequence, the piecemeal destruction of each.

CAMPAIGN IN YUNNAN IN EARLY 1944

On the Yunnan front, the Fifty-sixth Division was assigned in the east to do what the Eighteenth did in the west—support the Imphal operation. Before formal approval of the Imphal campaign, the division had a draft plan for the invasion of China through the back door of Burma to capture Baoshan and Kunming and preclude an Allies' counteroffensive from that region. Once Imphal was designated as the main strategic target, however, the division scaled down its original plan and limited its operational theater to the west of the Salween River.[22] Its objective was to safeguard this area, which served as a source of abundant food, by garrisoning forces in key cities such as Tengyue in the middle of a byway connecting Myitkyina with Baoshan, Lameng (a key city near the Burma Road), and Pingxia in the south. Longling, which was further inland on the Burma Road, was to be a liaison point for the coordination among these three. Offensive actions beyond these three points depended on the approval of the BAA—and later by the Thirty-third Army after its activation.[23] During the first half of 1944, the Fifty-sixth Division operated to the fullest extent within these restrictions to attempt to destroy Allied strongholds in the area and thereby preempt their counteroffensive.

As of 10 May 1944, the Fifty-sixth Division had approximately 11,000 men, and its main force was six and a half infantry battalions and two artillery battalions. The infusion of one infantry battalion detached from the Fifty-third Division as well as the Fifty-third reconnaissance regiment augmented the division's strength to 16,000. The division was vastly outnumbered by the Chinese, but the Japanese rank and file considered the combat capability of one Chinese division in the Yunnan Expeditionary Force the equivalent of only one Japanese battalion. Although the Salween campaign during the first half of 1944 vindicated this complacent analysis, the Allies' subsequent large-scale offensive effectively refuted it.

Once IGHQ authorized the Imphal operation in August 1943, the Fifty-sixth Division launched its operation on the Salween front in mid-October 1943. Its contingents wiped out all the outposts that the Chinese had established on the Japanese side of the Salween River. They even crossed the river for a quick raid against Chinese strongholds on the opposite bank.

Such aggressive military actions temporarily boosted morale because they were in line with the division's originally professed aim of advancing deep into the Chinese mainland. The division's success contributed to an increasingly observable tendency among its officers and soldiers to underestimate Chinese fighting effectiveness, and it led to their consequent neglect to strengthen garrison defenses because of their adherence to offensive-oriented campaign planning.[24]

Each of the Japanese garrisons—at Lameng, Tengyue, Longling, Pingchia, Mangshi, and Kunlong—was initially stockpiled with one hundred days' worth of ammunition. Later, however, these arsenals were removed from this Yunnan front to supply the Eighteenth Division in Hukawng when it was cut off from its supply base in the south by Wingate's airborne unit. This diversion of stockpiled munitions later proved to be a major cause of the ammunition shortages in these garrison posts.[25]

While the Japanese enjoyed partial success in the Salween campaign, the Chinese Expeditionary Force in Yunnan was steadily stepping up its preparations for a counteroffensive. Two events paved the way. First, on 14 April 1944, the United States and Chiang Kai-shek's Nationalist army reached an agreement when the American side accepted almost all the demands presented by Chiang previously.[26] Second, the Japanese offensive in the Imphal theater had stalled. Subsequently, the frontline Chinese troops maneuvered aggressively upon Chiang's approval of the Yunnan army's plan. A notable new development was that a part of the American air group in China— sixty fighter planes and forty heavy bombers flying from newly completed airstrips in Kunming and at the Yunnan station—were available to provide air support to the ground operations of the Chinese Yunnan force.

By late April, the intelligence team of the Fifty-sixth Division uncovered the imminent Chinese counterattack and predicted the opening date of this offensive, its principal targets, and the composition of the units scheduled to participate in the operation. Such intelligence prompted the Fifty-sixth Division command to summon garrison commanders to Mangshi to brief them on meeting the anticipated Chinese offensive. The Japanese would concentrate troops at locations along the Salween River close to the intended Chinese landing areas. Then they could counterattack the Chinese troops either in the midst of their river crossing or immediately after, when the Chinese were the most vulnerable. Defenders of fortified garrisons would hold their positions no matter what happened. In addition, the Fifty-sixth Division aimed to retain control of the road connecting Tengyue and Longling—a portion of which was surfaced highway—as well as the Burma Road.

Chinese advance detachments crossed the Salween River on 11 May, first north of Tengyue and later south of Lameng. The main contingent forded the river between these two points, as the Chinese were bent on enveloping the Fifty-sixth Division with a pincer movement from north and south that met in the Longling area. Then they would annihilate the encircled Fifty-sixth Division in the vicinity of Lameng.

Although the Eighteenth Division fought with a certain degree of success against the Chinese forces that had crossed the Salween in the north, the Japanese defense along the river crumbled in ten days after the commencement of the Chinese offensive. Starting around 20 May, fighting shifted westward from the Salween River estuary to the Gaoligong Mountains. The Chinese Fifty-third Army (Thirty-sixth, 116th, and 198th divisions as well as the newly formed Thirty-ninth and 130th divisions), advanced across the mountains. Major Hagio Isamu's battalion, originally supposed to deploy to Myitkyina, was reinforced by the 148th Regiment, Fifty-sixth Division led by Colonel Kurashige Yasumi. They attacked the Chinese force in coordination with the 113th Regiment, which came from Lameng. This pincer attack routed the Chinese Fifty-third Army by 6 June and forced it to retreat back across the Gaoligong Mountains. The main force of the northern pincer was a two-battalion force. By concentrating almost all its strength, the Fifty-sixth Division put together a powerful offensive thrust and temporarily repelled the Chinese army's attack.

On 10 June, however, the Chinese Eleventh Army Group crossed the Salween River farther south of Lameng by capitalizing on the weakened Japanese defenses debilitated by the extraction of troops to the north. Thus, the Chinese Eleventh Army Group struck the weakest point of the Japanese Fifty-sixth Division's defensive perimeter and dealt Japanese defenders in Longling a smashing blow. The Chinese intensified their offensive against Longling and captured all the Japanese mountain outposts on the outskirts of the city by early June. They even took some of the fortified positions in the city's suburb and fought their way into the city itself on 15 June. With the onset of the battle in Longling, the Fifty-sixth Division's headquarters in Mangshi in the east on the Burma Road almost lost contact with the garrisons in the north.

Lieutenant General Matsuyama, commander of the Fifty-sixth Division, rushed reinforcements to Longling. Most were small units, composed of some one hundred men, that had been deployed in the south of Mangshi. Matsuyama ordered most troops north of Tengyue to abandon their positions and mop up the enemy troops in the Longling-Mangshi area. This concerted effort by the Longling garrison and the relief force from the north and the south enabled the Fifty-sixth Division to lift the siege of Longling on 17 June.

The Japanese defended Longling only by diverting a substantial part of the 148th Regiment from Tengyue to the Longling area. The regiment had to abandon a wide area in the north. Its remaining contingent, a battalion-size force, including the regimental commander, entrenched itself within the city walls of Tengyue and posted a small number of troops in the mountains surrounding the city to pin down as many enemy troops as possible through a protracted siege defense and thereby to allow the division's main contingent to operate on the Longling front more effectively.[27] The Japanese tried to hold Tengyue despite an overwhelming numerical inferiority for two reasons. First, they hesitated to surrender the rich agricultural fields around Tengyue to the Chinese. Second, they feared Tengyue's loss would allow the Allies to open a new supply route from Ledo to China via Myitkyina.

Around the same time, the Chinese Twenty-eighth Division isolated the Lameng garrison. Matsuyama intended first to reinforce the garrison rather than completely lift the siege. The Matsui regiment (the 113th Infantry Regiment, commanded by Major General Matsui Hideji), augmented with other units, advanced on Lameng on 21 June, but the newly formed Chinese Thirty-ninth and Eighty-seventh divisions inflicted heavy losses on the Japanese and forced them to retreat to Longling. The Fifty-sixth Division was able to link up with a detachment in Ping-chia in early to mid-July while it successfully kept open a line of communication between Longling and Mangshi. Meanwhile, the garrison of Ping-chia, south of Lameng, continued its defense against Chinese attacks.

These continuous military engagements over a wide area reduced the Fifty-sixth Division's strength by about 40 percent, as some 2,000 men were killed in action and about 6,000 were wounded or hospitalized for illness. Lameng and Tengyue were isolated completely, while Ping-chia and Longling faced imminent encirclement. Such was the precarious situation on this northwestern front when IGHQ called off the Imphal operation in July 1944.

Battle for Myitkyina:
Watershed in the Burma Campaign

The Allies accelerated their offensive with a 17 May glider assault against Myitkyina. The ensuing fighting opened another major campaign for supply routes, much like the Hukawng and Yunnan battles already underway. Strategically, Myitkyina was an extremely important point in the Burma theater. If the Allies took Myitkyina, they would isolate Japanese forces between the Hukawng and the Yunnan fronts. An even more ominous eventuality was the doom of the Japanese defense of Burma because Myitkyina's fall would open the way for the Allies to threaten Mandalay, in central Burma, while control of the Myitkyina airfield also would allow U.S. supplies to be flown over a more southerly and less dangerous air route than the Hump along the Himalayas, which the Allies had been using.

Originally, the Myitkyina garrison was 300 strong, commanded by Colonel Maruyama Fusayasu, and subordinate to the Eighteenth Division. On 17 May, a joint Sino-American airborne assault enveloped the city. The Eighteenth Division headquarters concentrated minor units positioned on the outskirts to bolster the garrison holding Myitkyina. Following a meeting with Eighteenth Division commander Tanaka in Kamaing, Honda Masaki, commander of the Thirty-third Army, placed the Myitkyina garrison under his direct command in a symbolic gesture of his determination to hold the town whatever the cost. The BAA concurred and reinforced the defenders with the Fifty-third Division, which was directly attached to the BAA.

The Thirty-third Army reacted swiftly to the Allies' next offensive thrust, at least on the surface, by ordering a regiment-size force of the Fifty-sixth Division commanded by Major General Minakami Genzō on 18 May to destroy Wingate's troops, who had landed in the Namhkam area the previous day.[28] The Minakami regiment, however, had been assigned to guard the Burma Road, and its actual strength totaled only one battalion, the other two having been transferred elsewhere. Soon afterward, the Fifty-sixth Division moved a battalion of reinforcements, but without obtaining permission from the Thirty-third Army. This decision left Major General Minakami, newly appointed as the Myitkyina garrison commander, to enter the city with only one infantry platoon and one artillery company. The paucity of his own troops created discord over command issues between Minakami and Colonel Maruyama of the Eighteenth Division, who had so far been in charge of the garrison defense of Myitkyina.

The Thirty-third Army headquarters learned about this unauthorized troop movement only after trucks had transported the battalion to Tengyue. By then, however, it had little choice but to approve this action ex post facto, and it took no disciplinary action against the Fifty-sixth Division's commanders.[29] This lenient settlement resulted from Thirty-third Army's fear that harsh measures would strain an already fragile relationship between the Thirty-third Army and the Fifty-sixth Division. A source of this command relationship problem was professional jealousy: Honda and Matsuyama had graduated in the same class from the military academy, but Honda commanded an army, while Matsuyama commanded only a division and was subordinate to his classmate.

Besides the personal differences between these two commanders, the Japanese army failed to make the best use of available intelligence. Advance warning by its code-breaking team had enabled Fifty-sixth Division to anticipate an offensive by the Chinese Twentieth Army Group.[30] The division was unable, however, to exploit a similar intelligence report concerning another impending Chinese offensive, launched on 11 June, because "immediate countermeasures" were unavailable. Furthermore, intelligence that revealed an impending Allied offensive in the northern estuary of the Salween River prompted the division to pay closer attention to the defense of that area north of Tengyue at the cost of curtailing the troops available for Myitkyina, despite the latter's obvious strategic importance.

Notwithstanding the disproportionate emphasis that the Japanese army placed on the defense of the Tengyue area, the defenders in Myitkyina had sufficient munitions to meet their immediate needs because a substantial amount of the ammunition stockpiled in Lameng had been transported to Myitkyina. Yet this situation illustrates the Japanese army's inconsistency in its plan for Myitkyina; they did not provide enough manpower to make effective use of the available arsenal.

Dan Operation: July 1944–January 1945

TERMINATION OF THE IMPHAL OPERATION: ITS SIGNIFICANCE AND RESULTING TROOP REDEPLOYMENT

The Thirty-third Army's campaigns, under way at three locations and already complicated by command personality conflicts, were further affected by the termination of the Imphal operation and subsequent reshuffling of the senior leadership in Burma.

A 2 July SAG order redefined the BAA's primary mission to prevent the Allies from opening a communication route between India and China along the western bank of the Salween River and in northern Burma. Troops west of the Chindwin River were expected to hold their current positions. Thus, without explicit recognition of its failure, the SAG called off the Imphal operation by shifting the BAA's principal area of operations to northern Burma.[31] The Japanese strategy in the Burma theater thus reverted to the original defense plan of blocking of the Allies' supply route to China instead of the aggressive offense-oriented plan for the invasion of India. The Dan operation exemplified this shift as the campaigns in northern Burma and Yunnan, which the BAA had so far undertaken in support of the Imphal operation, now occupied the central stage in the BAA's entire spectrum of operations.

The BAA's strategic shift, which took effect on 2 July, did not immediately boost the Thirty-third Army's strength. Although the Second Division had a reputation as a crack division, it was rumored to have gone soft because of its "easygoing barracks life" during its occupation duty in Java, Netherlands East Indies. Thereafter, the division suffered heavy losses at Guadalcanal, and its morale apparently never recovered.[32] Furthermore, the Second Division was initially equipped with mountain artillery for operations along the swampy coastal region in southern Burma. But replacing those light guns with heavier field artillery pieces turned out to be a time-consuming process. The contrast with the Fifty-sixth Division, which had operated in the area as if it were its own backyard, was striking. The Second's unfamiliarity with the terrain and climate of northern Burma and Yunnan was a handicap as it improvised operations based on a few outdated maps and without adequate logistics. IGHQ also had a behind-the-scenes role in the redeployment of the Second Division because the BAA commander, Lieutenant General Kawabe, decided to transfer the Second Division from the Twenty-eighth Army in southern Burma to the Thirty-third Army in the north,[33] in response to the recommendation of an IGHQ staff officer visiting Burma on 15 June.

Thus, the BAA did not expect the Second Division to play much of a role immediately. Nevertheless, it deployed the division around Bhamo and Namhkam, where the Japanese expected an imminent offensive by the X-Force. The Second Division's orders were to hold its positions until the arrival of the Eighteenth Division. If the Allies, whose operations in this theater were stalled because of their own command problems, had advanced southward immediately after their capture of Myitkyina, they could have breached the Second Division's defenses much more easily.

FORMULATION OF THE DAN OPERATION PLAN

The Thirty-third Army's campaign in northern Burma and Yunnan was code-named the Dan operation. Although this plan was closely linked with the Ichigō operation (which was designed for the Japanese army in China to traverse the Chinese mainland from the north to the south), it had a considerable impact on the overall defense plan of Burma.

The debate over the Dan operation plan was whether or not the Japanese troops could accomplish two missions simultaneously, that is, (1) defend Burma by reconstituting their forces in the aftermath of the unsuccessful Imphal operation, and (2) prevent the Allies from opening their China-bound supply route through Burma. More precisely, could the Japanese army in Burma still retain sufficient combat effectiveness to fend off the simultaneous Allied offensives from the east and from the west? Those skeptical about the feasibility of achieving both objectives feared that the Dan operation would jeopardize the defense of Burma. Although naysayers were found within the military leadership even before the loss of Myitkyina, they voiced their opinion even more openly after its fall.

For example, Lieutenant General Tanaka Shin'ichi concluded that the BAA was "unwise" to place its priority on preventing the Allies from reopening the India–China route. When the Dan operation was underway, he recognized the need for a campaign against the Allies' supply route in addition to the need to defend southern Burma against a possible Allied landing. Nevertheless, he reasoned that the "reconsolidation of the Fifteenth Army's front" should be the "key in the campaign planning" because the Allies' capture of Myitkyina would enable them to airlift even greater amounts of supplies.[34] Major Sejima Ryūzō, a staff officer of the IGHQ's Second Section, was another doubter. After his inspection tour throughout Burma in early September, he reported to the army chief of staff, General Umezu Yoshijirō, that the "BAA would be unable to conduct the campaign for the blocking of the India–China route and the defense of southern Burma simultaneously." Sejima added that it would be "imperative for the BAA to prioritize either one of them clearly." Considering multiple factors such as the need to secure the BAA's rear, the coordination of operations in Burma with the overall campaign planning of the SAG, as well as "political implications," he concluded that the defense of southern Burma should receive top priority.[35] When Sejima recommended this to IGHQ, preparations for the Dan operation were already underway. Only after the commencement of the Dan operation and the annihilation of the garrisons of Lameng and Tengyue did the IGHQ finally adopt his idea.

The IGHQ's willingness to proceed with the Dan operation, even at the cost of the defense buildup in Burma, appears attributable to its decision to support the Ichigō operation. In July 1944, the IGHQ hoped that "the Dan operation would keep the Burma Road blocked until late September to facilitate the implementation of the Guilin campaign—a part of the Ichigō operation." Colonel Tsuji Masanobu, on the staff of the Thirty-third Army, felt this was no problem: "We can easily keep the Allies' route blocked until the target date of late September. But is that all that should be accomplished?" He believed that the Japanese army in Burma could do more than what the IGHQ expected.[36] In fact, the IGHQ offered a compromise to the Thirty-third Army by setting a limited time frame, until the end of September, for the blocking of the Burma Road. Nevertheless, the Thirty-third Army intended to do more than that.

On 12 July—ten days after the Imphal campaign ended—the BAA issued orders for the Dan operation, which envisaged defense in the west and offense in the east. There were three main elements in this operation order:

1. The BAA was to direct its main offensive to the west bank of the Salween River to secure Tengyue and its adjacent area in order to block the Allies' supply route connecting India and China. The Second Division was to become a part of the Thirty-third Army to facilitate the accomplishment of this goal.
2. The Fifty-third Division was to withdraw from the Hukawng front to the vicinity of Indaw, where the Irrawaddy River curves sharply, and there defend the west bank of the river under the command of the Fifteenth Army.
3. The Eighteenth Division was to march to the Yunnan area immediately.[37]

Tsuji visited the BAA headquarters in Rangoon on 9 July to coordinate operations with BAA staff officers. Tsuji had virtually dictated campaign planning within the Thirty-third Army headquarters because its chief of staff, Major General Yamamoto Kiyoe, had assumed the responsibility for logistics since August. Although Yamamoto had drafted a detailed campaign plan and submitted it personally to the BAA, Honda relegated to Yamamoto this rear-area duty so that Tsuji, who, in the eyes of Honda, was a more energetic and independently minded planner, could fully exercise his own initiative.[38]

Tsuji completed his own operation plan, based on Yamamoto's draft, by 20 July and code-named it the Dan operation. The plan called for the Thirty-third Army to concentrate in the Mangshi area to destroy the Chinese Yunnan Expeditionary Force, relieve the siege of the Lameng and Tengyue garrisons by reinforcing the Salween River line, and thereby prevent the Allies from reopening their India–China supply route.[39] Success depended on securing Myitkyina before completing defensive fortifications at Bhamo, Namhkam, and Wanting. A deception campaign to convince the Allies that these garrisons were well prepared was intended to buy additional time for the Japanese. Furthermore, instead of being deployed in the Longling area, the Second Division, which was arriving in piecemeal fashion from the south, found itself under orders to move eastward by night marches. It attacked the Yunnan Expeditionary Force as part of a delaying action to cover the withdrawal of the badly battered Eighteenth Division from Hukawng Valley. Therefore, the defense of Namhkam and Bhamo was undertaken by remnants of the Eighteenth Division and the under-equipped Second Division, which was unfamiliar with the terrain and had to defend poorly fortified positions.

Difficulties with logistics plagued the Dan operation from the beginning. Without wheeled transport, the exhausted men of the Eighteenth Division had to move on foot to their newly assigned position. Shifting the division's heavy equipment sparked a series of clashes with the Allied troops at multiple locations on the Burma Road as well as on the Lashio railway line running to Mandalay. Fighting intensified as the Thirty-third Army's area of operations shifted from the so-called Myitkyina line, which stretched along the railway line on the west bank of the Irrawaddy River to the Yunnan area. The Eighteenth Division also had to undertake a difficult logistic task of hastily evacuating its sick and wounded as well as ammunition, fuel, and other materiel through the Lashio line and the Burma Road.

The Dan operation depended on sustained logistic support. The Japanese high command hoped the garrison of Myitkyina—a transshipment point between the eastern and western fronts in Burma—would hold out. But the defense of Myitkyina crumbled by 31 July—some ten days after the formal adoption of the Dan operation plan. A contingent led by Major

General Maruyama Fusayasu of the Eighteenth Division escaped south-ward to Bhamo. Major General Minakami Genzō stayed behind, follow-ing Thirty-third Army's orders that he personally defend Myitkyina to the last. The implication of the order allowed Maruyama with the entire 800-man garrison to withdraw eastward across the Irrawaddy River. Faithful to his orders, Minakami committed suicide.

The premature fall of Myitkyina shocked the Thirty-third Army leader-ship and set off a serious debate over the Allies' next course of action. Some Thirty-third Army staff officers predicted that Stilwell's X-Force would strike southward from Myitkyina to the Bhamo-Namhkam area along the railway line or on the east bank of the Irrawaddy River. They recom-mended strengthening the defenses between Myitkyina and Mandalay and urged a reconsideration of the Dan operation, which was essentially an offensive in Yunnan. These officers reasoned that the Allies, having cap-tured Myitkyina, could now bring about the collapse of the entire Japanese defense in Burma by invading central Burma via the Myitkyina Railway. This action would wipe out the Fifteenth Army, already weakened in the Imphal fighting. An Allied occupation of Mandalay and other key points in central Burma would isolate the Japanese forces in Yunnan.

Tsuji dissented, insisting that the Allies' primary objective remained the opening of the Burma Road.[40] Based on his view of the Chinese, he foresaw that the X-Force in India, which included newly formed Chinese units, would be most likely to advance eastward to link up with the Yun-nan Y-Force on the Burma Road. Tsuji and other Thirty-third Army staff officers wanted to concentrate the Japanese defense along the Myitkyina Railway. Lieutenant General Honda accepted Tsuji's plan to concentrate in Yunnan to keep the Allies' India–China route blocked. He sought to stockpile ammunition and other materiel in Yunnan, where there were abundant foodstocks. Hence, even if the Japanese were cut off from their logistic support, they would be able to continue to fight by retreating to Thailand.

DAN OPERATION: FIRST PHASE

While all this was transpiring, the Japanese garrisons at Longling, Lameng, and Tengyue were once more fighting off repeated Chinese attacks. On 23 August, the Longling garrison commander urgently radi-oed the Fifty-sixth Division headquarters that his troops could hold out for only two more days. The defenders of Lameng were in logistic extre-mis, their perimeter shrinking, and their defense outposts falling one after another. General Matsuyama concluded that the garrison could not hold until September and that the fall of Longling was imminent. Faced with this crisis, Matsuyama initiated his relief of the Longling garrison.[41]

The news of the Fifty-sixth Division's initiative shocked Thirty-third Army headquarters.[42] Originally, it had envisaged that the Dan campaign in Yunnan would start in early September after the arrival of the entire Eighteenth Division, which would first consolidate its defensive positions at Namhkam and Bhamo to prevent an Allied attack from the west against the unprotected Japanese rear. The Fifty-sixth Division's unexpected move forced the Thirty-third Army to advance its timetable for the Dan operation and order the Second Division on 26 August to move secretly from Namhkam to Mangshi under the cover of night before the arrival of the main contingent of the Eighteenth Division.[43] Namhkam and Bhamo were thus temporarily undefended, and the strength of their garrisons was inadequate even after they later received reinforcements. One Thirty-third Army staff officer remembered that

Bhamo and Namhkam were like an air pocket in the Japanese defense since the units that were supposed to occupy Bhamo barely arrived in Maymyo on 28 July. The arrival of the main force of the Second and Eighteenth divisions was further delayed . . . Had the Allies capitalized on their victory in Myitkyina and started advancing to Bhamo and Namhkam immediately, they would have not only nullified the basic rationale of the Dan operation but would have also threatened the rear of the Fifty-sixth Division . . . Thus, a mood of frustration, uneasiness, and distress permeated the leadership [at Thirty-third Army Headquarters] for several weeks until Bhamo was firmly under their control on 17 August . . . Fortunately, their fears were not realized because the Allies showed no sign of making further advances after their victory in Myitkyina.[44]

On 30 August, the Thirty-third Army ordered the Dan operation to commence. The original plan scheduled the operation to begin in early September, but the starting date was advanced because of the Fifty-sixth Division's initiative, approved after the fact by the Thirty-third Army. The first phase of the Dan operation lasted until 14 September, when the Tengyue garrison fell, during which time the Lameng garrison also had collapsed a week earlier. The main fighting involved Japanese attempts to relieve Lameng and Tengyue as well as the battle at Longling, which was fought as a prelude to the attempted Japanese relief of the two beleaguered garrisons.[45]

These operations provoked debate and confusion in Thirty-third Army headquarters, in particular over the role of the Second Division. While the initial plan called for the Fifty-sixth Division to advance alone along the Burma Road to Longling, the Thirty-third Army command became anxious about the division's security and ordered the Second Division to make a parallel approach to the town.

On the south side of the Longling basin were seven hills, excellent artillery observation posts, which the Japanese numbered 1 through 7. Fierce fighting to control this high ground erupted between the Japanese and the Sino-American forces, which enjoyed American air support. The Fifty-sixth

Division captured a number of Chinese artillery outposts and, reaching Longling, prepared to advance to threaten Chinese positions to the south.

The Second Division attacked from the south and captured hill number 1, but failed to take hill number 2 because frontline troops mistook their assault objective. When Colonel Tsuji learned of this error, he personally led the attack on hill number 2, which they took on the evening of 9 September,[46] and with reinforcements consolidated their hold on the position by 14 September.

Meanwhile, the Japanese offensive caused serious reverberations within the Allied leadership. Stilwell's diary entry for 12 September records his feeling of an impending crisis in eastern China and along the Salween front of the Y-Force. Stilwell claimed that Chiang wished to divert manpower and resources from the Y-Force in order to bolster the eastern China front and even hoped to abort military efforts at the Salween front itself immediately.[47] When they met in Chongqing on 15 September, Chiang angered Stilwell by presenting two choices—either for the Y-Force to retreat from Longling or for the X-Force to commence its offensive within one week.

General Honda was unaware of such discord with the Allied camp and was shocked to learn about the fall of the garrisons at Lameng and Tengyue. After a three-month siege, the survivors at Lameng were annihilated during a 7 September banzai charge against enemy lines. At Tengyue, the 2,000 men of the 148th Regiment had withstood a siege since late June. By 1 September, house-to-house fighting was taking place within the town, and by 8 September only 300 Japanese were left. On 13 September, they all perished in a suicidal frontal attack.

These defeats forced Honda on 14 September to suspend the Dan operation. Several factors affected his decision. First, he wished to rescue the defenders of Ping-chia, who were also under siege and were likely to meet the same fate as the Lameng and Tengyue garrisons. Second, increasing signs were indicating that the battle for Longling was stalemated, as both the Fifty-sixth and Second divisions were unable to breach the heavily fortified Chinese defenses after the Japanese had taken hills number 2 and number 3. Third, the high command concluded that the Japanese would be forced to fight a battle of attrition that would further drain their strength. Casualties during the short-lived Dan operation were heavy on both sides. Chinese losses—killed, wounded, and missing in action, as computed from data available from decoded Chinese messages—were some 63,000.[48] The Japanese Thirty-third Army suffered 18,000 casualties (9,000 from the Fifty-sixth Division, 6,000 from the Second Division, and 3,000 directly assigned to the headquarters) of which 7,300 were killed in action. Even inflicting 3.5 Chinese casualties for each Japanese lost, since the Chinese outnumbered the Japanese 15 to 1,[49] the Japanese were fighting a battle of attrition that they could not win.

Fourth, reconnaissance reports on 13 September confirmed that fresh

Chinese reinforcements were moving into the Longling area, and decoded Chinese radio messages reported on the imminent arrival of the vanguard of the Chinese 200th Division, a mechanized division trained in India and composed of elite troops, at Longling across the Salween River.[50] The Japanese assumed that this crack division, the strategic reserve of the Chinese army, might be deployed to Guilin to check the Ichigō offensive. But Japanese code breakers discovered its advance on Longling after the capture of Lameng on 7 September. Summoning his divisional commanders to his command post on the next day, Honda ordered abandonment of the Thirty-third Army command post at Longling and the withdrawal of the Fifty-sixth Division toward Mangshi. This retreat left only the Second Division to defend Longling and the Burma Road.

The appearance of the Chinese 200th Division in Yunnan relieved pressure on the Ichigō operation but contributed to the end of the Dan campaign.[51] The Thirty-third Army, which had advanced as far as Longling, avoided a showdown with the fresh Chinese reinforcements. Furthermore, the Japanese were unaware of the schism in the Allied leadership and could not capitalize on the Allied command crisis. The relationship between Stilwell and Chiang was on the brink of a total breakdown because of the series of Chinese defeats during the Ichigō operation and Stilwell's possible takeover of the Allied command. On 15 September—the very day when the Japanese side called off the Dan operation—Chiang summoned Stilwell to Chongqing and threatened to withdraw the Chinese Y-Force from Longling unless the X-Force began its offensive from the west within one week. Recriminations continued into mid-October, when Roosevelt removed Stilwell from the theater. These problems at the top caused the Y-Force to suspend its offensive against Longling and prevented the X-Force from advancing southward from Myitkyina.

During the Allied standstill, the Japanese Thirty-third Army shifted its focus from interdicting the Burma Road to the defense of Burma proper. The Thirty-third Army ordered the Fifty-sixth Division to relieve the garrison of Ping-chia, a mission accomplished by 26 September, after which the division was redeployed in the Longling area while the Second Division pulled back to Namhkam to defend that town.[52] The Second Division was then placed under the BAA on 5 October and transferred to southern Burma starting in mid-October. Later orders from SAG moved the unit to Indochina.[53] The SAG willingness to remove a major unit of the BAA in the face of overwhelming enemy superiority demonstrated that the Japanese no longer intended to prevent the Allies from reopening the Burma Road.

The IGHQ was revising the Burma campaign plan when the first phase of the Dan operation ended. On 19 September, General Umezu Yoshijirō, chief of the army general staff, ordered the SAG to hold southern Burma and prevent the Allies from reopening the Burma Road. The initial Japanese objective had been to interdict the Burma Road.[54] Uemzu's orders arrived around the time of a general reshuffling of the Japanese leadership in Burma that reflected Tokyo's decision to reorient the Burma campaign to the defense of Burma proper.

For these reasons, Tsuji proposed transferring the Second Division to the BAA to contribute to the SAG's overall plan of concentrating its strength in the Pacific theater.[55] After the Thirty-third Army's chief of staff and his subordinates endorsed this proposal, the Second Division minus its Ichikari unit, under the command of Colonel Ichikari Yūsaku in charge of defending Bhamo, left the command of the Thirty-third Army. By early October, with the transfer of the Second Division to the BAA, the Fifty-sixth Division and several small units, numbering not quite 20,000 men, were the only Japanese forces in northern Burma, barely enough to prevent the reopening of the Burma Road.[56]

The Thirty-third Army had agreed to relinquish the Second Division because it assumed that deployment of the Chinese 200th Division in the Longling area had boosted the chances of Ichigō's success. In this con-nection, Tsuji accepted the loss of the Lameng and Tengyue garrisons as sacrifices for the greater objective—the success of Ichigō.[57]

Now the IGHQ's foremost concern was how to coordinate three major concurrent campaigns—the Ichigō operation in China, the Dan operation in northern Burma and Yunnan, and the Shō number 1 operation in the Philippines.[58] The Dan operation was redefined as a auxiliary campaign to support the anticipated battle in the Irrawaddy area for the defense of southern Burma. Lieutenant General Tanaka Shin'ichi, now chief of staff, BAA, urged that "the Thirty-third Army should wrap up its Dan operation at the earliest opportunity and complete the redeployment of the Second Division and other units from the Yunnan front."[59]

DAN OPERATION: SECOND AND THIRD PHASES

The second and third phases of the Dan operation now involved a gradual retreat to keep losses to a minimum while conducting a prolonged defense in southern Burma. In late October, however, X-Force launched its offensive from the west against Bhamo, followed by a full-scale offensive against Longling from the east on 1 November. The heavy artillery bar-rage on Longling created such thick smoke in the mountains where the Japanese were entrenched that they thought they were under a gas attack.

Simultaneous attacks from the west and from the east forced the Thirty-third Army to give ground. The Fifty-sixth Division abandoned Longling on 2 November, and the garrison completed its retreat to Mangshi by the night of 6 November. The Japanese evacuated Mangshi on 18 November, after learning from decoded Chinese messages that a full-scale offensive against the town was scheduled for the following day.

Before abandoning Mangshi, Honda wrote to Chiang Kai-shek and had the letter delivered by a Chinese lieutenant, released from Japanese captivity. The letter in part read:

Although Japan and China are neighbors and are supposed to be friends, an unfortunate twist of fate has pitted the two nations against each other. I have been a commander in Burma for six months and have fought against your crack troops during that time. As a fellow Asian, I was happy to be a witness to the bravery of your officers and soldiers with my own eyes and would like to extend my heartfelt congratulations to you. At present, strategic necessity has compelled me to relinquish Mangshi. I would like to extend my heartfelt condolences to the spirits of your 70,000 men who lost their lives in the service of their country.[60]

Having thought that the X-Force would push south from Myitkyina in early November, the Thirty-third Army had second thoughts and ordered the Eighteenth Division to redeploy from its fortified position at Namhkam, leaving one understrength regiment to defend the town. This overreaction by the Thirty-third Army, which incorrectly interpreted the advance of the X-Force as an attempt to overrun all of Burma rather than a limited offensive to reopen the Burma Road, considerably weakened the Thirty-third Army's strong points at Namhkam and Bhamo.[61]

Despite maldeployment of the Eighteenth Division, the Thirty-third Army conducted a gradual fighting withdrawal, suffering minimal losses while preventing the Allied reopening of the Burma Road for two more months.[62] In early December, when the Bhamo garrison was on the brink of annihilation in the face of encirclement by the X-Force, the Japanese initiated a relief operation. By capitalizing on the enemy's confusion at the appearance of the Japanese relief force on the southern side of the encircling pocket, the Bhamo garrison extricated itself from the tightening ring between 15 and 20 December.[63] Not only that, motorized transportation units from Thirty-third Army successfully forced their way through to the town and removed to the rear area the ammunition, fuel, and other materiel stockpiled for the Dan operation.[64]

Thus, the nearly 20,000 men of the Thirty-third Army evacuated Bhamo, Namhkam, and Mong Yu by 27 January 1945, and thus allowed the Allies to reopen the Burma Road.

Conclusion: Failure of the Dan Operation
and Its Effect on the Ichigō Offensive

Ichigō continued in China even after Dan was suspended. Tokyo's decision that the Japanese troops in Burma should not prevent the reopening of the Burma Road prompted the CEA to make its deepest penetration into western China, before the road was reopened. In this way, the CEA hoped that it could build up its forces for a later offensive against Chongqing and Kunming. Also under consideration were additional campaigns farther to the west to protect the flank of the land route through eastern China opened by the successful Ichigō operation. These proposed campaigns were designed to destroy the Chongqing regime before the Allies could make full use of the newly opened Burma Road.

General Okamura Yasuji, who had taken command of the CEA in November 1944, accelerated these plans. On 2 December, the Japanese moved westward to advance from areas that they had occupied during the Ichigō operation. When the Japanese captured Dushan in Guizhou Province, General A. C. Wedemeyer, who had replaced Stilwell, proposed that Chiang defend Kunming even at the cost of Chongqing,[65] and he was so alarmed by the Japanese advance on 10 December that he reported to General George C. Marshall, U.S. Army chief of staff, that the fall of both cities was imminent.[66]

The Japanese commanders in China, however, viewed the campaign for Dushan as a risk that might overstretch their military capability. Tokyo's initial plan of operations called for the capture of Guiyang and "strengthening of the strategic positions in the Sichuan and Yunnan areas" by a westward advance to seize Nationalist army supply bases and strongholds there. Yet logistic difficulties constrained the scope of the Japanese operation and permitted only the temporary occupation of Dushan, the gateway to Guizhou Province.[67]

Nevertheless, Okamura pressed Tokyo for a Sichuan campaign to take Chongqing,[68] thereby destroying the Chiang regime before any U.S. landing on the southwestern coast of China, which had been anticipated to take place after mid-1945.[69] Another objective was to support the military situation in Burma. Thus, the concept of a campaign to take Chongqing was formulated on the premise that the Allies would soon open the Burma Road. Moreover, the CEA intended to destroy the American air bases in Sichuan and Kunming before any U.S. landing on the Chinese mainland. At the same time, it recommended destabilizing the Chongqing regime by supporting the Communist regime in Yan'an into a national force."[70] The Operations Division, Army General Staff, adopted this CEA proposal on 16 January, and it was incorporated into the IGHQ's overall strategic concept.[71]

These recommendations were not implemented, however, because of the opposition from the "middle echelon" of the IGHQ, who argued that a "westward" campaign for Zhijiang and Kunming would have to be undertaken without air cover because of the depletion of the army's air strength during its defense of the Philippines.[72] Another reason for the cancellation of this plan was the opposition of conservatives in Japan—former prime minister Konoe Fumimaro in particular—that by aiding the Chinese Communists in Yan'an, the Japanese army would help strengthen Communist influence. Furthermore, deciphered Chinese radio intercepts pointed to the strengthening of Chinese defenses in Sichuan Province as Chiang withdrew some troops from the Yunnan area.[73] Thus, the sounder military option seemed to be for preparations against the anticipated U.S. landing on the Chinese coast rather than deeper penetration of China. These concerns finally led to the abandonment of the CEA plan.[74]

After January 1945, the Thirty-third Army devoted itself to the defense of southern Burma. The Fifteenth Army, now about 25 percent of its original strength after the Imphal operation, suffered another devastating defeat in the Mandalay area at the hands of the advancing British India army. The Thirty-third Army's defensive line in the Shan plateau to the east of Lashio saved the Fifteenth Army from complete destruction and allowed it to escape to the highland of the Shan. The Thirty-third Army also covered the extrication of the Twenty-eighth Army to avoid encirclement after the fall of Rangoon. Elements of Thirty-third Army held the far bank of the Sittang River, allowing the men of the Twenty-eighth Army, after their breakout, to swim across the monsoon-swollen river and escape to the Shan plateau. The Japanese army in Burma avoided catastrophic destruction and lived to see the end of the war in the Shan region thanks to the Thirty-third Army's successful retreat from northern Burma and Yunnan.

As for the Allies, they could not make full use of the Ledo Road, which they had opened at considerable cost, as a land supply route to China, because the war ended soon thereafter. Thus, the Chinese victory in the Burma-Yunnan theater has been remembered more as a military campaign that enhanced the prestige of Nationalist China rather than as one that contributed strategically to the overall Allied victory. The Chinese victory over the Japanese in Burma became the most effective propaganda tool for the Nationalists not only to impress the world with the birth of the newly trained Chinese military equipped with modern weaponry but also to argue that China had defeated Japan.[75] In Japan, the memory of the fleeting success of the Ichigō operation, which had been won at the cost of the campaign in Burma, escaped the attention of the Japanese public in the face of the devastation wrought by American bombardment of Japan's major cities. Likewise, that portion of the Burma Road running from Lameng to Lashio via Mangshi is largely remembered as an escape route for the Nationalists after their defeat by the Communists in the civil war. Today, the road that stretched from Ledo to Myitkyina and linked to the Burma Road at Namhkam is almost abandoned, invisible under thick jungle vegetation.[76]

15 Chinese Operations in Yunnan and Central Burma

ZANG YUNHU

Since the fall of Burma in 1942, the Allies had debated operational plans for the recovery of Burma. Little came of these plans at first because of military setbacks elsewhere and shortages of materiel and available troops. After the strategic balance turned in favor of the Allies, South East Asia Command (SEAC) was created and Lord Louis Mountbatten was appointed supreme allied commander. The Allies began to plan more concretely for a campaign to drive the Japanese out of Burma. Mountbatten presented detailed operational plans, which had the support of Chiang Kai-shek and provided for the deployment of sizable U.S. and British air, ground, and naval forces, to the Allies' Cairo Conference of November 1943. In a private evening conversation with Chiang Kai-shek, Roosevelt suggested his support, but after the U.S. and British discussions with Stalin at the Tehran Conference led to the decision to deploy maximum resources in the European theater, Roosevelt informed Chiang that the plan agreed to at Cairo had to be abandoned.[1] Despite Allied discord and a lack of overall planning, Allied forces, including Chinese, that had been preparing for the reinvasion of Burma, went into action in late 1943.

In early 1944, the Nationalist government dispatched the Chinese Expeditionary Force (also known as Y-Force), which had been trained in Yunnan, to enter north Burma to fight alongside China's British and U.S. Allies. Its offensive against the Japanese is referred to in China as the Battle of Western Yunnan and Northern Burma. This battle has attracted the attention of military historians ever since it was fought.[2] I seek to complement existing research through a close description of the military operations, tactics, organization, training, and equipment with which it was waged. I make use of available archival materials and memoirs.

Preparations

In 1943, Chiang Kai-shek appointed General Chen Cheng commander of the Chinese Expeditionary Force and charged him with preparing China's armies for the Burma campaign. On 23 March 1943, Chiang had sanctioned the plan of the Department of Military Operations, drawn up in collaboration with General Joseph Stilwell, for the training of thirty-one divisions for a total of around 400,000 personnel.[3] Chen left Chongqing for Kunming on 12 March and set up his command at Chuxiong in Yunnan Province. After Chen fell ill, General Wei Lihuang replaced him in October. After long delays, the Chinese Expeditionary Force began assembling troops in west Yunnan.

In Stilwell's original proposals for the reconstruction of the Nationalist army, which would become known as X-Force, 100,000 Nationalist army soldiers were to be trained in Ramgarh in India. Stilwell had also proposed the training of a further thirty divisions in both Yunnan and Guilin, with the former, as mentioned, to be known as Y-Force and the latter as Z-Force.[4] An important motivation for Chiang Kai-shek to agree to these proposals was that he desperately needed to acquire U.S. supplies and equipment.[5] The Taiwanese scholar Liu Fenghan has argued that Y-Force consisted of 189,000 men.[6] In reality, Y-Force was understrength; Stilwell stated that "there were 115,000 fewer soldiers than formally registered."[7] Wei Lihuang reported to Chiang Kai-shek that "our army is more than 100,000 troops short compared to the official establishment."[8] Despite strenuous efforts by Nationalist army authorities and frequent urgings from Stilwell, efforts to bring units up to strength failed. In 1943, desertion and death, according to He Yingqin, led to the loss of a third of the Nationalist army's strength.[9]

To overcome this problem, Chongqing began a mobilization drive among China's educated youth. On 19 December 1943, the Ministry of Military Administration promulgated Regulations for Student Voluntary Military Service to govern this mobilization effort.[10] The Military Training Department set up seven training camps to offer basic training for 19,000 students out of a registered 51,000. They were to serve in both the X-Force and the Y-Force.[11]

In November 1944, the KMT and its youth organization, the Three People's Principles Youth Corps, mobilized an additional 100,000 youths, who, after training, became the Youth Expeditionary Army. Songs expressed their hope: "Link up Yunnan and Burma, fight with our allies, and exterminate the Japs."[12] A total of 120,000 educated youths registered for service in the army, and 86,000 actually joined.[13] The background of these recruits greatly improved the quality of Nationalist army soldiers and alleviated troop shortages, at least as far as Y-Force was concerned.

As part of his proposals, General Stilwell had suggested that an army corps should consist of two rather than three divisions. Although General Chen Cheng had disagreed because he favored the three-three system—in which a corps consisted of three divisions, a division of three brigades, and so on down the hierarchy—in the end he accepted General Stilwell's suggestion. On 8 August 1943, he telegraphed Chiang Kai-shek and He Yingqin to state that a corps should have three divisions, but for now the reorganization would equip two divisions in accordance with the reform program for Y-Force and later the remaining units should be brought up to strength and equipped properly as well.[14] Not only was the personnel establishment based on the U.S. model, it also adopted American practices with respect to arrangements for artillery, intelligence, logistics, and medical affairs.[15]

Chongqing also made efforts to unify command for Y-Force. On 14 June 1943, Chiang Kai-shek ordered the amalgamation of the Military Affairs Commission's organs in Yunnan and Guilin and stated that all forces in an area of operations of an army group were subject to the orders of the relevant commander in chief.[16] To overcome the opposition of General Long Yun, the longtime ruler of Yunnan Province, General Chen Cheng proposed that Long Yun be appointed formally as the Commander of Y-Force. Chiang Kai-shek approved General Chen's proposal.[17] He informed Long Yun that he would establish the Kunming Field Headquarters Combat Plan in Yunnan with the task of defending southern Yunnan and facilitating Y-Force operations.[18] This step eased Long Yun's misgivings.

Not only did Y-Force pose command issues with local Chinese leaders, it also raised command problems with the United States and Britain. On 19 October, Chiang met generals Mountbatten and Stilwell in Chongqing. He confirmed that Y-Force would operate under General Mountbatten, assisted by General Stilwell once Y-Force entered Burma.[19] When in May 1944 Mountbatten sought to activate the arrangement, Chiang was hesitant because of concerns about the implications for China's historical position in northern Burma, which the British had traditionally recognized, and also because he was frustrated by U.S. and British failures to deliver on earlier promises of naval and ground support. On 11 May, Chiang gave instructions that Mountbatten could not command Y-Force. The conflict concerning command authority over Y-Force continued over the next few weeks, and Chiang Kai-shek never formally abandoned his position.

The United States supplied weapons to China through the Lend-Lease Act. After the spring of 1943, Chongqing used virtually all of this equipment to arm the X-Force and Y-Force.[20] By the spring of 1944, the equipping of Y-Force was complete. Although the weapons of Y-Force were inferior to those of X-Force at Ramgarh, they were nonetheless a great improvement.[21] In addition, the Americans introduced U.S. Army training methods and priorities with great effectiveness.[22]

Action

One lesson that Chiang Kai-shek drew from the 1942 Allied defeat in Burma was that the loss of operational control had been highly damaging to China's interests because the British had used Chinese forces to cover their retreat to India.[23] He was therefore determined to remain in charge of operational planning. Immediately upon the activation of Y-Force, he instructed General Chen Cheng and General Xu Yongchang, minister of Military Operations, to draft a plan stressing flanking movements to avoid frontal combat with the strong Japanese.[24] After the Cairo Conference and the beginning of operations by X-Force, the Ministry of Military Operations drew up a combat plan for Y-Force that focused on the crossing the Salween River and advancing toward Longling and Tengchong, with the subsequent goal of linking up with X-Force at Bhamo and taking Lashio.[25]

Only after the Japanese offensives in early 1944 hit the Allies hard and the Allies demanded urgent Chinese action did Y-Force move into action. On 13 April, the Military Affairs Commission decided to order Y-Force to attempt to cross the Salween River and move into northern Burma. Y-Force made plans, approved on the seventeenth, for crossing the river; the plans were emphatically endorsed by Chiang Kai-shek on 25 April.[26] In handwritten orders, he put the commanders of Y-Force, including Commander in Chief Wei Lihuang, on notice, stating, "The prestige of the Nationalist army is at stake, as is the outcome of the war."[27]

After General Wei Lihuang moved Y-Force's operational headquarters forward to Baoshan on 4 May,[28] Y-Force began to cross the Salween on 11 May and quickly reached its objectives.[29] The initial units crossed the river to test Japanese defenses. The Chinese high command soon realized that X-Force's attack on Myitkyina prevented the Japanese from sending reinforcements to the Salween front. The high command thereupon decided to dispatch the main strength of Y-Force against Longling, Tengchong, and Mangshi.[30] On 1 June, the Eleventh Army Group went into action.

After Y-Force units that had crossed the Salween reassembled, General Song Xilian led the major combat units of the Seventy-first Division and Second Corps against Longling. Although they succeeded in occupying the town, Japanese reinforcements from Tengchong evicted them. Song attributed the setback to the failure to strike simultaneously against Tengchong, enabling the Japanese to relieve Longling with 2,000 troops and large field guns. On 22 June, Chiang upbraided Commander in Chief Wei Lihuang as well as General Song Xilian and ordered them to redouble their efforts, threatening court-martial in case of failure.[31]

General Wei Lihuang rearranged his forces in the hope of advancing simultaneously to both Longling and Tengchong. However, the end of the Japanese advance to Imphal and Kohima prompted Lieutenant General

Kawabe Masakazu, the commander of Japanese forces, to shift the focus to west Burma. The resulting Dan operation, discussed by Asano Toyomi in chapter 14, aimed at preventing the opening of the Burma Road. The operational plans for the Dan operation called for "the concentration of major forces around Mangshi, the defeat of Y-Force at Longling, the advance toward the Salween River, and relief of the encirclement at Lameng and Tengyue, rescuing Japanese units at these two places and severing the Burma Road."[32] The Dan operation began on 5 September.

Two days later, Wei Lihuang advised Chiang Kai-shek that the Japanese had begun a large-scale offensive against Longling and Mangshi and that, after four months of tough combat, Chinese forces had lost numerous casualties and that their fighting strength had diminished by 70–80 percent.[33] Chiang insisted that the advance toward Longling and Tengyue continue. That same day, the Eighth Army Group took Songshan after a siege of two months, and the Twentieth Army Group occupied Tengchong a week later. Following these and subsequent successes, which left the Japanese with only one of their original four fortresses in western Yunnan,[34] Chiang Kai-shek approved special commendations. On 27 September, Xu Yongchang awarded the Blue Sky and White Sun medals to the army group's commanders.[35]

Faced with a setback there, as well as the loss of Myitkyina, the Japanese high command decided to concentrate on a campaign in the Irrawaddy Valley. It ordered the Thirty-third Group Army to continue the Dan operation against Y-Force and to offer relief to units facing X-Force.[36] On the Chinese side, Chiang Kai-shek ordered Wei Lihuang to continue the Y-Force offensive on 25 October and seize Longling and Mangshi, then to take up a defensive position.[37] On 3 November, the forces conquered Longling, and they took Mangshi on 20 November.

Although Wei Lihuang preferred a period of rest and recuperation, on 27 November Chiang ordered him to push on to Wanting. On 27 December, the attack on Wanting began with a three-pronged offensive, and the town was taken on 20 January. On 27 January, the Y-Force and X-Force linked up at Mangyou, and on 28 January, senior Chinese and U.S. commanders celebrated their successful campaigns.

Assessment

The Y-Force campaign in north Burma was the first in which Chinese forces took the offensive and won a decisive victory. It formed a contrast with the fortunes of Chinese forces in 1942 when Burma was lost to the Allies. Participation in the Burma campaign provided important opportunities for the Nationalist military to retrain and reequip its forces according to the U.S. model, opportunities that Chiang Kai-shek seized eagerly. Important to the success of Y-Force campaign was careful planning, by the Ministry of Military Operations, by local commanders such as Wei Lihuang, and by Chiang Kai-shek himself. The Chinese officers and soldiers fought bravely and recovered Tengchong and Longling. The Chinese victory was also the result of mistaken Japanese assessments of Chinese intentions. With great flexibility, Nationalist commanders exploited mounting Japanese difficulties in central and north Burma. In contrast to operations in China (for instance at Hengyang as discussed by Wang Qisheng in his account of the Ichigō campaign in Hunan in chapter 17), Chinese forces also cooperated effectively and assisted one another when the need arose.

TRANSLATED BY SHUXI YIN

16 *The Ichigō Offensive*

HARA TAKESHI

A Summary of the Ichigō Offensive

The Ichigō offensive (*Ichigō sakusen*: Operation number one) was the largest military operation carried out in the history of the Japanese army. It was undertaken by the China Expeditionary Army along the Peking–Hankou, Hankou–Guangzhou, and Hunan–Guangxi railways between mid-April 1944 and early February 1945. This was a time when Japan's military situation in the Pacific was deteriorating. Ichigō had the twin aims of destroying American air bases in China, which threatened the Japanese mainland with air raids, and forcing the opening of an overland route from central China to French Indochina.

It was a major operation, deploying approximately 500,000 troops (twenty divisions in all, representing about 80 percent of the 620,000 troops available to the China Expeditionary Army), 100,000 horses, 15,000 motor vehicles, and 1,500 pieces of artillery. It extended along a 900-mile line from the Yellow River in Henan Province through Hunan Province to Guangdong and the border with Indochina.[1] It involved the largest number of men ever mobilized in the history of the Japanese army. By comparison, the Japanese deployed in the Battle of Mukden (March 1905), the largest battle of the Russo-Japanese War, numbered about 250,000.

The Ichigō offensive was divided into two stages: the first stage was known as the Keikan (Ching-han) offensive (called the Kogō offensive for short), while the second stage was known as the Shōkei (Hsiang-kuei) offensive (called the Togō offensive for short).

During the initial Keikan offensive, carried out from mid-April to late May 1944, the North China Area Army deployed its Twelfth Corps (four infantry divisions, one tank division, and two brigades) and part of its First Corps (one division and one understrength brigade) to surround and destroy the Chinese forces along the southern Peking–Hankou Railway and in the vicinity of Luoyang, which the Japanese then occupied. At the same time, a brigade of the Eleventh Corps advanced north along the Peking–Hankou Railway, with a north–south linkup taking place at Queshan, thus clearing the Peking–Hankou Railway.

During the second stage, or Shōkei offensive, between late May and late December 1944, the Eleventh Corps (ten divisions) moved south along the Xiang River, taking Changsha and Hengyang, and then joined forces with the Twenty-third Corps (two divisions and two brigades) to capture Guilin, Liuzhou, and Nanning. These forces then made contact with the Twenty-first Corps, which had been advancing north from northern Indochina, thereby creating an overland route to Indochina. Then, between early January and early February of the following year, the Twentieth Corps (two divisions and one brigade) and the Twenty-third Corps (one division and one brigade) swept along the southern Hankou–Guangzhou Railway from both the north and the south, destroying American air bases at Suichuan and elsewhere. This Shōkei offensive is generally divided into three phases: the first Shōkei offensive (through early August), lasting until the occupation of Hengyang; the second Shōkei offensive (through late December), from the occupation of Guilin and Liuzhou to the formation of an overland route to Indochina; and the southern Ekkan (Yūeh-han) clearing operation, aimed at destroying American air bases along the southern Hankou–Guangzhou Railway.[2]

The losses incurred during the Ichigō offensive are shown in table 16.1.

Logistics Issues

As for the Peking–Hankou campaign, logistic support was not a major problem because operations were conducted within 60 miles of Japanese army supply bases. The Hunan–Guangxi operation saw major problems in supplying front-line units with weapons, ammunition, and food because they had advanced 600 miles from their logistic base.

Japanese forces used the Yangtze River as a waterway to transport supplies as far as their logistic base for the Hankou area, where they stockpiled essential military stores. Until the beginning of the Hunan campaign, the army moved 40,000 tons of military supplies each month to Hankou. Once the campaign began, heavy attacks by American aircraft gradually made waterborne and rail transport to Hankou difficult, and the monthly amount decreased to 8,000 tons. Large cargo carriers became targets for air attacks, and it was difficult to navigate the upper reaches of the Yangtze. Fortunately, the army was able to continue the delivery of emergency military supplies by using small boats and trucks to haul the materiel. Even when the Japanese repaired bomb-damaged railroads, rail capacity proved

TABLE 16.1

Losses incurred during the Ichigō offensive

Peking-Hankou Operation (Keikan offensive)				
	Killed	*Wounded*	*Sick*	*Total*
Japanese forces	850	2,500	—	3,300
Nationalist forces	37,500	15,000	—	52,500
First Hunan-Guangxi Operation (First Shōkei offensive)				
Japanese forces	3,860	8,327	7,099	19,286
Nationalist forces	93,915	66,468	27,447	93,915

NOTE: Imperial General Headquarters, Army Division estimated that Nationalist army losses (including sick and prisoners) in the Second Hunan-Guangxi campaign exceeded 750,000. Precise figures for the campaign are not clear, as documentation is lacking.
SOURCES: Bōeichō Bōkeikenshūjo, *Senshi sōsho* (BBS, SS), *Ichigō sakusen,* part 3, *Kōsei no kaisen,* 618; Yoshiwara Kane et al., *Nihon kōhei monogatari* (Hara shobō, 1980), 253; BBS, SS, *Ichigō sakusen,* part 3, *Kōsei no kaisen,* 681; Ibid., 679; BBS, SS, *Ichigō sakusen,* part 1, *Henan no kaisen,* 515; BBS, SS, *Ichigō sakusen,* part 2, *Hunan no kaisen,* 341, 418; BBS, SS, *Ichigō sakusen,* part 3, *Kōsei no kaisen,* 685.

TABLE 16.2

Transportation of Japanese military stocks, November 1944

Location	Distance in miles	Means of transport	Monthly tonnage
Wuhan	125	barge/truck	3,850
Yueyang	125	barge/truck	3,850
Zhuzhou	125	truck/light rail	3,850
Hengyang	125	truck/light rail	2,750
Quanxian	80	truck/light rail	1,325
Guilin	85	truck/light rail	—
Liuzhou	85	truck/light rail	330

insufficient, and because of the damage from American bombing, work on the lines south of Hankou did not make much progress. From Hankou, material first went by rail with steam locomotives pulling heavy freight trains between Hankou and Yueyang. Between Zhuzhou and Hengyang, only light rail was used, and tractors pulled light freight cars.

Table 16.2 shows Japanese military stocks, means of transportation, and tonnage transported in November 1944. It clearly demonstrates that the farther the Japanese moved from their main logistic base at Hankou, the fewer supplies they received.

Army headquarters expected field units to gather almost all their provisions and forage from the local area they occupied, but local procurement was insufficient. Despite the best efforts of each unit to live off the land, rations were poor. These logistic problems plagued the Japanese throughout the Ichigō campaign.

The Planning of the Ichigō Offensive

THE INCEPTION

In December 1942, when the situation in the Pacific had begun to deteriorate, Colonel Sanada Jōichirō, who had replaced Colonel Hattori Takushirō as head of the Operations Section, proposed a withdrawal from Guadalcanal. This retreat represented a major turnabout in strategy, and while taking a leading role in the implementation of this proposal, Sanada also felt keenly the need for a long-term strategic plan. Accordingly, in January 1943 he began research into future strategic planning with the cooperation of the Navy General Staff, the Army Ministry, and the military and naval staff colleges. By August, the Operations Section had produced a five-year "Long-Range Strategic Plan."[3]

These studies demonstrated that there was no prospect of winning the war. In the event the situation in the Pacific deteriorated still further and maritime links were cut between Japan and Southeast Asia, Japan had to secure an adequate foothold on the Chinese mainland. The strategic concept was to fight a long and drawn-out war by forging a direct link with Japanese forces in Southeast Asia. Toward this end, Japan had to open and secure a north-south route through China.[4]

In October 1943, when the situation in the Pacific worsened, Colonel Hattori was reappointed chief of the Operations Section. In mid-November, Hattori inspected the Southeast Asia theater and, as a result, pressed even harder for the China clearing operation. The clearing operation would allow Japan to carry out the war from mainland China regardless of what happened in the Pacific.[5]

Underpinning Hattori's thinking was his optimistic assessment that Japan would be able to halt enemy advances in the Pacific, while it would secure a line of communication with Southeast Asia by clearing an overland corridor through China. The line of communication, Hattori believed, would enable Japan to launch a major counteroffensive in the Pacific during 1946.[6]

In addition, as the Japanese fell back to the Pacific, in China American air support for the Nationalist army had also increased. U.S. aircraft and submarines were frequently sinking Japanese transports in the East China Sea, threatening Japan's sea link with Southeast Asia. In early November 1943, General Sugiyama Hajime, chief of the General Staff, who viewed this situation with concern, instructed Hattori to examine the possibility of attacking American air bases in southeast China in order to protect sea traffic in the East China Sea. Sugiyama also gave the same instruction to Lieutenant Colonel Miyazaki, staff officer in charge of operations with the China Expeditionary Army, who happened to be in Tokyo for liaison purposes.[7]

Then, on 25 November, just as Hattori, Sanada, and Sugiyama had all begun to consider a major military operation to clear an overland corridor through China, more than twenty American aircraft, both fighters and bombers, flew from Suichuan in southeast China and attacked the Hsinchu naval airfield in Taiwan. This attack foreshadowed air raids on the Japanese mainland, and the Imperial General Headquarters ordered the China Expeditionary Army to intensify its air operations. Using its Twelfth Air Division, the China Expeditionary Army tried to destroy American air bases at Suichuan and elsewhere in China. These attacks had little effect; on the contrary, the American air forces increased their predominance, securing command of the air in southeast China, attacking Japanese ships in the East China Sea, and inflicting unending damage on the Japanese facilities.[8]

At the end of November, after the air raid on Hsinchu, Sanada informed a Colonel Amano, Tokyo-based senior staff officer of the First Operations Section of the China Expeditionary Army, that Imperial General Headquarters intended to launch an offensive in early June of the following year. The twin aims were to establish a railway link with Southeast Asia by opening the Hunan–Guangxi, Hankou–Guangzhou, and Peking–Hankou railways and to destroy enemy air bases located along these railways, thereby forestalling any air raids on the Japanese mainland by the American air force stationed in China. Amano was instructed to undertake research for carrying out this operation.[9]

Concrete plans now began to be drawn up for an overland clearing operation to secure a link with Southeast Asia, an operation that Sanada had been considering ever since his appointment as head of the Operations Section. The main difficulty was that the army had to carry out the operation on its own because the navy would probably refuse to participate. True, at this time the China Area Fleet was responsible for operations along the Chinese coast, but the Combined Fleet had its hands full with operations in the Pacific. It had little interest in any offensive in mainland China and no flexibility to commit its air units to attack American air bases in southeast China. At the time, the 254th Naval Air Group was the only air unit attached to the China Area Fleet, and it was deployed at Sanā, a base on the island of Hainan, but it was responsible primarily for protecting maritime traffic and for providing air defense and thus had no latitude to releases forces to participate in the Ichigō offensive.[10]

RESEARCH UNDERTAKEN BY THE CHINA EXPEDITIONARY
ARMY AND IMPERIAL GENERAL HEADQUARTERS

On being informed by Sanada of the intentions of the Imperial General Headquarters, the China Expeditionary Army immediately set about studying the overland clearing operation. Although the China Expeditionary Army had about 600,000 troops at its disposal, since early 1943 it had been engaged chiefly in securing occupied areas and had been unable to launch any active offensives. Consequently, this new military operation galvanized the staff officers of the China Expeditionary Army, whose morale had been flagging. But the Tokyo high command and General Hata Shunroku, commander in chief of the China Expeditionary Army, took a more cautious approach.[11]

The Operations Section of the China Expeditionary Army undertook the planning for the offensive and on 7 December wired to Imperial General Headquarters a draft outline of a plan of operations. It proposed to begin with the first Shōkei offensive, aimed at capturing Hengyang and its environs in early June 1944. This would be followed by the Keikan offensive in early July to seize strategic areas along the southern Peking–Hankou Railway. The second Shōkei offensive would commence in early September to capture Guilin and Liuzhou, followed by the third Shōkei offensive in December to take important areas along the southern Hunan–Guangxi Railway.[12]

On receiving this draft outline, Hattori personally conducted war games with members of the army and navy staffs to examine the Ichigō operation within the context of overall future strategy. The aim of these war games was to impress upon the participants the need for a major plan of operations to clear an overland corridor through China, which both Hattori and Sanada had long contemplated; to examine its feasibility and relevance; and to advocate its execution.[13] When the exercises ended, all agreed the Ichigō offensive was necessary, and they drafted an outline of the campaign plan.[14]

After the war, Lieutenant Colonel Imoto Kumao, a former member of the Operations Section, recalled:

A distinctive feature of these exercises would seem to have been that they took a remarkably optimistic view of the war situation and aimed to give the participants hope for the future. In particular, the plan had as its final goal the launching of a major offensive in the Pacific from northern Australia or the southern Philippines in about 1946 to bring the war to an end. Yet there were no concrete prospects of this happening, and the sole objective seemed to be to keep hopes alive for the future.[15]

In addition, Imoto wrote that "One even felt that the Kogō war games were in fact carried out to promote the overland clearing operation."

In this fashion, on 4 January 1944 the China Expeditionary Army formulated a draft outline for the offensive and submitted it to Imperial General Headquarters. The stated objectives of the operation were (1) to destroy enemy air bases and thwart any plans to launch air strikes against the Japanese mainland, (2) to clear a corridor along the trunk railways traversing mainland China and secure an overland link with Japanese forces in Southeast Asia, and (3) to crush the Nationalist government's plans for continuing the war. The China Expeditionary Army also proposed to bring the Keikan offensive forward to late April, ahead of the Shōkei offensive.[16]

On the basis of this outline, the General Staff drew up a draft plan of operations, which was then presented to Army Minister Tojo Hideki. Tōjō, noting these several objectives, assented only to the single objective of destroying enemy air bases.[17]

Thus, on 24 January General Sugiyama reported the modified Ichigō plan to the emperor and received his sanction. On the same day, the chief of the General Staff ordered forces in China to execute the Ichigō offensive.

The operational order stated that Imperial General Headquarters intended to destroy the American air bases in southwest China by capturing strategic areas along the Hunan–Guangxi, Hankou–Guangzhou, and southern Peking–Hankou railways.[18]

The Objectives of the Ichigō Offensive

Though the imperial command sanctioning the Ichigō offensive had fixed on the single objective of the destruction of enemy air bases, in the General Staff's plan it retained the objective of securing an overland corridor. It is possible that this was due to the strong influence of Sanada and Hattori and their conviction about an overland clearing operation and the China Expeditionary Army's determination to conduct the campaign.

The General Staff plan acknowledged the need to destroy American air bases but expanded the mission to seize the railroads and instructed the China Expeditionary Army to open a line of communications running the length of China. Thus, the earlier idea of clearing an overland corridor was still viable.[19]

Sugiyama's earlier report to the emperor emphasized that Ichigō's prime objective was to destroy enemy airfields and ensure the security of the Japanese mainland and the East China Sea, but a subsidiary aim was to clear overland supply route links in case the maritime links were severed.[20] This meant that while the ostensible objective had been narrowed down to the destruction of enemy air bases, in actual fact the creation of an overland corridor was also one of the operation's objectives. .

In addition, the "Plan for the Ichigō Offensive," formulated by the

China Expeditionary Army on the basis of the imperial command, also gave as the operation's objectives the destruction of enemy air bases and the crushing of the Nationalist government's resolve to continue fighting. It also referred to the opening of the railways as far as Liangshan.[21]

When this plan was reported on 20 March to Tōjō, who had just taken over as chief of the General Staff, he reiterated his earlier comments. He again ordered the operation's objective to be restricted to the destruction of American air bases rather than succumbing to needless diversions. The Operations Section, however, argued that since an imperial command had already been issued, time was running out, and it decided to launch the offensive. Subsequent operational guidance would take Tōjō's views into account.[22] In this manner the operation's objectives were not consolidated into a unified objective, as directed by Tōjō.

On 27 May, the China Expeditionary Army launched the first Shōkei offensive. Even after it began, Tōjō expressed his dissatisfaction with the China Expeditionary Army's plan: "From what I hear, this plan remains the same as earlier operations. There is no plan to destroy the enemy's airfields in southwest China."[23]

He accordingly dispatched General Hata Hikozaburō, vice chief of the General Staff, to liaise with the China Expeditionary Army and to observe the operation. Hata arrived in China in early June and conveyed Tōjō's views to the commander in chief, General Hata Shunroku: "When looking at the Eleventh Corps' plan of operations, there seems to be an emphasis on the extermination of enemy forces. But because the Nationalist army is now totally an Anglo-American army, the prime objective of the operation is to destroy enemy airfields, and, if necessary, the clearing of the railways may be suspended. I hope that research will explore the means to destroy enemy airfields at Suichuan and Nanyang (Nan-hsiung)."[24]

The China Expeditionary Army responded that because the Nationalist army had suffered a 50 percent casualty rate in the Keikan offensive, it would have a difficult time recovering its combat effectiveness by the end of the year. This condition would ensure the success of the Shōkei offensive, since the Japanese then enjoyed absolute superiority, though logistic problems could arise in the future. As planned by the field army, the offensive continued without alteration.[25]

The Accomplishment of
the Overland Clearing Operation

Thereafter, the first Shōkei offensive proceeded satisfactorily, but at Hengyang the Nationalist forces resisted stubbornly, while Japanese supply lines were attacked by American planes. And it was only after a hard-fought battle that Hengyang was finally occupied on 8 August. (For Chinese resistance at Hengyang, see chapter 17 by Wang Qisheng.)

Around this time there was within the Army Ministry and the General Staff increasing opposition to the Ichigō offensive, or at least a growing perception that it ought to be postponed, because of preparations for Operation Victory (shōgō sakusen) in the Philippines and because of the failure of the Imphal campaign. Hattori argued that the only active offensive was the Shōkei offensive, and, after the loss of the Marianas, in order to make a decision about continuing the operation, in early September he set out for China with several staff officers on a hastily organized tour of inspection.[26] Following his discussions with officers in the field, Hattori told the China Expeditionary Army of his intention to proceed with the Ichigō offensive:

At the time the situation was unfavorable in the Pacific and northern Burma. Enemy pressure from east and west threatened the links between Japan and Southeast Asia. He made it clear that Imperial General Headquarters had higher expectations for Ichigō. The goal was to prevent the construction of enemy air bases closer to the China coast because that would disrupt maritime traffic and thus weaken Japan's homeland defense. Not knowing that the forces involved in the operation were inadequate, Hattori sought the wholehearted effort of the Expeditionary Army to make it a success.[27]

Hattori also called for the swift capture of the Guilin and Liuzhou airfields. And given the lessons of the Imphal Campaign that mere encirclement of enemy positions was inadequate, the Expeditionary Army advancing from the north, together with the Twenty-third Corps moving from the south, should take Guilin and Liuzhou simultaneously.[28]

Returning to Japan, Hattori recommended that the operation in China should be carried out as planned because, in contrast with the Imphal campaign, Japanese airpower was adequate, the offensive was progressing effectively, supplies were adequate, the state of the railways was sufficient, and the aerial war of annihilation would probably succeed.[29]

But the War Guidance Section of the Army General Staff raised several objections to Hattori's report: "It is difficult to consider any of the reasons to be appropriate as dispassionate observations. The actual situation on the ground is more serious. Future operations will coincide with the first stage of Operation Victory, which depends on concentrating air assets. Therefore, aircraft for operations in China will not be available, and the campaign should be suspended. If, despite these considerations, the China campaign is carried out, it simply will be a repeat of the Imphal campaign."[30]

This opinion was shared by the General Staff, except for its Operations Section and the Army Ministry.[31]

In order to face down this opposition, Sanada and Hattori put together materials for replying to any questions or objections that the emperor might raise concerning the offensive. They argued,[32] first, that since the Chinese strategic position had completely collapsed as a result of the battle of Hengyang, the pursuing Japanese forces could take advantage of this weakness. Moreover, because the Chinese could muster no more than twenty-odd divisions in Guilin and Liuzhou districts, it would be possible, with the help of the Twenty-third Corps, to take those two cities by early December. Second, the Ichigō offensive and the first stage of Operation Victory were closely connected. Air operations in the Philippines would be impossible if American air forces had free use of their air bases in southeast China. The two operations were mutually compatible because the first stage of Operation Victory involved chiefly airpower, while the Ichigō offensive involved mainly ground forces.

In this manner, Sanada and Hattori forcefully argued for the continued prosecution of the Ichigō offensive, which continued to be carried out according to plan. The subsequent second Shōkei offensive and the operation to clear the southern Hankou–Guangzhou Railway ended earlier than expected, the American air bases were also captured, and an overland route to Indochina was opened. Thus, the objectives of the Ichigō offensive appeared to be accomplished, at least on the surface.

Reflections on the Ichigō Offensive

In early February 1945 the Ichigō offensive, with its goals apparently accomplished, ended. The losses inflicted on Chinese forces during the Keikan and Shōkei offensives are estimated to have reached approximately 750,000.[33]

First, with regard to the prime objective of destroying American air bases in southern China, bases at Hengyang, Guilin, Liuzhou, Nanning, Suichuan, and Nan-hsiung, were captured, thereby preventing their use by the U.S. Fourteenth Air Force. As for the second objective, the clearance of an overland route to Indochina, so aggressively sought by the Operations Section at the Imperial General Headquarters and the China Expeditionary Army, was also achieved in December 1944 when the southward advancing Twenty-second Division met the Twenty-first Division, which had come north from north Indochina.

But did Ichigō really achieve its goals?

In response to the Ichigō offensive, the Americans evacuated their air bases in eastern China and moved them deeper into the interior. Medium-range B-25s were being replaced by B-29s, and on 15 June 1944, during the first Shōkei offensive, these long-range bombers flying from Chengdu struck the Yawata Iron and Steel Works in northern Kyushu.[34] B-29s struck Yawata again on 20 August, and they followed with four raids against the naval air depot at Ōmura in Nagasaki Prefecture.[35]

Furthermore, with the loss of Saipan and the defeat at Imphal, Japan's prospects dramatically worsened. A squadron of B-29s now based on Saipan began carrying out full-scale air strikes on major Japanese cities and factories. Thus, the original objective of the Ichigō offensive—to destroy American air bases in southern China and prevent air strikes against mainland Japan—had lost its purpose.

True, an overland route to the south was opened in December 1944, but American airpower had destroyed railways and roads, and there was a shortage of materials and equipment to repair them. In addition, with the American air forces in China having command of the skies, supplies could not be sent by road or rail, and the corridor could be used only as a temporary route of march for some ground forces. Although the Japanese had planned to fight a long, protracted war by using the overland route traversing China to send supplies from Southeast Asia to Japan and war materiel from Japan, the air raids on Japan led to a shortage of materiel, nor could strategic resources be sent from the south because of the catastrophic losses in Japanese merchant ships in those waters. Thus, the overland route, which had been cleared by the commitment of enormous military effort, no longer had any real strategic value when it was eventually completed.[36] It could be said to have been a flawed operation in which the true objectives were not achieved.

Yet the Ichigō offensive struck a massive blow against the Nationalist army, as a result of which the Americans were made painfully aware of the weaknesses of the Nationalists and lost faith in the Nationalist army.[37]

Furthermore, the Ichigō offensive inflicted an estimated 750,000 casualties on the Nationalist army and thus fatally weakened it for the postwar confrontation with its Communist rivals. The huge number of troops thrown into the Ichigō campaign forced the Japanese army to strip its local garrisons of manpower and thus diminished its control over local areas in northern China. For their part, the Chinese Nationalist forces, which had been engaged in sealing off Communist-occupied areas, now had to redeploy around Guiyang in order meet the Japanese onslaught. The Communists took advantage of the resulting military vacuum to launch a counterattack, gradually expanding their liberated areas and enhancing their military position.[38]

In sum, the Ichigō offensive was a disaster for both the Japanese army and the Nationalists. The only winners were the Communists.

17 The Battle of Hunan and the Chinese Military's Response to Operation Ichigō

WANG QISHENG

Japan began Operation Ichigō in April 1944 with 500,000 soldiers, making it not only the largest operation of the war but also the largest in the history of the Japanese army (see Hara Takeshi's chapter 16).[1] Ichigō inflicted huge damage on the Nationalists. Thousands of Chinese soldiers and civilians were killed. The Japanese north-south corridor cut in half the area under Nationalist government rule. One-fourth of China's manufacturing base was destroyed. Revenue dropped sharply because of the loss of manufacturing and because of the Japanese occupation of grain resource areas, aggravating an already desperate financial situation. Ichigō dealt a disastrous blow to the Nationalist regime on what would prove to be the eve of China's victory in war. Chiang Kai-shek wrote that "1944 is the worst year for China in its protracted war against Japan . . . I'm fifty-eight years old this year. Of all the humiliations I have suffered in my life, this is the greatest."[2]

Ichigō lasted about eight months and ended in December. The major battles were the Battle of Henan, also known as the Central China Battle; the Battle of Hunan, or the Changsha-Hengyang Battle; and the Battle of Guilin and Liuzhou. Japanese troops occupied the provinces of Henan, Hunan, Guangxi, and parts of Guangdong. The Battle of Hunan, lasting from late May to early September, was the longest and it witnessed the most determined Chinese efforts to resist the Japanese invaders. This chapter analyzes Nationalist efforts to respond to Japan's strategy and tactics during this battle. It also examines Nationalist strategic decision making, the intelligence system, the military officers and soldiers, the logistic supplies, military service and discipline, and civilian mobilization. It will show that although the Nationalists sought to resist Japanese forces strenuously, and even though it is not true that they focused their efforts on combating Communist expansion, they were unable to halt the Japanese advance because their combat strength had deteriorated badly.

Nationalist Assessments of Japanese Strategic Goals

Ichigō had multiple strategic goals. The first was to destroy the American air bases in China to prevent the U.S. Air Force from attacking the Japanese homeland. The second was to establish a north–south transportation line to Southeast Asia. The third was the destruction of the Nationalist army to end its resistance. For discussions of Ichigō's aims, see also chapter 18 by Tohmatsu Haruo and chapter 14 by Asano Toyomi. Guilin was an important Japanese objective because U.S. heavy bombers stationed at the city could strike Japan. To open up a line of communications to Southeast Asia, the Japanese attempted to secure the entire lengths of the Peking–Wuhan, Guangzhou–Wuhan, and Hunan–Guangxi railways.[3]

The Nationalist army only gradually developed an accurate assessment of Japanese aims. The Ministry of Military Operations (Junlingbu), under the Nationalist government's Military Affairs Commission and responsible for operational planning, had three departments. Its First Department was in charge of designing and assessing combat operations, deployment, and training. The Second Department collected and analyzed military intelligence. The Third Department was in charge of staff work.[4] Xu Yongchang, the minister of Military Operations, kept a personal diary during Ichigō in which he wrote down daily the deployment of both the Japanese and the Chinese troops. The diary allows us to examine the assessments of the military situation at the highest Nationalist levels.

Xu Yongchang learned as early as 25 February 1944 that the Japanese had deployed engineering troops to repair the Yellow River bridge on the Peking–Wuhan Railway, indicating its intention to open up this railroad. He also learned that the Japanese were moving forces from the Yangtze delta upstream to Wuhan and western Hubei. On 4 March, Xu further became aware that two groups of enemy aircraft had flown from Peking and Shanghai to Wuhan. Although Xu suspected that something might be afoot, he believed these moves to be Japanese feints and did not believe them important.

In mid-March, Chiang Kai-shek arrived at the conclusion that the Japanese intended to open up the Peking–Wuhan Railway. He ordered the First War Zone in Henan, with generals Jiang Dingwen and Tang Enbo as commander in chief and vice commander in chief, to make preparations to counter the Japanese offensive. He ordered the Ministry of Military Operations to draw up detailed combat plans for the First War Zone. On

21 March, based on the enemy's deployment, Xu Yongchang ordered the First War Zone to guard against Japanese attempts to secure the Guangzhou–Wuhan Railway. Xu also believed that the Japanese might focus on Hengyang in southern Hunan, as this would be strategically most advantageous to them. In late March, his ministry received intelligence that large numbers of Japanese units were moving from Manchuria and the lower Yangtze River to Wuhan and from north China to Henan province. The ministry thus concluded that the Japanese might be planning a large-scale offensive.[5]

According to Xu's diary, the Nationalist army was able to intercept and decode some highly classified Japanese telegrams. Intelligence stations were placed around the country. Military operation sections in different war zones also organized intelligence-gathering efforts. The Ministry of Military Operations synthesized various intelligence sources and sometimes reached accurate judgments, but at other times they were inaccurate. Japanese intelligence capabilities were far superior.

On 6 April, Xu Yongchang learned from a Shanghai intelligence source that the Japanese wanted to open up the "Greater East Asia Railway."[6] Xu concluded that the Japanese might want to open up the Guangzhou–Wuhan Railway to facilitate withdrawals from Southeast Asia and to harass U.S. air bases in southwestern China. But he believed that the Japanese would not be able to redeploy their forces and continued to worry that the Japanese posture of opening up the Peking–Wuhan Railway was a feint for an offensive in south China.[7] In reality, Japanese units troops were about to attack areas in Henan province along the Peking–Wuhan Railway.

Xu Yongchang underestimated Japanese ambitions. Although he was correct about Japanese intentions to secure the Guangzhou–Wuhan Railway, he did not realize that the Japanese planned to open up the Peking–Wuhan Railway first. Xu's misjudgment affected Chinese deployments along the Peking–Wuhan Railway. Xu did not dispatch enough units from other war zones to counter the Japanese offensive.

On 17 April, Xu Yongchang wrote in his diary that the Nationalist government should focus on the defense of Hunan. By this time, the Japanese had stepped up their preparations for campaigns in Hunan and Guangxi. Xu observed with much concern the transfer of Japanese forces into Hunan Province. He continued to believe that the Japanese attack along the Peking–Wuhan Railway was a feint and that the real goal of the Japanese was the Guangzhou–Wuhan Railway.[8] On 27 April, Xu received intelligence from sources in Vietnam considered reliable that the Japanese in reality aimed at securing both the Peking–Wuhan and Guangzhou–Wuhan railways. But he still did not accept that the Japanese were serious about operations in Henan. He thought that the purpose of those operations in Henan was to weaken Nationalist government forces in the First

War Zone, camouflage redeployments elsewhere, or remove the harvest.[9] Yet the Japanese offensive in Henan had already lasted half a month.

By May 1944, the Nationalists reached accurate conclusions about Japanese intentions. On 6 May, Chiang Kai-shek telegraphed General Xue Yue, commander in chief of the Ninth War Zone in south China, that "intelligence indicates overwhelmingly that the Japanese are about to attack Zhuzhou and Hengyang from northern Jiangxi. You must pay special attention to this possibility and construct fortifications." The next day, Xu Yongchang learned that ten Japanese divisions were prepared to strike south. On 14 May, Chiang telegraphed General Xue that "after opening up the Peking–Wuhan Railway, the enemy will advance along the Guangzhou–Wuhan Railway to open up a north–south transport line to improve its strategic position. You must make appropriate preparations." Chiang telegraphed General Yu Hanmou, commander in chief of the Seventh War Zone in Guangdong, to inform him of the Japanese design on the Guangzhou–Wuhan Railway and the possibility of Japanese troop increases in Guangzhou. He ordered Yu, too, to prepare for these eventualities.[10]

On 15 May, the First Department of the Ministry of Military Operations developed operations plans for the defense of the Guangzhou–Wuhan and Hunan–Guangxi railways. On 28 May, Chiang Kai-shek convened a top-level meeting to discuss military plans for Hunan and Hubei and China as a whole. He thought, "The enemy has nine divisions to attack northern Hunan and western Hubei. They are determined to secure the Guangzhou–Wuhan Railway. They have enough troops, but geographical and transport difficulties will present greater problems than they anticipate, while they are also short on air power. We should exploit the enemy's weaknesses to compensate for the inferiority of our forces."[11] The high command of the Nationalist army had arrived at a correct understanding of Ichigō's aims.

In May, the Ministry of Military Operations received intelligence from various sources that the Japanese were moving a significant number of troops toward Wuhan, southern Hubei, and northern Hunan, and would soon attack the Guangzhou–Wuhan Railway. After compiling and analyzing information from all sources, the Second Department of the Ministry of Military Operations concluded that during the previous month the Japanese, drawing men from various areas in China, had increased troop strength in Wuhan by about 240,000 men. But Xu Yongchang still underestimated the Japanese ability to attack. On 19 May, in response to questions from Chiang Kai-shek, Xu answered that the Japanese would not be able to maintain their offensive, because the Japanese had removed their best troops to other theaters, including the Pacific.[12]

The Japanese army had begun planning for operations in Hunan and Guangxi in late March and early April as part of Ichigō. The Tokyo high command wished to use successes in China to boost domestic morale after the increasingly discouraging news from the Pacific theater. The Japanese army was preparing to put 150 battalions into the offensive. Because seasoned Japanese forces had been deployed to the Pacific and Southeast Asia theaters, troops for Ichigō, though numerous, often had received little training. In other respects, however, Japanese plans for Ichigō were thorough, considering not only deployments but also matters of logistics, climate, and topography.[13]

Because of the slow understanding of Japanese intentions, the Nationalist army authorities found it difficult to develop timely responses. In mid-May, Chiang Kai-shek ordered Generals Xue Yue and Yu Hanmou in the Ninth and Seventh war zones to prepare countermeasures. But his instructions were vague, and he declined to send reinforcements from other war zones. Chiang was in the dark about the strength, imminence, and direction of the planned Japanese offensive. The Ministry of Military Operations failed to make detailed operational plans. Only after Ichigō had been under way for ten days did the Ministry of Military Operations produce a defense guideline. General Xue did not appreciate the seriousness of the Japanese plans and believed that the Japanese would not dare to attack Changsha after having been defeated there three times before.[14] He was also convinced that redeployments to the Pacific and Southeast Asia theaters had placed a limit on Japanese offensive capabilities. Moreover, the rainy season had begun, and the climate and topography of Hunan were disadvantageous to mechanized Japanese forces.[15]

On 26 May, as the Japanese struck into Hunan, General Tōjō Hideki, army chief of staff, reported to the emperor that the Nationalist army did not understand the objectives of Ichigō.[16] However, by this time, Chiang Kai-shek and Xu Yongchang had arrived at a correct assessment of Japanese intentions. Nonetheless, they underestimated the combat effectiveness and the determination of the Japanese. This mistake lay behind their failure to take adequate countermeasures.

The Strategic Deployment of the Nationalist Military

On 26 and 27 May, the Japanese Eleventh Army, discussed in chapter 8 by Tobe Ryōichi, attacked the flanks of the Nationalist army, initiating the Battle of Hunan. From the start of the battle, the Military Affairs Commission was divided. One group, represented by General Bai Chongxi, believed that since the Guangzhou–Wuhan Railway was doomed to fall, the Chinese should abandon it at the outset and withdraw to the Hunan–Guangxi Railway. It could then fight the decisive engagement at the Hunan-Guangxi border or at Guilin. Others, including Xu Yongchang, believed that the Nationalist army should concentrate along the Hunan–Guangxi Railway to blunt the Japanese offensive there.

On 28 May, Xu Yongchang reported to the Military Affairs Commission on the situation in Hubei. He argued that the Japanese forces engaged in Ichigō were more notable for their size than their quality. Thirty-four divisions were in China, even more than at the time of the Battle of Wuhan. He stated that he was deeply concerned by the decline in the Nationalist army's command capabilities and combat effectiveness, as illustrated by its performance in Henan. Chiang Kai-shek agreed. Xu wrote in his diary that the majority view in the Military Affairs Commission was in favor of abandoning the Guangzhou–Wuhan Railway and preparing to fight along the Hunan-Guangxi border. Xu opposed this view. He contended that the Hunan–Guangxi Railway was difficult to defend. He also advocated a counteroffensive in north China. Continuous retreat might sap the morale of Chinese forces. Xu wrote in his diary, "My anger silenced others at the meeting."[17]

The majority of the members of the Military Affairs Commission supported the abandonment of the Guangzhou–Wuhan Railway, indicating their lack of confidence in a hastily organized defense. Withdrawal to the Hunan–Guangxi Railway would free up a month for preparations for the defense of Guilin, including the redeployment of forces from other regions. Such a move might offer a chance of success. The distance between Hubei and Guilin was about 400 miles. Strung out over this distance, the Japanese advance would lose its momentum and become vulnerable to counterattack. General Bai Chongxi advocated this course of action.[18]

Xu Yongchang was firmly committed to the defense of the Guangzhou–Wuhan Railway for strategic reasons. On 3 June, Xu wrote that a majority of the Military Affairs Commission believed that the Japanese intended to open up a rail connection to Zhennanguan, a pass on the Chinese-Vietnamese border. Xu disagreed and argued that the Japanese would move against the U.S. air bases in south China only after the defense of the Guangzhou–Wuhan Railway. He was convinced that the Japanese would attack Chinese field armies to ward off a counteroffensive. Further, he held that the pace of Ichigō would be determined by the strength of the Nationalist army's defense. Xu Yongchang underestimated Japanese intentions and capabilities, believing that they had insufficient strength to operate on three fronts simultaneously.[19]

The defeat of generals Jiang Dingwen and Tang Enbo in the First War Zone had already aroused domestic and international comment. Xu thought that if the Nationalist army now abandoned the Guangzhou–Wuhan Railway without a fight, "what would be the prospect of the Sino-Japanese War?" Chiang Kai-shek concurred.

To secure the Guangzhou–Wuhan and Hunan–Guangxi railways, the

Japanese had to take Changsha, Hengyang, and Guilin. Changsha and Hengyang were located in General Xue Yue's Ninth War Zone and Guilin in General Zhang Fakui's Fourth War Zone. The Seventh War Zone of General Yu Hanmou in Guangdong and the Sixth War Zone under General Sun Lianzhong in western Hubei were located on the flanks of the Fourth and Ninth war zones. Following the defeat of the forces led by generals Jiang Dingwen and Tang Enbo in the First War Zone, withdrawal from the Guangzhou-Wuhan Railroad might lead to a general collapse.

The Japanese plan was to pass through the western part of the Ninth War Zone and then advance through the Fourth War Zone. The Japanese army considered that the key to winning Operation Ichigō was to conquer Changsha, and it decided to deploy greater strength than during the previous three attempts. The defeat of Chinese offensives from the flanks at Hengyang and Changsha would be critical. The army also believed that it would encounter the strongest resistance at Hengyang.[20]

A force of 150,000 men took part in the Japanese offensive in Hunan and Hubei. The first wave consisted of five divisions, and the second had three. On 26 and 27 May, the Japanese marched southward in three columns along a broad front seventy-five miles wide and thirty deep, using rail, road, and water. On 28 May, the Chinese Military Affairs Commission ordered General Xue Yue to prepare for decisive battle between Changsha and Liuyang. Because Chongqing underestimated the number of Japanese troops, it dispatched only a single division from the Sixth War Zone. Xue Yue requested reinforcements from other war zones, but Chiang Kai-shek ordered him to fight with locally available forces. Only after some time did Chiang realize the scale of the Japanese offensive and dispatch forces from the surrounding war zones.[21]

General Xue Yue's strategy for defending his zone was a managed withdrawal along the banks of the Xiang River in order to degrade the enemy as much as possible. His principal forces were deployed along the two flanks of the river. After drawing the Japanese south, he planned that Nationalist army forces would encircle the enemy near Changsha. But Xue Yue had used this strategy in the previous battles for Changsha, so the Japanese forces were prepared for it. Previously, the Japanese had attempted to take Changsha by narrow thrusts, but now they moved forward on a broad front and placed their strongest forces on the two wings. Thus, it was difficult for Xue Yue to take on the Japanese flanks.[22]

The Japanese marched south along the banks of the Xiang River to Changsha, which they besieged with two divisions, or 30,000 men, while Xue Yue had available only 10,000 men. The Japanese plan aimed at taking the strategic Mount Yuelu that rose up west of the city. General Zhang Deneng, commander of the Fourth Army in defense of Changsha, was ordered to hold Mount Yuelu with one division. Understrength, the division had to defend an area about fifteen miles in length with only 3,000 men. Seeing Mount Yuelu in danger, Zhang Deneng moved forces from Changsha city, but he lacked the necessary ferries, and the result was chaos. Morale plummeted, and Changsha was lost on 18 June.[23] Thus ended the first phase of the Battle of Hunan.

The Ministry of Military Operations had finished a defense plan for Hunan on 10 June, just one week before the loss of Changsha. This plan hoped to conduct strategic protracted warfare to safeguard Chongqing and Kunming.[24] By this time, Chinese at various levels clearly understood the intentions behind Ichigō, though they had continuing differences about the precise objectives.[25] Xu Yongchang's diary makes clear that although Chiang Kai-shek disagreed with Xu's assessment of Japanese plans, he did agree to offer determined resistance to the Japanese advance, withdrawing from Hunan altogether, abandoning Hengyang, and concentrating on the defense of Guilin, as General Bai Chongxi advocated.[26]

In late June, the Battle of Hunan entered its second stage. In frustration, the Japanese army had concluded that although it had tried to destroy the main force of the Ninth War Zone, it had been unable to bring the Chinese to battle, and therefore the Chinese military presence to the east would pose a threat during the Japanese second-stage efforts toward Guilin and Liuzhou. The Japanese decided to seek the destruction of these Chinese forces to prepare for the capture of Guilin and Liuzhou. They attempted to entice the Chinese forces to attack them.

Hengyang, situated at the intersection of the Guangzhou–Wuhan and Hunan–Guangxi railways, was a key strategic point, guarding lines of advance toward Guangxi, Guizhou, Sichuan, and Yunnan provinces. The Xiang River connected Changsha and Hengyang. The Japanese army anticipated that when it approached Hengyang, the Nationalist army would launch a major attack. So while launching their offensive, the Japanese planned to use major forces to counter flanking offensives by the Nationalist army, especially by the main forces of the Ninth War Zone in eastern Hunan.[27]

For its part, the Nationalist army had a plan for the second stage of the Battle of Hunan: to resist in the center while exerting pressure on the Japanese from both sides of the Xiang River and then to harass the Japanese rear. This strategy did not differ much from that of the first stage. During the second stage, the Nationalist army used only one army to defend Hengyang, but more than thirteen armies on the flanks.[28]

On 20 June, Chiang Kai-shek ordered various divisions to flank the Japanese to prevent them from reaching Hengyang.[29] However, the Japanese quickly overcame Chinese resistance and reached the vicinity of Hengyang on 23 June. The Japanese deployed two divisions to attack Hengyang, three divisions to attack eastern Hunan, and one division to

attack the region west of the Xiang River. Two days later, the Chinese
Military Affairs Commission ordered General Fang Xianjue's Tenth Division to defend Hengyang to the death. On the twenty-sixth, following the
Ninth War Zone plan to conduct a decisive engagement with the Japanese
at Hengyang, it moved forces to the vicinity. On the same day, Chiang Kai-
shek dispatched General Bai Chongxi to Guilin to coordinate the defense
of Hengyang.

On 1 July, Chiang Kai-shek, meeting with his staff, came to the conclusion that it was impossible to keep control of the Guangzhou–Wuhan Railway and the critical task was to defend Hengyang and strengthen the forces
along the Hunan–Guangxi Railway to safeguard air bases at Guilin.[30]
After many defeats in the preceding months, criticism of the Nationalist
government had mounted at home and abroad. As supreme commander
of the Nationalist forces, Chiang Kai-shek feared the loss of British and
American confidence. In mid-July, President Roosevelt telegraphed Chiang
Kai-shek, remarking that the Nationalist defeats in Henan and Hunan
had damaged China's credibility and suggesting the appointment of General Joseph Stilwell to command Allied forces in China, including those
of the Chinese Communists. This message deeply humiliated and angered
Chiang Kai-shek,[31] who stated to a gathering of high military officials that
"since our failures in Henan and Changsha, the prestige of our nation
and our military, including of those in the highest command, has been
shattered. Foreigners do not respect our soldiers or our commanders! This
disgrace is more unbearable than the Japanese occupation of our territory
by force of arms!"[32] According to Xu Yongchang's diary, Chiang Kai-shek
was "shaken to the core and pounding the table again and again."[33]

General Bai Chongxi, as always, advocated a different approach. On 26
July, he telegraphed from Guilin,

We should reexamine our strategy toward the enemy. The railway from Yueyang
to Hengyang is about 212 miles, the water passage is about 441 miles, and the
road is about 447 miles. The enemy has more than 100,000 soldiers. They are
short of supplies. As we are unable to defeat or stop the enemy at the front, I
suggest that we should change our strategy. We should shift our troops to the
enemy's rear to attack their supply and destroy their transport. Thus, our enemy
will become exhausted, run out of supplies, and will not be able to last.[34]

Xu Yongchang argued that, to the contrary, only stiffer resistance
would improve Nationalist prestige and reverse international perceptions,
an opinion that largely reflected that of Chiang Kai-shek.[35] Guerrilla wars
in the enemy's rear might be more immediately effective in degrading the
enemy but would not reverse China's battered international reputation.

The Tenth Army's defense of Hengyang lasted forty-seven days and
resulted in one of the most ferociously contested battles of World War

II. Despite determined efforts by the Nationalists, Hengyang was lost on 8 August. General Bai Chongxi thereupon suggested to Chiang Kai-shek that the Forty-sixth and Sixty-second armies be withdrawn to Guilin, since it was the obvious next objective of the Japanese. This move made sense, but upon seeking the opinion of Xu Yongchang, Chiang discovered that the minister of Military Operations advocated retaining forces near Hengyang. Xu feared that a withdrawal to Guilin would invite further Japanese advances, that it risked military collapse, and that it would further damage China's international reputation. He held out hope for success. He also recommended that General Bai Chongxi be instructed to visit Chongqing to illustrate his support for the decisions of the Central Command.[36] Chiang Kai-shek sided with Xu Yongchang. On 10 August, Chiang ordered counterattacks against Hengyang.[37]

Not until late August did Chiang order a halt to these counterattacks and a redeployment to the Hunan–Guangxi Railway. On 1 September, learning from reliable intelligence that the Japanese were indeed attempting to enter Guangxi, he ordered Ninth War Zone forces to resist along the Guangzhou–Wuhan Railway.[38] On 7 September, the Japanese conquered Lingling,[39] bringing the Battle for Hunan finally to a close.[40]

Debates within the Military Affairs Commission illuminate two important strategic views within the high command, one advocating a staged withdrawal in the face of the Japanese advance and the other urging that the Chinese army stand and fight. On 11 September, when the Military Affairs Commission discussed the defense of the Hunan–Guangxi Railway, General Bai once more advocated withdrawal. He believed that because it was impossible to defend the entire province, the Nationalist army should increase forces at Guilin for a defense of three or four months. Xu Yongchang, again in disagreement with Bai, pointed out that a stand at Guilin was possible because the army had enough ammunition for three months and the terrain in Guizhou Province was more suitable for military operations than it had been at Hengyang. But he suggested setting up a terminal date for holding out.[41] Chiang Kai-shek this time sided with Bai Chongxi. Liuzhou and Guilin fell on 10 November.

Lacking adequate intelligence assessments and too concerned with international reaction, Xu Yongchang was unable to deploy Nationalist army units in large enough numbers. The size of the Japanese forces and the broad fronts over which they advanced also posed serious problems. In both Changsha and Hengyang, the Nationalist army had insufficient forces to defeat the Japanese enemy. Strong Nationalist army units were kept as reserve forces in the rear, rather than being employed in key battles at a critical time.[42] In contrast, the Japanese could act when and where they wanted. They concentrated superior forces and advanced in depth. In Changsha and Hengyang, the Japanese forces possessed absolute numerical superiority.[43] In consequence, the Japanese defeated the Nationalist army piecemeal.

The Nationalist Army Command

The wartime command system of the Nationalist army was as follows: Under the Military Affairs Commission in Chongqing was the Supreme Command in charge of all war zones. The chairman of the Military Affairs Commission, Chiang Kai-shek, was the supreme commander, assisted by the chief of staff, General He Yingqin, and the vice chief of staff, General Bai Chongxi. Subordinate to the supreme commander were also General Xu Yongchang's Ministry of Military Operations and the Ministry of Military Administration, which was in charge of military training, political affairs, and logistics.[44]

According to the command system, as chairman of the Military Affairs Commission, Chiang Kai-shek should have sent orders to war zone commanders, but he often bypassed them. In some major battles, Chiang attempted to control combat minutiae from afar by means of telegrams and telephone calls directly to frontline commanders. Xu Yongchang wrote in his diary on 12 June 1944, "Local commanders dare not disobey Chairman Chiang's direct orders. They implement them because they will not be held responsible for their consequences. Frequent combat failure is the result. Chairman Chiang's instructions . . . amount to illogical interferences."[45] One consequence of Chiang's interference was that officers lacked initiative, waiting for Chiang's permission before taking action. Xu's diary entry of 6 May 1944 noted that during a meeting of the Military Affairs Commission, Lin Wei, the director of Chiang's powerful Personal Staff Office, passed on four or five telephone calls from the First War Zone. Even battalion-level orders needed Chiang Kai-shek's sanction.[46] Xu complained of a sense of futility in his diary and worried that Chiang's insistence on personally managing low-level details damaged China's war effort.[47]

Zhang Zhizhong had been the director of the Personal Staff Office from 1939 to 1940. He also objected to Chiang Kai-shek's centralization of power. He wrote that "whenever officers receive an order from Chiang, they look first at the end to see if it is from Chiang himself. If so, they regard it as of the utmost importance. If it is from someone in the Personal Staff Office, they will take it seriously. If it is from another organ, circumstances determine what they do with it. The ministries of Military Operations and Administration sometimes send orders over Chiang's name in the hope of securing their implementation that way . . . Here is one reason for our military failures."[48]

Chiang Kai-shek concentrated power in himself yet complained that he had no reliable people under him to push things forward. The vice minister of Military Operations, General Liu Fei, stated in a conversation with Xu Yongchang that "Chiang Kai-shek is personally responsible for this situation. Military leaders do not obey orders unless written by Chiang Kai-shek and ignore everybody except members of the Personal Staff Office. This wrecks our organizational cohesion."[49]

Nationalist army commanders with close connections to Chiang Kai-shek could ignore orders by commanders who were formally their superior but were less close to Chiang. Local commanders outside Chiang's clique might refuse orders in order to preserve their forces or because they received less funding. After Changsha was lost, Chiang Kai-shek ordered General Xue Yue to move the main forces of the Ninth War Zone to the west of the Xiang River. Xue Yue refused, arguing that they were needed to prevent the Japanese from securing the Guangzhou–Wuhan Railway. According to Xu Yongchang, "Xue Yue refused because he wants to protect his own area and fears a contingency."[50]

During the Battle of Hunan, units from the Third and Sixth war zones were deployed in the Ninth War Zone. There they were subject to orders from different war zone commanders, while at the same time they might receive orders from Chiang Kai-shek and Lin Wei, the latter as director of the Personal Staff Office. During the battle of Hengyang, Chiang Kai-shek sent Bai Chongxi, the vice chief of staff, to Guilin with the task of coordinating the defense of the city. As we have seen, Bai held to a different strategic view than Xu Yongchang, but he also disagreed with Xue Yue's operational plans.[51] Unsurprisingly, conflicting orders confused local combat units, and the Chinese forces were hamstrung by a lack of coordination.

A further problem was the lack of communication between frontline commanders. The Tenth Army defended Hengyang for more than forty days. If reinforcements had coordinated their operations with the Tenth Army inside the city, the defense of Hengyang might have been more effective. When the Tenth Army tried to force its way out of the city, units outside offered no support. When units outside attacked the enemy, the Tenth Army merely adopted a defensive position. The lack of coordination meant that the Japanese could defeat the defenders piecemeal.[52]

The Officers and Soldiers of the Nationalist Army

The Battle of Hunan lasted three months. The Nationalists deployed forty divisions, with 350,000 to 380,000 soldiers, while the Japanese used ten divisions with about 250,000 to 280,000 soldiers.[53] According to Japanese estimates, 66,468 Chinese soldiers died, 27,447 were captured, and

132,485 were sick or wounded, while the Japanese suffered 60,000 casualties.[54] Xu Yongchang's Ministry of Military Operations estimated that
90,557 Chinese soldiers were killed or wounded and that 66,809 Japanese
soldiers became casualties.[55] These estimates differ on China's losses, and I
will not attempt to reconcile them here. Although various reasons account
for the high Chinese casualty rate, here I focus on two: the will of the
Nationalist army to fight in Hunan and its combat effectiveness.

Zhang Xianwen, in his 2001 book *Zhongguo Kangri Zhanzheng shi*
(The history of the Sino-Japanese War), argues that the main reason for the
defeat at Hengyang was Chiang Kai-shek's wish to preserve his forces for
postwar confrontations with the CCP and other challengers to his authority.[56] During the past few decades, most PRC historians have argued this
position. However, this view does not accord with historical facts. Almost
400,000 Nationalist soldiers fought for Hunan, and the Nationalist army
incurred high casualties. Chiang put up determined resistance at Hengyang.
"The battle for Hengyang was the most protracted and fiercest defense of
a city with the greatest casualties during the entire war."[57] Two hundred
thousand Chongqing residents signed declarations of respect to encourage
the Tenth Army. The *Da gong bao* newspaper in Chongqing stated that the
Tenth Army represented "the spirit of China's resistance."[58] In his diary,
Wang Shijie called the Hengyang defense "absolutely the greatest achievement since the beginning of the Sino-Japanese War."[59] Some scholars claim
that the defense of Hengyang was conducted by Xue Yue, who was outside
Chiang Kai-shek's clique, and that Chongqing obstructed it.[60] This view
is incorrect.

Chongqing was of course concerned with Communist expansion, discussed by Yang Kuisong in chapter 12. According to Xu Yongchang's
diary entry of 8 June, when a large number of the Japanese moved south
from northern Hunan, the Chinese Military Affairs Commission had two
main items on the agenda of one of its meetings. One concerned possible
Japanese operations in Shanxi Province in north China and in Guangdong
Province in the south. The second was to "get prepared in case the Communists harass the rear."[61] On 10 June, Xu's ministry issued its Guidelines
for Future Combat of the Nationalist army. It ordered the Eighth War Zone
in north China to make efforts to contain the Communists. That same day
Chiang Kai-shek reiterated this order in instructions to the war zone's chief
commanders.[62] Even at a time of intensive combat against the Japanese, the
Nationalists were determined to prevent Communist expansion.

Still, the Nationalists deployed far greater numbers against the Japanese than against the Communists. In his diary entry of 3 July 1944, Xu
Yongchang noted that British and American commentators had criticized
the KMT for using hundreds of thousands of troops against Communists
and downgrading their efforts against Japan. According to Xu, only a few

divisions were deployed against the Communists, with little effect on the fighting against the Japanese.[63] In July, Chiang Kai-shek ordered a reduction of Nationalist army divisions from 321 to 240 to weed out ineffective units. According to the plan designed by Chief of Staff He Yingqin, the Nationalists planned to use 140 of the 240 divisions to fight Japan, 20 to contain the Communists, and 40 to defend the northwest border with the Soviet Union. The rest served as strategic reserves, were deployed in Burma, or were assigned to defend U.S. airbases.[64]

With respect to the combat effectiveness, at the beginning of the war Japanese forces were so superior that one Japanese battalion matched one Chinese division. The Japanese First Army defeated thirty Chinese armies in Shanxi.[65] By 1944, the combat effectiveness of the Nationalist army had declined further. The ratio of Japanese to Chinese soldiers in the First War Zone was 14:100, in the Second War Zone 13:100, and in the Third War Zone it was 20:100.[66] Xu Yongchang, who agreed with such estimates, believed that Chinese units might have some effectiveness in paddy fields or mountains but not on flat, dry land.[67] Yet, we must remember that most Nationalist army units were woefully understrength. A division with a theoretical strength of 10,000 men might actually be 2,000 to 3,000 men short.[68] The real ratio was probably more like 33:100 and, according to Xu Yongchang, perhaps even less.[69]

It is well known that General Joseph Stilwell believed that Chinese soldiers were tough and disciplined, that the quality of junior officers varied, and that division-level commanders were largely incompetent.[70] Chiang also criticized his senior commanders, although he may have done so partly to spur them on. On 18 August 1944, Chiang quoted a Soviet adviser as having stated that

the Nationalist army below battalion level is largely satisfactory. Many problems exist at regiment and division level. Few commanders know how to design operational plans or conduct sand table exercises . . . Above the regiment level, many officers are not professionals but friends of their superiors. Important responsibilities are assigned to outdated officers or literati without military expertise. Staff officers have no battlefield experience although they have graduated from a military academy. They do not know how to manage personnel or logistics . . . Engineers do not know even how to maintain an engine.[71]

Xu Yongchang expressed similar thoughts in his diary.[72]

Chinese soldiers suffered from malnutrition and bad health. Shortages of food rather than weapons formed the primary reason for the decrease in the fighting capabilities of Chinese soldiers in the later years of the war. In October 1944, General Albert Wedemeyer, who had succeeded General Stilwell, discovered that Nationalist army soldiers were too weak to march and fight because they were severely malnourished.[73] Transport problems prevented food deliveries from the rear, while soldiers frequently did not receive full pay. Rations were of poor quality, and uniforms went undelivered. Medicines were frequently unavailable, and the lack of medical care led to numerous deaths.[74]

During the war, Jiang Menglin, chairman of the Chinese Red Cross, investigated recruitment. Due to a lack of transportation, new recruits often had to march several hundred miles to reach their assigned units. Because of hunger and sickness, 80 to 90 percent of new recruits died on the way. Chiang Kai-shek was shocked by Jiang's report, and commented, "I must apologize to our people . . . recruitment problems are the biggest factor in the decline of our combat effectiveness."[75]

Ninety percent of the soldiers were illiterate.[76] The famous historian on the Ming Dynasty, Ray Huang, then a platoon leader, writes, "The Chinese soldier was not only physically weak, but also looked retarded like an idiot. It was impossible to bring them up to a proper standard. The approach was to train those who had basic skills with a cram course. The rest received little training. Officers only wanted these soldiers to show up during a battle to show the Japanese that we have a lot of people."[77]

Nationalist soldiers suffered from unreliable logistics and supply. Many units had to live off the land and therefore could not train properly. Half of all soldiers engaged in nonmilitary tasks. After six months' service, many soldiers did not know how to aim a gun, use sights, or judge distance. The Nationalist soldiers were inferior to Japanese personnel in marksmanship. Many fired randomly during combat or fired their weapons prematurely. They threw grenades prematurely, leaving the Japanese enough time to throw them back. Sometimes the enemy with loud shouts induced Nationalist soldiers to fire their weapons prematurely, wasting their ammunition and giving away their positions.

Yet Nationalist soldiers were tough and had high morale. Assaults and hand-to-hand combat were the most reliable ways for the Nationalist army to win. In the beginning of the war, the Japanese feared bayonet combat. But later, the bayonet skills of the Nationalist army declined due to malnutrition and lack of training. In close combat, Chinese soldiers were reduced to ineffectively shouting "attack" and "strike."[78] Xu Yongchang wrote in his diary, "I am unable to turn the situation around . . . if we have suffered too many defeats, it is because the training of our soldiers is bad and morale has deteriorated."[79]

During the Battle of Henan, when the province suffered from a severe famine, Chiang Kai-shek lamented, "The local population attacked our own forces and seized their arms, just as happened with the czar's army in imperial Russia during World War I. Such an army cannot win! Our military trucks and horses carry smuggled goods, not ammunition . . . During the retreat, some troops lost discipline, looting and raping women."[80] At

Changsha, officers engaged in commerce and attended banquets rather than being with their troops and fighting. Looting was endemic. Some troops played cards in their bunkers while the city was under attack.[81] Xue Yue made much the same comments after the Battle of Hunan, as did Xu Yongchang after the battles of Guilin and Liuzhou.[82]

Various factors determine victory or defeat. The Battle of Hunan was just one of many in the Sino-Japanese War. However, it reveals fundamental characteristics of the Nationalist army with respect to strategy and tactics, officers and soldiers, training, logistics, and mobilization of civilians. Chiang Kai-shek was especially dismayed about the latter. "Our biggest humiliation in the battles of Henan and of Hunan was that the Japanese used Chinese people as plain-clothes personnel, while we were not able to do so. With the exception of one general, no Nationalist army unit was able to mobilize our own people in our service."[83]

TRANSLATED BY SHUXI YIN

Photo 6.   Aerial photo of the Marco Polo Bridge

Photo 7.   Japanese Type 89 tanks attached to the Eleventh Mixed Brigade moving through a village near Nankou, Hubei Province

Photo 8.   Japanese Mistubishi Model 22, Type 96 medium bombers of the Kisarazu Naval Air Group on a mission over the Chinese interior

Photo 9. Men of the Japanese 108th Infantry Regiment returning in the rain from fighting outside Guangzhou, 1938

Photo 10. Japanese infantry clearing a village in central China

Photo 11.   Men of the Japanese First Battalion, Thirty-fourth Infantry Regiment counterattacking across the Peking–Wuhan rail line in central China

Part VI

HISTORICAL PERSPECTIVES

At the conference that was the genesis of this volume, the role of China in the outcome of World War II was a subject of genuine disagreement. This difference was not surprising, since China's proper place in Allied strategy and consequently the character and volume of Allied aid to the country were subjects of intense debate in Washington, London, Chongqing, and New Delhi.

In turn, China's role in Allied plans and Allied aid to that country were greatly influenced by the acrimonious relations between Chiang Kai-shek and General Joseph Stilwell, chief American representative to wartime China. Given General Stilwell's public image in the United States, given his acerbic temperament, and given his sulfurous view of the deficiencies of the Nationalist regime and its conduct of the war, we should not find it remarkable that his perspective on the Nationalists and wartime China have influenced American historiography on the China theater, most notably Barbara Tuchman's *Stilwell and the American Experience in China*. Following the logic of her critique of the many ills of the Chiang Kai-shek regime, it is easy to be dismissive of China's claim to a share of the Allied victory in Asia and the Pacific.

It is this view of wartime China, which privileges Western military standards for military effectiveness in modern warfare and sees Nationalist China as profoundly deficient in meeting those standards, that Hans van de Ven puts under vigorously critical analysis in chapter 19. Van de Ven argues that China's great strategic challenge, unlike that of its industrialized allies, was "how to mobilize a still largely agrarian economy for war against the modern military of an industrialized state." It met this challenge, van de Ven instructs us, by means that were largely nonmilitary and largely traditionally Chinese, such as use of the *baojia* system of communal effort and responsibility and exploitation of the traditional resources and advantages of its geographic frontiers. That China continued to exist as a nation and as a culture through its years of invasion and destruction was, in van de Ven's view, more deserving of recognition than it was ever given by its Western allies.

Another, more extreme, verdict on China's active wartime role was mentioned only in passing at the Maui conference but has been given full voice by certain spokespeople of the People's Republic. In this view, not only did China's forces decisively defeat Japanese armies on the continent, but by holding at bay so many Japanese divisions, they prevented the armies from being shifted elsewhere, most critically westward through India to link up with Hitler's legions driving east through Iran, a scenario that could have spelled the ultimate Allied defeat. In this perspective, the China theater was not merely important, it was *the* critical theater in World War II. In chapter 18 on the interrelationship between the China and Pacific theaters, Tohmatsu Haruo effectively demolishes this argument for the primacy of China in the Allied victory in 1945. Tohmatsu demonstrates that, for good or ill, Allied activities in other theaters affected the war effort in China, but seldom the reverse. He notes, for example, that the Japanese divisions that remained in China at war's end had been kept there not by the force of Chinese armies but by the fact that, given the shattered state of Japanese merchant shipping in the last years of the war, no way existed to transport them to the central and southwest Pacific where they were desperately needed. Most importantly, Tohmatsu concludes that Japan, including its forces in China, was brought to its knees not by Chinese armies but through the destruction of the Japanese homeland by aerial bombs, submarine torpedoes, and nuclear weapons.

The fact of the matter is that China was indeed a tertiary theater in World War II. Essentially, this was not a matter of indifference, racism, or American ineptitude. It involved, rather, a matter of basic national survival. For the United States, as well as Britain, this meant that Nazi Germany was the most dangerous of the Axis enemies and thus had to be defeated first. In consequence, Allied aid and assistance had to be apportioned accordingly to those theaters most critical to Germany's defeat. Moreover, as Japan's war against the West unfolded, two facts became clear: first, that the conflict against Japan was primarily a naval war, and second, as long-range bomber technology developed, the need for air bases in China to bombard Japan's home islands decreased.

All that having been said, two other facts are obvious. First, for four years, China, expending oceans of blood and undertaking huge material sacrifices, had carried on the struggle against Japan virtually alone, with a heroism and stoicism far too little appreciated in the West. As Ronald Spector confirms in chapter 20, China's contribution to the Allied effort— simply remaining in the war—was real enough.

Second, Americans need to be sensitive to China's claims about the importance of their theater to the Allied triumph in 1945. Of the import of Allied victories at Midway, El Alamein, Stalingrad, Kursk, and the Philippine Sea, the Chinese could only be dimly aware. For the government and for the people, the resistance against the Japanese invader *was* World War II. Understandably, they saw it as China's triumph alone. A recognition of this perspective should be incorporated into the judgments of an otherwise triumphalist West.

18 The Strategic Correlation between the Sino-Japanese and Pacific Wars

TOHMATSU HARUO

The Sino-Japanese and Pacific Wars and the Strategic Plans of the Combatants

By the time the Pacific War broke out on 8 December 1941, the undeclared war between Japan and China had already been fought on the Chinese mainland for some fifty-two months. On 9 December, the Chinese Nationalist Government in Chongqing finally declared war on Japan. It thereby made the Sino-Japanese conflict a formal war in light of international law and changed it from a regional conflict in East Asia to a component of a global war. Under those circumstances, Japan, China, and the United States each envisaged strategic plans for the China theater.

JAPANESE STRATEGIC PLAN

The Japanese based their strategic plan on an assumption of victory over the Anglo-American powers. After securing its victory in the war against the United States and Britain, Japan would completely cut off American and British assistance to China while isolating the Nationalist government. Then, augmented by forces which had just finished their missions in Southeast Asia, the China Expeditionary Army, Japan's main force in China, would launch an offensive into Sichuan Province (the Gogō operation) and militarily annihilate the Chongqing government. As it turned out, however, because the war against the United States turned downhill in the fall of 1942, the Gogō operation was abandoned. After 1943, the problem Japan had to face was how to wrap up or scale down its operations in the China theater so that it could transfer its military forces and materiel to the war in the Pacific.

AMERICAN STRATEGIC PLAN

To the United States, the meaning of the China theater in the war with Japan was primarily political rather than strategic. In other words, by incorporating the nonwhite, non-Christian China into the Allied camp, the United States could nullify Japanese propaganda about "Asia for Asiatics" and thus avoid turning WWII into a racial conflict.[1] In the pursuance of an American East Asian policy, it would be important to let a democratic as well as pro-American Republic of China win its war with Japan. Under such considerations, American strategic objectives for the China theater were, first, to tie up a considerable portion of Japanese ground forces and materiel, and second, to establish air bases in areas controlled by the Chongqing government in order to facilitate strategic bombardment of the Japanese home islands and Japanese-occupied territories on the Asian continent. The United States held strong expectations in relation to the second objective, particularly since it was unlikely that the Soviets would provide air bases in the Maritime Provinces or Kamchatka. To achieve these two strategic objectives, the problem of how best to assist China became an issue of strategic importance for the United States.

CHINESE STRATEGIC PLAN

To China, the outbreak of the Japanese-American War had mitigated, on the whole, the military pressure imposed by Japan. It also improved the prospects that China would eventually become one of the victorious powers. The preferable scenario for China was that the Chinese forces, strengthened by American assistance, could act in concert with the U.S. forces attacking from the Pacific. The United States and China looked to the defeat of Japanese forces in China and to the use of the Chinese mainland as a foothold to pin down the Japanese from the air and ground. This scenario was also what the Americans had in mind at the beginning of the Pacific War.

However, exhausted in the aftermath of its war with Japan, which had lasted for more than four years, and devoid of modernized military forces capable of defeating the Japanese, what China could do independently in the war against Japan was fairly marginal. Although it had become politically one of the "Big Four" alongside the United States, Britain, and the Soviet Union, China was hindered economically and militarily in its assumption of a big power role largely because of heavy dependence on American assistance.

Spread of the war into Burma the and Allies' defeat in the area in 1942 meant the loss of the Burma Road, a lifeline of Chinese resistance against the Japanese, and the increase of Japanese pressure on China from northern Burma and Yunnan Province. China faced a two-front war and struggled to maintain the fronts of east China and northern Burma-Yunnan simultaneously.

Basically, China was confronted with three sets of problems: (1) how to make the best use of military assistance from the United States; (2) how to make strategic choices that might improve its status within the Allied camp; and (3) how to survive Japanese military bludgeoning and then go on to defeat the bludgeoner.

This chapter outlines how from the viewpoints of the three belligerent nations—Japan, the United States, and China—the Sino-Japanese and Japanese-American Wars strategically related, or disconnected, during the period 1941–1945.

The Strategic Rear: The War in China, 1941–1943

THE OUTBREAK OF THE PACIFIC WAR
AND THE CHINA THEATER

At the start of the Pacific War, the Japanese field army (the China Expeditionary Army) comprised twenty-two divisions and twenty brigades, with a total of 680,000 men. This was almost 32 percent of the Japanese army's total strength of fifty-one divisions, twenty-two brigades, totaling 21 million men.[2]

Confronting the China Expeditionary Army, the Nationalist government had about 300 divisions with approximately 3 million men. Yet, except for those forces belonging directly to the central government, whose quality in terms of equipment and discipline was relatively high, the forces also included various warlord forces loosely allied to the Nationalist government and possessed of poor equipment, discipline, and morale. While these forces were no match for the Japanese they contributed to the numerical advantage of the Nationalist army, which was a continuing concern for the China Expeditionary Army.

On the other hand, by December 1941, the forces assigned for the war against Britain, the United States, and the Netherlands comprised ten divisions and three brigades, totaling 150,000 men—only 7 percent of the total personnel strength of the Japanese army.[3] Needless to say, the operations in the southwest Pacific and Southeast Asia were mainly sea and island campaigns in which naval and air forces were more significant than ground units. The Japanese navy had used nearly 90 percent of its warships and aircraft for operations in those theaters. When the Pacific War broke out the army's seventy-eight air squadrons with over 2,000 aircraft were used in these southern operations, while thirteen air squadrons with less than 400 aircraft remained in the China theater. Moreover, since the forces sent south by the army were well-trained units that received primarily new equipment, their combat readiness counted for more than the mere percentage they shared in the numerical totals.[4] Nonetheless, the Japanese army had to enter the war with Britain and the United States with two-thirds of its ground forces still deployed on the Chinese mainland, including Manchuria.

As for war expenditures, by 1941 the Japanese Army had spent 3.18 billion yen of extraordinary war expenditures in Manchuria and in the China theater (5.92 billion yen were used in Japan proper and 470 million yen in Southeast Asia, specifically in French Indochina). When the war with the United States and Britain became full-scale in 1942, the China expenditures were reduced to 2.44 billion yen in the same period, 6.42 billion yen were spent in Japan proper, and 890 million yen in Southeast Asia and the southwest Pacific.[5] As mentioned, the Japanese navy had sent most of its forces to fight the war with the United States in the Pacific. But still, in accordance with certain statistics, if the war expenditures invested in China by the navy from 1937 to 1945 had been used to build war vessels, they could have built one hundred *Unryu*-class medium-size aircraft carriers (17,000 tons with sixty-five carrier-borne aircraft).[6] From the viewpoint of force structure, as well as military expenditures, the China theater (including Manchuria) became a colossal burden for Japan after the outbreak of the Pacific War.

THE SECOND CHANGSHA OFFENSIVE

Almost simultaneous with the outbreak of the Pacific War, the Eleventh Army, a subsidiary command of the China Expeditionary Army, employed three divisions and one independent mixed brigade, totaling about 60,000 men, to wage the Second Changsha offensive.[7] Opposing them, the Nationalists had available twenty-two divisions with 190,000 men belonging to the Ninth War Area. This operation was designed as a feint to support the Twenty-third Army's assault on Hong Kong by drawing Chinese forces north toward Changsha and away from southern China. The Chinese and Japanese forces fought a number of ferocious encounters from late December till early January of 1942. Having briefly held Changsha and restrained Nationalist forces, the Eleventh Army pulled out of Changsha and withdrew to Hankow, completing the operation by 15 January 1942. The casualties of the Eleventh Army came to nearly 1,600 killed and nearly 4,500 wounded, while over 26,000 men of the Chinese Ninth War Area were killed or wounded, and about 1,000 were captured. Amid a series of Allied defeats in the winter of 1941–42, the Battle of Changsha had a certain propaganda value for the Nationalist government, since China had achieved the sole Allied "victory."[8] Yet the operation per se had no strategic impact on either the Battle of Hong Kong or the war between Japan and the United States in the Pacific.

THE FIRST AMERICAN AIR RAID ON THE JAPANESE HOMELAND AND THE ZHEJIANG-JIANGXI OFFENSIVE

However, the first aid raid on Japanese home islands on 18 April 1942, undertaken by sixteen B-25 bombers of the U.S. Army Air Force taking off from a U.S. Navy aircraft carrier on the Pacific under the command of Lieutenant Colonel James Doolittle exerted a direct influence on the China theater. The air raid itself caused little damage, and most of the B-25s were damaged in making emergency landings in areas controlled by the Nationalist government. But, after an unbroken string of Japanese victories, it had dealt a blow to Japanese military and civilian confidence. The Doolittle raid was an object lesson in the strategic threat to Japan by American airpower. If four-engined bombers such as the B-17s and B-24s, which had a greater operational radius and could carry more bombs than the two-engined B-25s, were ever based on the Chinese mainland, the Japanese home islands could come within easy reach of American air power.

It was in order to prevent such aerial bombardment from American bases in China that the Expeditionary Army undertook the Zhejiang-Jiangxi operation from May to August 1942. The operation was designed to destroy American air bases in Nationalist-occupied territory and was a precedent for the Ichigō operation two years later. Three divisions of about 45,000 men of the Eleventh Army stationed in the Wuhan area, together with five divisions and three brigades with about 130,000 men from the Thirtieth Army in Shanghai, were mobilized for the offensive. The Japanese operation thoroughly demolished a number of American air bases, nearby highways, and various military facilities from Zhejiang to Jiangxi while overwhelming the resistance of the 260,000 troops of the Chinese Third War Area army's thirty-four divisions and three brigades. Nevertheless, since the Japanese forces were not capable of holding the occupied areas, all Japanese units withdrew to their operational starting points by August. In the fighting, the Chinese lost about 30,000 men. Japanese casualties amounted to approximately 1,000 dead and about 10,000 wounded or sick.[9]

The Zhejiang-Jiangxi operation was the first example of how American initiatives in the Pacific War directly affected the China theater. Little realizing that the Doolittle raid on Japan proper would trigger a deadly Japanese offensive in the China theater, the Nationalists suffered a heavy blow. This, in turn, demonstrated the reality that, not withstanding its status as one of the Big Four in the Allied camp, China was still a secondary figure in the view of the main contenders in the Pacific War.

THE GUADALCANAL OPERATION AND THE CANCELLATION
OF THE INVASION OF THE SICHUAN PROVINCE

As soon as the offensive operations in Southeast Asia were successfully completed in the spring of 1942, Imperial General Headquarters (IGHQ), under the rubric of "reordering military deployments" *Gunyō sasshin*, withdrew a certain portion of Japanese forces in Southeast Asia and the southwest Pacific to prepare for the anticipated war with the Soviet Union and the invasion of Sichuan province.[10] In early April, IGHQ ordered the China Expeditionary Army to make plans for the attack on Sichuan. According to the plans, codenamed "Gogō" and completed in late August 1942, the operation would start in the spring of 1943, using about sixteen divisions or a total strength of about 300,000 men. The period of operations would be nearly five months, during which the key centers like Chongqing and Chengdu were to be occupied and the Chongqing government obliterated. In addition to the China Expeditionary Army, the invasion forces were to be reinforced by nearly 80,000 men transferred from Japan proper, from Manchuria, and from Southeast Asia. In early September 1942, IGHQ formally instructed the China Expeditionary Army to prepare for the operation, and selected units began to accumulate war materiel and to conduct mountain training.[11]

Then, as the battle escalated between Japanese and American forces on Guadalcanal, three elite divisions that were to have been used in the Gogō operation—the Second (in Java), the Thirty-Third (in Burma), and the Thirty-eighth (in Hong Kong) Divisions—were transferred to Southeast Asia and the Pacific, along with a large amount of war materiel.[12] Lacking sufficient forces, the Japanese army cancelled the Gogō operation on 10 December 1942. If the Guadalcanal campaign had not turned out to be such a relentless struggle and the Gogō operation had been conducted as scheduled, the Chongqing government might well have collapsed by the end of 1943, though there was no guarantee that such an event could have turned the tide of the war against the United States in the Pacific. At all events, the Guadalcanal campaign was another example of the way in which developments in the Pacific War exerted a critical influence on the China theater.

GROUND OR AIR? THE CHINA THEATER IN AMERICAN
STRATEGIC PLANNING

Before the war with Japan broke out, the United States had high hopes for the military potential of the Chinese army. The technological level of China might have been low, but the country's manpower was abundant. Thus the Americans thought that they could raise the quality of the Chinese Nationalist army to a level equal to the Japanese army in a relatively short time simply by providing the Chinese with enough weapons, equipment, materiel, and appropriate training.[13] By combining an offensive by refurbished and retrained Chinese ground forces with the landing of American ground units on the Chinese coast or Taiwan, the American high command believed that a pincer attack could be made against Japan in the China theater.[14]

It was Lieutenant General Joseph Stilwell, Commanding General of the United States Army Forces in the Chinese Theater of Operations, Burma, and India and chief of staff to Chiang Kai-shek, who strongly recommended the modernization of the Chinese Army to Chongqing and Washington after the Allied fiasco in Burma in early 1942.[15] Stilwell proposed that the current 300-plus Nationalist divisions be reduced to 90. Then, in a preliminary stage, thirty of these divisions, composed mainly of the battered Chinese units which had retreated into India after the defeat in Burma were to be rebuilt at Ramgarh in India. Collectively designated "X-Force," those divisions would each be reorganized and retrained as a crack unit with weapons, equipment, and discipline equal to that of an American light mechanized division. In a subsequent stage, thirty more divisions, gathering in western Yunnan province—to be collectively designated "Y Force"—would be similarly renamed, re-equipped, and retrained. The remaining thirty divisions were to be organized into internal security forces for the maintenance of public order.

In order to fulfill the refurbishment and redeployment of the Chinese forces it was necessary to secure a supply line through which material of every sort could be transported without interruption from India to China. The former ground supply route—the Burma Road—had been interdicted during the disastrous Burma campaign of 1942. To reopen a route from India to northern Burma and Yunnan province, the Allies established a new China-Burma-India (CBI) theater command (Chinese and Japanese involvement in the subsequent campaign to undertake this effort is discussed elsewhere in this volume by Zang Yunhu in chapter 15 and Asano Toyomi in chapter 14).

Yet from mid-1942 to early 1943, the United States was fully occupied with preparations for the counteroffensives in the southwest Pacific, as well as by the need to provide material assistance to Great Britain and the Soviet Union. Furthermore, while Britain was responsible for the recapture of Burma, it had to give higher priority to Europe and the Middle East as well as to the defense of India. Britain, therefore, could not afford to assign its limited forces to recover its lost Burmese colony. For those reasons, CBI soon became a rear area with the lowest priority in the Allied strategic scheme.

With the interdiction of the Burma Road, an air route was opened from India to China over the Himalayas—popularly known as the Hump—from air bases in Assam to Chinese air bases at Kunming and Chengdu. From the second half of 1942, the air transport squadrons of the U.S. Army Air Force began to undertake these Hump missions. But due to bad weather over the Himalayas there was a limit to the loads carried on such long-range missions, and operational losses in aircraft, air crew, and cargo were frequent.[16] Given the issue of the most effective use of materiel brought from India to China at such difficulty and peril, inevitable conflicts surfaced between the plans for the modernization of the Nationalist army and plans for the strategic bombardment of Japanese forces and installations on the continent and in the Japanese home islands.

THE AMERICAN PLANS FOR THE CHINA THEATER AND FOR THE STRATEGIC BOMBARDMENT OF JAPAN

From 1943, the United States gradually shifted from a plan to modernize the Nationalist army to plans for the strategic bombardment of Japanese targets. Underlying this change was an epochal innovation in technology: the Boeing B-29 bomber with a radius of 4,100 miles and a payload of more than five tons. The United States had already been pummeling Japanese forces in the southwest Pacific with long-range strikes by existing four-engine bombers such as the B-17 and B-24. As the larger, more powerful B-29s were scheduled to be deployed by mid-1943, the American high command considered that the most effective strategy to paralyze Japanese resistance was to concentrate on organized aerial bombardment by B-29s targeting manufacturing centers in Japan proper.[17]

Yet from 1943 to the first half of 1944, the U.S. government and the military had engaged in a debate over whether the air bases for strategic bombardment of Japan should be located on the Chinese mainland or in the Mariana Islands.[18] If it were possible to base B-29s in China, most of Japan proper could soon be included in the bombardment zone. Meanwhile, the bitter struggle over New Guinea and the Solomon Islands had delayed the offensive against and acquisition of the Marianas. Indeed, it was not until 12 March 1944 that the Joint Chiefs of Staff decided to use the Marianas as the base for B-29 raids against the Japanese home islands. Moreover, even then, the Joint Chiefs continued to consider plans for landing American forces on the China coast or on Taiwan for the purpose of acquiring bases to augment the aerial assault on Japan.

In the meantime, General Claire Lee Chennault recommended the strategic bombing plan from a slightly different viewpoint.[19] Having been training the Chinese Air Force as Chiang Kai-shek's adviser since 1937, Chennault had organized a volunteer squadron nicknamed the Flying Tigers, which had tortured the Japanese forces during the Sino-Japanese War. He was appointed as the Commander of the Fourteenth U.S. Air Force, newly founded in China after the outbreak of the Japanese-American War, to supervise the operations of the U.S. Air Force in the China theater. Chennault stressed that it was possible to quash Japanese military power by using the strengthened U.S. air forces in the China theater to systematically bomb supply bases, bridges, highways, railway facilities, barracks, and factories. In other words, he argued that the B29s should be used not only in air raids on Japan proper but also against military facilities of the Japanese forces in the China theater.

Chiang Kai-shek himself had been passionate about modernizing the army. However, persuaded by President Franklin Roosevelt, he started inclining toward supporting the use of China as the base for strategic bombing on Japan. To Chiang, reliance on U.S. air power also seemed to be the easiest way to achieve victory at a minimum cost to his ground forces. Moreover, the deterioration of his relationship with Stilwell, who, while promoting the army modernization plan, asked for supervisory power not only over the U.S. forces in the China theater but over the Chinese forces as well, was another reason for Chiang's becoming reluctant about army modernization.[20]

Furthermore, besides personal discord, the modernization of the army was difficult for political reasons inside his government.[21] Within the Chongqing government, which was a mixture of the Kuomintang and various local warlords, the division of political power was determined by the scale of military power directly held by each party. Therefore, the drastic reduction of the Chinese army met obstinate resistance from the warlord cliques. In addition, the creation of new forces trained and equipped in the American style potentially fostered new rivals against Chiang Kai-shek. What was more, the generalissimo and his protégés feared that, by allowing the new forces to operate under Stilwell's command, the Chinese forces in the China theater would become American puppet troops—an American-Chinese force much like the British-Indian Army, which had little autonomy.[22]

Due to the difficulty in acquiring the necessary materials to modernize the Chinese army, the internal problems of the Chongqing government that restrained army modernization, the confrontation between Chiang Kai-shek and Stilwell, and most importantly, the deployment of B29s, the emphasis of the strategy against Japan in the China theater thereafter shifted from the modernization of the army to strategic air bombardment. Stilwell, in light of his experience during the Zhejiang-Jiangxī Operation a year earlier, warned that without the existence of strong Chinese ground forces, there was a danger of losing air bases through Japanese ground attacks. But he was ignored, as it was thought that Japan, which was fighting hard on the Pacific theater, was unlikely to wage a considerable new offensive on the China theater.[23] A year later, however, Stilwell's prophecy came true.

Through discussions at the conference of the U.S.-Britain Combined Chiefs of Staff Committee held in Washington in May 1943 (the Trident Conference), it was decided at the meetings of American, British, and Chinese leaders in Cairo in November of the same year that the emphasis of the strategy against Japan in the China theater must be placed on strategic air bombardment. The air raids on Japan proper by B-29s based in China were codenamed Operation Matterhorn. As a result, the modernization of the Chinese army was downgraded.

Meanwhile, the U.S. air forces in China were gradually reinforced starting at the end of 1943. In February and March 1944, 357 and 657 transports respectively had lifted a large amount of air war materials from India to bases around Chengdu. Having mobilized labor forces numbering a total of 330,000, four airbases with 4,920-foot runways were rapidly constructed around Chengdu. The Twentieth Bombardment Group of the U.S. army was newly established to conduct strategic air raids against Japan from bases in China.[24]

The Twentieth Bombardment Group was not commanded by Stilwell or Chennault but was put under the direct supervision of General Henry Arnold, Commanding General of Army Air Force, in Washington. This was based on the understanding that the strategic air forces, with their predominant strength, should be utilized not in a regional framework like the China theater but from a higher standpoint: the comprehensive strategy against Japan. Despite this original purpose, such an action had given rise to disputes both between the United States and China and inside the U.S. forces in the China theater.[25]

On 24 April 1944, B-29s from Assam in India began to arrive in Chengdu and by mid-May, 130 B-29s were deployed in air bases around the city. On 15 June the same year, seventy-five B-29s taking off from bases in Chengdu undertook the first air raids on the Yawata Ironworks in north Kyushu in Japan proper. But in spite of America's physical supremacy, it was no easy task for the United States to maintain B-29 operations, which consumed large quantities of accumulated materials transported through difficult Hump airlifts.[26]

THE ESTABLISHMENT OF JAPAN'S ABSOLUTE NATIONAL
DEFENSE PERIMETER AND THE CHINA THEATER

While the United States and China were discussing their strategy against Japan on the China front, Japan, which suffered huge losses during the war of attrition in the southeast Pacific, started considering a drastic strategic change to turn the tide. In late September 1943, the IGHQ issued the proposal of an Absolute National Defense Perimeter, suggesting a shrinking of the defensive boundary to a line along Burma, Dutch East India, west New Guinea, the Mariana Islands, the Kurile Islands, and Manchuria. According to the proposal, the China theater was accurately defined as a front with only secondary significance, and military forces and materials in the China theater were to be transferred to reinforce the Pacific front of the Absolute National Defense Perimeter.[27]

In the first half of 1943, twenty-four Japanese divisions and sixteen mixed brigades, with a total strength of 600,000 men, were retained in the China theater. Although the numbers were somewhat reduced compared to the period from 1941 to 1942, more than 30 percent of the Japanese Army was still in the China theater. Subsequently, it was planned that five A type divisions would be reassigned to the south from the China theater, and then another five divisions would be gathered for transfer. The vacuum left by the withdrawal of these forces was to be filled by eight newly formed independent infantry brigades. This meant that more than half of the essential military power of the China Expeditionary Army was to be moved out and, if the plan was enacted, there would be no doubt that the Expeditionary Army would be downgraded to an occupation guard-force exclusively for the maintenance of security and order. As the first wave of the transfer, the advance units of the Third and Thirteenth divisions were to depart to Saipan and the Luzon Islands respectively within the year.[28]

Consequently, the army war expenditure invested in the southern theater nearly doubled, reaching 1.62 billion yen in 1943 (compared to 890 million yen in 1942). Yet, during the same period, the expenditures in Manchuria and the China theater rose surprisingly also, claiming 2.72 billion yen. (The amount for Japan proper in the same period was 5.46 billion yen.)[29] Because of the forthcoming implementation of a plan for a major offensive on the mainland (eventually the Ichigō operation), the pullout of forces from the China theater was terminated. Instead, from the end of 1943 to early 1944, forces in China were conversely strengthened by reinforcements from Manchuria and Japan proper. As a result, most of the forces dispatched to the war with the United States in the Pacific were from the Kwantung Army in Manchuria and troops recently mobilized in Japan proper. After all, it seemed common sense to reassign forces from Manchuria, where huge numbers of men were retained, rather than the China theater, where actual combat operations existed despite the stalemate.[30]

AMERICAN DESTRUCTION OF JAPAN'S MERCHANT MARINE AND DRASTIC INCREASE IN VESSELS LOST

During this period, the biggest threat to the augmentation of Japan's Absolute National Defense Perimeter were the considerable operations of the U.S. air forces and submarines aimed at destroying Japanese trade. The Japanese navy, which was strongly inclined toward decisive battles between fleets, paid for its negligence to make preparations to protect its nation's merchant fleets from air and underwater threats. Inferior in terms of radar, sonar, variable time fuses, and antisubmarine Asroc, the Japanese navy was unable to conduct efficient convoys at sea, leaving Japanese transport ships to fall prey to U.S. submarines and aircraft one after another.[31]

Ultimately in the Pacific War Japan lost 2,259 ships weighing more than 500 tons with a total tonnage of 8.14 million tons—80 percent of the total vessels held by Japan when the Japanese-American War started and those built during the war.[32] Thus, on average, only about 50 percent of the troops and facilities transferred from the Japan proper and Manchuria to the Pacific theater reached their destinations. For those troops that barely arrived at their destinations, it was impossible to provide consistent supply owing to the blockades of the U.S. naval and air forces. As mentioned, the majority of the forces sent to the Pacific theater to strengthen the Absolute National Defense Perimeter were from the Kwantung Army in Manchuria and from forces inside Japan proper. But even if a large number of troops and facilities had been transported to the Pacific theater as originally planned, most of them would probably either have disappeared at sea or become idle forces isolated on islands blockaded by the U.S. naval and air forces. The direction of the Japanese-American War could no longer be determined by the settlement of the Sino-Japanese War. At the end of 1943, it could be said that Japan was fighting two independent wars with marginal connections between them.

A Showdown Between Ground and Air Forces: The Japanese-American War in 1944 and the China Theater

THE ICHIGŌ OFFENSIVE

The year 1944 was a turbulent one in the course of the Japanese-American War. As Japanese forces forged a massive offensive campaign (the Ichigō operation) aimed at penetrating the Chinese mainland from north to south, the strategic relationships between Japan, the United States, and China regarding the China theater suffered a drastic change.

Notwithstanding the deterioration of the war in the Pacific, the objectives of the Ichigō operation were concentrated on two points: (1) with the sea traffic under attack around Japan proper and the occupied areas in the south falling into crisis, Ichigō was designed to connect Japan proper, Korea, Manchuria, China, and the occupied areas in the south by land, and (2) forestalling the forthcoming air raids on Japan proper by U.S. air forces from the Chinese mainland by destroying air bases in areas controlled by the Chongqing government. However, the IGHQ had been uncertain when trying to determine which one of these two objectives should be emphasized and, above all, whether the operation was worthwhile.[33] Ever since mid-1943, the IGHQ had been able to detect quite precisely the deployment of B-29s as well as the plan of strategic bombing against Japan, and now IGHQ was concerned about the possibility that locales in China under the control of the Chongqing government might be used as bases to launch such raids.[34] The haunting memory of the Doolittle mission in 1942 was still fresh. Eventually, under the direct instruction of Prime (and Army) Minister Tōjō Hideki, the main focus of the Ichigō operation was on the second point— the elimination of air bases.[35]

The offensive was scheduled to be set in motion in January 1944. In addition to the existing forces in the China theater, reinforcements were gathered from Manchuria and the homeland. In the spring of 1944, the total strength of forces belonging to the China Expeditionary Army was twenty-five infantry divisions, one tank division, eleven mixed brigades, and one cavalry brigade, altogether 620,000 troops. The strength of the Expeditionary Army had peaked after the outbreak of the Sino-Japanese War. Some 82 percent of the Expeditionary Army, about 510,000 men, now took part in the Ichigō operation, for which 100,000 horses, 1,550 artillery pieces, 800 tanks and armored cars, and 15,550 trucks were mobilized. Furthermore, the newly formed Fifth Air Army, with about 240 aircraft, was also assigned for backup missions from the air.[36] In that year, army expenditures in the China theater amounted to 5.33 billion yen, which greatly surpassed the 2.26 billion yen spent in the south and the 2.24 billion yen in Japan proper.[37]

It appears that the objectives of the Ichigō operation, which was undertaken from April 1944 to January 1945, were generally accomplished. (Regarding the details of the Ichigō operation, see Hara Takeshi's chapter 16.) While fighting bravely in certain areas such as the battle of Hengyang from June to August, the Chinese forces, which had failed to predict this Japanese offensive, collapsed throughout the theater.[38] The Chinese ground forces, which were being trained by Stilwell, were unable to stem Japanese ground attacks against the air bases. In the course of the offensive, the China Expeditionary Army attacked and destroyed thirteen bases in eight locales, causing the loss of more than 300,000 men on the Chinese side. In December, it successfully linked up with the Southern Army fighting northward from French Indochina.[39] The U.S. forces had lost a huge amount of war supplies accumulated via the difficult Hump, and the U.S. air forces in China were forced to withdraw from Kunming. Stilwell's 1943 admonition had come true.

DISPUTES BETWEEN THE UNITED STATES AND CHINA ON THE USE OF AIR POWER

In the wake of Japan's large-scale ground offensive, disputes escalated between China and the United States in relation to the use of the latter's air power on the China theater. Chennault's Fourteenth Army Air Force and the Chinese Air Force dispatched nearly 500 fighters and light bombers to attack the approaching Japanese ground forces, supply bases, river-crossing spots, and vessels while escorting the Chinese ground forces' retreat. Ground attacks by U.S. forces inflicted considerable damage on the Japanese, but they could not stop Japan's advance.[40] Japanese ground troops held their positions during the day and marched at night when the U.S. airplanes' activities were handicapped. Meanwhile, despite its numerical inferiority, the Japanese Fifth Air Army also contained the movements of the U.S. Air Force by backing up Japanese ground forces from the air and conducting twilight attacks against American air bases. (For the details of air battles, see Hagiwara Mitsuru's chapter 9.)[41] Accordingly, the Ichigō operation demonstrated that it was impossible to prevent offensives by powerful ground forces in a combat theater of vast terrain like the Chinese mainland merely by using air power on a tactical level.

While Chinese forces kept on retreating under the Japanese ground offensive and Chennault's U.S. air forces were trying hard to wage counterattacks, B-29s of the Twentieth Bombardment Group deployed around Chengdu continued to attack objectives outside the China theater. In May, B-29s from the Chengdu airport launched their first raid on Bangkok, and as mentioned earlier, the first air bombing from Chengdu was made on north Kyushu on June 15.

Facing the crisis of a collapse in the China theater, Chiang Kai-shek, Chennault, and Stilwell asked the U.S. government to transfer the materials for the B-29s of the Twentieth Bombardment Group to the Fourteenth Army Air Force's air operations within China offensives. They also repeatedly suggested systematic strategic bombardment by B-29s on Japanese rear supply bases in Hankow, Peking, and Shanghai, only to be turned down by Roosevelt and Arnold.[42] The U.S. government and military leaders were already convinced that strategic bombing on Japan proper rather than the China theater was the most efficient means to bringing Japan to its knees.

THE CAPTURE OF THE MARIANAS AND THE DECLINING IMPORTANCE OF THE CHINA THEATER

On 18 June, two months after the beginning of the Ichigō operation, U.S. forces landed on Saipan. About one month later, Tinian and Guam were also captured, placing the whole Mariana Islands in America's hands. The Twenty-first Bombardment Group of the U.S. Army Force, which was deployed on six airfields built in the Mariana Islands, held 120 B-29s in November 1944 and 400 by early 1945. On 24 November 1944, air raids on Japan proper from the Mariana Islands commenced.[43]

On the other hand, in the China theater, in the aftermath of a reiterated request from the Chongqing government, on 18 December 1944, the Twentieth Bombardment Group and the Fourteenth Army Air Force belatedly undertook a joint strategic bombing on Hankow. The U.S. air forces, with eighty-four B-29s and seventy fighter-bombers, made a heavy raid on the city of Hankow for three hours with regular and incendiary bombs. Ninety percent of the city was burned out and many material supplies of the Japanese forces were reduced to ashes. The China Expeditionary Army was stunned by the demolition of Hankow—the bastion for Japanese forces in central China ever since 1938.[44] If air raids of this scale could be made against military facilities in Hankow, Nanking, Peking, and Shanghai or against Japanese ground forces gathering in the early stage of the Ichigō offensive (and this was in fact possible), it was very likely that the ground offensive could have been either defeated at its outset or indefinitely postponed. But the strategic bombing of the Japanese ground forces and facilities in the China theater came too late.

Although the Ichigō operation gained a token victory, the fundamental strategic objective of Ichigō in terms of forestalling air raids on Japan proper was not achieved, as the U.S. forces moved the base for their strategic bombing against Japan to the Marianas. From June 1944 to January 1945, 3,058 B-29s from bases in China (including those from India via China) had made 10 raids on Japan proper, dropping 9,748 tons of bombs, whereas from November 1944 to August 1945, the number of air bombings on Japan proper from the Mariana Islands reached 128, with 27,059 planes dropping 155,253 tons of bombs.[45] As compared to raids from China, those from the Marianas boasted thirteen times the frequency, nine times the number of aircraft used, and fifteen times the quantity of bombs.

These figures vividly exhibit the decline of China's position as a base for strategic bombardment.

Reflecting that situation, in late February 1945, the Twentieth Bombardment Group in Chengdu also started moving from China to the Marianas to join the Twenty-first Bombardment Group in raiding Japan proper. In terms of defense and supply, the base group in the Marianas was much easier to maintain than that in Chengdu, which had to be supported by the tough Hump missions.[46]

Offensive or Retreat: The China Theater in 1945

LAHEKOU AND ZHIJIANG

In late 1944, the newly appointed commander in chief of the China Expeditionary Army, General Okamura Yasuji, suggested to the IGHQ that the army should attack Chongqing under the momentum of the Ichigō offensive. But this was not accepted due to the deterioration of the situation in the Pacific theater.[47] What surfaced instead were the Lahekou and Zhijiang operations.

As a result of the Ichigō offensive, U.S. air forces in China, which had lost many of their air bases, built new bases for fighters and medium bombers in Lahekou (185 miles northwest of Hankow) and Zhijiang (155 miles west of Hengyang). The China Expeditionary Army intended to obliterate these bases. From early March to early April, three divisions and one cavalry brigade of the Japanese Twelfth Army with 60,000 men succeeded in destroying the Lahekou base.[48]

However, despite the fact the operation should have been conducted by five divisions and four brigades, the Japanese Twentieth Army attacking Zhijiang had to rely on merely two divisions and one brigade due to the lack of forces. On 25 April, sixty-seven divisions of the Chinese army with 600,000 troops joined by 200 airplanes of the U.S. Air Force took on the 50,000 men of the Twentieth Army who were on their way from Paoching to Zhijiang 200 miles away. Five modernized divisions of the Chinese army, which were organized under the army modernization plan supervised by Stilwell's successor, General Albert Wedemeyer, from late 1944 to early 1945, and another fifteen partially modernized divisions were transferred from Burma and Yunnan to east China to engage in the defense of Zhijiang. The consequence was a miserably harsh battle for the Japanese forces. Having suffered the loss of more than 4,000 men, the Twentieth Army was unable to accomplish the objective of its operation and barely made its way back in late May, escaping the pursuit of Chinese forces. The last big operation of the Sino-Japanese War ended with the defeat of the Japanese army.[49]

The battle of Zhijiang demonstrated that with sufficient equipment and appropriate training, the Chinese Army could efficiently compete with the well-experienced Japanese Army. As for the Japanese forces, they learned that even in the China theater, troops short of firepower and lacking command of the air were doomed to defeat.

THE TRANSFER OF ARMY UNITS AND THE
CONCENTRATION OF FRONT LINES

With the threat of U.S. forces approaching Japan proper, the China Expeditionary Army also had to transfer some of its troops to Okinawa, Japan proper, and the weakening Kwantung Army. From May to June 1945, four divisions were reassigned to the command of the Kwantung Army, and the Fifth Air Army became part of the Korea Army.

A well-known force that had been transferred from the China theater to the war against the United States was the Sixty-second Division. The Sixty-sedond Division, which was transferred to the Thirty-second Army in Okinawa in August 1944, was a garrison division consisting of eight independent infantry battalions. While it could hardly be called a first-class unit originally, the division fought courageously during the Peking-Hankow penetration operation in the early stage of the Ichigō operation. After the battle of Okinawa opened on 1 April 1945, the Sixty-second Division, being the main force for the defense of the city of Shuri, had held its battle line for a whole month while continuing to inflict heavy casualties on the superior U.S. forces.[50] This was one example that makes one wonder what would have happened had the forces in the China theater been transferred to the war with the United States earlier. Yet the stubborn resistance of the Sixty-second Division in the defense of Shuri was possible only with the powerful backing of artillery and by concentrating on defensive battles while hiding in strong semiunderground positions, and therefore may not be considered appropriate as an example in demonstrating the effectiveness of moving forces from the China theater to the Pacific.

In May 1945, when the Sixty-second Division was on the brink of annihilation on the Shuri front, the China Expeditionary Army, under instructions from IGHQ, began to move eastward while giving up positions it had recently occupied in the aftermath of the Ichigō operation a year earlier in order to cope with the expected landing of the U.S. forces on the east Chinese coast.[51] When the war ended on 15 August, the total strength of the Expeditionary Army gathering in the Peking, Tientsin, Shanghai, Wuhan, and Canton areas reached 1.05 million. These troops were isolated from Japan proper due to the U.S. blockade of the sea lane. If Japan had not surrendered in August, and had the U.S. forces started their landing operations on Japan proper in November, the 1 million troops of the

China Expeditionary Army would have become a gigantic idle force just like the 100,000 Japanese troops left in Rabaul. The China Expeditionary Army made almost no contribution to the preparation for the showdown in Japan proper. Even without the conduct of major operations, the war expenditures in the China theater in 1945 still reached 3.02 billion yen. (The expenditures in the Southern theater were 390 million yen, and for Japan proper, 5.63 billion yen.)[52]

THE COUNTEROFFENSIVE PLAN OF THE CHINESE FORCES

While the China Expeditionary Army was vacillating between offensive and retreat, the Chinese forces were recovering from the damage inflicted by the Ichigō operation a year before. The surrender of Germany in May made possible the transfer of the Allied forces and material supplies hitherto used in the European theater. The reconstruction of the China theater was thus hastened. From November 1944, China's ground counteroffensive was planned under the initiative of General Wedemeyer, who had become commander in chief of the U.S. forces in China. In accordance with the plan, the Chinese forces would start their offensive in southern China in the end of 1945 and were to restore Canton and Hong Kong in January 1946.[53]

Summary and Analysis

It appears that after the Japanese-American War broke out on 8 December 1941, the war between Japan and China moved to the back burner and China was unable to make substantial contributions to the final result of the Asian Pacific War. Indeed, it was the U.S. Navy's thorough destruction of Japanese shipping, the U.S. Air Force's strategic raids launched from the Mariana Islands on Japan proper, and the atomic bombings of Hiroshima and Nagasaki that crushed Japan's economy and its ability to continue the war. And it was the Soviet Union's participation in the war that made the Japanese government and military authorities give up trying to negotiate an end to the war and to make up their minds to announce unconditional surrender. Moreover, engaging in the civil war between the Kuomintang and the Communists shortly after the Japanese defeat, China was also unable to join the Allied occupation of Japan, and this, in turn, made its presence in the Pacific War even more inconspicuous.[54]

My first conclusion is that even if Japan had been able to settle the Sino-Japanese War, it would still have been difficult for it to transfer its military forces left in China to combat operations against the United States given the number of transports Japan had lost and the limits to the Japanese

navy's escort capabilities at sea. And even if the transfer had material-
ized, it would not have been easy to replace the equipment and training
for troops conducting offensives and public order operations in temper-
ate climes (northern and central China) or subtropical regions (southern
China) with those for use in defensive battles and dilatory operations in
tropical jungles, solitary islands, or coral reefs, considering the equipment
and training system of the Japanese army at the time. In light of all these
difficulties, it seems impossible that a dramatic change could have taken
place between Japan and the United States similar to the military crisis in
World War I inflicted on the Allied forces in the spring of 1918 by the German army's transfer from Russia to the Western Front following the Russian Empire's collapse, or the Third Reich's military collapse in 1944–1945
due to the split of its ground forces in the east and west as a result of the
success of the Normandy landings.

On the other hand, if the Sino-Japanese War had been settled and the
war expenditures spent on the Chinese mainland had been transferred
to the war with the Americans, Japan might have been able to somehow
improve its relative ratio in terms of naval and air power against the United
States. But given the Japanese general level of innovation and industrial
power at the time, the extent of increase Japan could have achieved in its
production of naval vessels, ships, and airplanes during a short period of
time is doubtful.[55]

Consequently, Japan had engaged in two individual wars—a continental war, the Sino-Japanese War; and an oceanic and amphibious war, the
Japanese-American War—whose strategic correlations were extremely
marginal. This is ironic considering that in the end, the Japanese-American
War resulted in the failure to settle the Sino-Japanese War.

Fearing that China might drop out of the war against Japan by ultimately concluding a peace agreement with the Japanese, the United States
continued offering military and economic assistance to China while bear-
ing the subsequent hardships caused in other theaters. Inside the United
States, some argued that China must modernize its ground forces through
abundant economic and military aid from the United States and use those
forces to smash the Japanese army, but others insisted that China give
higher priority to its providing the U.S. Air Force with bases for strategic
raids on Japan. Since the Burma Road was shut down due to the Japanese occupation of northern Burma and southern Yunnan, the only way
to transport resources necessary to China was the air lane from bases in
India to Kunming and Chengdu across the Himalayas. But even with its
great resources, it was difficult for the United States to meet the demands
of both the modernization of Chinese ground forces and the maintenance
of air bases in China.

In the end, harboring fundamental doubts about the capability of the

Chinese army, the United States shifted its emphasis toward the provision of bases for strategic raids on Japan proper as the primary significance of China in American strategy against the Japanese. China's role was to contribute land and labor for the construction of air bases and to provide ground forces to protect those bases from the Japanese army's attack. The mission of the Chinese forces was the defense of the U.S. air bases instead of serving as a field army able to form independent offensives against the Japanese army.

Under such circumstances, apart from insufficient resources, China made little progress in modernizing its Chinese ground forces owing to factional infighting as well as a lack of efficiency within the Chinese government and among military authorities. Hence China was unable to nurture a military force by early 1945 that could fight squarely with the Japanese Army. The handful of modernized Chinese divisions, having been used on the operations to reopen the ground route in northern Burma and Yunnan, were not transferred to the front in east China until the spring of 1945.

As a result of the Ichigō operation from spring to winter of 1944, the military foundation of the Chongqing government was collapsing and this brought the conflict between China and the United States regarding the war against Japan to its climax. The Chinese argued that if forces and equipment, particularly the air forces, gathered by the United States for the offensive against the Mariana Islands and the Philippines had been moved to the China theater in the first half of 1944, the offensive of the Japanese forces could have been stopped. The United States, stressing the importance of detaching Japan proper from the resource areas in the south through counterattacks in the Pacific and strategic bombings by B-29s from the Marianas, responded negatively to China's demand. On 18 December 1945, due to the reiterated request from China, the U.S. air forces in China eventually launched strategic raids on Hankow and inflicted tremendous damage on the big rear bases of the Japanese army. Yet this was too late, as all major objectives of the Ichigō operation had already fallen into Japanese hands.

Debates concerning the significance of the China theater in the context of the landing operations on Japan proper continued between the United States and China thereafter until the defeat of Japan.[56] But in the end, to the United States, the meaning of China in the war against Japan was primarily political. China's strategic value was limited to the possibility of setting up bases for strategic bombing against Japan. Such strategic value also sharply declined with the implementation of the U.S. strategic raids on Japan by B-29s from the Mariana Islands. After 1945, debates on China inside the United States were no longer made in terms of the military operations against Japan but started shifting into the context of postwar arrangements in East Asia.

For China, then, what was the significance of the Japanese-American War? Immediately after the outbreak of that conflict, while Japan was still steadily advancing, Chiang Kai-shek, who declared war on Japan within the day, used the proverb "drinking poison to ease thirst" to present his optimism that the Japanese forces' momentum was temporary whereas the final victory of the Allies was unshakable.[57] He had no doubt that what would bring final victory to the Allies was the overwhelming productivity and military power of the United States.

Nevertheless, the Chongqing government was well aware of the fact that unless the Chinese forces could achieve certain victories in the war against Japan, the country would be unable to raise its status among the Allied powers during and after the war. In other words, the problem for the Chongqing government concerned the kind of strategic contribution it could make as one of the Big Four during the Allies' war against Japan under U.S. leadership. But in this sense, the foremost issues Chongqing had to confront were political rather than strategic: the augmentation of the power of Chiang Kai-shek and the Kuomintang inside the Chongqing regime, which was a scratch team made up of warlords, and the preparation for the coming civil war with the Communists, with whom cooperation had already started cracking after the New Fourth Army Incident in early 1941.[58]

Inevitably, as the military operations against Japan shrank to a secondary position, the Japanese and Chinese forces basically entered a stalemate from the end of 1941 to the spring of 1944. During this period, the Japanese and American forces had fought tough battles in the Solomon Islands, New Guinea, and the Central Pacific. Of course, as the seesaw game between the Chinese and Japanese forces in the wake of big and small campaigns continued in the China theater, the Chongqing government stressed its nation's contribution in confronting the colossal Japanese ground forces and making major war expenditures for the defense of China. Indeed, during that period, Japan's China Expeditionary Army did not transfer so many troops to the war against the United States. Yet, rather than being the result of the Chongqing government's strategy, this was due to internal conditions in Japanese forces.

In conclusion, from the end of 1941 to the summer of 1945, the China theater executed no substantial influence on the development of the Japanese-American War. But on the contrary, the enactment of the Zhejiang-Jiangxi operation, the cancellation of the Gogō operation, and above all, the Ichigō operation, the vicissitudes of the Japanese-American War in the Pacific had a direct impact on the China theater.

During the Ichigō operation, through their punishing attacks, the Japanese ground forces inflicted enormous damage upon the Chinese field army, smashing most bases of the U.S. air forces in China and occupying several key strategic spots. Given the effect of the belated strategic raids on Hankow made by the U.S. air forces in China in December 1944, it was possible that the political and strategic map of China during the year from the summer of 1944 to the summer of 1945 could have been considerably different if the United States had strengthened its assistance to China, even though it would have had to postpone the operations in the Marianas and the Philippines.

By the same token, if Chiang Kai-shek had not been persuaded by Roosevelt's insistence at the Cairo Conference giving higher priority to the strategic bombing and had committed himself to the army's modernization, he might have avoided suffering such a crushing defeat. Chinese forces might have been able to hold the key spots, moving the air bases to the east while increasing air raids waged from China on the Japanese homeland, thereby enabling them to forge a large-scale counteroffensive against the China Expeditionary Army. Accordingly, the prestige of the Chongqing government, which was slipping both within and outside the country, could have been restored as the Kuomintang established control over the recovered lands. But what really happened was the destruction of the Chinese field army in eastern and southern China as well as a decline in the prestige of the Chongqing government.[59] In this sense, in the long run, the Ichigō operation had a far more serious effect on the civil war between the Kuomintang and the Communist Party after WWII than it did on the outcome of the Japanese-American War.

Nonetheless, as seen in the attack in Yunnan Province and northern Burma during the second half of 1944, the heroic defense of Henyang in the course of the Ichigō operation in the summer of 1944, and the defeat of the Japanese forces in the defense of Zhijiang, the rapid progress in the battle-effectiveness and morale of some Chinese units was remarkable. From the spring to the summer of 1945, if the China Expeditionary Army had neglected the opposition of the General Headquarters and launched an attack against Chongqing, the Japanese army, whose supply line would have been cut off by the attack of the U.S. air forces, could have been besieged and then warded off by the American-equipped Chinese ground forces, thereby potentially repeating the tragedy of Imphal on the Chinese mainland. Furthermore, if Japan had not surrendered in August 1945, the China Expeditionary Army would have been gradually driven to the east under the joint operations of the U.S. air and Chinese ground forces and thereby could have lost Canton and Hong Kong to the Chinese.

On the other hand, had the U.S. forces' landing operations on Japan proper started after the autumn of 1945, similar to the Ichigō operation, strategic debates between the United States and China on the distribution of the Allies' military power in Japan proper and the China theater might have been rekindled. Moreover, when the Japanese and American troops were fighting hard against the Japanese, the civil war between the Kuomintang and the Communists might already have broken out in the Chinese mainland. Moreover, Soviet troops could have invaded not only Manchuria but also northern China. But on 15 August, the world war on the Chinese mainland came to an end, leaving behind a big "if."

19   The Sino-Japanese War in History

HANS VAN DE VEN

Dealing conceptually with the violence that engulfed China during World War II is an extraordinarily difficult task. First of all, we face the question of when the war began and when it ended. In this volume, we have held to the idea that what we call the Sino-Japanese War began with the Marco Polo Bridge Incident of 7 July 1937. Although one might argue that in reality all-out warfare commenced only with the Battle of Shanghai on 14 August and that therefore this date should be taken as the start date of the war, a far more fundamental revision of our understanding of World War II would become necessary were we to accept the commonly held view in the People's Republic of China (PRC) that what there is called the War of Resistance against Japan began with the Japanese occupation of Manchuria in 1931.

If we were to do so, China's conflict with Japan would have to be accorded a far greater significance in the "Nanjing Decade" (1927–1937). Warlord conflict and the struggle between the Communists and the Nationalists have been the dominant themes in Western scholarship on this period. For histories of World War II more generally, East Asia would have to receive more extensive treatment. Most histories produced in Europe and the United States still concentrate on British and American fighting in Europe and the Pacific, even though the critical role of Russia in crushing Germany is now commonly acknowledged.

The collapse of Japan in 1945 might at first glance seem an obvious marker for the end of the war. Whether the precise date should be 15 August 1945, when Japan declared that it accepted the Potsdam Declaration of the Allies, with its demand for unconditional surrender, or 2 September, when the formal surrender took place on board the USS *Missouri* anchored in Tokyo Bay, is only a minor quibble, although it is worth noting that the PRC authorities have decided to use the latter for commemorations of the end of the war. But peace did not break out in much of East, Southeast, and South Asia after Japan ceased to be a combatant. The Chinese Nationalists and Communists began an intensive civil war. China was not unique: in French Indochina, British Malaya, Burma, and the Dutch East Indies, huge national movements accumulated strong military forces during World War II and went on fighting after 1945 for a variety of purposes ranging from independence to radical social, political, and cultural change. Even if in Europe the collapse of Germany brought much unrest, East, Southeast, and South Asia were not stabilized until the end of the Vietnam War and the economic takeoff, first of Taiwan, Hong Kong, Singapore, and South Korea, and then of the PRC and other Asian countries.[1] Martial law was lifted in Taiwan only 1987.

If questions can be asked about the beginning and end dates of the Sino-Japanese War, interpretations of the war are difficult also because issues other than the defeat of Japan, no matter how important, were at stake. Various groups in China held to sharply divergent ideas about the future. I have already mentioned the Communists and the Nationalists. The Nationalists themselves were an amalgam of political forces, family alliances, regional interest groups, and military forces. Some of the great warlords such as Yan Xishan and Li Zongren had their own reasons to join Chiang Kai-shek in opposing the Japanese. The frontier regions surrounding China, including Tibet, Chinese Turkestan, Manchuria, Taiwan, and Mongolia, were home to a variety of military forces, ethnic groups, political structures, and religious movements with their own hopes about the outcome of the war. To term the fighting "the Sino-Japanese War" or the "War of Resistance against Japan" simplifies the complexity of the issues in play.

Raising such issues is useful to open up opportunities for questioning established interpretations. The trope of failure runs through Western academic writing about the Sino-Japanese War, with the China theater seen as irrelevant to the outcome of the war and the Nationalists as incapable or even unwilling to mount effective resistance against the Japanese invasion. This view is problematic not in the least because the belittling of China's war effort has led to ignorance not just about the enormous suffering caused by the destruction of the period, but also about its impact on China. I first discuss this dominant Western view and the political context in which it took hold. I also sketch the understandings of the best way to conduct war and conceptualizations of the nature of modern historical change that underpinned and sustained the Western assessment of the Nationalists.

In the second and third sections of this chapter, I discuss Nationalist China's military mobilization as well as the significance of frontiers. Attention to other aspects of China's approach to the war, including its international strategy and its moral mobilization of the home front, would be required to provide a fully rounded understanding of the fact that China ended World War II on the victorious side. Nonetheless, I focus on mobilization and frontiers, first of all to demonstrate that Nationalist China was committed to fighting the Japanese. As well, China was an agrarian and poor but modernizing bureaucratic state that had to take on a modern industrialized military force. Even if the Nationalists had some forces equipped with modern armaments, most were deficient in training and lacked logistic support. Tactics dated from the First World War. Another serious deficiency, exposed for instance during the Battle of Shanghai, was lack of cooperation between divisions and armies. This, and the lack of a modern navy and substantial air force, meant that the Nationalists were never able to take the war to Japan. But that did not mean that nothing could be done.

Nationalist China opted for defensive warfare, for trading space for time, and for drawing out the Japanese forces so as to wear them down and prevent them from translating their battlefield successes into a durable victory. The Nationalists turned to historically formed practices of military mobilization and warfare to continue resistance, forged accommodations with local political and military constellations, and marshaled imaginative resources from China's cultural traditions to keep going. Rather than seeing these aspects of Nationalist China's conduct of the war as evidence of irredeemable backwardness and incompetence, I suggest that the approach was in reality firmly grounded in local realities and indigenous practices. That doesn't mean that this approach formed a panacea. Although the Nationalists were able to resist Japan with a degree of success until 1941 and the Japanese were never able to force their surrender, the limits of the Nationalists' strategy became horribly clear during the last years of the war and especially after the 1944 Ichigō offensive.

The China Theater as a Failure: Explaining the Western Consensus

By the 1970s, a consensus view had emerged in Western studies of the Sino-Japanese conflict. It held that the Nationalists had formed an incompetent, corrupt, and militarist regime that had been unable to mobilize Chinese society effectively against Japanese aggression. It had failed to make use of U.S. support to reform its armies and take the war to Japan, preferring instead to ready itself for a postwar conflict with the Chinese communists. The consensus about the Nationalists was most clearly articulated in Barbara Tuchman's 1970 *Stilwell and the American Experience in China*,[2] in which General Joseph "Vinegar" Stilwell, commander of U.S. forces in the China theater and chief of staff to Chiang Kai-shek, figured as a quintessentially American hero—plain speaking, go-getting, dedicated, patriotic, honest, modern, and rational. The Nationalists, on the other hand, were a politically debilitated "husk" who had wasted the United States' "supreme try" in China.[3]

Tuchman built on criticism of the Nationalists by U.S. journalists such as Theodore White, of Henry Luce's *Time* magazine, and Brooks Atkinson, of the *New York Times*. During the last years of the War of Resistance, the journalists had reported negatively on the Nationalists and positively about the Communists. In 1946, Theodore White and Annalee Jacoby's *Thunder out of China* became a best seller.[4] It paved the way for U.S. Secretary of State Dean Acheson's "The China White Paper" of 1949 that sought to put an end to the China issue, which had figured prominently in the U.S. presidential elections of the year before, by arguing that the Nationalists had been an incompetent and militarist regime without popular support.[5] Tuchman's book was important: The trauma of Senator Joseph McCarthy's paranoid hunt for Communists in the U.S. government still lingered, especially with the senator's victims. Cold war fears about a Communist drive for world domination had caused the United States to intervene in Vietnam and elsewhere on behalf of nasty dictatorships. Tuchman's study of the American intervention in China during the Second World War formed an argument by proxy about why the United States could end up in such a position, and held open the possibility of an alternative and benign U.S. foreign policy—under democratic leadership.

The idea that the Communists had deserved their victory because of Nationalist incompetence and corruption became entrenched afterward. Frank Dorn's *The History of the Sino-Japanese War* and academic monographs by Lloyd Eastman, Hsi-sheng Ch'i, William Wei, and Parks Coble developed Tuchman's assessment further. These scholars argued that after the Nationalists came to power during the Northern Expedition of 1926–1928, their obsession with the Communists had led them to abandon reform and revolution. In essence, the Nationalist government had been stillborn. The Nationalist period in Chinese history was cast as an irrelevant detour because the Nationalists had declined to push through economic modernization and political reform along Western, liberal lines out of an obsession with the Communist threat.

Political expediency had something to do with the emergence of the view outlined above. President Roosevelt used it in the fall of 1944 to distance himself from Chiang Kai-shek just prior to the tightly contested U.S. elections of that year. The summer of 1944 was difficult for the Allies: German resistance proved tenacious; in Burma the Indian Army became encircled at Imphal and Kohima while Stilwell's Chinese forces were stalled at Myitkyina; and Japanese resistance against U.S. amphibious landings in the Pacific proved fierce. In China, Japan's Ichigō offensive had cut through

Nationalist defenses, and the fear that China might yet be knocked out of the war gripped U.S. political and military leaders.

With the conduct of the war an important issue in the 1944 presidential election, and with his lead in the polls slipping, Roosevelt had a problem in the bad news from Asia. General George Marshall, the U.S. Army chief of staff, had wanted Roosevelt to force Chiang to place Stilwell in command of all China's forces in the hope that battlefield setbacks could be reversed. Chiang agreed to hand overall command to an American officer, but he also insisted that Stilwell, with whom he, like many others, had a stormy relationship, be recalled. Roosevelt then decided to not only agree to Stilwell's recall but also to not appoint a U.S. officer to command Nationalist China's forces. He wrote Chiang that "a full and open explanation of the reasons for General Stilwell's recall will have to be made."[6] He personally gave approval, necessary because of censorship, for the publication of articles by Brooks Atkinson in the *New York Times*. Atkinson depicted the Nationalists as a moribund and antidemocratic regime with which the United States should have nothing to do.[7] If China should fall, the blame would be put firmly in Chiang's lap.

The depiction of the Nationalists as incompetent, corrupt, and militaristic had deeper origins than mere political expediency. Contemporary assumptions about the nature of modernity, the path toward progress in non-Western societies, and the role of the West and especially the United States in the world were influential. Stilwell himself articulated many of them in his briefings to U.S. journalists such as Theodore White and embassy personnel such as John Service and John Paton Davies, as well as in his private papers.

One assumption was that offensive warfare was modern, and defensive warfare was backward. If U.S. war planners had adhered to a cautious global strategy before Pearl Harbor, Marshall had instilled highly offensive tactics in the U.S. Army during the so-called Benning Revolution (named after Fort Benning, Georgia, home of the U.S. Army's infantry school, where Marshall was commandant) of the 1930s. These tactics involved the concentration of all possible resources for a single but overwhelming assault on one strategic point. The desire to avoid the men-wasting warfare of the American Civil War and World War I and the conviction that the American public would not support a long war shaped Marshall's views. Just after Pearl Harbor, Marshall called for an invasion of Europe with forty-eight divisions in 1943 and immediate emergency operations across the Channel, believing that anything else, including the North Africa operations preferred by Churchill, were of no consequence to the main task of striking at the heartland of the enemy with maximum force. In 1942, U.S. mobilization had still only just begun, and the United States had only a few divisions available for deployment abroad, not many of them ready to face highly professional and well-trained German units.[8] Churchill rejected Marshall's plans on the grounds that they could result only in a bloodbath. Stilwell, who had assisted Marshall as he reshaped the U.S. Army at Fort Benning, frequently bemoaned the lack of the "offensive spirit" in Nationalist armies. He explained the loss of Burma in 1942 not as the result of overwhelming Japanese superiority, especially in air and sea power, or a lack of Allied preparation, coordination, and commitment, but as the result of "stupidity, fear, and the defensive attitude" of the Nationalists.[9]

Marshall himself judged China by its capacity for large-scale offensives against the Japanese. Concluding that China lacked this capacity, he kept U.S. military resources from East Asia beyond what was necessary to maintain appearances.[10] He did not want to become involved in a long campaign in China, or anywhere else on the Asian mainland, including Burma. The Japanese experience had illustrated the difficulties of fighting a ground war on the Asian continent. In the works of Dorn (who had been Stilwell's aide-de-camp), Hsi-sheng Ch'i, and F. F. Liu, and to a lesser degree in that of Lloyd Eastman, a major theme was explaining why the Nationalists had been unable to prosecute offensive warfare characteristic of modern nation-states.

Characterizations of China as not a martial culture and one mired in corruption and backwardness contributed to dismissals of the Nationalists. Frank Dorn talked about "Confucian attitudes toward the settlement of difficulties" and wrote that the Chinese were "feudal in their thinking," people who lived "in a sort of dream world of correct words and resounding phrases" and whose strategy of "defense in depth presaged defeat."[11] Stilwell referred to Chinese politics as "Byzantine" and spoke of "the suspicious, jealous Oriental mind."[12] In 1942, he lamented that the "despised people [Chinese, Russians, Greeks, and Filipinos] are doing the best work for civilization."[13] He believed that "only outside influence can do anything for China—either enemy action will smash her or some regenerative idea must be formed and put into effect at once."[14]

Finally, in the academic literature of the 1950s and after, modernization theory provided the dominant framework for the construction of arguments about the Nationalists and the significance of the Sino-Japanese War. Practitioners of area studies believed that societies were on a developmental track first pioneered by the states of Western Europe and then the United States. The track's characteristics included the creation of a strong central state that penetrated local society deeply, the construction of articulated bureaucracies capable of mobilizing it efficiently, the emergence of autonomous and rational individuals who willingly committed themselves to the nation, the rise of the nuclear family, urbanization, and the erosion of particularistic social networks.[15]

Hsi-sheng Ch'i, Lloyd Eastman, Parks Coble, and others explained

China's failure as the result of the willful suppression by the Nationalists of China's development along liberal and modernizing lines. According to Eastman, the Nationalists under Chiang Kai-shek rapidly evolved into a "one man military dictatorship" dependent upon "old style bureaucrats and the army."[16] During the war, they were "unwilling to permit the people a meaningful role in politics" and "remained an elitist regime" that "relied on force or the threat of force."[17] Factionalism, corruption, and authoritarianism prevented social, military, economic, and political reform. As a result, the Nationalists were unable to gain the loyalty of warlord troops, tax the economy efficiently, create a modern military, and institute fair conscription, so that it quickly became incapable of "sustained effective military operations."[18] Hsi-sheng Ch'i argued that the inability of the Nationalists to mount offensive warfare was the consequence of the Nationalists' abandonment of Sun Yat-sen's revolutionary agenda soon after coming to power.[19] Such arguments about the Nationalists and the War of Resistance fitted views of China, articulated for instance by Joseph Levenson and John Fairbank, as a society that was held back by Confucian habits, the patterns of rule of the dynastic past, and landlord elites.

The interpretations of the Sino-Japanese conflict outlined above have proved remarkably tenacious, and this has made it harder to have serious discussions about the Nationalists. Until recently, the weight of the field lay not with republican history, but with studies of Chinese Communism and late imperial China. From this perspective, World War II was of little consequence, as it did not have a significant impact on history; hence the paucity of studies about the Sino-Japanese War from a military point of view or analyses of its broader historical consequences.

Mobilizing an Agrarian Society
against a Modern Army

The Japanese military was far superior to China's. As Edward J. Drea's chapter 4 makes clear, in mid-1937 Japan possessed one of the best land armies in the world, and like its navy, its air forces were first-rate. Japanese capabilities in amphibious operations—one of the most complex elements of modern warfare, requiring the close coordination of naval, air, and ground forces—were outstanding. Without these operations, Japan would not have been able to amass large numbers of troops with great speed at Shanghai and take the city, or later invade Southeast Asia.

Yet Japan also had weaknesses. Its industrial base remained limited, it lacked natural resources such as oil, and its logistic capacity was underdeveloped. Shortages in small arms and artillery ammunition hampered Japanese operations at Shanghai. A British military report noted that during the 1937 Battle of Shanghai, "the fighting troops have been compelled to live on biscuits, bully beef, and tinned plums for weeks at a stretch" and that "blankets have not been carried."[20] These material shortcomings, an army culture devoted to the offensive outrance,[21] and the government's failure to construct favorable international alliances at a time when the global nature of warfare required them, hindered Japan's ability to secure a quick and decisive military victory and translate its battlefield supremacy into a durable conquest.

The Nationalists survived the Japanese onslaught in part because of nonmilitary factors. Significantly, China had been invaded by overwhelmingly superior military forces in the past and had seen long periods of disunion and internal chaos, but something that could be called China had always reemerged. China's history provided powerful imaginative resources to inspire resistance against Japan. Chiang Kai-shek himself regularly referred to the great military strategists and commanders of China's past, such as Sunzi (Sun Tzu), Qi Jiguang, and Zeng Guofan. During the war, movies appeared about the legendary General Yue Fei, whose exploits during the Southern Song dynasty against northern invaders was the stuff of local storytelling and operas about heroic resistance against foreign aggression and loyalty to the Chinese state. Chang-tai Hung has shown how urban cosmopolitan artists turned to traditional themes and formats during the war as they promoted the cause of resistance among the populations of inland China.[22] Even if some, like Wang Jingwei, favored an accommodation, Chiang Kai-shek and many others continued to have the will to fight. When Wang Jingwei departed Chongqing, he no doubt expected that many Nationalists would join him; only a few did.

In 1937, international opinion quickly turned against Japan. That disapproval had been far less the case following Japan's occupation of Manchuria and its bombing of Shanghai in 1931 and 1932. The rise of fascism in Europe, the Spanish Civil War, the growing disrepute of European imperialism, and the consolidation of Nationalist rule helped change the climate of public opinion, as did the threat that Japan posed to European colonial possessions in East and Southeast Asia. Japanese bombing campaigns played into public anxieties of the mass bombing of civil populations that had been fueled by the German bombing of towns during the Spanish Civil War, as Pablo Picasso's painting *Guernica* illustrated.[23] The horrific mistreatment of civil populations and captive Chinese soldiers by the Japanese evoked memories of German barbarity in Belgium during the First World War. If the Japanese had aimed to impress the world with their modern army and longed for a glorious war,[24] their actions in the field turned the world against them.

Geopolitical developments worked out in favor of the Nationalists. Japanese control over China was a threat to the Soviet Union and the

white empires of Great Britain, the United States, France, and the Netherlands. The Nationalists first forged an alliance with the Soviets, who
shared a long border with the Japanese in Manchuria. As Zhang Baijia
makes clear in chapter 11, the Nationalists gained an enormous amount
of Soviet aid and the assistance of its air force volunteers. Although Japan
and the Soviet Union fought a five-month border war near Nomonhan in
1939, they concluded a nonaggression treaty in April 1941, after which the
Soviets did not again involve themselves in the war against Japan until the
last days before Japan's surrender. But after Japan's Southward Offensive,
the Nationalists became one of the Allies. Even if China was only a junior
partner with little impact on Allied strategy, the alliance nonetheless was
critical. Like Britain in its war against Germany, China could not have
defeated Japan on its own. An important element of Nationalist strategy
was to make sure that at the end of the war it would be in the camp of the
victors, and in this it was successful. The Versailles Peace Conference, at
which German rights in Shandong had been assigned to Japan, formed a
cautionary example for China of the dangers of failing to secure a significant voice at the post-war peace conference.

Nonetheless, the Nationalists had to mobilize their own society. Had
they failed, the Japanese might well have been able to reduce them to insig-
nificance as earlier invaders such as the Mongols and the Manchus had
done with their adversaries. The Nationalists adopted a mixture of modern
and historical practices. They certainly wanted to fight in a modern way.
That way would be much safer, given that modern bureaucracies are better
able to control a society's military forces. Having fought hard against warlordism throughout the 1930s, they were well aware of the advantages of a
unified military controlled through a centralized bureaucracy. They were
also ideologically committed to being modern. However, the Nationalists
found that in practice they had to develop accommodations with practices
that had emerged over time and with local realities.

The Nationalists began to prepare for a large-scale conflict with Japan
after the Japanese takeover of Manchuria and the attack on Shanghai in
the early 1930s.[25] They did so while internal warfare, including combat
against the Communists, continued and tensions with the Japanese were
always high and at times spilled over into armed clashes. As Zhang Baijia
has argued, one element of their approach consisted of recruiting German military advisers, retraining armies according to German military
models, building up military industries, and constructing defensive lines
around Shanghai and the main lines of communications in the north. The
Nationalists worked hard to reconstruct a centralized bureaucracy with
clear lines of authority in the provinces along the coast and the Yangtze
River over which they were able to exercise effective control. Socially, they
instituted the New Life Movement, which was inspired by models of social

mobilization from Europe, including those of Germany as well as Britain and France, but they also drew on China's moral-philosophical heritage, appealing to it as representing China's cultural uniqueness. They adopted modern fiscal and financial institutions, including a unified national currency. In areas affected by banditry and Communism, they reinstituted the *baojia*, a traditional system of local mutual responsibility and policing to bring militia under control, eliminate banditry, take the weapons out of society, construct new social relations, and control local elites. An important aim behind the reconstitution of the *baojia* was to lay the basis for the introduction of national military service and a modern conscription system.[26] Thus, the Nationalists sought to launch modern state capacities while at the same time rehabilitating or updating traditional mechanisms in that context, all in the hope of forging a new, modern, and Chinese nation-state.

Significant resistance to the *baojia* existed. The *baojia* never worked as idealized understandings required, and the Nationalists were no doubt unable to keep abusive elements out of its structures. Nonetheless, archival reports suggest that the *baojia* contributed to the gradual imposition of order and the removal of banditry after 1932. The *baojia* became the basis on which new local security organizations, including the provincial and local Peace Preservation Forces, were built. Following the introduction of a Military Service Law in 1933, the adoption of the National Army Reorganization Plan in 1934, and the creation of Divisional Conscription Commands in 1936, the Nationalists also began to use *baojia* structures to draw recruits into new divisions, of which thirty had been activated by the beginning of the War of Resistance. The revival of the *baojia* also had symbolic and normative aspects. He Yingqin, the minister of war, thought of the *baojia* as a means to revive Chinese military prowess, which he believed had been deliberately suppressed by dynasties that had been afraid to arm the population and had therefore relied on mercenary armies.

The *baojia* was a hallowed institution, even if in the 1930s it was also given new meaning and purposes. In an essay on Chinese military law, Robin Yates notes that during periods of crisis, including the Warring States Period, the Period of Disunion, the Song Dynasty, the Ming Dynasty, and of course during the Taiping Rebellion of the mid-nineteenth century, Chinese states turned to the *baojia*.[27] It regimented society into small units made up of men who were well known to one another and who would therefore support one another in battle. Yates says that important features of the Chinese military included the emphasis on just rewards and strict punishments, disdain of heroic action or individual initiative, control of religious practices, and insistence on truthfulness. During the War of Resistance, Chiang Kai-shek stressed the same themes in his lectures at military conferences.[28] Here then, we may well have an enduring feature of

Chinese military history quite relevant to understanding Nationalist war making during World War II. This feature stands in sharp contrast to the British practice of defining martial races or tribes in its colonies—the Sikhs and the Ghurkas—and relying on them.[29]

In 1937, the Japanese quickly drove the Nationalists from the areas in which they had built up new conscription structures. These structures had, in any case, lacked the capacity to remedy battlefield losses, bring divisions up to strength, and make up for large-scale desertion. Army and division commanders, desperate to fill up their ranks, went on an unregulated recruitment binge. The result was significant social unrest, widespread avoidance, the weakening of central control, and the strengthening of the powers of divisional and army commanders. The Nationalists responded by abandoning universal military service and modern conscription, which were hated precisely because they were blind to local conditions. They began to recruit in areas well known to have made good recruitment grounds in the past and sought accommodations with some regional or warlord forces.

In January 1938, the Nationalists issued new regulations in recognition of the fact that conscription on the basis of a national military service obligation was not practicable.[30] They required armies to report the number of recruits they needed to the Ministry of Military Administration. These numbers were then allocated to recruitment areas in provinces such as Henan, Anhui, Jiangxi, Hunan, Zhejiang, Shaanxi, and Sichuan. These regions tended to enjoy agricultural surpluses, unlike coastal provinces such as Jiangsu and Guangdong that had for centuries been grain-deficit areas. They also had large but relatively poor populations, with the result that for many poor families military service was attractive. Army recruiters were to cooperate with provincial and county officials, who received financial grants and who encouraged local society to develop local mechanisms to manage recruitment and provide benefits to families with members in the army. Salary increases in the army for the rank and file also made military service more attractive. From 1937 until 1941, the Nationalists recruited annually about 2 million men, something they could, of course, not have done by force alone.[31]

Even if the Nationalists continued to support some large modern armies capable of operations far from their bases, after the fall of Wuhan, these regions nonetheless became increasingly significant as zones from which to resist the Japanese invasion. The Nationalists faced three interconnected problems. First, control over recruitment could easily slip away from the center and end up in the hands of local satraps. Second, armies could become localized and so dependent on their base areas that they would refuse to operate at any distance away from them. And, third, the agricultural economy had to be kept going. The Nationalists attempted to deal with the first problem by stationing core divisions in each area, making central grants of money and materiel, appointing local leaders to high Nationalist posts, and insisting that representatives and sometimes family members were stationed at the center. Nationalist intelligence services were deployed to keep informed about the local situation, to prevent lateral alliances, and to intervene with extreme measures, even including murder, when subversion threatened to undermine central authority too far.[32]

To ensure sufficient supplies, the Nationalists implemented a program aimed at storing enough grains for a year. Three months' worth of grains were to be kept at the front, another three months' worth in granaries located in major centers in the Nationalists' war zones, and the final six months' worth were to be kept in large cities of unoccupied China. To balance available supplies and army size, after 1938 about one-third of the army was withdrawn from the front, officially to retrain them but also to lighten the pressure on the supply system. The Nationalist grain storage system was designed to ensure that even if armies could not move very far from their bases, they nonetheless could retain a degree of mobility and were never so tied to a particular region that they would refuse to move at all.

Although the Communists would be more successful in creating base areas and generating military forces from them, as Yang Kuisong makes clear in chapter 12, they too followed a policy of having a great number of local forces tied to a local area, while others were "divorced from production" and capable of operating at a distance. The Communists were a far more disciplined party whose close attention to local economic capacity and avoidance of major operations help explain their comparative success, while the Nationalist government, hampered by a chaotic bureaucracy, lost control of its initially far larger number of guerrilla forces. The fact that most Japanese military operations were directed against the Nationalists was also a factor; the chapters by Asano Toyomi (chapter 14), Hara Takeshi (chapter 16), Zang Yunhu (chapter 15), and Wang Qisheng (chapter 17) suggest that the Ichigō campaign was probably decisive, as it drove the Nationalists from their last resource areas outside Sichuan and crushed their morale, while Communist forces streamed into areas vacated by Japanese forces as they moved south.

In the first years of the war, the Nationalists were able to maintain agricultural production. They relied on bank loans, printing of money, and direct taxes, while they also reduced salaries and cut government expenditures. These measures affected urban areas and the rich far more than the peasantry in the countryside. The Nationalists provided fertilizers, promoted new seed varieties, settled refugee populations on fallow land, managed irrigation networks, protected transport networks, and bred draft animals, some of which were inoculated against disease. Even if the effect of these measures should not be overstated and the maintenance of agricultural productivity was possible because most marketing networks remained intact, nonetheless, until 1941, agricultural production was adequate, inflation low, and average calorie intake remained at the same level as before the war.

After 1941, the situation became much more difficult. China lost its last remaining international supply line in Burma. Arms and ammunition had flowed to China over its railroad and river networks. Burma was also important for its oil and rice exports. The Japanese further closed the Chinese coast and cut domestic trade networks. They occupied Yichang in 1940, thus severing the connection between Sichuan and war zones to the east. Following the inauguration of the Wang Jingwei national government in 1941, the Japanese drove the Nationalist currency, the fabi, out of the areas they had occupied. Already severely strained Nationalist revenues plummeted further as trade collapsed and tax officials fled to the rear. After 1941, inflation skyrocketed, food panics and real food shortages led to hoarding, and, by 1944, severe famine racked Henan Province.

The Nationalists' response to the growing crisis was to reinstitute the direct taxation of the land in kind, thus transferring the financial burden of the war onto the shoulders of the countryside population. Battles for the harvest followed between the Nationalists' state, its armies, local militaries, and the population, a struggle in which the Japanese also joined. The Nationalists sought to wind down the war in China, making most military units live off the land while keeping only a few elite forces for active campaigning. Recruitment was reduced, in part because of the lack of financial resources but also because the pools of recruitable men were exhausted. Sichuan, however, was put through the wringer: after 1941, recruitment there increased by 50 percent. The situation became even worse after the Ichigō offensive led to the Japanese seizure of Henan, Hunan, Hubei, and Guangxi provinces. Toward the end of the war, the Nationalists were reduced to dragooning recruits out of the countryside. The frequently reproduced photographs of young and old men tied together by ropes and being dragged away indicate the desperate plight of the Nationalists.

Mobilization offers, I believe, a perspective on Nationalist war making that is rooted in Chinese history and also takes into account China's geography and economy. During World War II, China could not recruit its armies through a national military service system. It had neither the required bureaucracy nor the logistic systems. Nor did it have the industrial base that modern offensive warfare required. What the Nationalists could do was base their resistance in China's traditional recruitment areas and grain baskets, develop accommodations with local society, and so draw the vast numbers they needed into their armed forces. As mentioned, after 1941, and especially during the last year of the war, the limits of this approach were reached. By this time, the Nationalists, the Communists, and the Japanese all lived off the land, competing pitilessly for scarce and eventually nonexistent resources. As in the Thirty Years' War of seventeenth-century Europe, armies crisscrossed a denuded continent in increasingly desperate attempts to keep their war machines going, spreading malnutrition, disease, brutality, famine, and death where they marched.

I believe mobilization also offers a lens through which to view the Nationalists' approach to the Sino-Japanese War that helps elucidate the problems they faced and recognizes that they possessed agency and understanding, but also does not ignore their shortcomings and failures or fall back on dubious characterizations of Chinese culture. Although in the first section of this chapter I questioned the appropriateness of the Western dismissal of the Nationalist war effort, I do not conclude from this discussion of mobilization that China must be seen, and absolved from criticism, as a special case. Obviously, the Nationalist war making had its limits. Even if informed by the past, it also was not unique. As Ronald Spector's chapter 20 shows, many parallels exist between the Nationalists' conduct of the war and premodern European warfare. Also, the Nationalists recognized the potency of modern bureaucratic, governmental, social, and military structures and worked hard to construct them. But during World War II, they had to mobilize a still largely agrarian society. After they found in the first year of the war that their newly activated modern divisions were unable to withstand the Japanese, the Nationalists turned to past mobilization practices, and these enabled them to keep up the resistance and wait for events to turn in their favor.

The Uses of Frontier Regions

At the time of World War II, China's borders were not clearly delineated. As with mobilization, I draw attention to the military opportunities and challenges inherent in large frontier regions not to argue that China was unique or special: before the rise of the modern nation-state, frontier regions were significant in European warfare as well. During the Napoleonic Wars, the Duke of Wellington's armies cooperated with hard-fighting local guerrillas on the Iberian Peninsula to draw Napoleon's overstretched armies into a quagmire and so prevent Napoleon from tightening his blockade of England and consolidating his continental empire. This cooperation created the time and the space for Wellington later to move against Napoleon in a decisive way.

Both the Japanese and the Nationalists sought to develop alliances with military forces, political leaders, and populations in frontier regions. Japanese policies in Manchuria, Mongolia, Taiwan, and Tibet aimed at doing so, while the Nationalists did the same, for instance when they instituted sacrifices to Genghis Khan for the purpose of attracting Mongol support or asserted the right to verify the Dalai Lama to enhance Chinese influence in Tibet. Frontier zones were useful to attract supporters, to offload unwanted troops, and to create trouble for enemies and domestic rivals. They also were full of danger, as the arming of a particular force at a frontier could easily backfire.

In Chinese history, frontiers have always been military and symbolically important. As Mark Lewis has shown, the military of the Han Dynasty, and its society, like that of subsequent dynasties, was shaped by the reality that frontier warfare required a professional standing army capable of operating against mounted nomads far away from the core areas of the Han Empire.[33] Nicola Di Cosmo has made clear that the northern frontiers shaped definitions of China and the Other.[34] At the end of the Period of Division, the Toba Wei generated new social structures in a frontier area that made it possible for their successors to obtain the material, manpower, and political resources to reunify China. Mark Elliot demonstrates that the Manchus were able to do the same in the seventeenth century.[35] These structures were hybrid in nature, drawing on tribal practices of the frontier as well as Chinese dynastic institutions, while cosmopolitan cultural and religious attitudes allowed their leaders to forge links with elites in core Chinese areas but also in peripheries.

During the Sino-Japanese War, frontiers were important not only militarily but also politically and culturally. Japanese pan-Asian imaginings of the future political shape of Asia required the forging of new boundaries and the fostering of new identities linked to an overarching Asian one.[36] The Japanese spent considerable energy to achieve this, for instance in Manchukuo, Taiwan, Mongolia, the areas under the Wang Jingwei national government, and South and Southeast Asia. Even if few welcomed Japanese overlordship and their military brutality alienated most, anti-imperialism provided the Japanese with real opportunities for their "Asia for the Asians" stance. The appeal of popular redemptive movements asserting deep roots in traditional Asian religious ideas and practices is something that only now is becoming clear. In 1938, Japanese political strategy was to deny that the Nationalists represented China.

As for the Nationalists, they laid claim, like their republican predecessors, to the territories conquered by the Qing Dynasty in the eighteenth century. Chiang Kai-shek argued in *China's Destiny* that China was made up of various clans of one racial stock.[37] He maintained that China included Tibet, Chinese Turkestan, Mongolia, and Manchuria and asserted that all these areas were critical to China's national defense. These were outlying frontier zones, inhabited by populations with strong cultural identities. Political forces there tended to aim at independence. Regions closer to China's heartland, such as north China (Hebei and Shandong), the northwest (Shaanxi and Shanxi), and the southwest (Guangxi and Yunnan) were inner frontier areas that were culturally less distinct. The militaries that inhabited these areas could be "guest armies" seeking refuge, or local forces brought together by a competent and charismatic local leader. In contrast to leaders on the outer frontiers, they usually aimed at national power in China.

China's frontier regions differed according to geographical, social, cultural, geopolitical, and economic conditions. Peter Perdue has suggested that China had six different frontiers: the northern maritime frontier from Shanghai to Liaoning; Manchuria; the northwest frontier of Mongolia and Xinjiang or Chinese Turkestan; the Tibetan frontier along the Himalayas; the southwestern frontier of Yunnan and Guangxi bordering Burma, Thailand, Laos, and Vietnam; and, finally, the southern maritime frontier.[38] As Perdue has noted, these descriptions can be refined and subdivisions can be made, and the situation was not historically constant. Nor were all frontiers in play equally or similarly during all conflicts. Yet to keep the idea of the frontier region in mind is useful in studying the Sino-Japanese War. Chiang Kai-shek developed his general military strategy with a clear eye on frontiers.

Frontiers had a variety of military functions. One was to trap the enemy and find powerful allies. Nationalist strategy aimed at exploiting the tensions between the Soviets and the Japanese sharing a long border around Manchuria. Even though the Soviets declined to participate in the war, during the first phase of the war the Nationalists nonetheless gained significant amounts of military aid, while the Japanese, fearful of the Soviets, were hampered by the belief that they needed to conclude the fighting in China in a short time. In addition, the Soviets believed that only the Nationalists could bring enough forces to bear to contain Japan and therefore supported them and put pressure on the Communists to participate in the United Front.[39] During the Xi'an rebellion of December 1936, Chiang Kai-shek was taken prisoner by a former Manchurian warlord and the Communists.[40] Possibly no united front would have been formed without Moscow's pressure on the Communists to arrange Chiang's release; in that case the Nationalists might have preferred to avoid war with the Japanese for longer. After the Battle of Nomonhan in 1939 and the Soviet-Japanese Nonaggression Treaty, the strategic value to China of the Soviet Union disappeared. With America isolationist and Europe engulfed in war, the Japanese could concentrate on China. They pushed south, advanced deeper into China, shored up their embargo, undertook massive bombing campaigns, and fostered Wang Jingwei as an alternative to Chiang Kai-shek, all in the hope of ending meaningful opposition in China before having to face the Western powers. The plan was first to attack Southeast

Asia in late 1941 and early 1942, and redeploy the bulk of those units to
Manchuria to take on the Soviet Union.

Japan's Southward Offensive, beginning with the attack on Pearl Harbor on 7 December, gave prominence to China's southwestern frontier and
opened up new possibilities for the Nationalists to draw strong allies into
its war with Japan. In this case, the allies were Britain and the United
States. As mentioned, the Nationalists' alliance with the United States and
Britain suffered from serious problems. Britain made use of Chinese forces
to protect its own armies and recover its colonial possession in Burma,
while in 1944 the United States compelled Chinese forces in Yunnan to
enter Burma at the same time that Japanese forces pushed deep into south
China. Nonetheless, the opportunities of fighting together with Britain
and the United States in Burma and for constructing new alliances were
politically, symbolically, and militarily critical to the Nationalists. These
affiliations allowed the Nationalists to become one of the Big Four among
the Allies.

Frontier regions had more purely military functions as well. They were
buffer zones. Before 1937, north China functioned as a buffer. The armies
of Yan Xishan, Feng Yuxiang, Song Zheyuan, Fu Zuoyi, the Chinese
Communists, and Zhang Xueliang's Fengtian Army stood between the
Nationalists and the Japanese. Even if it was difficult for the Nationalists
to make these armies stand and fight in 1937, the Japanese nonetheless
were never able to pacify north China fully. Chinese Turkestan, Tibet, and
the southwest also functioned as such a buffer at different times of the war.

Frontier regions could be used to offload unwanted forces or troops
that the Nationalists could not sustain. When Ray Huang, the eminent
historian of the Ming Dynasty, went to Yunnan to serve in the Fourteenth
Division, he noted that this once lavishly equipped unit was down to half
strength.[41] A report by He Haoruo, the head of the Material Resources
Bureau, remarked that troops in Yunnan cultivated their own land and
even dug coal in their own mines.[42] At military conferences after 1942 in
the northwest, Chiang Kai-shek urged his commanders to put their men to
work to grow food for themselves and their horses as well as to run their
own business because the center could not supply them and because it was
unlikely that the area would see large-scale fighting in the near future.
Although Chiang Kai-shek feared losing control over Chinese forces stationed at Ramgarh in India or fighting in Burma, a fear that proved realistic, nonetheless it also was a way to make one of his allies responsible for
their upkeep and obtain modern armaments. Frontiers were useful to keep
the war going, distract the Japanese, and sustain military forces at little
cost to the center.

The significance of frontier regions changed as the general war situation
developed. The Nationalists' removal to Sichuan in 1938 had profound

effects. They first had to secure Sichuan and did so partly by drawing the forces of Liu Xiang, a Sichuan warlord who until then had been promoted as the Nationalists' man in Sichuan, to the battlefields of north China and Shanghai. Liu became suspicious and formed an alliance with Han Fuju, the dominant warlord of Shandong who had allowed the Japanese to pass through his areas and had thus thrown the Nationalist strategy for the defense of north China into disarray. The two conspired to withdraw Han's forces to Sichuan and block the entrance of the Nationalists into his home province. The Nationalists then executed both.[43] To deal with Liu Wenhui, another powerful Sichuan warlord, the Nationalists created, in 1934, the new province of Xikang. This move had the advantage of giving Liu Wenhui a substantial stake in the Nationalist order while keeping him away from Sichuan's core area. The creation of Xikang also reduced the size of Tibet. The Nationalists kept the Panchen Lama and his retinue in Xikang to create trouble for Liu and maintain a stake in Tibetan politics.[44] Frontier politics were exceedingly complex and involved creating and nurturing intricate balances of power.

Frontier warfare required the forging of accommodations with local power holders in frontier zones. A certain Lo Zhengming had terrorized the Manglun state on the Sino-Burmese border with a ragtag force. After local Nationalist units incorporated Lo into their structures, he regularized his revenue stream by imposing a household tax, payable in opium. If, as was probably the case, the Nationalists received a cut of Lo's opium monopoly, they also benefited because Lo declared that the Burmese government had handed Manglun to China and that the Nationalists had appointed him military and civil administrator. With Lo having secured his financial base, his military forces also became less predatory and kept themselves busy with drilling and marching.[45]

If frontiers were full of opportunities for forging new alliances, trapping the enemy, off-loading troops, developing new sources of income, and creating a buffer shielding more-central areas against the main enemy, they were also dangerous. In frontier regions, adversaries could accumulate power and resources, as Anlushan had done during the Tang Dynasty and as the Communists would do during the War of Resistance. Another difficulty was how to make forces in frontier regions stand and fight, rather than avoid battle and preserve their forces. Although Nationalist strategy in 1937 had hoped to contain the Japanese in north China, they failed, in part because the armies of Han Fuju, Song Zheyuan, and Yan Xishan did decide to preserve their own forces.

Following the beginning of the Battle of Shanghai, the Communists and the Guangxi Clique did join the war. Both deployed in north China and helped stabilize the battlefield there. In return, they received from the Nationalists substantial military and financial aid, were allocated new recruitment areas, and built up their political capital. Although their contributions were important to the war, they also imposed limits on the efforts that would be demanded. When, after a tactical victory at Taier-zhuang in April 1938 Chiang Kai-shek pushed for a counteroffensive in north China, Li Zongren, the Guangxi Clique commander in charge of the war zone there, reminded Chiang that this course of action ran counter to the operational principles that they had agreed to earlier.[46] The Communists would never concentrate in large numbers at a single location during the war.[47] During the Battle of Shanghai, the forces guarding Hangzhou Bay offered no resistance to the Japanese landings there. The Japanese could then encircle Shanghai, thus dooming the Nationalist defense of the city. During the summer of 1938, the Nationalists had put much effort into strengthening the Madang barrier near Jiujiang along the Yangtze River in order to block a Japanese joint army-navy thrust toward Wuhan. German military advisers considered the barrier capable of resisting the Japanese for at least six months. Yet a Chinese division critical to the defense of the barrier abandoned its position as soon as the Japanese approached. Its commander was later shot.[48] The Nationalists were able to turn resistance against Japan into a broadly national effort, but some allies proved less than fully committed.

One school of thought regards the decision of post-1912 Chinese governments to claim the territories that the Qing had conquered as a liability. However, frontier regions were also often useful for the defense of China. They provided strategic and tactical options, as well as difficulties, that states with clearly marked borders did not have. As with mobilization, attention to frontier regions during World War II in China provides opportunities for deepening our understanding of China's conduct of its war against Japan.

A Reassessment of the Nationalists

In this chapter, I have sought to show that it is erroneous to maintain that the Nationalists were unwilling to fight the Japanese, as the English secondary-language literature has done. Historians in the PRC no longer do so. As this volume shows, their research bears out the fact that the Nationalists were determined to resist the Japanese. I have argued that the slighting of the Nationalists as militarist, backward, feudal, and incompetent derived partly from a Western-centric interpretation of the war and, more generally, from an understanding of warfare that judged societies by their ability to generate modern industrialized offensive warfare. It also was based on an understanding of Asian, or non-Western, societies as held back on a known developmental path by traditional belief systems, the modes of rule of the past, and large landholding.

For China itself, the Sino-Japanese War was all. China would either outlast Japan or be destroyed as an independent nation or even a culture. China did prevail, partly because of fortunate geopolitical developments, but also because various sides in China did manage to mobilize Chinese society with sufficient effectiveness to prevent the Japanese from securing a durable victory. The Nationalists had important cultural, political, and military resources in the Chinese past on which they could draw. The fight was extraordinarily difficult, and by the end of the Sino-Japanese War, all parties, including the Japanese, struggled to keep even limited forces supplied and combat ready; they resorted to desperate measures just to keep going. The dismissals of the China theater in World War II are problematic in part because they glance over this reality.

I have presented accommodations with local warlords, the exploitation of historically shaped methods of military mobilization, and the use of frontier regions not as evidence of feudal backwardness but as sensible ways of pursuing a difficult war against an overwhelmingly superior enemy in a largely rural society with limited industrial resources and a weak state. This evaluation should not lead to any reification of a Chinese way of warfare, or obscurantist interpretations about Chinese guile or patience, partly because these concepts are of dubious validity, partly because past practices too could be effective only to a degree, and also because the Nationalists were simply not blindly beholden to tradition. They built up or acquired modern forces when they could, sought to exploit geopolitical opportunities, worked to strengthen the state, and were utterly committed to bringing about modernity.

This line of thinking could be pushed further. China since the Opium Wars has been described as a decaying civilization or a failed state that was unable to generate modernity and nationalism and where ultimately a revolution was necessary to wipe away the political structures and the traditions that held it back. I find this dichotomous understanding of tradition and modernity, the presumptuous belief in superior insight and the patronizing assessments of successive national leaderships, problematic. Other ways of reconstructing the past can be found. Following the Taiping Rebellion, the Qing Dynasty, like other governments around the world that had faced enormous upheaval in the middle of the nineteenth century, found a way to recover and reconstitute itself. Past political structures and social hierarchies proved durable, but also an enormous amount of change and creativity was unleashed, witnessed in China by the beginnings of industrialization, the emergence of modern harbors, the laying down of a vast railway network, the rapid expansion of international trade, the introduction of new taxation regimes, the establishment of the modern press, the emergence of new social classes, and the flowering of intellectual creativity. Subsequently, further ruptures would occur, including of course the 1911 Revolution and the Northern Expedition that brought the Nationalists to power. Such ruptures were often followed by rapid changes in social formations, leisure, dress, consumption, transport, and the economy.

The regimes of Yuan Shikai, the Beiyang warlords, and the Nationalists, rather than suppressing such developments, often fostered them. At the same time, they sought to consolidate unified bureaucratic rule while drawing new constituencies into their worlds, devising new ideological constructions about China, and advancing interpretations of Chinese identities that drew from the past as well as from modernity. In such a reconstruction of China's recent past, rupture, hybridity, change, accommodation, and globalization come to the fore as important themes, while failure, decay, backwardness, and incompetence decline.

After coming to power in a brutalizing war against vastly larger forces in 1927, the Nationalists first sought to push through their anti-imperialist, nationalist, and modernizing agendas, only to become embroiled in debilitating civil wars against warlords and the Communists in the early years of the 1930s. Following the Japanese occupation of Manchuria, they used the sense of national crisis to build new alliances, reconstitute bureaucratic rule, and through their party, state, and social organizations, draw new constituencies into their world. At the same time, they modernized the fiscal, monetary, and financial systems, built new communications networks, promoted industrialization, and fostered a new Chinese identity, which reconstituted, updated, and Westernized Chinese cultural, moral, and philosophical traditions. The growth of large urban centers, especially around coastal and river ports with their transient populations, generated dynamic social formations. Open to the new but also not dismissive of the old, as the May Fourth generation had been, these populations forged novel, locally constructed and interpreted, Chinese modernities.

From this perspective, the Sino-Japanese War gains further meaning: as yet another rupture. Cities were destroyed, marketing and information networks ruined, and state structures wrecked, including ones responsible for keeping order. China turned inland and inward. While the Nationalists' approach enabled China to sustain resistance at greater or lesser levels of intensity throughout the war, they ended the war driven from their core regions and hated in many areas across China. They still had a vast military force, but they did not have the resources to sustain it, and many parts of it had ceased to be combat effective. Following the collapse of Japan in 1945, the Nationalists were unable to reestablish their state. Instead, the Chinese Communists, driven to the inhospitable northwestern frontier before the war, were able to seize power using the bases in the countryside and the military forces that they had accumulated during the war. Under their leadership, China turned inward and inland—temporarily.

20   *The Sino-Japanese War in the Context of World History*

RONALD SPECTOR

Writing shortly after the Nanjing Massacre, a German diplomat observed, "We Germans in Nanjing, including Mr. Rabe [a German civilian living in Nanjing at the time of the massacre], all think that the war in Asia is fundamentally different from the ones with which we are familiar. It seems as if we are back in the Thirty Years War."[1] Putting aside the irony of a servant of the Nazi regime deploring the savagery of war, this comparison encompasses much that readers of this book might find appropriate. Indeed for sheer scale, length, and destructiveness the Sino-Japanese War is in a class by itself. The German-Soviet struggle on the Eastern Front is the only really comparable event, and while that appalling marathon of destruction probably resulted in more deaths, it was much shorter than the catastrophic war over China.[2] How are we to conceptualize and represent such a conflict within the larger framework of our understanding of modern war?

With the aid of hindsight, we can easily see that the older-style wars like the Thirty Years War, with their indeterminate beginnings and endings and their indiscriminate destructiveness, had never really disappeared, even from Europe. They had simply been eclipsed by the color, precision, and power of the armies and navies of the Age of Reason, the French Revolution, and the industrial age. Strangely enough, the great Swiss strategist Antoine-Henri Jomini, the foremost celebrant of scientific warfare, was also the first theorist to recognize the survival of the older forms. And what he saw, he didn't like.

Jomini had served with Napoleon's armies in Spain. There, the French had forced the Spanish king to abdicate and taken control of the government. Yet the French soon found themselves facing a national insurrection. The Spanish army took the field against the French, sometimes aided by British troops. It brought in by sea and throughout the country thousands of civilians, often women and children, and waged a relentless war of terrorism and guerrilla operations against the French. The French responded with brutal reprisals that further alienated the population, and Napoleon's generals soon found that they controlled only those areas of the country physically occupied by their troops. The savagery, cruelty, and indecisiveness of the Peninsular War made a lasting impression on Jomini, who wrote that "the spectacle of a spontaneous uprising of a nation is rarely seen; and though there be in it something grand and noble which commands our admiration, the consequences are so terrible that, for the sake of humanity we ought to hope never to see it . . . As a soldier preferring loyal and chivalrous warfare to organized assassination I acknowledge that my prejudices are in favor of the good old times . . . preferring them to the frightful epoch when priests, women and children throughout Spain plotted the murder of isolated soldiers."[3]

For most of the next century, Europe managed to avoid the ordeal of "national wars," as Jomini called them, though the experience of continued French popular resistance even after the defeat of Napoleon III's armies in the Franco-Prussian War reportedly shocked and worried General Helmut von Moltke, who believed that the "improvised armies, irregular elements and appeals to popular passion" presaged "a return to barbarism."[4] That return was delayed during the First World War, where most of the unprecedented loss of life was confined to military men, but the debut of the bomber and the submarine in that conflict suggested a future in which the distinction between soldiers and civilians as targets was likely to fade. It took the Second World War to show what the consequences might be when Jomini's "national war" was superimposed on the new weapons, technology, and total mobilization of the twentieth century. And that potential was demonstrated first in China.

What makes the Sino-Japanese War difficult to accommodate within the normal discourse of modern war is not simply that it is a kind of return to the "frightful epoch" of pre-Clausewitzian warfare but that it combines these older elements with the most destructive aspects of industrial age military operations. If this is the case, it is probably insufficient to interrogate the China war simply by finding analogies to earlier modes and constructs of warfare. To try to comprehend the totality of that war, we may find it useful to borrow the construct of Sir Michael Howard, that warfare may be understood as having four "dimensions." They are the *operational*, the *logistic*, the *social*, and the *technological*. Of course, these four aspects of war continually influence and interact with one another, and Howard's essay, written almost twenty-five years ago primarily as a critique of the U.S. and NATO's obsession with the technological aspects of nuclear war and deterrence, was never intended to provide a formal theoretical model.[5] Nevertheless, I believe that Howard's framework is especially helpful in a discussion of the Sino-Japanese War, where an understanding of the operational dimension, that is the military strategies, operations, and tactics of the two sides, is, in itself, obviously insufficient to comprehend the dynamics and outcome of the conflict.

At the operational level what is most striking to a reader of these chapters is the way in which the Japanese and Chinese leadership completely misconstrued the kind of war they were about to enter. Neither side initially expected a protracted war of attrition. As Edward J. Drea makes clear, Japanese expectations were based on the doctrine of rapid war settlement, *sokusen sokketsu*. Only such a war was acceptable to a Japanese leadership that always had to keep an apprehensive eye on the Soviet Union. Indeed, some elements in the army, like Ishiwara Kanji, preferred to avoid a conflict with China in favor of a large-scale expansion and modernization of the armed forces. Yet even those generals who favored a showdown with Chiang did not view this as a decision to begin a major war but as a way of rapidly securing their rear areas for a confrontation with the Soviets. As Edward J. Drea points out in chapter 4, past experience led these men to assume that "the Chinese would quickly collapse once the actual fighting began."

If the Japanese completely misread the determination and ability of the Chinese to resist their aggression, Chiang Kai-shek perhaps misconstrued the Western powers' interest in aiding China and, while not optimistic about Soviet intervention, thought the threat to Japan's northern flank would curtail Japanese freedom of action. One of the revealing insights into Chiang's decision making, provided by Yang Tianshi's chapter 5, is the discussion of the surprising extent to which Chiang clung to such weak reeds as the 1937 Brussels Conference, convened under the Nine-Power Treaty in 1937. Apparently Chiang sincerely believed that this ludicrous and ineffectual gathering of representatives from countries that had repeatedly been chased under the bed by the ranting and saber rattling of fascist nations in their own neighborhood was going to result in serious measures to stop Japan's advance in China. More seriously, Chiang's decision to carry out the desperate and costly defense of Nanjing was based, at least in part, on the anticipation of Soviet intervention. This expectation was not as far-fetched as hope in the Brussels Conference and was apparently encouraged by statements by the Russians. Even after Chiang learned that Soviet support was unlikely, however, he still continued to encourage his commanders to believe that international assistance was coming, in much the same way that General Douglas MacArthur would later assure his doomed troops on Bataan, Philippine Islands, that "help is on the way from the United States."[6]

On the China battlefield, an army that believed in all-out attack at any cost faced one that believed in unyielding defense. The result might well have been the kind of bloody stalemate that the European armies confronted along the Western Front in 1914. Japan's superiority in fire-power—including the availability of naval gunfire, dominance in the air, and the superior mobility provided by their naval and amphibious forces—complemented its maneuver doctrine. China's vastness, however, facili-tated operational maneuver and mobility similar to that witnessed on the Eastern Front during World War I, when large armies executed double envelopments, and large swaths of territory changed hands during offen-sives and counteroffensives. In heavy weapons and individual weapons alike, Chinese Nationalist divisions were greatly inferior, though Chinese commanders were already beginning to employ the practices of moving and fighting at night, mass-wave counterattacks, and close-in combat that would serve Communist Chinese armies well twelve years later against the United Nations' forces in Korea.

Yet the battles in China, even in 1937 and 1938, were not between sym-metrical forces. The Imperial Japanese Army was a uniformly trained, equipped, and organized force under the control of a national government and a central military headquarters. The Nationalist Chinese "army" was a shifting federation of troops loyal to Chiang Kai-shek, plus warlord armies, provincial troops, and Communist units varying considerably in their training and equipment and in their willingness to collaborate with one another. Hans van de Ven suggests in chapter 19 that China's war effort has to be understood within the context of a largely agricultural "preindustrial" society that had to mobilize against the forces of a modern industrial state. Under these circumstances Chinese mobilization had to be regionally based and had to accommodate local realities and traditional practices. The European-style—or Japanese-style—universal conscript army, centrally organized and administered, was never a realistic option for China.

Although van de Ven draws attention to the indigenous origins of the Nationalist Chinese military system of World War II, the origins were not in any sense uniquely Chinese, as he acknowledges. The expedients adopted were those of any preindustrial state system. Specifically, the Chinese military system of 1937–1945 looks a great deal like the Euro-pean military institutions and practices of the sixteenth century. Indeed, Stephen MacKinnon's description in chapter 7 of how the great regional warlord generals for a time put aside their differences after the fall of Peking, Shanghai, and Nanjing to work with Chiang in the defense of central China brings to mind the wars in the Mediterranean in the age of Phillip II and Suleiman the Magnificent, fought by ever-shifting coalitions and uncertain alliances.

The protracted, savage fighting in the vicinity of Shanghai from August through November 1937 appears to have created the conditions for a protracted war and shifting Chinese coalitions. Earlier fighting in north China witnessed warlord armies ignoring the orders of central headquarters to preserve their own forces. But at Shanghai, Chiang used his best trained, equipped, and indoctrinated troops to bloody the Japanese. Both sides paid a terrible price in the battle of attrition whose indecisive outcome made a localized settlement impossible and an all-out war probable. Chiang's most loyal forces were shattered, forcing him to rely on coalitions and political deals to continue the struggle. The Japanese home front, incensed and confused by the long casualty lists, demanded tougher military action to crush the Chinese. Neither side could quit, having invested too much in a failed military solution. In strictly military terms, Japan's well-organized reserve system and mobilization doctrine enabled the army to replace losses. The Chinese lacked both features, forcing Chiang to look elsewhere for replacements.

Chinese success in temporarily checking the Japanese in the battles around Xuzhou, and particularly in the heralded victory at Taierzhuang, brings to mind the brief moment during the sixteenth century when Don Juan of Austria was able to bring together the navies of Spain, the Papal States, and traditional bitter rivals like Venice, Genoa, Savoy, and Naples to achieve victory at Lepanto. Like Lepanto, Taierzhuang had no decisive military effect, but the political and psychological impact was far-reaching.[7] As important, the Japanese army's inability to translate a succession of other battlefield victories into a strategy to defeat the Chinese left the war open-ended and enabled China to gain in international stature, particularly during the defense of the new capital at Wuhan in the summer of 1938.

The importance, perhaps the decisiveness, of logistic factors in the Sino-Japanese war is clearly demonstrated in many of the chapters in this volume. At the highest level, both Japan and China were poorly positioned, economically and socially, to carry on a protracted war. This statement may seem obvious in the case of China, a poorly integrated, largely pre-industrial society. But it is also true of Japan. Japan's economic, industrial, and technological lead over China was considerably reduced by Tokyo's excessive strategic commitments. These included the defense and development of Manchuria, preparation for possible war with the Soviet Union, and preparation for possible war with one, perhaps both, of the world's largest naval powers.

Japan's economy was modern in many sectors, and Japanese technology and engineering were nearly as advanced as in the West. Yet development in various sectors was uneven, a situation well illustrated by the story of the first Zero fighter plane being transported from the factory on an oxcart. The absence of mobile construction teams, equipment, and techniques severely hampered the establishment of forward air bases in

China, and the lack of air bases in turn limited the potential of Japanese airpower there, as it did in the southwest Pacific in World War II.[8] The Japanese army fielded modern weapons but few trucks. In this they had little choice for, as Edward J. Drea notes in chapter 4, in one year the entire Japanese automobile industry could have produced only about 4 percent of the trucks needed to motorize the army. Lack of motorization meant that Japan's fast-moving infantry columns would sooner or later outrun their supply lines, a condition that made unlikely the conquest of all China and made the Chinese strategy of trading space for time all the more effective. At the soldier's level, the Japanese infantryman frequently suffered from shortages of food and fresh water due to chronic supply problems. As Kawano Hitoshi observes in chapter 13, for lack of automobiles and trucks soldiers "ended up carrying heavy weapons and supplies on their shoulders." Tobe Ryōichi's account of the Wuhan campaign in chapter 8 and Hara Takeshi's account of the Ichigō offensive in chapter 16 underline Japan's shoestring logistic apparatus that collapsed under the pressure of time and distance.

If Japan faced formidable logistic problems, China's situation, at least from 1938 to 1944, was always dire. China's internal economic problems—seriously aggravated by the loss of its ports, major business and industrial centers, and millions of acres of agricultural land—are well known. What is surprising is the extent to which, according to Hans van de Ven in chapter 19, China was able successfully to cope with the problems of raising armies, maintaining food production, and controlling inflation, at least until the loss of Burma in 1942 cut China's last major land link with its allies. Asano Toyomi's description of combat in northern Burma and Yunnan Province in chapter 14 demonstrates the strategic value the Japanese army attached to blocking the Burma Road in order to keep keeping Chiang isolated from overland resupply. In chapter 15, Zang Yunhu examines Chinese attempts to reopen the route, noting the tremendous constraints the inhospitable terrain imposed on well-trained and well-equipped Nationalist forces. Numbers and conventional force structures counted little in jungle-clad mountains that fragmented large unit operations, logistics, and command and control. Small isolated armed bands, willing to fight desperately, often made the difference.

China's difficulties in obtaining external support were even more formidable. During the late 1930s, when the Soviet Union was China's major source of military assistance, it took eighteen days for a truck to cover the 1,800 miles from Soviet Kazakhstan to the remote Chinese province of Xinjiang. Stalin's investment in military aid to China was enormous, and in the end, he received little more political benefit than he had reaped from his earlier period of alliance with the Kuomintang in the early 1920s.

The geographic and logistic difficulties of U.S. and British aid to China were even greater. These were inextricably entangled with issues of politics and strategy among and between the wartime Allies fighting Japan. Because of the enormous symbolic and psychological role the fate of China was to play in U.S. domestic politics a decade later, the subject of military and economic support to China, from the American point of view, far transcends the question of its impact on the war.

Questions about the wisdom, effectiveness, and motives of American aid to China, and about the judgment and motives of those involved in it, are directly connected to the larger differences between those Americans who tend to emphasize America's failures in helping China, perhaps even betrayal of China, and those who emphasize the incompetence and ineffectiveness of Chiang's regime and the enormous waste of lives and money involved in trying to meet his wartime demands. As Hans van de Ven notes, the views of the latter group are well represented in Barbara Tuchman's *Stilwell and the American Experience in China* as well as other lesser-known but more scholarly accounts.

Although the United States provided China with Lend-Lease military supplies, they amounted to less than 2 percent of all U.S Lend-Lease aid to its Allies in every year except 1945. Much other aid, requested and promised, never reached China. Arguments still rage over American policy toward China, but these seem more about personalities, particularly those of Lieutenant General Joseph Stilwell and Chiang Kai-shek, concerning control and distribution of Lend-Lease supplies and strategy to defeat the Japanese.

Yet even had Washington appointed St. Francis or Robert E. Lee to Chongqing, nothing could have changed the fundamental logistic nightmare that confronted China in 1942. Nothing could fundamentally alleviate the problem except the recapture of Burma or the opening of a port on the China coast. Neither option would become realistic until well into 1944. In the meantime, supplies from the United States had to travel 12,000 miles to India, cross India by rail, and then be transferred to American transport planes operating from primitive airfields in Assam to be flown across the Himalayas (the Hump) to China. At the Cairo Conference, when Chiang Kai-shek declared that he had a right to expect greater tonnage deliveries over the Hump, even at the expense of other theaters, General George C. Marshall, army chief of staff, angrily replied, "You are talking about your 'rights' in this matter. I thought these were *American planes* and *American* personnel and *American* material. I don't understand what you mean by saying we can and can't do thus and so."[9]

Many Americans in Chongqing and a few in Washington soon began to wonder whether this enormous undertaking was worth the cost and effort. They saw Chiang's government as kind of kleptocracy and believed his principal aim was to acquire military equipment and weapons for a postwar conflict with the Chinese Communists. Whether these conclusions were accurate or the product of personal animosity or cultural bias may be still open to debate, as van de Ven's chapter 19 suggests. But the existence of such feelings ultimately had greater impact on U.S.-China relations than the military outcome of the war.

While the logistic dimensions of the Sino-Japanese War remain the subject of controversy, the social dimensions remain something of a mystery, at least to English-speaking readers. Unlike the American armed forces, the Chinese and Japanese conducted no systematic social and psychological studies of their soldiers, issued no "morale reports" as did the British and Commonwealth commands. Very few Japanese and Chinese memoirs of the war have been translated into Western languages.

During the Second World War and for many years afterward, the social and behavioral characteristics of Japanese soldiers were believed to be so radically different from those of other soldiers that they were considered unique. Japanese were seen as fierce, fanatical warriors, completely devoted to their divine emperor. They could endure any hardship and would fight to the end rather than surrender. As befitted the citizens of a highly disciplined, group-oriented authoritarian state, most had no ideas or thoughts of their own except to die honorably.

Research such as that by Kawano Hitoshi presented in chapter 13 provides a somewhat different perspective on the Japanese soldier's motivation and morale. Like Western soldiers of World War II, the Japanese soldier's primary motivation was to survive and see his friends survive. Solidarity with his unit, confidence in and loyalty to his officers and noncommissioned officers (NCOs) were most important in determining combat motivation. Fanatical devotion to the emperor and the Japanese state were distinctly secondary, if they existed at all. Asked by Kawano whether soldiers ever shouted "Long live the emperor!" one veteran replied, "There is no such idiot who says that!" Nor were Japanese soldiers immune from the stresses of combat. Kawano points out that the Japanese army in China had a rate of psychiatric casualties lower than, but comparable to, that for American troops.

The major difference in motivation between the Japanese soldier and his Western opponents in the war lies in the Japanese soldier's feeling of affection and loyalty toward his hometown and friends and family at home. American and British soldiers were often proud of their hometowns and of course felt affection toward their families. But they also believed that "the folks at home"—the newspaper writers and the politicians—had no real concept of what they were experiencing. They also frequently suspected that the civilians back home were taking advantage of the war to feather their own nests. This resentment of those leading safe, comfortable lives on the home front could easily turn to explosive anger when civilian countrymen appeared to act in an unpatriotic fashion. In the American Civil War,

Union troops expressed the desire to kill the draft rioters in New York. Similarly, World War II GIs frequently voiced a wish that they could shoot the members of the United Mine Workers Union who had gone out on strike. If the Japanese soldier harbored any resentment toward the home front, he did not voice it publicly. On the contrary, Kawano finds that affection for the family and community and concern for their honor were the most frequently mentioned combat motivations.

The Japanese soldier was the product of a nation with a strong national-ist ideology and thoroughly militarized social and educational institutions, all of which supported the idea of military service as an obligation and an honor. The Chinese soldier was the product of a society in which soldiers were viewed as low-status, even marginal, members of society. Most Chi-nese still shared the view embodied in the old saying "Good men do not become soldiers."[10] One of the major achievements of the Communists was that they were able to transform the image of the soldier from a degraded and predatory social outcast to one of a friend and partner of the ordi-nary citizen; to convince rural Chinese that the People's Liberation Army, as it came to be called in 1946, really was the *people's army.* "We ordi-nary village folk love the Eight Route Army and so does the village head-man." In chapter 12, Yang Kuisong reports one Shanxi farmer declaring, "When kids see the Eighth Route soldiers coming, they fight to walk their horses . . . Everyone comes out to do chores for them. The Eighth Route always pays for its food and never abuses folks . . . A lot of guys from here have joined the Eighth Route Army." (See chapter 12 by Yang Kuisong.)

While in China the poorest members of society sometimes enlisted to escape destitution, the Nationalist war effort, like the Japanese, relied mainly on conscripts. About 13.5 million men were conscripted between 1937 and 1945, according to one informed estimate.[11] As Chang Jui-te points out in chapter 3, the conscription system was chaotic, poorly administered, and corrupt. Sons of rich families largely escaped military service by fleeing to the towns and cities, where they enrolled in schools and received deferments. Civil servants were also exempt from military service. Bribes and personal connections could also be used by the well-to-do to escape conscription. Or substitutes could be hired. No reliable census figures existed for many areas of China, and conscription was haphazard and unsystematic. "Conscription comes to the Chinese peasant like famine and flood, only more regularly," observed an American commander in the China theater, General Albert C. Wedemeyer. "Famine, flood, and drought compare with conscription like chicken pox with plague."[12]

Conscripts would often be dragged away from working in the fields, "leaving their villages in utter turmoil."[13] Once in the army, recruits sel-dom received an adequate diet and sometimes starved to death. Medical care and hospitals were rare. Infantrymen might or might not receive at least some formal training before being committed to combat. A serious weakness was the paucity of any trained NCOs, a marked contrast to the Japanese army. A core of experienced and competent NCOs might have made an important difference in situations where new and only partially trained troops had to be sent into battle. The lack of noncommissioned officers, even more than the weaknesses in the officer corps, probably was a critical factor in limiting the military effectiveness of the Chinese military.

Still, the character of the two armies was not the most important component in the social dimension of the Sino-Japanese War. Like many other protracted conflicts of the twentieth century, the war completely erased the Clausewitzian distinction between the army and the people, the civilian and the military. This loss was largely due to the actions of the Japanese. As James E. Sheridan concludes in his older but still important assessment of the republican period in China, most rural Chinese did not share the intense anti-imperialism and nationalism of urban political activists and intellectuals. They might have remained only passively hostile to the presence of foreign occupiers had it not been for the harsh policies of the Japanese.

Even under the best of conditions, the Japanese soldiers often behaved with casual cruelty and brutality toward the rural Chinese, and in cases where the peasants appeared to pose a threat or to be aiding the Nationalists or Communists, entire villages could be destroyed, large numbers of civilians executed, and populations displaced.[14] Chinese in the cities and towns were also subject to bombing. Chongqing, as both Edna Tow in chapter 10 and Hagiwara Mitsuru in chapter 9 observe, became one the most bombed cities of World War II. In the course of the war, the Chinese capital was subjected to 141 air raids involving 6,000 sorties, which resulted in at least 10,000 civilian deaths and destroyed much of the city. (See chapter 9 by Hagiwara Mitsuru).

But if the ordinary people of China frequently became a target, they also became a weapon. In this sense, the Chinese Communists took the lead, mobilizing, indoctrinating, and organizing all segments of the community for a People's War. As Yang Kuisong shows in chapter 12, teenagers, women, and older men, in addition to guerrilla combatants, were all enlisted to support the anti-Japanese war by acting as scouts and spies, porters, propagandists, recruiters, and counterintelligence agents. Villages provided safe houses, provided food and other supplies, and served as a recruiting base. The People's War went well beyond guerrilla warfare to organize entire societies to resist the Japanese.[15]

The technological dimension of the war in China was narrower than that for most of the other World War II combatants. China lacked the means to develop and refine technological innovation for its armed forces and largely depended on what advanced weapons and equipment it could obtain from the Soviets and Americans. The Japanese developed some of the world's most advanced weapons systems, but these were not a product of the China war, nor were they always well adapted to it. As the China war widened into the Asia-Pacific war, some of the most potent weapons were moved out of China to other theaters. Mark Peattie has described how the Japanese navy progressively withdrew its air groups from China beginning in 1939, so that by the early autumn of 1941, the number Japanese naval aircraft in China had been reduced from over 300 to less than a dozen.[16] With the navy went some of Japan's most advanced planes like the Zero fighter and the Nell long-range bomber. In this sense, it could be argued that, rather than China tying down the Japanese war machine to the benefit of the Allies, it was the Allies who tied down a part of the Japanese war machine to the benefit of China.

In the air war, the Sino-Japanese conflict indeed demonstrated the power and limitations of technological innovation in war. It was the first war in which all-metal monoplanes engaged in combat, the first war in which bombers carried out long over-water air raids, the first war in which bombers received fighter protection, and the first war in which one of the belligerents attempted to cause the collapse of the opposing government through airpower alone.[17]

Both sides used state-of-the-art aircraft. The Chinese purchased them abroad or received them from the Soviets; the Japanese developed them at home. Japanese plans to modernize and expand their army and navy air forces were incomplete when the war broke out, but they had progressed just far enough to give Japan the means to retain the upper hand in the air war much of the time. Then, in 1940, the introduction of a second wave of advanced aircraft like the Zero enabled the Japanese to gain air superiority over the Chinese. But they could never completely destroy the Chinese air force, whose planes could always be moved to out-of-range bases when necessary, again demonstrating the time and space factors that affected even the most technologically advanced weaponry.

China might be said to have fought the war with three different air forces. The first was the air force with which it entered the war, which included Curtiss Hawk fighters and other advanced foreign aircraft types. After China lost most of these aircraft in the opening campaigns of the conflict, the second was a successor air force of advanced Soviet aircraft, including the I-15 fighter, sometimes flown by Russian pilots. In chapter 11, Zhang Baijia makes clear the enormous undertaking of the Soviet effort. More than 700 Soviet air force volunteers served in China, and more than a quarter of them died. The Soviets trained over 9,000 Chinese pilots and technicians. (See chapter 11 by Zhange Baijia.) Finally, the third was a potent American-supplied air force that fought as part of an Allied air organization that, by the end of 1943, had completely overmatched the Japanese air opposition.

The Japanese war in China was also the first war in which the doctrine of airpower as a weapon of shock and intimidation was applied in practice, with repeated Japanese mass bombings of China's cities, especially Chongqing. Such attacks produced plenty of shock and terror but had little effect on the war. Even after most of Chongqing had been reduced to rubble, the Nationalist government and bureaucracy continued to function, and people carried on their daily lives, even if they had to move underground.

We might have expected that the experience of China would play an important role in resolving the long debate about airpower as a means to "break the will of the enemy," a debate that had been carried on in the Western press and military staffs since the 1920s. It did not. Journalists, military analysts, and airpower advocates all saw what they wanted to see in bombing campaigns in China and in the nearly contemporaneous Spanish Civil War. Many writers derided the Japanese bombing of Chinese cities as stupid and brutal, something of which only a fascist nation would be capable. An article in *Colliers* argued that the bombings had demonstrated only that the incompetent Nationalist government was incapable of protecting its cities.[18]

In a world military history, the Sino-Japanese War would certainly rate a substantial place in the chapter on the theory and practice of protracted war. Like Napoleon's war in Spain and the United States' twenty-first-century war in Iraq, it can be numbered among those wars that began with the swift and decisive defeat of one side's conventional armies, only to be followed by a prolonged insurgency that deprived the victors of much of the fruits of their victories. It was in the end not only protracted but also indecisive. The Japanese could never completely conquer China or end China's national resistance, while the Chinese could never drive the Japanese out of China.

Despite the extravagant hopes and plans of Washington's leaders and military strategists and despite the commitment of men, material, and expertise by the Americans in order to sustain and strengthen China's war effort, the contribution of China to the Allied victory was, at best, secondary, although this interpretation is heatedly contested by Chinese military historians. They see China as the center of gravity of the war against Japan and regard Allied efforts in southwest Asia and the Pacific as supporting operations to regain colonial possessions. After all, the war against Japan was China's struggle for national survival, a fact less appreciated by Westerners, especially Americans, who assumed that Japan's defeat was a matter of time.

True, China tied down a number of Japanese troops, though not nearly so many as Chiang Kai-shek and his American boosters, much less Mao Zedong, were wont to claim. Rapid technological advances, especially in long-range heavy bombers and aircraft carrier task forces, diminished

China's value near the end of the war as a base to launch aerial assaults against the Japanese home islands. Yet the inability of the Japanese army to withdraw substantial numbers of troops by 1944 from the theater to more critical battlefields elsewhere was due less to the danger posed by Chinese military forces than to the relentless American and Allied submarine and air attacks that destroyed Japan's merchant marine fleet, leaving Tokyo without sufficient shipping to redeploy forces or move essential raw materials and finished goods.

This dire condition in part accounted for Japan's last major wartime offensive, the Ichigō offensive, launched in 1944, that eventually spread the length of China. Beyond any military value—and apparently there was very little—Hara Takeshi in chapter 16 and Wang Qisheng in chapter 17 stress that the interrelated campaigns caused enormous dislocation, forced the Japanese to abandon previously pacified zones to sustain the momentum of their offensive, and opened the way for the Chinese Communists to move into the vacated areas. Ichigō offers yet another case of a conventional army winning all the major battles and achieving its short-term operational objectives while committing an unintentional long-term strategic blunder. In short, warfare's destructive and chaotic nature invariably carries unintended consequences.

If the strategic impact of the war in China on the United States' war against Japan was small, this outcome was not true of the political and psychological contribution that China made to the Allied cause simply by staying in the war. The Japanese claim to be fighting a war to liberate all Asians from the Western imperialists could never be given full credence as long as Asia's most populous and largest nation was ranged on the side of the Allies. With India's forces, which despised imperialism as much as, if not more than, the Chinese Nationalists and Communists, fighting alongside the Allies, it became easy to cast Japan as a country ruled by barbaric militarists. In any case, millions of Chinese did not endure the hardships and losses of seven long years of war to ensure an Allied victory but to liberate their country from the Japanese. That this liberation was achieved was, for the Chinese, the vindication of their sacrifices and the ultimate victory of their cause.

Final Considerations

In a number of ways, the Sino-Japanese War of 1937–1945 illuminated developments in the conduct of war that were either unnoticed by the West at the time or which have been considered by historians only in the more than sixty years since.

Two salient features of the conflict were barely noticed by Western

political and military leaders during World War II. While Chinese Nationalist armies in doctrine, weapons, and tactics were not appreciably dissimi-
lar from Western models of 1914–1918, Chinese Communist forces, which
grew in size and complexity from 1937 to 1945, were strikingly different.
The consistent doctrine of those forces, from rudimentary militia units at
the beginning of the war to reasonably well-equipped armies at the end
of it, was, at every stage, a radically new operational doctrine: "People's
War," Mao Zedong's formula for the social, political, and economic mobilization of the rural masses as the basis of military operations. It was and
is today China's greatest contribution to the history of warfare. It stymied
Japanese efforts to pacify the countryside (though it did not "defeat" the
Japanese army as some have claimed); it weakened the Nationalist army
in the civil war that followed, and it invigorated a spate of anticolonial
insurgencies throughout Asia in the postwar world.[19]

The conflict also demonstrated the limitations as well as the capacities
of strategic airpower that were not fully appreciated in the West at the
time. Specifically, the war made evident that, by itself, airpower could
not bring about a final decision in land warfare, nor could it, by itself,
bring about desired political results. During the first four years of the war,
Japanese airpower, though challenged, remained generally dominant. It
proved unable, however, to break the stalemate that had solidified on the
ground as early as 1938. Despite relentless Japanese aerial bombardment
of Chongqing, as Edna Tow's chapter 10 indicates, Japan was never able to
bring the Nationalist government to the bargaining table. Yet if offensive
airpower proved less than decisive in the war in China, its logistic advantages were amply demonstrated. With most of its land and coastal communications interdicted, China was kept on logistic life support by Allied
air transport from India.

For a conflict so protracted and of such scale, a salient feature of the
Sino-Japanese War of 1937–1945 was the paucity of strategic planning by
either Japan or China. In large part this lack was due to the amorphous
nature of the strategic priorities on both sides. Without serious strategic
planning, Japan stumbled into the war in 1937. From 1938 to 1944, the
Japanese priority was to pacify the countryside by any means possible—
brute force, intimidation, the use of terror, subversion, and bribery—an
objective that involved Japan's armies in a constant struggle to consolidate
its control over those territories it had conquered during the first year of
the war. For Nationalist China the minimum acceptable "victory" was
simply the survival of China as a nation and, it hoped, a place at the postwar treaty table.

This lack of planning on the part of Japan's military leadership soon
led to the folly of letting Japanese ambitions outrun the nation's military
capacity to achieve them.

The reality was that, from the beginning of the conflict, and despite its vast expenditures of blood and treasure, Japan never had enough "boots on the ground" to pacify all the territory it had conquered. Nor did Japan's strategic folly stop there, for the Japanese decision to attack the world's most potent industrial power in December of 1941 with an earlier enemy still in the field was matched only by Hitler's fatal error in launching an attack against the world's largest land power while Britain, in its rear, was undefeated and still defiant.

· · ·

Turning to the diplomatic side of the conflict, the war amply demonstrated the difficulties of waging coalition war. This difficulty was less relevant for Japan, since the global distances between itself and its European partners would have made a coordination of Axis land operations nearly impossible in any event. But divergent expectations between Nationalist China and its Anglo-American allies over material assistance and strategic priorities provoked ongoing frustrations for all sides, a situation exacerbated by the abrasive personalities of the coalition's most forceful leaders, Chiang Kai-shek and Joseph Stilwell.

To return to the comparison of Japan's war in China, 1937–1945, and Napoleon's campaign in Spain, 1808–1818, the two conflicts are strikingly similar in their protracted conduct, in their generally indecisive outcomes, and in the horrific atrocities inflicted on the civilian populations by the two occupying powers. Like any historical analogy, one can point to major dissimilarities as well: no Western ground force was present in China akin to Wellington's expeditionary army, for example. Nevertheless, the Spanish example seems the most appropriate to comprehend the dynamics at work during the Sino-Japanese War and to appreciate the validity of Jomini's concerns.

REFERENCE MATTER

Notes

All Japanese citations were published in Tokyo unless otherwise noted.

NOTES TO CHAPTER I

1. "Jiang Weiyuanzhang dui diren zhanlue zhenglue de shikuang he wo jun Kangzhan huosheng yaodao xunci" [Generalissimo Chiang Kai-shek's instructions about the real military and political strategy of the enemy and the fundamental strategy for victory of our forces during the War of Resistance] (18 August 1937), in Qin Xiaoyi, ed., *Zhonghua Minguo zhongyao shiliao* [Preliminary collection of important historical sources for the Republic of China] (Taipei: Guomindang Zhongyang Zhixing Weiyuanhui Dangshi Yanjiu Weiyuanhui, 1981–1988), vol. 2, part 1, 44–48.

2. The following paragraphs on the Japanese air campaign in China are drawn from Mark R. Peattie, *Sunburst: The Rise of Japanese Naval Air Power, 1909–1941* (Annapolis, MD: Naval Institute Press, 2001), 102–124.

3. The cease-fire agreement following the First Shanghai Incident of early 1932 allowed Japanese special naval landing force units to garrison sections of Shanghai. See chapter 5 by Yang Tianshi.

4. Wang Daoping, *Zhongguo Kangri zhanzheng shi* [History of China's War of Resistance against Japan] (Peking: Jiefangjun Chubanshe, 1995), vol. 2, 141–160. (Hereafter *History of China's War of Resistance*.) "Deguo fu Hua junshi guwen guanyu 'Ba Yisan' zhanyi cheng Deguo Lujun Zong Silingbu Baogao" [Reports about the Battle of Shanghai by German military advisers in China to the German army high command], *Minguo Dang'an*, 1998, vol. 3, 33–41, 50–56, and 1999, vol. 1, 46–55; *Ba Yisan Song Hu Kangzhan—yuan Guomindang jiangling Kangri Zhanzheng qinli ji* [The Battle of Shanghai—the personal experiences of former Nationalist commanders] (Peking: Zhongguo Wenshi Chubanshe, 1987).

5. *Nanjing baowei zhan: Yuan Guomindang jiangling Kangri qinli ji* [The defense of Nanjing: The personal experiences of the former Nationalist commanders] (Peking: Zhongguo Wenshi Chubanshe, 1987).

6. Zhang Xianwen et al., eds., *Nanjing Da Tusha shiliao ji* [Historical sources for the Nanjing Massacre], 28 vols. (Nanjing: Fenghuang Chubanshe, 2005).

7. Wang, *History of China's War of Resistance*, 158–170; Xuzhou Huzhan: Yuan Guomindang jiangling Kangri qinli ji [The Battle of Xuzhou: The personal experiences of the former Nationalist commanders] (Peking: Wenshi Chubanshe, 1985).

8. Hata Ikuhiko, *Nitchū sensō* [The Sino-Japanese War] (Kawade shobo, 1972), 287.

9. Furuya Tetsuo, *Nitchū sensō* [The Sino-Japanese War] (Iwanami shinsho, 1985), 154.

10. Hata, *Nitchū sensō*, 288. Between 20 February and 10 May, the Fifth Division lost about 6,600 men, while the Tenth Division recorded around 5,000 casualties from 14 March through 12 May. The majority of the losses occurred during the Taierzhuang operation. Chinese losses were approximately 20,000 troops. Bōeichō Bōeikenshūjo, *Senshi sōsho, Shina jihen rijugun sakusen* [Army operations during the China incident], part 2, *Shōwa 14 nen 9 gatsu made* [To September 1939] (Asagumo shimbunsha, 1976), 41; Kojima Noboru, *Nitchū sensō* (Bunshun bunko), vol. 4, 329.

11. This reflected a name change from the Central China Area Army (CCAA), activated 30 October 1937. The substantive reorganizations of 12 September 1939 created the Headquarters, Central China Expeditionary Army (CCEA) activated 12 September 1939 to control Japanese army operations in China.

12. "1938 nian Huanghe juedi ziliao yi zu" [Some historical sources for the breaking of the Yellow River dike in 1938], *Minguo Dang'an*, vol. 3 (1997).

13. Diana Lary, "Drowned Earth: The Strategic Breaching of the Yellow River Dyke, 1938," *War and History* 8, no. 2 (2001), 198–202; and Diana Lary, "A Ravaged Place: The Devastation of the Xuzhou Region, 1938," in Diana Lary and Stephen MacKinnon, eds., *Scars of War: The Impact of Warfare on Modern China* (Vancouver: University of British Columbia Press, 2001), 112 table 4.3.

14. Furuya, *Nitchū sensō*, 172; Sheldon Harris, *Factories of Death: Japanese Biological Warfare 1932–45 and the American Cover-Up* (London: Routledge, 1994).

15. Second Historical Archives of China, eds., *Kang Ri zhanzheng zhengmian zhanchang.* [The regular fronts of the War of Resistance against Japan] (Nanjing: Jiangsu Guji Chubanshe, 1987), 648–779; Stephen MacKinnon, "The Tragedy of Wuhan, 1938," *Modern Asian Studies* 30, no. 4 (1986), 932. Qin Xiaoyi, *Preliminary Collection of Important Historical Sources*, vol. 2, 180–202; *Wuhan Huizhan: Yuan Guomindang jiangling Kangri zhanzheng qinli ji* [The Battle of Wuhan: The personal experiences of the former Nationalist commanders] (Peking: Zhongguo Wenshi Chubanshe, 1989); Qin Xiaoyi, comp., *Preliminary Collection of Important Historical Sources*, vol. 2, part 2, 287–314.

16. Wang Daoping, *History of China's War of Resistance*, vol. 2, 423–429; see also primary sources reprinted in Second Historical Archives of China, eds., *The Regular Fronts of the War of Resistance against Japan*, vol. 1, 22–36.

17. Handō Kazutoshi, *Nomonhan no natsu* [Nomonhan summer] (Bungei shunjū, 1998), 12.

18. Inaba Masao and Usui Katsumi, eds., *Gendaishi Shiryō* [Documents of contemporary history], vol. 9, *Nitchū sensō* [The Sino-Japanese War], part 2 (Misuzu shobō, 1964), xxxiv.

19. "Jiang Weiyuanzhang zhishi Dongji Kongshi ge zhanqu zuozhan renwu ji kaishi riqi shouling" [Personal order by Generalissimo Chiang Kai-shek assigning combat responsibilities to each war zone and setting a start date], in Qin Xiaoyi, comp., *Preliminary Collection of Important Historical Sources*, vol. 2, part 1: 196–197; Zhang Xianwen et al., *History of China's War of Resistance*, 643–659.

20. Eleventh Army staff, *Shōwa jūyonnen toki sakusen sakusen keika no gaiyō* [An overview of the 1939 winter season operation and the course of operations],

5 March 1940, *Gendaishi shiryō* [Contemporary historical documents], vol. 9, part 2, 440.

21. Huang Meizhen and Zhang Yun, *Wang Jingwei: Guomin Zhengfu chengli* [The establishment of the Wang Jingwei national government] (Shanghai: Shanghai Renmin Chubanshe, 1984).

22. But sometimes it ended up dependent on Chinese opportunists and careerists who amassed great power but whose brutality alienated local populations and so undermined Japan's purpose. See Brian Martin, "Shield of Collaboration: The Wang Jingwei Regime's Security Service, 1939–45," *Intelligence and National Security* 16, no. 4 (2001), 89–148.

23. Fujiwara Akira, *Nitchū zenmen sensō* [Full-scale Sino-Japanese War], vol. 5, *Shōwa no rekishi* [A history of the Shōwa reign] (Shogakkan, 1982), 288–289.

24. Fujiwara Akira, *Taiheiyō sensōron* [A theory of the Pacific War] (Aoki shoten, 1982), 124–125.

25. Lyman P. Van Slyke, "The Battle of the Hundred Regiments: Problems of Coordination and Control during the Sino-Japanese War," *Modern Asian Studies* 30, no. 4 (October 1996), 979–1005. Zhang Xianwen et al., *History of China's War of Resistance*, 731–750.

26. Mainichi shimbunsha, eds., *Ichiokunin no Showashi* [One hundred million people's Shōwa history] vol. 6, *Nitchū sensō* [The Sino-Japanese War] (December 1979), part 4, 81; Guofang Daxue [National Defense University], ed., *Zhanshi jianbian* [Brief combat history] (Peking: Jiefangjun Chubanshe, 1983), 283–384; Wang Daoping et al., *History of China's War of Resistance*, vol. 3, 53–115.

27. Wang Daoping et al., *History of China's War of Resistance*, vol. 3, 171–174.

28. Zhang Xianwen et al., *History of China's War of Resistance*, 815–835; Qin Xiaoyi, comp., *Preliminary Collection of Important Historical Sources*, vol. 2, part 2, 523–551.

29. Usui Katsumi, *Nitchū sensō* (Chuoko shinsho, 1967), 129.

30. Rikusen gakkai, eds., *Kindai sensōshi gaisetsu, shiryō hen* [An overview of modern war history—documents collection] (Kudansha, 1984), 99.

31. Northern Burma had also continued a formal relation of allegiance to China even after the British had colonized the country.

32. Wang Daoping et al., *History of China's War of Resistance*, vol. 3, 186–191; Qin Xiaoyi, *Preliminary Collection of Historical Sources*, vol. 2, part 2, 555–592.

33. Usui, *Nitchū sensō*, 144–146.

34. Ibid., 163.

35. Theodore White, *Thunder Out of China* (New York: William Sloane, 1946), 166–178.

36. Second Historical Archives, *Regular Fronts*, vol. 2, 1440–1502.

37. IGHQ had ordered the transfer of the Second Division from Burma to Saigon because of continuing defeats in the Pacific and southern Burma.

38. Usui, *Nitchū sensō*, 177–178; Qin Xiaoyi, *Preliminary Collection of Important Historical Sources*, vol. 2, part 2, 695–709.

39. Kuroha Kiyotaka, *Nitchū jugonen sensō* [The fifteen-year Sino-Japanese War] (Kyoikusha, 1979), vol. 3, 266.

40. Hsi-sheng Ch'i, "The Military Dimension, 1942–1945," in James C. Hsiung and Steven I. Levine, eds., *China's Bitter Victory: The War with Japan 1937–1945* (Armonk, NY: M. E. Sharpe, 1992), 180 table 3.

NOTES TO CHAPTER 2

1. The organization of this chapter has been drawn in part from Marius Jansen, *Japan and China: From War to Peace, 1894–1972* (Chicago: Rand McNally, 1975). Critically, my understanding of the political and military events in China discussed in the latter half of the chapter has been shaped by my reading of Parks Coble's superb study *Facing Japan: Chinese Politics and Japanese Imperialism, 1931 1937* (Cambridge, MA: Council on East Asian Studies, Harvard University, 1991).

2. This and the next three paragraphs are derived from the perspective offered by Hans van de Ven in his introduction to Hans van de Ven, *Warfare in Chinese History* (Leiden: Brill, 2000), 25–26.

3. This formula for Japan's strategic security—the control of concentric and outward radiating circles of national interest—was first worked out by Japan's soldier-statesman Yamagata Aritomo in the 1880s. Seemingly logical at the time it was conceived, Yamagata's dictum contained a fatal flaw: the inability to give finite limits to Japan's security requirements and, eventually, to Japan's imperial ambitions. See Marius B. Jansen, "Modernization and Foreign Policy in Meiji Japan," in Robert Ward, ed., *Political Development in Modern Japan* (Princeton, NJ: Princeton University Press, 1968), 182; and Mark R. Peattie, "The Japanese Colonial Empire, 1895–1945," in Peter Duus, ed., *The Cambridge History of Japan*, vol. 6, *The Twentieth Century* (Cambridge: Cambridge University Press, 1988), 218–222.

4. Foreign perspectives on the Sino-Japanese War at the turn of the century have recently been given detailed study by S. C. M. Paine in *The Sino-Japanese War of 1894–1895: Perceptions, Power, and Primacy* (Cambridge: Cambridge University Press, 2003).

5. For a detailed discussion of these military forces see Yoshihiro Hatano, "The New Armies," in Mary C. Wright, ed., *China in Revolution: The First Phase, 1900–1913* (New Haven, CT: Yale University Press, 1968), 365–382.

6. See Ralph L. Powell, *The Rise of Chinese Military Power, 1895–1912* (Princeton, NJ: Princeton University Press, 1955), 144–146.

7. Stephen R. MacKinnon, *Power and Politics in Late Imperial China: Yuan Shi-kai in Beijing and Tianjin, 1901–1908* (Los Angeles: University of California Press, 1980), 97–99.

8. The classic work on Sun's relations with the Japanese is Marius Jansen, *The Japanese and Sun Yat-sen* (Cambridge, MA: Harvard University Press, 1954).

9. See Alvin Coox, *Nomonhan: Japan against Russia, 1939* (Stanford, CA: Stanford University Press, 1985), vol. 1, 11–12.

10. The demands and the response by Yuan Shikai are discussed in Jerome Ch'en, *Yuan Shih-kai (1895–1916)* (Stanford, CA: Stanford University Press, 1961), 152–158.

11. Kwanha Yim, "Yuan Shi-kai and the Japanese," *Journal of Asian Studies* 25, no. 1 (November 1964), 63–75.

12. See Jansen, *The Japanese and Sun Yat-sen*, 213–222; and Alfred A. Altman and Harold Z. Schiffrin, "Sun Yat-sen and the Japanese: 1914–16," *Modern Asian Studies* 6, no. 4 (1972), 385–400.

13. Altman and Schiffrin, "Sun Yat-sen and the Japanese," 385.

14. Jansen, *Japan and China*, 206.

15. The best English-language explanation of the Japanese army command system in general and the right of supreme command in particular is still to be found in Yale C. Maxon, *Control of Japanese Foreign Policy: A Study in Civil-Military Rivalry, 1930–1945* (Westport, CT: Greenwood Press, 1973), 24–26.

16. Each Imperial Defense Policy consisted of three parts: a broad declaration of Japan's strategic objectives; a statement of the force structure required to achieve those objectives; and an operational statement outlining where and how those forces were to be used.

17. For a different, navy view of Japan's essential defense posture, see David C. Evans and Mark R. Peattie, *Kaigun: Strategy, Tactics, and Technology in the Imperial Japanese Navy, 1887–1941* (Annapolis, MD: Naval Institute Press, 1997), 149–150.

18. For a pathology of Japanese army bureaucracy see Kitaoka Shin'ichi's "The Army as a Bureaucracy: Japanese Militarism Revisited," *Journal of Military History*, Special Issue, 57 (October 1993), 67–86. The factionalism in the Japanese army in the 1920s is expertly analyzed in Leonard Humphreys, *The Way of the Heavenly Sword: The Japanese Army in the 1920s* (Stanford, CA: Stanford University Press, 1995). Discussions of Japanese army factionalism in the 1930s can be found in James Crowley, "Japanese Army Factionalism in the Early 1930's," *Journal of Asian Studies* 2, no. 3 (May 1962), 309–326; and Seki Hiroharu, "The Manchurian Incident, 1931," in James W. Morley, ed., *Japan Erupts: The London Conference and the Manchurian Incident, 1928–1932* (New York: Columbia University Press, 1984), 145–147.

19. A concise and expert overview of the Kwantung Army and its turbulent history can be found in Albert Coox's "The Kwantung Army Dimension," in Peter Duus, Ramon Myers, and Mark Peattie, eds., *The Japanese Informal Empire in China, 1895–1937* (Princeton, NJ: Princeton University Press, 1989), 395–428. Coox provides a more detailed discussion of its origins in his "The Genesis of the Kwantung Army, 1905–1929," which is the first chapter of volume 1 of his magesterial *Nomonhan*, 1–29.

20. There is no comprehensive history of the China Garrison Army in English or Japanese, though there is a rather generalized and anecdotal account by Yoshino Naoya, *Tenshingun shireibu* [Tianjin army headquarters], *1901–1937* (Kokusho Kankōkai, 1989).

21. North China is defined here as comprising the provinces of Hebei, Shandong, Shanxi, Suiyan, and Chahar.

22. See Lincoln Li, *The Japanese Army in North China, 1937–1941: Problems of Political and Economic Control* (New York and London: Oxford University Press, 1975), 15 n. 3; and Shimada Toshihiko, "Designs on North China," in James William Morley, ed., *The China Quagmire: Japan's Expansion on the Asian Continent, 1933–1941* (New York: Columbia University Press, 1983), 105–106.

23. See Mark R. Peattie, "Japanese Treaty Port Settlements in China, 1895–

1937," in Duus, Myers, and Peattie, *The Japanese Informal Empire in China*, 198–200.

24. Maxon, *Control of Japanese Foreign Policy*, 24–25.

25. Admittedly, when looked at from the perspective of the priorities of the high command in Tokyo, the military's policy in China can be viewed as more coherent and consistent than I have assessed it in these pages. For an authoritative treatment of the subject by a distinguished Japanese scholar, see Kitaoka Shin'ichi, *Nihon rikugun to tairiku seisaku, 1906–1918* [The Japanese army and Japan's continental policy, 1906–1918] (Tokyo daigaku shuppankai, 1978).

26. Akira Iriye, "The Failure of Economic Expansionism: 1918–1931," in Bernard Silberman and H. D. Harootunian, eds., *Japan in Crisis: Essays on Taishō Democracy* (Princeton, NJ: Princeton University Press, 1974), 246.

27. Barbara Brooks, "China Experts in the Gaimushō, 1895–1937," in Duus, Myers, and Peattie, *The Japanese Informal Empire in China*, 388–393.

28. Hisashi Takakhashi, "A Case Study: Japanese Intelligence Estimates of China, 1931–1945," in Lt. Col. Walter T. Hitchcock, ed., *The Intelligence Revolution: Proceedings of the Thirteenth Military History Symposium* (Colorado Springs, CO: U.S. Air Force Academy, 1988), 203–207.

29. Donald Jordan argues that the Kwantung Army's intelligence on the fragmented nature of the Chinese political scene in the late summer of 1931 was critical to the planning for the Japanese conquest of Manchuria, 1931–1932. Donald A. Jordan, "The Place of Chinese Disunity in Japanese Army Strategy during 1931," *China Quarterly* 109 (March 1987), 42–63.

30. My understanding of China specialists in the army is shaped by Ed Drea's comments in chapter 4 in this volume and by my reading of Kitaoka Shin'ichi, "China Experts in the Army," in *Japan's Informal Empire in China*, 331–369. Kitaoka admits that it is difficult to provide a precise or comprehensive definition of a Japanese army "China expert" by any objective measure and for this reason identifies as "China experts" those officers with extensive service in China.

31. The army's Special Service organs (*tokumu kikan*) were intelligence units operating under the direction of the General Staff and undertaking intelligence gathering, political agitation, economic subversion, and other clandestine operations in China.

32. These views are exemplified by the writings of General Ugaki Kazushige (1868–1951). While not a "China expert," Ugaki had made a number of inspection trips to China in the first two decades of the twentieth century and had given a good deal of thought to Japan's relations with that country. Masaru Ikei, "Ugaki Kazushige's Views of China and his China Policy," in Akira Iriye, ed., *The Chinese and the Japanese: Essays in Political and Cultural Interactions* (Princeton, NJ: Princeton University Press, 1980), 199–219.

33. Mark R. Peattie, *Ishiwara Kanji and Japan's Confrontation with the West* (Princeton, NJ: Princeton University Press, 1975), 288–289.

34. I am conscious of the problems in the use of the term *warlord* (in the subhead) in Chinese history, difficulties made clear by Hans van de Ven in his discussions of the term. Like Professor van de Ven, I have decided to employ it for the sake of convenience and for the lack of a single better word, and I rely on Professor van de Ven's more elegant and knowledgeable reasons for doing so. See Hans

van de Ven, *War and Nationalism in China, 1925–1945* (London and New York: Routledge Curzon, 2003), 72.

35. Jansen, *The Japanese and Sun Yat-sen*, 174–212.

36. Jansen, *Japan and China*, 221.

37. Ibid., 222.

38. Arthur Waldron, *From War to Nationalism: China's Turning Point, 1924–1925* (Cambridge and New York: Cambridge University Press, 1995), 266.

39. For perspectives on "informal empire" see Duus, Myers, and Peattie, *The Japanese Informal Empire in China.*

40. Waldron, *From War to Nationalism*, 207.

41. Ibid., 204–205.

42. Ibid., 207.

43. Ibid.

44. The most authoritative summary of the founding of the Whampoa Academy and the creation of the National Revolutionary Army is to be found in van de Ven, *War and Nationalism in China*, 79–88.

45. Jansen, *Japan and China*, 296.

46. For a discussion of the background to the formation of the National Revolutionary Army, Chiang Kai-shek's military reforms, and the domestic and international context in which they took place, see van de Ven, *War and Nationalism in China*, 183–188.

47. See, for example, Donald Jordan, *The Northern Expedition: China's National Revolution of 1926–1928* (Honolulu: University of Hawaii Press, 1976).

48. These points have been made by van de Ven in his chapter "Culture and Violence during the Northern Expedition (1926–28)" in his *War and Nationalism in China*, 94–130.

49. Feng's place in the warlord conflicts of the period is detailed in James E. Sheridan, *Chinese Warlord: The Career of Feng Yu-hsiang* (Stanford, CA: Stanford University Press, 1966).

50. See Donald G. Gillin, *Warlord: Yen Hsi-shan in Shansi Province, 1911–1949* (Princeton, NJ: Princeton University Press, 1967).

51. Ian Nish, *Japanese Foreign Policy in the Interwar Period* (Westport, CT: Praeger, 2002), 65–66.

52. The Jinan "Incident" and the Japanese military expeditions to the Shandong Peninsula in 1928 are given expert treatment by Akira Iriye in his *After Imperialism: The Search for a New Order in the Far East, 1931–1941* (Cambridge, MA: Harvard University Press, 1965), 146–147, 192–205, and 248–251.

53. For the plot to assassinate Zhang Zuolin, see Coox, *Nomonhan*, vol. 1, 14–16.

54. The most complete discussion of Ishiwara and his ideas can be found in Peattie, *Ishiwara Kanji.*

55. The execution of the Ishiwara plan is told in Peattie, *Ishiwara Kanji*, 87–139; and by Seki Hiroharu, "The Manchurian Incident, 1931," in James William Morley, ed., *Japan Erupts: The London Naval Conference and the Manchurian Incident, 1928–1932* (New York: Columbia University Press, 1984), 139–240.

56. Herbert P. Bix, *Hirohito and the Making of Modern Japan* (New York: HarperCollins, 2000), 250–251; The most complete account of the Shanghai con-

flict of 1932 is to be found in Donald Jordan, *China's Trial by Fire: The Shanghai War of 1932* (Ann Arbor: University of Michigan Press, 2001).

57. Jansen, *Japan and China*, 383–384. See also "The Manchurian Incident in Retrospect," which is chapter 5 of Coox, *Nomonhan*, vol. 1, 55–62.

58. For a discussion of the Japanese involvement in the Shanhaiguan crisis, see Shimada, "Designs in North China," 13–15.

59. Coble, *Facing Japan*, 90–102. The Kwantung Army's Jehol campaign is discussed in Shimada, "Designs on North China," 18–27.

60. Coble, *Facing Japan*, 90–92

61. Ibid., 106–111.

62. So argues Coble, ibid., 113.

63. The statement, couched in informal remarks made to Japanese reporters by Amō Eiji, head of the ministry's Information Division, raised a storm of protest in the West and China but was really only a more sharply worded assertion of a general policy that Japan had been pursuing for some years in China.

64. According to Parks Coble, the abject terms of the He-Umezu agreement were potentially so damaging to public support for the Nanjing regime that Chiang Kai-shek initially denied that the agreement really existed. Coble, *Facing Japan*, 205.

65. Fostered by Japan's field armies, two "autonomous" client regimes had by now emerged in north China: the East Hebei Anticommunist Council and the Hebei-Chahar Political Council.

66. Coble, *Facing Japan*, 303–309; and Shimada, "Designs on North China," 161–174.

67. The Japanese military's promotion of invasive economic schemes are set forth in Takafusa Nakamura, "Japan's Economic Thrust in North China, 1933–1938: Formation of the North China Development Company," in Akira Iriye, ed., *The Chinese and the Japanese*, 220–253.

68. Masatake Okumiya, "Lessons of an Undeclared War," Naval Institute *Proceedings* 93 (December 1972), 30.

69. Shimada, "Designs on North China," 180–195.

70. It is highly ironic that Ishiwara Kanji, the quondam plotter of the conquest of Manchuria, whose intransigent defiance of the Tokyo high command made it impossible to rein in the runaway Kwantung Army in 1931, was now chief of the Operations Division of the General Staff, traveling in north China but unable to stop the reckless operation by his former Kwantung Army colleagues. Peattie, *Ishiwara Kanji*, 277–279.

71. The finest work on this abortive mutiny is Ben-ami Shillony, *Revolt in Japan: The Young Officers and the February 26, 1936, Incident* (Princeton, NJ: Princeton University Press, 1973).

72. This point was made many years ago by James Crowley in his *Japan's Quest for Autonomy: National Security and Foreign Policy, 1930–1938* (Princeton, NJ: Princeton University Press, 1966).

73. Peattie, *Ishiwara Kanji*, 273–286.

74. Lieutenant Colonel Takahashi Tan of the China Section on the General Staff is said to have boasted that "as soon as the first trainload of Japanese troops passes through Shanhaikuan the Chinese will throw in the sponge." Quoted in

Bōeichō Bōeikenshūjo, *Dai Hon'ei Rikugun-bu* [General headquarters, army division], vol. 1, 430.

75. Ibid., 285; and Shimada, "Designs on North China," 226–227.

76. Peattie, *Ishiwara Kanji*, 285–286.

NOTES TO CHAPTER 3

This article is an abridged and revised version of a chapter published in Huang Zijin, ed., *Jiang Zhongzheng yu jindai zhongri guanxi* [Chiang Kai-shek and Modern Sino-Japanese Relations] (Taipei: Daoxiang Publishing Co., 2006), 219–256. The author wishes to express his thanks to the publisher for permission to translate this article into English.

1. Jiang Yongjing, "Cong Lugouqiao shibian dao Shanghai cheshou: Ju Xu Yongchang riji de ziliao" [From the Marco Polo Bridge Incident to the retreat in Shanghai: Documents from the Diary of Xu Yongchang], *Jindai Zhongguo*, vol. 99 (February 1994), 137.

2. Jia Tingshi, Ma Tiangang, Chen Sanjing, and Chen Cungong, *Li Zongren xiansheng fangtan jilu* [Records of interviews with Mr. Li Zongren] (Taipei: Institute of Modern History, Academia Sinica, 1989), 98–99; Tang Degang, *Li Zongren huiyilu* [Memoir of Li Zongren] (Hong Kong: Nanyue Press, 1986), 451.

3. Tang, *Li Zongren huiyilu*, 451–452.

4. Li Yunhan, *Lugouqiao shībian* [The Marco Polo Bridge Incident] (Taipei: Dongda Book Company, 1987), 407–408.

5. Ibid., 408. Long Yun also went to Nanjing after the conference. This was the first time that Long Yun had been to the capital in his ten years of governance in Yunnan. See Yang Weizhen, *Cong hezuo dao juelie: Lun Long Yun yu zhongyang de guanxi (1927–1949)* [From cooperation to rupture: The relations between Long Yun and the Nationalist Party central committee (1927–1949)] (Taipei: Guoshiguan [Academia Historica], 2000), 154–155; Ishijima Noriyuki, *Unnan to kindai Chūgoku: "Shuhen" no shiten kara* [Yunnan and modern China: From perspective of the periphery] (Aoki Shoten, 2004).

6. Jia et al., *Li Zongren xiansheng fangtan jilu*, 98–99.

7. Deng Hanxiang, "Liu Xiang yu Jiang Jieshi de gouxindoujiao" [The infighting between Liu Xiang and Chiang Kai-shek], *Wenshi ziliao xuanji* [Selections of historical records], issue 5, 1960, 70.

8. Cao Juren, *Jiang Baili pingzhuan* [Critical biography of Jiang Baili] (Hong Kong: Sanyu Books and Stationeries, 1963), 65.

9. Jiang Fangzhen, *Guofang lun* [Discussion of national defense] (Taipei: Zhonghua bookstore, 1962).

10. Yang Tianshi, "Lugouqiao Shibian qian Jiang Jieshi de dui shi moulue" [Chiang Kai-shek's strategy toward Japan before the Sino-Japanese War], *Jindaishi yanjiu*, no. 2, 2001, 5–6.

11. Xue Guangqian, ed., *Banian Kangri Zhangzheng zhong zhi Guomin Zhengfu (1937–1945)* [The Nationalist government in the eight years of the Sino-Japanese War (1937–1945)] (Taipei: Commercial Press, 1978), 24.

12. Liu Weikai, *Guonan qijian yingbian tucun wenti zhi yanjiu: Cong jiuyiba dao qiqi* [Research on managing contingency and striving for survival during the

national calamity: From the Mukden Incident to the Marco Polo Bridge Incident]
(Taipei: Guoshiguan, 1995), 222.

13. Second Historical Archive of China, "Deguo zongguwen Fakenhaosen
guanyu Zhongguo kangri zhanbei zhi liangfen yijian shu" [Two proposals of the
chief German consultant Falkenhausen concerning China's military preparation to
counter Japanese aggression], *Minguo dang'an*, no. 2, 1991, 25–27.

14. Ibid., 27.

15. Zhang Xianwen et al., eds., *Zhongguo kangri zhanzheng shi (1931–1945)*
[History of China's war against the Japanese aggression (1931–1945)] (Nanjing:
Nanjing University Press, 2001), 200.

16. Ma Zhendu, *Cansheng: Kangri zhanzheng zhengmian zhanchang daxieyi*
[Tragic and heroic victory: Front battlefield during the Sino-Japanese War] (Guilin: Guangxi Normal University Press, 1993), 51–52.

17. Chiang Kai-shek, "Diyu wairu yu fuxing Zhonghua" [Resist foreign aggression and revive China], part 2, in Qin Xiaoyi, ed., *Xian Zongtong Jianggong sixiang yanlun zongji* [General collection of the thoughts and speeches of
the late president Chiang Kai-shek] (Taipei: Guomindang Dangshihui 1984), vol.
12, 325–326.

18. Chiang Kai-shek, "Kangzhan jiantao yu bisheng yaojue" [Self-criticism of
the Sino-Japanese War and essential secret of success], in *Zongtong Jianggong
sixiang yanlun zongji*, 15, 45–46.

19. Shi Jian, "Kangri zhanzheng shiqī Zhongri liangguo lujun zhi bijiao [A comparison between the Chinese army and Japanese army during the Sino-Japanese
War], *Dangan shiliao yu yanjiu*, no. 1, 1997, 70–71.

20. Liu Fenghan (F. F. Liu), "Lun Kangri Zhanzheng qian riren dui Zhongguo
junshi zhi diaocha" [About Japan's military investigation of China before the Sino-
Japanese War], *Zhongyang Yanjiuyuan Jindaishi Yanjiusuo Jikan*, vol. 17 (1988).

21. Huang Runsheng, Peng Guangkai, and Yu Xianglin, "Kangzhan qianqi
Guojun paobing zhi biange ji dui zuozhan zhi yingxiang" [Nationalist artillery's
prewar evolution and its impact on combat] (paper presented at the academic
conference War and Military Revolution in the Twentieth Century, 3 November
2004), 21.

22. Long Shengwu, *Long Shengwu xiansheng fangtan jilu* [Record of Mr. Long
Shengwu's reminiscences], ed. Zhang Pengyuan (Taipei: Institute of Modern History,
1989), 111–112. For the Yunnan troops' equipment before the war, see Yang Wei-
zhen, *Cong hezuo dao juelie: Lun Long Yun yu zhongyang de guanxi (1927–1949)*
[From cooperation to rupture: The relations between Long Yun and the Nationalist
Party central committee (1927–1949)] (Taipei: Guoshiguan, 2000), 158–161.

23. Shi Jian, 65–66.

24. Ger Teitler and Kurt W. Radtke, eds., *A Dutch Spy in China: Reports on
the First Phase of the Sino-Japanese War, 1937–1939* (Leiden: Brill, 1999), 61.

25. Tao Peijing, "Kangzhan qian Guomindang tongxin budui jiqi jiaoyu
jigou qingkuang" [The Nationalist signal troops and their educational institutions before the Sino-Japanese War], in *Wenshi ziliao cungao xuanbian: Junshi
jigou* [Selections of remaining historical records: Military organizations] (Peking:
Zhongguo wenshi chuban she, 2002), part 2, 631.

26. Zhang Xianwen, ed., "Minguo dang'an yu Minguo shi xueshu yantaohui

lunwenji" [Proceedings of the academic conference of the archives of the Republic of China and history of the Republic of China] (Peking, 1989), 521.

27. Junshi weiyuanhui di sanshijiu ci huibao [Report of the thirty-ninth convention of the Nationalist military committee], in Shao-kang Chu, "On Chiang Kai-shek's Position on Resisting Japan: An Analysis of 'Domestic Stability Takes Precedence over Resisting Foreign Invasion' Policy, 1928–1936" (unpublished doctoral dissertation, University of British Columbia, 1999), 129.

28. General He Yingqin's chronicle compilation committee, *He Yingqin jiangjun jiuwu jishi changbian* [Preliminary chronicle of General He Yingqin when he is ninety-five years old] (Taipei: Liming Wenhua Press, 1984), part 1, 570.

29. Hu Jingru, *Dengyu Dongshi* [Fireside recollection] (Taipei: Longwen Press, 1994), 43–44.

30. He Yingqin, *Junzheng shiwu nian*, 143.

31. Wen Xianrui, "Guomindang jundui jingli qiantan" [Prelimintary discussion of the Nationalist military management], *Shehong wenshi ziliao*, vol. 4, 22.

32. He Zhilin, *Chen Cheng xiansheng huiyilu: Kangri Zhanzheng* [Chen Cheng memoir: The Sino-Japanese War] (Taipei: Guoshiguan, 2004), part 1, 65.

33. Chiang Kai-shek, "Daibing yaoling" [Essentials of commanding troops], in *Zongtong Jianggong sixiang yanlun zongji*, vol. 12, 325–326.

34. According to prewar estimates, the Nationalist troops needed 8,000 medical doctors, yet in 1936, the Nationalist troops had only 4,000 medical doctors. Documents after the Sino-Japanese War broke out in 1937 revealed that various Nationalist troops had 28,000 medical personnel, among which were only 2,000 qualified medical doctors and others who had received only some medical training. In contrast, during the World War II, the U.S. Army had 45,000 medical doctors. See F. F. Liu, *A Military History of Modern China, 1924–1949* (Princeton, NJ: Princeton University Press, 1956), 139–140.

35. General He Yingqin's chronicle compilation committee, *He Yingqin jiangjun jiuwu jishi changbian*, part 1, 570.

36. Teitler and Radtke, *A Dutch Spy in China*, 147.

37. Hu Jingru, *Dengyu Dongshi*, 153.

38. Chen Qianping, "Shilun Kangzhan qian Guomindang Zhengfu de guofang jianshe" [Preliminary investigation of the national defense construction of the Nationalist government before the Sino-Japanese War], *Nanjing University Academic Journal*, no. 1, 1987, 27.

39. Huang Zhenqiu, *Nanjing fangkong jingyan* [Experience of air defense in Nanjing] (Guiyang: Air Defense School, 1939), 113; Hu Chunhui and Lin Quan, *Yin Yifu xiansheng fangwen jilu* [Records of interviews with Mr. Yin Yifu] (Taipei: Modern China Press, 1992), 61–62; Jia et al., *Li Zongren xiansheng fangtan jilu*, 140–141; Li Junshan, *Wei zhenglue xun: Lun Kangzhan chuqi Jing Hu diqu zuozhan* [Sacrifice for the public: Combat in the Nanjing and Shanghai regions at the initial stage of the Sino-Japanese War] (Taipei: National Taiwan University Publishing Committee, 1992), 105–108.

40. Zhang Li, "Jindai guoren de kaifa xibei guan" [Views of developing northwest China in modern Chinese history], *Zhongyang yanjiuyuan jindaishi yanjiusuo jikan* [Collected papers of the Institute of Modern History at the Academia Sinica], vol. 18, June 1989, 177.

41. Yang Tianshi, "Lugouqiao shibian qian Jiang Jieshi de dui shi molue" [Chiang Kai-shek's strategy toward Japan before the Sino-Japanese War], *Jindaishi yanjiu*, no. 2, 2001.

42. Lü Shiqiang, "Kangzhan qian Jiang Zhongzheng xiansheng dui Sichuan jidi de jianshe" [Chiang Kai-shek's development of the Sichuan base before the Sino-Japanese War], in Compilation committee of the academic conference on Chiang Kai-shek and Modern China, comps., *Jiang Zhongzheng xiansheng yu xiandai Zhongguo xueshu taolun ji* [Collections of discussion papers on Chiang Kai-shek and modern China] (Taipei: Modern China Press, 1986), vol. 3, 263.

43. He Yingqin, *Junzheng shiwu nian*, 73–74.

44. Li Zhaoliang, "Wo suo zhidao de Guomindang bingyi qingkuang" [The Nationalist military recruitment as I know it], in *Wenshi ziliao cungao xuanbian: Junshi jigou*, part 2, 1.

45. Zhou Jiantao, "Wo suo zhidao de Zhejiang, Sichuan Guomindang bingyi qingkuang" [The Nationalist military recruitment in Zhejiang and Sichuan as I know it], in *Wenshi ziliao cungao xuanbian: Junshi jigou*, part 2, 26.

46. Li Zhaoliang, "Wo suo zhidao de Guomindang bingyi qingkuang" [The Nationalist military recruitment as I know it], in *Wenshi ziliao cungao xuanbian: Junshi jigou*, part 2, 2.

47. Diana Lary, *Region and Nation: The Kwangsi Clique in Chinese Politics, 1925–1937* (Cambridge: Cambridge University Press, 1974), 169.

48. Zhu Hongyuan, "1930 niandai Guangxi de dongyuan yu chongjian" [The mobilization and reconstruction in Guangxi in the 1930s], *Zhongyang yanjiuyuan jindaishi yanjiusuo jikan* [Collected papers of the Institute of Modern History at the Academia Sinica], vol. 17, December 1988, 336–337; Eugene William Levich, *The Kwangsi Way in Kuomintang China, 1931–1939* (Armonk, NY: M. E. Sharpe, 1993), 23–24.

49. Ge Mingda, "Guomin junxue ji Fuxingshe" [National military training and the Society of Rejuvenation], in *Wenshi ziliao cungao xuanbian: Junshi jigou*, part 2, 79.

50. Xiao Zuolin, "Fuxingshe shulue" [Brief account of the Society of Rejuvenation], in Pang Jingtang et al., *Jiangjia tianxia Chenjia dang* [The Chiang Kai-shek family's country and the Chen family's Nationalist Party] (Hong Kong: Zhongyuan Chubanshe, 1989), 172; Frederic Wakeman Jr., *Spymaster: Dai Li and the Chinese Secret Service* (Berkeley: University of California Press, 2003), 120–121.

51. Chen Jinjin, *Kangzhan qian jiaoyu zhengce zhi yanjiu* [Research on the educational policy before the Sino-Japanese War] (Taipei: Modern China Press, 1997), 211.

52. Deng Yuanzhong, *Sanmin zhuyi lixingsheng shi* [History of the Society of Earnest Practice of the Three People's Principles of Sun Yat-sen] (Taipei: Shijian Chubanshe, 1984).

53. Li Xiangqi, "Huiyi guomin junxun" [Recollection of national military training], in *Wenshi ziliao cungao xuanbian: Junshi jigou*, part 2, 76.

54. He Yingqin, *He Shangjiang Kangzhan qijian junshi baogao* [Military reports of General He Yingqin during the Sino-Japanese War] (Nanjing: Guofangbu, 1948), 146.

55. Army Officer Academy Committee of Academy History Compilation, *Lunjun junguan xuexiao xiaoshi* [History of the Army Officer Academy], 4.

56. Hsi-sheng Ch'i, *Nationalist China at War: Military Defeats and Political Collapse, 1937–45* (Ann Arbor: University of Michigan Press, 1982), 60. For German military advisers' influence on the Nationalist troops' education and training, see Donald S. Sutton, "German Advice and Residual Warlordism in the Nanking Decade: Influences on Nationalist Military Training and Strategy," *China Quarterly* 191 (September 1982), 389–397.

57. In 1938, the Ministry of Military Training was reorganized into the Ministry of Military Drilling of the Military Committee. Its nature did not change. Deputy chief of staff and Guangxi clique military officer Bai Chongxi served as the minister of this ministry concurrently. See Lan Xiangshan, "Bao Chongxi zai Junxunbu" [Bai Chongxi at the Ministry of Military Drilling], in *Wenshi ziliao cungao xuanbian: Junshi jigou.*

58. Nationalist military officer Guan Linzheng was good at utilizing education to support the war. In 1947 he became the president of the Army Officer Academy. After he assumed his post, he found that many courses used old books written before World War I. See Guan Linzheng, "Benxiao yinian lai zhi huigu" [Reflection on one year of our school], in Guan Linzheng, *Xiaozhang Guan xuehua ji* [Collections of academy president Guan Linzheng's instructive speeches] (Chengdu: Army Officer Academy, 1948), 176–177.

59. Military Committee Inspection Commission, *Lu hai kong jun jiaoyue shoubu* [Handbook of inspections of the army, navy, and air force] (n.p., n.d.).

60. It is noteworthy that after the war broke out, educational heads of various military schools were transferred to general headquarters or headquarters of war areas to serve as senior aides and commanders. Excellent instructive officers also served in the army. The successors in the schools did not have qualifications as good as their predecessors. Moreover, schools passed through many places. Many facilities were lost. As inflation was high, life was difficult. The educational level also declined. See Wan Yaohuang, *Wan Yaohuang jiangjun riji* [Diary of general Wan Yaohuang] (Taipei: Hubei Wenxianshe, 1978), part 2, 245–246.

61. Second Historical Archive of China, "Zhengjun jiangjun zhuanti baogao" [Special report of regrouping troops and founding troops] (1946), *Minguo dang'an*, no. 2, 1994, 54.

62. Compilation group of Chinese military history, comp., *Zhongguo junshi shi* [Chinese military history] (Peking: People's Liberation Army's Press, 1983), vol. 1, 274.

63. Bai Chongxi, "Bai zhuren weiyuan xunci" [Instructive speech of chief committee member Bai Chongxi], part 2, in Military Committee Inspection Commission, *Lu hai kong jun jiaoyue shoubu* [Handbook of inspections of the army, navy and air force] (n.p., n.d.), 61; Jia Tingshi, Ma Tiangang, Chen Sanjing, and Chen Cungong, *Li Zongren xiansheng fangtan jilu*, 535–536.

64. Chen Cheng, "Jinhou budui xunlian zhi yaoling" [Essentials of military training from now on], in Chen Cheng, *Dierqi Kangzhan guanyu zhengxun gongzuo zhi zhishi* [Instructions concerning political instruction during the second stage of the Sino-Japanese War] (Chongqing: Nationalist government military committee political ministry), 1939.

65. Chiang Kai-shek, "Junguan xunlian tuan xunlian zhi mudi yu shoufa" [Goals and measures of the training of military officer training camp], in *Zongtong Jianggong sixiang yanlun zongji*, vol. 22, 83; Chiang Kai-shek, "Junshi xunlian fangzhen yu yaozhi" [Guidelines and essentials of military training], in ibid., vol. 12, 391–392.

66. Fan Chengyuan, "Lun xiandai junshi jiaoyu yingyou zhi gaizao" [About the necessary reform of the current military education], *Xiandai junshi*, vol. 2, no. 7 (July 1947), 15.

67. Wan Yaohuang, *Wan Yaohuang jiangjun riji*, part 2, 294.

68. Liu, *A Military History of Modern China, 1924–1949*, 150–151.

69. "Guojun zuozhan jingyan jieyao" [Summaries of battle experiences of the Nationalist army], in Military Committee Ministry of Military Command, *Kangzhan cankao congshu* [Reference book series of the Sino-Japanese War] (Chongqing, 1940), bound vol., part 1, 126.

70. Chiang Kai-shek, "Canmouzhang huiyi xunci" [Instructive speech at the staff conference], part 2, in *Zongtong Jianggong sixiang yanlun zongji*, vol. 15, 308.

71. Second Historical Archive of China, "Deguo junshi guwen Fuocaier guanyu zhengdun Zhongguo jundui zhi Jiang Jieshi chengwen liangjian" [German military adviser Georg Wetzell's two proposals to Chiang Kai-shek concerning reforming Chinese troops], *Minguo dang'an*, no. 4, 1988, 39.

72. Chiang Kai-shek, "Kangzhan jiantao yu bisheng yaojue" [Self-criticism of the Sino-Japanese War and secret of success], *Zongtong Jianggong sixiang yanlun zongji*, vol. 14, 72–73.

73. Tang, *Li Zongren huiyilu*, 539. For strengths and weaknesses of Japanese military officers, see Alvin D. Coox, "The Effectiveness of the Japanese Military Establishment in the Second World War," in Allan R. Millett and Williamson Murray, eds., *Military Effectiveness*, vol. 3, *The Second World War* (Boston: Unwin Hyman, 1988), 36–38.

74. Liu Fuxiang, "Xiaoweiyuanzhang Chen Cheng" [Little Chairman Chen Cheng], in Wang Weili, ed., *Jiang Jieshi de wenchen he wujiang* [Chiang Kai-shek's officials and officers] (Zhengzhou: Henan People's Press, 1989), 239.

75. Ministry of Defense History and Politics Compilation and Translation Bureau, *Huangpu junxiao xiaoshi jianshi jianbian* [Brief history of the Whampoa Military Academy] (Taipei, 1986), 180.

76. F. F. Liu, *A Military History of Modern China, 1924–1949*, 149.

77. Zhou Zhirou, *Ruhe jianli xiandai junshi jiaoyu zhidu* [How to establish a modern military education system] (Taipei: Shijian Xueshe, 1951), 18.

78. Chen Ruian, "Kangri Zhanzheng zhong de Chen Mingren jiangjun" [General Chen Mingren in the Sino-Japanese War], *Hunan wenshi ziliao* [Hunan historical records], vol. 28, December 1987, 130; Qiu Zhongyue, *Yuanzheng* [Long-distance march] (Taipei: Baoxin Cultural Enterprise, 1988), 74. In some units, it was even a tradition that if the company commander was promoted from a soldier, the platoon commander of the first platoon must be a graduate from a military academy to facilitate daily education and training. See Xu Zhen, *The Story of Ah-Mao's Joining the Army* (Taipei: Fuji Culture Press, 1987), 152.

79. "Report: Statement on Commissioned Personnel Strength and Classifica-

tion as to Training, January 28, 1936," in U.S. War Department, *U.S. Military Intelligence Reports: China, 1911–1941*, Reel V, 524. For the psychological distance between military academy graduates and military officers promoted from the ranks, see Xu Zhen, *The Story of Ah-Mao's Joining the Army*, 130.

80. Feng Yuxiang, *Jiang Feng shujian* [Correspondence between Chiang Kai-shek and Feng Yuxiang] (Shanghai: Chinese Culture Trust Press, 1946), 123; Xu Zhen, *The Story of Ah-Mao's Joining the Army*, 1531.

81. Liu, *A Military History of Modern China*, 149.

82. Tao Menghe, "Yige jundui bingshi de diaocha" [A survey of soldiers in one force], *Shehui kexue zazhi*, vol. 1, no. 2 (June 1930), 115.

83. Feng Yuxiang, "Feng Yuxiang zhi Weiyuanzhang zhihai dian" [Feng Yuxiang's telegram to Chiang Kai-shek], in Feng Yuxiang, *Jiang Feng shujian* [Correspondence between Chiang Kai-shek and Feng Yuxiang] (Shanghai: Chinese Culture Trust Press, 1946), 70.

84. Liu Zhi, "Jianjun de jiben tiaojian" [Basic conditions of establishing troops], *Jianjun daobao*, vol. 1, no. 2 (August 1944), 6.

85. Cao Juren, Shu Zongqiao, eds., *Zhongguo Kangzhan huashi* [Pictorial history of China's war of resistance against the Japanese aggression] (Shanghai: United Pictorial Newspaper Press, 1947), 120.

86. According to the survey of 946 soldiers in one Xianshi unit conducted by Tao Menghe in 1929, 73 percent of soldiers reported that they came from poor families, 24 percent reported that they came from families that could make ends meet, and 3 percent reported that they came from well-off families. See Tao Menghe, "Yige jundui bingshi de diaocha" [A survey of soldiers in one force], *Shehui kexue zazhi*, vol. 1, no. 2 (June 1930), 115.

87. Tan Jiyu, *Rongma suoyi* [Trivial recollections of military life] (n.p., n.d.), 7. Hu Jingru, *Dengyu duoshi*, 48.

88. Tao Menghe, "Yige jundui bingshi de diaocha," *Shehui kexue zazhi*, vol. 1, no. 2 (June 1930), 99. According to the estimate of Ta-chung Liu and Kung-chia Yeh, in 1933, 79.1 percent of the national working population (from seven years old to sixty-four years old) was in the agricultural sector; 74.9 percent of male working population was in the agricultural sector. See Ta-chung Liu and Kung-chia Yeh, *The Economy of the Chinese Mainland: National Income and Economic Development, 1933–1959* (Princeton, NJ: Princeton University Press, 1965), 182.

89. Bai Chongxi, *Xiandai lunjun jiaoyu zhi qushi* [Trends of modern army military education] (n.p., 1945), 107.

90. U.S. War Department, *U.S. Military Intelligence Reports: China, 1911–1941*, No. 8231, 1 March 1932.

91. Ibid., Reel V, 30 April 1928.

92. Xin Damo, "Deguo waijiao dang'an zhong zhi Zhong De guanxi" [Chinese-German relations reflected in the German diplomatic archives], *Zhuanji wenxue*, vol. 41, no. 6.

93. Second Historical Archive of the Republic of China, "Zhengjun jianjun zhuanti baogao" [Special report of regrouping and establishing units] (1946), *Minguo dang'an*, no. 2 (1994), 55.

94. Xu Naili, "Kangzhan shiqi Guojun bingyuan de buchong yu suzhi de bianhua" [Replacement of Nationalist enlisted personnel and change in Nationalist

military quality], *Kangri zhanzheng yanjiu* [Research on the Sino-Japanese War], no. 3, 1992, 53. For evaluations of the combat effectiveness of various Nationalist units before the Sino-Japanese War, see Morimatsu Toshio et al., "Bōeichō Bōeikenshūjo Senshishitsu" [Military History Department, Defense Research Institute, Japanese Defense Ministry], *Shina jihen Rikugun sakusen* [Japanese army's combat during the China Incident] (Asagumo Shinbunsha, 1975), 104–105. See also Liu Fenghan, *Lun Kangri Zhanzheng qian riren dui Zhongguo junshi zhi diaocha*, 368–383; Evans Fordyce Carlson, *The Chinese Army: Its Organization and Military Efficiency* (New York: Institute of Pacific Relations, 1940), chapter 6.

95. Xu Naili, "Kangzhan shiqi Guojun bingyuan de buchong yu suzhi de bianhua" [Replacement of Nationalist enlisted personnel and change in Nationalist military quality], *Kangri zhanzheng yanjiu*, no. 3 (1992), 12–13.

96. General He Yingqin's chronicle compilation committee, *He Yingqin jiangjun jiuwu jishi changbian* part 1, 563.

97. Chiang Kai-shek, *Zongtong Jianggong dashi changbian chugao* [Preliminary draft of the journal of President Chiang Kai-shek) (Taipei: Zhongguo Guomindang zhongyang weiyuanhui dangshi weiyuanhui, 1978), vol. 4, part 1, 265.

98. Hsi-sheng Ch'i, *Nationalist China at War*, 16–17.

99. In 1939, the Nationalist government's expenditures accounted for only 9 percent of the GNP in that year. See Chang Kai-ngau, *The Inflationary Spiral: The Experience in China, 1939–1950* (New York and London: MIT Press and John Wiley, 1958), 145–150.

100. Chiang Kai-shek, "Guofu qian Yu yu Kangzhan qiantu" [Nationalist government's move to Chongqing and prospects for the Sino-Japanese War], in *Zongtong Jianggong sixiang yanlun zongji*, vol. 14, Speech 654.

101. Bruce A. Elleman, *Modern Chinese Warfare, 1795–1989* (London: Routledge, 2001), 185.

NOTES TO CHAPTER 4

1. Kojima Noboru, *Tennō* [The emperor] (Bungei shūnjū, 1974), vol. 3, 196–197.

2. Rikugun daigaku, "Kita Shina sakusen shiyō," Shōwa 12/7/8–13/12/30, 1 of 3, April 10, 1943 [Important historical points of north China operations, 8 July 1937–30 December 1938], Bōeichō Bōei kenshūjo, senshibu shiryōkan, Tokyo, Japan. Hereafter cited as JDA (Japan Defense Archives).

3. Hata Ikuhikō, "Rokōkyō jihen no saikentō" [Reappraising the Marco Polo Bridge Incident], *Seiji keizai shigaku* 333 (March 1944), 4.

4. Shimada Toshihikō, "Designs on North China, 1933–1937," trans. by James B. Crowley, in James William Morley, ed., *Japan's Road to the Pacific War: The China Quagmire: Japan's Expansion on the Asian Continent 1933–1941* (New York: Columbia University Press, 1983), 11–230; Parks Coble, *Facing Japan: Chinese Politics and Japanese Imperialism, 1931–1937* (Cambridge, MA: Harvard University Press, 1991); Youli Sun, *China and the Origins of the Pacific War, 1931–1941* (New York: St. Martin's Press, 1993); and the more narrowly focused work of Marjorie Dryburgh, *North China and Japanese Expansionism 1933–1937* (Richmond, Surrey, UK: Curzon Press, 2000).

5. Hata Ikuhikō, *Rokōkyō jiken no kenkyū* [An inquiry into the Marco Polo Bridge Incident] (Tokyo daigaku shūppansha, 1996), 9.

6. Bōeichō Bōei kenshūjō senshibu, eds., *Senshi sōsho, 8, Daihon'ei rikugunbu (1) Shōwa jūgonen gogatsu made* [Official military history, vol. 8: Imperial General Headquarters, army division, vol. 1, to May 1940] (Asagumo shimbunsha, 1967), 398. Hereafter DRB (1).

7. Itagaki Seishirō, "Kantōgun no ninmu no motozuku taigai shomondai ni kansuru gun no iken" [The opinion of the army regarding external problems relating to the mission of the Kwantung Army] 28 March 1936, in Gaimushō, ed., *Nihon gaikō nenpō narabini shūyō bunsho* [Japan foreign affairs chronology and important documents] (Hara shobō, 1965), part 2, 333.

8. Sun, *China and the Origins*, 54.

9. Usui Katsumi, *Nitchū sensō* [The Sino-Japanese War], rev. ed. (Chūkō shinsho, 2000), 58; Hata, *Rokōkyō*, 9.

10. Cited in Ôsugi Kazuo, *Nitchū jūgonen sensō* [The fifteen-year Sino-Japanese War] (Chūkō shinsho, 1996), 16.

11. Hata Ikuhikō, *Nitchū sensōshi* [A history of the Sino-Japanese War], rev. ed. (Kawade shobō, 1972), 135, 137 n. 6; Ōsugi, *Nitchū jūgonen sensō*, 243; Hata, *Rokōkyō*, 9; "Tai Sō, tai-ka senryaku ni kansuru Kantōgun no iken gushin" [Reporting the Kwantung army's opinion concerning Soviet and China strategy], 9 June 1937, in Hata, *Nitchū sensōshi*, documentary appendix, no. 22, 351.

12. Nomura Minoru, *Taiheiyō sensō to Nihon gunbu* [The Pacific war and Japan's military] (Yamakawa shūppansha, 1983), 251, 268.

13. Ibid., 280 n. 9, 267.

14. Shimanuki Takeji, "Nichi-Rō sensō igo ni okeru kokubō hōshin shoyō heiryoku, yōhei kōryō no hensen" [Changes to national defense policy, matters of force structure, and operational employment of troops after the Russo-Japanese War], part 1, *Gunjishi gaku* 8, no. 4 (March 1973), 13.

15. DRB (1), 319.

16. Ibid., 329.

17. Bōeichō Bōei kenshūjō senshibu, eds., *Senshi sōsho, 86, Shina jihen rikugun sakusen (1) Shōwa jūsannen ichigatsu made* [Official military history: Army operations during the China incident, vol. 1, to January 1938] (Asagumo shimbunsha, 1982), 100. Hereafter SJRS (1).

18. DRB (1), 370; Yasui Sankichi, *Rokōkyō jiken* [The Marco Polo Bridge Incident] (Kenbun shūppan, 1993), 118. Also see DRB (1), 322–323.

19. SJRS (1), 101–102; DRB (1), 369–370.

20. DRB (1), 403–404, 407.

21. SJRS (1), 64; Sanbō honbu dai 1 ka [First section, army general staff], "Jōbun an" [Report to the throne: draft], 21 May 1936, "Rikugunshō mitsu dai nikki" [Army ministry confidential great record], vol. 1, JDA.

22. SJRS (1), 103.

23. Sanbō honbu dai 2 ka, "Sensō keikaku" [War plans] (1st draft), August 1936, in Nihon kokusai seiji gakkai, eds., *Taiheiyō sensō e no michi*, 8, bekkan, shiryōhen [The road to the Pacific war: Documentary appendix] (Asahi shimbunsha, 1963), vol. 8, 227, 230. Hereafter TSM (8).

24. DRB (1), 412–413; Hata, *Rokōkyō*, 47; Shimanuki Takeji, "Dai 1 ji sekai daisen igo no kokubō hōshin, shoyō heiryoku, yōhei kōryō no hensen" [Changes to national defense policy, matters of force structure, and operational employment of troops after the First World War], *Gunjishi gaku* 9, no. 1 (June 1973), 74.

25. Hata, *Rokōkyō*, 47, 48.

26. Nagai Kazuo, "Nihon rikugun no kahoku senryō toji heikaku ni tsuite" [Concerning the Japanese army's administrative plan for the occupation of north China], *Jinbun gakuhō* 64 (March 1989), 110.

27. Shina chūtongun shireibu [Headquarters China Garrison Army], "Shōwa 11 nendō kita Shina senryōchi tōchi keikakusho" [1936 administrative plan for the occupation of North China], 15 September 1936, Microfilm Reproductions of Selected Archives of the Japanese Army, Navy, and other Government Agencies, 1868–1945, T 784, Reel 109, Frame 18802, Library of Congress.

28. Shina chūtongun shireibu, "Kita Shina senryōchi," f 18804; Nagai, "Nihon rikugun," 111.

29. Cited in SJRS (1), 91; DRB (1), 418–419.

30. DRB (1), 414.

31. Kageyama Kōichirō, "Shina jihen to Nihon kaigun" [The China incident and the Japanese navy], 96RO-7H, 1966, 55, JDA. The phrase appears in Teikokugun no yōhei kōryō [Operational principles for imperial military forces].

32. DRB (1), 413.

33. Maebara Toru, "Nihon rikugun no 'kōbō' ni kakawaru riron to kyōgi" [The effects of theory and doctrine on the Japanese army's "offense and defense"], *Kenkyū shiryō* 86RO-5H, mimeo., 1986, 147, JDA.

34. Leonard A. Humphreys, *The Way of the Heavenly Sword: The Japanese Army in the 1920s* (Stanford, CA: Stanford University Press, 1995), viii; Maebara, "Nihon rikugun," 201, 257.

35. Ōe Shinobu, *Shōwa no rekishi* [A history of the reign of the Shōwa emperor] vol. 3, *Tennō no guntai* [The emperor's army] (Shōgakkan, 1982), 218.

36. Maebara, "Nihon rikugun," 204–205.

37. Humphreys, 106; Maebara, "Nihon rikugun," 215–216.

38. Maebara, "Nihon rikugun," 208.

39. Rikugunshō [Army ministry], "Sentō kōryō" [Combat principles], 6 February 1929 (Ikeda shoten, repr. 1977), 12, 65, 69, 128; Maebara, "Nihon rikugun," 220, 226.

40. Kyōiku sōkanbu [Inspector general of military education], "Hohei sōten sōan hensan riyūsho" [Reasons for revisions to draft infantry manual], 1928, 9, JDA.

41. Bōeichō Bōei kenshūjō senshibu, eds., *Senshi sōsho*, 27, Kantōgun (1) [Official military history, vol. 27, The Kwantung Army, part 1] (Asagumo shimbunsha, 1969), 28.

42. Kyōiku sōkanbu, "Hohei sōten" [Infantry manual], 25 January 1928, 2–3; Kyōiku sōkanbu, "Hohei sōten sōan" [Draft infantry manual], May 1937, 2–3.

43. Kyōiku sōkanbu, "Hohei sōten sōan hensan riyūsho" [Reasons for revisions to draft infantry manual], 21 January 1937, 61, JDA. For a recent analysis of lessons of World War I and the revision of the infantry manual, see Endō Yoshinobu,

Kindai Nihon guntai kyōikushi kenkyū [A study of the history of military education in the modern Japanese army] (Aoki shoten, 1994), 165–177.

44. Hohei sentōhō no sui-i gaikenhyō [Overview chart of the transition of infantry tactics], n.d., mimeo., JDA.

45. Maebara, "Nihon rikugun," 278.

46. Rikugun gakkai senshibukai, comp., *Kindai sensōshi gaisetsu, Shiryō hen* [Overview of modern war history: Documents section] (Rikugun gakkai senshibukai, 1984), 39.

47. Ôe, *Tennō*, 72.

48. Momose Takase and Itō Takashi, eds., *Jiten Shōwa senzenki no Nihon: seidō to jittai* [Dictionary of prewar Shōwa Japan: system and practice] (Furukawa kōbunkan, 1990), 271–272. Category A conscripts were taller than 5 foot 1 inch (155 cm) and in the best physical condition. B 1 and B 2 were similar in height but the next level down from A. Ohama Tetsuya and Ozawa Ikurō, eds., *Teikoku rikukaigun jiten* [Dictionary of the imperial army and navy] (Dōseisha, 1984), 38; *Kindai sensōshi gaisetsu*, 35. Only a few thousand conscripts served in the navy, which depended on volunteers to fill the ranks of its smaller, more selective service.

49. Kawano Hitoshi, *Gyokusai no guntai, seikan no guntai* [An army that fought to the death, an army that returned alive] (Kōdansha, 2001), 28–29; *Kindai sensōshi gaisetsu*, 35.

50. I am indebted to Tachikawa Kyōichi and Hara Takeshi of the National Institute of Defense Studies, Military History Department, for this information.

51. Maebara, "Nihon rikugun," 215.

52. Fujiwara Akira, *Uejinishita eiyūtachi* [Starving heroes] (Aoki shoten, 2001), 186–187; Edward J. Drea, "In the Army Barracks of Imperial Japan," *Armed Forces and Society* 15, no. 3 (1989). Humphreys, *Heavenly Sword*, 80, 171; Yoshida Yutaka, "Nihon no guntai" [The Japanese military], in Ohama Tetsuya et al., eds., *Iwanami kōza: Nihon tsūshi*, dai 17 kan, Kindai 2 [Iwanami lectures on Japan's common history, 17, Modern, 2] (Iwanami shoten, 1994), 169–170.

53. Yoshida Yutaka, *Nihon no guntai* [The Japanese military] (Iwanami shinsho, 2002), 182; Humphreys, *Heavenly Sword*, 106.

54. "Gundōin no seidō to jissai" [The theory and practice of military mobilization], *Kenkyū shiryō*, 95 RO-4H, mimeo., 1994, 85–87, 93, JDA; Yoshida, *Nihon no guntai*, 143.

55. Tanaka Keishii, "Rikugun jinji seidō gaisetsu," [An overview of the army personnel system], part 2, *Kenkyū shiryō*, 80RO-1H, mimeo., 1980, 34–35, JDA.

56. Yoshida, *Nihon no guntai*, 73; Kumagai Tadasu, "Kyūriku kaigun shōkō no senbatsu to kyōiku" [Officer selection and education in the former imperial army and navy], *Kenkyū shiryō*, 80R-12H, mimeo., 1980, 129, JDA. Kumagai's revised work was later published as *Nihongun no jinteki seidō to mondaiten no kenkyū* [Research concerning the Japanese military's personnel system and its controversial points] (Kokusho kankōsho, 1994).

57. The school was initially restricted to infantry branch, but it expanded in 1933 to cavalry and artillery. Other branches had their own preparatory schools or specialized training units for the purpose. Tanaka, "Rikugun jinji," 113.

58. Yoshida, *Nihon no guntai*, 88, 91.

59. Tanaka, "Rikugun jinji," 113.

60. Hata, *Rokōkyō*, 95, has an organizational chart.

61. The army reductions of 1923 had eliminated the fourth company from the peacetime force structure of each infantry battalion to avoid closing any military installations. Humphreys, *Heavenly Sword*, 62.

62. Bōeichō Bōei kenshūjō senshibu, eds., *Senshi sōsho*, 27, *Kantō gun* (1) [Official military history: The Kwantung Army, vol. 1] (Asagumo shimbunsha, 1969), 167. (Hereafter KG [1].) Kuwada Etsu and Maebara Toru, eds., *Nihon no sensō: chizū to dêta* [The wars of Japan: Maps and data] (Hara shobō, 1982), appendix 6, 10; HQ U.S. Army Forces Far East and Eighth Army (Rear), "Japanese Studies on Manchuria," vol. 5, "Infantry Operations," 14 December 1956, 25.

63. Three divisions, the Fifth, Eleventh, and Twelfth, had amphibious assault missions and were equipped with the lighter and more easily transportable mountain artillery.

64. Katogawa Kōtarō, *Rikugun no hansei* [Reflections on the army], part 1 (Bunkyō shūppan, 1996), 19.

65. KG (1), 559; Rikujō bakuryō, ed., "Nomonhan jiken no hōheisen" [Artillery battles during the Nomonhan incident], mimeo., 1965, 53–59, JDA.

66. Wada Kazuo, "Nihon rikugun heiki gyōsei seidōshi no kenkyū," part 2, [Research on the administrative and organizational history of the Japanese army's weaponry], *Kenkyū shiryō*, 83 RO-4H, mimeo., 1983, 14, JDA.

67. Alvin D. Coox, *Nomonhan: Japan against Russia, 1939* (Stanford, CA: Stanford University Press, 1985), vol. 2, 1085.

68. Katogawa Kotarō, *Teikoku rikugun kikō butai* [Imperial army armored corps], rev. ed. (Hara shobō, 1981), 43, 72, 77, 239.

69. SJRS (1), 96.

70. Alvin D. Coox, "The Rise and Fall of the Imperial Japanese Air Forces," *Aerospace Historian* 27, no. 2 (Summer 1980), 81; Alvin D. Coox, "The Effectiveness of the Japanese Military Establishment in the Second World War," in Allan R. Millett and Williamson Murray, eds., *Military Effectiveness* (Boston: Allen and Unwin, 1988), vol. 3, 6.

71. Humphreys, *Heavenly Sword*, 61; DRB (1), 402; KG (1), 145.

72. DRB (1), 402–404; KG (1), 145, 167.

73. DRB (1), 402.

74. Sanbō honbu dai 1 ka, Jōbun an, May 21, 1936, JDA.

75. KG (1), 245.

76. A day of supply was the predetermined quantity of ammunition, rations, and supplies a unit would consume during a single day's operations.

77. Ôkada Ikuhikō, "Rikugun no kōbō, heitan seidō gaisetsu" [An overview of the army's rear area logistics system], *Kenkyū shiryō*, 83 RO-2H, mimeo., 1983, 195–201, JDA.

78. Mainichi shimbunsha, eds., *1 Okunin no Shōwashi: Nihon no sensō* (3), *Nitchū sensō* (1) [100 million's Shōwa history: vol. 3, The wars of Japan, part 1, The Sino-Japanese War] (Mainichi shimbunsha, 1979), 191.

79. Fujiwara, *Uejinishita eiyūtachi*, 141–142.

80. Ibid., 195–197. Not a single transport officer rose to the rank of full general

in the history of the Japanese army, and the number who attended the staff college was 0.01 percent of all students.

81. Matsuzaki Shōichi, "Shina chūtongun zōkyō mondai" [The problem of the reinforcement of the China Garrison Army], part 1, *Kokugakuin zasshi*, 96, no. 2 (February 1995), 28.

82. Shiraishi Hiroshi, "Manshū jihen ni okeru Kantōgun no kōyū nimmu to sono kaishaku-unyō mondai" [The Kwantung Army's inherent mission in the Manchurian Incident and problems of execution], Special Issue, "Saikyō: Manshū jihen," *Gunji shigaku* 37, nos. 1 and 2 (October 2001), 192–193. Also Matsumoto Keisuke, "Shina jihen ni kakudai yōin ni tsuite" [Primary factors in the expansion of the China incident], *Kenkyū shiryō* 95RO-2H, mimeo., 1995, 4–5, JDA.

83. Hata, *Nitchū senso*, 86 n. 3; SJRS (1), 73–74; Etsu and Maebara, *Nihon no senso*, plate 17.

84. Furuya Tetsuo, *Nitchū senso* [The Sino-Japanese War] (Iwanami shinsho, 1985), 114.

85. Coble, *Facing Japan*, 244; Hata, *Nitchū senso*, 61.

86. Matsuzaki Shōichi, "Uemzu-Ho Yong-chin kyōtei" [The Umezu-Ho agreement], Special Issue, "Nitchū senso no shosō," *Gunji shigaku* 130 (December 1997), 48.

87. Matsuzaki, "Shina chūtongun" part 1, 32–33.

88. Ibid., 30.

89. Yasui, *Rokōkyō jihen*, 98; SJRS (1), 71; Matsuzaki, "Shina chūtongun" part 1, 28.

90. Nagai, "Nihon rikugun," 143 n. 24; Hata, *Rokōkyō*, 55.

91. Usui, *Nitchū senso*, 43; SJRS (1), 77.

92. Kuda and Maebara, *Nihon no senso*, plate 17; Hata, *Rokōkyō*, 53; Matsuzaki Shōichi, "Shina chūtongun zōkyō mondai" [The problem of the reinforcement of the China Garrison Army, part 2] *Kokugakuin zasshi* 96, no. 3 (March 1995), 55; SJRS (1), 71.

93. Rikugun daigaku, "Kita Shina sakusen shiyō," JDA; Headquarters, First Infantry Regiment was at Peking along with the unit's First Battalion. The Second Battalion was placed at Tianjin, and the Third Battalion at Fengtai.

94. Yasui, *Rokōkyō jihen*, 100–101.

95. Rikugun daigaku, "Kita Shina sakusen shiyō," JDA.

96. Hata, *Rokōkyō*, 54.

97. Rikugun daigaku, "Kita Shina sakusen shiyō," JDA. The reference to Zhangjiakou suggests the 1937 operational plan.

98. Furuya, *Nitchū senso*, 117–118; Ôsugi, *Nitchū jūgonen senso*, 205; Kojima, *Nitchū senso*, 2, 1932–1937 [The Sino-Japanese War, vol. 2, 1932–1937] (Bungei shūnjū, 1984), 350–351.

99. Sanbō honbu 2 ka, "Tai-Shi seisaku no kentō" (draft) [Examination of China policy], 1 September 1936, TSM (8), 227. See Mark Peattie, *Ishiwara Kanji and Japan's Confrontation with the West* (Princeton, NJ: Princeton University Press, 1975), 275, for Ishiwara's views on China.

100. "Tai-Shi jikyoku taisaku," 15 September 1936.

101. Kojima, *Nitchū senso*, vol. 2, 351; Hata, *Nitchū*, 125.

102. Hata, *Rokōkyō*, 59.

103. "Ishiwara Kanji chūshō kaisō otoroku" [Lt. Gen. Ishiwara Kanji retrospective interview], fall 1939, in Usui Katsumi and Inaba Masaō, eds., *Gendaishi shiryō* (9) [hereafter *GSS* (9)], Nitchū sensō (2) (Misuzu shobō, 1964), 304. Prince (Captain) Takeda Tsuneyoshi, who was assigned to the general staff War History Office, conducted the interview.

104. Hashimoto Gun chūshō kaisō otoroku [Lt. Gen. Hashimoto Gun's retrospective interview], fall 1939, *GSS* (9), 326–327; Kageyama, "Nihon kaigun," 9; Hata, *Rokōkyō*, 59.

105. Ishiwara otoroku, 307.

106. Rikugun daigaku, "Kita Shina sakusen shiyō," JDA; Coble, *Facing Japan*, 303.

107. Rikugun daigaku, "Kita Shina sakusen shiyō," JDA; Hata, *Rokōkyō*, 68; Coble, *Facing Japan*, 303.

108. Hata, *Rokōkyō*, 68.

109. Rikugun daigaku, "Kita Shina sakusen shiyō," JDA.

110. Yasui, *Rokōkyō*, 108; Shina chūtongun hohei dai ichi rentai [First infantry regiment, China Garrison Army], "Rokōkyō fukin sentō hōkoku" [Report of combat near the Marco Polo Bridge], S 12-7-8–12-7-9 [8–9 July 1937] 1:4, JDA.

111. Ishiwara otoroko, 307.

112. Peattie, *Ishiwara Kanji*, 262–263; Hata Ikuhikō, *Gun fashizumu undōshi* [The military fascist movement], rev. ed. (Kawade shobō, 1972), 192–194.

113. Shimada, "Designs on North China," 251; Peattie, *Ishiwara Kanji*, 292.

114. Takahashi Hisashi, "Military Friction, Diplomatic Suasion in China, 1937–1938," *Journal of Intelligence Studies* 19 (July 1987), 72; John Hunter Boyle, *China and Japan at War 1937–1945* (Stanford, CA: Stanford University Press, 1972), 44; Humphreys, *Heavenly Sword*, 178.

115. Hata, *Rokōkyō*, 25.

116. In a postwar interview, Mutaguchi remarked that Kawabe was "unfit as a commander," but the cause of his complaint was likely the Imphal disaster of mid-1944. Handō, *Shikkan to sanbō* [Commanders and staff officers] (Bungei shūnjū, 1992), 66.

117. Kojima Noboru, *Eiyū no tani* [Valley of heroes] (Bungei shūnjū, 1973), 53; Fujiwara, *Uejinishita eiyūtachi*, 72; Handō Kazutoshi, *Shikkan to sanbō*, 66–68.

118. Matsuzaki, "Shina chūtongun," part 2, 60, 67.

119. Terasaki Hidenari and Mariko Terasaki Miller, eds., *Shōwa tennō dokuhakuroku-Terasaki Hidenari goyōgakari nikki* [The Shōwa emperor's monologue: Court official Terasaki Hidenari diary] (Bungei shūnjū, 1991), 35.

120. Imoto Kumao, *Shina jihen sakusen nisshi* [Journal of China incident operations], rev. ed. (Fūyō shobō, 1998), 55, 61–62.

121. Ibid., 61.

122. SJRS (1), 134.

123. DRB (1), 428–429; Tobe Ryōichi, *Nihon Rikugun to Chūgoku* (Kōdansha, 1999), 197–198. On Ishiwara's attitude see Peattie, *Ishiwara Kanji*, 289.

124. Hata, *Rokōkyō*, 61.

125. Matsuzaki, "Shina chūtongun," part 2, 58.

126. Rikugun daigaku, "Kita Shina sakusen shiyō," JDA.

127. Shina chūtongun, "Rokōkyō fukin sentō hōkoku," JDA.

128. Rikugun daigaku, "Kita Shina sakusen shiyō," JDA; Shina chūtongun, "Rokōkyō fukin sentō hōkoku," JDA.

129. Shina chūtongun, "Rokōkyō fukin sentō hōkoku," JDA.

130. Hata, *Rokōkyō*, 55, 63; Shina chūtongun, "Rokōkyō fukin sentō hōkoku," JDA.

131. Coble, *Facing Japan*, 366; Hata, *Rokōkyō*, 62–63; Hata Ikuhikō, "Rokōkyō jihen no saikentō," *Seiji keizai shigaku* 333 (March 1994), 8; Sun, *China and the Origins*, 43, 54; Tobe, *Rikugun to Chūgoku*, 29.

132. Ôsugi, *Nitchū jūgonen sensō*, 22; Sun, *China and the Origins*, 68, 75; Hata, *Nitchū sensō*, 57.

133. Tobe, *Rikugun to Chūgoku*, 178–181.

134. Fujiwara, *Uejinishita eiyūtachi*, 148; Hayashi Saburō, "Senjka no rikugun chūōbu" [Army headquarters during wartime], *Rekishi to jimbutsu* (winter 1986), 249–250; "Kisō chōsa Nihon rikukaigun no jōhō kikō to sono katsudō" [Basic research: Japan's army and navy intelligence organizations and their activities], *Kenkyū shiryō* 84RO-2H, 1984, 144–145, JDA; Sugita Ichiji, *Jōhō naki sensō shidō* [War guidance without military intelligence] (Hara shobō, 1987); Tobe, *Rikugun to Chūgoku*, 6, 225; Kitaoka Shin'ichi, "China Experts in the Army," in Duus, Myers, and Peattie, *The Japanese Informal Empire in China*, 367.

135. Hisashi Takahashi, "A Case Study: Japanese Intelligence Estimates of China and the Chinese, 1931–1945," in Lt. Col. Walter T. Hitchcock, ed., *The Intelligence Revolution: A Historical Perspective*, Proceedings of the Thirteenth Military History Symposium, U.S. Air Force Academy, Colorado Springs, CO, 12–14 October 1988 (Washington, DC: U.S. Government Printing Office, 1991), 205–208.

136. SJRS (1), 141; Shina chūtongun, "Rokōkyō fukin sentō hōkoku," JDA.

137. Rikugun hohei gakkō [Army infantry school], ed., "Tai Shinagun sentōhō no kenkyū" [Studies of tactics against the Chinese armies], January 1933, 6, JDA.

138. Ibid.

139. Ôsugi, *Nitchū jūgonen sensō*, 266.

140. Ibid., 276–277.

141. "Hashimoto otoroku," 335.

NOTES TO CHAPTER 5

1. Chiang Kai-shek, *Kunmian ji* [Anthology of encouragement amid difficulties] (draft), *Jiang Zhongzheng Zongtong dang'an* [Archive of President Chiang Kai-shek], eds. Wang Yugao and Wang Yuzheng (Taipei: Guoshiguan). This draft is abridged and compiled from the diary of Chiang Kai-shek. There are minor deviations from the original text of Chiang's diary.

2. Chiang Kai-shek, *Zongtong Jianggong dashi changbian chugao* [Draft of the extended compilation of major events during the presidency of Chiang Kai-shek] (Taipei: Zhongguo Guomindang zhongyang weiyuanhui dangshi weiyuanhui, 1978), vol. 4, part 1, 1120.

3. Xu Yongchang, *Xu Yongchang riji* [Diary of Xu Yongchang], 14 July 1937 (Taipei: Zhongyang yanjiuyuan jindaishi yanjiusuo, 1991).

4. Ibid., 16 July 1937.

5. Ibid.

6. Ibid. Xu repeated this sentiment in a speech at a meeting on 19 July.

7. *Hu Shizhi xiansheng nianbu changbian chugao* [Draft of the extended compilation of the chronology of Mr. Hu Shi] (Taipei: Lianjing chuban shiye gongsi, 1984), vol. 5, 1598–1612.

8. "Dui Lugouqiao shijian zhi yanzhen biaoshi" [Solemn resolution on the Marco Polo Bridge Incident], in *Zongtong Jianggong dashi changbian chugao*, vol. 4, part 1, 1131.

9. Chiang, *Kunmian ji*.

10. Ibid.

11. Wang Shijie, *Wang Shijie riji* [Diary of Wang Shijie], 7 August 1937 (Taipei: Zhongyang yanjiuyuan jindaishi yanjiusuo, 1991).

12. Huang Dejin, "JingHu guofang gongshi de shexiang" [Design of the defenses of Nanjing and Shanghai], in *Bayaosan Songhu Kangzhan* [Battle of Shanghai of 13 August] (Peking: Zhongguo wenshi chubanshe, 1987), 40–41; and Liang His-huey, "Alexander von Falkenhausen," in Bernd Martin ed., *Die Deutsche Beraterschaft in China* [The German adviser group in China] (Dusseldorf: Droste, 1977), 141–142.

13. *Bayaosan Songhu kangzhan*, 40.

14. Zhang Zhizhong, "Jiekai Bayaosan Songhu kangzhan de xumu" [Unveiling the initial stage of the Battle of Shanghai of 18 August]," in *Bayaosan Songhu kangzhan*, 17. See also Yu Zhanbang, *Zhang Zhizhong jiyao mishu de huiyi* [Zhang Zhizhong: Memoir of the secret secretary of Zhang Zhizhong] (Changchun: Jilin wenshi chubanshe, 1992), 27.

15. Chiang Kai-shek, *Jiang Jieshi milu* [Secret records of Chiang Kai-shek] (Changsha: Hunan renmin chubanshe, 1988), vol. 4, 24.

16. Office of Military History, Japanese Ministry of Defense, *Zhongguo shibian lujun zuozhan shi* [History of Japanese army's operations during the China Incident] (Peking: Zhonghua shuju, 1981), vol. 1, part 2, 1.

17. *Zhongyang ribao* [Central newspaper], 10 August 1937.

18. *Shanghai zuozhan riji* [Journal of the military operations in Shanghai], in Zhongguo dier lishi dang'an guan, *Kangri zhangzheng zhengmian zhanchang* [The frontal warfare during the Sino-Japanese War] (Nanjing: Jiangsu guji chubanshe, 1987), 263.

19. There is no consensus about the number of Japanese forces in Shanghai. The number cited in this paper is from the Office of Military History, Japanese Ministry of Defense, *Zhongguo shibian lujun zuozhan shi*, vol. 1, part 2, 4.

20. Wang Shijie, *Wang Shijie riji*, 12 Auguest 1937.

21. Zhongguo dier lishi dang'an guan [China Second Historical Archive], *Kangri Zhanzheng zhengmian zhanchang* [The front battlefield of the Sino-Japanese War] (Nanjing: Jiangsu guji chubanshe, 1987), 265.

22. *Kangri zhanzheng zhengmian zhanchang*, 336.

23. Chiang, *Kumian ji*.

24. Chen Cheng, "Chen Cheng siren huiyi ziliao" [Chen Cheng's personal memoirs], *Minguo dang'an*, vol. 1, 1987.

25. Chiang, *Kunmian ji* .

26. Ibid.

27. Wang, *Wang Shijie riji*, 12 October 1937.

28. *Cong Lugouqiao shibian dao Nanjing zhanyi*, 373.

29. Ibid., 374.

30. *Bayaosan Songhu kangzhan*, 95.

31. Wang, *Wang Shijie riji*, 6 September 1937.

32. *Bayaosan Songhu kangzhan*, 96.

33. Liu Fei, "Kangzhan chuqi de Nanjing baoweizhan" [The battle in defense of Nanjing], in Quanguo zhengxie, *Wenshi ziliao xuanji* [Documents of literature and history], vol. 12, 3–4.

34. Chiang, *Kunmian ji*.

35. Wang, *Wang Shijie riji*, 21 September 1937. Li Zongren also tried to persuade Chiang Kai-shek to limit the Shanghai fighting: "The Shanghai Triangle is indefensible. We should not defend it at all costs. To avoid unnecessary sacrifice, we should stop when our initial goals have been achieved." Li Zongren, *Li Zongren huiyilu* [Memoirs of Li Zongren] (Nanning: Zhengxie Guangxi Zhuanzu zizhiqu wenshi zilian yanjiu weiyuanhui, 1980), vol. 2, 692–693.

36. Chiang, *Kunmian ji*.

37. *Zhonghua minguo zhongyao shiliao chubian* [Preliminary compilation of the important historical documents of the Republic of China], vol. 2, *Zuozhan jingguo* [The progress of the fighting], part 1 (Taipei: Guomindang lishi weiyuanhui, 1981), 55.

38. Chiang Kai-shek, "Jiang weiyuanzhang dui Long Yun shiyue jingdian" [Telegram from Chairman Chiang Kai-shek to Long Yun in October], *Geming wenxian: Songhu huizhan yu Nanjing cheshou* [Revolutionary documents: The Battle of Shanghai and the retreat to and defense of Nanjing], *Jiang zhongzheng Zongtong dang'an*.

39. *Kangri zhanzheng zhengmian zhanchang*, 281.

40. Chiang, *Kunmian ji*.

41. Chen Cheng, "Chen Cheng zhi Jiang Jieshi midian" [Secret telegram from Chen Cheng to Chiang Kai-shek], in *Kangri zhanzheng zhengmian zhanchang*, 372.

42. Gu Zhutong, "Gu Zhutong zhi He Yingqin midian [Secret telegram from Gu Zhutong to He Yingqin]," in *Kangri zhanzheng zhengmian zhanchang*, 373–374.

43. Chiang, *Kunmian ji*.

44. Chiang, *Zongtong Jianggong dashi changbian chugao*, vol. 4, part 1, 1148.

45. Ibid., 1167.

46. Ibid., 1179.

47. Chiang, *Jiang Jieshi milu*, vol. 4, 28.

48. *Kangri zhanzheng zhengmian zhanchang*, 294.

49. Xu, *Xu Yongchang riji*, 12 November 1937.

50. Chiang, *Kunmian ji*, 2 February 1938.

51. *Cong Lugouqiao dao Nanjing zhanyi*, 554–555.

52. Chiang, *Kunmian ji*.

53. *Kangri zhanzheng zhengmian zhanchang*, 282.

54. "Disan zhanqu Songhu huizhan jingguo gaiyao" [Abstract of the process of the Battle of Shanghai in the Third War Zone], *Kangri zhanzheng zhengmian zhangchang*, 381.

55. Chiang, *Kunmian ji*.

56. Xu, *Xu Yongchang riji*, 7 November 1937.

57. Ibid., 5 November 1937.

58. Chiang, *Kunmian ji*.

59. Ibid.

60. *Bayaosan Songhui kangzhan*, 252.

61. *Cong Lugouqiaon dao Nanjing zhanyi*, 555.

62. Xu, *Xu Yongchang riji*, 5 November 1937.

63. *Cong Lugouqian shibian dao Nanjing zhanyi*, 601.

64. Wang, *Wang Shijie riji*, 19 November 1937; Liu Fei, "Kangzhan chuqi de Nanjing," [Nanjing in the initial stage of the Sino-Japanese War], in *Nanjing Bao-weizhan Bianshenzu* [Editorial Committee for "The Siege of Nanjing"], *Nanjing baoweizhan* (Nanjing: Zhongguo Wenshi Chubanshe, 1987), 8–9.

65. Chiang, *Kunmian ji*.

66. Wang, *Wang Shijie riji*, 19 November 1937. See also Tang Shengzhi, "Wushu Nanjing zhi jingguo" [The process of defending Nanjing], *Nanjing bao-weizhan*, 3–4.

67. Xu, *Xu Yongchang riji*, 6 November 1937.

68. Chiang, *Kunmian ji*.

69. Ibid.

70. Ibid.

71. Wang, *Wang Shijie riji*, 21 November 1937.

72. Chiang, *Kunmian ji*.

73. "Songhu zuozhan disanqi zuozhan jihua" [The combat plan for the third stage of the Battle of Shanghai], in *Kangri zhanzheng zhengmian zhanchang*, 331.

74. Ibid., 333–334.

75. Xu, *Xu Yongchan riji*, 3 December 1937.

76. Chiang, *Kunmian ji*.

77. One source is "Tairikumei dai hachi go" [Imperial army order number 8], 1 December 1937, in Usui Katsumi and Inaba Masao, eds., *Gendaishi shiryō*, vol. 9, *Nitchū sensō*, part 2 (Misuzu shobō, 1964), 216. A *tairikumei* was issued over the seal of the emperor and normally was general in nature. A *tairikushi* (imperial army instruction) was issued by the chief of staff based on the *tairikumei* and contained specific details and instructions for commanders.

78. Ibid.

79. In his diary on 9 December 1937, Chiang Kai-shek wrote, "In this war of resistance, even if all China is occupied by the enemy, we will regard it only as the temporary setback in the second stage of our revolution. We should not regard it as our country was conquered by the enemy. We should not regard it as our nation perished. We should boost our national spirit to revive." See Chiang, *Kunmian ji*.

80. Wang, *Wang Shijie riji*, 1 September 1937.

81. Ibid., 28 September 1937.

82. Chiang Kai-shek, "Jiang weiyuanzhang zhi Jiang Tingba, Yang Jie qing Fu yuanshuai zhuan Sidalin xiansheng dian" [Telegram from Chairman Chiang Kai-Shek to Jiang Tingbi and Yangjie (Please ask Marshall Voroshilov to pass it on to Mr. Stalin)], *Geming wenxian: Duisu waijiao* [Revolutionary documents: Diplomacy toward the Soviet Union], *Jiang Zhongzheng zongtong dang'an.*

83. Stalin and Voroshov, "Sidalin, Fuluoximofu zhi Jiang weiyuanzhang shieryue dian" [Telegram from Stalin and Voroshilov to Chairman Chiang Kai-shek in December] *Geming wenxian: Duisu waijiao, Jiang Zhongzheng zongtong dang'an.* The original telegram was not dated. The date was derived from Xu, *Xu Yongchang riji.*

84. Chiang, *Kunmian ji*, 5 December 1937.

85. Xu, *Xu Yongchang riji*, 6 December 1937.

86. Chiang Kai-shek, "Jiang weiyuanzhang zhi Li Zongren, Yan Xishan deng dian" [Telegram from Chairman Chiang Kai-shek to Li Zongren, Yan Xishan, and others], *Geming wenxian: Songhu huizhan yu Nanjing tuishou, Jiang Zhongzheng zongtong dang'an.*

87. "Nanjing baoweizhang zhandou xiangbao" [Detailed report of the battle in defense of Nanjing], in *Kangri zhanzheng zhengmian zhanchang*, 413.

88. Chiang Kai-shek, "Jiang weiyuanzhang zhi Tang Shengzhi, Liu Xing, Luo Zhuoying dian" [Telegram from Chairman Chiang Kai-shek to Tang Shengzhi, Liu Xing, and Luo Zhuoying], *Geming wenxian: Songhu huizhan yu Nanjing tuishou, Jiang Zhongzheng zongtong dang'an.*

89. "Xianbing silingbu zhandong xiangbao" [Detailed report of the combat by the headquarters of the police], in *Kangri zhanzheng zhengmian zhanchang*, 433.

90. "Lujun di qishiba jun Nanjing huizhan xiangbao" [The detailed report of the Battle of Nanjing by the Seventy-eighth Army], in *Kangri zhanzheng zhengmian zhanzheng*, 424–425.

NOTES TO CHAPTER 6

1. Hando Katzutoshi, *Showashi* [A history of Shōwa] (Heibonsha, 2004), 179–185; see also Hata Ikuhiko, *Ryokōkyō jihen no kenkyū* [An inquiry into the Marco Polo Bridge Incident] (Tokyo daigaku shuppankai, 1996).

2. Air squadrons of the Japanese army maintained twenty planes in a fighter squadron, fifteen in a light bomber squadron, and ten in a heavy bomber squadron. Air regiments consisted of two air squadrons. An air group had about one hundred fighters and bombers.

3. Ronald Haiferman, *Nitchū kōkū kessen* [Decisive air battles of the Sino-Japanese War], trans. Sakai Fumiya (Sankei shimbunsha), 1973, 8–11.

4. The Type 92 heavy armored vehicles and Type 94 light armored vehicles were equipped with caterpillar tracks and were in fact tanks.

5. Bōeichō Bōeikenshūjō, ed., *Senshi sōsho* (hereafter BBS, SS), *Chūgoku hōmen kaigunsakusen* (1) *Shōwa 13 nen 3 gatsu made* [Naval operations on the China front through March 1938] (Asagumo shimbunsha, 1974), 36.

6. Kojima Noboru, *Nitchū sensō* (Bunshun bunko ed., 1988), vol. 4, 92.

7. Japanese doctrine called for a division to defend a six- to nine-mile frontage, depending on terrain. Kyoiku sōkanbu honbuncho, "Renshūyo sūryo hyo" [Table

of measures for use in field training exercises] 19 January 1941, in Rikusen gakkai, ed., *Kindai sensishi gaisetsu (shiryo hen)* (Rikusen gakkai, 1984), 192.

8. Kojima, *Nitchū sensō*, vol. 4, 93–94.

9. BBS, SS, *Chūgoku hōmen rikugun kōkū sakusen* [Army air operations on the China front] (Asagumo shimbunsha, 1974), 36–37.

10. Kojima, *Nitchū sensō*, vol. 4, 94–95.

11. Ibid., vol. 4, 95–98, quotation, 98.

12. BBS, SS, *Chūgoku hōmen kaigunsakusen*, vol. 1, 255–256.

13. BBS, SS, *Shina jihen rikugun sakusen (1) Shōwa 13 nen 1 gatsu made* [Army operations during the China incident through January 1938] (Asagumo shimbunsha, 1975), 325.

14. My account is adapted from Kojima, *Nitchū sensō*, 108.

15. BBS, SS, *Chūgoku hōmen rikugun kōkū sakusen (1)* Up to March 1938, 367–372.

16. BBS, SS, *Shina jihen rikugun sakusen*, vol. 1, 363–365.

17. Ibid., 365–367.

18. Ibid., 384–396.

19. Kageyama Koichirō, "Oyama jihen no hitotsu kosatsu—dai niji Shanhai jihen no dokasen no shinsō to gunreibu ni ateta eikyo" [A reconsideration of the Oyama incident: the facts about the fuse for the second Shanghai incident and the effect it exerted on the naval general staff], *Gunji shigaku*, 32, no. 3 (December 1996), 14. Kageyama acknowledges that the incident remains shrouded in mystery, but on the basis of Japanese documentary and first-person accounts, he concludes that radical Central Army troops, recently arrived in Shanghai, ambushed the Japanese automobile. Kojima, *Nitchū sensō*, 66–67.

20. BBS, SS, *Chūgoku hōmen kaigunsakusen*, vol. 1, 340–352.

21. Usui Katsumi, *Shinhan Nitchū sensō* (Chūkō shinsho, 2000), 79.

22. Ibid., 79–80; Kojima, *Nitchū sensō*, 80.

23. BBS, SS, *Shina jihen rikugun sakusen*, vol. 1, 267.

24. Ibid., 258.

25. Ibid., 294.

26. Ibid., 278.

27. Kojima, *Nitchū sensō*, 140.

28. Hata Ikuhiko, *Nitchū sensōshi* [A history of the Sino-Japanese War] (Kawade shobō, 1972), 281.

29. BBS, SS, *Shina jihen rikugun sakusen*, vol. 1, 279.

30. BBS., SS, *Daihon'ei rikugunbu (1), Shōwa 15 nen 5 gatsu made* [Imperial General Headquarters army division to May 1940] (Asagumo shimbunsha, 1967), 489.

31. BBS, SS, *Shina jiken rikugun sakusen*, vol. 1, 387.

32. Hata Ikuhiko, *Nankin jihen* (Chūkō shinsho, 1986), 65.

33. Hata, *Nitchū sensōshi*, 280–281.

34. A division in frontal attack was assigned a frontage of 1.5 to 2.5 miles. Kyoiku sokanbu honbuncho, "Renshūyō sūryōhyō" [Table of measures for use in (field training) exercises] 19 January 1941, in Rikusen gakkai, ed., *Kindai sensishi gaisetsu (shiryō hen)*, 192.

35. Dai 9 shidan sanbō [Ninth Division staff], "Dai 9 shidan sakusen keika no gaiyō" [A summary of the source of the Ninth Division's operations], January 1938, in Usui Katsumi and Inaba Masao, eds., *Gendaishi shiryō* 9, *Nitchū senso* 2 [Documents on contemporary history, vol. 9, the Sino-Japanese War, part 2] (Misuzu shobō, 1964), 225.

36. BBS, SS, *Shina jiken rikugun sakusen*, 379–380, 400 map; Hata, *Nitchū sensōshi*, 281.

37. Dai 9 shidan sanbō, "Dai 9 shidan sakusen keika no gaiyō," 226.

38. BBS, SS, *Shina jiken rikugun sakusen*, 381.

39. This account is drawn from Hibino Shirou, "Wuusun kuriiku" [Wusong creek], in Agawa Hiroyuki et al., eds., *Shōwa senso bungaku zenshū* [Complete works of Shōwa war literature] vol. 2, *Chugokū e no shingeki* [The advance into China] (Shueisha, 1964), 47–49, 64, 77. Hibino, a thirty-four-year-old reporter for a Sendai newspaper, was recalled to active duty as a corporal with the 101st Division. He was severely wounded in fighting at Wusong Creek. His account first appeared in the February 1939 issue of *Chūō kōron*.

40. Hata, *Nitchū sensōshi*, 65; BBS, SS, *Shina jihen rikugun sakusen*, 380.

41. Dai 9 shidan sanbō, "Dai 9 shidan sakusen keika no gaiyō," 226.

42. Ibid., 248.

43. Morimatsu Toshio, moderator, "Dai kyu shidan no funsen" [The bitter struggle of the Ninth Division], *Rekishi to jimbutsu* (December 1985), 244.

44. Morimatsu, "Dai kyu shidan no funsen," 247–248.

45. Dai 9 shidan sanbō, "Dai 9 shidan sakusen keika no gaiyō," 227.

46. BBS, SS, *Shina jihen rikugun sakusen*, 387.

47. Dai 9 shidan sanbō, "Dai 9 shidan sakusen keika no gaiyō," 227.

48. Hata, *Nitchū sensōshi*, 282.

49. Dai 9 shidan sanbō, "Dai 9 shidan sakusen keika no gaiyō," 252.

50. Ibid., 228.

51. BBS, SS, *Shina jihen rikugun sakusen*, 381.

52. Hata, *Nankin jihen*, 93.

53. Ibid., 71.

54. See "Shimomura Sadamu taishō kaisō ōtō roku" [Record of questions and answers with Gen. Shimomura Sadamu], in Usui Katsumi and Inaba Masao, eds., *Gendaishi shiryo* 9, *Nitchū senso* 2 [Documents on contemporary history, vol. 9, the Sino Japanese War, part 2] (Misuzu shobō, 1964), 389; Hata Ikuhiko, "The Marco Polo Bridge Incident, 1937," in James William Morley, ed., *Japan's Road to the Pacific War: The China Quagmire: Japan's Expansion on the Asian Continent 1933–1941* (New York: Columbia University Press, 1983), 278; Kojima, *Nitchū senso*, 283–284.

55. Kojima, *Nitchū senso*, 158–160, 173–174.

56. Hata, *Nitchū sensōshi*, 278; "Shimomura taishō kaisō ōtō roku," 391; Masahiro Yamamoto, *Nanking: Anatomy of an Atrocity* (Westport, CT: Praeger, 2000), 50.

57. Kojima, *Nitchū senso*, 165–167; BBS, SS, *Shina jihen rikugun sakusen*, 420.

58. BBS, SS, *Shina jihen rikugun sakusen*, 422–423; BBS, SS, *Chūgoku hōmen rikugun sakusen*, 416–28; Kojima, *Nitchū senso*, 175–176.

59. Yamamoto, *Nanking*, 55.

60. Hata, *Nankin jihen*, 70; Kojima, *Nitchū sensō*, 151.

61. BBS, SS, *Chūgoku hōmen kaigunsakusen*, 402–407.

62. Kojima, *Nitchū sensō*, 111; Morimatsu, "Dai kyu shidan no funsen," 253.

63. Morimatsu "Dai kyu shidan no funsen," 253.

64. Kojima, *Nitchū sensō*, 175.

65. Ibid., 210–211.

66. Ibid., 222.

67. Hora Tomio, *Nankyo daigyakusatsu* [The great massacre at Nanking] (Tokuma shoten, 1982), 125.

68. Kojima, *Nitchū sensō*, 228; Yamamoto, *Nanking*, 134.

69. Dai 9 shidan sanbō, "Dai 9 shidan sakusen keika no gaiyō," 233.

70. Nakajima, "Nankin korakusen Nakajima dai 16 shidanchō nikki" [Diary of Sixteenth Division commander Nakajima], *Zokan rekishi to jimbutsu*, December 1984, 261.

71. Yang Daqing, "Atrocities in Nanking: Searching for Explanations," in Diana Lary and Stephen MacKinnon, eds., *Scars of War: The Impact of Warfare on Modern China* (Vancouver: University of British Columbia Press, 2001), 84, 86–88, 90; Hata Ikuhiko, among others.

NOTES TO CHAPTER 7

1. Wei Hongyun, *Kangri zhanzheng yu Zhongguo shehui* [Chinese society during the Anti-Japanese War] (Liaoning, 1997), 163–176; and Lao She's reports in *Da gong bao*, October–December 1937, for discussion of civilian panic in Shandong.

2. Standard accounts and relevant documents on the fall of Jinan and Qingdao are to be found in Zhongguo dier lishi dang'an guan, *Kangri zhanzheng zhengmian zhanchang* [Documents from the front lines of the Anti-Japanese War] (Nanjing: Second Historical Archive, 1987), vol. 1 (hereafter *Documents from the front lines)*; Ministry of Defense, *Kangrizhanshi: JinPu Tielu* [History of the Anti-Japanese War: JinPu Railway campaign] (Taipei, 1962), 75–84; and Zhang Xianwen, *Kangri zhanzhengde zhengmian zhanchang* (Front battlefield of the Anti-Japanese War) (Henan, 1987), 86–96.

3. *Da gong bao*, 20, 24, 25, 26 January 1938. There are many conflicting accounts of General Han's actual execution. I have chosen one of the more dramatic versions told me at the Changjun temple at Wuchang. See Wang Yimin, "Guanyu Han Fuju tongzhi Shandong he bei busha de jianwen" [Accounts of Shandong under Han Fuju, his imprisonment, and his execution], *Wenshi ziliao xuanji*, no.12 (1960), 59–67; and Sun Dongxuan, "Han Fuju beike qianhou" [Events surrounding the execution of Han Fuju] *Wenshi ziliao xuanji* 54, no. 6 (1962), 99–109. Chen Qinghua, "Jiang Jieshi chujue Han Fuju zhenxiang" [Real story behind Chiang Kai-shek's execution of Han Fuju], *Gong Ming* (Guangzhou), no. 52. Also, in English, Tang Te-kong and Li Tsung-jen, *The Memoirs of Li Tsung-jen* (Boulder, 1979), 338–340; and Frank Dorn, *The History of the Sino-Japanese War: From Marco Polo Bridge to Pearl Harbor* (New York, 1974), 138–145, for different accounts. At about the same time, Liu Xiang, the most important militarist in Sichuan, like Han Fuju with a history of defiance of Nanjing, died mysteriously in

a Wuhan hospital. At the 2004 conference Liu Fenghan insisted that Feng Yuxiang had everything to do with the execution of Han Fuju and the death of Liu Xiang.

4. The Communists did not participate directly in the 16 January tribunal decision, but by the end of the month Zhou Enlai had joined the united front government at Wuhan, becoming the vice head of the political section of the Military Affairs Commission under Chen Cheng. See *Kangzhanzhong de Wuhan* [Wuhan during the Anti-Japanese War] (Zhengxie, 1985), 60–80; and Mao Lei et al., *Wuhan Kangzhan shiyao* [Important points in history of Anti-Japanese War in Wuhan] (Hubei, 1985).

5. A definitive work on this subject is Hans J. van de Ven, *War and Nationalism in China, 1925–1945* (London, 2003).

6. On the planning for the defense of Xuzhou and then Wuhan, as well as Japanese strategies, see a book by a leading Chinese military historian, Xu Yong, *Zhengfu zhi Meng: Riben qinhua zhanlue* [Pacification dreams: Japanese war strategies in China] (Guilin, 1993), 147–156, 179–228; and an article by Ao Wenwei, "Wuhankangzhan shiqi Jiang Jieshi de zhanlue zhanshu sixiang" [Chiang Kai-shek's battle strategies and tactics during the Battle of Wuhan period], *Jindai shi yanjiu*, 1999, no.6, 128–156. *Chijiu zhan* as a strategic concept had its roots in the writings of Jiang Baili and others in the 1920s but can be traced earlier, some say back to the Song Dynasty. See the classic article on the subject by Wu Xiangxiang, "Total Strategy Used by China and Some Major Engagements in the Sino-Japanese War of 1937–45," in Paul Sih, ed., *Nationalist China during the Sino-Japanese War, 1937–45* (Hicksville, NY, 1977), 37–80, later published in Chinese in *Zhuanji wenxue*, no. 302 (July 1987), 61–70.

7. John Dower, "Lessons of Another Occupation," *Nation* 277, no. 1 (7 July 2003), 11–14.

8. Mark Peattie, *Sunburst: Rise of Japanese Naval Air Power, 1909–1941* (Annapolis, MD, 2002), chapter 5, "Attacking a Continent: The Navy's Air War in China, 1937–41."

9. See chapter 8 by Tobe Ryōichi in this volume.

10. See, for example, *New York Times* reportage for early 1938 and a book by its China correspondent, Hallett Abend, *Chaos in Asia* (New York, 1939).

11. Sun Youli, "Chinese Military Resistance and Changing American Perceptions, 1937–38," in Robert David Johnson, ed., *On Cultural Ground* (Chicago, 1994), 81–96.

12. Stephen MacKinnon and Oris Friesen, *China Reporting: An Oral History of American Journalism in the 1930s and 1940s* (Berkeley, 1987).

13. Indeed, Wuhan raises the wider question: was not the defense of the central Yangtze in 1938–1939 a precursor to later prolonged anticolonial struggles in Algeria, Vietnam, Afghanistan, Chechnya, and elsewhere in which the colonizer won on the battlefield but was otherwise trapped by an increasingly difficult political quagmire?

14. Liu Fenghan, "Wuhan huizhan yanjiu," *Kangzhan jianguo shi yantaohui lunwenji* [Conference essays on the War of Resistance and national construction] (Taipei, 1985), vol. 1, 99–154.

15. Chang Jui-te, *Kangzhan shiqi de guojun renshi* [Nationalist army's personnel during the Sino-Japanese War] (Taipei, 1993).

16. See Lyman Van Slyke, "The Battle of the Hundred Regiments: Problems of Coordination and Control during the Sino-Japanese War," *Modern Asian Studies* 30, no. 4 (1996), 979–1005.

17. Liu, "Wuhan huizhan yanjiu."

18. Ibid.

19. On the strategic importance historically of Xuzhou as the gateway to the central Yangtze Valley, see Diana Lary, "Defending China: The Battles of the Xuzhou Campaign," in Hans van de Ven, ed., *Warfare in Chinese History* (Boston, 2000), 398–427.

20. Besides the detailed study by Liu Fenghan, "Wuhan huizhan yanjiu," see also the classic earlier work by F. F. Liu, *A Military History of Modern China* (Princeton, NJ, 1956), chapters 13 and 17.

21. Van de Ven, *War and Nationalism in China*; and on lack of good intelligence, Dorn, *History of the Sino-Japanese War.*

22. Dorn, *History of the Sino-Japanese War,* 6–10. This assessment has not been contested, even by Hans van de Ven.

23. Western military observers, be they European, North American, German, or Russian seem to agree on these points. See works discussed in Diana Lary, "Defending China." Chinese forces under different leadership pursued a similar strategy in Korea, 1950–1952. Full citation in note 19.

24. Chang Jui-te, "Chiang Kai-shek's Coordination by Personal Direction" in Steven MacKinnon, Diana Lary and Ezra Vogel, eds., *China at War: Regions of China, 1937–45* (Stanford, CA, 2007), 65–90.

25. See Liu, *A Military History of Modern China,* chapter 17; and Ray Huang, "Chiang Kai-shek and His Diary as a Historical Source," *Chinese Studies in History* 29, no. 1 (1996).

26. *Baoding lujun junguan xuexiao* [Baoding Military Academy] (Shijiazhuang, 1987); and Lin Dezheng, "Baoding junguan xuexiao zhi yanjiu" [A study of Baoding Military Academy], master's thesis, Institute of Modern History, Taipei, 1980.

27. On Jiang Baili, Jiang Fucong and Xue Guangqian, *Jiang Baili Xiansheng Quanji* [Collected works of Mr. Jiang Baili] (Taipei, 1971); and Tao Juyin, *Jiang Baili* (Peking, 1985). Also see Liu Shipin, *Jiang Baili junshi sixiang yanjiu* [Study of Jiang Baili's military thought] (Peking, 2005).

28. See, for example, Agnes Smedley, *Battle Hymn of China* (New York, 1943).

29. See Mao Lei, *Wuhan kangzhan shi* for the connection on the Chinese side and chapter 8 in this volume for the Japanese side.

30. See Dorn, *History of the Sino-Japanese War* and reports by Carlson and Stilwell cited in detail in note 38; General Falkenhausen as quoted in Liu, *A Military History of Modern China,* 162–166; also in Martin and Bernard, eds., *Dei deutsche Beraterschaft in China, 1927–38* (Dusseldorf: Droste, 1980); Liang Hishuey, "General Alexander von Falkenhausen," in *Die Deutsche Beraterschaft,* 175–186; Aleksandr Ya Kalyagin, *Along Alien Roads,* trans. Steven I. Levine (New York, 1983); as well as Mowrer, *Mowrer in China* (New York, 1938); Chinese historians sharing this view include Xu Yong, *Zhengfu zhi Meng,* and Liu, *A Military History of Modern China,* especially chapter 17.

31. See chapter 8 in this volume.

32. See relevant documents in *Documents from the front lines*, vol. 1, 558–569 (first cited in note 2); and Ao Wenwei, "Wuhan kangzhan shiqi Jiang Jieshi de zhanlue zhanshu sixiang."

33. Troop allocation changes and personnel changes are clear from Tobe Ryō-ichi's chapter 8. What the politics were in Tokyo behind these moves is less clear. Nevertheless, the minister of war was changed in early April and replaced by General Itagaki Seishirō, a veteran of the Shanghai campaign.

34. The best thorough account in Chinese of both the Xuzhou and Wuhan campaigns can be found in Mao Lei, *Wuhan kangzhan shi*. See also *Documents from the front lines*, 558–778, about individual campaigns. Useful memoir accounts edited by People's Political Councils (*guomin canzhenghui*) at the provincial level include *Xuzhou Huizhan* [Battle of Xuzhou] (Peking, 1985) and *Wuhan huizhan* [Battle of Wuhan] (Peking, 1989). Kuomintang (Taiwan-based) archival documents, focusing on Chiang Kai-shek as well as giving the official Kuomintang postwar analysis, are the standard Ministry of Defense multivolume publication, *Kangri zhanshi* [History of the Anti-Japanese War] (Taipei, 1962); *Wuhan huizhan* (vol. 10 in three parts); and *Xuzhou huizhan*. A good, more contemporary summary for the Battle of Wuhan is by the senior Taiwan military historian, Liu Fenghan, "Wuhan baowei zhan yanjiu" [Study of the defense of Wuhan], in *Kangzhan jianguoshi yantaohui lunwenji* (Taipei, 1985), 99–162. Liu pays special attention to evaluating casualties and the use of chemical weapons by the Japanese.

35. Wang Mingzhang's heroics are chronicled in *Kangri zhanzheng guomindang zhenwang jianglinglu* [Chronicle of the front-line heroic sacrifices of Kuomintang generals in the Anti-Japanese War) (Peking: Jiefang jun chubanshe, 1987), 99–103.

36. Sun Youli, "Chinese Military Resistance and Changing American Perceptions," 81–96.

37. Two years later Zhang Zizhong died in battle defending Yichang and became the most celebrated fallen hero of the war on the Chinese side. The literature on Zhang Zizhong is considerable. For a summary see Arthur Waldron, "China's New Remembering of World War II: The Case of Zhang Zizhong," *Modern Asian Studies* 30, part 4 (October 1996), 945–978.

38. Note the careful wording by Tobe Ryōichi in chapter 8 saying that the Japanese were not defeated at Taierzhuang. The battle for Taierzhuang is well known. While the area remained in Chinese hands, the foreign press corps was taken there for a tour. I have based the preceding and following narrative on the fine summary by Diana Lary, "Defending China," in *Warfare in Chinese History*, 398–427; and celebratory Chinese accounts in *Taierzhuang huizhan* and *Xuzhou huizhan*. Also useful were detailed eyewitness military attaché reports by Evans Carlson and Joseph Stilwell in U.S. War Department, *U.S. Military Intelligence Reports: China, 1911–41* (Frederick, MD: University Publications of America, 1983), Reel 10, 16 March, 6 and 22 April (Carlson's 3–10 April visit), 5, 13, and 21 May, 25 June. For French attaché reports, *Rapports des attachés militaires, 1938*, files 7N3290, 91 (Chine), Chateau Vincennes, Paris.

39. Diana Lary, "Drowned Earth: The Strategic Breaching of the Yellow River Dyke, 1938," *War in History* 8, no. 2 (2001), 191–207; and Bi Chunfu, *Kangzhan Jianghe juekou mishi* [Secret history of the breach of the dike during the War of Resistance) (Taipei, 1995).

40. For details see chapter 8 by Tobe Ryōichi in this volume.

41. It is for this reason that Chinese historians have at times dealt separately with the battles for Xuzhou and Wuhan—separating the more positive story from the more negative one. But, as argued earlier, in terms of military history and the minds of the commanders on both sides at the time, the Xuzhou and Wuhan campaigns were closely connected.

42. See Wu Xiangxiang, "Total Strategy Used by China," in *Nationalist China during the Sino-Japanese War*; as well as Hsu Lung-hsuan and Chang Ming-kai, *History of the Sino-Japanese War, 1937–45* (Taipei, 1971); and Ao Wenwei, "Wuhan kangzhan shiqi Jiang Jieshi de zhanlue zhanshu sixiang." This view is argued forcefully by Hans van de Ven in *War and Nationalism in China*.

43. Lary, "Defending China."

44. See military attaché reports of Carlson and Stilwell cited in note 38. Also in books by Evans Carlson, *Chinese Army* (1939) and *Twin Stars of China* (New York, 1940); Dorn, *History of the Sino-Japanese War*; and Israel Epstein, *People's War*, London, 1939; and others. Typical was Stilwell in his 13–14 May report on Taierzhuang, which especially praised the Thirty-first Division commander, Chi Fengcheng, for his bravery and brilliance. General Zhi was thirty-four years old, a northerner who worked his way up through the regional armies connected to Feng Yuxiang (graduating from the Nanjing Staff College in 1933). Accolades repeated in Dorn, *History of the Sino-Japanese War*, 152–158. Note critique by Hans van de Ven in chapter 19 in this volume.

45. See book-length elaboration of this argument in van de Ven, *War and Nationalism in China*.

46. What happened to General Li at this point remains a mystery. His leadership of troops and participation in the war were never again at the same level. He did return to his troops in the Dabieshan area before the fall of Wuhan and remained there throughout most of the rest of the war. From 1939 on, he was involved in directing only relatively light engagements in answer to Japanese probes west of the Pinghan Railway. I have benefited from discussions with Diana Lary of Li's malaise. See Li Zongren's memoir: Te-Kong Tong and Li Tsung-jen, *Memoirs of Li Tsung-jen* (Boulder, CO, 1979); and Diana Lary's chapter in in MacKinnon and Lary, *China at War*.

47. For details see chapter 8 in this volume.

48. For the relevant documents see *Wuhan huizhan*, 6–29; and/or *Documents from the front lines*, vol. 1.

49. The best popular history of the Battle of Wuhan, with a focus on the personalities and peccadilloes of the commanders, is Fang Zhijin, *Jianghan Aige* [Elegy for Jianghan] (Peking, 1995). The most authoritative scholarly text is Mao Lei, *Wuhan kangzhan shi*.

50. In May the preparations at Madang were well publicized. International observers and journalists were invited to inspect the defenses, which included cables cutting across the river and the sinking of ships to further block movement upstream. In Chinese, see *Wuhan huizhan*, 30–43.

51. The question of Japanese use of chemical weapons is highly controversial. Doubts were raised by the Japanese participants at the 2002 conference. Tobe

in chapter 8 does not address the question. Chinese scholarship (mainland and Taiwanese) on the war has dealt at length with the subject, using for the most part Chinese sources. See, for example, an essay focused on the Wuhan campaign by Bi Junfu, "Qinhua rijun Wuhan huizhan qijian huaxue zhan shishi gaikuang" [The employment of chemical weapons by invading Japanese troops in the Wuhan campaign], *Minguo dang'an*, 1991, no. 4, 134–138, citing Japanese and Chinese sources. Also Liu Fenghan, "Wuhan baowei zhan yanjiu."

52. See chapter by Peter Merker in MacKinnon and Lary, *China at War*, 288–313.

53. *Wuhan huizhan*, 94–114; see also chapter 8 in this volume on the Japanese thrust into Lushan.

54. Fang, *Jianghan Aige*; *Wuhan huizhan*, 184–198.

55. *Wuhan huizhan*, 167–183.

56. Ibid., 246–263; Mao Lei, *Wuhan kangzhan shi*.

57. *Wuhan huizhan*, 1–5 (from Li Zongren's memoir, a searing attack on Hu Zongnan), also 231–245; also Fang, *Janjiang Aige*.

58. Mao Lei, *Wuhan kangzhan shi*.

59. Zhang Zhizhong spent the rest of his career trying to live down the Changsha fire. He continued as a trusted associate of Chiang, in the 1940s playing a major role in the civil war negotiations. See Yu Zhanbang, *Zhang Zhizhong: Zhang Zhizhong jiyao mishude huiyi* [Zhong Zhizhong: Recollections of Zhang Zhizhong's secretary] (Changchun, 1992), 43–64; and Zhang Zhizhong, *Zhang Zhizhong huiyi lu* [Memoir of Zhang Zhizhong] (Peking, 1985).

60. Ao Wenwei, "Wuhankangzhan shiqi Jiang Jieshi de zhanlue zhanshu sixiang"; see also van de Ven, *War and Nationalism in China*.

61. Key communications for both campaigns are in *Documents from the front lines*, 781–823 and 1027–1080, respectively.

62. Dorn, *History of the Sino-Japanese War*, chapter 10; see also Merker chapter in MacKinnon and Lary, *China at War*, 288–313.

63. See *Documents from the front lines*, vol. 2, 781–823; *Min Zhe Gan Kangzhan* [Anti-Japanese War in Fujian, Zhejiang, and Jiangxi] (Peking, 1995). Frank Dorn, *History of the Sino-Japanese War*, chapter 10, is especially clear and detailed on the Nanchang and Changsha campaigns of 1939.

64. Editorial Committee for "The Four Battles of Hunan" of the National Political Consultative Conferrence, *Documents from the front lines*, vol. 2, 1027–1080; *Hunan sidahuizhan* [The four big battles in Hunan] (Peking, 1995); Feng Zhengjian, *Xiangshui susu: Hunan huizhan ji* [Record for the battles of Hunan] (Peking, 1995), 43–113; Gao Jun, *Xue zaishao: Zhongri Changsha sici huizhan jiyao* [Blood and Fire: Record of important events in the four Chinese-Japanese battles] (Changsha, 1993). Dorn, *History of the Sino-Japanese War*, is again especially good; see chapter 12.

65. *Wuhan huizhan*, 319–449; on Zhang Zizhong, see note 37.

66. On the importance of the loss of Yichang to Chongqing and last-minute efforts to salvage the situation, see Van de Ven, *War and Nationalism in China*, 243–246. For the Japanese side see chapter 8 in this volume.

NOTES TO CHAPTER 8

1. Yet the IJA did prevail in most battles against the Chinese. The Eleventh Army was always victorious, even though it often had to fight hard and was severely tested. Certainly, the Chinese fought admirably, not only as guerrilla forces in the occupied areas but also as regular forces. The reason they adopted retreat tactics was not that they wanted to avoid battles but that they fully understood the Japanese pattern of advance followed by withdrawal. But the Chinese could not defeat the IJA, either. The winter offensive in 1939 was their only full-scale counteroffensive. The Japanese were unable to carry out major strategic offensives; China's armies were equally incapable of a full-scale counteroffensive to drive Japan from China. In this way both were caught in a stalemate. After the Pacific War began, the battlefields in China became a secondary theater of war. By that time, neither the Japanese nor the Chinese wanted to change the situation of stalemate in this secondary theater. "Rikugun Sakusen Shidō Yoko" [Main principles of the army's operational strategy] in November 1938," cited in Bōeichō Bōeikenshūjo, *Senshi-sōsho: Shina jihen rikugun sakusen* [Official war history series: The army's operations in the Sino-Japanese War] (Asagumo shimbunsha, 1976), vol. 2, 295–296.

2. Hata Ikuhiko, "Nitchū sensō no Gunji-teki Tenkai [The military development of the Sino-Japanese War], 1937–1941," in Nihon Kokusai-seiji Gakkai Tai-heiyo Sensō Gen'in Kenkyū-bu [Research group to study the causes of the Pacific War, the Japan Association of International Relations], *Taiheiyo Sensō eno michi* [The road to the Pacific War] (Asahi shinbunsha, 1963), vol. 4, 54.

3. For details of the operations, see Bōeichō Bōeikenshūjo, *Senshi-sōsho Shina jihen rikugun sakusen*, vols. 2 and 3; Frank Dorn, *The Sino-Japanese War, 1937–41: From Marco Polo Bridge to Pearl Harbor* (New York: Macmillan, 1974).

4. "Hashimoto Gun Chujo Kaisō-ōtō-roku" [Reminicences of Lt. Gen. Hashimoto Gun], in Usui Katsumi and Inaba Masao, comps., *Gendaishi Shiryō: Nitchū sensō* [Archives of contemporary history: the Sino-Japanese War] (Misuzu shobō, 1964), vol. 2, 342–343.

5. Inada Masazumi, "Senryaku-men kara Mita Shina-jihen no Sensō-shidō" [Japan's war strategy of the Sino-Japanese War], *Kokusai-seij*, March 1961, 158.

6. Japanese detachments were frequently referred to by their commanders' names. Their strength was usually equivalent to a brigade.

7. Morimatsu Toshio, "Nihon-gun Taijiso Taihai'no Shinsō" [The truth of so-called Japanese complete defeat at Taierzhuang]," *Rekishi to Jinbutsu*, August 1978, 181.

8. Kuo Mo-jo, Japanese tran., *Konichi-sen Kaisō-roku* [Recollections of Anti-Japanese War] (1959); repr. Chūōkōron-shinsha, 2001, 70.

9. Sankei-shinbun-sha, *Sho Kaiseki Hiroku* [Secret memoir of Chiang Kai-shek] (Sankei-shuppan, 1976), vol. 12, 136.

10. Hata Ikuhiko, *Nihon Riku-kaigun Sōgō Jiten* [Encyclopedia of the Imperial Japanese Army and Navy] (Tokyo Daigaku Shuppankai, 1991), 705.

11. Okamura Yasuji, *Okamura Yasuji Taishō Shiryō: Senjō Kaisō-hen* [Materials of General Okamura Yasuji: Memoirs of battlefields], ed. Inaba Maseo (Hara shobo, 1970), 308.

12. Sawada Shigeru, *Sanbō-jichō Sawada Shigeru Kaisō-roku* [Memoirs of Sawada Shigeru, vice chief of Army General Staff], ed. Morimatsu Toshio (Fuyo-shobo, 1982), 111.

13. Sasaki Harutaka, *Chōsha Sakusen* [The Changsha operation] (Tosho-shuppan-sha, 1988), 86.

14. Kumamoto Heidan Senshi Hensan Iin-kai [Editorial committee of war history of army corps organized in Kumamoto], ed., *Kumamoto Heidan Senshi: Shina-jihen Hen* [War history of army corps organized in Kumamoto: Period of the Sino-Japanese War] (Kumamoto: Kumamoto Nichinichi Shinbun-sha, 1965), 234.

15. Sankei-shinbun-sha, *Sho Kaiseki Hiroku*, vol 12, 152.

16. Kojima Noboru, *Nitchū sensō* [The Sino-Japanese War] (Bungei Shunjū, 1984), vol. 3, 395–399.

17. Ibid., 338.

18. Tani Torao, "Bukan Kōryaku-sen oyobi Kanton Kōryaku-sen" [The Wuhan campaign and Canton campaign], in Kono Osamu, ed., *Kindai Nihon Sensō-shi* [War history of modern Japan] (Dodai-keizai-konwa-kai, 1995), vol. 4, 389.

19. Okamura, *Okamura Yasuji Taishō Shiryō*, 308.

20. Rikujō-jieitai Dai-10-shidan Shirei-bu [The Tenth Division headquarters, ground self-defense force], *Dai-9-shidan senshi* [War history of the Ninth Division] (Kanazawa, 1966), 190.

21. These figures on the Eleventh Army's casualties and achievements are based on its reports. The same will apply hereinafter. However, the number of the enemy's abandoned corpses could not be counted during the combat, so a number several times larger than killed Japanese was usually reported as the Chinese abandoned corpses. We should regard these numbers as inflated ones. See Sasaki, *Chosa Sakusen*, 153.

22. Cited in Matsumoto Keisuke, *Shina-haken-gun no Sakusen to Daitoa-sensō no Kaisen* [The operations of the China Expeditionary Army and the outbreak of the Pacific War], Bōeichō Bōeikenshūjo Senshi-bu Kenkyū shiryō [Research material of War History Branch, National Institute of Defense Studies, National Defense Agency], 98RO-13H, 1998, 13.

23. "Shōwa 13-nen Aki Iko Tai-shi Shōri Hoshin" [Policy for dealing with China after the autumn of 1938], in Bōeichō Bōeikenshūjo, *Senshi sōsho: Shina jihen rikugun sakusen*, vol. 2, 289.

24. Kono Osamu, "Jikyu Taisei-ka no Rikugun Sho-sakusen [Army's campaigns in the protracted stage of the war], in Kono, *Kindai Nihon Sensō-shi*, vol. 4, 449.

25. Okamura, *Okamura Yasuji Taishō Shiryō*, 345.

26. Ro-shudan Sanbō-bu [The staff of the Eleventh Army], "Bukan Kōryaku-sen-go ni okeru Ro-shudan Tōmen Tekigun Ippan no Josei" [The general situation of the enemy forces confronting the Eleventh Army after the Wuhan campaigns], in *Gendaishi Shiryō: Nitchū sensō*, vol. 2, 420–430. *Ro* is the code name of the Eleventh Army.

27. Okamura, *Okamura Yasuji Taishō Shiryō*, 334–335.

28. Lt. Gen. Okamura, "Nisshi-jihen Sokketsu ni Kansuru Sakusen-jo no Iken" [A military opinion to bring the Sino-Japanese War to a quick settlement], *Ro-*

shudan Shō-Keikaku Kyotei narabi-ni Iken-to Tsuzuri [The file of the Eleventh Army's plans, agreements, and opinions], Bōeichō Bōeikenshūjo Toshokan.

29. Bōeichō Bōeikenshūjo, *Senshi sōsho: Dai-hon'ei Rikugunbu* [Official war history series: The Army Department of the IGHQ] (Asagumo shimbunsha, 1967), vol. 1, 626.

30. Okamura, *Okamura Yasuji Taishō Shiryō*, 350–351.

31. Imoto Kumao, *Sakusen Nisshi de Tsuzuru Shina-jihen* [The Sino-Japanese War told by operation diary] (Fuyo-shobō, 1978), 343.

32. Sawada, *Sanbō-jichō Sawada Shigeru Kaisō-roku*, 159, 157.

33. Kono, "Jikyū Taisei-ka no Rikugun Shō-sakusen," 452.

34. Ro-shudan Sanbō-bu, "Shōwa 14-nen Toki Sakusen Sakusen-keika no Gaiyō" [Summary of development of the operation in winter 1939], in *Gendaishi Shiryō: Nitchū sensō*, vol. 2, 436–451.

35. Sawada, *Sanbō-jichō Sawada Shigeru Kaisō-roku*, 159.

36. Ibid., 160.

37. Imoto, *Sakusen Nisshi de Tsuzuru Shina-jihen*, 428.

38. Sawada, *Sanbō-jichō Sawada Shigeru Kaisō-roku*, 56, 177.

39. For the death of General Zhang, see Morikane Chiaki, *Kachu Dai-issen* [The front line in central China] (Sobun-sha, 1977), 58–71.

40. Imoto, *Sakusen Nisshi de Tsuzuru Shina-jihen*, 431–432.

41. Sawada, *Sanbō-jichō Sawada Shigeru Kaisō-roku*, 46.

42. This is what a Chinese military leader in Taiwan told Sawada when he visited Japan after the Pacific War. Ibid., 57.

43. Liu Da-nian and Bai Jie-fu, eds., *Chūgoku Ko-Nichi Sensō-shi* [History of China's Anti-Japanese War] (Sakurai-shoten, 2002), 220.

44. Ro-shudan Shirei-bu [The Eleventh Army headquarters], "Jōsei Kakuho ni Kansuru Iken" [Opinion on securing the west area of the Han River], in Okamura, *Ro-shudan Shō-Keikaku Kyōtei Narabi-ni Iken-to Tuzuri*.

45. Imoto, *Sakusen Nisshi de Tsuzuru Shina-jihen*, 482.

46. Bōeichō Bōeikenshūjo, *Senshi-sōsho: Shina jihen rikugun sakusen*, vol. 3, 328–329.

47. Ibid., 333.

48. Morikane, *Kachu Dai-issen*, 153.

49. Liu and Bai, *Chūgoku Ko-Nichi Sensō-shi*, 320.

50. Kono, "Jikyū Taisei-ka no Rikujō Shō-sakusen," 457–458.

51. Liu and Bai, *Chugoku Ko-Nichi Sensō-shi*, 321.

52. Kumamoto Heidan Senshi Hensan Iin-kai, *Kumamoto Heidan Senshi: Shina-jihen Hen*, 337.

53. *Senshi-sōsho: Honkon Chōsa Sakusen* [Official war history series: Hong Kong and Changsha operations] (Asagumo shimbunsha, 1971), 352.

54. Sankei-shinbun-sha, *Shō Kaiseki Hiroku* (1977), vol. 13, 47–48.

55. Dai-11-gun Shireikan [Commander, the Eleventh Army], "Gunjo Hokoku" [Report of the Eleventh Army's conditions], *Gendaishi Shiryō: Nitchū sensō*, vol. 12, 411.

NOTES TO CHAPTER 9

1. Within the Japanese literature that deals systematically with the air war in China, 1937–1945, the following works are particularly noteworthy: the relevant volumes of the Bōeichō Bōeikenshūjo [Defense Research Center, War History Office, eds.] (hereafter cited as BBS), *Senshi sōsho* [War history series] (hereafter cited as SS) (Asagumo shimbunsha); Nihon Kaigun Kōkūshi Hensan Iinkai hen [History of Japanese Naval Aviation Editorial Committee, eds.], *Nihon kaigun kōkūshi* [History of Japanese naval aviation], vol. 4 (Jiji Tsūshinsha, 1969); Nihon Kōkū Kyōkai hen [Japanese Aviation Association, eds.], *Nihon kōkūshi* [History of Japanese aviation] (Jiji Tsūshinsha, 1975). In addition to popular works on the subject, there are various memoirs and recollections of air crews who served in the conflict. Studies on the war in the air over China have occasionally appeared abroad by non-Japanese. A representative work of this type is the study by Mark R. Peattie, *Sunburst: The Rise of Japanese Naval Air Power, 1909–1941* (Naval Institute Press, 2001), which devotes a chapter to the China air war.

2. Tsutsui Mitsuru, "Shina jihen boppatsuji ni okeru rikukaigun kōkō heiryoku" [Japanese military and naval air strength at the outbreak of the China war], *Gunji Shigaku*, no. 42 (September 1975), 27.

3. Aizawa Jun, *Kaigun no sentaku* [Japanese navy's road to war] (Chūō Kōron Sha, 2002), 96.

4. Editor's note: In reference to the status of military aircraft, the term *operational* can have one of two meanings, for which there are two different Japanese terms. The first meaning is any aircraft that is not a combat aircraft (in Japanese, *jissenki*); the second meaning is any aircraft that is operable (i.e., undamaged, no engine trouble, and so forth, *jitsudōki*). The author's use of *jissenki* makes it clear that he uses the term *operational* in the first sense.

5. The figures on China's air strength are taken from Kūgun Sōshireibu Jōhōshō, *Kūgun kōnichi senshi* [Air combat against Japan] (1950), vol. 1, table 15. The other numerical estimates are derived from Kaigun Yūshūkai, eds., *Kaigun yōran* A survey of the Japanese navy, 1937.

6. See Peattie, *Sunburst*, 27–28.

7. These figures are taken from Tsutsui, "Shina jihen boppatsuji ni okeru rikukaigun kōkō heiryoku."

8. BBS, SS, vol 74, *Chūgoku hōmen rikugun kōkū sakusen* [Army air operations in the China theater] (Asagumo shimbunsha, 1974), 25.

9. Nihon Kōkū Kyōkai hen, *Nihon kōkūshi*, 159.

10. BBS, SS, vol. 95, *Kaigun kōkū gaishi* [Historical overview of Japanese naval aviation] (Asagumo shimbunsha, 1976), 115.

11. "Shina jihen kōkū sakusen ni okeru shotōkei" [Statistics concerning air combat in China], document in possession of the Map Library of the War History Office of the Defense Research Center of the Defense Agency.

12. Nakayama Masahirō, *Chūgoku-teki tenku chimmoku no kōkū senshi* [China skies: An untold account of aerial combat] (Sankei Shuppan, 1981), 207–221.

13. Nihon Kaigun Kōkūshi Hensan Iinkai hen, *Nihon kaigun kōkūshi*, vol. 4, 280–281.

14. Ibid., 271–272.

15. Nakayama, *Chūgoku-teki tenku chimmoku no kōkū sanshi.*

16. Nihon Kōkū Kyōkai hen, *Nihon kaigun kōkūshi*, vol. 4, 429.

17. Wang Zhenghuo, *Kangzhan Qianqi de Sulian Kongjun Zhiyuandui* [The Soviet volunteer group in the early period of the War of Resistance], in Guoshiguan [Academia Historica], ed., *Zhonghuo Minguo Shi Zhuanti Lunwen Ji* [Collected articles on special topics in the history of the Republic of China] (1993), vol. 2, 684–685.

18. Zhuo Wenyi, "Kangzhan Chuqi Wuhan Zhikong Baowei Zhan zhi Yanjiu" [Research on the struggle for air supremacy at Wuhan in the early period of the War of Resistance], 462.

19. According to Zhuo, "Kangzhan Chuqi Wuhan Zhikong Baowei Zhan zhi Yanjiu," 450, the Japanese lost twenty-one aircraft compared to the Chinese total of twelve. On the other hand, a leading Japanese source, Nihon Kōkū Kyōkai hen, *Nihon kaigun kōkūshi*, vol. 4, 388, claims that the Japanese lost only two. The kills claimed by each side in the April battle over Wuhan do indeed differ greatly. But it seems clear that if we use the "admitted losses formula" (see Peattie, *Sunburst*, 115), it is clear that the Chinese lost more aircraft than did the Japanese and that the Japanese were left in control of the air over Wuhan after the battle. Thus, it was a Japanese victory, though not on the grand scale trumpeted by the Japanese navy.

20. Zhuo, "Kangzhan Chuqi Wuhan Zhikong Baowei Zhan zhi Yanjiu," 462, states that during the defense of 1939 the Japanese lost 56 aircraft compared to the Chinese total of 40. But according to the Japanese BBS, SS, *Kaigun kōkū gaishi*, 117, between April and late October 1939, as opposed to the loss of 61 Japanese aircraft, the Chinese lost 660, of which 379 were destroyed in the air and 281 on the ground.

21. Dong Liang and Jiang Yuxiang, "Kangzhan shiqi Zhongguo kongzhong zhanchang shuping" [An assessment of the air war in China during the war of resistance], *Minguo Dang'an* 3 (1993), 91.

22. Nihon Kōkū Kyōkai hen, *Nihon kaigun kōkūshi*, vol. 4, 637.

23. Maeda Tetsuo, *Senryaku bakugeki no shisō* [The concept of strategic bombing] (Asahi shimbunsha, 1988), 192. Editor's note: Professor Hagiwara fails to note the most serious deficiency in all Japanese aircraft, a defect particularly serious in the G3M bomber: highly inadequate armor protection, especially for aircraft fuel tanks. Such a deficiency repeatedly caused Japanese bombers to explode in flames when their fuel tanks were hit. See Peattie, *Sunburst*, 86–87 and 106–107.

24. Tang Zhurong, ed., *Kangzhan shiqi Chongqing di fangkong* [Air defense at Chongqing during the War of Resistance] (Chongqing Press, 1995), 31–32, 50, 59.

25. Ibid., 31–32, 50, 59. This figure does not include the some 10,000 victims of the great Chongqing air raid shelter disaster of June 1941, an indirect result of a Japanese air raid on the city.

26. Yanagizawa Hiroshi, "Chunkin bakugeki—1938–1941" [The bombing of Chongqing, 1938–1941], *Hōyū* 4 (November 2002), 56.

27. BBS, SS, vol. 74, *Chūgoku hōmen rikugun kōkū sakusen*, 302, 378, 382.

28. Ibid., 394.

29. Ibid., 545.

30. Xie Benshu and Wen Xianmei, eds. *Kangzhan shiqi di xinan da houfang* [The great rear area of southwest China during the War of Resistance] (Peking Press, 1997), 247.

31. Jin Guanghui, "Shilun Chennade de kongzhong zhanlue" [A preliminary account of Claire Chennault's air strategy], *Jindaishi Yanjiu* 5 (1988), 206.

NOTES TO CHAPTER 10

1. With the Nationalist capital at Nanjing under imminent threat by Japanese forces, the Kuomintang regime of Chiang Kai-shek formally declared on 20 November 1937 that the city—more familiarly known by its Western appellation Chungking—would serve as the country's provisional capital (*peidu*). All government ministries and official personnel were ordered to transfer there immediately.

2. The cities of London, Dresden, Hamburg, and Tokyo come readily to mind, though they are by no means the only examples of urban centers that were subject to aerial bombardment during World War II.

3. By way of comparison, the German Luftwaffe's air campaign against England lasted roughly eight months and was spread across many English cities, though London bore the brunt of the Blitz.

4. These figures are based on estimates provided by military authorities to the Administrative Yuan's investigative committee on war losses in May 1946, cited in Chi Jingde, *Zhongguo duiri kangzhan sunshi diaocha shishu* [China's damage during World War II] (Taipei: Academia Historica, 1987), 238–239. Other sources provide slightly different estimates. For example, the compilation Kangzhan Shiqi de Chongqing Congshu Bianweihui [Editorial Committee for "Collectanea of Chongqing during the War of Resistance period], *Kangzhan shiqi Chongqing de fangkong* [Air defense in wartime Chongqing] (Chongqing: Chongqing chubanshe, 1995) quotes 11,889 deaths and 14,100 injuries (192). According to figures found in *Chongqing fangkong zhi* [Air Defense Gazetteer for Chongqing] (Chongqing: Southwest China Normal University, 1994), 9,166 Japanese bombers dropped 17,812 bombs on the city, resulting in an aggregate death and injury toll of 24,004 (2); Tang Shourong, *Chongqing dahongzha* [The great bombing of Chongqing] (Chongqing: Chongqing chubanshe, 1992), Southwest China Normal University History Department and Chongqing Municipal Archives, comp., provides the following figures: 5,940 Japanese planes dispatched, 15,677 bombs dropped, more than 9,990 people killed, and roughly 10,200 people injured (26).

5. One of the first demonstrations of Japan's aerial firepower occurred during the Shanghai War of 1931–1932, when the districts of Zhabei and Wusong were bombed by Japanese naval air units. The bombardment lasted only a few weeks but still exacted a serious toll: civilian casualties numbered in the thousands while major industrial, railway, and publishing facilities were leveled.

6. Chiang Kai-shek, "Relocating the national government to Chongqing and prospects for the Anti-Japanese War," 29 October 1937, quoted in Zhang Guoyong, "Qianlun Guomindang zhengfu zeqian Chongqing de sange wenti" [A cursory discussion of three topics on the KMT's decision to relocate to Chongqing],

Dang'an shiliao yu yanjiu, no. 1 (1996), 66. Zhang's essay provides an overview of the decision-making process leading up to the transfer of the capital; see 63–67.

7. "Chongqing fangkong silingbu diaocha eryue shi'er ri diji xiyu qingkuang ji shangwang sunhai gaikuangbiao (zhailu)" [Figures from the Chongqing Air Defense Command's investigation into injuries, deaths, and losses from Japan's bombing of Chongqing on 18 February (extracts)], compiled in *Chongqing dahongzha* [The great bombing of Chongqing] (Beibei: Xinan shifan daxue chu-banshe, 2002), 26–27.

8. Tairikumei 241 go, 2 December 1938, cited in Bōeichō Bōeikenshūjo, eds., *Senshi sōsho* [Official military history], vol. 89, *Shina jihen rikugun sakusen* [Army operations during the China incident], part 2, Shōwa 14 nen 9 gatsu made [To September 1939] (Asagumo shimbunsha, 1976), 296–297; "Tairikushi dai 345 go," 2 December 1938 and "Atch Kōkū ni kansuru rikukaigun chūō kyōtei," December 1938, in Usui Katsumi and Inaba Masao, eds., *Gendaishi shiryō* [Docu-ments on contemporary history], vol. 9, *Nitchū sensō* [The Sino-Japanese War], part 2 (Misuzu shobō, 1964), 402–404, respectively.

9. Bōeichō Bōeikenshūjo, ed., *Senshi sōsho* [Official military history], vol. 8, *Dai hon'ei rikugunbu* [Imperial General Headquarters, Army Department], part 1 (Asagumo shimbunsha, 1967), 571–574.

10. Usui Katsumi, *Shinhan: Nitchū sensō* (Chūkō shinsho, 2000), 130.

11. *Kangzhan shiqi Chongqing de fangkong*, 105–106.

12. Mark Peattie, *Sunburst: The Rise of Japanese Naval Air Power, 1909–1941* (Annapolis, MD: Naval Institute Press, 2002), 109.

13. These figures were compiled from the following documents: "Chongqing fangkong silingbu diaocha wuyue sanri diji xiyu qingkuang ji shangwang sunhai gaikuangbiao" [Investigation by the Chongqing Air Defense Supreme Command of the 3 May Japanese raid on Chongqing and the death, injury, and losses suf-fered]; "Chongqing fangkong silingbu diaocha wuyue siri diji xiyu qingkuang ji shangwang sunhai gaikuangbiao" [Investigation by the Chongqing Air Defense Supreme Command of the 4 May Japanese raid on Chongqing and the death, injury, and losses suffered], reprinted in *Chongqing dahongzha 1938–1943*, 65–66, 68–69.

14. Peattie, *Sunburst*, 118.

15. *Chongqing dahongzha*, 15.

16. Bōeichō Bōeikenshūjo, ed., *Senshi sōsho* [Official military history], *Daihon'ei rikugunbu* [Imperial General Headquarters, Army Department] (Asa-gumo shimbunsha, 1975), vol. 2, 419.

17. Concrete measures for air defense began in 1931. In that year, the Nan-jing government promulgated the "Draft plan for Nanjing's air defenses," which detailed the various preparations needed to ensure the capital's protection against aerial attacks. Among the items addressed were the following: potential launch-ing sites for enemy aircraft; the deployment of reconnaissance planes, antiaircraft guns, and lookout towers in the surrounding region; a comprehensive commu-nications network composed of radio, cable, and railway lines; the construction of defensive fortifications; and, finally, on-site tasks and responsibilities for the police and civil defense corps. See Nanjing shi difangzhi biancuan weiyuanhui

[Compilation Committee for the Nanjing City Gazetteer], *Nanjing renmin fang-kongzhi* [Gazetteer on people's air defense in Nanjing] (Shenzhen: Haitian chu-banshe, 1994), especially 49–50.

18. For an overview of these developments, see Mark Peattie's chapter "Soar-ing: Japanese Naval Aircraft and the Japanese Aircraft Industry, 1937–1941," in *Sunburst*, 77–101. Xu Guangqiu, in his monograph *War Wings: The United States and Chinese Military Aviation, 1929–1949* (Westport, CT: Greenwood Press, 2001), reproduces a chart (116) estimating numbers and types of Japanese aircraft deployed to the China theater—roughly 450—based on figures taken from *Air Operations in the China Theater, 1937–1945* (Japanese Monograph No. 76, prepared by Headquarters, United States Army Forces Far East and Eight U.S. Army, 1956), 17.

19. He Yingqin, *He Shangjiang kangzhan qijian junshi baogao (shangce)* [Military reports of General He during the Anti-Japanese War] (Taipei: Wenxin shudian, 1963), vol. 1, 38. A Japanese estimate of China's air forces gives a more conservative accounting: 170 fighter aircraft, 148 reconnaissance aircraft, 79 light bombers, and 668 pilots, according to figures cited in *Kangzhan shiqi Chongqing de fangkong*, 104, based on a translation of a Japanese monograph produced by the Japan Defense Research Institute entitled *The Japanese Navy's War in China*. Xu Guangqiu, *War Wings*, points out that estimates vary from 300 to 700 air-craft, though he uses the larger number in his discussion of China's air force at the outset of the war.

20. Xu, *War Wings*, 116. Xu includes a chart breaking down the number of military aircraft and their origins. The Chinese military aviation sector was virtu-ally undeveloped before 1932 but underwent a dramatic expansion in the years preceding the war as the Nationalist government established aircraft factories, air training schools, and airports. Kuomintang authorities also consolidated a preex-isting patchwork of regional air units to form a national air force. China's progress in these areas relied heavily on American support and technical assistance. For a discussion of these developments, see Xu, *War Wings*, chapter 3, "The Expansion of Chinese Military Aviation, 1932–1936," 57–114.

21. *Kangzhan shiqi Chongqing de fangkong*, 104–105.

22. Xu, *War Wings*, 125. By mid-1940, Soviet airmen were being dispatched to China in smaller and smaller numbers until finally, in late spring 1941, this flow stopped altogether as the Soviet Union began redeploying military forces to defend the Eastern Front.

23. Even with the moratorium, the sale of U.S. aircraft and other forms of technical and financial assistance continued, albeit at decreased levels compared to prewar figures. In addition, despite its formal stance, the Roosevelt adminis-tration remained sympathetic to the Chinese cause and tacitly encouraged such exchanges. Xu Guangqiu's *War Wings*, chapters 4–6, provides a good summary of such efforts by U.S. companies to provide aircraft to China. For an account of the role of American officials—including Chennault—in expanding U.S. air inter-ests in the China theater, see Michael Schaller, "American Air Strategy in China, 1939–1941: The Origins of Clandestine Air Warfare," *American Quarterly* 28, no. 1 (Spring 1976), 3–19.

24. Xu, *War Wings*, 137–138.

25. After the particularly devastating air campaigns in the summer of 1940, in the fall Chiang Kai-shek instructed Chennault to seek American pilots and aircraft to counter Japan's bombing raids. Claire Chennault, *Way of a Fighter: The Memoirs of Claire Lee Chennault, Major General, U.S. Army (Ret.)* (New York: G. Putnam's Sons, 1949), 90–91.

26. Chennault returned from the United States in the summer of 1941, and training for the AVG continued through the fall, at which point Japan had already ended its bombing campaign for the year. Chennault, *Way of a Fighter*, 105–106.

27. *Kangzhan shiqi Chongqing de fangkong*, 105.

28. Chennault, *Way of a Fighter*, 82.

29. "Chongqing fangkong silingbu gaoshebudui 1939 nian zuozhan pingjun danyao xiaohao shuliang biao" [Average number of shells used by the Chongqing Air Defense Command's antiaircraft units for the year 1939], Chongqing Municipal Archives, files of the Air Defense Command, 47 *juan*. Chart reprinted in *Kangzhan shiqi Chongqing de fangkong*, 118.

30. *Kangzhan shiqi Chongqing de fangkong*, 99–100.

31. *Chongqing dahongzha*, 375.

32. *Kangzhan shiqi Chongqing de fangkong*, 100.

33. For example, on 13 May 1939, the Chinese newspaper *Chongqing gebao lianheban* [United Daily of Chongqing] published a report on the previous day's bombing raid, citing the downing of three Japanese planes by Chinese antiaircraft fire. However, a newspaper item in the *Tokyo Daily News* from the same day makes no mention of the losses suffered by the Japanese side. For newspaper excerpts, see *Chongqing dahongzha*, 40–42. As for losses suffered by the Chinese, such information was closely guarded by military authorities, who took care not to disclose details for fear that they might embolden the Japanese air services further.

34. "1938–1941 Chongqing fangkong silingbu gaoshe budui zhanguo tongji" [Combat results of the Chongqing Air Defense Command's antiaircraft units for 1938–1941], cited in Chongqing renmin fangkong bangongshi, comp., *Chongqing fangkong zhi*, 137. These figures are based on statistics from the Chongqing Municipal Archives, files of the Air Defense Command, 47 *juan*.

35. Peattie's *Sunburst* discusses the concurrent challenges faced by the Japanese air services in stemming attrition rates due to the dogged resistance put up by Chinese interceptors. See chapters 4–5 for an overview of Japan's efforts to strengthen and update its naval aviation sector during the war.

36. Figure cited in *Kangzhan shiqi Chongqing de fangkong*, 87.

37. Ibid., 87.

38. Cheng Yuchen, "Jiang Jieshi yu Chongqing de fangkongdong," in *Dang'an shiliao yu yanjiu*, no. 4 (1993), 92.

39. *Kangzhan shiqi Chongqing de fangkong*, 88.

40. Ibid., 88–89.

41. Chongqing renmin fangkong bangongshi, *Chongqing fangkong zhi*, 13.

42. Total construction in 1938 amounted to 166 structures with a capacity of 33,300 people. Total construction in 1939 amounted to 951 structures with a capacity of 256,000 people. Figures cited in *Kangzhan shiqi Chongqing de fangkong*, 88–89.

43. Ibid., 94–95.

44. Private air raid shelters were differentiated between fee-based shelters, which charged anyone who wished to enter, and those belonging to government and military organizations, companies, and work units, which did not charge but were for the exclusive use of their employees and, if living nearby, their families. These differed from the public shelters, which were for general population use, and at least in the beginning, did not discriminate or limit the number of people who could enter. Stricter regulation, however, was imposed after the tunnel tragedy of 5 June 1941.

45. In 1942, the number of private shelters rose to 1,330. *Kangzhan shiqi Chongqing de fangkong*, 94–95.

46. "Chongqingshi jinji shiqi juliuzheng, churuzheng faji banfa" [Chongqing municipality's emergency procedures for distributing resident and exit cards], cited in *Kangzhan shiqi Chongqing de fangkong*, 79.

47. *Kangzhan shiqi Chongqing de fangkong*, 80.

48. "Chongqingshi nanmin diaocha dengji ji anzhi banfa" [Refugee registration and resettlement procedures for Chongqing municipality], reprinted in *Kangzhan shiqi Chongqing de fangkong*, 81–82.

49. Chongqing Air Defense Command, "Jingcha fangkong xuzhi" [Essential knowledge for police forces about air raids], January 1938, 15.

50. Chongqing Bureau of Public Works, *Chongqingshi jianzhu guize: fu feichang shiqi Chongqingshi jianzhu buchong guize* [Construction regulations for Chongqing municipality: Emergency supplemental construction guidelines for Chongqing municipality] (May 1941), 27.

51. Chongqing Bureau of Public Works, *Chongqing jianzhu guize*, 160–162.

52. In addition to being broadcast and transcribed in Chinese, Chiang's speech was translated into English as well, and copies of the translation were made available by the Kuomintang's Central News Agency and Ministry of Information. This was common practice for all of Chiang Kai-shek's speeches made during the war.

53. Chiang Kai-shek, *China Fights On: War Messages of Chiang Kai-shek, Volume I, October 1938–January 1940*, trans. Frank Wilson Price (Chungking and Hong Kong: The China Publishing Company, n.d.), 157, 158.

54. Ibid., 158–159.

55. Ministry of Information of the Republic of China, "A Growing Air Force," in *China after Seven Years of War* (New York: Alliance-Pacific Press, Inc., 1942), 74.

56. Supervisory Department, Aviation Commission, comp., *Di yijie fangkongjie jinian tekan* [Commemorative volume of the first Air Defense Day], 15 November 1940.

57. The details of the tragedy and its aftermath have been reconstructed from several sources: Xie Zaosheng, "Chongqing da suidao zhixi can'an qinli" [An eyewitness account of the Chongqing tunnel suffocation tragedy], in *Chongqing dahongzha*, 179–182; and Guo Weibo, "Chongqing da suidao zhixi can'an qinli ji" [An eyewitness recollection of the Chongqing tunnel suffocation tragedy], in "Chongqing kangzhan jishi," *Chongqing wenshi ziliao* (1985), 183–190.

58. War orphans and infectious disease control were two of the more visible issues that emerged as public concerns.

59. Adet Lin was seventeen at the time and the oldest daughter of Lin Yutang, a prominent Chinese intellectual who had moved his family to Beibei, a suburb of Chongqing, in 1939. She, along with her two sisters, wrote an account of their three months in the locale and the countless air raids they experienced. Adet, Anor, and Meimei Lin, *Dawn over Chungking* (New York: The John Day Company, 1941), 41.

60. Han Suyin, who would later become a noted author, worked in Chengdu for an American missionary hospital before moving to Chongqing in 1940 to reunite with her husband, a Nationalist military officer. Han Suyin, *Destination Chungking* (Sydney: Halstead Press, 1942), 251.

61. Israel Epstein, "The May Third Chungking Bombing," in *United Relief Series No. 1* (Chungking: China Publishing Company, 1941), 4.

62. Throughout the war years, inflation posed a serious challenge to Nationalist authorities. Chiang Kai-shek expressed his concern on numerous occasions over soaring food prices and the anxiety it provoked among the people.

63. Due to health problems, Wang traveled to Japan to seek medical treatment, where he died in 1944.

NOTES TO CHAPTER 11

1. Zhou Huimin, *Deguo Guwen Chechu Zhongguo Shimo*, in Chinese Modern History Society in conjunction with the Lianhe Bao Cultural Fund, *Qingzhu Kangzhan Shengli Wushi Zhounian Liang'an Xueshu Yantao Hui Lunwen Ji* [Proceedings of the Cross-Strait Scholarly Conference Commemorating the Fiftieth Anniversary of Victory in the War of Resistance] (Taipei: Modern History Society, 1996), 423.

2. For the work of the successive German military advisers, see chapter 3 of Ma Zhendu and Qi Rugao, *You hu? Di hu? Deguo yu Zhongguo Kangzhan* [Friend or enemy? Germany and China's War of Resistance] (Guilin: Guangxi Normal University Press, 1997).

3. Ibid., 184.

4. China Second Historical Archive, *Zhongde Waijiao Midang 1927–1947* [Secret files of Chinese-German relations, 1927–1947] (Nanning: Guangxi Shifan Daxue Chubanshe, 1994), 324–326.

5. Ibid., 329–330.

6. Ma Zhendu and Qi Gaoru, *You hu? Di hu?*, 316–317.

7. Ibid., 312–313, 317.

8. William Kirby, *Germany and Republican China* (Stanford, CA: Stanford University Press, 1984), 222–223.

9. Qin Xiaoyi, *Zhonghua Minguo zhongyao shiliao chubian: Zhanshi Wajiao* [Compilation of important historical materials of the Republic of China: Wartime foreign relations], second collection (Taipei: Guomindang lishi weiyuanhui, 1986), vol. 3, 687.

10. *Sulian Duiwai Zhengce Wenjian Ji* [Selected documents on Soviet foreign policy], vol. 20, 743 n. 167, cited in Li Jiagu, *Hezuo yu Chongtu: 1931–1945 Nian*

de *Zhongsu Guanxi* [Cooperation and conflict: Sino-Soviet relations from 1931 to 1945] (Guilin: Guangxi Normal University Press, 1996), 82.

11. Yang Jie, *Yang Jie riji* [Diary of Yang Jie], cited in Li, *Hezuo yu Chongtu*, 82.

12. Qin Xiaoyi, *Zhonghua Minguo zhongyao shiliao chubian: Zhanshi Wajiao*, vol. 3, 486–491.

13. The first two Soviet loans to China were concluded without being formally signed because Chinese representative Yang Jie, after a long delay, had still not received written plenipotentiary authority to sign treaties. These two loan agreements were not formally signed until 11 August 1938.

14. Li, *Hezuo yu Chongtu*, 81. In the past, Chinese and Soviet historians have had many differences of opinion concerning the actual amounts of the Soviet loans to China during the war of resistance to Japan. The Chinese historian Li Jiagu, using the documents of the Executive Yuan of the Nationalist government preserved in the Chinese Second Historical Archive, has basically solved this problem.

15. V. K. Wellington Koo, *Gu Weijun Huiyi Lu* (the Chinese version of the memoirs of V. K. Wellington Koo) (Peking: Zhonghua Shuju, 1985), vol. 3, 136.

16. Li, *Hezuo yu Chongtu*, 85–99. Concerning the quantity of munitions provided by the Soviet Union, previously Chinese and Russian scholars each had relied on their own historical documents, and their conclusions were inconsistent. In this paper, I used Li Jiagu's calculations, which were based on *Guomin Zhengfu Xingzheng Yuan Duiwai Yihuo Weiyuanhui guanyu dongyong Sulian daikuan xiang Sulian goumai wuqi de zhanglue* [Summary account of the use of Soviet loans to purchase Soviet munitions by the National Government Executive Yuan Foreign Barter Commission] (4 March 1941). Some items missing in this document were filled in by the use of Russian-language materials.

17. Regarding the circumstances of the aid to China by the Soviet volunteer air force, see Wang Zhen, *Dongdangzhong de Tongmeng, Kangzhan Shiqi de Zhongsu Guanxi* [Allied amid Turbulence: Sino-Soviet relations during the War of Resistance] (Guilin: Guangxi Normal University Press, 1993), 118–126; and Li, *Hezuo yu Chongtu*, 140–154.

18. Qin Xiaoyi, *Zhonghua Minguo zhongyao shiliao chubian: Zhanshi Wajiao*, vol. 3, 341.

19. Regarding the circumstances of the work of the Soviet military advisers in China, see Wang, *Dongdangzhong de Tongmeng*, 106–118; and Li, *Hezuo yu Chongtu*, 128–139.

20. Vasilii I. Chuikov, *Zai Hua Shiming, yige Junshi Guwen de Biji* [Mission to China: Notes of a military adviser] (Chinese translation from the Russian original), 140–146.

21. Chuikov, *Zai Hua Shiming*, 35.

22. Qin Xiaoyi, *Zhonghua Minguo zhongyao shiliao chubian: Zhanshi Wajiao* vol. 3, 335.

23. "Sulian fu waijiao renmin weiyuan zhi zhu Hua quanquan daibiao dian" [Telegram from the Soviet deputy people's commissar for foreign affairs to the Soviet plenipotentiary representative in China], 18 September 1938, in the journal *Lishi Dang'an*, 1995, no. 4, 74.

24. After Chuikov left China, the Soviet Union did not send a new chief adviser to replace him, but only sent an acting chief adviser. This was because of Chiang

Kai-shek's order in June 1942 that "advisers cannot be replaced on Soviet initiative without the Chinese government's invitation, and afterward, if China needs advisers, it must be at China's request, and if there is no request, then they will not be able to send replacements. From now on, if new Soviet advisers are to replace current advisers or current advisers resign, these appointments and resignations shall not be valid if I as chairman do not approve." See Qin et al., *Zhanshi Waijiao*, 396–397.

25. See Li, *Hezuo yu Chongtu*, 130–131.

26. Wang Zhenghua, *Kangzhan Shiqi Waiguo dui Hua Junshi Yuanzhu* [Foreign military aid to China during the Sino-Japanese War] (Taipei: Huanqiu shuju, 1987), 187, 204.

27. Zhang Qiyun, *Dang Shi Gaiyao* [Outline of party history] (Taipei: Zhonghua Wenwu Gongyingshe, 1979), vol. 3, 973.

28. On 8 July 1937 Kong Xiangxi (H. H. Kung), vice premier of the Executive Yuan of the Nationalist government and minister of finance, and United States Secretary of the Treasury Henry Morgenthau Jr. signed the Silver-Gold Exchange Agreement. Under this agreement, in the first year of the war China sold $138 million worth of silver to the United States. In spring 1938, the United States allowed China to use an appropriate proportion of the proceeds from this agreement for purposes other than currency stabilization, and this authorization created the de facto purchase credit. See Tao Wenzhao, Yang Kuisong, and Wang Jianlang, *Kangri Zhanzheng Shiqi Zhongguo Duiwai Guanxi* [China's foreign relations during the war of resistance to Japan] (Peking: Zhonggong Dangshi Chubanshe, 1995), 139.

29. According to the Tung Oil Loan Agreement, the United States Export-Import Bank would advance loans totaling $25 million to Chinese companies, to be repaid in five years at an annual interest rate of 0.45 percent, and during this period the Chinese companies would sell 220,000 tons of tung oil to American companies. According to the Chinese Tin Credit Loan Agreement, the Chinese parties were to deliver 40,000 tons of tin within seven years to pay off the loan at an annual interest rate of 0.4 percent, and the other terms were also more favorable than the tung oil loan. The Tungsten Ore Agreement also had an annual interest rate of 0.4 percent, and its terms were even more favorable, only specifying that the loan would be repaid by deliveries of tungsten ore within a five-year period. See Tao Wenzhao, *Zhongmei Guanxi Shi (1911–1950)* [History of Sino-American relations (1911–1950)] (Chongqing: Chongqing Chubanshe, 1993), 204–213.

30. On 19 December 1938 Great Britain announced a loan of £500,000 to China, which was spent on motor vehicles to carry cargo on the Yunnan–Burma road; and on 18 March of the following year Great Britain announced the award to China of £5 million in equilibrium fund loans, to stabilize the value of the Chinese currency. See Tao, Yang, and Wang, *Kangri Zhanzheng Shiqi Zhongguo Duiwai Guanxi*, 150.

31. Zhongguo Shehui Kexueyuan Jindaishi Yanjiusuo Zhonghua Minguoshi Zu [Republic of China History Group of the Modern History Research Institute at the Chinese Academy of Social Sciences], comp., *Zhonghua Minguoshi Ziliao Conggao* [Draft series of documents on the history of the Republic of China], *Zhuanti Ziliao Xuanji* [Selected documents by subject], series 3, *Hu Shi Ren Zhumei Dashi*

Qijian Wanglai Diangao [Incoming and outgoing telegrams from the period of Hu Shi's ambassadorship to the United States] (including *Hu Shi Diangao* [Hu Shi's telegrams]) (Peking: Zhonghua Shuju, 1978), 76–78.

32. Ibid., 79–80.

33. Tao, *Zhongmei Guanxi Shi*, 218–219. The large loan mentioned here was partly the Treasury Department stabilization fund loan and partly the Export-Import Bank loans to be repaid with raw metal imports that were discussed and settled shortly afterward.

34. Qin Xiaoyi, comp., *Zongtong Jiang Gong Dashi Changbian Chugao* [Preliminary draft compilation of the great achievements of H. E. President Chiang Kai-shek], vol. 4, part 2 (1978), 672–673, cited in Wang Zhenghua, *Kangzhan Shiqi Waiguo dui Hua Junshi Yuanzhu* [Foreign military aid to China during the Sino-Japanese War] (Taipei: Huanqiu shuju, 1987), 230.

35. United States Department of State, *United States Relations with China, with Special Reference to the Period 1944–1949* (Washington, DC: U.S. Government Printing Office, 1949), 26.

36. Claire Lee Chennault, *Way of a Fighter: Memoirs of Claire Lee Chennault*, Robert Hotz, ed. (New York: G. P. Putnam and Sons, 1949), 26.

37. See Liang Jingchun, *Shidiwei Shijian* [The Stilwell incident] (Peking: Shangwu yinshu guan, 1973), 21, 26.

38. Wang, *Kangzhan Shiqi Waiguo dui Hua Junshi Yuanzhu*, 231.

39. Ren Donglai, "Ping Meiguo dui Hua Junshi 'Zujie' Yuanzhu" [Commentary on the American "Lend-Lease" military aid to China], in Zhong Mei Guanxi-shi Congshu Bianweihui [History of Sino-American Relations Series Compilation Committee] and Fudan Daxue Lishi Xi [Fudan University History Department], comp., *Zhong Mei Guanxishi Lunwenji* [Collected research papers on the history of Sino-American relations] (Chongqing: Chongqing chubanshe, 1988), vol. 2, 329–330.

40. Ibid., 333.

41. Michael Schaller, *The U.S. Crusade in China* (New York: Columbia University Press, 1979), 89.

42. Liang, *Shidiwei Shijian*, 65.

43. Ibid., 66, 68, 70.

44. Ibid., 118–119.

45. See chapter 7 of Niu Jun, *Cong Yan'an Zouxiang Shijie—Zhongguo Gongchandang Duiwai Zhengce de Qiyuan* [From Yan'an to the world—the origins of the foreign policy of the Chinese Communist Party] (Fuzhou: Fujian Chubanshe, 1992).

46. Liang, *Shidiwei Shijian*, 118; Schaller, *The U.S. Crusade in China*, 109, 115.

47. Ren, "Ping Meiguo dui Hua Junshi 'Zujie' Yuanzhu," 333.

48. Wang, *Kangzhan Shiqi Waiguo dui Hua Junshi Yuanzhu*, 251.

49. Ibid., 262.

50. Shi Yuanhua et al., eds., *Zhonghua Minguo Waijiaoshi Cidian* [Dictionary of the diplomatic history of the Republic of China] (Shanghai: Shanghai guji chubanshe, 1996), 484, 488; Wang, *Kangzhan Shiqi Waiguo dui Hua Junshi Yuanzhu*, 254, 269, 276.

51. Wang, *Kangzhan Shiqi Waiguo dui Hua Junshi Yuanzhu*, 281–282. This book cites the archives of the Taiwan Guofangbu Shizheng Bianyiju [Taiwan Defense Ministry Historical and Political Documents Compilation and Translation Bureau], and gives a detailed account of the number of aircraft that the Nationalist government requested for China on each occasion, the number approved for delivery by the United States, and the number actually delivered.

52. Liang, *Shidiwei Shijian*, 169–170.

53. Ibid., 91–92; Wang, *Kangzhan Shiqi Waiguo dui Hua Junshi Yuanzhu*, 285–287; Du Yuming et al., *Yuanzheng Inmian Kangzhan, Yuan Guomindang Jiangling Kangri Zhanzheng Qin Liji* [Expeditionary campaign in India and Burma, from personal experiences of the former Nationalist military officers during the Sino-Japanese War] (Peking: Zhongguo Wenshi Chubanshe, 1990), 117.

54. Liang, *Shidiwei Shijian*, 92; Wang, *Kangzhan Shiqi Waiguo dui Hua Junshi Yuanzhu*, 289.

55. Du Yuming et al., *Yuanzheng Inmian Kangzhan*, 72–73, 116–120, 323–324.

56. Because the archives are incomplete and the officers in charge did not refer to the units in a consistent manner, at present there is no unified opinion as to which units received training and equipment on the American model. A Taiwanese scholar has concluded that the following Chinese army corps received American-style equipment and training: New First, New Sixth, Fifth, Second, Eighth, Thirteenth, Fifty-fourth, Fifty-third, Seventy-third, Seventy-fourth, Seventy-first, Ninety-fourth, and Eighteenth, each corps consisting of three divisions, for an overall total of thirty-nine divisions. See Wang, *Kangzhan Shiqi Waiguo dui Hua Junshi Yuanzhu*, 299–300.

57. Ren, "Ping Meiguo dui Hua Junshi 'Zujie' Yuanzhu," 343–344.

58. Wang, *Kangzhan Shiqi Waiguo dui Hua Junshi Yuanzhu*, 304.

59. Arthur Young, *China and the Helping Hand, 1937–1945* (Cambridge, MA: Harvard University Press, 1963) 350.

60. Great Britain, the Soviet Union, and France accounted for 94.45 percent of the total amount of American Lend-Lease aid. Great Britain received 64.65 percent, the Soviet Union 23.20 percent, and France 6.60 percent of the total amount of Lend-Lease aid, compared to China's 3.20 percent. See Ren, "Ping Meiguo dui Hua Junshi 'Zujie' Yuanzhu," 328.

61. United States Department of State, *United States Relations with China*, 1046.

62. Meng Mowen, *Mei Jiang Guojie Shiliao* [Historical documents on the conspiracy between the United States and Chiang Kai-shek] (Yangzhou: Xinchao chubanshe, 1951), 318, 346, 352.

63. Ren, "Ping Meiguo dui Hua Junshi 'Zujie' Yuanzhu," 335.

64. Schaller, *The U.S. Crusade in China*, 209.

65. United States Department of State, *United States Relations with China*, 1051.

NOTES TO CHAPTER 12

1. Mao Zedong, *Mao Zedong junshi wenji* [Military works of Mao Zedong] (Peking: Junshi kexue chubanshe, 1993), vol. 2, 5, 18.

2. Ibid., vol. 2, 5.

3. "Dabenying ban diyi zhanqu zuozhan zhidao jihua xunling" [Instructions by the Chinese Nationalist military headquarters concerning the combat plan of the First War Zone], 8 August 1937, *Zhonghua Minguo shi dang'an ziliao huibian* [Compilation of archives of the Republic of China], vol. 5, sec. 2, *junshi* [military] (1) (Nanjing, Jiangsu guji chubanshe, 1998), 616.

4. For inner-party controversies early in the war surrounding the responsibilities of armed warfare, see Yang Kuisong, "Kangzhan chuqi ZhongGong Zhongyang duiRi junshi zuozhan fangzhen di yanbian," [Evolution of the Chinese Community Party Central Committee's military strategy during the initial stage of the Sino-Japanese War], *Jindaishi yanjiu*, 1988, no. 1.

5. See Mao, *Mao Zedong junshi wenji*, vol. 2, 217.

6. "Mao Zedong zhi Peng Dehuai dian" [Telegram from Mao Zedong to Peng Dehuai], 11 April 1940.

7. Cheng Zihua, "Jizhong pingyuanshang de minbing douzheng" [Militia's combat on the central Hebei plain] (November 1942), in ZhongGong Hebei shengwei dangshi yenjiushi, ed., *Jizhong kangri zhengquan gongzuo qixiang wunian zongjie (1937–1942)* [Five-year work summary of five tasks of anti-Japanese aggression regime in central Hebei] (Peking: ZhongGong dangshi chubanshe, 1994), 304.

8. Wang Enmao, *Wang Enmao riji—kangri zhanzheng* [Diary of Wang Enmao] (Peking: Zhongyang wenxian chubanshe, 1995), part 1, 222.

9. Ibid., 300.

10. This refers to dispersed harassment by individual soldiers who fired shots then move to another location.

11. Cheng Zihua, "Jizhong pingyuanshang de minbing douzheng," 305–309.

12. See Li Gongpu, *Huabei dihou—JinChaJi* [Rear in north China: Shanxi, Chahar, and Hebei] (Peking: Sanlian shudian, 1979), no. 27, 31.

13. For example, the core of the central Hebei base was "practically surrounded by the enemy. It lay between the Jinpu, Pinghan, and Beining rail lines and the Cangshe highway." The Japanese occupied "towns and between-towns" in corridors from ten to thirty li (three to nine miles) wide. "We and the enemy surround one another, like a jigsaw puzzle or a *weiqi* [go] board." Guan Xiangying, "Lun jianchi Jizhong pingyuan yuji zhanzheng" [On persisting guerrilla warfare on the central Hebei plain] (1939), in *JinChaJi kangri genjiudi shiliao xuanbian* [Selections of historical materials on Shanxi-Chahar-Hebei bases of anti-Japanese aggression] (Shijiazhuang: Hebei renmin chubanshe, 1983), part 1, 110.

14. Mo Yueyun and Guo Tielun, "Shilun GuoGong liangdang dihou kangri youji zhanzhong di guanxi" [On the relationship of Nationalists and Communists in anti-Japanese guerrilla warfare], *Kangri zhanzheng yanjiu* [Research on the Sino-Japanese War], no. 1 (1997), 173–174.

15. See Jiang Weiguo, *Kangri zhanzheng zhidao: Jiang Weiyuanzhang lingdao kangri guan zhuoyue shisi nian* [Fourteen tough years of resistance under the leadership of central committee chairman Chiang Kai-shek] (Hong Kong: Yuanliu chubanshe, 1989), 311.

16. See Tang Liguo, "Guanyu KMT kangri youjizhan di jige wenti" [Several

issues on KMT's guerrilla warfare during the Sino-Japanese War], *Kangri zhan-zheng yanjiu*, no. 1 (1997), 194–195.

17. Qin Xiaoyi, ed., *Zhonghua Minguo zhongyao shiliao chubian* [Compilation of important historical materials of the Republic of China], second collection, vol. 3 (Taipei: Guomindang lishi weiyuanhui, 1986), 149.

18. Mo and Guo, "Shilun GuoGong liangdang dihou kangri youji zhanzhong di guanxi," 175.

19. Peng Ming, ed., *Zhongguo xiandai shiliao xuanbian* [Selected historical sources for modern China], (Peking: Renmin daxue chubanshi, 1989), vol. 5, 10.

20. See Jiang Weiguo, *Guomin geming zhanshi (3)—kangri yuru* [History of national revolution: Anti-Japanese aggression] (Taipei: Liming, 1978), vol. 7, 152.

21. Chiang Kai-shek expressed it clearly: "Guerrilla warfare is but one form of conventional warfare. It must be undertaken by regular forces." Chiang Kai-shek, *Collected works of President Jiang*, ed. Zhang Qiyuan (Taipei, 1993), 996.

22. Riben fangweiting zhanshishi, ed., *Huabei zhian zhan shang* [North China security war] (Tianjin: Tianjin renmin chubanshe, 1982), 201.

23. Wang, *Wang Enmao riji—kangri zhanzheng*, part 1, 463–464.

24. "Zhongyang Junwei guanyu muqian xingshi he renwu di zhishi" [Instructions by the Central Military Committee of the Chinese Communist Party concerning the current situation and assignments] (10 February 1940), in Zhongyang Dang'anguan, ed., *Zhonggong zhongyang wenjian xuanji* [Selections of documents of the Chinese Communist Party Central Committee] (Peking: Zhonggong Zhongyang Dangxiao Chubanshe, 1990–1991), vol. 12, 184–187.

25. Tang Liguo, "Guanyu KMT kangri youjizhan di jige wenti" [Several issues concerning KMT's guerrilla warfare during the Sino-Japanese War], *Kangri zhan-zheng yanjiu*, no. 1 (1997), 194–195.

26. See Qin, *Zhonghua minguo zhongyao shiliao chibian*, vol. 5, part 4, 227–230. Also see "He Yingqin Bai Chongxi zhi Peng Dehuai fuzongsiling Ye Ting junzhang dian" [Telegram from He Yingqin and Bai Chongxi to vice chief commander Peng Dehuai and army commander Ye Ting], 19 October 1940, in Zhongyang dang'an guan, ed., *Wannan shibian (ziliao xuanji)* [Selected documents of Southern Anhui Incident] (Peking: Zhonggong zhongyang dangxiao chubanshe, 1982), 87–88.

27. "Zhongyang guanyu ge kangri genjudi nei sheng renli wuli jianchi changqi kangzhan di zhishi" [Instructions from the Chinese Communist Party Central Committee concerning saving human and financial resources and persisting in long-term resistance] (20 August 1940), in *Zhonggong zhongyang wenjian xuanji*, vol. 12, 469–470.

28. These recruits were viewed by the CCP as peasant soldiers who still bore signs of feudal superstition.

29. Wang, *Wang Enmao riji*, 209–291.

30. Ibid., 354–355. "Within a few months, the phenomenon of absent without leave (AWOL) soldiers in the 359th Brigade basically ended."

31. See Riben fangweiting zhanshishi, *Huabei zhian zhan*, vol. 1, 235–245.

32. *Quick-strike operations* (*poxi zhan*, literally "destroy-attack operations") refers to operations aiming to destroy transportation lines, communications sys-

tems, mines, wharves, and so forth and to attack scattered Japanese or puppet outposts and strong points.

33. *Mobile operations* refers to a form of combat using flexible maneuvering to assemble forces capable of annihilating the enemy.

34. *Assault operations* refers to attacks on pillboxes, blockhouses, barricades, walls, and other such installations.

35. *Positional operations* refers to reliance on one's position on the battlefield to fight defensively.

36. "Zhongyang geming junshi weiyuanhui guanyu kangri genjudi junshi jian-she di zhishi" [Instructions from Central Revolutionary Military Committee con-cerning the construction of bases of resistance], 7 November 1941, in *Zhonggong zhongyang wenjian xuanji*, vol. 13, 124–125, 212–213. See also Liu Shaoqi, *Liu Shaoqi xuanji* [Selected works of Liu Shaoqi] (Peking: Renmin chubanshe, 1981), part 1, 253–257.

37. Ibid., "Guanyu Huazhong jingbing-jianzheng wenti di zhishi" [Instructions about better staff and simpler administration in central China] (4 August 1942) *Zhonggong zhongyang wenjian xuanji*, 213–214; "Zhongyang guanyu jiaqiang tongyi lingdao yu jingbing-jianzheng gongzuo di zhishi" [Instruction from Chi-nese Communist Party Central Committee about unifying leadership, better staff and simpler administration] (1 December 1942) *Zhonggong zhongyang wenjian xuanji*, 424, 466.

38. Li Bingxin, ed., *Xuese di Jizhong* [Bloody central Hebei Province] (Shijia-zhuang: Hebei renmin chubanshe, 2002), no. 13, 236–241.

39. Lü Zhengcao, "Zai dikou fanfu qingjiao xia di Jizhong pingyuan youji zhanzheng" [Guerrilla warfare despite the enemy's repeated offensive on central Hebei plain] (July 1943), in *JinChaJi kangri genjudi shiliao xuanbian* [Selections of historical materials of Shanxi-Chahar-Hebei bases of anti-Japanese aggression] (Shijiazhuang: Hebei renmin chubanshe, 1983), part 2, 377–380.

40. Li Yunchang, Li Zhongquan, Zeng Kelin, "Jidong de kangri youji zhan-zheng" [Guerrilla warfare in eastern Hebei], in *JiReLiao renmin kangri douzheng* [People's struggle against Japanese aggression in Hebei, Rehe and Liaoning] (Tian-jin: Renmin chubanshe, 1987), part 2, 122–123.

41. Cheng, "Jizhong pingyuanshang de minbing douzheng," 318.

42. Lü, "Zai dikou fanfu qingjiao xia di Jizhong pingyuan youji zhanzheng," 380–381.

43. See Zhu De, *Zhu De xuanji* [Selected works of Zhu De], ed., Zhonggong Zhongyang Wenxian Yanjiushi (Peking: Renmin Chubanshe, 1983), 133; also Peng Dehuai, *Peng Dehuai junshi wenxuan* [Selected military works of Peng Dehuai] (Peking: Zhongyang Wenxian Chubanshe, 1988), 188; *Shandong junqu guanyu diren shousuo bingli he wo junshi douzheng fangzhen gei ge junchu di zhishi* [Instructions of Shandong Military Region to various military areas concerning the enemy's shrink and our military strategy]. See also Mao, *Mao Zedong junshi* 2, 711, 715.

44. Mao Zedong, "Mao Zedong guanyu duoda shengzhang gonggu ziji jixiao diren di zhishi" [Instructions from Mao Zedong concerning winning more com-bat, consolidating ourselves, and shrinking the enemy] (30 September 1944), in *Mao Zedong xuanji* [Selected works of Mao Zedong] (Peking: Renmin Chuban-

she), bound volume, 455, 458; *ZhongGong zhongyang wenjian xuanji* vol 14, 377–378; Zhang Pinghua, *Duidi douzheng yu lianbing yundong* (17 December 1944).

NOTES TO CHAPTER 13

1. Cited in Kazutaka Kikuchi, *Nihonjin hansen heishi to Nitchū sensō* [Antiwar Japanese soldiers and the Sino-Japanese War] (Ochanomizu-Shobō, 2003), 17–18. The images of irrational and incomprehensible behavior of Japanese soldiers abound in Peter Schrijvers, *The GI War against Japan* (New York: New York University Press, 2002); and Eric Bergerud, *Touched with Fire: The Land War in the South Pacific* (New York: Viking Press, 1996).

2. Schrijvers, *The GI War against Japan,* 175.

3. For further stereotypical views on the Japanese soldiers, see Robert Edgerton, *Warriors of the Rising Sun* (New York: W. W. Norton, 1997); and Allison Gilmore, *You Can't Fight Tanks with Bayonets* (Lincoln: University of Nebraska Press, 1998).

4. Edward J. Drea, "The Imperial Japanese Army, 1868–1945," in Jeremy Black, ed., *War in the Modern World since 1815* (London: Routledge, 2003), 75–115.

5. I use the term *combat motivation* to describe drives and incentives for individual soldiers to fight, while using *morale* to refer to the collective level of psychological readiness for combat among soldiers. The classical literature on the issue of combat morale and motivation includes the following: John Dollard, *Fear in Battle* (Washington DC: The Infantry Journal, 1944); Roy Grinker and John Spiegel, *Men under Stress* (New York: McGraw-Hill, 1945); Samuel A. Stouffer et al., *The American Soldier* (Princeton, NJ: Princeton University Press, 1949); S. L. A. Marshall, *Men against Fire* (New York: William Morrow, 1947); Edward A. Shils and Morris Janowitz, "Cohesion and Disintegration in the Wehrmacht in World War II," *Public Opinion Quarterly* 12 (1948), 280–315.

6. For further methodological details, see Kawano Hitoshi, *Nitchūsensō ni okeru Sentō no Rekishishakaigakuteki Kōsatu* [An historical sociology of combat in the Sino-Japanese War: Combat morale in the Thirty-seventh Division], Gunji-shi Gakkai, ed., *Nitchūsensō no soshō,* special issue *Gunjishi,* no. 130–131, vol. 33, no. 2–3, 197–216.

7. The sociological term *primary group* defines a small group with intimate face-to-face relations like a family or a peer group. According to Shils and Janowitz, analysis of ordinary German soldiers during World War II on the Western Front demonstrated that as long as the primary group structure of the component units of the German army persisted, attempts by the Allies to cause disaffection by invoking secondary and political symbols (e.g., about ethical wrongfulness of the National Socialist system) were mainly unsuccessful. Shils and Janowitz, "Cohesion and Disintegration," 281.

8. In order to achieve optimum combat performance, a soldier has to maximize his motivating factors while minimizing disturbing factors by, for instance, effectively coping with fear, preserving his physical strength, and keeping his weapons operable. Among various studies, see Anthony Kellett, *Combat Motivation: The Behavior of Soldiers in Battle* (Boston: Kluwer-Nijhoff, 1982); Stasiu Lubac, "Cul-

tural and Societal Factors in Military Organizations," in *Handbook of Military Psychology* (New York: John Wiley and Sons, 1991), 471–489; Kawano Hitoshi, "A Comparative Study of Combat Organizations: Japan and the United States during World War II," PhD dissertation, Northwestern University, 1996; Kawano Hitoshi, *Gyokusai no Guntai, Seikan no Guntai* [An army of death before dishonor, an army that returns home] (Kodansha, 2001).

9. The Twentieth Division went back to Japan in January 1940. Bōeichō Bōeikenshūjo, *Senshi sōsho* (hereafter BBS SS), *Hokushina Chiansen* [Security operation in north China] (Asagumo shimbunsha, 1968), vol. 1, 141.

10. The Twentieth Division was one of the nine Type A divisions mobilized for the war in 1937. The division was under the command of the Kwantung Army before it was assigned to the First Army.

11. Hata Ikuhiko, ed., *Nihon Riku-kaigun Sōgō Jiten* [Encyclopedia of the Imperial Japanese Army and Navy] (Tokyo daigaku shuppansha, 1991), 705.

12. The Thirty-seventh Division's assigned 2,640 (2,040 available) horses and 89 trucks were fewer than one-third of the 7,800 horses and 300 trucks authorized for the Twentieth Division.

13. Fujita Yutaka, ed., *Haru otozureshi daikōga* [Spring has come to the great Yellow River] (The Thirty-seventh Division History Publishing Committee, 1977), 44.

14. The North China Area Army had a total strength of 354,160, including direct command of 145,669 personnel, the Twelfth Army of 48,380, and the Garrison Army in Mongolia of 27,294. BBS, SS, *Hokusino Chiansen*, vol. 1, 234.

15. As of May 1939, the Thirty-seventh Division's 14,343 troops were dispersed over 105 base camps and 129 outposts, covering 7,000 square miles with a population of 709,000. In gross terms, this meant 2 Japanese soldiers per each square mile were facing 13.9 Chinese soldiers, 101 local residents, plus Communist guerrillas who had penetrated the area. Fujita, *Haru otozureshi daikōga*, 144.

16. The general staff of the North China Area Army evaluated combat readiness of the Chinese forces with three categories: A (high: actively engage in combat), B (medium), and C (low: quite inactive, retreat when attacked). All but one division of the Central Force were considered as A divisions, while the Shaanxi Army units were rated as B and C, and the other forces were all rated as C. Fujita, *Haru otozureshi daikōga*, 71.

17. BBS, SS, *Hokusino Chiansen*, vol. 1, 302.

18. Fujita, *Haru otozureshi daikōga*, 255.

19. Cited in ibid., 319.

20. A breakdown shows that the Thirty-seventh Division lost 451 men killed in action (KIAs) in 1939, 712 in 1940, 653 in 1941, 291 in 1942, 472 in 1943, and 86 in 1944, before joining the Ichigō offensive. A total 2,665 KIAs were lost in the north China theater, while an additional 2,929 men were lost in the central and southern China theaters, and 1,744 KIAs in the French Indochina theater as well. See Yutaka Fujita, ed., *Kōjin Sekijin* [Yellow dust red dust] (The Thirty-seventh Division History Publishing Committee, 1986), 426.

21. BBS, SS, *Hokusino Chiansen*, 1968, vol. 1, 472.

22. Cited in Saburo Sōda et al., trans., *Chūgoku Kōnichi Sensōshi* [The History of Anti-Japanese War in China] (Sakurai-shoten, 2002), 323.

23. Besides the Thirty-seventh Division, the Sixty-second Division, 110th Division, and Third Tank Division, as well as three brigades were mobilized for the offensive. BBS, SS, *Ichigo Sakusen (2) Kōnan no Kaisen* [Official military history series, Ichigō offensive, the Battles in Hunan] (Asagumo Shinbunsha, 1967), 27–28. See also chapter 16 by Hara Takeshi in this volume.

24. The Chinghang operation is called Yuzhong Huizhan in China. It lasted for two months, from 18 April to 12 June 1944, when the Twelfth Army eventually occupied Loyang. The Thirty-seventh Division left about 2,500 new recruits in Shanxi for further training. Fujita Yutaka, *Yuhi wa Akashi Menamu-gawa* [Red Sunset over the Menam River] (The Thirty-seventh Division History Publishing Committee, 1980).

25. BBS SS, *Ichigo Sakusen (1) Kanan no Kaisen*, 600.

26. According to Fujita's estimate, there were 1,776 KIAs in the first phase (14 June–7 November 1944) and 992 KIAs in the second phase of the Shōkei offensive. Fujita, *Yuhi wa Akashi Menamu-gawa*, 601.

27. The Thirty-eighth Army, with its headquarters in Saigon, was officially created on 20 December 1944, upgraded from the former Indochina Expeditionary Army. Three divisions were assigned to the north area. Replacing the Twenty-first Division, the Thirty-seventh Division was in charge of securing the northern part (Tong-King) of the French Indochina area east of the River Rouge, while the Twenty-first Division was assigned to the west of the river. The Twenty-second Division was monitoring the China–French Indochina border. The Thirty-fourth Mixed Brigade was in the middle, and the Seventieth Mixed Brigade and the Second Division were in charge of the south. The First Battalion of the 227th Regiment was attached to the Seventieth Mixed Brigade near Saigon. See Fujita, *Yuhi wa Akashi Menamu-gawa*, 476–481.

28. The Japanese army estimated the total strength of the French forces at about 90,000, while actual strength was about 50,000. About half of the total strength was supposed to be in the north area. See ibid., 537.

29. As for the strength of the Thirty-seventh Division, it was 10,400 as of 9 March 1945. Ibid., 483–485.

30. What made the offensive operations against the modern strongholds even more difficult was the obvious lack of ammunition and logistic support. The Thirty-eighth Army limited the supply of ammunition during the Meigo offensive as follows: 70 rounds per cannon, 1,000 rounds per machine gun, and 50 rounds per rifle. It seemed to a soldier as if he was fighting with a bayonet and hand grenades. Ibid., 486.

31. The breakdown is as follows: 389 KIAs in the battle near Luoyang (Chinghang offensive), April–June, 1944; 1,722 and 637 KIAs in the battles in the Guilin area (Hsiankuei offensive), June–November 1944 and November 1944–January 1945; 1,079 in French Indochina, January–May 1945; and 677 in Thailand and the Malayan peninsula. See Fujita, *Haru otozureshi daikōga*, 534.

32. It was 6,500 miles from Yuncheng to Bangkok. They moved about 2,900 miles on foot and 3,600 miles on train and ship. Fujita, *Yuhi wa Akashi Menamu-gawa*, 591.

33. The code name was changed to *Hikari* (light) after belonging to the Twelfth Army in April 1944.

34. Manning contends that morale is a function of cohesion and esprit de corps. He further elaborates *esprit de corps*: "By establishing relatively demanding expectations of combat behavior, and by linking the soldier's self-esteem to the reputation of the unit, the secondary group provides additional motivation for enthusiastic participation in combat by its members." Frederick Manning, "Morale, Cohesion, and Esprit de Corps," in *Handbook of Military Psychology* (New York: John Wiley and Sons, 1991), 458.

35. Their perception of the soldiers from Okinawa was slightly different from the image of Kyushu soldiers. Although some Okinawa soldiers showed exceptional valor, the stereotypical image of them was that they were naive and pacifist.

36. Nish refers to the fact that the Osaka regiments were less fit and less obedient than those from farming areas because of their urban and industrial backgrounds. Ian Nish, "Japan, 1914–18," in A. Millet and W. Murray, eds., *Military Effectiveness* (Columbus: Mershon Center, Ohio State University, 1988), 246. A captured Chinese officer allegedly told the Japanese interrogator of the Ninety-fourth Independent Infantry Battalion, Fifty-eighth Division, in November 1944 after the battle of Guilin castle, that fighting against ordinary Japanese army troops would require five times more troops than the Japanese strength, but if against a Kyoshu unit, it would need ten times more. See Haruhiko Kawasaki, *Nitchū sensō Ichi Heishi no Shōgen* [The Sino-Japanese War: Testimony of a soldier] (Kobunsha, 2001), 137.

37. Fujita, *Yūhi wa Akashi Menamu-gawa*, 472–476.

38. N. Balchin, *Some Aspects of Psychological Warfare* (London: United Kingdom War Office, 1945), cited in Lubac, *Handbook of Military Psychology*, 472.

39. Stanislav Andreski, *Military Organization and Society* (Berkeley: University of California Press, 1971), 186.

40. Kawano, "A Comparative Study of Combat Organizations," 51–63.

41. Morris Janowitz, *The Professional Soldier: A Social and Political Portrait*, expanded ed. (New York: The Free Press, 1971), 17.

42. A made-up name. All other names are also made up unless noted as real.

43. Veteran of the Thirty-seventh Division, IJA, interview by author no. 25, 30 July 1992.

44. Nemoto was a third-grade expert in kendo, and a self-claimed "first-grade expert" in judo. The skill in kendo later allowed him to save his own life in New Guinea. Veteran of the Thirty-seventh Division, IJA, interview by author no. 25, 30 July 1992.

45. Kawano, *Gyokusai no Guntai*, 137.

46. Kawano, "A Comparative Study of Combat Organizations," 85. Although the uncle told the new recruit not to quit the army, he later asked the unit leader to let him quit, a request that was denied.

47. Ibid., 84.

48. Grinker and Spiegel, *Men under Stress.*

49. The textbook for the first grade Japanese was used 1933–1940. War stories were included in Japanese and ethics textbooks. Toshio Nakauchi, *Gunkoku Bidan to Kyōkasho* [Militarist stories and textbooks] (Iwanami shinsho, 1988).

50. For the historical process of development, see Theodore Cook, "Heishi to kokka, heishi to shakai: Yōbei sekai e Nihon no Sannyū," [Soldiers and the state, soldiers and society: Japan joins the Western world], in Junji Banno, ed., *Nihon Kin-Gendaishi* [A history of modern and contemporary Japan], vol. 2, *Shihonshugi to "Jiyūshugi"* [Capitalism and "liberalism"] (Iwanami Shōten, 1993), 257–298.

51. Masato Hyūga, born in 1922, graduated from an advanced course of a primary school in Miyazaki, then engaged in farming with his family while attending· a youth school three or four days a week until he was inducted in January 1943. Interview by author, no. 2, 15 July 1992.

52. Veteran of the Thirty-seventh Division, IJA, interview by author no. 37, 10 August 1992.

53. Ibid.

54. According to Gilmore's summary of literature on the Japanese soldier's morale, three factors—(1) the central role of the imperial institution, (2) the prestige and power of Japan's armed forces, and (3) the duty-bound nature of the citizenry—are identified as most important. See Gilmore, *You Can't Fight Tanks with Bayonets*, 40.

55. According to Yoshida, it was a common practice to visit a local shrine before the examination to pray for no draft call. Some even tried to evade military service by using various tactics to physically disable themselves, or to convince the inspector that they were not fit for active duty. See Yoshida Yūtaka, *Nihon no Guntai* [The Japanese military] (Iwanami shinsho, 2002).

56. Sometimes, the party could last for two or three nights with different guests.

57. The symbolic meanings of those coins are "going beyond the line of death" (5 cent coin) and "overcoming a tough battle" (10 cent coin).

58. An induction party held in 1916, in Mito, Ibaragi, after which more than 150 people sent the inductee off to the barracks, cost 150 yen, according to the father's diary, while a bridal party for his niece whom he had been taking care of since her mother, who is his sister, lost her husband in the Russo-Japanese War, cost 170 yen. Cited in Shinobu Ohe, *Chōheisei* [Conscription system] (Iwanami-shoten, 1981), 117.

59. By the term *latent ideology*, Moskos refers to general acceptance of the worth of the social system for which the soldiers are fighting, though it is not necessarily a strong sense of patriotism, or in the Japanese case, imperialism. See Charles Moskos, *The American Enlisted Man* (New York: Russell Sage Foundation, 1970).

60. Kawano, "A Comparative Study of Combat Organizations," 104. The case of Toshio Shimada is an exception to the rule. On 20 February 1942, when he made a farewell speech in front of the people gathered for his induction ceremony at a local community center, he told the audience: "I will do my best, and will be a good enough soldier so that you won't ashamed of me." He was most concerned about not disgracing the family honor. However, he clearly stated that he did not like the idea of militarism and did not want to mention that he would die for the country. Interview by author no. 33, 5 August 1992.

61. Many local shrines offered prayers for the soldiers not to get killed in

action. Mothers kept a *Kagezen* every day, that is, a meal prepared for the absent son, which meant that they wanted their sons to get back home alive. Lining up the son's pair of wooden sandals inward also meant that he would come home later. Given the social pressure of militarist ideology, the parents managed to send a strong message to their sons through such symbolic actions.

62. Fujita, *Haru otozureshi daikōga*, 50.

63. As of 1 August 1938, 45.2 percent of the soldiers in the China theater were the second reserves (*Kōbieki*), aged 29–38, 22.6 percent were the first reserves (*Yobieki*) aged 24–28, and 20.9 percent were the supplements (*Hōjūeki*) aged 21–44. The 21- to 23-year-old active-duty soldiers constituted 11.3 percent to be exact. Ibid., 43.

64. Seventh Company, 226th Regiment, *Seishun Kaiko* [Reminiscences of the youth] (1988), 188–193. Interestingly, the combat units for the battle of 13 April had no private second class, whereas those for the battle of 29 April had fourteen private second class soldiers.

65. The Thirty-seventh Engineer Regiment, with eighty-three new recruits, including Private Imada, left Hakata, Fukuoka, on 5 May 1939 and arrived at Yuncheng on 22 May. Each company was separately assigned to a different regiment. Teruo Yuasa, ed., *Kōhei Dai 37 Rentai Shōshi* [A history of the Thirty-seventh Engineer Regiment] (37P Association, 1988), 30.

66. "What impressed me most when I joined the regiment was the fact that I was beaten almost every night. I wondered why they beat me that much. Sundays were supposed to be holidays, but I got beaten up on some Sundays. Thus, I was beaten almost every day." Veteran of the Thirty-seventh Division, IJA, interview by author no. 10, 20 July 1992.

67. "Informal Social Organization in the Army," *American Journal of Sociology* 51, no. 5 (1946), 365–370.

68. For a more detailed account of barracks life in the 1930s, see Edward J. Drea, "Trained in the Hardest School," in *In the Service of the Emperor* (Lincoln: University of Nebraska Press, 1998), 75–90.

69. Drea cites three criteria identified by Japanese army medical doctors for success in battle based on their observation of the Twenty-third Division, which fought in Khalkin Gol against the Soviet army: men in units fought well (1) when their commanders were present, (2) when the men believed that other units continued to support them, despite temporary isolation, and (3) when closely knit emotional ties existed among soldiers in small units. Drea, *In the Service of the Emperor*, 89–90.

70. Those specializations for infantry soldiers, for example, include radio/telephone/code operator, blacksmith, field observer, truck driver, trumpeter, sewer, cook, mechanic, carpenter, shoe repairman, and so forth.

71. Takeshi Yamada was inducted to the Sixth Engineer Regiment in Kumamoto in February 1942. He joined the Thirty-seventh Engineer Regiment in March. He passed the exam to be an officer candidate in June, and he became private first class on 30 August 1942. In October, while being promoted to private superior class, he became a Type B officer candidate due to his health problem. Interview by author no. 7, 17 July 1992.

72. Yutaka Yoshida, *Nihon no Guntai* [The Japanese military] (Iwanami shoten, 2002), 31–32.

73. Kumao Imoto, *Shinajihen Sakusen Nisshi* [Operation diary during the Sino-Japanese War] (Fuyo-shobo, 1998), 177.

74. "It was too long, so that when we threw it to the enemy, they'd throw it back to us, and it would then explode. The enemy used the four-second fused hand grenades, but we tried to pick them up and throw them back to the enemy." Veteran of the Thirty-seventh Division, IJA, interview by author no. 10, 20 July 1992.

75. Noriyuki Ishijima, *Chūgoku Kōnichi sensōshi* [China's Anti-Japanese War history] (Aoki shoten, 1984), 55.

76. The Infantry Gun Battery, 226th Regiment, Thirty-seventh Division, *Hoen* [Gun smoke] (Private publication, 1984), 237.

77. Etsu Kuwada, *Kōbō no Ronri* [Doctrines of offensive and defensive operations] (Hara shobō, 1991), 222.

78. Michael Howard, "Men against Fire: The Doctrine of the Offensive in 1914," in Peter Paret, ed., *Makers of Modern Strategy* (Princeton, NJ: Princeton University Press, 1986), 510–526.

79. Veteran of the Thirty-seventh Division, IJA, interview by author no. 33, 5 August 1992. The night they killed the Chinese POW, the new recruits were asked if they would volunteer for cutting his head off to see who had courage to do so. Private Shimada volunteered, though no one actually had to do it.

80. Veteran of the Thirty-seventh Division, IJA, interview by author no. 5, 16 July 1992.

81. According to the Thirty-seventh Division's history, the Battle of Zhongyuan, May 1941, alone accounted for 35,000 Chinese POWs of the South Route Army in the Second War Area. Fujita, *Haru otozureshi daikōga*, 390.

82. For instance, similar cases of a company commander of the Thirty-ninth Division (Tominaga Shōzō), who ordered his men to bayonet the Chinese POWs as "a finishing touch to training for men and a trial of courage for the officers." Haruko Cook and Theodore Cook, eds., *Japan at War: An Oral History* (New York: The New Press, 1992), 42. The men in the Twentieth Division, Forty-first Regiment (the Fifth Division), also engaged in similar acts.

83. According to the Thirty-seventh Division's own analysis of the Chinghang operation, 6 April–13 June 1944, when attacking at an enemy position which has a strong will to resist, the attack should start in the early morning while still dark and destroy the enemy position at daybreak. On the other hand, when the enemy force is withdrawing, the attack should be prepared in daytime, and start at sunset and seek the enemy in the dark, or get behind the enemy position in the dark and attack them in the early morning. "Dai 37 Shidan Senkun" [Lessons learned by the Thirty-seventh Division], a document at National Institute for Defense Studies, 501.

84. Maj. Gen. Nakajima, "Yakan Kogeki ni kansuru Shokan" [Thoughts on the night attacks], July 1942, a document at National Institute for Defense Studies.

85. Yuasa, *Kōhei Dai 37 Rentai Shōshi*, 83–93.

86. Ibid.

87. Veteran of the Thirty-seventh Division, IJA, interview by author no. 34, 6 August 1992.

88. He failed to successfully finish the job, so he was ordered to try it again a few times. Later in 1944, after being dismissed from the Thirty-seventh Division because of disease, he witnessed the beheading of the Chinese POWs at another unit. Veteran of the Thirty-seventh Division, IJA, interview by author no. 34, 6 August 1992.

89. Veteran of the Thirty-seventh Division, IJA, interview by author no. 34, 6 August 1992.

90. Veteran of the Thirty-seventh Division, IJA, interview by author no. 39, 19 August 1992.

91. During the Keikan operation, the Thirty-seventh Division lost 862 soldiers, including 242 KIAs, while capturing 3,350 POWs and counting 9,473 of the enemy's dead. The division maneuvered about 630 miles in total in sixty days of combat, or 11 miles a day, while fighting five division-level, and twenty-one regiment-level, battles. Fujita, *Yuhi wa Akashi Menamu Gawa*, 278.

92. Later during the operation his ear was injured by explosion of a shell, and he was hospitalized. Veteran of the Thirty-seventh Division, IJA, interview by author no. 8, 18 July 1992.

93. Kawano, "A Comparative Study of Combat Organizations," 351.

94. Veteran of the Thirty-seventh Division, IJA, interview no. 36, 9 August 1992.

95. After the war, he also joined the Self-Defense Forces. This suggests that his morale was not based on the imperialist ideology but simply on nationalism. Veteran of the Thirty-seventh Division, IJA, interview no. 36, August 9, 1992.

96. When he was a green lieutenant newly assigned to the Thirty-seventh Division, a sergeant told him not to do too much in combat and asked him, while smoking a cigarette, to watch how they fought for the first three months.

97. Veteran of the Thirty-seventh Division, IJA, interview by author no. 28, 2 August 1992.

98. Ibid.

99. Combat in the seasoned Israeli army also underlines the foremost importance of this principle. Kellett, *Combat Motivation*, 359.

100. Veteran of the Thirty-seventh Division, IJA, interview by author no. 19, 25 July 1992.

101. Alvin Coox, *Nomonhan* (Stanford, CA: Stanford University Press, 1988), vol. 1, 36–38.

102. Veteran of the Thirty-seventh Division, IJA, interview by author no. 38, 7 August 1992. In military science, *combat power* is the equivalent of the number of combatants squared.

103. Ibid.

104. Shinji Imada remembers the regimental commander's performance in combat clearly: "Yes, Commander Ueda. That's him. We used to be with him as a guard. In the combat field, with bullets flying all over, he stood up with his binoculars. He was watching the enemy position. He said to us, 'Don't put your heads up because nobody replaces you guys,' whereas another regimental commander would need three or four helmets in combat." Interview no. 10, 20 July 1992.

105. Veteran of the Thirty-seventh Division, IJA, interview by author no. 8, 18 July 1992.

106. Veteran of the Thirty-seventh Division, IJA, interview by author no. 42, 23 August 1992.

107. Heavy drinking or even illicit drug use by the unit members would facilitate the bonding between them. Manning, "Morale, Cohesion, and Esprit de Corps," 463.

108. Veteran of the Thirty-seventh Division, IJA, interview by author no. 12, 20 July 1992.

109. An expression used by George Sharp, *Brothers beyond Blood* (Austin, TX: Diamond Books, 1989).

110. Veteran of the Thirty-seventh Division, IJA, interview by author no. 33, 5 August 1992.

111. S. Noy, "Combat Stress Reactions," in *Handbook of Military Psychology*, 507–530; Erica Sharkansky et al., "Coping with Gulf War Combat Stress: Mediating and Moderating Effects," *Journal of Abnormal Psychology* 109, no. 2 (2000), 188–197; Richard Rahe, "Combat Reaction, Chronic," *Encyclopedia of Stress* (San Diego: Academic Press, 2000), vol. 1, 491–494.

112. John Dollard, *Fear in Battle* (New Haven, CT: The Institute of Human Relations, Yale University, 1943), 12–13.

113. Albert Glass, "Lessons Learned," *Neuropsychiatry in World War II* (Washington, DC: Office of the Surgeon General, U.S. Army, 1973), vol. 2, 1015–1023.

114. BBS, SS, *Hokusino Chiansen*, 452.

115. In 1939, an analysis of the psychiatric patients shows, out of 970 patients hospitalized at Kobudai Hospital, 42.9 percent schizophrenia, 14.1 percent hysteria, 11.4 percent epilepsy because of head injuries, 9.0 percent nervous breakdown. Toshimasa Asai, ed., *Uzumoreta Taisen no Giseisha* [Unknown victims of the war] (Private publication, 1993), 34.

116. Fujita, *Haru otozureshi daikōga*, 533, table 1.

117. Ibid., 533, table 3.

118. In the European theater, the U.S. Army, 1942–1945; if the ratio includes "neurological disorders," it increases to 38.3 per 1,000 men, including 2.0 "psychosis" patients per 1,000 men. See Glass, "Lessons Learned," 1015.

119. The company commander was kept at First Battalion HQ, 225th Regiment, which Imada witnessed five days later. Veteran of the Thirty-seventh Division, IJA, interview no. 10, 20 July 1992.

120. Hamada Toshiharu, "Kakoku na Senjo" [Severe battlefield], in Seventh Company, 226th Regiment, *Seishun Kaiko*, 27.

121. Veteran of the Thirty-seventh Division, IJA, interview by author no. 26, 1 August 1992.

122. Stouffer et al., *The American Soldier*, 201. Similar symptoms with less frequency were observed among the U.S. volunteers in the Spanish Civil War. Dollard, *Fear in Battle*, 19.

123. Raymond Corsini, "Defense mechanism," in *Encyclopedia of Psychology* (New York: John Wiley and Sons, 1994), 390.

124. "I believe that most of the soldiers have become fatalists. We'd die some-day. We couldn't do anything with it. It was the dominant trend at that time." Interview no. 7, 17 July 1992.

125. Fujita, *Haru otozureshi daikōga*, 534 n. 2.

126. According to statistics of the Eighth Route Army, from September 1937 to May 1944, a total of 2,407 Japanese POWs were captured, among whom 115 voluntarily surrendered to the Chinese force. Hata estimates that the total number of the Japanese POWs captured by the Eighth Route Army and the New Fourth Army from September 1937 to October 1945 is 6,959, which includes 747 voluntary surrenders. Hata Ikuhiko, *Nihonjin Horyo* [The Japanese POWs] (Hara shobo, 1998), 1:117.

127. When Sugino Rintaro was a squad leader, his platoon leader, a forty-eight-year-old reserve first lieutenant, told him, "Squad leader, please take it over. I'll step back for a while." The platoon leader kept silent during combat. Veteran of the Thirty-seventh Division, IJA, interview no. 40, 19 August 1992.

128. Veteran of the Thirty-seventh Division, IJA, interview by author no. 22, 29 July 1992.

129. Veteran of the Thirty-seventh Division, IJA, interview by author no. 19, 25 July 1992.

130. Samuel Huntington, *The Soldier and the State* (Cambridge, MA: Harvard University Press, 1957), 74–75.

131. Matsushige Tamio, "Guntai no Sokuseki" [Footprints in the army]," in Seventh Company, 226th Regiment, *Seishun Kaiko*, 48–52.

132. Veteran of the Thirty-seventh Division, IJA, interview by author no. 14, 21 July 1992.

133. Fujita, *Yuhi wa Akashi Menamu-gawa*, 83–102. Later, in the battle of 24 May 1944, against the retreating Chinese 110th Division, the lost artillery piece, though it was no longer operable, was recovered by the 225th Regiment.

134. The more atrocities (rape and killing) committed together, the stronger the bonding. However, when the bonding is so strong, the destruction of the group can lead to mass suicide, for example, banzai and kamikaze attacks. We also cannot underestimate the powerful demand of legitimate authority. Even ordinary citizens would inflict the maximum penalty on a total stranger under the demand of a seemingly legitimate authority figure. Stanley Milgram, "Behavioral Study of Obedience," *Journal of Abnormal and Social Psychology* 67 (1963), 371–378. It would be extremely difficult to refuse an order in the Japanese army, even when the order seemed illegitimate.

NOTES TO CHAPTER 14

1. Some Japanese army leaders proposed, as part of a grand political offensive, to invade India. The navy, however, looked to an invasion of Australia, hoping that such an operation would deprive the United States of a staging base for a future counteroffensive against Japan. In reality, the need to face an anticipated landing by U.S. forces on the southeast China coast not only blunted the achievements of the Ichigō operation but foreclosed the possibility of a westward military campaign in China.

2. As of October 1943, a plan was already drafted for the capture of Baoshan as an operation preliminary to a later campaign to Dali. See Rikusenshi Kenkyū Fukyūkai, ed., *Rikusenshi-shu 16: Unnan shomen no sakusen* [Land battle history series 16: Campaigns in the Yunnan front] (Hara Shobō, 1970), 27. Although staff officers of the Southern Army proceeded with the planning of the Dali campaign, the Imperial General Headquarters in Tokyo did not approve it. See Fuku-inkyoku, comp., *Biruma sakusen kiroku: hokumen homen dai-33-gun no sakusen* [Records of the Burma campaigns: Operations of the Thirty-third Army in the northern Burma theater] (Military History Division, Defense Agency of Japan), 13. In 1944, Noguchi Seiki, a staff officer of the Fifty-sixth Division, privately drafted a campaign plan to occupy Baoshan. Noguchi Seiki, *Kaisō Biruma sakusen: dai-33-gun sanbō tsukon no shuki* [Reminiscences of the Burma campaign: Regretful memoir of a Thirty-third Army staff officer] (Kojinsha, 1995), 41–42. Noguchi later became a staff officer of the Thirty-third Army.

3. The operation is often mistakenly referred to as the Tachi operation.

4. Sugie Isamu, *Fukuoka rentai-shi* [History of the Fukuoka regiment] (Akita Shoten, 1974).

5. Bōeichō Bōeikenshūjo (hereafter BBS), *Senshi sōsho* (War history series, hereafter SS): *Imparu Sakusen* [The Imphal operation] (Asagumo Shinbunsha, 1968), 78.

6. Ibid., 280.

7. Ibid., 632.

8. For details concerning the creation of the Thirty-third Army, see Rikusenshi Kenkyū Fukyukai, *Rikusenshi-shu*, 29.

9. Ibid., 381.

10. Fukuinkyoku, *Biruma sakusen kiroku*, 33.

11. Ibid., 42.

12. Rikusenshi Kenkyū Fukyukai, *Rikusenshi-shu*, 38.

13. Ibid., 112; Fukuinkyoku, *Biruma sakusen kiroku*, 67.

14. Mizumoto Kenjirō, "Watashi no Biruma Senki" [My record of the war in Burma], in *Watashi tachi no Isho* [Our final testaments] (Life Planning Center, 2001).

15. Tsuji Masanobu, *Jugo tai ichi* [Fifteen to one] (Kantosha, 1950; repr. Hara Shobō, 1979), 94.

16. Shōwa 20-nen 5-gatsu Jojun Tokushu Junpo (shi) [Special intelligence report on China for early May 1945], 11 May 1945, 3A/14/25–1, National Archives of Japan. This source material is also available at the Japan Center for Asian Historical Records. According to this document, which the Hanoi branch of the SAG's special intelligence unit compiled to summarize the code-breaking activities of the Japanese army against the Chinese, the Chinese forces adopted different keys for their codes depending on their organizations and force levels, such as army group, army, provincial government, war district, and the army high command. They gave a unique code name to each key and frequently changed it. The Japanese intelligence teams also attached their own nickname to each when deciphering it.

17. BBS, SS, *Imparu sakusen*, 272–275. The Japanese leadership seriously considered an advance farther into the Assam region following the Imphal operation

to occupy the Bengal Province and recruit Indian nationals there to form units of the Japanese-sponsored Indian National Army.

18. Ibid., 115.

19. While these events were in progress, the Eighteenth Division was transferred from the Fifteenth Army to the Thirty-third Army to support the Imphal operation.

20. Tsuji, *Jugo tai iIchi,* 141.

21. Chang Jen-chung, *Inmen Sensen nite* [On the Indian-Burmese front], trans. into Japanese by Hayashi Hiroaki (Jiji Tsushinsha, 1946).

22. BBS, SS, *Imparu sakusen,* 208–209.

23. Rikusenshi Kenkyū Fukyūkai, *Rikusenshi-shu,* 73.

24. Ibid.

25. Ibid., 78.

26. The conditions that the U.S. side accepted were for the U.S. force to (1) support cross-river operations, (2) provide air cover for the Chinese ground operations, (3) reinforce the Chinese with a U.S. artillery battalion, (4) extend logistic support to the Chinese, and (5) share command responsibility with the Chinese. See ibid., 79.

27. Ibid., 95.

28. BBS, SS, *Irawaji kaisen—Biruma boei no hatan* [The battle on the Irrawady—collapse of the defense of Burma] (Asagumo shimbunsha, 1969), 36.

29. Ibid., 35.

30. Ibid.

31. Ibid., 116–117.

32. Fukuinkyoku, *Biruma sakusen kiroku,* 17.

33. Ibid., 118–123. Kawabe took his initiative because the SAG was overwhelmed with operations in the Pacific theater, the Philippines in particular. This virtually allowed the BAA to dictate the planning and execution of military campaigns in Burma.

34. BBS, SS, *Imparu sakusen,* 675.

35. Rikusenshi Kenkyū Fukyūkai, *Rikusenshi-shu,* 103.

36. Tsuji, *Jugo tai iIchi,* 79.

37. Rikusenshi Kenkyū Fukyūkai, *Rikusenshi-shu,* 103–04; BBS, SS: *Iwaraji kaisen,* 122.

38. BBS, SS, *Iwaraji kaisen,* 233.

39. Rikusenshi Kenkyū Fukyūkai, *Rikusenshi-shu,* 109.

40. BBS, SS, *Iwaraji kaisen,* 227.

41. Ibid., 235.

42. Rikusenshi Kenkyū Fukyūkai, *Rikusenshi-shu,* 127.

43. BBS, SS, *Iwaraji kaisen,* 246.

44. Noguchi, *Kaisō Biruma sakusen,* 142.

45. Ibid., 163.

46. Ibid., 164; BBS, SS, *Iwaraji kaisen,* 257 states that the Second Division occupied hill number 2 on 13 September. It does not mention Tsuji's activity. Neither does Rikusenshi Kenkyū Fukyūkai, *Rikusenshi-shu,* 135. Nevertheless, it is beyond any doubt that Noguchi "at a frontline command post at Yun-lung-shan clearly witnessed at a distance" Tsuji's "death-defying commandership."

47. Joseph W. Stilwell, *Chugoku nikki* [China diary], trans. into Japanese by Ishido Kiyotomo (Misuzu Shobō, 1966), 290. The original was Joseph W. Stilwell, *The Stilwell Papers*, ed. Theodore H. White (New York: W. Sloane Associates, 1948).

48. Rikusenshi Kenkyū Fukyūkai, *Rikusenshi-shu*, 193.

49. Tsuji, *Jugo tai iIchi*, 112.

50. Rikusenshi Kenkyū Fukyūkai, *Rikusenshi-shu*, 117.

51. Ibid., 74–75.

52. Ibid., 187.

53. Ibid., 190–192.

54. BBS, SS, *Iwaraji kaisen*, 308.

55. Tsuji, *Jugo tai iIchi*, 128; Noguchı, *Kaisō Biruma sakusen*, 227.

56. BBS, SS, *Iwaraji kaisen*, 394.

57. Tsuji, *Jugo tai iIchi*, 95; ibid., 96; Rikusenshi Kenkyū Fukyūkai, *Rikusenshi-shu*, 136.

58. BBS, SS, *Ichigō sakusen* [The Ichigō operation (Asagumo shimbunsha, 1968),], part 2, 552, 556.

59. BBS, SS, *Iwaraji kaisen*, 341.

60. Tsuji, *Jugo tai iIchi*, 144.

61. Ibid., 135–39; BBS, SS, *Iwaraji kaisen*, 365–370.

62. Ironically, however, the battle along the Irrawaddy ended in defeat, nullifying the Thirty-third Army's mission to protect the Japanese line of retreat. See BBS, SS, *Iwaraji kaisen*, 545 ff.

63. Ibid., 386. By that time, the Thirty-third Army had retreated as far as Lashio.

64. Ibid., 395–396.

65. Memorandum, Wedemeyer to Chiang Kai-shek, no. 272, 2 December 1944, in Keith E. Eiler, ed., *Wedemeyer on War and Peace* (Stanford, CA: Hoover Institution Press, Stanford University, 1987), 92.

66. Wedemeyer to Marshall, 10 December 1944, in ibid., 84.

67. BBS, SS, *Ichigo Sakusen* (Asagumo Shinbunsha, 1969), part 3, 592–593.

68. Okamura Yasuji, *Okamura Yasuji Taishō Shiryō: Senjo Kaisō-hen* [Source materials of General Okamura Yasuji: Memoirs on military operations] (Hara Shobo, 1970), 214.

69. Gunjishi Gakkai, ed., *Daihon'ei rikugunbu sensō shidō-han kimitsu sensō nisshi* [Confidential war diary of the war guidance section, Imperial General Headquarters, army department] (Kinseisha, 1988), vol. 2, 643–644.

70. Ibid.

71. Ibid., 651.

72. Okamura, *Okamura Yasuji Taishō Shiryō*, 214.

73. Tsuji, *Jugo tai iIchi*, 141.

74. Barbara W. Tuchman, *Shippai-shita Amerika no Chūgoku Seisaku* [The failure of America's China policy], trans. by Suginobe Toshihide of *Stilwell and the American Experience in China, 1911–45* (Asahi Shinbunsha, 1996), 16.

75. Chang Jen-chung's Japanese translation was published by Jiji Tsushinsha as early as 1946. In Taiwan, there was a photo exhibition on the India-Burma campaign at a Taipei public hall named Chung-shan Hall on 1–5 January 1948. See the Taipei newspaper *He-ping*, 1 January 1948.

76. I would like to thank many people for various forms of assistance to me in writing this article. In particular, Professor Tōmatsu Haruo of Tamagawa University, Professor Nemoto Takashi of the Tokyo University of Foreign Studies, and Professor Chu Hung-yuan of the Taipei Research Institute who made some suggestions on source materials and made several available to me. I would like to express special thanks for these individuals.

NOTES TO CHAPTER 15

1. Hans van de Ven, *War and Nationalism in China, 1925–1945* (London: Routledge Curzon, 2003).

2. Regarding research by military scholars on this battle, see Song Guangshu and Xie Benshu, "Yunnan kangri zhanzheng shi zhushu jieshao" [An introduction to writers on the Anti-Japanese War of Resistance in Yunnan], *Kangri zhanzheng yanjiu* [Research on the Anti-Japanese War of resistance], 1995, no. 1, 83–85; Song Guangshu, "Mianxi zhanyi tushu yanjiu" [A study of maps and books on the battle of western Yunnan], in Fu Zongming and Lin Chaomin, eds., *DianMian kangzhan lunwen ji* [A collection of essays on the war of resistance in Burma and Yunnan] (Kunming: Yunnan daxue chubanshe, 1999), 409–418; Zeng Jingzhong, "Zhongguo kangri zhanzheng zhengmian zhanchang yanjiu shuping" [Comments on research on battles during China's War of Resistance against Japan], *Kangri zhanzheng yanjiu*, 1999, no. 3, 77–101; Li Songlin, "Taiwan guanyu kangri zhanzheng shi de yanjiu" [Research on the history of battles of the Anti-Japanese War of Resistance in Taiwan], in Guo Dehong, ed., *Kangri zhanzheng shi yanjiu shuping* [Research comments on the history of the Anti-Japanese war of Resistance] (Peking: Zhonggong dang shi chuban she, 1995), 441–467; Liu Fenghan, "Kangzhan shi yanjiu yu huigu" [Reflections and research on the history of the war of resistance], *Jindai Zhongguo*, no. 108 (August 1995), 127–164.

3. But later twelve corps were transferred to Yunnan. They were the Second, Fifth, Sixth, Eighth, Thirteenth, Eighteenth, Fifty-third, Fifty-fourth, Seventy-first, Seventy-third, Seventy-fourth, and Ninety-fourth corps. Tian Xuan, *Tiexue Yuanzheng: Zhongguo yuanzhengjun yinmian kangzhan* [An expedition of blood and iron: The War of Resistance of the Chinese Expeditionry Army in India and Burma] (Nanning, Guangxi Shifan Daxue Chubanshe, 1994), 56.

4. Barbara Tuchman, *Shidiwei yu Meiguo zai Hua jingyan* [Stilwell and the American Experience in China, 1911–1945] (Peking: Xinxing Chubanshe, 2007), 455, 494; *Yuanzheng YinMian Kangzhan*, 115–116.

5. According to the "Lujun bingli tongjibiao" [Army statistical table] by the Chinese Department of Military Command, the first bureau, second office, before 1 April 1944, the Chinese Expeditionary Force had two group armies, five corps, and thirteen divisions. See *Zhonghua minguo shi dang'an ziliao huibian* [Compilation of the archives of the Republic of China], issue 5, vol. 2, *Junshi*, no. 1 (Nanjing: Jiangsu guji chubanshe, 1998), 768–770. Obviously, these statistics do not include the units (three divisions in one corps and another division) that were under the direct command of the Chinese Expeditionary Force.

6. Liu Fenghan, "Guojun ru Mian zuozhan yanxi" [Study and analysis of the Nationalist army's combat in Burma], in *Qiqi shibian liushi zhounian guoji xue-*

shu yantao hui [The international academic conference commemorating the six-tieth anniversary of the Marco Polo Bridge Incident] (Peking, July 1997), 46–48.

7. Tuchman, *Shidiwei yu Meiguo zai Hua jingyan*, 520, 654.

8. "Jiang Jiesh zhi Junzhengbu, Bingyubu dai diangao" [Chiang Kai-shek's tele-grams to the Department of Military Command and Department of Military Ser-vice], 19 December 1944, in *Zhonghua minguo shi dang'an ziliao huibian*, 425.

9. Tuchman, *Shidiwei yu Meiguo zai Hua jingyan*, 520.

10. *Zhonghua minguo shi dang'an ziliao huibian*, 444–446.

11. Bingyibu yizheng yuekan she [Monthly military service affairs journal of the Military Service Department], *Kangzhan banian lai bingyi xingzheng gongzuo song baogao* [General report on military administration in the eight years of the Sino-Japanese War], 40–41, cited in Dai Xiaoqing, *Zhongguo yuanzheng jun ru Mian kangzhan jishi* [Historical records of combat of the Chinese Expeditionary Army in Burma] (Chongqing: Xinan Shifan Daxue Chubanshe, 1990), 204.

12. *Zhongyang ribao* [Central daily news, Chongqing], 12 December 1944.

13. Bao Zunpeng, *Zhongguo qingnian yundong shi* [A history of Chinese youth movements] (Chengdu: Shidai chubanshe, 1948), 132.

14. For the Second Corps, these would be the Ninth and Seventy-sixth divi-sions; for the Sixth Corps, the Ninety-third and reserve Second divisions; for the Eighth Corps, the honorary First and 103rd divisions; for the Fifty-third Corps, the 116th and 130th divisions; and for the Seventy-first Corps, the Eighty-seventh, Eighty-eighth, and Thirty-sixth divisions. *Zhonghua minguo zhongyao shiliao chubian: duiri kangzhan shiqi*, issue 2, vol. 3, *Zuozhan jingguo*, 381.

15. Chen Cheng, "Chen Cheng siren huiyi ziliao" [Chen Cheng's memoir], *Minguo dang'an*, 1987, no. 2, 32; Wang Wenxuan, "Zuijin shinian junwu jiyao, 1933–1943" [A summary of the military affairs of the last ten years, 1933–1943], *Mingguo dang'an*, 1989, no. 1, 65.

16. *Zhonghua minguo shi dang'an ziliao huibian*, issue 5, vol. 2, *Junshi*, no. 1, 61.

17. *Zhonghua minguo zhongyao shiliao chubian: duiri kangzhan shiqi*, issue 2, vol. 3, *Zuozhan jingguo*, 381–382.

18. *Zhonghua minguo shi dang'an ziliao huibian*, issue 5, vol. 2, *Junshi*, num-ber 4, 403–404.

19. *Zhonghua minguo zhongyao shiliao chubian: duiri kangzhan shiqi*, issue 2, vol. 3, *Zuozhan jingguo*, 388.

20. Wang Zhenghua, *Kangzhan shiqi waiguo duihua junshi huanzhu* [Military foreign aid to China during the Sino-Japanese War] (Taipei: Huanqiu shuju, 1987), 290; *Yuanzheng YinMian kangzhan*, 56; Chen Cheng, "Chen Cheng siren huiyi ziliao," 32; Meng Xiangfen, "Meishi wuqi zhangbei de Guomindang di bajun" [The American military equipment of the Nationalist Eighth Corps Army], in Zhongguo renmin zhengzhi xieshang huiyi quanguo weiyuan hui wenshi ziliao weiyuanhui, ed., *Wenshi ziliao cungao xuanbian: Kangri zhanzheng* [Selections of literary and historical documents of the Sino-Japanese War] (Peking: Zhongguo wenshi chuban she, 2002), part 2, 521–522.

21. *Yuanzheng YinMian kangzhan*, 57–58.

22. Chen Cheng, "Chen Cheng siren huiyi ziliao," 33; Yang Zhaoxiang, "Jun-

weihui zhu Dian ganbu xunlian tuan zuozhan ban" [The combat class of the Military Affairs Committee's cadre training team in Yunnan], in *Wenshi ziliao cungao xuanbian*, 526–538; Chen Cheng, "Chen Cheng siren huiyi ziliao," 33.

23. *Zhonghua minguo zhongyao shiliao chubian: duiRi kangzhan shiqi*, no. 2, *Zuozhan jingguo*, no. 3, 336.

24. Ibid., 373.

25. Jiang Weiguo, *Guomin geming zhanshi*, part 3, *Kangri yuwu* [History of national revolution: Anti-Japanese aggression] (Taipei: Liming, 1978), vol. 9, 170, 251.

26. Jiang, *Guomin geming zhanshi*, part 3, *Kangri yuwu*, vol. 9, 171–176.

27. *Zhonghua minguo zhongyao shiliao chubian: duiRi kangzhan shiqi*, issue 2, vol. 3, *Zuozhan jingguo*, vol. 3, 472–474.

28. Jiang, *Guomin geming zhanshi*, part 3, *kangri yuwu*, vol. 9, 216.

29. "Wei Lihuang zhi Jiang Jieshi dian," 480–482.

30. Xu Yongchang, "Xu Yongchang chenggao" [The draft submitted by Xu Yongchang], 20 May 1944, in *Zhonghua mingguo shi dang'an ziliao huibian*, issue 5, vol. 2, *Junshi*, no. 4, 416–417.

31. Song Xilian and Wei Lihuang, "Song Xilian, Wei Lihuang guanyu Longling de er fu shi qingxing yu Jiang Jieshi laiwang midian" [Song Xilian and Wei Lihuang's secret telegrams with Chiang Kai-shek on the situation in which the Chinese Expeditionary Army gained Longling and then lost it], in *Zhonghua minguo shi dang'an ziliao huibian*, issue 5, vol. 2, *Junshi*, vol. 4, 418–419.

32. Bōeichō Bōeikenshūjo, eds., Senshi sōsho [Military history series 25], *Irawaji kaisen: Biruma bōei no hatan* [The Battle of the Irrawaddy River, Japan's failure in the defense of Burma] (Asagumo shimbunsha, 1969), 221, 227–229.

33. *Zhonghua minguo shi dang'an ziliao huibian*, issue 5, vol. 2, *Junshi*, no. 4, 421.

34. He shaozhou, "He Shaozhou baogao weigong Songshan zuozhan jingguo midian" [A secret telegram from He Shaozhou reporting on the battle in the besieging of Mount Songshan], 10 September 1944, and Song Xilian, "Song Xilian baogao suo bu zuozhan jingguo midian" [A secret telegram from Song Xilian reporting on the battle of his forces], in *Zhonghua minguo shi dang'an ziliao huibian*, issue 5, vol. 2, *Junshi*, no. 4, 421–428.

35. *Zhonghua minguo zhongyao shiliao chubian: duiRi kangzhan shiqi*, issue 2, *Zuozhan jingguo*, vol. 3, 508–509.

36. Ibid., 327–333.

37. *Zhonghua minguo shi dang'an ziliao huibian*, issue 5, vol. 2, *Junshi*, no. 4, 421.

NOTES TO CHAPTER 16

1. Hattori Takushirō, *Daitōa sensō zenshi* [A complete history of the great East Asia war] (Hara shobō, 1965), 618.

2. Bōeichō Bōeikenshūjo, eds., (hereafter BBS), *Senshi sōsho* (War history series, hereafter SS), *Ichigō sakusen* [The Ichigō operation], part 1, *Kanan no kaisen* [The Battle of Henan] (Asagumo shimbunsha, 1967); BBS, SS, *Ichigō sakusen*, part 2, *Kōnan no sakusen* [The Battle of Hunan] (Asagumo shimbunsha,

1968); BBS, *SS*, *Ichigō sakusen*, part 3, *Kōsei no kaisen* [The Battle of Guangxi] (Asagumo shimbunsha, 1969); and BBS, *SS*, *Shōwa 20 nen no Shina hakkengun*, part 1 [The China Expeditionary Army in 1945] (Asagumo shimbunsha, 1971).

3. Sanada Jōichirō, *Sanada Jōichirō shōshō shūkki* [Major General Sanada Jōichirō's journal], Japan Defense Archives (hereafter JDA).

4. BBS, SS, *Daihonei Rikugunbu* [Imperial General Headquarters, army department] (Asagumo shimbunsha, 1973), part 7, 548.

5. Ibid. 549.

6. BBS, SS, *Ichigō sakusen*, part 1, *Kanan no kaisen*, 3–4.

7. Ibid., 2–3; BBS, SS, *Daihonei rikugunbu*, part 7, 549.

8. BBS, SS, *Hondo bōkū sakusen* [Homeland air defense operations] (Asagumo shimbunsha, 1968), 232–233.

9. BBS, SS, *Ichigō sakusen*, part 1, *Kanan no kaisen*, 10.

10. BBS, SS, *Chūgoku hōmen kaigun sakusen* [Naval operations on the China front] (Asagumo shimbunsha, 1975), part 2, 394.

11. BBS, SS, *Ichigō sakusen*, part 1, *Kanan no kaisen*, 12.

12. Ibid., 13.

13. BBS, SS, *Daihonei rikugunbu*, part 7, 545; Imoto Kumao, *Sakusen nikki de tsuzuru daitōa sensō* [Operations journal of the great East Asia war] (Fūyō Shobō, 1979), 498–499.

14. Hattori, *Daitōa sensō zenshi*, 524.

15. Imoto, *Sakusen nikki de tsuzuru daitōa sensō*, 498.

16. BBS, SS, *Ichigō sakusen*, part 1, *Kanan no kaisen*, 24–25.

17. Ibid. 28–29.

18. Morimatsu Toshio, ed., *Daihonei rikugunbu dairikumei dairikushi sōshū-sei, shōwa 19* [Collected imperial orders and imperial guidance issued by Imperial General Headquarters] (Emutei Press, 1994), 34.

19. Ibid., 341.

20. BBS, SS, *Ichigō sakusen*, part 1, *Kanan no kaisen*, 31.

21. Ibid., 52.

22. Ibid., 57–58.

23. Sanada, *Sanada shūki*; BBS, SS, *Ichigō sakusen*, part 2, *Konan no kaisen*, 174.

24. Zoku Gendaishi Shiryō, *Rikugun Hata Shunroku nikki* [The army: Journal of Hata Shunroku] (Misuzu Shobō, 1983), 473.

25. Gunjishi Gakkai, ed., *Daihonei rikugunbu sensō shidōhan kimitsu Sensō Nikki* [Imperial general headquarters, army department, war guidance section, confidential wartime journal], vol. 2 (Kinsei-sha, 1998), 545–546; BBS, SS, *Ichigō sakusen*, part 1, *Kanan no kaisen*, 175.

26. BBS, SS, *Ichigō sakusen*, part 1, *Kanan no kaisen*, 549.

27. Lieutenant Colonel Miyazaki Shun'ichi, *Shina hakkengun no tōsui* [Command and control of the China Expeditionary Army], JDA; BBS, SS, *Ichigō sakusen*, part 2, *Konan no kaisen*, 550.

28. Ibid.

29. Gunjishi, *Daihonei Rikugunbu Sensō Shidoban Kimi Sensō Nikki*, vol. 2, 584.

30. Ibid.

31. Zoku, *Rikugun-Hata Shunroku Nikki*, 487.

32. Sanbō honbu, ed., *Shōwa 19 Nen jōsō kankei Shorui Tsuzuru* [Miscellany of documents related to reports to the throne, 1944], vol. 2, JDA; BBS, SS, *Ichigō sakusen*, part 1, *Kanan no kaisen*, 554–555.

33. BBS, SS, *Ichigō sakusen*, part 3, *Kōsei no kaisen*, 685.

34. BBS, SS, *Hondo Bōkū Sakusen*, 307.

35. Ibid., 371–372.

36. BBS, SS, *Ichigō sakusen*, part 3, *Kōsei no kaisen*, 655.

37. Barbara. W. Tuchman, *Stilwell and the American Experience in China, 1911–45* (New York: Macmillan, 1971).

38. Ishijima Noriyuki, *Chūgoku KōNichi sensōshi* [A history of China's Anti-Japanese War of Resistance] (Aoki Shoten, 1984), 184; BBS, SS, *Ichigō sakusen*, part 3, *Kōsei no kaisen*, 696.

NOTES TO CHAPTER 17

1. Bōeichō Bōeikenshūjo [Japan Defense Agency, Defense Research Institute, Office of Military History], *Yihao Zuozhan zhier: Hunan huizhan* [Ichigō sakusen, or Ichigō operation], vol. 2, *Konan no kaisen* [The Battle of Hunan], trans. from Japanese into Chinese by Tianjin shi Zhengxie bianyi weiyuanhui (Peking: Zhonghua shūjū, 1984), part 1, 7. (Hereinafter *The Battle of Hunan*.)

2. Chiang Kai-shek, "Duiyu zhengjun gean zhi xunshi" [Instruction on various cases in the regrouping of troops], 28 July 1944, in *Xian Zongtong Jianggong sixiang yanlun zongji* [General collection of the thoughts and speeches of former president Chiang Kai-shek], vol. 20 (Taipei, 1966), 455–471; Xu Yongchang, *Xu Yongchang riji* [Journal of Yongchang Xu] (Taipei: Zhongyang yanjiuyuan jindaishi yanjiusuo, 27 July 1944), vol. 7, 387; *The Battle of Hunan*, part 1, 2.

3. *The Battle of Hunan*, part 1, 7, 11.

4. Junshi Weiyuanhui Junlingbu zuzhi fa [The organization law of the Ministry of Military Operations of the Military Commission], "Junshi Weiyuanhui Junlingbu fuwu zhangcheng" [The service protocol of the Ministry of Military Operations of the Military Commission], March 1942, both in Zhongguo dier lishi dang'an guan [China Second Historical Archive] (in Nanjing), comp., *Zhonghua minguo shi dang'an ziliao huibian* [Compilation of the archival documents of the history of the Republic of China], issue 5, vol. 2, Military, part 1 (Nanjing: Jiangsu guji chubanshe, 1998), 95–96.

5. Xu, *Xu Yongchang riji*, vol. 7, 252, 255, 260, 264, 265.

6. According *Ichigō sakusen* [Ichigō operation], the military history compiled by Bōeichō Bōeikenshūjo, the Japanese military General Headquarters did have a plan to build the "Greater East Asia Railway." The railway would have started from Pusan (Korea); pass through Shenyang (Mukden), Peking, Hankou, and Hengyang; join the Hunan–Guangxi Railway; go through Guilin, Liuzhou, Liangshan (Vietnam); pass through French Indochina; reach Bangkok; cross the Malay Peninsula; and reach Singapore. The total length would be nearly 5,000 miles. Later, after evaluation, this plan was abandoned. See *The Battle of Hunan*, part 1, 6.

7. Xu, *Xu Yongchang riji*, vol. 7, 274.

8. Ibid., 285, 288.

9. Ibid., 293.

10. Chiang Kai-Shek, "Jiang Weiyuanzhang zhi dijiu zhanqu siling zhangguan Xue Yue zhishi diqing panduan dian" [Chairman Chiang Kai-shek's telegram to Xue Yue, commander in chief of the Ninth War Zone, asking an assessment of the enemy's situation], in Qin Xiaoyi et al., eds., *Zhonghua Minguo zhongyao shiliao chubian: Kangri zhanzheng shiqi* [The preliminary compilation of the important historical documents of the Republic of China], vol. 2, part 2 (Taipei: Zhongguo Guomindang zhongyang weiyuanhui dangshi weiyuanhui, 1981), 643, 644.

11. Chiang Kai-shek, *Zongtong Jianggong dashi changbian chugao* [The preliminary draft of the compilation of the important events of former president Chiang Kai-shek] (Taipei: Zhongguo Guomindang zhongyang weiyuanhui dangshi weiyuanhui, 1978) vol. 5, part 2, 526.

12. Xu, *Xu Yongchang riji*. vol. 7, 311–312.

13. *The Battle of Hunan*, part 1, 10–33.

14. The first Changsha battle took place from September to October 1939, the second Changsha battle took place from September 1941 to October 1941, and the third Changsha battle took place from December 1941 to January 1942.

15. Zhao Zili and Wang Guanglun, "Chang-Heng Zhanyi" [The Battle of Changsha and Hengyang] and Xiang Yanri and Chen Dezhao, Chaling and "Anren zhandou" [The engagements of Chaling and Anren], both in *Hunan sida huizhan: Yuan Guomindang jiangling Kangri Zhanzheng qinli ji* [The four battles in Hunan province: The experience of former Nationalist military officers in the Sino-Japanese War] (Peking: Zhongguo wenshi chubanshe, 1995), 399–403, 438.

16. *The Battle of Hunan*, part 1, 32–33.

17. Xu, *Xu Yongchang riji*, vol. 7, 320–321.

18. Zhao Zili and Wang Guanglun, "Chang-Heng Zhanyi," 399–403, 438.

19. Xu, *Xu Yongchang riji*, vol. 7, 324.

20. *The Battle of Hunan*, part 1, 12–14.

21. "Hunan Huizhan zhandou yaobao" [Key combat reports of the Hunan battle], in Zhongguo dier lishi dang'an guan [China Second Historical Archive] (in Nanjing), *Kangri Zhanzheng zhengmian zhanchang* [Front battlefields of the Sino-Japanese War] (Nanjing: Jiangsu guji chubanshe, 1987), part 2, 1256–1258.

22. Ibid., 1293; *The Battle of Hunan*, part 1, 34–35.

23. "Junshi Weiyuanhui fu canmou zongzhang Bai Chongxi cheng di sijun zai Changsha shoucheng jingguo deng baogao" [The report submitted by deputy chief of staff Bai Chongxi about the Fourth Army defending Changsha and other issues], in Qin Xiaoyi et al., *Zhonghua Minguo zhongyao shiliao chubian: Kangri zhanzheng shiqi*, vol. 2, part 2, 646–648. Zhao and Wang, "Chang-Heng Zhanyi."

24. "Junlingbu ni Guojun jinhou zuozhan zhidao jihua dagang gao" [The draft of the future combat plan made by the Ministry of Military Operations for Nationalist forces], in *Zhonghua Minguo shi dang'an ziliao huibian*, issue 5, vol. 2, "Military," part 1, 714–715.

25. Xu, *Xu Yongchang riji*, vol. 7, 335; ibid., vol. 7, 339–341.

26. Ibid., vol. 7, 339, 342.

27. *The Battle of Hunan*, part 1, 12–15, 78.

28. Ke Yufang, "Lun Changheng Huizhan dier jieduan zhanyi" [On the second stage of the Changsha-Hengyang battle], in *Kangri Zhanzheng yanjiu* [Research on the Sino-Japanese War], issue 4, 1996.

29. "Dijiu zhanqu Hunan Huizhan zuozhan zhidao fang'an" [The combat plan of the Hunan battle of the Ninth War Zone], in *Kangri Zhanzheng zhengmian zhanchang*, 1258.

30. Chiang, *Zongtong Jianggong dashi changbian chugao*, vol. 5, part 2, 551.

31. Xu, *Xu Yongchang riji*, vol. 7, 374, 379, 383.

32. Chiang Kai-shek, "Zhi chi tuqiang" [Recognizing humiliation and making the country strong], 21 July 1944, in *Xian Zongtong Jianggong sixiang yanlun zongji* [General collection of the thoughts and speeches of former president Chiang Kai-shek], vol. 20 (Taipei, 1966), speech 444–453.

33. Xu, *Xu Yongchang riji*, vol. 7, 380.

34. Bai Chongxi, "Junshi Weiyuanhui fu canmou zongzhang Bai Chongxi cheng zhanlue guanjian dian" [Telegram from deputy chief of staff Bai Chongxi concerning his ideas about strategy], in Qin Xiaoyi et al., eds., *Zhonghua Minguo zhongyao shiliao chubian: Kangri zhanzheng shiqi*, vol. 2, part 2, 649, 650.

35. Xu, *Xu Yongchang riji*, vol. 7, 383.

36. Ibid., vol. 7, 405.

37. "Dijiu Zhanqu Changheng Zuji zhan zhandou xiangbao" [The detailed combat report of the Changsha-Hengyang battle of the Ninth War Zone], in Zhongguo dier lishi dang'an guan [China Second Historical Archive] (in Nanjing), comp., *Zhonghua minguo dang'an ziliao huibian*, issue 5, vol. 2, Military, part 4, 209–210.

38. Ibid., 212–214.

39. Now Yongzhou, Hunan Province.

40. "Dijiu Zhanqu Changheng zuji zhan zhandou xiangbao." The time covered in this document is from 25 May to 10 October 1944. From early September to early October, the Nationalist forces still fought the Japanese enemy in Liuyang, Liling, Youxian district, Chaling, Anren, Leiyang, Changning, Shaoyang, and other places. On 3 October, Shaoyang fell. See Zhongguo kexueyuan lishi yanjiusuo disan suo Nanjing shiliao zhengli chu [The Chinese Academy of Sciences, Institute of Historical Research, third institute, Nanjing Bureau of Compilation of Historical Documents], comp., *Zhongguo xiandai zhengzhi shi ziliao huibian* [Compilation of the historical documents of modern Chinese politics], issue 3, vol. 40, 1957.

41. Xu, *Xu Yongchang riji*, vol. 7, 430.

42. "Dijiu Zhanqu Changheng zuji zhan zhandou xiangbao," 216–217.

43. "Dijiu Zhanqu Hunan Huizhan zuozhan jiantao" [Self-criticism of the combat in the Hunan battle by the Ninth War Zone], in *Kangri Zhanzheng zhengmian zhanchang*, 1293.

44. There had been *juntuan* (formation) under the army group and above the army. There had been brigades under the division and above the regiment. But these units were abolished after a year. See Liu Fenghan, "Kangzhan qianqi Guojun zhi kuozhan yu yanbian" [The expansion and evolution of the Nationalist

forces at the initial stage of the Sino-Japanese War], in *Zhonghua Minguo jian-guo bashi zhounian xueshu taolun ji* [The anthology of academic papers on the eightieth anniversary of the foundation of the Republic of China], (Taipei: Jindai Zhongguo chubanshe, 1992), vol. 1, 481–484.

45. Xu, *Xu Yongchang riji*, vol. 7, 332.

46. Ibid., 298.

47. Ibid., 300.

48. Zhang Zhizhong, *Zhang Zhizhong huiyi lu* [The memoir of Zhang Zhi-zhong] (Peking: Zhongguo wenshi chubanshe, 1985), 298–300.

49. Xu, *Xu Yongchang riji*, vol. 7, 286.

50. Ibid., 416.

51. Zhao and Wang, "Chang-Heng Zhanyi."

52. "Dijiu Zhanqu Hunan Huizhan zuozhan jiantao," in *Kangri Zhanzheng zhengmian zhanchang*, part 2, 1296–1297; Huang Tao et al., "Di liushier jun canjia Hengyang Zhanyi de jingguo" [The process of the Sixty-second army's par-ticipation in the Hengyang battle].

53. Ke Yufang, "Changheng Huizhan rijun canzhan bingli shukao" [A study of the input of Japanese forces in the Changsha battle and Hengyang battle], *Kangri Zhanzheng yanjiu*, issue 3, 1998.

54. *The Battle of Hunan*, part 2, 71; Riben Fangweiting Zhanshishi [War His-tory Office of the Japanese Defense Department], ed., *Riben diguo zhiyi qinhua ziliao changbian* [An extensive compilation of documents concerning the Japanese invasion of China] (Chengdu: Sichuan renmin chubanshe, 1987), part 2, 314.

55. "Hunan Huizhan dijun shangwang panduan biao" [A table concerning an assessment of the enemy's casualties during the Hunan battle] and "Hunan Hui-zhan Guojun shangwang tongji biao" [The statistical table of the casualties of the Nationalist forces during the Hunan battle], both in the archives of the Zhanshi hui, Zhongguo dier lishi dang'an guan [China Second Historical Archive] (in Nan-jing); Zhang Xianwen, et al., eds., *Zhongguo kangri zhanzheng shi* [History of the Sino-Japanese War, 1931–1945 (Nanjing: Nanjing daxue chubanshe), 2001], 1089.

56. Zhang et al., *Zhongguo kangri zhanzheng shi*, 1090–1091.

57. Ge Xiancai, "Hengyang gujun kangzhan shishi" [The history of the iso-lated units defending Hengyang during the Sino-Japanese War], *Zhonghua zazhi*, vol. 17, no. 217 (1981).

58. "Ganji Hengyang shoujun" [To thank the forces defending Hengyang] and "Xiang Fang junzhang huanhu" [Hailing General Fang], *Da gong bao* (Chong-qing), 4 August 1944, 13 December 1944, respectively. See also "Hengyang tuwei" [Breaking the siege of Hengyang], 39–42; "Zhanshi wenhua gongying she" [War-time Cultural Supplies Union] (n.p., n.d.).

59. Wang Shijie, *Wang Shijie riji* [Journal of Shijie Wang] (Taipei: Zhongyang yanjiuyuan jindaishi yanjiusuo, 1990), vol. 4, 365.

60. John King Fairbank, *Jianqiao Zhongguo shi*, trans. of *The Cambridge His-tory of China*, vol. 13, *Republican China 1912–1949*, part 2 (Shanghai: Shanghai renmin chubanshe 1992), 636; Zhang et al., *Zhongguo kangri zhanzheng shi*, 1090–1091.

61. Xu, *Xu Yongchang riji*, vol. 7, 328.

62. Ministry of Military Operations, "Junlingbu ni Guojun jinhou zuozhan zhidao jihua dagang gao" [The future combat plan for the Nationalist forces] and Chiang Kai-shek, "Guanyu diba zhanqu junshi bushu midian gao" [Draft of the telegram concerning the military deployment of the Eighth War Zone], both in *Zhonghua Minguo shi dang'an ziliao huibian*, issue 5, vol. 2, Military, part 1, 714–718.

63. Xu, *Xu Yongchang riji*, vol. 7, 356.

64. Ibid., vol. 7, 397.

65. See Liu Fenghan, "Lujun yu chuqi Kangzhan" [The Army and the initial stage of the Sino-Japanese War], in Liu Fenghan, *Kangri zhanshi lunji* [Anthology of the history of the Sino-Japanese War] (Taipei: Dongda tushu gongsi, 1987), 252–257.

66. Chiang Kai-shek, "Dui Huangshan zhengjun huiyi shencha xiuzheng gean zhi xunshi" [Instructions concerning investigating and correcting various aspects of the Mount Huangshan Conference on military reorganization], cited in *Zhonghua Minguo shishi jiyao* [Keynotes of the historical events of the Republic of China], July to September 1944 (Taipei: Guo shi guan, 1994), 365.

67. Xu, *Xu Yongchang riji*, vol. 7, 388.

68. Zhang Ride, "Kangzhan shiqi lujun de jiaoyu yu xunlian" [The education and training of infantry forces during the War of Resistance], in *Zhonghua Minguo jianguo bashi zhounian xueshu taolun ji* [An anthology of academic papers at the eightieth anniversary of the foundation of the Republic of China] (Taipei: Jindai Zhongguo chubanshe, 1992), vol. 1, 532.

69. Xu, *Xu Yongchang riji*, vol. 7, 400.

70. Cited in Zhang Ride, *Kangzhan shiqi de Guojun renshi* [Nationalist forces during the Sino-Japanese War] (Taipei: Zhongyang yanjiuyuan jindaishi yanjiusuo, 1993), 39.

71. Chiang Kai-shek, Duiyu zhengjun huiyi gean zhi zhishi [Instructions on various aspects of the conference on military rectification], cited in *Zhonghua Minguo shishi jiyao*, 493.

72. Ibid., 432.

73. Fairbank, *Jianqiao Zhongguo shi*, 625.

74. Chiang Kai-shek, "Dui Huangshan zhengjun huiyi shencha xiuzheng gean zhi xunshi" [Instructions concerning investigating and correcting various aspects of the Mount Huangshan Conference on military reorganization], "Budui shou junxu junxi yu bingzhan bu zhi kutong shiqing" [The reality of troops' suffering from poor military supplies, military medical services, and military depots], and "Junxu bu jianquan junxu yewu ji bu hefa you bu heli shiqing" [The reality: military supply system is flawed and its business is illegal and unreasonable], all cited in *Zhonghua Minguo shishi jiyao*, 370–373.

75. Chiang Kai-shek, "Zhi chi tuqiang" [Recognizing humiliation and making the country strong], cited in ibid., 151–152.

76. Liu Zhi, "Jianjun di jiben tiaojian" [The basic conditions for establishing forces], *Jianjun daobao*, vol. 1, no. 2, August 1944.

77. Ray Huang, *Dibei tiannan xu gujin* [Various thoughts on history] (Taipei: Shibao wenhua chubanshe, 1991), 141.

78. Chen Cheng, "Zhengzhi bu Chen buzhang xunci" [Instructional speech by Minister of Politics Chen Cheng] (Ministry of Military Training, Military Commission, 1939), 23; Gu Zhutong, "Dui zuozhan renyuan yanjiu ban diwuqi xunhua" [Instructional speech to the fifth research course for combat personnel] (Command of the Third War Zone, 1944), 10–11; Zhang, "Kangzhan shiqi lujun de jiaoyu yu xunlian," in *Zhonghua Minguo jianguo bashi zhounian xueshu taolun ji*, vol. 1, 547–548.

79. Xu, *Xu Yongchang riji*, vol. 7, 447.

80. Chiang Kai-shek, "Zhi chi tuqiang" [Recognizing humiliation and making the country strong], cited in *Zhonghua Minguo shishi jiyao*.

81. "Di sijun Changsha disici huizhan zuozhan jingguo diebao canmou baogaoshu" [Staff report on combat procedures of the Fourth Army in the fourth Changsha battle], in *Kangri Zhanzheng zhengmian zhanchang*, part 2, 1263–1264.

82. "Dijiu Zhanqu Hunan Huizhan zuozhan jiantao" [Self-criticism of the combat in the Hunan battle by the Ninth War Zone], in *Kangri Zhanzheng zhengmian zhanchang*, part 2, 1297; "Guiliu Huizhan zhandou yaobao" [Key combat reports of the Guilin and Liuzhou battle], archive of Zhanshi hui, in Zhongguo dier lishi dang'an guan [China Second Historical Archive] (in Nanjing), archive number 25/4884.

83. Chiang Kai-shek, "Duiyu zhengjun huiyi gean zhi zhishi" [Instructions on various aspects of the conference on military rectification], cited in *Zhonghua Minguo shishi jiyao*, 493–494.

NOTES TO CHAPTER 18

1. Arthur Young, *China and the Helping Hand* (Cambridge, MA: Harvard University Press, 1963), 420.

2. Morimoto Tadao, *Mashono Rekishi: Mikurokeieigaku kara Mita Taiheiyosenso* [A study of the Pacific War from the viewpoint of macro business analysis] (Tokyo: Bungeishunjusha, 1991), 49.

3. For the deployment of the Japanese Army units at the time of the outbreak of the U.S.-Japan war, see Morimoto, *Mashono Rekishi*, op. cit., 59–60.

4. For example, the three mechanized divisions that the Japanese Army possessed in 1941 (the Imperial Guard Division, the Fifth, and the Forty-eighth) and all sixty of the latest type of army fighter planes Type 1 "Oscar" were deployed in operations in the south.

5. Morimoto, *Mashono Rekishi*, op. cit., 50–51.

6. Ibid., 60.

7. Bōeicho Bōeikenshūjō Senshishitsu, *Honkon Chōsa Sakusen* [Hong Kong and Changsha operations] (Tokyo: Asagumo Shinbunsha, 1971), 535 ff.

8. Shō Kaiseki, *Makuro historii-shikan kara yomu Shō Kaiseki Nikki* [Chang Kai-shek Diary read from macro historic view] (Tokyo: Tōhō shoten, 1997), 279.

9. Bōeicho Bōeikenshūjō Senshishitsu, *Shōwa Jushiochihachinen no Shinahakengun* [China Expeditionary Army in 1942–1943] (Tokyo: Asagumo Shinbunsha, 1972), 97–298.

10. For the "Gunyōsasshin keikaku" see *Daihonei Rikugunbu (4)*, op. cit., 162–165.

11. *Shōwa Jushiochihachinen no Shinahakengun*, op. cit., 9–96; *Daihonei Rikugunbu (4)*, op. cit., 255–253, 558–573.

12. The Second and Thirty-eighth divisions were sent to Guadalcanal in the autumn of 1942 and completely destroyed. The Thirty-third division was sent to the Burma front and seriously damaged in the Imphal campaign of spring 1944.

13. Evans Fordyce Carlson, *The Chinese Army: Its Organization and Military Efficiency* (New York: Institute of Pacific Relations, 1940), 77–79.

14. Young, *China and the Helping Hand*, op. cit., 408.

15. Charles Romanus and Riley Sunderland, *Stilwell's Mission to China* (Washington, DC: Department of the Army, Office of the Chief of Military History, 1953), chapters 8 and 10; Hsi-sheng Ch'i, *Nationalist China at War: Military Defeats and Political Collapse* (Ann Arbor: University of Michigan Press, 1982), 67–68, 108–113.

16. Young, *China and the Helping Hand*, op. cit., 245–251; Charles Romanus and Riley Sunderland, *Stilwell's Command Problems* (Washington DC: Department of the Army, Office of the Chief of Military History, 1956), 11, 25, 168.

17. See Carl Burger, *B29* (Japanese edition), Masui Kōichi, *Chōku no Yosai B29* [Super Fortress B29] (Tokyo: Mainichi Shinbunsha, 1971). For theoretical development of strategic bombing including the B-29 operations, see Maeda Tetsuo, *Senryakubakugeki no Shisō: Gerunika, Jukei, Hiroshima eno Kiseki* [The theory of strategic bombing: the road to Guernica, Chungking, and Hiroshima] (Tokyo: Asahi Shinbunsha, 1988).

18. For the controversy regarding the location of B-29 airbases between the Marianas and China, see Burger, *B29*, op. cit., 138–140.

19. Robert Holz, ed., *Way of a Fighter: The Memoirs of Claire Lee Chennault* (New York: Putnam, 1949).

20. Barbara Tuchman, *Sand against the Wind: Stilwell and the American Experience in China 1911–1945* (New York: Macmillan, 1970). Ch'i, *Nationalist China at War*, op. cit., 107–108.

21. Ch'i, *Nationalist China at War*, op. cit., 83–131; T'ien-wei Wu, "Contending Political Forces During the War of Resistance," in Hsiung and Levine, *China's Bitter Victory*, op. cit., 51–78.

22. *Shōkai Kaiseki: Makuro historii-shikan kara yomu Shō Kaiseki Nikki*, op cit., 283.

23. Tang Tsou, *American Failure in China* (Chicago: Chicago University Press, 1963), 82.

24. Burger, *B29*, op. cit., 83–89; Masui, *Chōku no Yōsai B29*, op. cit., 138–140.

25. Tsou, *American Failure in China*, op. cit., 83–84.

26. Young, *China and the Helping Hand*, op. cit., 301–303.

27. Bōeichō Bōeikenshūjō Senshishitsu, *Daihonei Rikugunbu (7) Shōwa Juhachinen Junigatsu made* [Imperial General Headquarters Army Section (7) Up to December 1943] (Tokyo: Asagumo Shinbunsha, 1973), 179–216.

28. Ibid., 315–317, 324, 545–548.

29. Morimoto, *Mashono Rekishi*, op. cit., 54.

30. Number of units transferred from the Kwantung Army in Manchuria to elsewhere between January 1944 and March 1945: 19 infantry divisions, 2 tank

divisions, over 700 aircraft. This figure amounted to nearly 90 percent of the Kwantung Army strength at its peak. Ito Masanori, *Teikokurikugun no Saigo 5 Shūmatsuhen* [The end of the Imperial Japanese Army 5 the final phase] (Tokyo: Kadokawashoten, 1973), 146–154.

31. Bōeichō Bōeikenshūjō Senshishitsu, *Kaijō Goeisen* [The maritime protection war] (Tokyo: Asagumo Shinbunsha, 1971), 289–296, 408–416, 549–560. Morimoto, *Mashono Rekishi*, op. cit.

32. Bōeichō Bōeikenshūjō Senshishitsu, *Kaijō Goeisen*, op. cit., 545 and appendix chart no. 8.

33. Ch'i, *Nationalist China at War*, op. cit., 69–74.

34. The IGHQ and the China Expeditionary Army in earlier stages had already detected the American deployment of B-29 bombers. Masui, *Chōku no Yōsai B29*, op. cit., 53–56, 174–188.

35. Ibid., 72. Tōjō was rather more concerned about the destruction of American airbases in the vicinity of Xi'an.

36. For the number of units mobilized for the Ichigō operation and its overall plan, see Bōeichō Bōeikenshūjō Senshishitsu, *Ichigō Sakusen (1) Kanan no Kaisen* [Ichigō Operation (1) The Honan phase] (Tokyo: Asagumo Shinbunsha, 1967), 1–57.

37. Morimoto, *Mashono Rekishi*, op. cit., 55–56.

38. Hsi-sheng Ch'i, "The Military Dimension 1942–1945," in Hsiung and Levine, *China's Bitter Victory*, op. cit., 163.

39. For Chinese casualties in the Ichigō operation, see Ch'i, *Nationalist China at War*, op. cit., 80–81; Ch'i, "The Military Dimension 1942–1945," op. cit., 165.

40. For Japanese casualties caused by American air attacks, see Masui, *Chōku no Yōsai B29*, op. cit., 117–118. Japanese loss of trucks and tanks amounted to 15 percent of the whole number mobilized.

41. For the operations of the Fifth Air Army during the Ichigō operation, see Bōeichō Bōeikenshūjō Senshishitsu, *Rikugun Kokugunbi no Unyō* [Use of army air power] (Tokyo: Asagumo Shinbunsha, 1976), 168–171; *Chūgokuhomen Kokusakusen* [Air operations in the China theater] (Tokyo: Asagumo Shinbunsha, 1974), 406 ff.

42. Young, *China and the Helping Hand*, op. cit., 304; Tsou, *American Failure in China*, op. cit., 83; Romanus and Sunderland, *Stilwell's Command Problems*, op. cit., 325, 366, 368.

43. For the American bombing operations from the Marianas, see Burger, *B29*, op. cit., 138–159; Maeda, *Senryakubakugeki no ShisōShisō*, op. cit., 469–471.

44. Holz, *Way of a Fighter*, op. cit., 328–329; Burger, *B29*, op. cit., 121–124; Masui, *Choku no Yosai B29*, op. cit., 227–230.

45. These figures are based on the United States Strategic Bombing Survey, "The Strategic Air Operation of Very Heavy Bombardment in the War Against Japan (Twentieth Air Force) Final Report" (Washington DC: Government Printing Office, 1946), reprinted in *The United States Strategic Bombing Survey*, Volume 9 (New York: Garland, 1976).

46. Maeda, *Senryakubakugeki no Shisō*, op. cit., 469.

47. Bōeichō Bōeikenshūjō Senshishitsu, *Shōwa Nijūnen no Shinahakengun (2) Shūsenmade* [The China Expeditionary Army in 1945 (2) Up to the Termination

of War] (Tokyo: Asagumo Shinbunsha, 1973); Ito, *Teikokurikugun no Saigo 5, Shumatsuhen*, op. cit., 32–34.

48. For the battle of Lahekou, see Bōeichō Bōeikenshūjō Senshishitsu, *Shōwa Nijunen no Shinahakengun (2) Shusenmade*, op. cit., 379–432.

49. For the battle for Zhijiang, see ibid., 53–378.

50. For the performance of the Sixty-second division in Okinawa, see Bōeichō Bōeikenshūjō Senshishitsu, *Okinawahomen Rikugun Sakusen* [Army operations in Okinawa] (Tokyo: Asagumo Shinbunsha, 1968), 314 ff.

51. For the transfer of units to the east coast, see Bōeichō Bōeikenshūjō Senshishitsu, *Shōwa Nijunen no Shinahakengun (2) Shusenmade*, op. cit., 461 ff.

52. Morimoto, *Mashono Rekishi*, op. cit., 58.

53. Ch'i, "The Military Dimension," op. cit., 165–166.

54. Nationalist China forces were originally designated to take part in Allied occupation of Japan, chiefly deployed in Shikoku.

55. Morimoto, *Mashono Rekishi*, op. cit.

56. In correspondence with the fall of the Marianas the weight of the China theater declined. In such circumstances China tried hard to keep U.S. commitment in the China theater by emphasizing the possibility of Japan continuing its resistance by moving the Imperial Household and the Government to the Asian mainland. For example, on 11 April 1945, in a conversation with Admiral William Leahy, the U.S. Joint Chief of Staff, Wellington Koo, the Chinese Ambassador to Washington, warned that the Japanese military intended to move the center of resistance to China in the event of an American invasion of the Japanese homeland. "Notes on Conversation with Admiral Leahy, 12 a.m., Wednesday, April 11, 1945 at White House," Box 77, File 2, Wellington Koo Papers, Butler Library, Columbia University.

57. Usui Katsumi, *Shinban Nitchū sensō* [New Edition: The Sino-Japanese War] (Tokyo: Chuokoronsha, 2000), 149.

58. For wartime Communist activities and Nationalist Government's reaction, see T'ien-wei Wu, "The Chinese Communist Movement," in Hsiung and Levine, *China's Bitter Victory*, op. cit., 79–106.

59. Young, *China and the Helping Hand*, op. cit., 421–426; Ch'i, *Nationalist China at War*, op. cit., 82.

NOTES TO CHAPTER 19

1. On this point and the implications for Southeast Asia, see Christopher Bayly and Tim Harper, *Forgotten Wars: The End of Britain's Empire* (London: Allen Lane, 2007).

2. Barbara Tuchman, *Stilwell and the American Experience in China* (New York: Bantam Books, 1972).

3. Tuchman, *Stilwell*, 678.

4. Theodore White and Annalee Jacoby, *Thunder out of China* (New York: William Sloane, 1946).

5. Department of State, *The China White Paper*, introduction by Lyman Van Slyke (Stanford, CA: Stanford University Press, 1970).

6. "Draft of Message from the President to the Generalissimo" (16 October

1944), in George C. Marshall, *The Papers of George Catlett Marshall*, ed. Larry Bland (Baltimore: Johns Hopkins University Press, 1991), iv, 627.

7. Hans van de Ven, *War and Nationalism in China, 1925–1945* (London: Routledge, 2003), 19–63.

8. Mark Stoler, *Allies and Adversaries: The Joint Chiefs of Staff, the Grand Alliance, and U.S. Strategy in World War II* (Chapel Hill: University of North Carolina Press, 2000), 74–76.

9. White, *Stilwell Papers*, 77.

10. Van de Ven, *War and Nationalism in China*, introduction and chapter 1.

11. Frank Dorn, *The History of the Sino-Japanese War: From Marco Polo Bridge to Pearl Harbor* (New York: Macmillan, 1974), 65, 120, 128.

12. White, *Stilwell Papers*, 61, 77, 115–116, 128, 202–203, 220–221, 231, 332–334.

13. Ibid., 115–116.

14. Ibid.

15. Leila Fawaz and Christopher Bayly, "Introduction," in Fawaz and Bayly, eds., *Modernity and Culture: From the Mediterranean to the Indian Ocean* (New York: Columbia University Press, 2002), 3–4.

16. Lloyd Eastman, "The Nanking Decade," in Dennis Twitchett and John Fairbank, eds., *The Cambridge History of China* (Cambridge: Cambridge University Press, 1987), vol. 14, 119, 123

17. Lloyd Eastman, "Nationalist China at War," in *The Cambridge History of China*, vol. 14, 603.

18. Lloyd Eastman, *Seeds of Destruction: Nationalist China in War and Revolution* (Stanford, CA: Stanford Univerisity Press, 1984), 156

19. Hsi-sheng Ch'i, *Nationalist China at War: Military Defeats and Political Collapse* (Ann Arbor: University of Michigan Press, 1982), 236.

20. "Report by Major G. T. Wards on a visit to Shanghai," 15 December 1937, WO 106/5576, National Archives, London.

21. Edward J. Drea, "The Imperial Japanese Army (1868–1945): Origins, Evolution, Legacy," in Jeremy Black, ed., *War in the Modern World since 1815* (London: Routledge, 2003), 79, 84.

22. Chang-tai Hung, *War and Popular Culture: Resistance in Modern China, 1937–1945* (Berkeley: University of California Press, 1979).

23. For an example of the emotional impact of Japanese aerial bombing, see Hallett Abend, *My Years in China* (London: John Lane The Bodley Head, 1944), 257–267; *Four Months of War* (Shanghai: North China Daily News and Herald, 1938); Joly, "Confidential report on occurrences Preceding and Following the Fall of Kiukiang," file 679(1)/31526, Chinese Maritime Customs Service Archives, The Second Historical Archives of China; W. J. Gorman (fire brigade chief) to the harbor master Shanghai (23 August 1937), 679(1)/32230, Chinese Maritime Customs Service Archives, The Second Historical Archives of China; and H. D. Hilliard (commissioner of Chinese Customs, Nanjing) to Frederick Maze (inspector general), 3 and 9 December, 679/32187, Chinese Maritime Customs Service Archives, The Second Historical Archives of China.

24. Henry de Fremery, "Report No. 11," n.d., in Ger Teitler and Kurt Radtke,

A Dutch Spy in China: Reports on the First Phase of the Sino-Japanese War (1937–39) (Leiden: Brill Academic Publishers, 1999), 193, 200.

25. On Manchuria, see Prasenjit Duara, *Sovereignty and Authenticity: Manchukuo and the East Asian Modern* (Lanham, MD: Rowman and Littlefield, 2003); and Rana Mitter, *The Manchurian Myth: Nationalism, Resistance, and Collaboration in Modern China* (Berkeley: University of California Press, 2000); on Shanghai, see Donald A. Jordan, *China's Trial by Fire: The Shanghai War of 1932* (Ann Arbor: University of Michigan Press), 2001.

26. This and the following paragraphs are based on van de Ven, *War and Nationalism*, 140–151.

27. Robin Yates, "Law and the Military in Early and Imperial China" (paper presented at the conference Military Culture in Imperial China, University of Christchurch, January 2003).

28. Chiang's speeches at military conferences during the War of Resistance can be found in Ch'in Hsiao-i, ed., *Zhonghua Minguo Zhongyao Shiliao Chubian—Dui Ri Kangzhan Shiqi* [A preliminary collection of historical sources for the Republic of China—The period of resistance against Japan], part 2, *Zuozhan Jingguo* [The battles], vol. 1, 57–100 (First and Fifth war zones), 126–179 (First Nanyue), 189–196 (Second Nanyue), 205–251 (Liuzhou), 351–397 (Third Nanyue), 403–419 (Xinglongshan), 419–477 (Xi'an), 478–469 (Enshi), 469–527 (Fourth Nanyue) (Taipei: Guomindang Zhongyang Zhixiang Weiyuanhui Dangshi Yanjiu Weiyuanhui, 1981–88).

29. Douglas Peers, "South Asia," in Black, *War in the Modern World*, 50–51.

30. Van de Ven, *War and Nationalism*, 256.

31. Ibid., 253–258.

32. This and the following paragraphs draw from van de Ven, *War and Nationalism*, 253–287.

33. Mark Lewis, "The Han Abolition of Universal Service," in Hans van de Ven, ed., *Warfare in Chinese History* (Leiden: Brill, 2000), 33–76.

34. Nicola Di Cosmo, *Ancient China and Its Enemies* (Cambridge: Cambridge University Press, 2002), 294–312.

35. Mark Elliot, *The Manchu Way: The Eight Banners and Ethnic Identity in Late Imperial China* (Stanford, CA: Stanford University Press, 2001), 39–132.

36. Prasenjit Duara, *Sovereignty and Authenticity*, 89–130.

37. Lin Hsiao-ting, "A Re-examination of Nationalist China's Frontier Agenda: A Case Study of Tibet" (PhD dissertation, Oxford University, 2003), 176–177. I am grateful to Dr. Lin for giving me permission to refer to his work.

38. Peter Perdue, "Coercion and Commerce on Two Chinese Frontiers" (paper presented at the conference Military Culture and Imperial China, Christchurch, New Zealand, 10–12 January 2003).

39. Yang Kuisong, *Shiqu de Jihui: Zhanshi Guo Gong Tanpan Shilu* [Lost Chance: The true history of KMT-CCP negotiations during the war] (Guilin: Guangxi Shifan Daxue Chubanshe, 1992), 4–59.

40. Jiang Tingfu, *Jiang Tingfu Huiyilu* [Memoirs of Jiang Tingfu] (Changsha: Yuelu Chubanshe, 1923), 199–216.

41. Ray Huang, "Chiang Kai-shek and His Journal," *Chinese Studies in History* 29, no. 1 (1996), 118–119.

42. He Haoruo, "Ri Yong Bixupin Gongying Jihua yu Wu Wu Jiaoyi" [A Plan for the supply of daily necessities and barter trade], June 1942, file 055/1267, Academia Historica.

43. Ma Zhendu, *Cansheng: Kangzhan Zhengmian Zhanchang Daxieyi* [Bitter victory: Impressions of the battlefields at the front during the War of Resistance] (Guilin: Guangxi Normal University Press, 1993), 163–169.

44. Lin Hsiao-ting, "A Re-examination of Nationalist China's Frontier Agenda," 64–68.

45. "Report on Chinese Guerrilla Activities in Relation to the Kengtung and Manglun States, 1942–45," in "China General; Chungking General; Guerrillas," (PRO), HS 1/180, National Archives, London.

46. Van de Ven, *War and Nationalism,* 224.

47. Lyman Van Slyke, "The Battle of the Hundred Regiments: Problems of Coordination and Control during the Sino-Japanese War," *Modern Asian Studies* 30, no. 4 (1996), 979–1005.

48. C. H. B Joly, "Confidential Report on Occurrences Preceding and Following the Fall of Kiukiang" (1938), in "Confidential and IGS (Inspectorate General Series) Correspondence with Kiukiang, Nanjing, Chinkiang, Soochow, Hangchow, and Wuhu," file 679(1)/31526, Chinese Maritime Customs Service Archives, Second Historical Archives of China, Nanjing.

NOTES TO CHAPTER 20

1. Joshua A. Fogel, ed., *The Nanjing Massacre in History and Historiography* (Berkeley: University of California Press, 2000), 120.

2. Gerhard Weinberg gives an estimate of close to 25 million Soviet deaths and over 4 million German deaths in World War II. The majority of the German deaths and almost all Soviet deaths were on the Eastern Front. For China, his estimate is 15 million dead. Gerhard L.Weinberg, *A World at Arms: A Global History of World War II* (Cambridge: Cambridge University Press, 1994), 894. To these should be added an undetermined percentage of the 2.7 million Japanese who died in the war.

3. Antoine-Henri Jomini, *The Art of War* (San Francisco: Presidio Press, 1992), 26, 31.

4. Gunther Rothenberg, "Moltke, Schlieffen and the Doctrine of Strategic Envelopment," in Peter Paret, ed., *Makers of Modern Strategy* (Princeton, NJ: Princeton University Press, 1986), 305.

5. Michael Howard, "The Forgotten Dimensions of Strategy," *Foreign Affairs,* Summer 1979.

6. On this message, see Ronald Spector, *Eagle against the Sun: The American War with Japan* (New York: Free Press, 1984), chapter 5.

7. On Lepanto, see John F. Guilmartin, "The Tactics of Lepanto Clarified: The Impact of Social, Economic, and Political Factors," in Craig L. Symonds, ed., *New Aspects Of Naval History* (Annapolis, MD: U.S. Naval Institute Press, 1981), 41–65.

8. See the discussion of this issue in Mark Peattie, *Sunburst: The Rise of*

Japanese Air Power, 1909–1941 (Annapolis, MD: Naval Institute Press, 2001), 127–128.

9. Quoted in Robert Dallek, *Franklin D. Roosevelt and American Foreign Policy, 1932–1945* (New York: Oxford University Press, 1981), 427

10. Li Huang, oral history interview, vol. 6, 656, Chinese Oral History Collection, Columbia University, New York.

11. Li Huang, interview, 654.

12. Charles F. Romanus and Riley Sunderland, *The United States Army in World War II: The China Burma India Theatre*, vol. 3, *Time Runs Out in CBI* (Washington, DC: Office of the Chief of Military History, 1959), 369.

13. Li Huang, interview, 657

14. James E. Sheridan, *China in Disintegration: The Republican Era in Chinese History* (New York: Free Press, 1975), 264–265.

15. I am grateful to Edward J. Drea for suggesting this observation.

16. Peattie, *Sunburst*, 122.

17. See ibid. for an expanded discussion of these themes.

18. Michael S. Sherry, *The Rise of American Airpower* (New Haven, CT: Yale University Press, 1987), 70.

19. For a detailed discussion of Mao's strategy see Chalmers Johnson, *Peasant Nationalism and Communist Power: The Emergence of Revolutionary China* (Stanford, CA: Stanford University Press, 1962); M. Elliot Bateman, *Defeat in the East: The Mark of Mao Tse-tung on War* (New York: Oxford University Press, 1967); and S. M. Chao, ed., *Chinese Communist Revolutionary Strategy, 1945–1949* (Princeton, NJ: Woodrow Wilson School of International Affairs, Princeton University, 1961).

Bibliographies: Explanatory Note

Serious research in the military history of the Sino-Japanese War of 1937–1945 requires the use of sources in at least two of the three relevant languages: Chinese, Japanese, and English. The three bibliographies prepared for this volume are introductory and selective rather than exhaustive and inclusive. They do not necessarily contain all the titles cited in this collection of essays but do list works not mentioned in the narratives. Our purpose and assumptions in organizing this volume and the scholarly conference that preceded it also shaped the form and content of the bibliographies.

Our goal is to introduce the subject to a Western readership, and we assume that most readers will be younger scholars, probably graduate students interested in modern Chinese or Japanese history, in the history of Sino-Japanese relations, in the history of modern warfare generally, or in the history of World War II specifically. We further assume that such persons already have acquired some facility in the Chinese and/or Japanese language for thesis, dissertation, or postdoctoral research.

The military historiography and literature of the Sino-Japanese War is immense, especially in the Chinese and the Japanese languages. Even to list major sources and collections would take dozens of pages. Our brief bibliographies instead offer a guide that introduces a few of the rich and varied studies of the military history dimension of the conflict. Researchers will undoubtedly discover significant major and minor works and unexplored archival collections on their own. The purpose of our recommendations is to identify some basic introductory sources that may encourage the study of one of the major conflicts of the twentieth century that remains controversial, highly emotional, and still little understood in the West.

We wish to thank Steven Phillips of Towson University for his significant contributions in the compilation of these bibliographies.

A Selected Bibliography of English-Language Sources

STEVE PHILLIPS

Barrett, David D. *Dixie Mission: The United States Army Observer Group in Yenan, 1944*. Berkeley: University of California Center for Chinese Studies, 1970. One of the most detailed accounts of military discussions between the United States and the Chinese Communists. Barrett was a participant in the Dixie Missions to the Communist headquarters at Yan'an. His personal papers are held at the Hoover Institution at Stanford University.

Belden, Jack. *Retreat with Stilwell*. New York: Knopf, 1943. Highlights the resilience of the Allied forces and the personal qualities of the American general. Belden's personal papers are held at the Hoover Institution.

Benton, Gregor. *New Fourth Army: Communist Resistance along the Yangtze and the Huai, 1938–1941*. Berkeley: University of California Press, 1999. Exhaustive study of the New Fourth Army and its defeat at the hands of the Nationalists. He illustrates the conflict between local and national elites and the role this competition played in the larger war effort. Massive bibliography that is vital for anyone interested in the New Fourth Army.

Carlson, Evans Fordyce. *Twin Stars of China: A Behind-the-Scenes Story of China's Valiant Struggle for Existence by a U.S. Marine Who Lived and Moved with the People*. New York: Dodd, Mead, 1940. One of the best first-person accounts of the early years of the China war, including guerrilla warfare, the Eighth Route Army, and the Nationalists' retreat. Generally sympathetic to Mao Zedong's efforts.

Chang Jui-te. "Nationalist Army Officers during the Sino-Japanese War, 1937–1945." *Modern Asian Studies* 30, no. 4 (1996), 1033–1056. Overview of the officer corps, and an introduction to the author's vital Chinese-language works.

Chennault, Claire Lee. *Way of a Fighter: The Memoirs of Claire Lee Chennault*. Edited by Robert Horz. New York: G. P. Putnam's Sons, 1949. Chennault, who served as major general, United States Army Air Forces; commanding general, American Volunteer Group, 1941–1942; commanding general, China Air Task Force, 1942–1943; and commanding general, United States Fourteenth Air Force, 1943–1945, offers a generally positive appraisal of the Nationalists' war effort.

Ch'i, Hsi-sheng. "The Military Dimension, 1942–1945." In James C. Hsiung and Steven I. Levine, eds. *China's Bitter Victory*. Armonk, NY: M. E. Sharpe, 1992, 157–184. Brief overview. Updates chapter 2 ("Military Disasters, 1937–

45") of his *Nationalist China at War: Military Defeats and Political Collapse, 1937–1945*. Ann Arbor: University of Michigan Press, 1982.

Chinese Military Studies and Materials in English Translation. Prepared under the auspices of the Office of the Chief of Military History, Department of the Army. Washington, DC: Library of Congress Photoduplication Service, 1974. This ten-reel microfilm collection includes works mostly prepared for or by the Office of the Chief of Military History, Department of the Army, which were issued in limited numbers. These items were prepared by Nationalist military officers specifically for the Americans, or are translations of Chinese-language materials. Includes a 500-page history of the Sino-Japanese War from the Nationalist perspective.

Coox, Alvin D. *Nomonhan: Japan against Russia, 1939*. 2 vols. Stanford, CA: Stanford University Press, 1985. While Coox's efforts focus on Japanese military disasters on the Manchurian-Mongolian border, the work has detailed information on the Japanese army's tactics, doctrine, weapons, and leadership. Vital bibliography for anyone interested in this topic.

———. "The Kwantung Army Dimension." In Peter Duus, Ramon H. Myers, and Mark R. Peattie, eds. *The Japanese Informal Empire in China, 1895–1937*. Princeton, NJ: Princeton University Press 1989. Introductory history of the Kwantung Army's rise as a military and political force.

Crowley, James B. "A Reconsideration of the Marco Polo Bridge Incident." *Journal of Asian Studies* 22, no. 3 (May 1963), 277–291. Concludes that the incident was not the result of a Japanese conspiracy, and that the Japanese army was not responsible for the "steady drift toward war." See also his *Japan's Quest for Autonomy: National Security and Foreign Policy, 1930–1938*. Princeton, NJ: Princeton University Press, 1966.

Dorn, Frank. *The Sino-Japanese War, 1937–1941: From Marco Polo Bridge to Pearl Harbor*. New York: Macmillan, 1974. Dorn's work is among the most prominent first-person accounts of interest to scholars of the 1937–1941 period. He served with the U.S. Army in China during the war. Includes Chinese and Japanese orders of battle in an appendix.

Drea, Edward J. *In the Service of the Emperor: Essays on the Imperial Japanese Army*. Lincoln: University of Nebraska Press, 1998. While not specifically focused on the China war, this is a key study of the Japanese Army's organization and internal politics. This volume's bibliographic essay is a first step for any researcher in the field.

Dryburgh, Marjorie. *North China and Japanese Expansion, 1933–1937: Regional Power and the National Interest*. Richmond, VA: Curzon Press, 2000. Focuses on Song Zheyuan, a Nationalist military commander, and his interaction with both Chiang Kai-Shek and Japanese generals. Gives insight into Nationalist leadership and problems of mobilization.

Eastman, Lloyd. *Seeds of Destruction: Nationalist China in War and Revolution, 1937–1949*. Stanford, CA: Stanford University Press, 1984. Key overview of the Nationalists' state and nation-building efforts during the war, with particular focus on the role of the military.

Gordon, David M. "Historiographical Essay: The China-Japan War, 1931–1945."

Journal of Military History 70 (January 2006), 137–182. Useful state-of-the-field article.

Harries, Meiron, and Susie Harries. *Soldiers of the Sun: The Rise and Fall of the Imperial Japanese Army.* New York: Random House, 1991. Broad overview from the Meiji era through 1945 based on English-language sources.

Hsu, Lung-hsuan and Chang Ming-k'ai. *History of the Sino-Japanese War, 1937–1945.* Translated by Wen Ha-hsiung. Taipei: 1971. Among the best of the detailed accounts based on the Nationalists' interpretation of the war and its campaigns. Good maps.

International Military Tribunal for the Far East records on microfilm. Much of the material in the U.S. National Archives, Record Group 331, is available on microfilm. Some of these items contain information on the war in China.

Japanese Monographs. The 187 Japanese Monographs consist of a series of operational histories written by former officers of the Japanese army and navy under the direction of General Headquarters of the U.S. Far East Command beginning in 1945. See U.S. Department of the Army. *Guide to Japanese Monographs and Japanese Studies on Manchuria.* Washington, DC: Office of the Chief of Military History, 1962, 1980.

Johnson, Chalmers A. *Peasant Nationalism and Communist Power: The Emergence of Revolutionary China, 1937–1945.* Stanford, CA: Stanford University Press, 1962. Using Japanese sources, this work examines how the Communists melded socioeconomic revolution and nationalism. Chapters 2 and 3 examine the Japanese army and the development of Mao's forces.

Jordan, Donald A. *China's Trial by Fire: The Shanghai War of 1932.* Ann Arbor: University of Michigan Press, 2001. Most detailed account of this preview of all-out war in 1937. Detailed account of military actions and extensive bibliography.

Kitaoka, Shin'ichi. "China Experts in the Army." In Peter Duus, Ramon H. Myers, and Mark R. Peattie, eds., *The Japanese Informal Empire in China, 1895–1937.* Princeton, NJ: Princeton University Press, 1989. Provides insight into how Japanese officers understood China, and the bureaucratic challenges they faced. The essay also explains the organization of expertise within the army.

Lary, Diana. "Defending China: The Battles of the Xuzhou Campaign." In Hans van de Ven, ed. *Warfare in Chinese History.* Boston: Brill, 2000. The author seeks to remind us of battles that "did not reflect well on either the GMD or the CCP." See also her "A Ravaged Place: The Devastation of the Xuzhou Region, 1938." In Diana Lary and Stephan MacKinnon, eds., *Scars of War: The Impact of Warfare on Modern China.* Vancouver: UBC Press, 2001, 98–117.

———. "Drowned Earth: The Strategic Breaching of the Yellow River Dyke, 1938." *War in History* 8, no. 2 (2001), 191–207. Story of the Nationalists' desperate attempt to slow the Japanese advance, and the cost borne by China's civilians.

Lee, Chong-sik. *Counterinsurgency in Manchuria: The Japanese Experience.* Santa Monica, CA: Rand Corporation Research Memorandum RM-5012-ARPA, 1967. Includes a 70-page narrative and almost 300 pages of translated Japanese documents on "Collective Hamlets" and other pacification operations.

Lindsay, Michael. *The Unknown War: North China, 1937–1945*. London: Bergstrom and Boyle Books, 1975. Photos and account by Lord Lindsay, who traveled with Communist guerrillas in Shanxi and Hebei. Personal papers at the Hoover Institution.

MacKinnon, Stephen R. "The Tragedy of Wuhan, 1938." *Modern Asian Studies* 30, no. 4 (October 1996), 931–943. Details the gradual Japanese victory and slaughter of the Chinese because of superior technology and discipline, while noting the "sobering effect" that this victory had on the Japanese military.

Miles, Milton. *A Different Kind of War: The Little-Known Story of the Combined Guerrilla Forces Created in China by the U.S. Navy and the Chinese during World War II*. Garden City, NY: Doubleday & Company, 1967. A valuable and sympathetic first-person account of the Sino-American Cooperative Organization (SACO) and warfare along the China coast.

Morley, James W, ed. *Japan Erupts: The London Naval Conference and the Manchurian Incident, 1928–1932*. New York: Columbia University Press, 1984; and *The China Quagmire: Japan's Expansion on the Asian Continent 1933–1941*. New York: Columbia University Press, 1983. Hata Ikuhiko's article in the *China Quagmire* volume, "The Marco Polo Bridge Incident, 1937," is key. See also "Designs on North China, 1933–1937" by Shimada Toshihiko in *Japan Erupts*. These two books, and three other Morley volumes focused on diplomatic relations or the advance into Southeast Asia, consist of translations from the seven-volume *Taiheiyō sensō e no michi*.

Peattie, Mark R. *Ishiwara Kanji and Japan's Confrontation with the West*. Princeton, NJ: Princeton University Press, 1975. The biography of an officer instrumental in the seizure of Manchuria. General survey of the region in Japanese military-strategic thinking, with particular attention to military attitudes toward China offered in chapter 8.

———. *Sunburst: The Rise of Japanese Naval Air Power, 1909–1941*. Annapolis, MD: Naval Institute Press, 2000. See chapter 5, "Attacking a Continent: The Navy's Air War over China, 1937–1941." How did the war in China prepare the Japanese for later struggles?

Peck, Graham. *Two Kinds of Time*. Boston: Houghton Mifflin, 1950. Very detailed on the 1940–1945 period in central and southern China. Focuses on the failures of Chiang's regime.

Peterkin, W. J. *Inside China, 1943–1945: An Eyewitness Account of America's Mission in Yenan*. Baltimore: Gateway Press, 1992. The personal papers of Peterkin, commanding officer of the Observer Mission with Chinese Communist forces, Yan'an, China, 1944–1945, are held at the Hoover Institution.

Pritchard, John R. "Reassessment of Changkufeng as a Japanese Victory." In Gordon Daniels, ed., *Proceedings of the British Association for Japanese Studies*, vol. 3. Part 1, *History and International Relations*. Sheffield, UK: Sheffield Centre for Japanese Studies, 1978.

Romanus, Charles F., and Riley Sunderland. *Stilwell's Mission to China*. Washington, DC: Department of the Army, Historical Division, 1953. Part of the seventy-eight-volume collection *The U.S. Army in World War Two*. Washington, DC: U.S. Government Printing Office, 1949–1993. The classic volumes on America's role in Chongqing's anti-Japanese struggle. Starting point of all research into official sources. Each volume concludes with a valuable bibliographic essay.

———. *Stilwell's Command Problems*. Washington, DC: Department of the Army, Historical Division, 1956.

———. *Time Runs Out in the CBI*. Washington, DC: Department of the Army, Historical Division, 1959.

Sih, Paul K. T., ed., *Nationalist China during the Sino-Japanese War, 1937–1945*. Hicksville, NY: Exposition Press, 1977. Although limited in the range of sources used, this is a good introduction to the state of the field in the 1970s for a wide range of topics related to the war.

Snow, Edgar. *The Battle for Asia*. New York: The World Publishing Company, 1941. Famous and sympathetic observations of Mao Zedong at Yan'an.

Spector, Ronald, *The Eagle and the Sun: The American War with Japan*. New York: Macmillan, 1985. Chapters 15, 16, and 17 offer an excellent overview of the China conflict in the context of the larger war.

Teitler, Ger, and Kurt W. Radtke, eds. *A Dutch Spy in China: Reports on the First Phase of the Sino-Japanese War (1937–1939)*. Leiden, Netherlands: Brill, 1999. Comments on Japanese strategy and tactics in the first years of the war by a Dutch intelligence officer sent from the Netherlands East Indies to observe the fighting.

Tuchman, Barbara. *Stilwell and the American Experience in China, 1911–1945*. New York: Macmillan, 1970. Devastating critique of Chiang Kai-Shek's leadership and commitment to the anti-Japanese struggle.

United States Department of State. *United States Relations with China: With Special Reference to the Period 1944–1949*. Washington, DC: Department of State, 1949. Famous "white paper" that seeks to explain the collapse of the Nationalist regime and justify American policy through narrative and documents. Includes information on the Nationalists' wartime failures.

Van de Ven, Hans. "Stilwell in the Stocks: The Chinese Nationalists and the Allied Powers in the Second World War. *Asian Affairs* 34, no. 3 (November 2003), 243–259. Reviews the rise of the "Stilwell myth," that Chiang's refusal to follow American advice during the war was the primary factor in the regime's inability to resist the Japanese.

———. *War and Nationalism in China, 1925–1945*. London: Routledge, 2003. Key background on the origins and development of the Nationalist army. Notes that Chiang's forces had to contend with superior Japanese training and technology. The Nationalists had no choice but to remain on the defensive after the initial Japanese invasion in 1937. Exhaustive bibliography of Chinese- and English-language sources.

Van Slyke, Lyman P., ed. *The Chinese Communist Movement: A Report of the United States War Department, July 1945*. Stanford, CA: Stanford University Press, 1968. Report prepared by the Military Intelligence Division in 1945. Chapter 7 describes the organization of the Communist military.

———. "The Battle of the Hundred Regiments: Problems of Coordination and Control during the Sino-Japanese War." *Modern Asian Studies* 30, no. 4 (October 1996), 979–1005. The author emphasizes that the August–December 1940 campaign was not centrally controlled or coordinated.

Wartime Translations of Seized Japanese Documents: Allied Translator and Interpreter Section Reports, 1942–1946. California: CIS, 1988. Includes a two-volume index. Over 2,200 microfiches on a wide variety of war-related topics. These 7,200 documents, usually interrogation reports or translations of captured documents, can provide detail for scholars who are interested in specific events, locations, or battles.

Wedemeyer, Albert. *Wedemeyer Reports.* New York: Holt, 1958. Generally favorable account of the Nationalist war effort, almost a mirror image of Stilwell's accounts. Wedemeyer was commanding general, United States Forces, China theater, and chief of staff to Chiang Kai-Shek, 1944–1946.

White, Theodore, and Annalee Jacoby. *Thunder Out of China.* New York: William Sloane, 1946. Vital work in the field, and perhaps the best example of the sympathetic treatment Communists forces received from American observers.

Yu, Maochun. *OSS in China: Prelude to Cold War.* New Haven, CT: Yale University Press, 1996. Vital work in the field. Sources are a useful guide to materials at the National Archives and Hoover Institution.

A Selected Bibliography of Chinese-Language Sources

STEVE PHILLIPS

东北抗日联军史料编写组. 东北抗日联军史料 [Historical materials on the united anti-Japanese forces in northeast China]. 北京: 中共党史资料出版社, 1987. 2 册. Documents from Chinese and Japanese sources, including personal reminiscences, military reports, and Communist Party directives. Most of the materials focus on the 1931 to 1937 period. Some of these items have been published elsewhere.

东北抗日联军斗争史编写组编. 东北抗日联军斗争史 [A history of the struggle of united anti-Japanese forces in northeast China]. 北京: 人民初版社, 1991. Extremely detailed narrative history by Communist Party members in the three northeast provinces. For example, this book offers information to the level of examining the formation of guerrilla forces in eastern Jilin in 1932. Offers only a few useful footnotes to assist scholars.

国人民解放军军事科学院, 毛泽东军事思想研究所年谱组编. 毛泽东军事年谱, 1927–1958 [A chronicle of Mao Zedong's military affairs, 1927–1958]. 南宁: 广西人民出版社, 1994. Incredibly detailed research tool that includes the major events, meetings, and publications related to Mao.

中国新四军和华中抗日根据地研究会编. 华中抗日根据地史 [A history of the anti-Japanese base area in Central China]. 北京: 当代中国出版社, 2003. A lengthy account with limited documentation. Can be read in conjunction with the same organization's 新四军的组建与发展 [The New Fourth Army's organization and development], very useful reference work published in 2001.

中共中央党案馆编. 中共中央文件选集 [A collection of Chinese Communist Party Central Committee documents]. 北京: 中共中央党校出版社, 1982–. 第11册至第15册 cover the war era. The best easily accessible authoritative collection of documents on policy decisions and directives related to the war at the top level of the party.

中共中央党校科研局编. 卢沟桥事变和平津抗战资料选编 [An edited selection of materials on the Marco Polo Bridge Incident and the War of Resistance in Peking and Tianjin]. 北京: 中共中央党校科研办公室, 1986. Besides the content, this is a useful introduction to the types of documents available to researchers.

中国人民政治协商会议全国委员会文史资料委员会编辑. 从九一八到七七事变: 原国民党将领抗日战争亲历记 [From 18 September to the 7 July incident: The personal stories of former Nationalist generals' anti-Japanese resistance]. 北京: 中国文史出版社, 1987. Part of a series of books reprinting the personal narratives of military conflict in China offered by "patriotic" Nationalist officers. The book is designed to emphasize the importance of the united front during the War of Resistance. Other volumes in the series focus on fighting around Wuhan, Xuzhou, Nanjing, Burma, and elsewhere.

中国人民解放军历史资料丛书编审委员会. 新四军文献 [Documents on the Eighth Route Army]. 北京: 解放军出版社, 1992–1995. Four-volume collection of documents and articles related to the Eighth Route Army. Volume 4 contains telegrams and documents from Peking's Central Archives, the People's Liberation Army Archives, and the Nanjing Military District Archives. Documents include helpful explanatory footnotes.

中国人民革命军事博物馆. 百团大战历史资料选编 [An edited selection of historical materials on the Hundred Regiments Campaign]. 北京: 解放军出版社, 1991. Wide variety of documents and supplementary material on the Hundred Regiments, including party directives, descriptions of specific battles, and materials from generals Ye Jianying and Peng Dehuai. The documents include helpful explanatory footnotes to introduce less-familiar individuals and events.

中国第二历史档案馆编辑. 中华民国史档案汇编 [Archival materials on the history of the Republic of China]. 南京: 江苏古籍出版社, 1994–1998. See 第五辑, 第一编 (南京国民政府的建立与十年内战), 第六到第十分册 (军事); 第二编 (第二次国共合作与八年抗战), 第六到第十分册 (军事). Famous compilation of documents, including materials on the Military Affairs Commission, the organization of the Nationalist military, reports on the war effort, and some key cables from Chiang.

中国第二历史档案馆编辑. 抗日战争正面战场 [The frontline battlefield of the Anti-Japanese War of Resistance]. 南京: 凤凰出版社, 2005. 3 册. One of the most comprehensive collections related to the Nationalists' war efforts. Includes Chiang Kai-shek's orders to his generals for all major military campaigns and offers a great introduction into the materials available at the archives. Includes over 1,000 pages of documentation on air force and navy matters.

万仁元主编. 中国第二历史档案馆编辑. 抗日战争时期国民党军机密作战日记 [The secret battlefield logbooks of the Nationalist military during the Anti-Japanese War of Resistance]. 北京: 中国档案出版社, 1995. 3 册. Extremely detailed and useful material for advanced researchers who know the dates and military units they wish to investigate. Materials from the Nanjing Second Historical Archive.

中華民國重要史料初編編輯委員會.　中華民國重要史料初編：對日抗戰時期 [An initial edited collection of important historical materials on the Republic of China: The Anti-Japanese War of Resistance]. 臺北: 中國國民黨中央委員會黨史委員會. See 第二編:作戰經過 [part 2: The course of the war] (1981) and 第五編: 中共活動 [part 5: Communist activities] (1985). Vital collection of orders and reports on the war as seen from the perspective of top Nationalist leaders. Also includes memoranda of conversations for events such as Chiang's talks with British generals concerning the China-Burma-India theater.

刘德军主编. 抗日战争研究述评 [A review of Anti-Japanese War of Resistance research]. 济南: 齐鲁书社, 2005. A comprehensive and up-to-date overview of the secondary source literature on every topic related to the war. Includes an introduction to all the major document collections.

劉鳳翰. 抗日戰史論集—紀念抗戰五十周年 [A collection of essays on the Anti-Japanese War commemorating the fiftieth anniversary of the War of Resistance]. 北京：東大圖書公司, 1987. Series of essays on the Nationalists at war prepared by a prominent scholar from the Academia Sinica. For example, he offers an important counterpoint to mainland scholarship on the Hundred Regiments Campaign. Includes detailed time lines and footnotes vital for anyone wishing to learn about Nationalist archival material and historiography.

何應欽. 八年抗戰之經過 [The course of the eight-year War of Resistance]. 南京：南京政府陸軍總司令部, 1946. Overview of the war from the perspective of one of Chiang's top generals. Key example of how the Nationalists wished to portray the conflict. Included are some useful appendices on Nationalist losses.

何理. 中国人民抗日战争史 [A history of the Chinese people's Anti-Japanese War of Resistance]. 上海：上海人民出版社, 2005. Overview from an instructor at China's National Defense University and chair of the Chinese Anti-Japanese War of Resistance Study Society.

何理等编. 百团大战史料 [Historical materials on the Hundred Regiments Campaign]. 北京：人民出版社, 1984. Reprints lengthy battle reports from 1940 and translations from Japanese military sources.

侯坤宏. 粮政史料. 第六册：軍糧, 戰後糧政, 統計資料 [Historical materials on provisions policies. Volume 6: Military provisions, postwar administration, statistical data]. 台北縣：国史馆, 1988. Materials from the Nationalist archives on how Chiang's military was supplied and led. Good collection of documents that can guide future research.

全国中共党史研究会编. 抗日民主根据地与敌后游击战争 [Anti-Japanese democratic base areas and the guerrilla war behind enemy lines]. 北京：中共党史资料出版社, 1986. Essays on Communist leaders and their military strategies, regional guerrilla forces, and 张宏志, "八路军挺进敌后的决策与战略实施" [The determination and strategic implementation of the Eighth Route Army pressing forward behind enemies].

全国政协闽浙赣抗战编写组编. 闽浙赣抗战 [The War of Resistance in Fujian, Zhejiang, and Jiangxi]. 北京, 中国文史出版社, 1995. An entry in the extensive series 北京, 中国文史出版社, which documents the views of Nationalist generals.

全国政协湖南四大会战编写组编. 湖南四大会战 [Four decisive battles in Hunan]. 北京：中国文史出版社, 1995. Part of the 原国民党将领抗日战争亲历史 series.

曾景忠. "抗日战争正面战场研究述评" [A review of research on the frontline battlefield of the Anti-Japanese War of Resistance]. 抗日战争研究 vol. 33, no. 3 (1999), 77–101. This useful article includes information on document collections and secondary literature.

军事历史. Bimonthly journal filled with valuable short articles on topics related to the war, such as the air war over China, railroad transportation, military administration, and reminiscences of soldiers and generals.

军事科学院军事历史研究所. 中国抗日战争史 [A history of China's Anti-Japanese War of Resistance]. 北京：解放军出版社, 2005. 3 卷. 修订版. Vital work that includes footnotes for secondary sources, maps, and timelines.

郭汝瑰, 黄预玉章主编. 中国抗日战争正面战场作战记 [The front lines of China's Anti-Japanese War of Resistance]. 南京：江苏人民出版社, 2002. 2 册. Detailed endnotes to assist future scholars. One of the best volumes on military conflict. Includes maps, charts detailing orders of battle, and selections from official documents.

郭雄等编写. 抗日战争时期国民党正面战场 [The Nationalists' frontline battlefield during the Anti-Japanese War of Resistance]. 成都: 四川人民出版社, 2005. This volume is most useful for its short biographies of Nationalist generals.

荣维木. "抗日战争史" [A history of the Anti-Japanese War of Resistance]. 在曾业英主编. 五十年来的中国近代研究. 上海: 上海书店出版社, 2000. Describes the state of the field with a particular focus on recent works.

抗日战争研究 [The journal of studies of China's resistance war against Japan]. 中国抗日战争史学会, 中国社会科学院近代史研究所. 1991–. Quarterly journal covering all aspects of the conflict. Offers an annual bibliography of works published in Chinese.

董栋, 江羽翔. "抗战时期中国空中战场述评" [A review of books on China's air war during the War of Resistance]. 军事历史 2(1993): 34–38. The starting point for research on the air war. Includes a review of the secondary source literature and an introduction to the relevant document collections.

山西新军历史资料丛书编审委员会编. 山西新军决死第一纵队 [The life-and-death struggle of the Shanxi New Army First Corps]. 北京: 中共党史出版社, 1993. See volumes on the Second and Third corps, and a collection of historical materials, also published in 1993.

广东省档案馆编. 东江纵队资料 [Materials on the lower Yangtze River corps]. 广东人民出版社, 1984. 2 券. Focuses on guerrilla forces in Guangdong. Consists of documents and reprints of scattered reports on combat and other materials. Provides a clear picture of how these forces were organized. No source notes.

庹平. 长江作证: 新四军抗战纪实 [Bearing witness on the Yangtze: a record of the New Fourth Army's War of Resistance]. 北京: 团结初版社, 1995. Extremely detailed but undocumented account of the war in central China. Focuses on the successful leadership of the Communist Party.

张宏志. 抗日战争的战略防御 [Strategic defense during the Anti-Japanese War of Resistance]. 北京: 军事学院出版社, 1985. Focuses on comparing the Nationalists and Communists on the battlefield, including their strategies and discipline. Covers the outbreak of war up through the fall of Wuhan. Some footnotes. See also subsequent volumes by the same author: 抗日战争的战略反攻, *1944–1945* [Strategic counterattack during the Anti-Japanese War of Resistance, 1944–1945] (1990) and 抗日战争的战略相持 [Strategic stalemate during the Anti-Japanese War of Resistance] (1990).

张宪文等主编. 中国抗日战争史 *(1931–1945)* [A history of China's Anti-Japanese War of Resistance (1931–1945)]. 南京: 南京大学出版社, 2001. Huge volume with extensive footnotes and bibliography of secondary works, including archives and books from Taiwan. Can be used as an introduction to the kinds of materials available in China's archives.

张宪文等主编. 南京大屠杀资料集 [A collection of materials on the Nanjing Massacre]. 南京: 江苏人民出版社, 2006. This massive twenty-eight-volume collection of oral histories, documents, and memoirs is by far the best way to begin research on any aspect, including military, of the Nanjing Massacre.

张宪文主编. 抗日战争的正面战场 [The frontline battlefield of the Anti-Japanese War of Resistance]. 郑州: 河南人民出版社, 1987. Perhaps the best single-volume overview on military aspects of the war, based on documents from the Second Historical Archive in Nanjing. Extensive footnotes. This work is a revision and expansion of 中国抗日作战史. The work seeks to correct what is defined as the "influence of leftist thought" that prevented thorough and systematic research in the past.

張瑞德. 抗戰時期的國軍人事 [The Nationalist Army's personnel system during the War of Resistance]. 台北: 中央研究院近代史研究所, 1993. Along with 役政史料 below, explains all the major aspects of the topic.

王晓辉. 东北抗日联军抗战纪实 [A record of northeast China's united anti-Japanese forces during the War of Resistance]. 北京: 人民初版社, 2005. Written by officers at the National Defense University. The most detailed chronological account of the conflict in Manchuria. Includes a short bibliography, orders of battles, and maps.

王秀鑫, 郭德宏主编. 中共中央党史研究室第一研究部编著. 中华民族抗日战争史 [A history of the Chinese people's Anti-Japanese War of Resistance]. 北京: 中共党史出版社, 2005. A revision of the 1995 version. A comprehensive overview of the war that includes an eight-page bibliography.

朱汇森主编. 役政史料 [Historical materials on military service policies]. 台北縣: 国史馆, 1990. 2 册. A huge collection of documents that offers a road map for more in-depth research on Nationalist manpower policies.

李文. 八路军115师征战实录 [A record of the battles of the 115th division of the Eighth Route Army]. 长沙: 湖南人民出版社, 2005. 2 册. Part of a series of short books focusing on top Communist generals, such as Lin Biao or Chen Yi. No documentation.

杨奎清. "抗日战争敌后战场研究述评" [A review of research on battles behind enemy lines in the Anti-Japanese War of Resistance]. 抗日战争研究 Vol. 33, no. 3 (1999), 50–76. Offers guidance on documents and secondary sources related to guerrilla warfare.

毛泽东军事文集 [A collection of Mao Zedong's military writings]. 北京: 军事科学出版社, 1993. Volume 2 of this six-volume collection, which covers the war years, offers information on Mao's justification for military policies and strategies. For example, volume 2 includes Mao's lengthy 1938 essay "Strategic Problems of the Anti-Japanese Guerilla War."

新四军征战史编辑室编. 新四军征战日志 [A daily record of the New Fourth Army's campaigns]. 北京: 解放军出版社, 2000. Extremely detailed time line. This volume is a supplement to the 新四军战史 by the same editorial group.

胡璞玉编, 李震等修编. 抗日戰史 [A history of the Anti-Japanese War]. 臺北, 國防部史政局, 1962–9. 101 册. Published to commemorate the sixtieth anniversary of the founding of the Republic of China, this massive collection includes volumes on every major military campaign of the war. Although focused on the Nationalists' frontline battlefield efforts, the collection includes volumes on guerrilla warfare. Also includes maps.

欧阳植梁. 陈芳国主编, 武汉抗战史 [A history of the War of Resistance in Wuhan].

武汉: 湖北人民出版社. This volume examines all aspects of the war around Wuhan, but only part 1 focuses on military conflict. Extensive footnotes assist scholars interested in further research.

罗焕章, 高培编. 中国抗战军事史 [A military history of China's War of Resistance]. 北京: 北京出版社, 1995. Prepared under the auspices of the People's Liberation Army and the Chinese Anti-Japanese War of Resistance Study Society. Includes Japanese, Russian, and American sources. Detailed work with some maps, but limited in documentation.

魏汝霖編纂, 張其昀主編. 抗日戰史 [A history of the Anti-Japanese War]. 陽明山: 國防部研究院, 1966. One of the best single-volume overviews of the war from the Nationalist perspective. Includes useful maps, photos, and charts, but no source notes.

A Selected Bibliography of
Japanese-Language Sources

EDWARD J. DREA AND TOBE RYŌICHI

All entries are published in Tokyo unless otherwise noted.

PRIMARY SOURCES

Bōeicho Bōei Kenshujō, eds., *Senshi Sōsho* [War history series]. Fourteen volumes of the Japan Defense Agency's official 102-volume military history series deal directly with the China war, while another five have extensive coverage of the conflict. Volumes 18 and 50 offer one of the few treatments of counterguerrilla operations in north China; volumes 86, 89, and 90 detail operations in China from 1937 through 1941, mainly at the strategic and operational levels; volume 74 treats army aviation in China; volumes 72 and 79 examine naval aviation; volumes 55, 42, and 64 narrate the China Expeditionary Army's operations between 1942 and 1945; and volumes 4, 16, and 30 deal with the Ichigō offensive of 1944–1945. Policy and operational developments related to China appear in volumes 8, 20, 35, 69, and 65, which examine Imperial General Headquarters' role in the conflict. Written by former imperial army and navy staff officers, the official histories reflect their viewpoints and biases. As a consequence, tactical detail is slighted in favor of high-level operational or strategic military policy issues. The authors' tendency to reprint complete documents, some unavailable elsewhere, adds to the value of the series. Overall, however, it is uneven, and omission of controversial topics is the norm.

Gendaishi Shiryō [Documents of contemporary history] series (Misuzu Shobō, 1964–). In this collection of documents, volumes 8, 9, 10, 12, 13, and 38 deal with strategic and operational issues of the Sino-Japanese War, commencing in 1931. Each volume contains primary documents, including imperial orders, army operational planning, war diaries, contemporaneous interviews with senior officers, and so forth. Among individual works, volume 8 has extensive material on the Manchurian Incident (1931) and subsequent Japanese planning, policy, and operational activities in Manchuria and north China. Volume 9 continues the chronology with documentation dealing with the outbreak of full-scale warfare in 1937 and carries it through 1939. Volume 10 treats the Nomonhan Incident of 1939, policy related to the Tripartite Pact (1940), and the army's push into Indochina (1940–1941), while volume 11 returns to the Manchurian Incident, beginning with the London naval conference (1930). Volumes 12 deals with Japanese activities in Inner Mongolia, the Xi'an Incident

(1936), and events after the Marco Polo Bridge Incident, while volume 13 is more diplomatic- and political policy–related, focused on the Wang Jingwei regime and the Tianjin blockade of 1939. Volume 38 covers military operations in China and Imperial General Headquarters during the early stages of the Pacific War (1941–1945) of the Asia-Pacific War (1931–1945).

SECONDARY SOURCES

Chūō Daigaku Jinbunkagaku Kenkyūjō, ed., *Nitchū Sensō: Nihon, Chūgoku, Amerika* [The China war: Japan, China, and the United States] (Chūō Daigaku Shūppankai, 1993). The results of joint research on the China war conducted at Chūō University, Tokyo. Essays consider various aspects of the war, including Japanese soldiers' atrocities and the use of poison gas during operations.

Eguchi Keiichi, *Jūgonen Sensō Shōshi, shinpan* [A short history of the fifteen years' war, new edition] (Aoki Shoten, 1991). A concise history of Japan's policies from 1931 to 1945. It contains chapters on the outbreak of the China war and its escalation, on its military deadlock, and on the campaigns and battles in China during the Pacific War period.

Fujiwara Akira, *Taiheiyō Sensōron* [A theory of the Pacific War] (Aoki Shoten, 1982). An intriguing reevaluation of the place of the China war in Japan's military thinking and the larger context of the Pacific War.

——. *Shōwa no rekishi, 5, Nitchū zenmen sensō* [A history of the Shōwa reign], vol. 5 [Total war between Japan and China] (Shōgakkan, 1982). Weaves Japan's military campaigns in China into the political, social, and economic developments in Japan and the world between 1937 and 1941.

——. *Chūgoku Sensen Jugunki* [Record of field duty on the front line in China] (Ōtsuki Shoten, 2002). Fujiwara's superb anecdotal account of his service as a junior officer in China. He offers insights into the daily lives of young officers and soldiers fighting an endless, dreary war.

Furuya Tetsuo, *Nitchū Sensō* [The Sino-Japanese War] (Iwanami Shinsho, 1985). A good account of the Manchurian Incident and its aftermath with a solid general treatment of military operations from 1937 to 1945.

Hata Ikuhiko, *Nitchū Sensōshi* [A history of the Sino-Japanese War] (Kawade Shobō, expanded, rev. ed., 1972). A classic account of the political, diplomatic, and military initiatives from 1931 through 1940. Chapter 7 is an excellent description of military operations from the outbreak of the north China fighting through the Battle of the Hundred Regiments (1940).

——. *Rokōkyō jihen no kenkyū* [Research about the Marco Polo Bridge Incident] (Tokyo Daigaku Shūppankai, 1996). The single best source on the incident. Hata describes in exquisite detail the month from the outbreak of fighting to the decision to escalate.

Hatano Sumio, *Daitōa Sensō no jidai* [The era of the great East Asia war] (Asahi Shuppansha, 1988). Superb explanation of Japan's political and strategic policies from the Manchurian Incident to the outbreak of the Pacific War. Hatano explains convincingly the army and navy staff officers' judgments and expectations that promoted the war's escalation.

Imai Takeo, *Shina Jihen no kaisō* [Recollections of the China incident] (Misuzu shobō, 1964). A Japanese staff officer's view that concentrates on attempts to negotiate a settlement to the fighting between 1937 and 1940.

Imoto Kumao, *Sakusen nisshi de tōjiru Shina jihen* [An operational diary of the China incident] (Fūyō Shobō, 1978). A midlevel staff officer's account of policy and operations.

Itō Takahashi, *Jūgonen sensō* [The fifteen years war], (*Nihon no rekishi 30*) [A history of Japan, vol. 30] (Shōgakkan, 1976). A wide-ranging analysis of political, diplomatic, social, and economic aspects of Japan's long war. Military operations receive broad, general coverage within that context.

Kasahara Tokushi, *Nitchū zenmen sensō to Kaigun: Panai gō jiken no Shinsō* [Escalation of the China war and Japan's navy: The truth of USS *Panay* incident] (Aoki Shoten, 1997). A good study on the navy's role in the war-escalation process. It treats in detail the reasons and circumstances of the naval air attack against the U.S. Navy gunboat *Panay*.

Kita Hiroaki, *Nitchū kaisen* [The beginning of the Sino-Japanese war] (Chūkō Shinsho, 1994). A treatment of the legal implications of an undeclared war.

Kojima Noboru, *Nitchū Sensō* [The Sino-Japanese War], 3 vols. (Bungei Shūnjū, 1974; repr. in 5 volumes Bunshūn Bunkō, 1988). Contains detailed information on combat operations through 1939. Kojima has no footnotes but clearly relied on official war diaries and archival documents to write the trilogy.

Kono Shu, eds., *Kindai Nihon sensōshi* [A history of modern Japan's wars], vol. 3, *Manshū Jihen, Shina Jihen* [The Manchurian Incident and the China war] (Dōdai Keizai Konwakai, 1995). A volume of essays by military historians dealing with Japan's political and military strategies from 1931 to 1941, focused on the role of the army. Various operations in the China war are analyzed compactly from the military point of view.

Kuroha Kiyotaka, *Nitchū Jūgonen Sensō*, 3 vols. [The fifteen-year Sino-Japanese War] (Kyōikusho Shinsho, 1979). A series of brief accounts of significant events in China and Japan, often using excerpts from the period. Interspersed with statistics and information on the period, it is helpful in understanding the Japanese soldiers stationed in China.

——, *Nitchū Sensō zenshi* [Prehistory of the China war] (Sanseidō, 1983). Focused on the Manchurian Incident and the first Shanghai Incident of 1932. The last chapter examines the circumstances leading to the Marco Polo Bridge Incident.

Kuwada Etsu and Maebara Toru, eds., *Nihon no sensō-zukai to dēta* [The wars of Japan; maps and data] (Hara Shobō, 1982). This covers the period from 1894 through 1945. The numerous detailed campaign maps of China operations are accompanied by brief overviews of the operation, order of battle information, and statistics.

Mainichi Shimbunsha, eds., *Ichiokunin no Shōwashi* [One hundred million people's Shōwa history], *Nihon no Sensō* [The wars of Japan] (Mainichi Shimbun, 1979). Volumes 3 through 5 deal with the Sino-Japanese War. Although this is a photographic account of the war, each volume contains excellent short essays written by top Japanese military historians or participants and has detailed order of battle data.

Minō Kazuo, *Wakari yasui Nitchū sensō* [The Sino-Japanese War made intelligible] (Kojinsha, 1998). A well-balanced overview of the war in its various aspects, providing, moreover, adequate coverage of the political-military background to the conflict and its legacies. The author is a well-read and well-published amateur historian.

Nihon Kokusai Seiji Gakkai, eds., *Taiheiyō Sensō e no michi* [The road to the Pacific War], 7 vols. and documents volume (repr., Asahi Shimbunsha, 1987). The classic and still standard account of Japan's political, military, and diplomatic actions on the Asian continent between 1928 and 1941. The documentary volume remains unsurpassed. Several of the essays are available in English language translations in James Morley's *The Road to the Pacific War.*

Ōsugi Kazuo, *Nitchū jūgonen sensōshi* [A history of the fifteen-year Sino-Japanese War] (Chūkō Shinsho, 1996). Despite the title, this deals mainly with political and diplomatic developments to 1937.

Sasaki Harutaka, *Chōsa Sakusen* [Changsha operations] (Tōsho Shuppansha, 1987). A junior officer's personal experience during the two Changsha operations, 1941–1942. Not only a firsthand account but also an excellent and critical analysis of the operations. The author later became a general officer in Japan's postwar Ground Self-Defense Force and a professor of military history at National Defense Academy.

Tobe Ryōichi, *Nihon Rikugun to Chūgoku: Shina-tsu ni miru yume to satetsu* [The Japanese army and China: The failure of the China expert's vision] (Kōdansha, 1999). An excellent analysis of the evolution and changing views of Japan's military China experts in the first half of the twentieth century.

Usui Katsumi, *Shinpan Nitchū Sensō* [New edition: The Sino-Japanese War] (Chūkō Shinsho, 2000). A revised and updated version of Usui's 1967 work of the same name that includes fresh material on the role of the emperor in decision making. Military operations, particularly in 1937–1938 and 1944–1945 (the Ichigō campaign), receive general coverage.

Yasui Sankichi, *Rokōkyō jiken* [The Marco Polo Bridge Incident] (Kenbun Shūppan, 1993). Another first-rate treatment and examination of the military and political events surrounding the incident with extensive use of Chinese language materials to develop both sides' perspectives of the event.

Character List

Anami Korechika 阿南惟幾
angohan 暗号班
Anhui 安徽
annei rangwai 安内攘外
Araki Sadaō 荒木貞夫
Asegawa Sei (see Hasegawa Kiyoshi)
Bai Chongxi 白崇禧
Bainianqiao 百年橋
baoan dui 保安隊
baoanhui 保安会
baojia cun 保甲村
baojia ziweituan 保甲自衛團
baojia 保甲
baozhang 保障
Battle of Taierzhuang 臺兒莊之戰
Battle of Xinkou 忻口抗
bingma wei dong; liangcao xian xing 兵馬未動, 糧草先行
Bushido 武士道
Chahar 察哈爾
chajin liangshi zidi 查禁糧食資敵
Changsha 長沙
chankoro チャンコロ
chanliang zhongdian xian 產糧重點縣
Chen Anbao 陳安寶
Chen Cheng 陳誠
Chen Cunren 陳存仁
Chen Gongbo 陳公博
Chen Shaomin 陳少敏
Chen Yi 陳儀
Chiang Kai-Shek (Jiang Jieshi) 蔣介石
Chihli clique 直系軍閥
chijiu zhan 持久戰

chijō zettai koku yusen 地上絶対航空優先
chiyu or yuchi 敕諭 or 諭敕
choki-jikyu 長期持久
Chongqing 重慶
chukun aikoku 忠君愛国
Cun Xingqi 寸性奇
cun 村
da gong chang 打公場
Dahoufang 大后方
Dai Li 戴笠
Daidogakuin 大同學院
daikōri 大行李
Damin hui 大民會
dan 擔 (equals 110.2 lbs.)
Danyang 丹阳
dao 道
Datong zueyuan (Japanese Daido gakuin) 大同学院
Deng Yuxian 鄧雨賢
dishao renduo 地少人多
Doihara Kenji 土肥原賢二
dokudan senkō 独断専行
dokudan 独断
dou 斗
Du Yuming 杜聿明
Duan Qirui 段祺瑞
ducu ban 督促班
East Chahar Incident 东察哈爾事件
Eighth Route Army 八路軍
Emperor Puyi 溥儀
Ererba Incident 二二八事件
Executive Yuan 行政院
fabi 法幣

587

Fang Xianjue 方先觉
fangkong 防空
fanzhan junren 反战军人
Feng Yuxiang 馮玉祥
Feng Zhanhai 馮占海
fengsuo 封锁
Fengtian clique (Feng xi) 奉系軍閥
fenshe 分社
Fu Zuoyi 傅作义
Fujian 福建
Gansu 甘肅
gaoliang 高粱
Gassaku Sha (Chinese xingnong hezuo
  she) 行农合作社
genchi chohatsu 現地調達
Gengsheng jinian ri Rebirth
  Commemoration Day 更生纪念日
genro 元老
Gijutsu Kyōkai 技術教會
gongshu 公书
gongsi 公司
Greater East Asia Co-Prosperity
  Sphere (Kyujitai) 大東亞共榮圈
Gu Weijun 顧維鈞
Gu Zhutong 顧祝同
guancang 灌倉
Guandong jun 関東軍
Guangdong 广东
Guangxi 广西
Guangzhou 廣州
Guilin shounan 桂林受难
gun 軍
gun'yō sasshin 軍容刷新
Guo Dejie 郭德洁
Guofang lun 《國防論》
Guofang Zui Gao Weiyuanhui 国防
  最高委員會
guohuo 国货
*guomin shenghuo (kokumin
  seikatsu)* 国民生活

Guomindang weisheng weiyuanhui 国
  民党卫生委員會
Guowu yuan 國務院
Guoyi huiyi 國医會议
guoyi ji 國醫记
Guoyi xuehui 國医学会
gutoujia 骨頭架
gyokusai 玉砕
Hagio Isamu 萩尾勇
Hamamoto Sosaburo (Hamamoto
  Kisaburo) 浜本喜三郎
Han Deqin 韓德勤
Han Fuju 韩復榘
Hanatani Sei (Hanaya Tadashi) 花谷正
hanjian 漢奸
Hasegawa Kiyoshi (Asegawa Sei) 長
  谷川清
Hashimoto Gun 橋本群
Hata Hikozaburō 秦彦三郎
Hata Shunroku 畑俊六
Hattori Takushirō 服部卓四郎
He Haoruo 何浩若
He Jian 何鍵 (何健)
He Yingqin 何應欽
Hebei 河北
hefa hua 合法化
Heian shidai 黑暗时代
Heilongjiang 黑龙江
Henan 河南
hezuo 合作
Hirata Kenkichi 平田健吉
Hirose Takeo 広瀬武夫
Hirota Kōki 広田弘毅
hisshoō shinnen 必勝信念
Hohei sōten sōan 《步兵操典草案》
Hohei sōten 《步兵操典》
hōmen gun 方面軍
Honda Masaki 本多政材
hou sheng ke 厚生科
Hu Shi 胡適

Hu Zongnan 胡宗南

Huabei hezuo shiye zonghui 華北合作事業總會

Huabei zonghe diaocha yanjiusuo 華北綜合調查研究所

huandu 还都

Huang Tao 黃涛

huangse youjidui 黃色游擊隊

Hubei 湖北

hukou (Japanese *koseki*) 戶口

Hunan 湖南

Ichigō offensive 大陸打通作戰

Ichikari Yūsaku 一刈勇作

Ichiki Kiyonao 一木清直

Imai Kiyoshi 今井清

Imoto Kumao 井本熊男

Inada Masazumi 稲田正純

ippatsu-ichimei 一発一命

Ishiwara Kanji 石原莞爾

Isogai Rensuke 磯谷廉介

Itagaki Seishiro 板垣征四郎

Jasakh Prince Demchugdongrub (Prince De) 德穆楚克栋鲁普

jianbi qingye 堅壁清野

Jiang Dingwen 蔣鼎文

Jiang Fangzhen 蔣方震

Jiang Jingguo 蔣經國

(Jiang Baili 蔣百里)

Jiang Menglin 蔣夢麟

Jiang Zizhong (Zhang Zizhong) 張自忠

Jiangnan 江南

Jiangsu 江苏

Jiangxi *funū shenghuo gaijin hui* 江西妇女生活改进會

Jiangxi 江西

jiao gong ziwei 剿共自衛

jibi 冀幣

jiecun zhi 街村治

jiji 積極

jin 斤 (equals 500 grams)

Jinan 冀南

jinanbi 冀南幣

jingbeidui 警備隊

Jinjiluyu 晋冀魯豫

jiti dachang 集体打場

jituan liangchang 集團麥場

jiu lao piao 就勞票

junfu 军服

Junshi weiyuan hui 軍事委員會

kaisen 会戦

kakushin kanryo 革新官僚

Kanai Shōji 金井章次

kanbu kōhosei seidō 幹部候補生制度

Kang Ze 康澤

Kawabe Masakazu 河辺正三

Kazuki (Kasuki) Kiyoshi 香月清司

Kempeitai Military Police 憲兵隊

kensei butai 建制部隊

Kinshi kunsho 金鵄勲章

Kita Sei'ichi 喜多誠一

Kita Shina homengun 北支那

Kōa-in 興亜院

Kobayashi Seizo 小林躋造

Kōdō 皇道

kōgun 皇軍

kokugun 国軍

Kong Xiangxi (H.H. Kung) 孔祥熙

kono gassaku sha 興農合作社

Konoe Fumimaro 近衛文麿

kuaishe 會社

kuilei 傀儡

kuli 苦力

Kunisaki Noboru 国崎登

Kurashige Yasumi 藏重康美

Kyōwa Kai (Chinese Xiehehui) 協和會

Lai He 賴和

laobaixing juede hen taiping 老百姓觉得很太平

Lei Zhong 雷忠
Li Jishen 李濟深
Li Shouxin 李守信
Li Xiannian 李先念
Li Youbang 李友邦
Li Zongren 李宗仁
lianbao zhuren 聯保主任
lianbao 聯保
Liang Hongzhi 梁鴻志
liang 兩 (equals 50 grams)
liangmo weiyuanhui 糧秣委員會
liangshi douzheng 糧食斗爭
liangzhang 粮長
lianhe she 聯合社
lianluo chun 聯絡村
lianzuo 联作
Liao Lei 廖磊
Liaodong peninsula 辽东半岛
Lin Biao 林彪
Lin Wei 林蔚
Lin Xiantang 林獻堂
lishi zhang 理事長
Liu Fei 劉斐
Liu Kan 劉戡
Liu Lianren 劉連仁
Liu Mao-en 刘茂恩
Liu Xiang 劉湘
Liu Ziqing 劉子清
Long Yun 龍云
Longmen 龍門
Lu Han 盧漢
Lu Zhongling 鹿鐘麟
Lugou qiao 盧溝橋
Luo Zhuoying 羅卓英
luoshi zhengce 落实政策
luoshui 落水
Luoyang 洛陽
Ma Fuxiang 馬福祥
Ma Hongkui 馬鴻逵
mafu 马夫

Manchukuo (Manzhouguo/
   Mashukoku) 滿洲國
ManMō 満蒙
Mao Zedong 毛澤東
Maruyama Fusayasu 丸山房安
Matsui Iwane 松井石根
Matsuyama Yūzō 松山祐三
Mengjiang 蒙疆
Minakami Genzō 水上源蔵
Minde zhongxue 民德中学
minde zhuyi 民德主义
minzhong yundong (mass
   movements) 民众运动
Mitsubishi 三菱
Mitsui 三井
Miyamoto Takenosuke 宮本武之助
Miyazaki Shuichi 宮崎周一
mu 亩 (equals 666.6 m²)
Mukden (modern Shenyang) 瀋陽
Mutaguchi Renya 牟田口廉也
Mutō Akira 武藤章
Nagatsu Sahishige (Sadashige) 永津
   佐比重
Naka Shina homengun 中支那
Nakajima Kesago 中島今朝吾
Nakamura Kōtarō 中村孝太郎
Nanjing 南京
nashui cun 納稅村
Nishihara Kamezō 西原亀三
Nishio Toshizo 西尾寿造
Nisshin 日清
nobori 幟
nongmin cangku 農民倉庫
North China Labor Association 華北
   労働會
Obata Toshishirō (Obata Toshiro) 小
   畑敏四郎
Okamoto Kiyotomi 岡本清福
Okamura Yasuji 岡村寧次
omamori 御守

Oyama Isao 大山勇夫

Ozaki Hotsumi 尾崎秀樹

pai gou 派售

Pang Bingxun 龐炳勛

Peking (Beijing) 北京

Peng Dehuai 彭德懷

Peng Xuefeng 彭雪峰

pingfan 平反

Prince Kan'in (Kan'in-no-miya Koto-
hito Shinnō) 閑院宮載仁親王

qi 旗

qiang zheng 強征

qiangliang douzheng 搶糧斗爭

qiangliang hui 搶糧會

Qin Dechun 秦德純

Qing bang 青幫

Qingdao 青島

qu lian 區聯

*Quanguo yiyao tuanti daibiao
dahui* 全國医药团体代表会

Rehe Province 熱河

rikusentai 陸戰隊

rinji hikōdan 臨時飛行団

Sanada Jōchirō 真田穣一郎

Sawada Shigeru 沢田茂

seinen kunrensho 青年訓練所

Sejima Ryūzō 瀬島龍三

senbetsu 餞別

senbu kōsaku 宣撫工作

Senda Sadaō 千田貞雄

senshin shichō 先進輜重

Sentō kōryō 戦闘綱領

Shandong 山東

Shanxi 陝西

Shen Honglie 沈鴻烈

sheng lian 省聯

shengliang 省糧

shi shi qiu shi 实事求是

Shi Yousan 石友三

shichōhei 輜重兵

shicongshi 侍從室

Shidehara Kijuro 幣原喜重郎

shifan diqu 示范地區

Shikan Gakkō 士官学校

shike 食客

shiliang quebao ban 食糧確保班

Shimizu Setsurō 清水節郎

shin kanryō 新官僚

Shina 支那

shinkō zaibatsu 新興財閥

Shōgō sakusen 捷号作戦

shōkōri 小行李

shouling 手令

shouyu 手諭

Shuidong duli tuan 水東獨立團

shūmai ban 收買班

Sichuan 四川

sokusen sokketsu 速戦即決

Song Xilian 宋希濂

Song Zheyuan 宋哲元

Songjiang 松江

Sonobe Waichirō 園部和一郎

South Manchurian Railway
(Mantetsu) 満鉄

Sugiyama Hajime 杉山元

Suiyuan 绥远

Sun Dianying 孫殿英

Sun Ke 孫科

Sun Liangcheng 孫良誠

Sun Lianzhong 孫連仲

Sun Liren 孫立人

Sun Tongxuan 孫桐萱

Sun Yat-sen 孫逸仙

Sunzi (Sun Tzu) 孫子

Suzuki Yormichi 鈴木率道

Tada Hayao 多田駿

Taicang 太倉

Taihang Mountain 太行山

Taiwan shibao 台灣时报

Taiyuan 太原

Tanaka Giichi 田中 義一

Tanaka Shin'ichi 田中新一

Tang Enbo 湯恩伯

Tang Huaiyuan 唐淮源

Tang Junwu 唐聚五

Tang Shengzhi 唐生智

tanki-kessen 短期決戰

tanpai 攤派

Tao Xisheng 陶希聖

Tashirō Kan'ichirō 田代皖一郎

tenno heika banzai 天皇陛下万歲

Terauchi Hisaichi 寺内寿一

Terauchi Masatake 寺内正毅

Tianjin 天津

ting 廳

Tōjō Hideki 東條 英機

Tokumu bu 特務部

tōkumu kikan 特務機関

tonarigumi 隣組

tongfei 通匪

Tongmenghui 同盟會

tongxiangren 同乡人

tongzhi shoumai 统治收買

Tōsei-ha 統制派

Tōsui kōryō 統帥綱領

Tsuji Masanobu 辻政信

Ueda Kenkichi 植田謙吉

Umezu Yoshijirō 梅津美治郎

Ushiroku Jun 後宮淳

Wan Fulin 万福麟

Wang Chonghui 王寵惠

Wang Jingjiu 王敬久

Wang Jingwei 汪精衛

Wang Jingyu 王靖宇

Wang Jun 王鈞

Wang Kemin 王克敏

Wang Ming 王明

Wang Mingzhang 王銘章

Wang Shijie 王世杰

Wang Yaowu 王耀武

Wang Ying 王英

Wei Lihuang 衛立煌

wei 伪

weian suo 微安所

Weng Junming 翁俊明

wenshi ziliao 文史资料

Whampoa Military Academy 黃埔軍校

Wu Huawen 吳化文

Wu Peifu 吳佩孚

Wu Shimin 武士敏

Wuhan 武汉

wuzhuang shoumai 武裝收買

Xiamen 厦门

xian lian 縣聯

xian zhengfu 縣政府

xiang gongsuo 鄉公所

xiaoji 消極

Xie Dongmin 謝東閔

Xikang 西康

Xinan lianda (Southwest United University) 西南联大

Xing'an 興安

Xinhai revolution 辛亥革命

Xinhua ribao 新華日報

Xinjiang 新疆

Xinmin hui 新民會

Xinxing hui 新興會

Xu Yongchang 徐永昌

xuanfu (Japanese *senbu*) 宣撫

Xue Yue 薛岳

Xuzhou 徐州

yakkai na 厄介な

Yamamoto Kiyoe 山本清衛

Yamato damashii 大和魂

Yan Daogang 晏道剛

Yan Xishan 閻錫山

Yan'an 延安

Yanagawa Heisuki 柳川平助

Yang Hucheng 楊虎城

Yang Kui 楊逵

Yang Sen 楊森

yanghang 詳行

Yangtze (Yangzi) River 揚子江

yaofang 药方

yasen sokō 野戰倉庫

Yasukuni Shrine 靖國神社

Ye Ting 葉挺

yen 円

yi hua zhi hua 以華制華

yimian baohu 一面保護, 一面協助農
民收割

Yonai Mitsumasa 米内光政

Yong'an (Wing On) Department
Store 永安

yosegaki 寄せ書き

Yoshida Shigeru 吉田茂

Yu Hanmou 余漢謀

Yu Huai'an 于怀安

Yu Jishi 俞濟時

Yu Xuezhong 于學忠

Yuan Shikai 袁世凱

yuan 元

yukai na 愉快な

zaibatsu 財閥

zaliang 雜糧

Zeng Guofan 曾國藩

zenpō kōri 前方行李

zeren shuliang 責任數量

zeren zhenggou 責任征購

Zettai kokubō ken 絶対国防圏

Zhang Fakui 張發奎

Zhang Jia'ao (Chang Kai-ngau)
張嘉璈

Zhang Xueliang 張學良

Zhang Yinwu 張蔭梧

Zhang Zhizhong 張治中

Zhang Zuolin 張作霖

Zhangjiakou 張家口

Zhao Qi 趙琪

zhaochi 昭敕 詔敕

Zhejiang 浙江

zheng liang 征糧

zhengtong 正統

zhengwushu 政务书

zhenwuhui 鎮务會

zhian weichi hui 治安维持会

zhiben 治本

Zhongyang guoyi guan 中央國医管

Zhongyi tiaoli 中医调理

Zhongzheng Shican (directive written
by Chiang's personal staff) 中正
侍参

Zhongzheng shouqi (personal directive
written by Chiang himself) 中正
手启、

Zhou Enlai 周恩來

Zhou Fohai 周佛海

zhou 州

Zhu De 朱德

Zhu Huaibing 朱怀冰

Zhu Shaoliang 朱紹良

zhuanbo qingge 輪番清剿

zhuyu 硃諭

ziwei tuan 自衛團

ziweituan (Japanese *jieitan*) 自卫团

zizhi weiyuanhui 自制委员會

zongshu 總署

Zongwu ting 總務廳

Zou Zuohua 鄒作華

zougou 走狗

Index

Page numbers followed by *t*, *m*, and *p* indicate tables, maps, and photographs.

Abe Norihide, 313

Absolute National Defense Perimeter (Japanese), 433–434

accommodation. See Appeasement

Acheson, Dean, 449

aerial campaigns. See also Chongqing; Ichigō offensive: Chahar and, 164; changing balance of airpower and, 250–253; effects of, *p*4, 478; Japanese aircraft and personnel performing, 239–240; against Japanese mainland, 427, 430–432; Japanese plans for at beginning of war, 241–242; limitations and capabilities of, 480; during 1939–1941, *m*12, 40, 246–249; north China campaign and, 162; over Nanjing, 177; over Wuhan (summer 1938), 244–246; overview of, 253–255; Shanghai campaign and, 169; structure of Japanese forces performing, 160, 237–238; during summer of 1937, 242–244; United States assistance and, 249–250

air bases. See also Ichigō offensive: destruction of American, 45–46, 427, 443–444; destruction of Chinese, 42–43, 242; in Taiwan, 396

air defense systems, 233–234, 247, 249, 263–277, 312

air forces. See Japanese Army Air Force; National Air Force (Chinese); United States Air Force

Air Transport Command (ATC), 298

aircraft: B-29 bombers, 252, 430, 436–437; Curtiss, 240, 243, 244, 250–251; decline of Japanese; superiority of Chinese, 252, 477; from Germany, 286, 301; of Japanese army and navy, 239–240, 252, 477; Mitsubishi B2M1 Type 89 carrier attack bombers, 240, 243; Mitsubishi G3M2 Type 96 medium bombers, *p*9, 240, 243, 247, 254; Mitsubishi G4M Type 1 medium bombers, 29, 249, 254; Mitsubishi Ki-21 Type 97 bombers, 249; Nakajima fighter planes, 240, 243, 251; overview of use of, 477; P-51 Mustangs, 252; Polikarpov I-12, 245; from Soviet Union, 289–291, 301; from United States, 300–301; weaknesses of during beginning of war, 243

Akagi, 239

Amau Statement, 70

American Military Mission to China (AMMISCA), 296

American Volunteer Group (AVG; Flying Tigers), 250, 265, 300, 431

Anami Korechika, 41–42, 226

Andreski, Staniskav, 332–334

annihilation, war of, 112, 115, 159, 400

Anqing, 197, 212, 245

antiaircraft artillery, *p*1, 92, 247, 266–267

antiaircraft facilities, 87, 264, 276

Anti-Comintern Pact, 156, 287

appeasement policy, 72, 143–144, 155–156, 205–206, 453

Araki Sadao, 111–112

Armed Forces Bureaus, 311, 323

armies. See Communist forces; Japanese army; Nationalist Army

Army of India (Chinese). See X-Force

Army Reorganization Bureau, 103

artillery: Chinese fortresses and, 92; defense of Chongqing and, 266, 267; of Japanese Army, 88–89, 119, 134; lack of in Nationalist army, 88–89; Principles of Operations and, 112

Asaka, Prince, 177

ATC. See Air Transport Command

Atkinson, Brooks, 449, 450

autonomous military zones, 94, 106

B-29 bombers, 252, 430, 436–437

BAA. See Burma Area Army

Bai Chongxi: execution of Han Fuju and, 182; guerrilla warfare and, 155, 313–314; Hangzhou Bay and, 154; Hengyang and, 411–412; Ichigō offensive and, 407–408, 411–414; Ministry of Military Education and, 96; Nationalist military strategy and, 83–84, 407; Shanghai campaign and, 150, 153; strength of regional army of, 185, 186, 189; Wuhan and, 197; Xuzhou and, 192, 195, 196

Baishiyi, 266

banzai tactics, 235–236, 328, 380

Baoding, 50, 162–164

Baoding Military Academy, 99, 100t, 101t, 188–190, 201, 205–206, 421, 455–456

baptism of blood, 341

Bauer, Max, 284

bayonet training, 236, 341, 343

Beijing. See Peking

Beiyang Army, 50

Bengbu, 192

Benning Revolution, 450–451

Bhamo garrison, 379, 383

Bias Bay, 213

blockades, 39–40, 46, 148, 224, 259, 434, 439

Boeing B-29 bombers, 252, 430, 436–437

bomb shelters, 234, 249, 264, 268–275, 277

bombing campaigns. See Aerial campaigns

Boxer Protocols, 48–49, 68, 124

Brussels Conference, 151, 153–157, 469

brutality, 236, 460, 476

buffer zones, 68, 462

Burma. See also Yunnan-northern Burma theater: Allied counteroffensive in, 44–45; Chinese progress in, 46; Imphal campaign and, 364–367; Lend-Lease Act and, 297–298; map of Chinese operations in (1943–1945), *m*14; occupation of by Japanese army, 362–365; Y-Force and, 386–391

Burma Area Army (BAA; Japanese), 362–365. See also *Specific units*

Burma Road, 39–40, 44, 46, 246–250, 381–382. See also Dan operation

CACW. See Chinese American Composite Wing

Cairo Conference, 444

Canton. See Guangzhou

Carlson, Evans, 195, 196

causes of war: changes in Japanese military priorities, 75–78; Chinese factions and regionalism, 62–64; Chinese warlordism, 58–62; Japanese aggression, Nanjing defensive strategy, 70–74; Japanese China policy dysfunctions, 52–55; Japanese encroachments in China, 49–52, 67–70; Japanese military attitudes towards China, 56–58; Japanese seizure of Manchuria, 64–67; overview of, 48–49; Young Officers' Rebellion of 1936, 74–75

C.C. Clique, 63

CCP. See Chinese Communist Party

Central China Area Army (Chinese), 35, 45–46, 162, 166–167, 283–285

Central China Area Army (Japanese), 30, 155, 176–177

Central China Battle (Battle of Henan), 392, 403–411, 417–418

Central China Expeditionary Army (CCEA; Japanese). See also

Eleventh Army: end of, 217; Nanjing and, 155–156; reorganization of, 210–211; Wuhan and, 196, 210–215; Xuzhou and, 33, 191–192; Yichang and, 203; Zuhou and, 209

Central Committee of the Nationalist Party (KMT). See Kuomintang

Central Military Academy, 96, 100, 100t

Central Plains (Zhongyuan) Operation, 226, 331, 342, 349

Chahar Expeditionary Force (Japanese), 164, 166

Chahar Province, 29, 70–71, 161–167, 310–324

Chang Kai-ngau (Zhang Jia'ao), 84

Changde, 44

Changkuofeng (Zhanggufeng), 34

Changsha: attacks on, 41–42; burning of, 197, 200, 202; Ichigō offensive and, 393, 403–404, 407–414

Changsha, First Battle of, *p*2, 202, 204, 217–218

Changsha, Second Battle of, 226–227, 291–292, 426–427

Changsha, Third Battle of, 88

Changsha-Hengyang Battle, 403, 407–414

Changzhou forts, 92

Chekan Railway, 216

Chekiang Province. See Zhejiang Province

Chen Anbao, 202

Chen Cheng: Army Reorganization Bureau and, 103; Burma campaign and, 386, 387–389; Changsha and, 200, 202, 206; China Expeditionary Force and, 302, 387; Military Affairs Commission and, 182; Ninth War Zone and, 186, 202; on problems of Chinese army, 91, 97; Wuhan and, 189, 196, 200; Yangtze campaign and, 147–149, 185, 188, 201, 206; Yichang and, 41

Chen Gongbo, 205

Chengdu, 94, 247, 252, 261, 401, 428, 430–438

Chennault, Claire, 160, 265–266, 299–300, 430–431, 436

Cherepanov, A.I., 291

Ch'i, Hsi-sheng, 449, 451–452

Chiang Kai-shek: defense of Chongqing and, 268–269, 273–274, 276, 280; defense of Shanghai and, 139, 145–153; defense of Xuzhou and Wuhan and, 205–206; distribution of weapons by, 90–91; expectations of regarding foreign intervention, 469; German advisors and, 284–285, 304; Great Britain and, 295–296, 299; guerrilla warfare and, 87–88, 314; Hangzhou Bay and, 153–154; Ichigō offensive and, 403–407, 410–414, 415–416; indecision of about Nanjing, 139–140, 154–158; indecision of on Chinese policy after Marco Polo Bridge Incident, 143–145; on inferiority of Chinese forces, 104; Japanese-American War and, 443; lack of support of, 184; loss of Manchuria and, 67; military hierarchy and, 99, 188; Ministry of Military Education and, 96; modernization and, 431; National Military Reorganization Conference and, 103; National Salvation Movement and, 77; Nationalist military strategy on eve of war and, 83–84; Northern Expedition and, 61–62; as prisoner, 461; protracted warfare and, 85; relocation of government to Chongqing and, 257–258; shifting alliances and, 63–64; Soviet Union assistance and, 288–289, 291–293, 305; Stilwell and, 296–299, 381, 431–432; United States and, 296–297, 299; Wusong and, 149–150; Xuzhou and, 195; Y-Force and, 388; Zhang Xueliang and, 72–73

Chih-chiang operation, 438–439, 444

Chihli Clique, 60

China Air Task Force (CATF). See Tenth Air Force

China Expeditionary Army (Japanese): creation of, 177, 217; Ichigō offensive and, 45–46, 392, 396–400, 435–436; Nanjing and, 176–178; in Pacific War, 438–440, 443–444; reductions in, 39

China Garrison Army (Japanese): code breaking by, 56–57, 132; independence of, 55; Marco Polo Bridge Incident and, 159, 161; north China campaign and, 161–163; overview of on eve of war, 105–106, 108, 124–127; role of air units of, 241; structure of on eve of war, 115; training of, 130; war plans on eve of war and, 108, 110, 114

China Section, 56, 131–132

"The China White Paper" (Acheson), 449

Chinese air force. See National Air Force (Chinese)

Chinese American Composite Wing (CACW), 44, 300

Chinese Aviation Commission, 264–265

Chinese Communist Party (CCP), 61, 308–313, 317–327

Chinese Expeditionary Force. See Y-Force

Chinese National Aviation Corporation (CNAC), 298

Chinese navy, 148, 160, 302–303

Ching-han (Kogō) offensive, 392–393, 394t, 397–398, 401

Chōōshū Clique, 54

Chongqing: abandoned plans for attack on, 384–385; air defense systems of, 233–234, 247, 263–268, 276–277; cutting off supply lines to, 39–40, 204; division of political power in government of, 431; Japanese-American War and, 424; loss of Yichang and, 203–204; as new base of Chinese operations, 258; victory celebration in, p5

Chongqing Air Defense Command, 276–277

Chongqing campaign. See also

Operations 101 and 102: Chinese air defense system and, 233–234, 247, 263–268; civil defense system during, 268–275, 269t; effects of, p4, 38, 233, 275–282, 476, 478; overview of, 248–249, 256–263, 263t; planning for, 36, 42, 43

Chuanshakou landing, 148

Ch'üeh-shan (Queshan), 393

Chuikov, Vasilii, 291, 293

chūkun aikoku, 328

Churchill, Winston, 450–451

civil defense system. See Air defense systems

civilians. See also Chongqing campaign: air raids and, 478; burning of Changsha and, 200; clashes of with Nationalist forces, 53; defection of, 205; estimates on total casualties of, 46; evacuation of from Xuzhou, 194–195; flooding and, 34, 195; genro and, 53; in Hebei, 322; mobilization of, 403, 418; in Nanjing, 179, 182, 242–243; soldiers disguised as, 133–134, 176, 179

CNAC. See Chinese National Aviation Corporation

coalition war, difficulties of, 481

code breakers, 56, 132, 365–366

cohesion, 329, 332–334, 347–348, 353

Combined Fleet (Japanese), 160

command and control, 127, 133–134, 139–140, 179, 245, 358–359, 472

communication facilities: attacks on Chinese, 32, 40, 44, 246, 253–254; defense of Chongqing and, 266, 271; Japanese intelligence and, 132; of Nationalist Army on eve of war, 90

Communism. See also Chinese Communist Party: after end of World War II, 446–447; United States and, 449

Communist forces. See also Chinese Communist Party: Battle of the Hundred Regiments and, 39, 235, 320–321, 326; doctrine of, 480;

guerrilla warfare and, 308–313, 317–327; Ichigō offensive and, 402; in north China, 463–464; overview of on eve of war, 185; soldiers of, 475; United States and, 299, 306; Xi'an rebellion and, 77, 461

conscription: Japanese army and, 115–117, 130, 332–339, 353; Nationalist army and, 83, 94–95, 189, 452, 455–456, 475–476

Cun Xingqi, 315

Curtiss aircraft, 240, 243, 244, 250–251

Dabie Mountains, 194, 196, 197–199, 211, 213, 314–317

Dachang, 172

Dahong Mountains, 203

Dan operation: failure and effects of, 383–385; first phase of, 378–382; goal of, 357, 362, 390; Imphal campaign and, 374–375; overview of, 390; planning for, 365, 375–378; second and third phases of, 382–383

Datong, 150, 164

Dayingzhen Pass. See Pingxingguan Pass

defections, 73, 205, 206

defensive warfare, 87, 448, 450–452

demilitarized zone, 69

depots, 87, 123, 457

desertion: after execution of Han Fuju, 183; Baoding generals and, 189; Chinese army and, 205; Japanese army and, 335, 350; military expansion and, 320; Nationalist army and, 91, 387, 456

Dexian, 162, 163

dikes, breaching of, 34, 195, 204, 209–210, 211, 212

dimensions of warfare, overview of, 468–479

disobedience: by Chinese soldiers, 139, 188, 413; Han Fuju and, 182; by Japanese soldiers, 66, 168, 179, 351–352

Doihara Kenji, 71, 73–74, 191, 194

dokudan senkō, 55, 112

Doolittle, James, 42–43, 427, 435

Doolittle raid, 42–43

Dorn, Frank, 196, 449, 451

drafts. See Conscription

Dratwin, M.I., 291

drilling. See Training

Duan Qirui, 59

Duliuzhen, 162

Dushan, 384

East Operation, 330–331

education. See also Training: Germany and, 284; of Japanese soldiers, 117, 206, 240, 333–334, 337–339, 475; of Nationalist soldiers, 95–102, 100t, 101t, 205; Soviet Union and, 291

Eighteenth Army (Chinese), 100

Eighteenth Division (Japanese): Burma and, 363, 365; Dan operation and, 375, 377–379; Hangzhou Bay and, 176; Hukawng and, 367–369; Myitkyina and, 373, 383

Eighth Route Army (Chinese): Battle of the Hundred Regiments and, 320–321, 326; guerrilla forces and, 316–317, 318, 319, 323–325; overview of, 185; Pingxingguan and, 165, 310–313

Ekkan clearing operation, 393

Eleventh Army Group (Chinese), 45, 371, 388–389

Eleventh Army (Japanese). See also Central China Expeditionary Army: assessment reports of, 218–219; central China campaigns (1938–1941) and, 140–141; Changsha and, 41–42, 46, 226–227, 426; Chongqing and, 42; Han River and, 224–225; Hebei-Shanxi border and, 43; Henan Province and, 43; Hunan and, 407; Ichigō offensive and, 45–46, 407; Jin River and, 225–226; Nanchang and, 43, 216–217; overview of, 207–208, 227–229; reorganization of, 210–211; Taierzhuang and, 208–209; Wuhan

Eleventh Army (Japanese) *(continued)* and, 34–36, 196, 203, 207–208, 210–215; Xuzhou and, 191–192, 209–210; Yichang and, 38, 203, 221–224; Yichang operation and, 38; Yunan and, 225

Eleventh Division (Japanese), 148–149, 169–172, 175, 175t

Emergency Evacuation Committee, 271

encirclement operations: as Chinese strategy, 324–325, 383, 390; as Japanese strategy, 27, 29, 112, 159; of Nanjing, 158, 178–179; north China campaign and, 162; Principles of Operations and, 112; Shanghai and, 30–31, 176; Wuhan and, 200; Xuzhou and, 33, 209

encroachments into China, 48, 49–52, 67–70

Epstein, Israel, 195, 279–280

equipment: of Chinese forces, 88–91, 89t, 160, 245; from Germany, 285–286; of Japanese forces, 118–121, 120t, 134, 160, 187, 239–240, 339–340, 340t; from Soviet Union, 289–290; from United States, 295, 300–301, 302–303

escorts, bombing campaigns and, 243–245, 247, 267

Essentials of Guerrilla Warfare, 314

executions, 179, 181–183, 198, 200

expansionism: Japanese interest in North China, 67–70; Japanese seizure of Manchuria, 64–67; military attitudes towards China and, 56–58; Nanjing's defensive strategy and, 70–74; problems with Japanese policy of, 52–55

Fabian tactics, 32, 73, 81

factionalism: as problem for Chinese, 61, 62–64, 442, 452; as problem for Japanese, 53–54, 128, 140

famines, 46, 417–418, 458

Fan Zhuxian, 315

Fang Xianjue, 411

fangkong. *See* Air defense systems

fear, coping with, 342, 348–350

Feng Chan-hai, 162

Feng Yuxian, 63, 72, 102, 182, 462

Feng Zhanhai, 162

Fengtai, 105, 127, 130–131

Fengtien Clique, 59–60, 313

field initiative, right of, 55, 112

Fifteenth Army Group (Chinese), 148–149, 346

Fifteenth Army (Japanese), 45, 362–365, 367, 385

Fifth Army (Chinese), 67

Fifth Division (Japanese), 29, 33, 161, 164, 209

Fifth War Zone: Japanese supply lines in, 41; Li Zongren and, 32, 36; redefinition of, 186; Tauhu and, 198–199; Wuhan and, 203–204; Xuzhou and, 196–197; Yichang and, 38, 222–225; Zaoyang-Yichang and, 315

Fifty-sixth Division (Japanese), 45, 363–367, 369–373, 378–382

Fifty-third Army (Chinese), 314, 369, 371, 373

First Air Group (Japanese), 162

First Army (Japanese), 28, 30–31, 161–163, 168, 330, 416

First Fleet (Japanese), 160

First Replenishment Plan, 122

First Special Combined Air Group, 241

First War Zone, 309, 314, 404–405, 408–409, 416

Five June Great Tunnel Tragedy, 263t, 274–275

Flying Tigers, 250, 265, 300, 431

foreign aid. *See also* Germany; Soviet Union; United States: overview of, 234–235, 254, 283, 304–307; problems of, 472–474; unrealistic expectations regarding, 469

Fourteenth Air Force (U.S.), 250–252, 300, 436

Fourteenth Army (British), 45

Fourth Air Group (Japanese), 162

France, 38, 48, 224, 239, 301

Franco-Prussian War, 468

French Concession, 30, 172
frontier regions, 459–464
Fujita Akira, 346

Galahad unit (Merrill's Marauders), 367, 368
Gan River, 217–218
Gansu Province, 319. See also Lanzhou
Gan-Xiang operation, 217–218
Gaoligong Mountains, 362, 371
garrison area system, 94
General Defense Guideline, 86
genro, 53
geography, Chinese: effect of on Japanese attacks, 28–29, 40, 121, 214, 229; impacts of, 197; Shanghai campaign and, 169–170, 173
German Military Advisers Group, 103
Germany: advisors and munitions experts from, 86, 92, 184, 283–288, 304–305; attacks of on Europe, 36, 184, 224; Chinese artillery from, 92; Chinese training and, 81, 97, 99, 102–103
Gogō operation, 423, 428, 443
Goh Koji, 334–335
Gongda airfield, 242
Great Bombing of Chongqing. See Chongqing
Great Britain: aid from, 292, 294–296, 301; Burma Road and, 39–40; Chongqing campaign and, 261; mediation and, 148; Southward Offensive and, 462; Y-Force and, 388
Great Tunnel Tragedy (6/5), 263t, 274–275
group ties, 329, 332–334, 347–348, 353
Gu Zhutong, 147, 268, 317
Guadalcanal Operation, 43, 364, 374, 395, 428
Guandong Army. See Kwantung Army
Guangdong Province, 86, 103, 186, 246, 253, 325
Guangxi Clique, 83, 317, 463–464

Guangxi Province, 37, 250, 403, 458. See also Hunan-Guangxi Railway
Guangyangba, 266
Guangzhou (Canton): attacks on ports of, 40; capture of, 35, 200, 205, 213–214; Japanese army in, *p10*; opposition to Chiang kai-shek in, 71; Sun Yat-sen in, 58–59, 61
Guangzhou-Wuhan Railway, 85, 404–409
guerrilla forces, Eighth Route Army and, 316–317, 318, 319, 323–325
guerrilla warfare: agrarian society and, 308, 311–313; Bai Chongxi and, 155, 313–314; Battle of Pingxingguan and, 310; Battle of the Hundred Regiments and, 326; Communist forces and, 308–313, 317–327; expansion and consequences of, 313–319; importance of to Chinese, 35, 87–88, 201, 235, 308–309, 313–316; Military Affairs Commission and, 315, 323–324; origins of, 309–313; overview of, 308–309, 326–327; Pingxingguan Pass and, 165–166, 310; "point and line" strategy vs., 37
Guilin: American air bases in, 250–251; capture of airbases in, 46; Ichigō offensive and, 376, 381, 393, 397, 400–403, 408–412
Guiyang, 384, 402
Guizhou Province, 94, 384, 410, 412. See also Dushan
gyokusai ideology, 328

Hōsho, 239
Hagio Isamu, 371
Han Deqin, 313, 314, 317
Han Fuju, 181–183, 189, 205, 463
Han River, 203, 222–225
Hangzhou, 242–243
Hangzhou Bay, 87, 110, 153–154, 175–176, 287, 464
Hangzhou-Nanchang Railway, 43, 197
Hankou, 86, 200, 210, 214–215, 229, 393. See also Keikan offensive; Peking-Hankou Railway

Hankou-Guangzhou Railway, 394, 396, 398, 401
Hanoi-Yunnan Railway, 40
Hanyang, 210, 214
HAPRO (Handelsgesellschaft für industrielle Produkte), 286
Hasegawa Kiyoshi, 146
Hashimoto Gun, 135, 208
Hata Hikozaburō, 399
Hata Shunroku, 191, 194, 196, 200, 397
Hattori Takushirō, 395–401
hazing, 337, 353
He Haoruo, 462
He Yingqin: on air forces, 264; appeasement and, 144; on attrition in Nationalist army, 387; baojia and, 455; command structure of army and, 413; Hebei Province and, 71; on inferiority of Chinese forces on eve of war, 103–104, 145; Ministry of Military Education and, 96–97; reorganization and reduction in forces and, 318, 388, 416; Sichuan Military Reorganization Conference and, 93–94; Suzhou Creek and, 154; Whampoa Military Academy and, 206; Zhongtiao area and, 316
heat, 34, 105, 211, 214, 229
Hebei Province, 69–73, 86, 309–310, 313–315, 319–323. See also Shanxi-Chahar-Hebei area; Shijiazhuang
Hebei-Chahar Political Council, 73
Henan, Battle of, 392, 403–411, 417–418
Henan Province. See also Huayuankou; Zhengzhou: Eleventh Army in, 43; famine in, 46, 417–418, 458; Fengtien Clique and, 60, 63; Ichigō offensive and, 392, 403–411, 417–418; war zones and, 86, 186; Zhang Xueliang and, 72–73
Hengyang. See also Changsha-Hengyang Battle: air bases in, 250, 251; Battle of Hunan and, 403, 407–415; conferences at, 201, 202–203; Ichigō offensive and, 393–394, 394t, 397, 399–402, 409

hierarchies, military, 99–102, 311
Himalaya Mountains, 250, 251, 254, 372, 430
Hindenburg Line, 156, 284–285, 287
Hirata Kenkichi, 329
Hirose Takeo, 334
Hirota Kōki, 76, 151
The History of the Sino-Japanese War (Dorn), 449
Hizen, 54
Hohei sōten. See Infantry Manual
Honda Masaki, 365, 373, 377, 381, 382–383
Hong Kong, 42, 280, 426
honor, 334–335, 343–344
Hopei Province. See Hebei Province
Howard, Michael, 468–469
Hsiang-kuei offensive, 45–46, 251–252, 392–394, 394t, 397–399, 403–404, 407–415
Hu Shi, 144, 155
Hu Zongnan, 181, 185, 199, 206
Huang, Ray, 462
Huangchuan, 199
Huangmei, 199, 212–213
Huayuankou, 34, 195, 204
Hubei Province, 38, 404–409. See also Peking-Wuhan Railroad; Suixian; Xiangyang; Yichang
Hukawng campaign, 367–369, 376–377
Humen forts, 92
Hunan, Battle of, 45–46, 251–252, 392–394, 394t, 397–399, 403–404, 407–415
Hunan Province, 218, 220. See also Changde; Changsha; Hengyang
Hunan-Guangxi Railroad, 45–46, 251–252, 331, 392–399, 404–412
115th Division (Communist), 165–166
Hundred Regiments, Battle of, 39, 235, 320–324, 326

Ichigō offensive: Changsha and, 409; Dan operation and, 375, 376, 383–385; Japanese-American war and, 434–436, 443–444; logistics issues of, 393–395, 394t; map of, *m*13; Nationalist army and, 407–418; objectives of, 251–252, 398–399, 404–407, 437; overview of, 45–46, 358, 392–393, 394t, 401–404; planning of, 395–398; results of, 399–402, 442–444, 479; Thirty-seventh Division and, 331

Ichikari Yūsaku, 382

Ichiki Kiyonao, 127

illiteracy, 100, 102, 417

Imada Shinji, 337, 339, 348–349

Imagawa Setsuo, 345–346

Imai Kigoshi, 128

Imamura Detachment, 213

Imamura Katsuji, 199

Imoto Kumao, 129–130, 397

Imperial army (Japanese), national army vs., 116–117

Imperial Defense Policy, 54, 107, 110, 115

Imperialism, 343–344, 460, 474, 479

Imphal campaign, 45, 364–370, 374

improvised procurement, 340

Inada Masazumi, 208

incendiary bombs, 176, 248–249, 260–261, 272, 437

India, 102, 301–302, 362, 364. See also X-Force

induction ceremonies, 335–336

infantry: Japanese, *p*10–12; Japanese army before the war and, 118, 121–122, 123; Japanese riverine, 55; Principles of Operations and, 112, 113–114; training of in Nationalist army, 100, 101t

Infantry Manual, 113, 130–131

initiative, right of, 55, 112

insubordination: by Chinese soldiers, 139, 188, 413; by Japanese soldiers, 66, 168, 179, 351–352

intelligence capabilities: Chinese, 90, 186–187, 210, 266, 405–406; Japanese, 56–58, 131–134, 365–366, 373–374

international aid. See Foreign aid

International Settlement, 30, 127, 152, 169–170

Ishiwara Kanji, 57, 66, 75–76, 106, 111, 128, 469

Isogai Rensuke, 191, 193

Itagaki Seishirō, 106, 164, 166, 191, 193

Izumo, 147, 242

JAAF. See Japanese Army Air Force

Jacoby, Annalee, 449

Japanese army. See also Soldiers; *Specific units*: air units of, 44, 241–242; autonomy of on Asian mainland, 54–55; Battle of the Hundred Regiments and, 235, 320–321; Chongqing and, 260; conflict of with Japanese navy, 53–54; conscription and, 475–476; development of firepower of over time, 114t; doctrine of on eve of war, 111–115; high command and field officers of on eve of war, 128–129; intelligence capabilities of, 131–134; logistics of on eve of war, 122–124; in Manchuria, 65; modeling of Beiyang army on, 50; national security policy, north China and, 106–107; new formations of on eve of war, 121–122; organization, weapons, and logistics of, 88, 89t; organization of, 336–340, 338t; overview of on eve of war, 28–29, 105–106, 129–130, 134–135; reductions in, 39; structure and personnel of on eve of war, 115–118; structure of air units of, 237–239; tensions of on eve of war, 127–128; training of, 105–106, 130–131; war plans of, 107–111; weaknesses of, 452–453; weapons and equipment of on eve of war, 118–121, 120t

Japanese Army Air Force (JAAF), 121, 160

Japanese navy: air units of, 237–242; bombardment of civilians by, 31–32; Chongqing and, 248–251, 258–260, 281–282; conflict of with Japanese army, 53–54; decline of, 252–255; in early air battles,

Japanese navy: *(continued)*
242–247; expenditures of, 426;
goals and priorities of, 31–32,
53–54; main responsibilities of,
29; naval landing parties of, 55;
Operation 101 and, 38; Pacific War
and, 425–426, 434, 477; smuggling
and, 72; superiority of, 160; United
States assistance to, 302–303
Japanese-American War: air raids
on Japanese homeland and, 427;
American strategic plan for, 424,
428–432; Chinese strategic plan
for, 424–425; destruction of
Japanese merchant marine and,
434; Guadalcanal Operation and,
428; Ichigō offensive and, 434–436,
443–444; Japan's absolute national
defense perimeter and, 433–434;
Mariana Islands and, 437–438;
overview of, 440–445
Japan-Imperial China Garrison Army,
124. See also China Garrison Army
Jehol Province, 68–69
Jiang Baili, 85, 188–189
Jiang Dingwen, 404, 408, 409
Jiang Fangzhen, 85, 188–189
Jiang Menglin, 144, 417
Jiangning forts, 92
Jiangsu Province, 92, 94, 147, 186,
202, 314, 317–318
Jiangxi Province, 42–43, 216, 427.
See also Nanchang; Shanggao;
Xuzhou
Jiangyin Fortress, 92, 156, 318
Jiaochangkuo, 274–275
Jin River, 225–226
Jinan, 65, 181
Jingmen, 203
Jinguan, 167
Jinpu railway. See Tianjin-Pukou
Railway
Jinshanwei, 176
Jiujiang, 40, 197–198, 212
Jomini, Antoine-Henri, 467–468
Ju Zheng, 155
June fifth Great Tunnel Tragedy, 263t,
274–275

Kachanov, K.M., 291
Kaga, 239, 242, 243
Kaifeng, 195, 331
Kamaing, 367–368
kamikaze tactics, 235–236, 328–329
Kanoya Air Group, 241, 243
Kao-li-kung Mountains. See Gaoli-
gong Mountains
Katsuki Kiyoshi, 161–163, 164
Kawabe Masakazu, 127, 129,
389–390
Kawabe Shōzō, 363, 375
Kawasaki Ki-10 Type 95 fighters, 240
Kayama Seiji, 343–344
Kazuki Kayoshi, 131
Keikan operation, 392–393, 394t,
397–398, 401
Kiangsi Province. See Jiangxi Province
Kisarazu Air Group, 241, 243
Klein, Hans, 285
KMT. See Kuomintang
Kobayashi Eiji, 347
Kobayashi Saburō, 344
Kogō offensive, 392–393, 394t,
397–398, 401
Kohima, 45, 389, 449
kokugun, 116–117
Konoe Fumimaro, 42, 107, 151, 259,
384
Korea, 48–49
Kuangtung. See Guangdong Province
Kuei-lin. See Guilin
Kuei-yang. See Guiyang
Kunisaki Brigade, 155
Kunisaki Noboru, 155
Kunming, 280, 300, 302, 369–370,
384
Kunming Field Headquarters Combat
Plan, 388
Kuomintang (KMT): Doihara Kenji
and, 73; five-year plan of, 106;
guerrilla warfare and, 308,
313–316, 326; Northern Expedition
and, 61–62; Sun Yat-sen and, 58,
61–63
Kwangsi Province. See Guangxi
Province
Kwantung Army (Japanese): air

campaigns and, 238–239, 241;
autonomy of, 54–55; Chahar and,
29, 163–167; China Garrison Army
and, 124–126, 161; collapse of
territorial schemes of, 73; on eve of
war, 106–111; in Hebei and Chahar
provinces, 70–71; Jehol Province
and, 68–69; Manchuria and,
65–66; Pacific War and, 433–434,
439; Pingxingguan Pass and, 166
Kwantung Leased Territory, 54
Kweichow. See Guizhou Province
Kyushu, 245, 252, 332, 339, 402, 432

Lameng, 365, 367, 370–372, 377–382,
390
landscape. See Geography, Chinese
Lanzhou, 87, 246, 247, 280, 290–291
Lao-ho-kuo operation, 438
Lashio, 46, 366, 377, 385
Lattimore, Owen, 296
Le Han, 97
leadership: Japanese army and, 329,
344–348, 350–353; Nationalist
army and, 100, 133, 140, 183, 204
Ledo Road, 357–358, 368, 385
Lend-Lease Act, 296–304, 388, 473
Li Zongren: assistance to Nationalist
army from, 182, 447; background
of, 189; as commander of Fifth War
Zone, 32, 185–186, 193; Huang-
chuan and, 199; Hubei Province
and, 36; Nationalist military
strategy on eve of war and, 83–84;
Xuzhou and, 191–192, 195–196;
Yichang and, 205; Zuhou and, 194
Liao Lei, 151–152, 314
Lin, Adet, 278
Lin Biao, 165–166, 310
Linyi, 193
Liu, F.F., 451
Liu Fei, 150, 155, 414
Liu Wenhui, 463
Liu Xiang, 84, 98–99, 463
Liu Yujing, 202
Liu Ziqing, 98–99
Liuzhou, 46, 213, 400–401, 403. See
also Shōkei offensive

Lo Zhengming, 463
loans: from Germany, 285; Nationalist
agricultural production and, 457;
from Soviet Union, 289–290; from
United States, 295–304, 388, 473;
warlord factions and, 59
logistics: improvised procurement and,
340; of Japanese army, 122–123,
134, 340; of Nationalist army on
eve of war, 91; overview of, 468,
471–474; supply depots and, 87,
123, 457
Lone Battalion, 152
Long March, 71, 93
Long Yun, 84, 185, 388
Longhai Railway, 32, 191–192,
194–195, 209, 314
Longling, 363, 369–372, 378–382,
388–391
loyalty: to Chiang Kai-shek, 184–189;
Japanese army and, 328, 343–344,
474–475; Nationalist army and,
189, 205; to warlords, 183, 452
Loyang, 45
Luo Zhuoying, 41, 189, 201–202, 301
Luodian, 149, 169–170, 171
Luogouqiao. See Marco Polo Bridge
Incident
Lushan, 144–145, 212
Lytton Commission report, 67

Madang, 197–198, 464
Magruder, John, 296, 298
Manchukuo, 66, 67, 74, 109–110,
163–164
Manchuria: Japanese interest in, 51,
64–67; Kwantung Leased Territory
and, 54; warlords in, 59–60, 63;
Zhang Zuolin and, 59–60
Manchurian Incident, 66, 85, 238
Mangshi, 366, 371, 379, 382–383, 390
Manzhouguo. See Manchukuo
Mao Zedong, 63–64, 309–310, 321,
323–326, 480
Marco Polo Bridge Incident, *p6*,
143–145, 159–161, 446
Mariana Islands, 430, 437–438, 442
Marshall, George, 450–451

Maruyama Fusayasu, 373, 378

Matouzhen, 199, 212, 214

Matsui Hideji, 372

Matsui Iwane: Nanjing and, 157, 177, 179, 182; Shanghai and, 148, 155, 169, 176; Suzhou Creek and, 172–173

Matsuyama Yūzō, 365, 371

Matterhorn Operation, 432

Meigo offensive, 331

Mengjian (Menguko), 71

merchant marine, 434, 479

Merrill, Frank, 367

Merrill's Marauders, 367, 368

Methods for Adjusting Guerrilla Forces, 318

Military Affairs Commission: Chongqing branch of, 93, 263, 268; conflicting opinions on strategy and, 412; defense plan of, 85–86; fortress construction and, 92; guerrilla warfare and, 313–316, 318, 323–324; Ichigō offensive and, 407–409; leadership of, 181–182, 413; Ministry of Military Operations and, 404; Sichuan and, 93; Y-Force and, 388

Military Service Law, 94, 455

Minakami Genzō, 373, 378

Ministry of Military Affairs, 94

Ministry of Military Training, 96, 97

Mitsubishi A5M4 Type 96 carrier fighters, 240, 245

Mitsubishi A6M "Zero" fighters, 38, 248, 254–255, 471, 477

Mitsubishi B2M1 Type 89 carrier attack bombers, 240, 243

Mitsubishi G3M2 Type 96 medium bombers, *p9*, 240, 243, 247, 254

Mitsubishi G4M Type 1 medium bombers, 29, 249, 254

Mitsubishi Ki-21 Type 97 bombers, 249

Miura Keiji, 164–167

Miyazaki Shūichi, 219, 396

mobilization, 311–313, 332–334, 387, 452–457

Model Forces (Nationalist army), 283

Model Units (Communist forces), 323

modernization: agrarian society and, 50, 452–457; German advisors and, 304; of Japanese army, 82, 111, 122, 221; lack of in Nationalist forces, 84–85, 444, 450–452; United States assistance and, 430–432, 441

Morita Tetsuo, 129

motivation, 236, 332–336, 343–344, 474–475. See also Leadership

Mountbatten, Louis, 386, 388

Mukden, 66, 288, 294, 392

Munitions Assignments Board, 298–299

Mutō Akira, 128, 135

Mutaguchi Renya, 105, 127–132, 362–363

Mutual Nonaggression Treaty, 288–289

Myitkyina, 44–45, 365, 372–374, 377–379

Myitkyina Line, 377

Nagano Shin'ichi, 344

Nakahara operation, 40

Nakajima fighter planes, 240, 243, 251

Nakajima Kesago, 179

Namhkam, 379, 383

Namita Detachment, 210–215

Nanchang, 35–36, 87, 201–202, 216–218. See also Hangzhou-Nanchang Railway

Nanjing: bombing of, 242–243, 248; causes of war and, 70–74; Central Army losses in, 287; Chinese defense of, *p1*, 154–158; Han Fuju and, 182; Japanese control of, 37; Nationalist military strategy on eve of war and, 83–84; Tenth Army attack on, *m6*, 31, 176–178

Nanjing Decade, 62–64, 446

Nanning, 46, 219–220, 401

Napoleon Bonaparte, 98, 459, 467–468, 481

National Air Force (Chinese), 147–148, 169, 244–245, 264–265, 300–301

National Defense Plans, 85–86, 103
National Military Reorganization Conference, 93–94, 103
National Revolutionary Army, 61, 96
National Salvation Movement, 73, 77
National Total Mobilization Law, 333–334
nationalism, 52, 84, 446–447
Nationalist army. See also *Specific units*: air bases of as targets of Japanese bombers, 241–242; command chain of, 413–414; conscription and, 475–476; defense of Nanjing by, 31; defense projects and rear bases of on eve of war, 92–94; on eve of Yangtze campaign, 184–188; formation of, 50; guerrilla warfare and, 235, 308–309, 313–316; Ichigō offensive and, 407–418; military education and training of, 95–98, 100t, 101t; New Fourth Army Incident and, 319, 321; officers and soldiers of, 414–418; organization, weapons, and logistics of, 88–91, 89t; overview of on eve of war, 27–28, 83–85, 103–104; personnel in military hierarchy of on eve of war, 99–102; prewar reorganization and combat effectiveness of, 102–103; reasons for consensus as incompetent, 448–452; reassessment of, 464–466; recruitment, military system and, 94–95; staff system of, 98–100; strategy, national defense planning, and tactics of, 85–88; strategy of after fall of Wuhan, 35; war zones of (map), *m*11
Naval Landing Party, 55, 67, 146–148
Nazi-Soviet nonaggression pact, 36
NCAA. See North China Area Army
Nemoto Kenji, 333, 342–343
Neutrality Act, 295
New Armies, 50
New Fourth Army (Chinese), 43, 185, 186, 205, 235, 293, 317–319
New Fourth Army Incident, 319, 321
New Life Movement, 94, 454–455

night attacks, 112, 341–342
Nine-Power Treaty, 151, 157, 292, 294, 469
Nineteenth Route Army (Chinese), 67
Ninth Division (Japanese), 172–175, 175t, 178, 211–215
Ninth War Zone, 41, 186, 197, 202–204, 409–414
Nishihara Kamezō, 59
Nishio Toshizō, 125, 161, 191
Nomonhan, 36, 141, 217, 221, 293
Nomura Yasushi, 336
nonaggression pacts, 36, 39, 157, 288–289, 454, 461
noncommissioned officers: in Japanese army, 115–117, 134, 337, 339, 474; lack of as weakness of Chinese army, 96, 476
nonexpansion policy, 208
North China Area Army (NCAA; Japanese). See also Fifth Division; First Army; Second Army: Chahar and, 164; Ichigō offensive and, 45–46, 392–393; insubordination in, 168; north China campaign and, 28, 161–163; Shanghai campaign and, 170; Taierzhuang and, 33; Three-All Policy of, 39; Wuhan and, 196; Xuzhou and, 33, 191–192
North China campaign, overview of, 28–29, 70–77, 161–163
North China Incident, 85, 92
North of the Yangtze operation, 226
Northern Expedition, 61–62, 65, 449
Northwest Development Bill, 93

Obata Toshishirō, 112
Ogawa Tetsuo, 345, 349
Okamoto Kiyotomi, 130
Okamura Yasuji: Changsha and, 36, 202; Chongqing and, 384, 438; Hankou and, 229; Nanchang and, 201, 216; Three-All Policy and, 39; Wuhan and, 210, 214; Yichang and, 220, 222
Okinawa, soldiers from, 116, 329, 339
101st Army (Japanese), 173, 175t
115th Division (Communist), 165–166

Open Door Policy, 151, 294
Operation 100, 36
Operation 101, 38, 248, 261
Operation 102, 38, 248–249
Operation Matterhorn, 432
operational dimensions, overview of, 468–470
Oyama Isao, 146
Oyama Tarō, 347

P-51 Mustangs, 252
Pacific War. See also Japanese-American War: invasion of Sichuan Province and, 428; Japanese strategic plan for, 423; Japan's absolute national defense perimeter and, 433–434; operations in China and, 251–255, 323–324; outbreak of, 425–426; second Changsha offensive and, 426–427
Pang Bingxun, 193, 313, 316
"peace and order first" policy, 215, 219–220, 224
Peace Preservation Forces, 145–146, 148, 455
Peking, 69–70, 161
Peking-Hankou (Pinghan) Railway: flooding of Yellow River and, 195; Ichigō offensive and, 331, 392–398, 394t; north China campaign and, 162; Shanghai campaign and, 151; Tengxian and, 192; Wuhan and, 197, 199–200; Yunnan and, 225
Peking-Hankou Operation, 392–393, 394t, 397–398, 401
Peking-Wuhan Railway: Chinese attacks on, 36; Chinese fortresses protecting, 92; Ichigō offensive and, 45–46, 404–406; importance of to Chinese, 85; Japanese attacks on, 28, 30–31; Japanese infantry at, p12; protracted warfare and, 86–87; supplies to Fifth War Zone forces using, 32; War Plan of 1937 and, 86–87
Pengze, 197–198
People's War, 476, 480
Ping-chia, 372, 381

Pinghan Railway. See Peking-Hankou Railway
Pingxingguan Pass, m4, 29, 164–167, 180, 310
poison gas, 34, 197–198, 201, 212
Polikarpov I-12 aircraft, 245
positional warfare, 88, 187, 188, 320
Poyang, Lake, 36, 197–198, 216
Principles of Command, 111–112, 133
Principles of Operations, 112
prisoners of war, 341, 350–351
protracted warfare: avoidance of confrontation and, 187; as basic strategy, 85–86, 153, 410; Japanese forces and, 329; Shanghai and, 470–471; success of strategy, 140; von Falkenhausen and, 285
Pukou. See Tianjin-Pukou Railway
puppet armies, 185, 312, 322–324
puppet regimes: Kwantung Army and, 163–164, 167; Manchukuo and, 66, 67, 163–164; Mengukuo and, 74; Wang Jingwei and, 37, 288, 296
Puyi, Henry, 66

Qin Qirong, 313, 317
Qing Dynasty, 49–51, 96–97, 465
Qingdao, 65, 182–183, 237

railways. See *Specific railways*
rapid war, 54, 112, 159, 180, 469
recruitment, 94–95, 417, 456, 458–459
reformed divisions, 89, 103
regionalism, 62–64, 93, 96
revolution, Sun Yat-sen and, 51
right of supreme command, 53
Roosevelt, Franklin, 294–297, 299, 386, 449–450
Ruichang, 198, 212–213

Sakamoto Detachment, 209
Salween River, 45, 363, 369–371, 374–377, 388–389
Sanada Jōichirō, 395–398, 401
Sawada Shigeru, 211, 220–222
scorched-earth tactics, 197, 200, 202
SEAC. See South East Asia Command
Second Air Group (Japanese), 164, 225

Second Army (Chinese), 162
Second Army Group (Chinese), 209
Second Army (Japanese), 28, 30–31, 161–163, 168, 374–375. See also 109th Division; Sixteenth Division; Tenth Division
Second Expeditionary Fleet (Japanese), 40
Second Fleet (Japanese), 160
Second Revolution, 58
Second Special Combined Air Group (Japanese), 241
Sejima Ryūzō, 376
Senda Sadaō, 131
Setani Detachment, 209
Seventh Company (Japanese), 127
Shandong Peninsula, 51, 59, 87
Shandong Province, 65, 168, 181, 313–319
Shanggao, 41, 225–226
Shanghai, 55, 67, 242–243, 258
Shanghai, Battle of: Central Army losses in, 287; core central forces in, 103; lack of Chinese resistance to, 85; logistics of National Army during, 91; overview of, *m5*, 29–30, 145–153; student military training and, 95
Shanghai campaign, 168–176, 175t, 283
Shanghai Expeditionary Force (Japanese): losses suffered by, 30; Nanjing and, 155; naval landing party and, 148; Shanghai campaign and, 169–172, 175, 175t, 179
Shanghai-Hangzhou Railway, 156
Shanghai-Wusong Railway, 169, 170–171
Shanhaiguan, 68
Shanxi Province, 30–31, 167, 330–331. See also Datong; Ping-xingguan; Tiayuan; Xinkou
Shanxi-Chahar-Hebei area, 310–324
Shen Honglie, 313, 314, 317
Shi Shuo, 148–149
Shibayama Kenjirō, 130, 135
Shidehara Kijurō, 56
Shijiazhuang, 168

Shimada Toshio, 341, 348
Shimizu Setsurō, 105–106
Shimura Yasuo, 349
Shinan, 168
Shinatsu, 132
Shipai fortress, 44
Shōkei offensives. See Hunan, Battle of
Sian. See Xi'an
Sichuan Military Reorganization Conference, 93–94, 103
Sichuan Province. See also Chengdu; Chongqing: bombing of air bases in, 246, 300; cancellation of invasion of, 423, 428; execution of warlords in, 463; as main Chinese base, 86, 93–94, 285, 462–463; relocation of capital to, 35, 93–94, 256; Tengxian and, 192–193; warlord armies and, 463
signal intelligence. See Intelligence capabilities
Silver-Gold Exchange Agreement, 295
Sinkiang Province. See Xinjiang Province
Sixteenth Division (Japanese), 159, 176–179
Sixth Division (Chinese), 149
Sixth Division (Japanese), 176–179, 211–214
Sixth War Zone, 44, 227, 409
Sixty-second Division (Japanese), 439–440
smuggling, 72, 124
Society for the Implementation of the Three People's Principles of Sun Yat-sen, 95
sokusen sokketsu (rapid war; rapid conclusion), 54, 112, 159, 180, 469
soldiers (Chinese), 94–102, 414–418, 475–476
soldiers (Japanese). See also Thirty-seventh division: combat and, 340–343; coping with fear and, 348–350; group ties and, 347–348; Imperialism vs. family and community honor and, 343–344; individual testimonies of, 334–336; institutional role of, 336–340;

soldiers (Japanese) *(continued)*
    leadership and, 344–347, 350–
    352; overview of, 328–329; social
    process of mobilization and social
    construction of, 332–334
Song Xilian, 389
Song Zheyuan, 28, 63, 73, 462–463
Sonobe Waichirō, 203, 222, 226
South East Asia Command (SEAC),
    386
South Manchuria Railway, 54, 65–66
Southward Offensive, 454, 461–462
Soviet Union: importance of supply
    lines to Chinese from, 150; influ-
    ence of on Japanese interests in
    China, 75–77, 106–107; military
    aid to China from, 157, 250,
    264–265, 288–293, 305; military
    buildup of, 108–109, 111; Nazi
    invasion of, 41; Nomonhan Inci-
    dent and, 217, 221; volunteer pilots
    from, 245, 264–265, 290–291, 477
Spain, 467–468, 481
sparrow warfare, 312
special intelligence, 132. See also Intel-
    ligence capabilities
special smoke (poison gas), 34,
    197–198, 201, 212
special trade, 72, 124
square divisions, 121–122, 210
Stalin, Joseph, 290, 292–293, 305
standardization, lack of, 81, 90, 133
Stilwell, Joseph: conflict of with
    Chiang Kai-shek, 296–299, 381,
    431–432; Imphal operation and,
    368; modernization and, 429;
    perception of China as backward
    and, 450–451; perspective of, 196,
    416, 421; Tuchman on, 448–449;
    X-Force and, 301–302; Y-Force
    and, 386–388
*Stilwell and the American Experi-
    ence in China* (Tuchman), 421,
    448–449, 473
Stilwell Road, 298
Sugiyama Hajime, 128, 151, 395–396,
    398
Suixian, 203, 222

Sun Dianying, 91, 313, 316
Sun Liangcheng, 316
Sun Lianzhong, 192, 193, 195, 198,
    409
Sun Tongxuan, 313
Sun Yat-sen, 51, 52, 58, 61
supply depots, 87, 123, 457
supreme command, right of, 53
Suzhou Creek, 30, 152–156, 172–176
Suzuki Yorimichi, 112, 129

Tada Hayao, 124
Taierzhuang, *p3*, 33, 97, 192–194,
    208–209, 471
Taihu, 198–199
Taiwan, 48, 245, 252, 396
Taiwan Garrison Army (Japanese), 115
Taiyuan, 167, 242
Tanaka Shin'ichi, 363, 368, 375–376,
    382
Tang Enbo: favoritism and, 188; Han
    River operation and, 224; Ichigō
    offensive and, 404, 408–409;
    Ruichang and, 198; success of, 201;
    Taierzhuang and, 193; Xuzhou and,
    192, 195; Yichang and, 222
Tang Shengzhi, 31, 96, 155, 158, 189
Tanggu Truce, 69–70
tanks, *p7*, 119, 160, 162
Tao Menghe, 102
tariffs, 72, 458
Tashirō Kan'ichirō, 129
Tengxian, 192–193
Tengyue, 369–374, 378–380, 382
Tenth Air Force (U.S.), 265, 300
Tenth Army (Chinese), 41, 411–415
Tenth Army (Japanese): Battle of
    Taierzhuang and, 33; Hangzhou
    Bay and, 153–154, 175; Nanjing
    and, *m6*, 31, 155, 176–178, 179;
    Shanghai and, 30
Terauchi Hisaichi, 161, 163, 168, 170
Terauchi Masatake, 59
terrain. See Geography, Chinese
Third Division (Japanese), 170–175,
    175t, 178, 217, 222–227
Third Fleet (Japanese), 146–147, 160,
    241

Third War Zone, 146–148, 317–319, 416
Thirteenth Air Group (Japanese), 241
Thirteenth Army (Japanese), 42–43, 172–173, 175t
Thirteenth Division (Chinese), 41
Thirty-first Army Group (Chinese), 40
Thirty-seventh Division (Japanese): combat leadership and, 344–347; failed leadership and authority conflict in, 350–352; fear and, 342, 348–350; group ties in, 347–348; individual soldiers of, 334–336; military operations of, 330–332; organization and institutional roles of, 336–340, 338t, 340t; overview of, 328–330, 352–353; soldiers in combat and, 340–343
Thirty-third Army (Japanese): Burma and, 44, 46, 363, 373; Dan operation and, 357, 374–385, 390; Imphal campaign and, 365–367
Three People's Principles Youth Corps, 387
Three-All Policy, 39, 313, 321
Thunder Out of China (White and Jacoby), 449
Tianjiazhen, 199, 213–214
Tianjin, 69–70
Tianjin Garrison, 55, 68, 71, 124. See also China Garrison Army
Tianjin-Pukou (Jinpu) Railway: as axis of Japanese attack, 28, 182; Chinese fortresses protecting, 92–93; guerrilla warfare along, 314; north China campaign and, 162; supplies to Fifth War Zone forces using, 32–33; Xuzhou and, 192, 194–195, 209
Tin Loan Agreement, 295
Tinian, 437
Toba Wei, 460
Tōjō Hideki: Chahar and, 163–164; Ichigō offensive and, 398–399, 407, 435; militarism and, 332–334; preemptive war and, 42, 107, 129
Tokyo, aerial attack on, 42–43

Tōsui kōryō. See Principles of Command
training: air raid defense systems and, 272, 274; bayonet training and, 236, 341, 343; Chinese air defense system and, 266–267; defense of Chongqing and, 272; Germany and, 81, 97, 99, 102–103, 283–288, 304–305; of Japanese troops, 116–117, 128, 130–131, 134, 240, 334, 337–341; of Nationalist Army, 92, 95–102, 100t, 101t, 265–297, 302; Soviet Union and, 291–292; United States and, 250, 301–302
Trautmann, Oskar, 156–157, 179, 287, 294
triangular divisions, 121–122, 125, 169, 211
Trident Conference, 432
Tripartite Pact, 295
Truman, Harry S., 303
Tsinan. See Jinan
Tsingtao. See Qingdao
Tsuji Masanobu, 365, 376–378, 380–382
Tuchman, Barbara, 421, 448–449, 473
Tung Oil Loan Agreement, 295
Tungsten Ore Loan Agreement, 295
tunnels, 263t, 268–270, 274–275
Twelfth Air Group, 241
Twentieth Army (Chinese), 45
Twentieth Bombardment Group (U.S.), 432, 436, 437–438
Twentieth Division (Japanese), 167
Twenty-eighth Army (Japanese), 364
Twenty-first Army (Japanese), 34–35, 46, 213
Twenty-first Army Group (Chinese), 151–152
Twenty-fourth Army Group (Chinese), 43
Twenty-ninth Army (Chinese), 63, 127–128, 132–133, 159–163
Twenty-one Demands, 51–52, 59–60

Ueda Kenkichi, 128–129
Umezu Yoshijirō, 71, 127, 128, 381–382

United Nations Declaration, 294
United States. See also Flying Tigers; Fourteenth Air Force; Japanese-American War: air bases of, 42, 45–46; air raids on Japanese homeland and, 427; Chinese-American alliance and, 293–296, 462; destruction of Japanese merchant marine and, 434; Galahad Force and, 367; Ichigō offensive and, 434–436; Lend-Lease Act and, 296–304; military aid to China from, 305–306; problems of aid from, 436–437, 473–474; strategic plan of, 424, 428–432; Y-Force and, 388
United States Air Force: assistance to Chinese air forces from, 249–250, 265, 429, 477; Changde and, 44; Flying Tigers, 250, 265, 300, 431; Fourteenth Air Force, 250, 251, 252, 300, 436; Tenth Air Force, 265, 300
Ushiroku Jun, 227

Vanguards to Resist Japan, 323
Versailles Peace Conference, 59
volunteer pilots, 245, 264–265, 290–291, 477
von Falkenhausen, Alexander, 86, 103, 196, 284–287
von Moltke, Helmut, 468
von Schiefflen, Alfred, 112
von Seeckt, Hans, 102–103, 284–285
Voroshilov, Marshall, 157

Wakamiya, 237
Wan Fulin, 162, 313
Wang Jingjiu, 149
Wang Jingwei: appeasement policy and, 72, 453; defection of, 205–206; opposition of to Chiang kai-shek, 63, 259; puppet regime of, 37, 43, 217, 280, 288, 296
Wang Ming, 183
Wang Mingzhang, 90, 193
Wannan Incident, 293
war of annihilation, 112, 115, 159, 400
war plans, 76, 86–87, 107–111

war zones, map of, *m*11. see also *Specific war zones*
warlord armies: after fall of Yichang, 203–204; effect of on Japanese attacks, 29; Japanese army and, 43, 57, 95–96; Nationalist army and, 28, 29, 98–99, 425; Nationalist relations with, 62, 463, 464–465; rise of in China before war, 58–62, 63–64
Warlord of Manchuria (Zhang Zuolin), 59–60, 63, 65
warlords. See also Li Zongren; Yan Xishan; Zhang Xueliang: Feng Yuxian, 63, 72, 102, 182, 462; Han Fuju, 181–183, 189, 205, 463; Liu Wenhui, 463; Liu Xiang, 84, 98–99, 463; Song Zheyuan, 28, 63, 73, 462–463; Xi'an rebellion and, 77, 461; Zhang Zuolin, 59–60, 63, 65
weapons. See also *Specific weapons*: Battle of Shanghai and, 147; of Japanese Army on eve of war, 89t, 118–121, 120t; of Nationalist Army on eve of war, 88–91, 89t; power and limitations of, 476–479; of Thirty-seventh Division, 339–340, 340t
Wedemeyer, Albert, 302, 384, 416, 440, 475
Wei Lihuang, 41, 387, 389–390
Wei Rulin, 195
Wetzell, Georg, 284
Whampoa Military Academy, 61, 96, 100–101, 100t, 101t, 201, 205–206
White, Theodore H., 104, 449, 450
Wingate, Orde, 357, 368, 370, 373
Winter Troops, 331–332
World War I, 51, 56, 468
World War II, 235–236, 303, 421–422, 446–447, 478–479. See also Japanese-American War; Pacific War
Wuchang, 87, 195, 199
Wuhan. See also Guangzhou-Wuhan Railway; Peking-Wuhan Railway: aerial attacks over, 244–246; as central area of defense, 32, 182;

Chinese defense of, 196–201; forts of, 92; isolation of Japanese units at, 36–37; occupation of, 203, 204

Wuhan, Battle of: Eleventh Army and, 34–36, 196, 203, 207–208, 210–215; Japanese attacks during, 33–35; overview of, *m8*

Wuhan-Guangzhou (Yuehan) Railway, 45–46, 214

Wusong, 92, 146–149, 169–171

Wusong Creek, 173

Wuxian. See Suzhou

X-Force: Burma Road and, 44–45; Dan operation and, 382–383; Hukawng and, 366–368; overview of, 301–302, 429; size of, 387

Xi'an, 77, 93, 461

Xiang River, 216–218, 409, 410–411

Xiangjang operation, 217–218

Xiangyang, 222–225

xiaoji, 264

Xie Weiying, 198

Xinjiang Incident, 293

Xinjiang Province, 48, 362

Xinkou, 30

Xinyang, 87, 199, 213, 217

Xu Yongchang, 83, 144, 389, 404–408, 410–418

Xue Yue: Baoding Military Academy and, 205, 206; Guangji and, 199; Ichigō offensive and, 406–409, 414–415; Jiujiang and, 198; Nanchang and, 201–202, 315; regional army under, 185, 186

Xuzhou, *m7*, 32–34, 190–196, 209–210

Yamada Takeshi, 336

Yamada Yoichi, 352

Yamamoto Kiyoe, 377

Yan Xishan: Chiang Kai-shek and, 72, 84, 447; Datong and, 150–151; forces of as buffer, 462–463; Japan and, 37; Nationalist military strategy on eve of war and, 84; overview of, 63; regional army under, 185; Shanxi Province and, 313, 317

Yanagawa Heisuke, 153, 176, 179

Yang Hucheng, 77

Yang Jie, 157, 289, 291

Yang Sen, 185, 197

Yangtze River Valley. See also Changsha; Nanchang; Wuhan; Xuzhou; Yichang: breaching of dikes and, 212; destruction of Wusong forts and, 92; fighting along, 34, 155; as focus of Chinese defense, 86, 184–188; Japanese naval landing parties and, 55; movement of Chinese economic center away from, 93

Ye Ting, 186, 189, 205–206, 319

Yellow River dikes, 33–34, 195, 204, 209–210, 211

Y-Force, 45–46, 302, 357–358, 380, 386–391, 429

Yichang, 38, 41, 202–208, 219–228

Yonai Mitsumasa, 146, 151

Yoneda Shingo, 346, 351

Young Men's Military Training Corps, 117

Young Officers' Rebellion of 1936, 74–75

Youth Expeditionary Army, 387–388

Yu Hanmou, 84, 406, 407, 409

Yu Huai'an, 316

Yu Jishi, 199, 205, 206

Yu Xuezhong, 316

Yuan Shikai, 50–52, 58, 60, 466

Yuanpingzhen, 167

Yue Fei, 453

Yuehan (Wuhan-Guangzhou) Railway, 45–46, 214

Yuelu, Mount, 409–410

Yueyang, 214–215

Yunan operation, 225

Yunnan Province, 250, 369–372

Yunnan-northern Burma theater: Burma occupation and, 362–365; Dan operation and, 374–385; Hukawng campaign and, 367–369; Imphal campaign and, 364, 367, 369–370, 374; Myitkyina and, 372–374; overview of, 361–362; Y-Force and, 386–391; Yunnan campaign and, 369–372

Yunzaobin River, 149, 151–152

Zero fighters, 38, 248, 254–255, 471, 477
Zhang Chong, 288–289
Zhang Deneng, 409–410
Zhang Fakui: background of, 189; Hangzhou Bay and, 153–154; Ichigō offensive and, 409; Jiujiang and, 198; regional army under, 185–186; Shanghai and, 148; Wuhan and, 200, 206
Zhang Xianwen, 415
Zhang Xueliang: accommodation of by Chiang Kai-shek, 72–73; Fengtian army and, 313, 462; Japanese invasion of Manchuria and, 85; Jehol and, 68–69; opposition to Chiang kai-shek by, 77; overview of, 63
Zhang Zhizhong: air war and, 153; burning of Changsha and, 200,

204; centralization of power by Chiang Kai-shek and, 413; Fifth War Zone and, 186; Huangchuan and, 199; Linyi and, 193; performance of, 206; Shanghai and, 146–149; Tahui and, 198; Xuzhou and, 192, 195; Yichang and, 203, 222
Zhang Zuolin, 59–60, 63, 65
Zhanggufeng, 34
Zhejiang Province, 42–43, 86, 147, 250. See also Hangzhou Bay
Zhejiang-Jiangxi operation, 147, 427, 443
Zhengzhou, 34, 352
Zhenjiang forts, 92
Zhijiang, 252, 384
Zhongtiao Mountains, 41, 315–316, 330
Zhongyuan, Battle of, 226, 331, 342, 349
Zhou Enlai, 183, 318
Zoumatang Creek, 173–175

Made in the USA
Las Vegas, NV
08 January 2023